A FORCE MORE
POWERFUL

A CENTURY OF
NONVIOLENT CONFLICT

Peter Ackerman and Jack DuVall

palgrave

First published 2000 by
PALGRAVE™
175 Fifth Avenue, New York, N.Y.10010 and
Houndmills, Basingstoke, Hampshire RG21 6XS.
Companies and representatives throughout the world

PALGRAVE is the new global publishing imprint of St. Martin 's Press LLC Scholarly and Reference Division and Palgrave Publishers Ltd (formerly Macmillan Press Ltd).

ISBN 0-312-22864-3 hardback
ISBN 0-312-24050-3 paperback

Library of Congress Cataloging-in-Publication Data
Ackerman, Peter.
    A force more powerful : a century of nonviolent conflict / Peter Ackerman, Jack DuVall.
    p. cm.
    Includes bibliographical references and index.
    ISBN 0-312-22864-3 (hardback) 0-312-24050-3 (paperback)
    1. Nonviolence. 2. Social conflict. 3. Ethnic relations. 4. Social action. 5. Social justice.
I. DuVall, Jack. II. Title.

HM1281 .A25 2000
303.6'1--dc21

                                                                00-040512

A catalogue record for this book is available
from the British Library.

Design by planettheo.com

20 19 18 17 16 15 14 13 12 11

Printed in the United States of America.

To Nate Ackerman and Elliot Ackerman
who will help shape the future

and

In memory of Margaret Clark DuVall (1911–1999)
who had faith in us all

CONTENTS

PART ONE
MOVEMENT TO POWER

PART TWO
RESISTANCE TO TERROR

LIST OF PHOTOGRAPHS

LIST OF MAPS

ACKNOWLEDGMENTS

The great English man of letters V. S. Pritchett, in writing about Leo Tolstoy, said that his novels illustrated "the crucial Russian difficulty . . . there seems to be no such person as a Russian alone. Each one appears in a crowd of relations and friends, an extravagantly miscellaneous and declaiming tribal court."[1] That too has been our experience, in preparing, writing, revising, and editing this book—but for us it was no difficulty; it was a privilege and a pleasure. We stand on the shoulders of our colleagues, both those who produced the documentary television series that was the occasion for this book and those whom we asked to participate in the research and preparation of its chapters and other content. Without their contributions to this project, ours would not have been adequate to the task.

Steve York produced and wrote the documentary television series *A Force More Powerful,* as well as the feature-length documentary film of the same name that was released in 1999. His incisive interviews of many participants and eyewitnesses who played a role in eight of the conflicts featured in the book made him our most-cited source. Without his assistance, this book could not have made a new contribution to the historical literature. Steve's mastery of the subject matter of nonviolent conflict has been much deeper and more far-ranging than any other documentary filmmaker could have brought to this work, and we learned much from the rhythm and structure that he found and amplified in the stories featured in the series.

Jonathan Mogul was our senior research and editorial associate. With a doctorate in history from the University of Michigan and much fine scholarly work to his credit, he gathered the empirical material and furnished first draft narratives for what became the chapters or chapter sections on the conflicts in Russia, India, Poland, the American South, South Africa, Eastern Europe, and Sri Lanka. He also redeveloped material on the El Salvador story, performed supplemental research on the Chile and Philippines stories, and assisted with the conclusion. His conceptual judgment about the structure of our stories lent clarity to several chapters, and his keen sense of what would stand up to historiographical scrutiny helped discipline our speculative instincts.

Jeff Heynen, a graduate student at Georgetown University's School of Foreign Service and fluent in both German and Dutch, was our editorial associate on the *Ruhrkampf* and World War II resistance conflicts, providing first draft narratives for those stories. His responsive and unflagging research helped harvest the ripest material from many diverse sources. Jeff was also our intrepid aide in verifying and correcting end notes and creating the index.

Carl Posey was our editorial associate on the Argentina and Chile conflicts, doing first draft narratives for those stories. He also assisted us in reshaping and revising the chapters and chapter sections on the conflicts in Russia, India, Poland, South Africa, China, Eastern Europe, and Mongolia. He often helped levitate the merely factual to the level of what offers a sense of human texture and color.

Greg Michaelidis was our editorial associate on the *intifada* and the conflicts in the Basque country, Burma, and Serbia, providing first draft narratives for those stories. His interviews of subjects and diligent pursuit of elusive information were invaluable. Michael Connelly was our editorial associate on the people power revolution in the Philippines and provided a first draft narrative for that story, helping us to identify the right moments to highlight in that densely paced conflict.

To prepare the China and Mongolia stories, we were fortunate to have the help of Morris Rossabi, one of the nation's foremost academic authorities on the Far East. He provided first draft narratives on those two conflicts, and his rich familiarity with the events and people in Ulaanbaatar was crucial in making the Mongolia account a fresh addition to the growing literature on nonviolent conflict.

We are also greatly obliged to Miriam Zimmerman, who completed our photographic research and compilation and was a partner in all phases of this project. Felicia Widmann, our photographic coordinator, was indefatigable in identifying and bringing back a towering collection of images. Jan Camp's contributions to the early effort in gathering this material were also most appreciated, as was the help of Heather Rush and Matthew Richardson. Alex Tait of Equatorial Graphics rendered our clear and informative maps.

Our gratitude also goes to Rosemary Umaru, Rosalyn Abraham, Valerie Cunningham, and Bridget Durand for their patience and hard work in coordinating the communications between the two of us; to Channing Walker for his timely support; to Sandy Goroff, our publicist, and to Susan Rumberg at WETA for her assistance in facilitating our contacts with PBS.

Particular thanks are due Bruce Jenkins of the Albert Einstein Institution, Sidney Tarrow of Cornell University, and Doug McAdam of Stanford University for their thoughts and reflections about the subject of the book and the series in informal conversations. They pointed out useful ideas in a way more valuable to us than it may have been apparent to them at the time. We are also thankful for the interviews conducted by Tom Weidlinger for several stories featured in the series and represented by excerpts in the book.

Of special help was Joanne Leedom-Ackerman, whose vision and perspective, bred of long involvement in the field of nonviolent conflict, gave us confidence to know that this book's distinctive purpose could be fulfilled. Also, no work even remotely related to this subject should lack an acknowledgment of the intellectual leadership of Gene Sharp, who has done more to advance the ideas at the root of modern nonviolent action than any living person.

Finally, we are very grateful to our editor at St. Martin's Press, Karen Wolny. Her enthusiasm for the book's concept and her shrewd advice about how to focus and abridge the longer stories made her the ideal shepherd in helping us find the way to a full expression of the vision that has motivated the book from the outset. Alan Bradshaw and Jennifer Simington were indispensable (and amazingly serene) in the copy editing process.

The documentary television series *A Force More Powerful* was made possible by the enlightened support of Susan and Perry Lerner, the Albert Einstein Institution, Elizabeth and John H. van Merkensteijn, III, Abby and Alan Levy, and the Arthur Vining Davis Foundations. Initial series research was funded by the U.S. Institute of Peace. Without the generosity of each of these individuals and organizations, neither the series nor the book would now be available to millions in North America and throughout the world.

This book spans five generations of political struggle, social upheaval, and military action that took place in twenty-four nations on five continents. While our research effort has been exhaustive, errors of fact, description, and interpretation are probable, and we accept the sole responsibility for any mistakes. Our aim has been to produce a truthful, even definitive account of the great nonviolent conflicts of the past one hundred years—but more than that, to portray emblematically how the people of the last century developed the power to secure equal rights, justice, and democracy, without using violence. If this book has lasting value, it is because that achievement has extraordinary importance for the future of us all.

Introduction

Justice and power must be brought together, so that whatever is just may be powerful, and whatever is powerful may be just.

—Pascal

The Stories

ONE FRIDAY NIGHT in December 1981, Lech Walesa and other leaders of Solidarity were arrested after a meeting in Gdansk. For sixteen months, their free trade union movement had shaken the foundation of communist power in Poland by occupying factories and staging strikes. Now martial law had been imposed, and Solidarity was looking down a gun barrel at defeat. But when he was taken away, Walesa challenged his captors. "At this moment, you lost," he told them. "We are arrested, but you have driven a nail into your communist coffin . . . You'll come back to us on your knees."[1]

If only violence is power, and if repression has no answer, then Walesa's words were foolish. But he knew that Solidarity had already defined the course of the conflict, by stripping the regime of the Polish people's consent. When the state had run out of ways to coerce their compliance, it would have to come to terms. Seven years later General Wojciech Jaruzelski, who had jailed Walesa, invited him and other Solidarity leaders to join roundtable talks that led to elections and the formation of a new government. In 1990 Walesa, a shipyard electrician only ten years before, became president of Poland. He had never fired a shot, nor had anyone in Solidarity. But together they threw back the shroud of authoritarian power and gave freedom to every Pole.

In the century's last decade, Walesa joined the ranks of many other heads of state who gathered each September in New York to attend the opening of the United Nations General Assembly. The great majority of these men and women were democratically elected presidents and prime ministers. Had such a meeting been held one hundred years before, all but a few would have been kings, emperors, generals, or other rulers who had reached power by violent force or dynastic inheritance. This was the most important political change that the twentieth century wrought, but it would not have come to pass without the actions of ordinary people who defied oppressive rulers through nonviolent power rather than by force of arms. How that power was developed and applied is the subject of this book.

This is a tale of ten decades, of popular movements battling entrenched regimes or military forces with weapons very different from guns and bullets. In each of these conflicts, disruptive actions were used as *sanctions,* as aggressive measures to constrain or punish opponents and to win concessions. Protests such as petitions, parades, walkouts, and demonstrations were used to rouse public support for movements. Forms of noncooperation such as strikes, boycotts, resignations, and civil disobedience helped subvert the operations of governments. And direct intervention such as sit-ins, nonviolent sabotage, and blockades frustrated many rulers' will to subjugate their peoples.[2]

The historical results were massive: Tyrants were toppled, governments were overthrown, occupying armies were impeded, and political systems that with-held human rights were shattered. Entire societies were transformed, suddenly or gradually, by people using nonviolent resistance to destroy their opponents' ability to steer events. How this happened and the ideas lying at the root of nonviolent action are at the heart of this book and the companion documentary television series that we helped produce.

It all started in Russia. Eighty-six years before Boris Yeltsin stood on a tank in Moscow in 1991, shouting scorn for a coup attempt, Russians marched to the Winter Palace in St. Petersburg to present petitions to the Tsar. In between those moments unfolded a tumultuous, worldwide march toward a fresh understanding of power: that real power derives from the consent of those it would control, not from the threat of violence against them. The emergence of this concept, in the great struggles against dictatorship, invasion, and the denial of human rights, is represented in the decisions of extraordinary individuals and their victories and failures:

- In 1905 an Orthodox priest, Georgii Gapon, persuaded 150,000 workers to walk the icy streets of Russia's ancient capital in the century's first public challenge to autocratic power. He ignited mass action nationwide that led to the country's first popularly elected national parliament.
- After the world war that opened the door to the Bolshevik takeover in Russia and imposed reparations on Germany, miners and railway workers in the Ruhr in 1923 confronted invading French and Belgian soldiers who were sent to extract German resources. They refused to cooperate and thwarted the invaders' goals until the British and Americans pressed for the troops' withdrawal.
- In 1930-1931 Mohandas Gandhi led mass civil disobedience against the British in India. He convinced his followers to stop paying salt taxes and cease buying cloth and liquor monopolized by the raj, intensifying his nation's long, successful drive to independence.
- Danish citizens during the German occupation in World War II refused to aid the Nazi war effort and brought their cities to a standstill in the summer of 1944, forcing the Germans to end curfews and blockades; other European peoples under Nazi domination resisted nonviolently as well.
- Salvadoran students, doctors, and merchants, fed up with the fear and brutality visited on their country by a longtime military dictator, organized a civic strike in 1944. Without picking up a single gun, they detached the general from his closest supporters, including members of the military, and forced him into exile.
- Less than ten years after the British left India, a Baptist preacher from Georgia, the Reverend Dr. Martin Luther King, Jr., following Gandhi's teachings, led his fellow African Americans on a fifteen-year campaign of marches and boycotts to overthrow racial segregation in the American South.
- A few years after Dr. King was assassinated, Polish dissidents defied communist rule by initiating new forms of social action rarely seen in the Soviet bloc. Later workers struck and won the right to organize, giving rise to Solidarity and eventually the end of communism.
- As change was brewing in Poland, a group of Argentine mothers, outraged by their government's silence about the disappearance of their sons, started marching in the central plaza of Buenos Aires. They did not stop until the legitimacy of the country's military junta was undermined, leading to its downfall after the debacle of the Falklands War.

- As the generals fell in Argentina, General Augusto Pinochet, across the Andes in Chile, faced a surging popular movement that mounted a series of protests of his dictatorship. Ultimately they overturned him through a plebiscite he was not supposed to lose.
- Half a world away, after Ferdinand Marcos stole an election in the Philippines in 1986, the widow of an assassinated opposition leader led hundreds of thousands into the streets. Supporting a rebellion by reform-minded military officers, they deprived the dictator of any chance to hold power by force, and he fled the country.
- Not long after Filipinos reclaimed their democracy, Palestinians challenged Israeli military occupation of the West Bank and Gaza by organizing protests and boycotts and by building their own network of social services. This wave of nonviolent resistance became the largest if least visible part of the *intifada*.
- While Solidarity continued its fight, boycott organizers, trade unions, and religious leaders in South Africa joined to wage a nonviolent campaign against apartheid. Along with international sanctions, they helped force the freeing of Nelson Mandela and negotiations for a democratic future.
- Days after the Berlin Wall fell, thousands of Czech students sat down at the edge of Wenceslas Square in Prague chanting, "We have no weapons . . . The world is watching." In weeks the communist regime and others like it in East Germany, Hungary, Bulgaria, and even Mongolia were gone.
- In the 1990s a Burmese mother, Aung San Suu Kyi, led her country's democracy movement while under house arrest, as young Burmese were bolstered in their struggle by a new worldwide cohort of nonviolent activists and practitioners.
- In 1999-2000, a student-led resistance movement, with support from pro-democratic groups abroad, and a unified political opposition mobilized to defeat President Slobodan Milosevic at the polls. With his security forces neutralized by a nonviolent uprising, and facing a general strike, Europe's last dictator capitulated.

The potential for victory without violence was present in all these conflicts, and the interplay among each story's vivid characters determined whether it was realized. From a German steel baron to a Chilean photographer, from Leo Tolstoy to Desmond Tutu, and from a Danish king to a Tennessee mayor: They, and dozens more with whom these stories are studded, all played a part. It is, after all, the words and works of individuals that we recount: the passion of those who sparked or led the campaigns; the arrogance, guile, and eventual disgrace of the autocrats they overcame; and the native genius, foolish blunders, and stunning sacrifice seen throughout the century's cavalcade of "people power."

In 1936 Mohandas Gandhi was visited by a well-known African American minister and his wife, who asked him at one point whether nonviolent resistance was "a form of direct action." Gandhi replied vigorously, "It is not one form, it is the only form . . . It is the greatest and the activist force in the world . . . It is a force which is more positive than electricity, and more powerful than even ether." It was as if he conceived of it, not as the product of beliefs, but as a kind of science with laws to be applied, yielding power that was predictable.[3]

It is often assumed that the choice of nonviolent resistance is made for moral reasons, but the historical record suggests otherwise. Most who used nonviolent action in the twentieth century did so because military or physical force was not a viable option. Some simply lacked sufficient arms to mount a violent revolt; others had recently seen a violent insurrection fail, with devastating results for life and property. But since people's most vital interests were at stake, and because they were determined to take down the rulers or laws that withheld their rights, they were impelled to take up other, nonviolent weapons. Those who used nonviolent action in our stories did not come to make peace. They came to fight.

The Conflicts

Before, during, and after the great ocean-spanning wars of the last century, a series of other conflicts took place, not between nations but within them, and not about conquest or ideology but about self-determination, freedom from domination by one party or racial group, and democracy. These conflicts have been overshadowed in the news and entertainment media and thus in our collective memory by wars, genocide, carpet bombing, and terror. But the nonviolent sanctions used in the stories we tell may be far more pertinent to the strategy and tactics of conflicts in the twenty-first century than were battles in the trenches against the German kaiser, naval showdowns in the Pacific, or guerrilla fighting in the jungles of Indochina.

This book is not a comprehensive history of all the century's clashes in which nonviolent action played a part. Instead each of the stories is emblematic of how nonviolent sanctions can be the cutting edge of a strategy to undermine and displace a seemingly intractable opponent. And through all these conflicts can be traced the century-long progression of ideas about nonviolent power and practice. The first three parts of the book are organized to show how nonviolent action was used in three major types of conflict.

Part I, Movement to Power, tells how nonviolent sanctions were pivotal in three of the century's great nation-changing popular movements for self-rule: the campaigns against imperial dynasty in turn-of-the-century Russia, against British colonial command of India, and against the Soviet-style system in Poland.

Part II, Resistance to Terror, shows how civilian resisters confronted military occupiers or rulers in midcentury, when state violence reached a crescendo. It tells how Germans hindered the invading French and Belgians in the 1920s, how Danes and other Europeans under German occupation subverted the Nazis during World War II, and how the Salvadoran people ousted General Martínez in 1944. And it traces how Argentines and Chileans weakened rulers who also wore uniforms and terrorized their people, in the 1970s and 1980s.

Part III, Campaigns for Rights, charts how, in the second half of the century, nonviolent sanctions were used against a variety of governments to obtain specific rights: how the American civil rights movement opened the fist of segregation in the American South, how the black majority in South Africa upended apartheid, how Filipinos ejected a dictator and restored democracy, how the Palestinians confronted Israeli control of the Occupied Territories, and how popular forces in China, Eastern Europe, and Mongolia contested the one-party regimes in their countries.

Part IV, Violence and Power, examines two reverse cases, in which movements that opted for violent insurrection or terror often spawned far more social chaos and political losses than they reaped power. It also explores how advanced technology, international sanctions, and other changing conditions may empower or limit those who use nonviolent power in the twenty-first century.

Along the spine of each story is a series of engagements between those who use nonviolent action and their adversaries. Some of our stories are about slow-building movements that display great momentum and dexterity in the use of nonviolent power but forsake short-term gains for long-term dreams. Other stories are about rapidly organized campaigns headed by brilliant amateurs who seem to triumph quickly against all odds. But in all cases, it is the strategy inherent in each side's choice of sanctions that decides its fate.

The continuity represented by these stories was not visible only at the century's end. The leaders who drove events often learned from earlier experience. Gandhi was inspired by what happened in Russia in 1905. African American leaders traveled to India to study Gandhi's tactics. When Chileans organized against the dictatorship of General Augusto Pinochet in the 1980s, and Filipinos organized against Ferdinand Marcos, they were influenced by Richard Attenborough's motion picture *Gandhi.*

Gandhi confronted the British raj, an adversary quite different from the German Wehrmacht faced by the Danes. Civil rights leaders in America had the law and U.S. Constitution on their side, an advantage not available to Solidarity in Poland. Yet all the nonviolent protagonists in these conflicts adopted remarkably similar approaches to secure different objectives, and their experience yields lessons that flout the conventional wisdom:

- The use of nonviolent sanctions has been far more frequent and widespread than usually supposed. They were crucial elements of history-making struggles in every part of the world and in every decade of the century.
- Nonviolent action has worked against all types of oppressive opponents— and there is no correlation between the degree of violence used against nonviolent resisters and the likelihood of their eventual success. Some who faced the greatest brutality prevailed decisively.
- A nonviolent movement's potential for success degenerates when it tries to incorporate violence into its strategy. Once a regime is attacked with deadly force, its ability to rally internal support and apply repression is enhanced.
- Mobilizing and maintaining a popular movement geared to nonviolent action go hand in hand with strengthening a civil society and establishing or sustaining democracy.

Notwithstanding these realities, the popular mind has persistently held onto two misconceptions of nonviolent conflict. First, since the century's two most celebrated leaders of nonviolent movements—Gandhi and Martin Luther King, Jr.—emerged from religious callings, nonviolent action has been stereotyped as a moral preference rather than a pragmatic choice, thereby obscuring its strategic value in conflicts. Second, since the fall of Marcos in 1986, news coverage of mass nonviolent action has left the impression that "people power" comes from the size or energy of crowds who agitate in city streets. While physically confronting an opponent can be necessary, the true rhythm of effective nonviolent action is less spontaneous than it is intentional, less theatrical than technical. It has little to do with shouting slogans and putting flowers in gun barrels. It has everything to do with separating governments from their means of control.

Many predict that the twenty-first century will feature a procession of fierce but parochial conflicts, in which irredentists try to seize old lands, ethnic partisans strive for independence, or aggrieved minorities seek a place at the table. Yet any provincial interest usually is voiced as the desire for rights. The great democracies believe that if power is predicated on self-government, rights can be freely petitioned. If assuring democracy is always the answer, what should have greater priority, freezing in place the parties to a conflict or promoting ways to engage in conflict so that it is more likely to yield a democratic outcome?

In a world in which vital human interests are in constant competition, conflicts will occur, and violence will be used in conflicts as long as people believe it will help them win. If another, more effective way to succeed, without the costs of violence, were more widely appreciated, violence would begin to seem less sensible as the way to fight for a cause. Most policymakers have been enamored of either arms reduction or conflict resolution as the primary methods of reducing deadly violence, assuming that all conflicts are prone to be violent. But in each of more than a dozen major conflicts in the twentieth century between two sides vying for control of a nation's destiny, strategic nonviolent action rather than violence was the decisive mode of engagement. Since violence can be supplanted as the means of conflict, the goal of curtailing violence need not always be encumbered by the separate task of resolving a conflict's cause.

"Capable of Wielding Great Power"

This book is an account of how the people of the twentieth century developed the ability to take power without using violence. Each of our stories focuses on the use of nonviolent action in a larger conflict. To show what nonviolent power accomplished, we have necessarily chosen to highlight certain events and individuals more important for our stories than they were for the full histories of their time or place. But we have not consciously understated the impact of other people or episodes that were significant in a broader historical context. We do not, for example, presume to give a complete history of how apartheid fell in South Africa. We do venture to provide a fair and instructive report of how nonviolent action was used to help make that happen.

All works of history are influenced by the perspectives of their writers, and ours is no exception. In parts I, II, and III we have tried to let the facts speak for themselves and to reserve most of our analytical thoughts for the concluding section of each chapter. The book's final part represents a blend of expository material and interpretive ideas about the larger questions raised by the way that nonviolent action has transformed the world. We make no apology for having a point of view: Nonviolent sanctions, if used effectively, can end oppression and liberate nations and peoples, and they can do so with less risk and more certainty than resorting to violent revolt or terror. But they have not always worked, and this book does not avoid mention of those moments when they are relevant to our stories.

We also believe that nonviolent resistance deserves more attention than it has generally received. In our time violence generates more news because, for many, history is perceived as a spectacle. But if it were understood more commonly as a process, then the dynamic effect of nonviolent sanctions would be more easily appreciated. This form of power is not arcane; it operates on the same level of reality that most people live their lives, and it is comprehensible for that reason. Contrary to cynical belief, the history of nonviolent action is not a succession of desperate idealists, occasional martyrs, and a few charismatic emancipators. The real story is about common citizens who are drawn into great causes, which are built from the ground up. It is about people staying home from work or occupying their factories and offices, refusing to carry identity papers, printing newsletters in their basements, and not leaving when they are told to go.

Indians who broke the British salt monopoly, Danes who obstructed Nazi military shipments, Chileans who organized against dictatorship: Many who used nonviolent action instinctively recognized that power derived from what *they* did, not only from what was done by those who sat in palaces or presidential mansions. In the words of the great theoretician of nonviolent power, Gene Sharp, "Nonviolent action is possible, and is capable of wielding great power even against ruthless rulers and military regimes, because it attacks the most vulnerable characteristic of all hierarchical institutions and governments: dependence on the governed."[4]

At the end of the last century, the world's airwaves and bookstores were full of material that looked back at what was called the most destructive hundred years in history. In reel after reel, and on page after page, we were shown the carnage, the awful cost, it was said, of defeating evil. But told only that way, the history of the century's conflicts would reinforce a terrible fallacy: that only violence can overcome violence, that the struggles with the highest stakes have to be settled by force of arms. Yet if that were true, how was it possible that in the same century, rulers and oppressors having every conceivable advantage in violent force were pushed aside on every continent by people who did *not* resort to violence?

The greatest misconception about conflict is that violence is always the ultimate form of power, that no other method of advancing a just cause or defeating injustice can surpass it. But Russians, Indians, Poles, Danes, Salvadorans, African Americans, Chileans, South Africans, and many others have proven that one side's choices in a conflict are not foreclosed by the other side's use of violence, that other, nonviolent measures can be a force more powerful. If the great sacrifice of lives and honor exacted by the last century is requited in the next one hundred years, it will be because that truth becomes more fully understood.

PART ONE

MOVEMENT TO POWER

Even so tyrants . . . the more is given them, the more they are obeyed, so much the more do they fortify themselves, become stronger and more able to annihilate and destroy. If nothing be given them, if they be not obeyed, without fighting, without striking a blow, they remain naked, disarmed and are nothing—like as the root of a tree, receiving no moisture or nourishment, becomes dry and dead.

—Etienne de la Boétie, 1577

CHAPTER ONE

Russia, 1905: The People Strike

The Silent Tanks

IN THE DARKNESS OF A SUNDAY NIGHT, in the second summer after the Cold War was over and when Russia was at peace, Major Sergei Evdokimov was awakened by the clanging of an emergency alarm. By three in the morning he was with his armored unit, based outside Moscow, waiting for instructions. They were not long in coming. As the eastern sky began to pale, Evdokimov's battalion commander ordered them to motor down the Minsk highway into Moscow and take up positions blocking two bridges across the Moscow River, which meanders through the center of the city. There were no explanations, but the major and his men followed orders without question—even when they pointed force at the civilian heart of Russia. So at eight o'clock sharp that Monday morning on August 19, 1991, Evdokimov signaled his column of tanks to move out.[1]

In the same dawn, Valerii Zavorotnyi, a computer scientist from Leningrad, was awakened by his ringing phone. "Gorbachev has been arrested," said the voice on the other end. "Emergency rule has been introduced." Zavorotnyi turned on his television and found classical music playing on all three channels, a familiar sign from years past that a major state event had occurred. Later an announcer came on and read "an Appeal to the Soviet People," issued by a group of high officials calling themselves the State Committee for the State of Emergency. "Compatriots, Citizens of the Soviet Union," it began, "a mortal danger looms large over our great Motherland." The Committee promised to end the "crisis" facing the country, and its "Resolution No. 1" banned strikes and demonstrations, asserted control over the mass media, and suspended the activities of parties and organizations that interfered with "normalization."[2]

All across the vast country, people awoke to the same news, delivered by telephone, by jittery neighbors, by radio and television. But no one was terribly surprised. For months there had been rumors that hard-line communists were preparing a coup to reverse the political and economic reforms introduced by Soviet President Mikhail Gorbachev. Now, it appeared, the nightmare had come true. The breathing room given to Soviet citizens over the last five years was about to be revoked, at gunpoint.

No sooner had the coup leaders begun issuing commands, however, than people disobeyed them. The first to do so was Gorbachev himself, who, after refusing to give his approval to the State of Emergency, was held prisoner at his summer home. Boris Yeltsin, the elected president of the Russian Federation, was not so easily contained. Eluding the KGB officer sent to arrest him, Yeltsin raced to the White House, the headquarters of his government. At noon he climbed on top of a tank outside and read his own appeal, addressed to the "Russian People," declaring all acts of the junta illegal and calling for a nationwide general strike. Then he went on the radio: "At this difficult hour of decision," he reminded the country's soldiers, "remember that you have taken an oath to your people, and your weapons cannot be turned against the people . . . The honor of Russian arms will not be covered with the blood of the people."[3]

By what he did as well as what he said, Yeltsin urged defiance of the coup. By early afternoon Muscovites were holding small demonstrations outside the Kremlin walls and posting photocopies of Yeltsin's appeal in the Metro. Soon men and women converged on the White House and built barricades out of construction materials, phone booths, and anything else they could lay their hands on. Cab drivers even donated their cars to fortify the ramparts.

When a line of tanks rumbled down Kalinin Prospekt on its way to the White House, people formed a human chain across the road. "Be with the People!" they yelled. "Don't shoot at your own people!" An old man shouted, "I've worked my whole life, you see, all my life I've paid for this army, and now you've turned against me, you're shooting at me." The argument carried the moment; the commander cut off his engine, and the other tanks in the convoy followed suit. People climbed all over them, offering candy, bread, and milk to the soldiers inside.

When Major Evdokimov and his company pulled up near the Kalininskii Bridge, right by the White House, they learned about the coup from people putting up barricades. A few demonstrators swore at them, calling them fascists, and others, including an acquaintance of the major, tried to convince him to defect to Yeltsin's side. The thirty-six-year-old career military officer was not sure what to do. It was no easy thing to contemplate disobeying orders; but he had made up his mind on the way downtown that he would not attack unarmed civilians. "I'm going to stay here, I've received an order," he declared. "But we will not shoot or crush anyone. I give my word."[4]

For several hours Evdokimov and his men stayed put. Around seven in the evening, a deputy from the Russian parliament appeared and asked the major to come talk to Vice President Aleksandr Rutskoi, a veteran of the war in Afghanistan, who was organizing the defense of the White House. Rutskoi told him about Gorbachev's arrest and Yeltsin's call to disobey the junta, and he asked him to help protect the White House. "Give me an order," Evdokimov replied. "We'll help." With that Evdokimov went back out to his company and led the tanks, now flying the Russian tricolor, rather than the Soviet hammer and sickle, through the cheering crowd to the White House.

Many journalists also refused to knuckle under. On Monday evening the junta held its first (and last) press conference. Tatiana Malkina, a young reporter, raised her hand and, with one question, destroyed the veil of legality that the junta was struggling to create. "Could you please say whether or not you understand that last night you carried out a coup d'état?" That night the whole country heard about the barricades in Moscow and Yeltsin's appeal on the tank from a five-minute report on an official news program, *Vremia*. Banned newspapers got the news out by faxing reports to activists, who distributed them on the streets.

The coup plotters expected that a show of force would unnerve any opposition. Indeed, most people, even the majority in Moscow and Leningrad, were passive; they went on with their daily lives, enjoyed their vacations, and paid scant attention to the news. Yeltsin's call for a national strike met with little response. But enough people came to the White House, as similar strongholds of resistance materialized in other cities, so that the junta was denied the acquiescence it needed. By posting leaflets, going to rallies, building barricades, and scrawling graffiti on tanks, these ordinary citizens showed that they would not be intimidated.

On Tuesday around 100,000 people were emboldened to go to a rally at the White House; by then more military units had joined the shield around the building. High military commanders, such as Pavel Grachev and Aleksandr Lebed, declared their support for Yeltsin, and even top KGB officers made it clear they would not take part in a bloodbath. In the end, the junta never ordered the attack prepared for Tuesday night. By early Wednesday the coup had collapsed.

The men and women who took to the streets in August 1991 had written a new chapter in the long Russian struggle to make government reflect the people's will. Although many of them may not have known it, they were not the first Russians to throw up civilian barricades in central Moscow and dispute arbitrary rule. Eighty years earlier, just a flew blocks from where the White House now stands, at the end of a year-long popular upheaval that shook the government of Tsar Nicholas II, Muscovites by the thousands had confronted armed soldiers in December 1905. But when they brandished guns, the troops mowed them down, killing scores—and stalling Russia's first democratic revolution. Until that moment, Russia had been the scene of the century's first sustained use of nonviolent action to achieve basic rights. But it started as it ended: on a day of violence.

BLOODY SUNDAY

The Priest and the Workers

On a cold, clear Sunday morning in January 1905, in the industrial outskirts of St. Petersburg, a young long-haired priest stood before several thousand factory workers. Father Georgii Gapon read a prayer, said a blessing over everyone, and then asked if anyone was armed. When the answer was no, he was pleased: "Good. We will go unarmed to our Tsar." A little after eleven, the crowd set off for the center of town, singing prayers as it went. In the front row, marchers carried a cross, icons, portraits of the country's rulers, and a banner reading "Soldiers! Do not shoot the people!" Their destination was the royal family's Winter Palace, where they would be joined by similar processions from other points in the city, over 100,000 in all. Then, on the spacious, classically proportioned square outside the palace, in the heart of the capital of the Russian empire, they would present a petition to Nicholas II.[5]

The petition they carried, entitled "A Most Humble and Loyal Address," had been drafted by Gapon. "We, the workers and inhabitants of St. Petersburg," it began, " . . . come to Thee, O Sire, to seek justice and protection. We are impoverished; we are oppressed, overburdened . . . Do not turn Thy help away from Thy people . . . Allow them to determine their own future; deliver them from the intolerable oppression of the officialdom. Raze the wall that separates Thee from Thy people and rule the country with them . . . "[6]

Gapon's followers were approaching their ruler not in revolt but in supplication. The petition listed more than a dozen requests, such as a minimum wage and an eight-hour day, yet it looked beyond workers' grievances and also embraced a political agenda that would touch every person in the empire. It called for freedom of speech, press, worship, and association;

the release of all political prisoners; and equality before the law for all people. Most important, it called for a constituent assembly, elected by universal and equal suffrage. "This is our principal request, upon which everything else depends," the petition insisted.

In effect, the marchers were asking the Tsar to dissolve an entire era of Russian history. Article 1 of the Fundamental Laws of the Russian Empire, still in effect in 1905, defined it succinctly: "To the Emperor of all the Russias belongs the supreme autocratic and unlimited power." A good Tsar would consult with his subjects and take their interests to heart, but he would not share his power with the people, or let it be constrained by civil liberties that would stand regardless of his will. His subjects felt the hand of the state everywhere: Censors decided what appeared in newspapers and journals, governors could order anyone detained without trial, and associations or clubs of the most innocent kind could be forbidden. Autocracy, in short, meant that there were no rights.

The Tsar's love for this system was more than a desire for personal power; he believed he had a divine mandate, reflected in hallowed traditions. Russia had industrial workers and capitalist entrepreneurs, modern political thinkers and artistic movements, but Nicholas surrounded himself with the trappings of an earlier time. He insisted that official documents use archaic spelling, and he held costume balls where everyone wore replicas of two-hundred-year-old outfits. He preferred to spend time in Moscow, with its traditional wooden architecture and winding streets, rather than among the massive stone palaces in the newer, more European St. Petersburg. In his imagination if not in reality, Nicholas stood before his subjects like a father before his children, bound by mutual affection and obligation before God.[7]

But some Russians wanted to sweep away that fantasy, and much of educated society had hungered for political change for the better part of a century. Beginning with a rebellion by military officers in 1825, small groups had from time to time hatched conspiracies to liberate the country from absolutism. The "People's Will" had managed to assassinate Tsar Alexander II in 1881 (Nicholas, then thirteen, had seen his grandfather die), and a new terrorist group, the "Battle Organization" of the Socialist Revolutionary (SR) Party, had become active after the turn of the century.

Other radicals rejected terrorism and tried instead to organize peasants or workers for popular uprisings. Marxist ideas tempted many young people, and socialists had agitated among workers in St. Petersburg, Moscow, and elsewhere since the 1890s. Still others were bent on persuading the government to reform itself. In the first years of the new century, a liberal movement emerged among many landowners, professionals, and intellectuals, who used public meetings and publications, both legal and illegal, to call for a constitution and some form of representative government.

Thus the demands in Father Gapon's petition—free unions, civil liberties, democracy—had all appeared before, in the appeals of revolutionary and liberal groups. What made the Gapon petition unprecedented was that tens of thousands of people took to the streets to show they supported it. For the first time demands for an end to autocracy came from an incipient mass movement rather than from educated circles. But the movement was also, ironically, aided by the state's own policies.

One of the policymakers was Sergei Zubatov, head of the political police in Moscow. Zubatov, who had once consorted with radicals and then been a police spy, feared that the state would lose ground to revolutionaries in the battle for workers' allegiance. He attacked the complacent view, popular among top officials, that since Russia's workers came mostly from peasant families, they would reflect the conservatism commonly found in the countryside. Strikes in St. Petersburg, and the involvement of Marxist activists in organizing them, collapsed this myth and provoked Zubatov to come up with a novel plan. He argued to his bosses that workers had real complaints, that their loyalty would last only as long as they believed that the state was not the enemy—and he won approval from the Ministry of Interior for state-sponsored mutual aid societies among workers in several cities, under the supervision of police agents. The state, not the revolutionaries, would lead workers to a brighter future.

Zubatov's strategy proved to be explosive. His associations became embroiled in disputes between workers and employers and actually organized strikes in a number of places. Outraged employers complained bitterly to V. K. Plehve, the Minister of the Interior, who transferred Zubatov to St. Petersburg late in 1902. But Zubatov was not to be deterred, and he established a new organization in the capital, the St. Petersburg Mutual Aid Society of Workers in the Machine Industry.[8]

One of the young men attracted to that society was a twenty-eight-year old worker by the name of N. M. Varnashev. From the age of twelve he had been working in factories in a city that had been flooded during the past decade by thousands of rural migrants who had put down their plows and taken up the tools of industry. Most of these workers were barely literate and still quite rustic, and they were crammed into tenements and grim barracks. But there were no unions to look out for their interests, and strikes were illegal and therefore risky. Still, some felt the yearning for something better.[9]

Often while daydreaming at his lathe, Varnashev would ask himself, "And what should become of you, if you lose this job and you can't immediately find a new one? And if you get hurt, or you grow sick and exhausted in your old age?"

Unlike many of his fellow workers, Varnashev took the time to think about his situation; he was an avid reader and saw himself as an urban, even cosmopolitan man. As a skilled metal worker, he was among the best paid in the city, and he had managed to find rooms near the city's statelier neighborhoods. He had even spent some of his earnings on a newfangled device called a bicycle.[10]

One autumn day in 1902, Varnashev (who was still learning to ride) pedaled over to visit his friend and co-worker Stepanov, who lived across the Neva River. After a few scrapes on his hands and knees and one collision with an apple-seller, Varnashev arrived at his friend's apartment. There he was introduced to a man named Kladovikov, who told him about a plan brewing among workers to organize a mutual aid fund, similar to one in Moscow. Kladovikov invited him to its second meeting, to be held the next week—and with that small step Varnashev started down a path that would bring him, together with thousands of other St. Petersburg workers, into open conflict with the government of Tsar Nicholas II.[11]

One of the leaders whom Zubatov had recruited for the St. Petersburg society was Georgii Gapon, who had arrived in the capital a few years earlier from his native province, after the death of his wife. Gapon, who came from a peasant family, showed a great concern for the poor people he met in the city, and while studying at the Theological Academy, had worked at an orphanage. His growing popularity among the city's less fortunate eventually came to Zubatov's attention.[12]

Gapon was a charismatic and complicated character. His personal charm helped him win the trust of almost everyone he met, from Tsarist officials to their seditious opponents. His sermons could reduce listeners to tears, and his eyes "burned with some inner light." Generous to the workers he met at the Zubatov society, he treated them without the condescension shown by many revolutionary intellectuals. But Gapon's passion was not harnessed to a disciplined sense of purpose. He had an impulsive and mercurial personality, which led him repeatedly to betray the trust that he persuaded others to place in him.[13]

Gapon had become a regular at meetings of the Zubatov society, listening carefully, encouraging workers to speak their minds, and occasionally offering a comment. By the spring of 1903 he had made friends with a few of the key members, including Varnashev, who urged him to take a more active role. But Gapon had declined, and many St. Petersburg workers were too leery of the authorities to join an organization operating under police control. By late 1903 the society was moribund. Gapon, Varnashev, and a few others, however, were busy setting up a new organization, which they called the Assembly of Russian Factory and Mill Workers in the City of St. Petersburg.

Like the Zubatov societies, the Assembly enjoyed the approval of officials, who saw it as something that might divert workers' attention from labor conflict and agitation by revolutionaries. In one crucial respect, however, it was different: Gapon convinced officials that the presence of police agents had deterred workers from joining the society in St. Petersburg, and they agreed to keep the police out of day-to-day operations of the Assembly. Gapon alone would oversee its affairs and guarantee that workers' energies were channeled in wholesome directions.[14]

The priest's initial intentions were probably not political. Earlier he had mingled with dockworkers on the city's wharves. "They got to trust me," he said later, "and some of them confessed to having become infected with political ideas. I did not at that time think that political change was necessary." Patriotism motivated the Assembly, he explained in a memorandum to the police: "Essentially the basic idea is to build a nest among the factory and mill workers," he told them. "From thence healthy and self-sacrificing fledglings could fly forth to defend their tsar and country and aid their fellow workers."[15]

The Assembly's leaders, known as the Responsible Circle, were mostly skilled, married, and relatively well-off metal workers. They set up a clubhouse in an industrial district, and members brought in furniture and books, found a cheap piano, and hung a portrait of the Tsar. Some nights there would be meetings, on others there were lectures, concerts, or dancing, or people just sat around reading or playing chess. The Assembly also organized a mutual aid fund and represented members in disputes with employers. Unlike the Zubatov societies, however, the Assembly steered clear of strikes. It seemed on the surface to be about anything except politics, justifying the confidence that officials placed in Gapon's judgment and reliability.[16]

These same officials, however, would have been appalled had they known what was going on behind this façade of self-help. While Gapon's early views oscillated between personal allegiance to the Tsar and disapproval of autocracy, the catalyst for entangling the Assembly in politics was someone else: Aleksei Karelin, a self-educated lithographer and former member of the Marxist Russian Social Democratic (SD) Workers' Party, who had been arrested and exiled for a time in the 1890s. Karelin and his associates had become disenchanted with the SD's tactics and welcomed the chance the Assembly offered to reach workers under legal cover and without fear of police harassment. They brought with them years of organizational experience and, in Varnashev's words, "unshakeable authority" among the city's factory workers, an influence that Gapon did not yet enjoy.[17]

After some initial distrust, Gapon eventually won the confidence of Karelin and the other radicals, just as he had the regime's officials. After meetings of the Responsible Circle, around ten at night, Gapon would invite a smaller number of workers, including the Karelin group, to his apartment, where they smoked, drank tea, and talked. In these midnight sessions, Gapon showed that he was inching toward the politically subversive views of the new members, who took key posts in the Assembly.[18]

In March 1904, Gapon invited Karelin, Varnashev, and two other members of the Assembly's inner circle to his apartment, swore them to secrecy, and pulled out a sheet of paper. On it was written, in red ink, a program for political and social change in the Russian empire. Political demands included civil liberties, equality of everyone before the law, and the "immediate pardon of all those who suffered for their convictions." Social demands included legalization of trade unions, an eight-hour work-day, a minimum wage, worker participation in drafting social insurance laws, and land redistribution for peasants. This was the sort of program that the Karelin clique had been urging on Gapon, and it was accepted as the Assembly's "Secret Program."[19]

"Senseless Dreams"

The "Secret Program" built a bridge between the workers and a broader opposition stirring in St. Petersburg. For over a decade, people of property and learning had been offering polite criticism of the government, advocating reform in journals and other sedate forums. But in 1904 the liberal movement had started reaching out to other potential opponents of the regime. This became evident at two congresses, of educators and doctors. With their doors opened to students and workers, these meetings were quickly turned into political forums. Speakers called for civil liberties and the right to unionize. The police closed the education congress and arrested its organizers, and the doctors' congress ended in chaos when participants, angry that it was being closed early, threw chairs at a military band that tried to drown out their protests.[20]

As this happened, delegates were arriving in the capital for the first congress of the Union of Liberation, an unlikely alliance between wealthy noblemen and radical intellectuals. The aristocrats had spent years trying to turn provincial (*zemstvo*) assemblies into a springboard for constitutional reform. Not only had Nicholas ignored all their appeals, he had labeled them "senseless dreams." But futility can inspire a change in methods, and a number of former revolutionaries, who had dropped the Marxist belief in class struggle, also were ready to join this new movement. "Our task is not to divide but to unite," said the mission statement of the Liberationists' journal.[21]

In 1904 two events had helped galvanize latent discontent and awaken a readiness for change among educated, upper-class Russians. At the end of January, the Japanese attacked Russia's Pacific fleet at Port Arthur, culminating years of rivalry between the two countries in the Far East. Almost immediately, the war brought a string of humiliating defeats for Russia, exposing the technical backwardness of the military and the ineptitude of its commanders. Public opinion, already frustrated by the regime's rigidity and repressiveness, now chewed on military disaster as another rag of complaint.

Amid this brewing disaffection, terrorists had assassinated Plehve, the widely hated minister of the interior, in July. His replacement, Prince Sviatopolk-Mirskii, recognized the chasm of hostility that yawned between the government and the country's elite, and felt strongly that the government must "make peace" with moderates. Word of Mirskii's conciliatory attitude had raised hope that reform might be possible, while his relaxation of control over public life gave liberals fresh opportunities to speak out and organize. In this newly enlarged political theater, the Liberationists took center stage.[22]

After staking out a wider tent for opposition with the simple demand for representative, constitutional government, they now enlisted prominent leaders in the zemstvo assemblies to get behind this position. The First Zemstvo Congress, held in Moscow in early November, passed a resolution favoring a national assembly with real powers, which went against the very essence of the autocracy.[23]

To diversify the movement and also provide innocuous cover for dissent, the Liberationists organized a series of banquets in cities across the empire, beginning in late November, to mark the fortieth anniversary of judicial reform. "There were more than 600 diners—writers, lawyers, 'zemstvo men,' in general, the intelligentsia," the prominent writer Maxim Gorkii said in a letter to his wife about one banquet. "Outspoken speeches were made, and people chanted in unison, 'Down with the autocracy!' 'Long live the constituent assembly!' and 'Give us a constitution' . . . It was all very heated and very democratic." Everywhere the banquets deepened the passion for change and gave many their first exposure to uninhibited speech.[24]

Having reached out to moderate liberals on its right and to its own natural constituency of urban professionals, the Liberationists now extended a hand to the socialists. To do this, the Union committed itself to a fully democratic rather than merely constitutional reform program. By the end of the year, the Liberationists could justifiably claim to speak for a wide cross-section of Russian society, including many of the country's most respected citizens.[25]

Nicholas seemed oblivious to the mounting disquiet. The Tsar spent his days immersed in court ceremonies and petty administrative matters, and since he was wont to appoint officials on the basis of personal manners and connections to the imperial court, the government tended to pitch back and forth from one policy to another, as ministers gained and lost the Tsar's favor. But his interior minister was well-focused on the causes of dissension, and he worked out a plan to deal with it. "As I see it," Mirskii told the Tsar, "the aspirations of the huge majority of well-intentioned people are . . . to establish Russian legality, broad tolerance of beliefs, and participation in legislative work in order to prevent the issuing of laws that are totally unsuitable or issued at some minister's whim." At the end of November he sent the Tsar a reform package, proposing an expanded franchise for zemstvo elections, the lifting of pre-publication censorship, and, above all, creation of an elected consultative assembly. None of these, Mirskii believed, would unravel the basic fabric of Tsarist rule, but the reforms would be sufficient to split the opposition and quiet the outcry for political change.[26]

But the decree Nicholas finally issued on December 12 fell far short of Mirskii's suggestions. Instead of guaranteeing reform, it offered vague promises to consider certain changes and left out any mention of an assembly; "never, under any circumstances, will I agree to a representative form of government," the Tsar insisted. The next day a second decree threatened repression if there were any further public disturbances or anti-government demonstrations. Mirskii submitted his resignation and told the Tsar, "it is inconceivable to run the country without the support of societal forces."[27]

Shutting the door on moderates and their hopes for orderly progress toward a reformed system, the December edicts also exposed the limits of the Liberationists' strategy. As long as the Tsar believed that he could disregard what his most respected citizens thought, and as long as he was adamantly opposed to any weakening of autocratic powers, then protest alone, no matter how articulate or loud, would not produce meaningful reform. It was not enough to object to the autocracy; the opposition had to push the regime to change. What the Tsar, his ministers, and their liberal opponents alike did not recognize as the year faded was that a new form of power was quickening under their very feet, one that, like a surprising winter thaw, would dissolve the ice on which they stood in the new year.

"To Be Heard . . . by All of Russia"

Compared to the conspicuous dissent of lawyers, professors, landowners, and intellectuals, the efforts of Father Gapon and his friends to build their Assembly had created hardly a ripple. Yet beneath the waterline of events, the Assembly had grown apace: By the fall, it had over 7,000 members and eleven district branches, all the while keeping on its apolitical public face—even as the turbulent waves in political thought that had washed over educated society broke over the Assembly. Newspapers reported on the country's shameful military defeats and on the political demands made by the Union of Liberation, the Zemstvo Congress, and, eventually, the banquet campaign. "All this," wrote Varnashev, "gave the Assembly's branches fully legal and gratifying material for agitation

Father Georgii Gapon, members of the Assembly of Russian Factory and Mill Workers,
and the mayor of St. Petersburg, 1905.

Credit: ©David King Collection

and propaganda." Liberationists came to the Assembly to read lectures, and several of them met privately with Gapon. Both the Karelin group and the liberals urged the same thing: Workers must join the campaign against the autocracy.[28]

On November 28, the evening after a bloody assault by soldiers on student demonstrators, about thirty-five people, including leaders of the Assembly's district branches, crammed into Gapon's stuffy, dimly lit apartment. The priest introduced his "Secret Program" and asked those who differed with it to leave the meeting and keep silent. Many who stayed wanted to take immediate, dramatic action rather than only issue a statement or send a delegation to the government. "But all agreed on one idea," Varnashev remembered. "If the workers were to add their voice, then it should be done in such a way as to be heard not only by the government, but by all of Russia." So they decided that Gapon should work out the content for a petition and devise some way to present it in public.[29]

The meeting in Gapon's apartment led to more debate rather than rapid action. But soon something unexpected happened to force the Assembly's hand. In early December four Assembly members who worked at the giant Putilov metal factory, the largest industrial plant in Russia, were fired or threatened with firing. Gapon took this as a challenge: If he could not get the workers reinstated, the organization's authority would be damaged, and it might be hit with other arbitrary measures. In the final days of December, Assembly leaders paid visits to the city's chief factory inspector, the director of the Putilov factory, and the city's governor. All but the governor greeted them rudely, and their demands were rejected. The only thing left was the sanction of last resort: a strike.[30]

On Sunday, January 2, 6,000 Putilov workers met at the Assembly's Narva branch and voted to strike the next day to protest the firings. By Tuesday they had closed down the plant and idled over 12,000 workers. Their demands: rehiring the fired workers, a board of workers' representatives to oversee pay rates, an eight-hour day, the end of overtime work, and free medical care. Putilov strikers began to make the rounds of other factories, and by the end of the week, over 110,000 workers at more than 400 factories in St. Petersburg had joined the strike.[31]

The Assembly leaders now saw a chance not merely to defend their organization but to take the offensive and put across their new political agenda. The timing could not have been better, since word of a new military failure— the fall of the naval fortress at Port Arthur—had just reached the capital, dropping the government's prestige to a new low. On Thursday, January 6, Gapon announced his plan: He would lead a peaceful but mammoth procession of strikers to the majestic square outside the Winter Palace, in the center of St. Petersburg, where they would present a petition to the Tsar himself. The march would take place that coming Sunday, January 9.[32]

Gapon's petition contained, essentially unchanged, the reform proposals of the "Secret Program" including civil liberties, the right to organize unions, and an eight-hour work-day. Gapon attached an introduction addressed to the Tsar, incorporating one further, cardinal demand: a representative assembly, elected by universal and equal suffrage. Reflecting the movement in Gapon's thinking over the previous year—under the influence of the Karelin group, liberal activists, and the exhilarating atmosphere of political unrest—this agenda came very close to the Liberationists' goal of a democratic political order.[33]

By midweek the Assembly's offices had become nerve centers of the strike. At the Vyborg branch, where Varnashev was in charge, packs of strikers jammed the office, and Assembly members helped them draft demands to present to their bosses. On Thursday branch leaders began to tell people about the procession and asked them to sign sheets of paper to be handed to the Tsar along with the petition. Assembly members mingled with strikers on the streets outside the offices to promote linking the fight for better working conditions to the larger movement for political rights. The discreet political lobbying that Varnashev and other Assembly leaders had done among the members since the previous spring was now paying off.[34]

An electric mood gripped strikers and Assembly leaders at meetings indoors all over the city during the next few days. "A kind of mystical, religious ecstasy reigned the whole time," wrote a Social Democrat of one meeting. "Thousands of people stood side by side for hours in the dreadful heat and closeness and thirstily devoured the artless, strikingly powerful, simple, and passionate speeches of their exhausted worker orators." At one branch a speaker asked the crowd, "And what, comrades, if the Ruler will not receive us and does not want to read our petition—how shall we answer this?" In response came a deafening roar: "Then we have no Tsar! . . . No Tsar! . . . No Tsar!"[35]

Nicholas did not hear of the restlessness until Wednesday. News of the planned procession reached the government on Thursday, and Gapon sent the petition in advance to various officials. The Tsar's ministers decided that under no circumstances would Nicholas personally receive the petition; in fact, he vacated the capital for his palace in nearby Tsarskoe Selo. They also opted not to declare martial law, since the minister of finance was negotiating with French and German bankers for a badly needed loan and wanted to avoid anything that might rattle potential lenders. Instead, the government planned an imposing show of military force, with troops blocking routes to the Winter Palace. They persuaded themselves that marchers would retreat when they saw soldiers barring the way, obviating the need for either concessions or bloodshed. On Saturday, a warning was posted that "no gatherings or processions on the streets will be tolerated, and . . . the most resolute measures prescribed by law will be used to avert mass disorders."[36]

On Saturday night Gapon, Varnashev, and others met to go over their preparations. Gapon was concerned that revolutionaries would try to co-opt the march, carrying red flags and provoking violence. So they decided to forbid the carrying of weapons, to deprive the regime of any excuse for a violent attack. Gapon wrote a letter to be delivered that night to the Tsar, guaranteeing his safety if he would come himself to receive the petition. But the leaders did make contingency plans in the case of violence and asked Karelin's wife to organize women members of the Assembly to care for the wounded. Finally, they went to a photographer and had their picture taken together.[37]

Aware that the procession could end in martyrdom, the planners exchanged the names of relatives to be informed in case they were killed and wrote parting letters to their families. "Niusha!" began the letter that Ivan Vasil'ev, chairman of the Assembly, left for his wife. "If I fail to return, and if I am killed, then, Niusha, do not cry . . . Raise Vaniura and tell him that I died a martyr for the freedom and happiness of the people." They were also braced for the loss of other marchers. "All clearly acknowledged their moral responsibility for the sacrifice in the making," Varnashev wrote about the Saturday night meeting, "because no one was under any doubt" that the authorities might use violence. "Better short-term, temporary suffering at an operation," wrote another, "than century-long pain."[38]

"The Beginning of the Popular Struggle"

Varnashev woke before dawn on Sunday, drank a cup of tea, said good-bye to his family, and set off for the Vyborg branch in the crisp, frigid air. When he got there, a swarm of people was waiting at the branch office. He told those who arrived before eleven to head for the Palace Square on their own, so they could make it before the bridges across the Neva River were blocked by troops. At noon he and the several hundred workers who arrived after eleven started off down Dvorianskaia Street, toward the palace.

As they approached the end of the street, they saw foot soldiers and cavalry waiting. When they had come within 500 paces, a signal sounded. With unsheathed sabres flashing in the sunlight, the horsemen charged and scattered the marchers into the cross streets. People scrambled over fences and unlocked the gates to courtyards, which filled with workers seeking refuge. When the horsemen had passed, Varnashev noticed about twenty people down on the street, hurriedly crawling to the sides, leaving behind caps and galoshes. Soon the horsemen were charging back down the street in the opposite direction, knocking down those who remained with the flat sides of their sabres. After about ten minutes, when it was apparent the troops had moved elsewhere, the courtyards began to empty out. Many left for home, while Varnashev and others started back toward the square, some crossing over the frozen Neva to bypass further skirmishes.[39]

Meanwhile Gapon was leading the largest group of marchers from the Assembly's Narva branch. At the bridge crossing the Tarakanovka River they were confronted by the 93rd Irkutsk Infantry Regiment, which had just arrived in town and been told that a revolutionary plot was afoot. The soldiers were nervous and became even more so when the lead marchers, ignoring the pleas of police to turn back, instead locked arms and advanced toward the troops. "The crowd moved toward the square at first," one striker remember later. "Then, seeing the soldiers readying their rifles, the leaders began to run toward them, followed by the crowd. Three times the bugle sounded; twice the soldiers fired into the air. The crowd still ran and was almost at the entrance to the bridge when the third volley, fired point-blank at close range, knocked down the gonfalon bearer . . . Shouts, wails, and groans were heard . . . The soldiers, due to the confusion·or the cruelty of their commander, fired seven more volleys into the crowd until both companies, firing in turn, had emptied their clips." People scattered for cover into the nearby streets, leaving dozens of killed and wounded lying in pools of blood. Gapon, dazed and muttering to himself, went into hiding, ending up later that day shorn of his long hair and beard, at the apartment of the writer Maxim Gorkii.[40]

Similar scenes were played out at points across the city where marchers encountered troops. But thousands did make it to the Palace Square before two, where they stood around awaiting the Tsar. As news of the massacres spread and mixed with rumors that Gapon had been killed, anger overtook expectation. Two o'clock struck and the Tsar did not appear. Finally troops began to clear the square, firing on demonstrators and striking at them with whips and the flats of their swords. Violent clashes continued all day and evening, mostly in the neighborhoods near the Winter Palace and across the river on Vasilevskii Island.[41]

Making hollow the Tsar's claim that he adored his people, the regime's violence on Bloody Sunday accomplished what revolutionary agitation could not. The hope of St. Petersburg's workers that their ruler heard their cries for justice or would act on their behalf was ravaged. No one voiced his outrage more plainly than Father Gapon. Sunday night Gorkii took the beardless Gapon to a meeting at the Free Economic Society, where many intellectuals had gone to weigh the day's events. Gorkii rose and delivered a statement from Gapon, saying that between the Tsar and the people lay the blood of their comrades. Next Gapon himself shouted out, "Peaceful means have failed! . . . Now we must go over to other means!" After appealing for money for the workers' struggle, he was recognized, the meeting flew into an uproar, and he fled through the back door—and then into foreign exile, no longer part of the movement he had helped create.[42]

Until January 9, opposition to the Tsar had been mainly a matter of words from politically motivated people. From that day on both the government and its opponents would have to reckon with a new and unpredictable force: dynamic, popular resistance. The march on the Winter Palace changed everything: The public's acquiescence to autocracy was ruptured, and the country would soon begin the greatest convulsion of its history. In the eyes of its organizers, the march was a victory: The honor and legitimacy of the Tsar did, as they predicted, "drown in blood." But the working men and women who marched that day had taken the meaning of their action at face value, as a humble request for justice, not as a deliberate act of conflict with their lives on the line. They had been drawn into a movement many were not aware of joining.

Gapon's Assembly had another lasting effect, which was hard to detect while the rifle volleys and cavalry charges of January 9 still echoed in people's ears. Thousands of workers in St. Petersburg had gained the experience of acting independently, something that was at odds with the old way of living under the autocracy. For the rest of the year, workers in the capital and elsewhere would build on this and develop other organizations, often collaborating with more educated people to fight for political rights and economic gains. The Assembly also brought forward a few ambitious and articulate characters, such as Aleksei Karelin, who would take key roles in working-class politics. When the Assembly had become just a memory, the habits of mind and the leaders that it developed gave ballast to the new popular front.

Unable to differentiate between a national crisis and his personal routine, Nicholas reduced it all to a brief diary entry: "A grievous day! Serious disorders occurred in St. Petersburg because workers sought to reach the Winter Palace. Troops were compelled to fire in several parts of the city; many were killed and wounded. God, how painful and heartbreaking! Mama came from the city straight to church. Had lunch with everyone. Went for a walk with Misha. Mama stayed overnight."[43]

In the days and weeks that followed, the Tsar lacked the political sense to realize that the bonds of loyalty linking him to his subjects had snapped. The common people, he thought, had been led astray by "small groups of scoundrels," and the turmoil could have been averted had his government been firmer. So Nicholas named Dmitrii Trepov, a military man reputed for his toughness, as governor-general of St. Petersburg and gave him powers consistent with martial law. Trepov tried to restore order by arresting strike organizers and Assembly leaders, clamping down on the press, and posting troops at striking factories. All this reinforced the message of Bloody Sunday: that the regime stood in the way of the people.[44]

A few of Nicholas's advisors, at least, realized that he had to offer some sort of conciliatory gesture to reestablish popular faith in the benevolent "Tsar-father." Mirskii and A. S. Ermolov, Minister of Agriculture, urged the Tsar to declare his concern for workers' welfare. The minister of finance added that if the Tsar did nothing to acknowledge workers' grievances and calm the commotion in the capital, Russia's credit with foreign lenders would suffer.

Nicholas agreed to make a gesture. He invited thirty-four handpicked workers, known for conservative views, to Tsarskoe Selo—where they were lined up, strip-searched, and lectured by the Tsar, who warned them not to participate in further disturbances. "I believe in the honorable feelings of the working people and in their unshakeable devotion to Me," the Tsar deigned to say, "and therefore I forgive them their guilt." Beyond this piece of gall, the government did appoint a new commission, including elected worker representatives, to investigate labor conditions in the capital—and, on February 18, under pressure from both ministers and his family, Nicholas reluctantly granted the right of individuals and institutions to petition the Council of Ministers and announced vague plans for an elected assembly.[45]

Had the Tsar issued these reforms back in December, as Mirskii had recommended, he might have won back a measure of loyalty from the educated elite. But by February even moderates were no longer satisfied with such changes, and the regime squandered any advantage they conferred by canceling the commission, after what it deemed excessive demands by workers' delegates. It was clear that a public crisis could force the regime to react but not actually to do much.

As the Tsar had dithered, the greatest surge of labor unrest in Russia's history hit the country. In St. Petersburg and other cities, workers walked out and demanded more pay, shorter hours, and better treatment by supervisors. They affronted the state as they challenged their employers, by ignoring the laws that forbade them from striking in the first place. On a vastly larger scale and over more territory than ever before, they defied a regime that had prohibited them from organizing and acting together. In all, more than 400,000 workers went on strike in January and close to 300,000 in February.[46]

Defiance of oppressive rulers would become common in the twentieth century, wherever popular discontent with practical conditions first was suppressed and thus became fuel for a wider political fire. A movement to change how a country is ruled can be spontaneous or carefully organized. But once on the march, it rarely can be stifled without being divided or appeased, or before it eventually triumphs. The Russians who marched on the Winter Palace in January 1905, by having audacious goals and going unarmed to the very seat of power, had changed the terms of the people's relationship with the state. Initiative no longer lay with the Tsar and his ministers. The people now began to set the pace of change.

AN EMPIRE OF CONFLICT

All over the empire during the spring and summer of 1905, people began to confront the power structures that had controlled their everyday lives. High-level protests and high-minded calls for political reform did not diminish, but at issue in the most heated clashes was authority at the roots of the autocratic system, not in its highest branches. Landlords and employers, local officials and military officers, all found their prerogatives and their position under attack from below.

During much of this period, the authorities were gripped by inertia. The Tsar was unwilling to offer major reforms, while his soldiers and police were unable to suppress the people. Two new defeats by the Japanese—on land at the Battle of Mukden, and at sea in the Tsushima Straits—only aggravated the sense of impotence. Tsushima Straits was especially mortifying: After months in transit, Russia's Baltic Fleet was completely destroyed within a few hours, and peace talks began soon after.

In this climate of failure, soldiers showed little enthusiasm for carrying out their assignments, especially when they had to restore order in factory districts or on estates hit by peasant disruptions. The men in some units went to political meetings and read revolutionary propaganda, and insubordination swept through the ranks: One infantry regiment obstructed the arrest of a soldier, and a rifle company refused to take target practice until a member of the unit was released from jail.[47]

There was no single cause of the disorders that erupted in the military, in cities and villages, in the heart of Russia, and in the borderlands of the empire. Every group had its own grievances. Soldiers' pay was so low that many had to sell part of their bread ration in order to get by, and off-duty soldiers were forbidden from riding in first- or second-class train carriages, visiting bars or restaurants, and walking on certain streets or in public gardens. Peasants resented the taxes they had to pay and the huge imbalance in landholdings between themselves and local nobles. And the non-Russian peoples of the empire objected to the subordination of their languages and cultures and wanted autonomy.[48]

None of these complaints was new, but what made them all explosive was that now the dissenters confronted a government that had defamed itself by brutalizing its own people on the streets of St. Petersburg. The Tsar was no longer trusted, and his generals and admirals had been disgraced in a losing war. From the helm of state, the old guard saw a sea of conflict.

In Kursk province, part of the empire's agricultural heartland, peasant uprisings began on February 8. Cued by church bells and bonfires, hundreds of peasants lined up with their carts and went off to the local manor, where they broke into storehouses and carted away the grain, later dividing it among themselves according to the number of mouths to feed in each household.[49]

On February 18 the government declared martial law in Georgia and sent in 10,000 soldiers. Since 1903 peasants in the remote Guriia region had not been heeding any government authority. They refused to pay taxes and burned portraits of the Tsar; they also killed a few officials (whom the gravediggers would not bury, as part of the boycott). All power in Guriia was in the hands of the Guriian Social Democratic Committee, which held weekly public meetings featuring unrestrained debate. In effect, Guriia had become a self-governing

Russian Empire, 1905

peasant republic. The great novelist Leo Tolstoy, who had long preached noncooperation with state power, wrote to a Georgian follower, telling him that the Guriians were doing exactly what he had been writing and thinking about for over twenty years. Rather than looking to the government to help them, Tolstoy said, or attacking the authorities, they were simply making themselves independent of their rulers.[50]

In Kherson province, in the village of Talashino, peasants met and drafted a petition that they sent to the government in St. Petersburg. "Our needs are great, Your Majesty!" it read. "For many centuries we peasants have endured all the adversities, all the blunders of the state: our ancestors spilled their blood for the expansion of Russia; for two and a half centuries we endured servitude and thereby made it possible for the privileged classes to live in clover . . . for many centuries we have had to pay an unbearable amount of taxes and dues." The petition then demanded a democratically elected assembly, civil liberties, redistribution of land, reform of local government, and amnesty for political prisoners.[51]

In Ivanovo-Voznesensk, a major textile center, more than 30,000 workers went out on strike on May 12. Workers from each factory elected representatives to an Assembly of Delegates, which conducted negotiations for the strikers. It drew up a list of demands, including an eight-hour day, higher wages, maternity leave, and freedom of speech and assembly, and it formed a militia to prevent violence. Only after troops attacked workers at a meeting in late May, whipping many and killing a few, did the strike turn violent: For eight days workers rioted, looted, and scuffled in the streets with police and soldiers. The strike dragged on until the end of June, when employers, under pressure from authorities, offered a few minor concessions and exhausted strikers returned to their jobs.[52]

On June 14 sailors on the battleship *Potemkin,* in the Black Sea, sent representatives to meet with officers to complain that they were being served meat infested with worms. An outraged officer shot the sailors' spokesman. The sailors mutinied, killed several officers, and hoisted a red flag over the ship. They elected a committee to take command, and that night, the *Potemkin* steamed into Odessa, a major port then caught up in a furious strike wave. The ship's arrival provoked a demonstration that degenerated into rioting, looting, and arson. Officials declared martial law, and the *Potemkin* headed back out to open sea and eventually landed in Romania, where the sailors surrendered.[53]

All over the Russian empire, people from the lower classes besieged institutions of authority and large holders of property. Much of this was provoked by state violence, and many outbreaks prompted a crackdown by authorities. But events such as the establishment of the Guriia republic and the Ivanovo-Voznesensk Assembly also revealed a new dimension to popular ferment: Even as they took direct action against employers, landowners, or local officials, peasants and workers claimed their own space in the civil order.

Organizing trade unions was the most common way to appropriate this space, even though they remained illegal. Unions often emerged out of spontaneous strikes. Typesetters in St. Petersburg struck after Bloody Sunday to get employers to agree to new wage rates. But when the strike failed because other workers in the industry refused to go along, organizers decided that all workers in the printing trades should be united, and they started a union in June. In all, there were forty attempts to launch unions between January and September, although most did not go beyond a small core of activists.[54]

The new flow of popular energy also ran through educated people in the cities. During the early months of 1905, first lawyers, then doctors, teachers, pharmacists, agronomists, writers, engineers, academicians, and veterinarians established national unions, which drew up liberal political programs. In Moscow peasant organizing climaxed in the summer, when elected peasant delegates from more than twenty provinces convened. Meeting secretly in a hospital, then in a barn, the delegates passed resolutions calling for the abolition of private property in land, the confiscation of land belonging to the church and the royal family, and the establishment of a constituent assembly.[55]

All this opposition overstretched the state's capacity for repression. While the Tsar's agents and provincial governors did not hesitate to arrest strike organizers or other activists when they could be found, they simply lacked the manpower to control every corner of the empire. Russia had far fewer police per capita than either Britain or France, for example; in the countryside the typical constable was responsible for an area of 2,000 square miles with about 50,000 people. The regime could be ruthless, but it could not be everywhere.

Besides organizing themselves and dodging the police, opponents of the Tsar endeavored to mobilize popular support where it was not spontaneous and sustain it where it was. Workers had become a potent but unruly political force, and socialists and liberals alike saw the need to corral and exploit that vitality. The Social Democrats, with years of underground experience and strong ideological motivation, approached this task with zeal. They handed out leaflets and newspapers at factories and threw themselves into union organizing. But while their leaders and ideas became familiar to many more workers, neither faction of the Social Democrats, the Bolsheviks or the Mensheviks, succeeded in attracting many members, and neither came close to co-opting the labor movement.[56]

As for Liberals, despite their professed solidarity with workers, they were blinded by the assumption that, as prominent men and women, they were the natural leaders of society and simply could count on workers to follow their lead.

As a consequence they remained, in the words of one historian, "a band of generals without sergeants."[57]

But there was no shortage of sergeants in the spring and summer of the Russian opposition. Every element of society—peasants, workers, soldiers, students, professionals—became involved. Newspapers defied censorship by reporting on protests and by condemning the government. Unauthorized meetings were held, and unsanctioned groups proliferated. In the face of this, the government failed to maintain even rudimentary public order, as ordinary crime soared, and hooligans carried out vicious attacks, including pogroms against Jews. The state, quite simply, was losing its grip. What allowed it to hang on was the lack of coordination among its opponents. No common organization, cutting across ethnic and class lines, ever emerged. A worthy if late effort to combine disparate groups and mount a determined campaign against the autocracy came finally in the fall, and it won the opposition's greatest victory.

STRIKE FOR POWER

"Comrades, Stop Work!"

After months of inaction, on August 6 the Tsar approved a consultative assembly, or Duma. It would convene by January 1906, after indirect elections. Suffrage would be so restricted, however, that in St. Petersburg, a city of over a million people, only about 7,000 would be eligible to vote. Workers would be virtually excluded. And the Duma would be limited to preliminary review of legislation. The Tsar's manifesto said the new body would preserve "inviolate the Fundamental Law of the Russian Empire about the essence of Autocratic Power," offering fresh evidence of his unwillingness to accept genuine democratic reform. A new confrontation would not be long in coming.[58]

As in January, workers went to the front lines. On September 19 printers at a plant in Moscow walked out and presented a list of demands. By the end of the week strikes had shut down most of the city's printing industry, and workers had elected deputies to a council, called a "soviet," to coordinate the strike. Soon bakers, carpenters, and metal workers walked out. By the beginning of October the strikes had jumped to St. Petersburg.

What motivated strikers at first was money, not politics. They asked employers for higher pay, shorter hours, parity for men and women workers, and polite treatment by bosses. But the physical act of striking brought workers face to face with troops. On September 22 strikers who had broken print shop windows and threatened non-strikers were surrounded by police and soldiers at a monument to the poet Sergei Pushkin. "The cossacks closed in," an eyewitness reported. "Shots suddenly rang out from the crowd, and a gendarme tottered on his horse and fell. The crowd . . . turned and ran. Mounted cossacks set out after them." Metal workers and bakers were entangled in similar clashes, leaving dozens wounded and several dead.[59]

As on Bloody Sunday, the regime's reaction politicized labor conflict. In the words of a leaflet issued by the printers' union, "Our peaceful economic struggle has led us straight to the very thing that some had previously wanted to avoid— it has led us to political struggle, to struggle with the autocracy." By early October the printers approved a resolution declaring that "only when the entire people govern the country through its representatives, elected by universal, equal, direct, and secret suffrage, will we be protected from police tyranny in our struggles with employers."[60]

But unlike Bloody Sunday, workers did not stand alone. Now their struggle took place within a broad revolt against the autocracy. The regime understood the threat without knowing how to respond. In late August Trepov had urged the Tsar to restore autonomy to the universities, suspended for the past twenty years. Doing so meant the faculty could give permission to students to hold meetings. Trepov— who one colleague said "probably never read a serious book in its entirety"— thought this would draw students back to classroom buildings and away from the streets and politics, subtracting one force from the opposition.[61]

The students made the governor-general rue his decision. They returned to school in early September, and the same rooms that held lectures and classes by day were packed with students and party activists for political meetings at night. Workers also flocked to the universities, holding huge meetings that often were regaled by speakers from revolutionary parties. Officials, who would not have hesitated to send troops to break up such meetings anywhere in the factory districts, had to tolerate them on campus and hope the excitement would taper off.[62]

Out on the streets, workers and educated Russians began to fraternize. On October 2 students, professionals, and workers turned a funeral procession for a university rector into a political parade. As they marched down Nevskii Prospekt into the center of town, scuffling at times with troops, many carried red flags and sang revolutionary songs. At the Admiralty Square, next to the Winter Palace, they knelt down, removed their hats, and sang a hymn for the martyrs of Bloody Sunday.[63]

This mixture of social classes and political motives made the opposition more forceful, and a microcosm was the All-Russian Union of Railroad Employees and Workers. Founded in April 1905, the union had steered away from economic issues and focused on political goals that could knit together the entire 700,000-strong railroad workforce, both white and blue collar. In July the Union had decided to push for a political strike. For months little was done to prepare, but in early October, as the strike wave that began in September was waning, union leaders in Moscow finally called for a labor action on all rail lines to begin on October 4.[64]

The rank-and-file were slow to respond, but on October 6 engine drivers on the Moscow-Kazan' line took matters into their own hands. That evening, after refusing to make freight runs, a band of drivers hijacked an engine to the Perovo station, where they sent a telegram proclaiming a national rail strike. In the next two days engine drivers, administrative employees, and crews from the line's workshops went from terminal to terminal, rallying workers on other lines that converged on Moscow. Soldiers guarding the stations did little to interfere. Reminding workers that any economic gains they hoped to win would be meaningless unless they also won "political freedoms," the union issued a list of demands on October 9, including freedom of speech and assembly, the right to organize unions, a constituent assembly based on universal suffrage, and amnesty for religious and political prisoners.[65]

As word of the strike flashed over telegraph lines, rail workers in one city after another shuttered their terminals and stopped the trains. In Kaluga, south of Moscow, the strike began when trains headed from Moscow to Kiev failed to appear. That night telegraph operators on another line passing through Kaluga sent out strike messages of their own and then walked out, cascading the strike to other towns. That halted mail service to the town of Samara, from which the strike extended to yet another line. In Ekaterinoslav, a southern industrial center, employees and craftsmen from railroad workshops walked out on October 10 and assembled in the main terminal. When troops arrived, workers dispersed. Some took over a train and steamed to the town of Nizhnedneprovsk, bringing the strike to workshops there. In less than two weeks, these chain reactions had choked off service on nearly every kilometer of railroad track in the empire.[66]

As it propagated from city to city, the rail strike acted as a catalyst for a general strike that suspended urban life in much of the Russian empire. In Moscow, teams of railway men fanned out into the industrial districts and convinced workers there to join the fray. Meanwhile, white-collar workers in the city's center abandoned their offices, with municipal employees leading the way. Service was blocked from the gasworks, waterworks, electric stations, and slaughterhouses, and the city administration was crippled. Pharmacy clerks and telephone operators went out too.[67]

This was not an ordinary labor action, confined to outlying factory districts, which respectable citizens in prosperous neighborhoods could easily ignore. It became impossible for anyone, even those not on strike themselves, to lead a normal life. Meat prices soared, grain supplies dwindled, and milk

Demonstration in St. Petersburg, Russia; October 1905.
Credit: ©David King Collection

ran out altogether. "Neither gas nor electric lights work," reported one newspaper on October 16. "The movement of trams, either horse-drawn or electrical ones, has not resumed. The telegraph system, telephones, and post offices do not work. A majority of the stores is closed, and the entrances and windows are boarded up."[68]

Instead of going about their daily routines, Muscovites of all kinds congregated at the university and the Technical Institute, where workers, socialist agitators, students, and professionals hobnobbed with tradesmen, police spies, and peddlers. "Merchants from the Zamoskvorech'e shot glances of fellowship at workers, who responded in kind," reported one observer, "while the wildly rapturous students were ready to embrace anyone who cried 'Down with autocracy!'"[69]

From all over the empire reports streamed into the capital about new strikes and disturbances. In Kharkov, people in the streets called for shutting down the mills and factories. In Batum, in the Caucasus, all shops were closed and all electricity was out. In all, more than a million factory workers struck in October, joined by hundreds of thousands of railway men, government employees, clerical workers, and students.[70]

Finally, on October 11 railroad workers in St. Petersburg voted to join the strike, and by the next day they had stopped traffic on all four lines into the capital. Workers from the large metal factories walked out the following day and began to make the rounds of smaller plants nearby. Strikers from the Obukhov steel mill showed up at the gates of the Rasteriaev factory and asked workers there to join in. Inside, workers dropped their tools and went around the factory crying "Comrades, stop work!" Within minutes the motors and machines fell silent, and the men took off their work shirts and went to their bosses with political demands.[71]

While workers were carrying the strike from one enterprise to another in the factory districts, others were delivering the strike to the center of the city. In the ensuing days printers, watchmakers, clerical workers, telephone operators, and even actors and grade-school students deserted their places. The university was the hub of it all, where people from different walks of life met, debated their options and needs, and decided whether or not to join the movement.[72]

D. Sverchkov, a clerical workers' union leader, went to the university on the evening of October 12 and found the assembly hall, the auditoriums, and the staircases and landings all jammed with people. He plowed through to the hall, and, once there, as he was urging several thousand to strike, he was handed a note that the city's electric stations were about to close and the building would go dark. Sverchkov had students hand out candles broken in half. "Someone lit a candle, then another, next a third," he wrote later. "Thousands of little flames began to burn around the hall. I looked out from the high platform and a feeling of rapture bubbled up in my chest: it seemed as if we were celebrating . . . the requiem for the dead autocracy." Once the meeting had ended and the hall had been cleaned up for the next group, Sverchkov left, crossed the Neva, and headed for home. Nevskii Prospekt—usually a colorful, bustling street—was empty. The lights were doused, the windows on the stores boarded up. The silence was broken only by the clatter of horse hooves from a passing patrol. It was the calm before a greater storm.[73]

"With Sword in Hand"

Even as they were acting together with other citizens in the general strike, the workers of St. Petersburg were setting themselves apart, as a force to defy the regime. The Menshevik faction of the Social Democrats had been pressing workers since the summer to form grass-roots organizations. Instead of waiting for the state to grant reforms, the Mensheviks wanted workers to take the initiative and develop their own institutions, as popular movements would do in nonviolent conflicts later in the century. On October 10 they called on workers in the capital to elect deputies to form the Petersburg General Workers' Committee. Three days later 40 deputies went to the Committee's first meeting; by the third meeting two days later, there were 266 deputies from almost 100 factories as well as a number of unions. On October 17 the Committee voted to rename itself the St. Petersburg Soviet of Workers' Deputies.[74]

When deputies from the revolutionary groups, including the Mensheviks and Bolsheviks, feuded with each other about who should be chairman, the Soviet elected Georgii Nosar', a young lawyer not affiliated with any party. Nosar'—who had twice been exiled to Siberia—was well off but showed great sympathy for those who were not; he had given legal advice to workers and helped them draft petitions. The Soviet also decided to put deputies from the main revolutionary organizations on the executive committee. The many years these activists had spent underground, printing illegal leaflets, organizing small circles of "enlightened" workers, all the while risking arrest, prison, and exile, finally seemed to be bearing fruit. At last, the socialists found themselves in the forefront of a people's movement.[75]

None of them had a higher profile than Leon Trotsky, a Menshevik. Born Lev Bronshtein to a Jewish family on the steppes of southern Russia, Trotsky had disappointed his father who wanted him to become an engineer. Instead he had plunged into the radical underground, only to wind up in a Tsarist prison cell by his twentieth birthday. After having been exiled to Siberia, he escaped to western Europe, where he joined circles of émigré Russian Marxists in London and Geneva. When word of Bloody Sunday reached him, he re-entered the empire with a false passport; thereafter he hid out in Finland and then arrived in St. Petersburg during the height of the October strike. A brilliant and charismatic man, Trotsky became a leader among the city's revolutionaries and a key strategist in the Soviet.

Heady with a sense of power they had never before felt, the vanguard of the opposition—for that is how the Soviet saw itself—began to issue threats not only to the regime but to others in society who stood in their way. The deputies asked factory and shop owners in the city to join the general strike by closing their businesses. But a warning came attached to the appeal: "If you don't fulfill this demand, your stores will be smashed, your machines destroyed . . . Close the factories, mills and stores . . . close them before it's too late, before you make yourselves victims of the people's wrath." That the strike had spread easily because it was nonviolent was not apparent to the deputies, and as they were soon to be reminded, the regime brought far more experience and resources to the game of violence.[76]

In other ways the Soviet was more effective in gaining control of events. Each night deputies arrived without warning at a different print shop, seized the premises, and, with the help of sympathetic printers, published an edition of the newspaper *Izvestiia*. On October 19, as the strike was winding down, the Soviet moved to end censorship in St. Petersburg. Deputies warned that typesetters and other workers would refuse to print any newspaper that observed restrictive press laws and submitted its contents to state censors before publication. Printers who refused to go along with this were to be ostracized by other workers. The Soviet had, in effect, decreed a new press law in the city, and almost all newspapers complied.[77]

While the Assembly had been run from the top by Father Gapon and his circle, the Soviet's members were enamored of doing things democratically. After first convening at the Technological Institute, they moved to the nearby building of the Free Economic Society, an illustrious club for intellectuals. Each evening the deputies, still in their work clothes, gathered in this grandiose but decrepit building, decorated with gilded pilasters and allegorical paintings. Leaving their galoshes at the entrance, they went up to the main assembly room, hung with portraits of generals, dignitaries, and the Tsar himself. After hearing reports at a long green table, the executive committee would retire to a room upstairs to hammer out resolutions and then return to the main hall to present them for debate and approval.[78]

Along with trade unions, professional groups, and the headlong action of hundreds of thousands of ordinary people, the Soviet helped make the October general strike into a vibrant nonviolent campaign, the century's first. Instead of launching a frontal assault on the regime, or—as Gapon's workers had tried in January—petitioning the Tsar to grant their requests, they simply stopped doing their jobs and announced that they would not start again until the government met their demands. The state could suppress demonstrations and arrest their leaders—in fact, it frequently did so—but it could not compel people to go to work; nor could it function very long if the railroad, telegraph, banks, and power plants were idle.

By immobilizing the transportation and communications networks that connected the capital to the rest of the country, the general strike plunged the state into confusion. Local officials had no clear instructions from the center to guide their response, while high officials lacked good information about events in the provinces and often acted on the basis of rumor. Not even the domestic routine of the Tsar, who was staying at his seafront palace in Peterhof, was exempt from the strike's impact. The interruption of rail traffic meant that his officials had to take boats from the capital to go speak with him, which at least once—as he recorded in his diary on October 12—delayed his lunch.[79]

Nicholas had given little thought to the escalating conflict between the people's movement and his regime. The Tsar, according to a close associate, was living "in an utter fool's paradise, thinking that He is strong, all-powerful as before!" When he finally became alarmed, his first impulse was to use force, but his ministers realized by then that little could be done to restore service on most rail lines: The colossal scale of the strike simply exceeded the grasp of the armed forces. So the Tsar told Trepov to put down unrest in the cities. On October 12 the governor-general instructed police chiefs to stifle all disruptions, and two days later he had a notice posted on the streets: "I have ordered the troops and police to suppress any such attempt [to create disorders] immediately and in the most decisive manner [and] upon a show of resistance to this on the part of the crowd—not to fire blank volleys and not to spare cartridges."[80]

The public was not intimidated. In St. Petersburg, on the very day Trepov's warning went up, 40,000 people demonstrated in the streets, while the usual political meetings filled the university's auditoriums. Police and troops never appeared to carry out Trepov's threats. In Moscow and other cities across the country there were violent incidents, not always provoked by the authorities. But repression could not still the maelstrom of protest. Signs of violence by the regime, as on Bloody Sunday, only inflamed its opponents.[81]

As coercive force seemed to fail, reform voices within the government became audible. The most influential was that of Sergei Witte, president of the Council of Ministers, who had won favorable terms in the peace talks with Japan. An intelligent, arrogant man and a skilled politician, Witte was not a foe of autocratic government; he was partly responsible, in fact, for sinking Mirskii's reform proposals the year before. Now, however, Witte saw that only by offering serious concessions could the government redeem itself. The government had failed to distinguish between reasonable calls for change and extremist sedition, he argued in a report to the Tsar. The rational, moderate parts of society were striving for freedom, and the government must not block the way. The state must "put itself under the banner of liberty," by extending the franchise for the upcoming Duma elections to all social groups and by granting a constitution guaranteeing citizens' civil liberties. The only alternative, he argued, was a dictatorship willing to bathe the country in blood.[82]

But the Tsar did not like either option. He could "appoint an energetic military man and try to crush the rebellion with all available force," he told his mother later. But "then there would be a breathing spell and after several months we would again be compelled to apply force but that would have cost rivers of blood . . . The other path was to grant the population civil rights—freedom of speech, press, assembly, and association, and the inviolability of person; furthermore, the obligation to guide every legislative project through the State Duma—that, in essence, is a constitution."[83]

For several days the Tsar agonized. He consulted Trepov, who counseled him to do what Witte had recommended. But on October 17 Nicholas opted for a crackdown and asked the Grand Duke Nikolai to assume the responsibil-

Count Sergei Witte, President of the Tsar's Council of Ministers
(photograph taken at the Portsmouth, New Hampshire peace conference
between Russia and Japan)
Credit: ©CORBIS

ities of military dictator. Only when the Duke melodramatically threatened to shoot himself in the head in front of the Tsar if he followed such a course did Nicholas change his mind and decide to sign a manifesto promising reforms. The document was issued immediately, and in the evening Nicholas recorded in his diary: "After such a day my head became heavy, and my thoughts began to get confused. Lord help us, save and pacify Russia."[84]

The October Manifesto was brief—the government would undertake three key reforms: It would grant the "foundations of civic freedom based on the principles of real personal inviolability, freedom of conscience, speech, assembly, and association;" it would enlarge the electorate for Duma elections, with the ultimate goal of universal franchise; and it would grant the Duma the power to approve laws and supervise the government. The manifesto ended with a call to "the faithful sons of Russia . . . to aid in putting an end in the unprecedented disturbances, and together with Us to make every effort to restore peace and quiet in our native land." The Tsar had made his concessions, and he would no longer tolerate disarray in his empire.[85]

"Thank God, the Manifesto has been signed. Now a new life will begin," wrote Trepov. Despite his reputation as a defender of the autocracy, he had come to believe that reform could succeed where repression had failed. At first Trepov's optimism seemed warranted. In Moscow and St. Petersburg people celebrated in the streets, and the Moscow city council adopted a resolution in support of the manifesto; its counterpart in the capital sent a telegram to Nicholas hailing him as "Tsar of a free nation." One newspaper exulted: "Let us embrace as free people, as citizens of a free, constitutional Russia."[86]

Before the end of the day, however, there were signs that the manifesto might not fully placate the opposition. In Moscow, at the founding congress of the liberal Kadet Party, speakers contended that the changes did not go far enough toward a democratic order. Socialists denounced the manifesto more stridently, as a ruse designed to trick the working class into ending the strike. From a university balcony, Leon Trotsky insisted to a horde of workers and students flying red banners that the struggle was not over. "Citizens! Now that we have got the ruling clique with its back against the wall, they promise us freedom," Trotsky bellowed. "Is the promise of liberty the same as liberty itself? . . . With sword in hand we must stand guard over our freedom. As for the Tsar's manifesto, look, it's only a scrap of paper. Here it is before you—here it is crumpled in my fist. Today they have issued it, tomorrow they will take it away and tear it into pieces, just as I am now tearing up this paper freedom before your eyes!"[87]

It was not only radicals that were still in a fighting mood; from the right came a torrent of violence. Right-wing crowds called "Black Hundreds" roved Moscow and St. Petersburg for days, smashing shop windows, and beating and sometimes killing students, workers, and others suspected of revolutionary activity. The police tolerated and, in some cases, encouraged them. Outside the two largest cities, the mayhem was even worse. Non-Russians and non-Christians were the main targets. In the Caspian Sea oil town of Baku, Black Hundreds staged attacks on Armenians (who were Christian but not Orthodox) in the hope of driving them out, killing more than sixty. Especially bloody were assaults on Jews. Twelve were killed in Kiev, 34 in Rostov-on-Don, 54 in Minsk, and over 500 in Odessa. As in St. Petersburg and Moscow, there was evidence of complicity by local authorities and police.[88]

As radicals gained confidence by the day and were unwilling to settle for less than the destruction of the autocracy and establishment of a republic, reaction-aries were not willing to leave the streets to the regime's enemies and fought back ferociously. The manifesto marked the beginning of a new and remorseless stage in the conflict that had started on the streets of St. Petersburg in the ice and snow of January.

"Almost No Restraints"

Within days of October 17, an editorial in *Izvestiia* captured the contradictions in the wake of the manifesto. "We have been given freedom of assembly," the paper admitted, "but our assemblies are encircled by troops. We have been given freedom of speech, but censorship remains . . . We have been given freedom of study, but the universities are occupied by troops . . . We have been given Witte, but we still have Trepov. We have been given a constitution, but the autocracy remains."[89]

The manifesto had promised a new relationship between the government and the governed, but the document, by itself, could not create this new order. While the Tsar and his ministers squabbled over how to implement it, the people of St. Petersburg appropriated new freedoms on their own. Newspapers reported and commented on events with new boldness, and people in the cities snapped up publications espousing every political viewpoint. Most provocative of all were satirical journals like *Pulemet* (machine gun), which printed blood-drenched, savage caricatures of officials and the Tsar. Authorities occasionally raided a publishing house, but there was no systematic attempt to stamp out the new de facto freedom of the press.

At the Rasteriaev metal factory, workers no longer hid their underground newspapers under their machines. They read proclamations from the Soviet in the open, and they posted resolutions by the revolutionary parties. Scores of public meetings took place each week in St. Petersburg during late October and November. People lined up and filled auditoriums to hear lectures about the principles of government and law. New unions sprang up in the fall of 1905 among everyone from tailors and bakers, to chimney sweeps, domestic servants, and policemen.[90]

These "days of freedom," as they became known, were not confined to the cities. In villages peasants met to talk about the manifesto and invited teachers, agronomists, or others in the "rural intelligentsia" to address them. In Markovo, just 150 kilometers (93 miles) from Moscow, the village assembly voted to withhold taxes, stop providing recruits to the army, and ignore the authority of local officials until demands for democracy, universal public education, amnesty for political prisoners, and land redistribution were met. They declared themselves the "Republic of Markovo," elected a president, and took control over schools and criminal justice.[91]

Soldiers and sailors also took the October Manifesto as a signal that the old rules no longer applied. At the Kronstadt naval base, on an island in the Baltic Sea, enlisted men demanded shorter military service, higher pay, permission to attend public meetings and walk in public places, the right to drink alcohol and to elect disciplinary courts. The sailors believed the Tsar had granted the right to gather "in open assembly" in order to "express their desires and state their needs," so they were outraged when an infantry company was arrested after presenting demands to their commander. Several thousand sailors rioted, demolishing stores, shooting into the air, and attacking officers and civilians. Twenty-six were killed, and over 2,000 were arrested.

In the six weeks following October 17, there were well over a hundred military mutinies. Most, unlike Kronstadt, ended peacefully, when officers conceded at least some demands made by enlisted men—tacitly acknowledging that the normal state of military discipline, in which officers command and soldiers obey, no longer held. This was ominous news for Tsarist officials. As Minister of War General Aleksandr Rediger recalled, "Dozens of reports on disorders in various units were received daily! It was obvious that the time was approaching when it would prove impossible to rely even on the army, and desolation would set in!"[92]

Never before had Russians felt such freedom to speak, publish, gather, and organize. They enjoyed these freedoms not because they were guaranteed by law but because they took them, and the authorities were too flummoxed to stop them. "We live as though in a state of intoxication; the revolutionary air affects people like wine," wrote F. I. Dan, a Menshevik leader, in letter to the German socialist Karl Kautsky. "There are in actuality almost no restraints on freedom of speech and assembly. The mood is splendid."[93]

But the "days of freedom" were also days of danger. Although the worst raids by right-wing extremists ended in October, occasional violence persisted and a new storm threatened. At the beginning of November, the right-wing movement took organized shape, through the new Union of the Russian People (URP). The URP attracted merchants who wanted stability, professionals who had prospered under the old order, state officials, and some peasants and workers. It also dripped the slime of a conspiracy theory over its defense of autocracy. Basing their ideas on the fabricated *Protocols of the Elders of Zion,* URP members believed that an international Jewish plot had engineered the revolution in Russia to create disarray in a Christian land and bring about Jewish supremacy. The URP asked the regime for repression, and hit squads were created to assassinate opposition leaders.[94]

The Tsar took heart from right-wing appeals. The "whole mass of loyal people," he wrote to his mother on October 27, were lashing out against the small number of "bad people" who had led them astray, including "the kikes" but also Russian intellectuals and agitators. The flood of telegrams that reached Nicholas convinced him that popular opinion had turned against the revolutionaries. Witte had assured him that reforms would bring peace; they had not, and now it was time to end the pandemonium.[95]

As Nicholas grew restive, Witte's influence declined. Despite a distinguished career, he had always been an outsider at the imperial court—thanks in part to having married a divorced woman who was rumored to be Jewish. Now that the Tsar was losing confidence in reforms, Nicholas began to rely more on Trepov, who had become palace commandant. To Nicholas, Trepov seemed resolute and absolutely loyal. But to educated society, Trepov symbolized the brutality and folly of the Russian military. "To Trepov, as to every ignoramus," Witte wrote later, "everything seemed simple: if people riot, you beat them . . ."[96]

A cataract of new freedoms, resurgent violence, and a government privately shifting from reform to reaction placed the opposition at a turning point. In forcing the October Manifesto, the Tsar's opponents had won more than they could have dreamed only months before, but many were tempted to press for even more. Pushing too hard could discredit Witte further and prod the Tsar toward a crackdown that could erase what had been won. But if they stopped fighting as the Tsar was on the ropes, they could forfeit the chance for an even larger victory. And, whatever course they took, it would be crucial to maintain the sense of common cause that had animated the October strike.

"A Violent Clash . . . Was Approaching"

No single party, union, or other organization had propelled the October strike, and no individual emerged as a rallying point or strategic pilot. What enabled the regime's adversaries to act together during the October days was work done earlier by a constellation of groups to rally behind the prime goals of civil liberties and representative government. There was much that split journalists from printers, or engineers from metal workers, but the events of the past year had taught them to stay focused on their common goals. Now that freedom seemed at hand, their solidarity would be tested as never before.

The Kadet party, formed during the October strike in Moscow, was the main organized force among liberals during the "days of freedom." Their objectives now were to feed the robust opposition that had ripened in October, persuade the regime to honor its promises, and work within the new order to achieve further political and social reform. The revolution had ended, as far as the Kadets were concerned, and what remained was to consolidate and build on its progress.

The Kadets, like the Union of Liberation, spoke in the name of a movement that transcended the boundaries of class and party. They expressed values such as democracy and constitutionalism that they thought could hold together landowners and liberals, workers and socialists. But, like the Liberationists, the Kadets actually represented a narrow layer of the population, mostly landowners and the urban elite. The lawyers and professors who led the party became increasingly isolated from both workers and revolutionary socialists, who were unwilling to follow their lead.

Within a week of October 17, St. Petersburg workers showed that they had other things on their mind besides political reform. On October 24 workers at the Nevskii Ship and Machine Works voted to shorten their work-day by the simple device of leaving after eight hours. All over town workers in other industries followed suit. The militance that had been aimed at the regime during the October strike was now trained on factory owners and bosses.[97]

During the October strike, employers had tolerated workers' protests, and many even had continued to pay a portion of their wages. But their reaction to the eight-hour campaign was different. By November 10 factory owners were locking their gates, and within a few days tens of thousands of workers were turned away. At a few enterprises workers compromised with bosses and returned to the line. At others they refused any settlement short of an eight-hour day and remained on the streets.[98]

The eight-hour campaign not only antagonized employers, it also drew criticism from liberals. Workers' aggressive pursuit of their own interests now isolated them from political activists who, just weeks before, had joined them in striking for dramatic change. Workers got sympathy, on the other hand, from the Soviet, which passed a resolution backing the campaign on October 29. But revolutionary leaders shared the liberals' sense that economic action was sapping energies that could better be applied to political struggle. "We are not yet done with absolutism, and you want to take on the bourgeoisie," admonished one socialist leader to Soviet deputies who endorsed the eight-hour movement. As the campaign dragged on, the lock-outs took their toll on workers' morale, and on November 13, the deputies called for a halt.[99]

The radicals had another role in mind for the working class: to be the infantry in a decisive battle to incinerate the regime. Over the previous months, the socialists had collaborated in various forms of nonviolent action—strikes, demonstrations, underground publishing—but they had never given up their conviction that violence was the ultimate revolutionary sanction. While liberals could live with the Tsar as long as he was tamed by a constitution, the socialists yearned to throw out the regime—lock, stock, and barrel. And there seemed to be plenty of historical evidence that only drastic means could produce a drastic

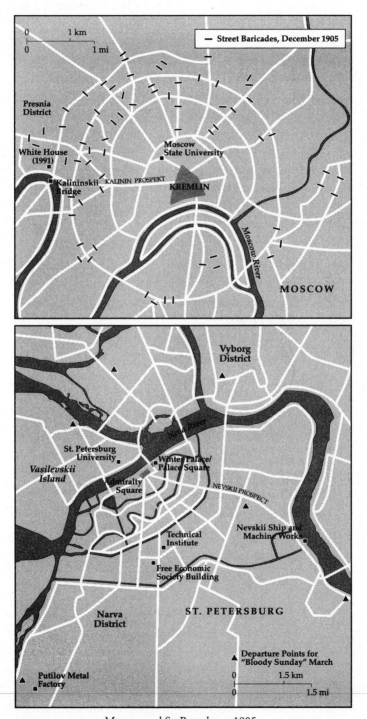

Moscow and St. Petersburg, 1905

result—the French Revolution was the great example—and little to suggest that a regime ready to use violence could be deposed without it.

For many young Russians, moreover, the image of a popular armed revolt had intense emotional resonance. "I believed that a violent clash between the people and the government was approaching," wrote Vladimir Voitinskii, a law student, decades later, "and I felt the urge, if not the moral obligation, to be with the people in the decisive hour . . . " He joined the Bolsheviks, who thought that violence would work. While knowing that they were certain to be badly outgunned by government troops, they believed that soldiers would disobey when ordered to shoot. Trotsky had noticed that some soldiers fired into the air rather than at civilians. "The same soldier who yesterday fired his shots in the air," he asserted, "will tomorrow hand over his weapon to the worker."[100]

In the wake of Bloody Sunday, Trotsky's bitter rival within the Marxist camp, V. I. Lenin, had arrived at the same conclusion. "Only an armed people can be the real bulwark of popular liberty," Lenin wrote from Geneva. "The sooner the proletariat succeeds in arming, and the longer it holds its fighting positions as striker and revolutionary, the sooner the army will begin to waver; more and more soldiers will at last begin to realize what they are doing and they will join sides with the people." The ragged discipline observed among troops during the summer, and the outright mutinies of the fall, only reinforced this reasoning, which undercut the incentive to take fresh nonviolent action.[101]

All year the Bolsheviks had importuned workers to take up arms. In January revolutionaries had circulated leaflets among the strikers in St. Petersburg, imploring them not to follow Father Gapon to the Winter Palace. "Freedom is bought with blood, freedom is won with weapons in fierce battle," said one handbill. The workers turned a deaf ear to this in January, and they spurned similar appeals in the spring and summer. In October Bolshevik speakers at university meetings called for converting the general strike into a full insurrection, and they asked workers to bring weapons to the university on October 16. Only 200 men, brandishing knives, brass knuckles, and small revolvers, turned out, and the organizers decided to send them home rather than provoke a fight with better-armed troops.[102]

After the October Manifesto, revolutionaries took their bid for an armed uprising to the Soviet. The very next day, Nosar' read deputies an executive committee resolution proposing that they arm themselves "for the final struggle," and Trotsky alerted them to prepare for "an even grander and more impressive attack on the staggering monarchy, which can be conclusively swept away only by a victorious popular uprising." The Soviet endorsed both the Nosar' and Trotsky statements, but asking for the Tsar's downfall inevitably separated the revolutionaries from their erstwhile allies the liberals, who disavowed any desire to overthrow the government. The loss of the liberals was a price the Bolsheviks were happy to pay; Trotsky refused to credit the role that they had played in the October strike. It was the workers who had forced the autocracy to offer concessions in October, he claimed, and it was armed workers who would deliver the final blow.[103]

Yet workers who prepared to fight perhaps were prompted less by revolutionary zeal than by wanting to defend themselves from the Black Hundreds. In the last week of October, rumors swirled around St. Petersburg that right-wing groups were planning a fresh onslaught against Jews and other subversives. At the Rasteriaev factory, workers bought guns and patrolled nearby streets. All over the city, they got hold of pistols or rifles and made knives and bludgeons. At a Soviet meeting on October 29, thousands of weapons were laid out. In the end, no pogrom occurred, but the weapons and armed squads remained.[104]

Throughout November the Soviet kept beating the drum for an armed revolt, but the revolutionaries did little to prepare for it besides reminding workers to get weapons. The growing arsenal, no secret to the regime, only brought closer the day of a crackdown. Moreover, workers were still more interested in the struggle against factory owners than an armed crusade against the state. And the Soviet—an open, deliberative body, with democratic procedures—was hardly the perfect vehicle for planning a military operation. Isolated by its fiery rhetoric, it waited like a tethered goat for the Tsarist tiger.

On November 26 the police arrested the Soviet's chairman, Nosar'. The remaining deputies continued to meet and elected a new presidium, with Trotsky as chairman, but the deputies grew increasingly tense and despondent as they waited for the regime's next move. In their passion to incite an uprising, they had only amplified repression. Police had already arrested the leaders of the All-Russian Peasants' Union and the Union of Postal and Telegraph Employees, and Nicholas had dismissed his liberal minister of justice. Then martial law was imposed in several provinces where peasant unrest had flared again. In late November and early December, the emergency powers of local officials were bolstered, and rail, postal, and telecommunications strikes were banned. In Moscow, the police raided a meeting place for labor organizers and arrested leaders of the Union of Ticket Collectors on one of the railroad lines. The "days of freedom" were disappearing like birch leaves in the taiga.[105]

On December 2 the Soviet resorted to one last, nonviolent gambit. By the late fall the government was in dire financial straits. The costs of waging the war against Japan and coping with domestic tumult were colossal, while a poor harvest and incessant strikes further impaired the economy and reduced government income. The budget deficit had ballooned and gold reserves had dwindled. Only a large foreign loan, which Witte had been negotiating with a

French banking syndicate, could avert financial catastrophe. The Soviet's leaders glimpsed an opportunity: If they could strike a sudden blow at the government's precarious financial position, that might persuade French bankers that the Russian empire was too marginal a credit risk, thus derailing Witte's loan and perhaps tumbling the government into bankruptcy.

Together with the Peasants' Union and several left-wing parties, the Soviet issued a Financial Manifesto, which urged citizens of the empire to withdraw their savings from banks and demand all payments in gold. "It is necessary," the document declared, "to cut the government off from the last source of its existence: financial revenue." But it was not the government's existence that the broader popular movement opposed, it was autocratic rule. So the sanction, promoted this way, was unlikely to be adopted by sufficient depositors to cut deeply. Still, during the next few weeks, 90 million rubles were withdrawn from savings banks.[106]

The Financial Manifesto provoked a swift response from the regime: On the same day it was issued, the authorities confiscated the eight newspapers that printed the document in St. Petersburg and arrested their editors. The next evening, December 3, the Soviet's deputies arrived as usual at the Free Economic Society building. After discussing several items of business, the executive committee learned that the building was surrounded by foot soldiers, mounted Cossacks, and police. Trotsky instructed the deputies not to resist, but the committee kept working as soldiers entered the room. Finally he declared the meeting closed—and all of them, the executive committee plus 200 deputies, were arrested. The St. Petersburg Soviet, which had howled for armed rebellion, succumbed without firing a shot.[107]

"Act Ruthlessly"

Revolutionaries in Moscow, like their counterparts in the capital, had been spoiling for a fight since October. "To Arms! To Arms!—That was the slogan of all revolutionaries," recalled V. M. Zenzinov, a socialist leader. Many pinned their hopes on support expected from troops in the Moscow garrison, where a wave of mutinies had just ebbed. But some doubted they would gain these allies, realizing that soldiers' rancor came more from their mistreatment than from hostility to the regime. Others felt they had to go it alone if necessary. It was "better to perish . . . than to be bound hand and foot without engaging in a struggle," Zenzinov remembered.[108]

Drunk with pride and their own violent rhetoric, members of all three radical groups—Bolsheviks, Mensheviks, and SRs—held meetings and voted to call for a general strike, as the prelude to an insurrection. On December 7 the

Moscow Soviet (formed two weeks earlier) endorsed the strike call, and the response was impressive: Within two days, 80,000 workers had walked off the job, stores were boarded up, and ordinary life, once again, came to a standstill.[109]

General fighting did not break out until the night of December 9, when troops shelled a building where 100 armed men were holed up. To avoid concentrating their numbers, revolutionaries circulated armed squads known as *druzhinniki* around the city, appearing out of nowhere to disarm small groups of police and soldiers. When the druzhinniki took shots at troops, the army responded by firing into crowds. In the Presnia district, home to textile factories, everyone seemed to be building barricades: Old women brought bed frames, concierges hauled out gates, and telephone poles and street lamps were dragged into the streets. "The ring of barricades around the city continues to tighten," wired the city's governor-general to St. Petersburg, asking for reinforcements.[110]

Although the revolutionaries took control of factory districts, they never tried to seize key points in the city's center. This made sense if soldiers were expected to disobey orders and join the insurgents. In the first days these hopes appeared justified, as soldiers fraternized with strikers and seemed to identify with their cause. But little had been done to harden that identification or recruit real partisans among the sons of the working class and peasantry that were serving in uniform—and hoping for a result and organizing to achieve it are two different things. As soon as the shooting began, the soldiers' mood shifted palpably. Spoiling Lenin's prediction, they felt no compunction about firing at workers who were pointing guns at them.

The tide turned on December 15. Just as troops from the capital were arriving in Moscow, the rebellion began to disintegrate in most parts of the city, as many workers headed to the countryside to celebrate Christmas with their families. One center of defiance remained: the Presnia district, where troops and police were still blocked by barricades. The 1,500-man Semenovskii Regiment from St. Petersburg got the assignment to dislodge the holdouts, and its commander was ordered to "act ruthlessly," to "exterminate the gangs of insurgents and seize the leaders of the insurrection." The following morning worker-occupied factories were hit with an artillery barrage. Despite little return fire, the regiment kept up the fusillade for two full days, killing hundreds of resisters and ordinary residents.[111]

By the eighteenth, both the Bolsheviks and the Moscow Soviet had conceded defeat, and the uprising sputtered out. Seven hundred or more revolutionaries and civilians had been killed, but just seventy police officers and soldiers. From the beginning, the firebrands in Moscow grasped that their cause was doomed unless they could spark an all-out revolution. But the tinder of a wider conflagration was damp by mid-December. St. Petersburg's workers did stage a brief general strike, but they never took up arms. There were small rebellions in a few other cities, but these were not enough to dictate redeployment of troops.[112]

As the government smashed the rebellion in Moscow, it also intensified the crackdown begun all over the country in late November. Even Witte beckoned for the army to deal "decisively and mercilessly" with armed adversaries. Nicholas enthusiastically endorsed every sign of truculence from his officials and commanders. "Terror must be answered by terror," he had come to believe. Commanders were given free reign to do anything necessary to subdue opposition. The governor-general of Kiev received orders that "insurgents be annihilated and their homes burned in the event of resistance." Forces sent to Siberia to end a railroad strike hanged and horsewhipped people. Troops descending on the Baltic provinces carried out summary executions, public beatings, and arson.[113]

The wolves of repression uncaged by the regime in late 1905 cowed the population and filled the jails with radicals. By early 1906 the government no longer had reason to fear revolution; it had pinched off a bloody revolt by bloodletting of its own. Throughout the repression Witte also had been doggedly working to circumvent financial calamity. After months of hard bargaining, on April 16 he landed a loan of over five billion francs from a group of foreign and domestic banks. The Tsar said this was the best achievement of Witte's whole tenure, and for once on a matter of supreme importance, he was right.

The revolutionaries in Moscow, St. Petersburg, and elsewhere had made a costly miscalculation. By resorting to arms in place of nonviolent action, they stopped doing what had most destabilized the regime and gave the government the kind of foe it knew how to trounce. Writing shortly afterwards Leo Tolstoy, who rejoiced about the political achievements of the revolution, said he had to "grieve for those who, imagining that they are making it, are destroying it. The violence of the old regime will only be destroyed by non-participation in violence, and not at all by the new and foolish acts of violence which are now being committed."[114]

Even before it finished wiping out resistance, the government issued laws that circumscribed the new order. On December 11 election procedures for the Duma were published. The franchise would be neither universal nor equal, two key demands of the opposition. Women, landless peasants, soldiers, and some artisans and laborers would be excluded. And, in indirect elections, the vote of one landowner would count the same as that of fifteen peasants and forty-five workers. While trade unions were later legalized, their activities were curbed, and any political action was forbidden.

On April 23, 1906, the new Fundamental Laws of the Russian Empire were promulgated, defining the Duma's powers. For any legislation to become law, as promised in the October Manifesto, it would have to be approved by the Duma. But the Duma would control only about 60 percent of the budget, had no say in military matters or foreign policy, and ministers would answer to the Tsar. Lawmaking power also was given to the State Council, consisting partly of the Tsar's appointees and partly of those elected under a narrow franchise. And when the Duma was not in session, the Tsar could legislate by issuing decrees.

The new order fell short of what the regime's opponents, liberals and revolutionaries alike, had hoped to achieve during the heady days of October and November. Elections were far from democratic, and Nicholas still called himself an autocrat. The government had fulfilled the letter of the October Manifesto while not going further. All the same, if the Russian empire was not yet a constitutional monarchy, neither was it any longer an unlimited despotism. Political parties, trade unions, a bolder press, and real limits, however modest, on the ruler's power: These all remained—the achievements of a movement that took its greatest strength not from armed militants in the streets but from the people's refusal to cooperate with a discredited government.

৯   ৯   ৯

Near the end of the century, Russians challenged a different kind of autocratic principle—a renascent party dictatorship—and again captured the world's attention with nonviolent resistance. The people's victory in 1991 was quick and stunning. Boris Yeltsin, the President of Russia, promptly opposed the junta that tried to seize control, and he offered citizens and soldiers a stark choice: They could support their own elected government, or they could obey the communist old guard. Once it met popular resistance, the half-baked junta folded. Nonviolent force, and the denial of military support, sealed its fate.

The divergent groups that opposed the Tsarist monarchy in 1905 faced a more imposing adversary: a dynasty that had ruled Russia for centuries and grew out of an even older absolutist tradition. This was no band of self-appointed usurpers; the autocracy, while blundering and vulnerable, would fight for its life, would appeal to tradition and religious authority. It would offer tactical concessions, deploy its soldiers and police, and exploit the resources of an empire to keep power in its hands. Only unrelenting pressure applied on many different fronts over an extended period could have forced the Tsarist state to break.

Yet with a suddenness that surprised everyone, the Tsar's opponents rose up and threw off the presumption of his authority. With more spontaneity than deliberate planning, they sapped the state's finances, confounded its police, disrupted its communications, demoralized its administrators, and defied its edicts at every chance. Opposition came from the top of society, from the bottom, and from all groups in between. Peasants set up their own "republics." Workers left their jobs and marched in the streets. Soldiers disobeyed their commanders. Students turned universities into political sanctuaries. Journalists exposed the government's incompetence and condemned its excesses. Lawyers, doctors, and engineers demanded reforms.

Time and again nonviolent action gave the Tsar's ministers only bad options. When the regime used force to subdue protestors or shut down newspapers, the public was incensed. When it swung the other way and offered concessions, opponents pressed for more reform even as they exploited new chances to organize and publicize their views. Then, after months of action and sacrifice, workers, white-collar employees, and professionals hit upon a sanction that struck at vital state interests without exposing themselves to an assault by the Tsar's forces. Rather than storming the regime head-on, people across the empire simply dropped their work and went home, destabilizing the regime more than any insurrection could have.

But the forces that strove to win new rights and a share of real power never amalgamated into a unified and disciplined movement. Unlike the people of Moscow in 1991, they lacked symbols around which all could rally—an elected leader or (ironically) the Russian tricolor flag—and they had no commonly accepted leadership to orchestrate their sanctions. There was no shortage of organizations in 1905 vying to head the opposition—revolutionary socialists, liberal democrats, and moderate constitutionalists all staked their claims—but they never put aside their political differences long enough to marshal decisive popular support.

It was not just political will that was divided. The revolution also gave vent to class and ethnic enmities, pitting peasants against landlords, workers against employers, and Christians against Jews. Often unable to work together, the Tsar's opponents could not plan and build on each successive sanction. They failed to capitalize on the regime's weaknesses, and they were flustered when it finally took the initiative and curtailed the days of freedom. The political change that came in the wake of mass nonviolent action in 1905 was real, but had that action been steered by a unified movement with a perceptive strategy, the Russian century might well have started down a different road.

In 1905 nonviolent action occurred in a stream of events marked by substantial violence. What started out as a peaceful demonstration often turned into a riot or a street fight between protestors and police. Most of the violence occurred incidentally, beyond the full control of any organization and often provoked by the regime's brutality. One group, however, consciously planned to use violence to overthrow the Tsar. For months they beseeched their followers to arm themselves. There was no need to fear his weapons, they claimed, because soldiers would join the uprising. Then, just as the government was regaining its balance, the revolutionaries launched an insurrection. When it was over, in little more than a week, an entire section of Moscow lay in ruins, and the regime was not only triumphant but primed for more repression.

The barricades from which Moscow's workers shot at troops in 1905 lay just blocks from the site of the Russian White House of 1991, where unarmed civilians cajoled soldiers like Major Evdokimov to join their cause. The contrast between the two lines of action and the two outcomes speaks volumes. The nonviolent citizen force of 1991 outclassed the junta in the eyes of many soldiers and turned them into either neutral bystanders or active defenders of the White House. The guns brandished against the Tsar's troops in December 1905 were answered by the full fury of a regular army facing hostile fire.

Trotsky and Lenin came to the moment convinced that real change required a revolution and that revolutions were violent. Blinded by this vision of what should happen, they did not see the possibilities of what could be made to happen. Changing a country by drawing on the power of the people, as the new century was to demonstrate at many times and in many places, was rarely a straight-line progression from a system predicated on autocratic whim to a new order based on the people's will. It required from a popular movement the skill of knowing when to consolidate gains and regroup for later phases in the conflict, as well as when to press for immediate advantage and not settle too soon.

If the movement against the Tsar had capitalized on certain key opportunities, Nicholas might have been pressed to enlarge the scope of reform, averting the sequence of events that led to the Bolshevik revolution twelve years later. In particular, if more of the regime's opponents had embraced the October Manifesto as the breakthrough it was—an admission that the people possessed power and inherent rights—rather than as a set of half measures to be disdained, then the friends of reform inside the palace might have persuaded the Tsar that repression was unneeded. But the temperature among the radicals was too hot for that, and violence from the right and overconfidence on the left sabotaged this opening.

If soldiers and sailors had been recruited methodically to join the opposition in 1905, the government's means of coercion might have been less reliable when it chose to crack down, and if the Financial Manifesto had been promoted aggressively on a broader front, the regime's fiscal lifeblood might have been gravely weakened. With internal and external support at greater risk, the government might not have been able to regroup and enfeeble its promised constitutional changes.

If the Soviet and its followers had not heeded the call to take up arms—if the movement had abjured violence at this crucial moment instead of embracing it, and if it had applied sanctions that the regime did not know how to counter— then the ultimate test of strength with the regime might have been measured in loans defaulted and kilowatts extinguished instead of blood spilled and lives lost. The regime needed solvency and control of daily life, and the movement was capable of wrecking both. People's movements need to sustain popular support and deliver on tangible goals, but they cannot do either if their followers are being killed in the streets and the concessions they win from the regime are being rejected by their leaders.

Not all or perhaps any of these alternatives were likely to have been seized, given the disjointed nature of the movement against the Tsar. Those who took nonviolent action at the outset of the century knew far less about the kind of conflict they had ignited than those who came later. But the consequences of the course they followed, of what they did and did not do, were fateful in the extreme.

When Trotsky denigrated the October Manifesto, called it "nothing," and demanded a people's republic, he was deaf to what the movement had already accomplished and made the desire for immediate satisfaction the enemy of eventual victory. When Lenin wrote from Geneva before the march on the Winter Palace that the people had to be armed to secure their liberty, he would soon be disproved, as strikes and nonviolent resistance frustrated the regime at almost every turn and opened the way for constitutional change. But he and his party went right on believing it.

The Marxists were wrong, of course. The sponsors of violence in 1905 derailed the Russian people's first genuine assertion of democratic power in their history. Moreover, violence in 1905 sowed the seeds for violence in 1917, creating then a new regime dedicated even more systematically than the Tsar's to violence as the basis for state power. Violence did not endow the Russian people with liberty. It gave them another eight decades of political desolation, which ended only when a new chapter of nonviolent resistance overcame an attempt to reverse democratic change.

Had he been granted a vision of what would happen in 1991, Tolstoy would have exulted, because he would have known what would make it possible: "the fundamental force which moves men and nations," he called it in 1905—the expression of the people's will that needs no violence to turn the clock-hands of history. Had the movement against the Tsar understood that mechanism, had its nonviolent action been strategic and not erratic, the century would surely have been different, in Russia and throughout the world. But as a lever just long enough can move a world, the Russians of 1905 still moved the century, in ways they could never have dreamed.[115]

CHAPTER TWO

India:
Movement for Self-Rule

A Remedy More Powerful

AMONG THE FAR-FLUNG MILLIONS who followed newspaper accounts of the Russian revolution in 1905, no reader was more avid than an unassuming Indian lawyer in South Africa. To thirty-six-year-old Mohandas Karamchand Gandhi, the events in Russia were the harbinger of a new world. Knowing that Russians had tried earlier to end autocracy by assassinating a ruler, he believed that now they had "found another remedy which, though, very simple, is more powerful than rebellion and murder." Russians had "declared a general strike and stopped all work," Gandhi wrote. "They left their jobs and informed the Czar that, unless justice was done, they would not resume work. What was there even the Czar could do against this? . . . It is not within the power of even the Czar to force strikers to return at the point of the bayonet."[1]

This was not the only time Gandhi had heard of people using nonviolent sanctions to oppose a government. As a law student in London in the late 1880s, he had paid close attention to the Irish campaign for home rule, including a rent strike. He knew that both Africans and Indians in South Africa had resisted restrictions and taxes imposed by white rulers. And at the time he was writing about Russia, he also read about a boycott of English cloth by Bengali Hindus to protest British plans to partition their province.[2]

In each of these cases, Gandhi noted, people had challenged the state not by attacking it but by refusing to cooperate with it, and their experience revealed that "even the most powerful cannot rule without the cooperation of the ruled." What was true in Russia was surely also true in his native land, where Indians were struggling against British rule. "The governance of India is possible only because there exist people who serve," Gandhi concluded. "We also can show the same strength that the Russian people have . . . " But while the young solicitor's mind was ranging from what had happened in Russia to what might happen in his native India, he was, in 1905, still very much a part of what was happening in South Africa.[3]

GANDHI IN SOUTH AFRICA

"No Place for a Self-Respecting Indian"

Mohandas Gandhi had been born to a Gujarati-speaking family in one of the small princely states on India's west coast, a relative backwater compared to cities like Bombay and Calcutta. His family expected him to follow in his father's footsteps and become a local administrative official, which is why they had sent him to London to study law. But his British studies had left Gandhi ill-prepared to practice law in India, and after he returned in 1891, he proved to be so hopelessly timid in the courtroom that during his first case he became tongue-tied and gave up in the middle of a cross-examination. He was soon reduced to making a living by drafting legal papers back in his home town of Rajkot. When he was offered a job representing an Indian company's traders in South Africa, he seized on it—leaving India as a professional failure, looking for a new start on a new continent.[4]

Tens of thousands of Indians had made this passage before. Most went as indentured laborers who worked off debts cutting sugar cane or picking coffee beans. Once they earned their freedom, many remained, toiling as traders, gardeners, or servants. Indian merchants from Gandhi's own Gujarat region had also immigrated. By the turn of the century there were 50,000 Indians in Natal alone, roughly the same as the white population, though far less than the 400,000 Africans, with smaller but fast-growing Indian communities scattered elsewhere.[5]

Indians in South Africa included Hindus, Muslims, and Christians, rich and poor, educated and uneducated, high caste and low. In the eyes of whites, they

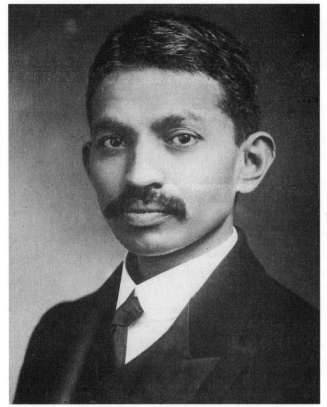

Mohandas Gandhi as a young lawyer in South Africa, 1906.
Credit: ©Dinodia/The Image Works

were all "coolies" or "Asiatics"—a lesser race. Prejudice against them had been codified in a network of laws (contravening Queen Victoria's Proclamation of 1858 that had guaranteed freedom from religious or racial discrimination throughout the British empire). Their rights to vote, to enter the country and travel within it, to do business, and to choose where to live were all restricted.[6]

It had not taken long for Gandhi to feel these restrictions himself. After just a week in Durban, he booked rail passage to Pretoria to argue a case there, traveling first class, as any respectable barrister would. When a white passenger complained about his presence, he was asked to leave the first-class wagon; when he refused, he was kicked off the train. Later in the same trip, he was not allowed to ride inside a stagecoach with the European passengers but had to sit outside with the driver. "I saw that South Africa was no place for a self-respecting Indian," he later wrote.[7]

In Durban, Gandhi built a thriving legal practice and was known for high ethical standards—but also for a willingness to compromise. Meanwhile the Indian community suffered under a barrage of discriminatory laws. When the Natal government proposed denying them voting rights, Gandhi organized Indians to oppose the legislation. In the coming years—first in Durban, later in Johannesburg—he would wage new battles, via lawsuits, petitions, and the press, against a head tax on former indentured laborers, limitations on immigration, licensing procedures for Indian merchants, and restraints on where Indians could trade and live. He won some temporary victories, but he could not stem the anti-Indian tide.[8]

A year after the events in Russia that so impressed Gandhi, laws were passed in Transvaal (where Gandhi then lived) further curbing Indian immigration and making Indians carry registration cards. Outraged, Gandhi felt they had to take new forms of action. At a meeting in Johannesburg's Empire Theatre in September 1906, Gandhi asked everyone to swear not to comply with the new law, and when it went into effect, a "Passive Resistance Association" that he set up picketed registration offices. What followed was a bonfire of registration cards outside a mosque, mass illegal border crossings into Transvaal, and a miners' strike. Thousands went to jail—Gandhi himself three times. Finally, in 1914, the government relented and withdrew the registration act along with other statutes that Indians found offensive. Hindus and Muslims, miners and merchants, had all joined a campaign behind Gandhi's leadership and, by breaking unjust laws and going to prison, had forced change.[9]

"Passive Resistance"

The years of struggle in South Africa molded the halting, unsuccessful young lawyer that Gandhi had been in India into a confident political man operating in another roiling, diverse society. But there was a second, equally important transformation also under way in the diminutive Indian. Almost as soon as he had arrived in South Africa, Gandhi had embarked on a search for spiritual understanding, which lasted the rest of his life. While he remained a Hindu, he had met and mixed with Muslims, Christians, Parsis, and Jains, in his parents' household, in London, and in South Africa—and he was particularly influenced by Rajchandra Ravjibhai Mehta, a Jain jeweler and poet with whom he corresponded and who emphasized to Gandhi the "many-sidedness of truth," which no individual or religion could ever know perfectly. "Religions are different roads converging to the same point," Gandhi wrote in 1909. "What does it matter that we take different roads so long as we reach the same goal?"[10]

For Gandhi, who saw all life as arising from a unity of being, there was no division between spiritual and practical activity, and he tried to live that way. One spiritual principle that had practical value for him was that of *ahimsa* or (loosely translated) "nonviolence." If no individual or group could claim absolute knowledge of the truth, no one should use violence to compel others to act against their different but also sincere understanding of it. Ahimsa had deep roots within Jain, Buddhist, and Hindu thinking, but Gandhi also found vigorous expressions of the same precept in Christian thought, especially in the Sermon on the Mount and in the writings of Leo Tolstoy. He read Tolstoy's book *The Kingdom of God Is Within You* in 1894 and found himself "overwhelmed" by the Russian's argument against violence.[11]

Ahimsa had clear implications for political conflict. Violence used against oppression, Gandhi believed, was not only wrong, it was a mistake. It could never really end injustice, because it inflamed the prejudice and fear that fed oppression. For Gandhi, unjust means would never produce a just outcome. "The means may be likened to a seed, the end to a tree," he wrote in 1909, "and there is just the same inviolable connection between the means and the end as there is between the seed and the tree . . . We reap exactly as we sow."[12]

Yet Gandhi had to find methods of political action that would also be effectual. In South Africa his actions as an Indian leader had been nonviolent, but speeches, petitions, letters, and meetings with officials had barely dented racist attitudes and laws. What he sought was a way to compel whites to see the truth that Indians would have to be treated as equals, and in the protest campaigns that followed the oath in the Empire Theatre, he found it.

At first he called it "passive resistance" (a term he disavowed in later years). The technique was simple: Declare opposition to an unjust law (such as restrictions on free movement), break the law (by crossing a border illegally), and suffer the consequences (arrest, physical abuse, prison). Resisters' calm and dignified suffering, Gandhi believed, would open the eyes of oppressors and weaken the hostility behind repression; rather than adversaries being bullied to capitulate, they would be obliged to see what was right, and that would make them change their minds and actions. Gandhi named this concept of action *satyagraha* (combining the Hindu words for "truth" and "holding firmly").[13]

But satyagraha soon took on a larger dimension, one that was less a function of its spiritual provenance than its feasibility. Gandhi recognized that there were limits to the exemplary value of personal sacrifice: Even the most committed resisters could absorb only so much suffering, and the pride and prejudices typical of entrenched regimes could not be dissolved quickly. If satyagraha was to become a practical political tool, Gandhi realized, it had to bring pressure to bear on its opponents. "I do not believe in making appeals," he wrote, "when there is no force behind them, whether moral or material."[14]

The potential of satyagraha to change an opponent's position, Gandhi believed, came from the dependence of rulers on the cooperation of those who had the choice to obey or resist. While he continued to argue that satyagraha could reveal the truth to opponents and win them over, he often spoke of it in military terms and planned actions that were intended not so much to convert adversaries but to jeopardize their interests if they did not yield. In this way he made satyagraha a realistic alternative for those more interested in what could produce change than in what conscience could justify.[15]

So Gandhi did not make ahimsa an absolute credo. He drew distinctions between organized violence by the authorities, which he excoriated, and the spontaneous violence of downtrodden people. While he did not condone the latter, he said it was "understandable" and might even serve the purpose of asserting dignity—and throughout his life he insisted that resorting to violence was preferable to abject cowardice. Gandhi's ahimsa and satyagraha were not reserved for saints; they were conceived for people who had to reconcile a passion for justice with a calculation of how to spur change.[16]

A trip to Britain in the summer of 1909 was the catalyst for thinking more about how to apply satyagraha to India. Although Gandhi went to London to lobby for Indians in South Africa, he became embroiled in debates about his homeland. Just days before he arrived, a young Indian living in London had assassinated a British official, Sir William Curzon-Wyllie. The act appalled Gandhi, as did the views of expatriate Indians who believed that terrorism was the surest route to liberation. To counter that belief, he spent ten days on his return trip aboard the *Kildonan Castle* preparing an essay on the ship's stationery, writing so quickly and with such urgency that when his right hand tired he simply switched to his left.[17]

The work that resulted, *Hind Swaraj,* appeared first in Gujarati in Gandhi's South African weekly, *Indian Opinion.* It was a dialogue between a "Reader," who seemed to express the views of Indian terrorists, and an "Editor," who spoke for Gandhi. Condemning terror as a tactic of nationalist struggle and advocating nonviolent satyagraha, it went well beyond the debate about violence to consider what Indian nationalists were after. They claimed that they wanted *swaraj,* a word used as if it were equivalent to the English concept of political independence, or home rule. Gandhi said that he too wanted swaraj for India, but he defined it as *self*-rule: "It is swaraj when we learn to rule ourselves."[18]

What would be the point, Gandhi asked, of ejecting the British from India by violence, as the terrorists intended, if the nation did not free itself from the violent, profane way of life that he said the British had implanted? Gandhi asked Indians to return to their authentically Indian roots; once this kind of swaraj came about, he insisted, the question of political independence would resolve itself. "If we keep our house in order, only those who are fit to live in it will remain. Others will leave of their own accord."

But swaraj meant more than repudiating Western ways. He admitted there were serious "defects" in Indian life—the marriage of children, for example— that could not be blamed on imitation of the county's foreign rulers. Swaraj, he explained, also meant reforming Indian ways. It was not a mere political condition, to be gained by driving the British out. It was also a social and personal condition, to be gained by first driving out one's own demons.[19]

During his two decades in South Africa, Gandhi practiced this kind of swaraj. Shedding many of the emblems of the West, he adopted simple Indian peasant clothes, he had his children educated at home rather than in European-style schools, and he rejected Western medicine when he or family members became ill. Gandhi also set aside certain deeply embedded Indian practices, particularly caste-related rules: He and other members of his household per-formed all domestic chores, including some—washing clothes, cutting hair, emptying chamber pots—that were thought to be polluting to all but the lowest castes. The hallmarks of how he lived were manual labor, simplicity, and purification, signified most clearly by his ascetic eating habits and the vow of sexual abstinence that he made in 1906.[20]

It was his outward work, though, that led him back to India. After the government in South Africa decided to repeal the registration act, Gandhi decided that it was time to close what had become a kind of political and spiritual laboratory and to apply the experimental knowledge gained there to India. He turned homeward with unique credentials: Living abroad had given him the perspective to see India whole, and the distance had kept him out of the stale air of political debate and helped him develop his own ideas. In July 1914, following his vision of a self-reliant and free India, he sailed for home.

THE RAJ

Overlords

The British had first gone to India in the sixteenth century as traders, not conquerors, setting up fortified stations along the coasts and leaving the interior to the Muslim Mughal emperors, whose ancestors had invaded India from Central Asia. But the Mughals had established no central government, instead making deals with local rulers, who collected revenues and provided soldiers for them. This system disinte-grated during the eighteenth century, as conflicts erupted among rival Indian powers.

As political instability jeopardized commerce, the East India Company—with a monopoly on British trade with India—raised an army and, in 1765, took control of Bengal, around its Calcutta headquarters. Over the next fifty years the Company expanded its writ south and west to cover most of the subcontinent, its army growing to over 250,000 men. Its domains were divided into three "Presidencies": Calcutta, Madras on the southeast coast, and Bombay on the west. The British *raj* had taken root. But ruling India—the size of Europe excluding Russia—was an enormous task. The Company made treaties with princely dynasties that held sway over large areas in return for military protection—saving itself the cost of direct administration.[21]

The British had always known that they depended on their Indian allies. "Our inexperience, and our ignorance of the circumstances of the people," wrote Tomas Munro, a Company official in Madras, in 1817, "make it more necessary for us to seek the aid of regular establishments to direct the internal affairs of the country, and our security requires that we should have a body of head men of villages interested in supporting our dominion." For the Indians who served the British, the benefits were many: salary, status, influence, rights to revenue, and other material and symbolic rewards.[22]

Where they failed to suborn consent, the British resorted to force. In1857 there were rebellions by Indian soldiers and civilians across northern India, and subduing them took more than a year as well as reinforcements from overseas. The trouble had taken hold in places where local potentates had long-standing grievances with the raj. But where rural magnates owed their positions and wealth to the British, they kept order and there was no unrest. The loyal princes, a government report conceded, were "breakwaters to the storm which would otherwise have swept over us in one great wave."[23]

After the East India Company was disbanded and India became a crown colony, the government took over the task of keeping influential Indians loyal—rewarding them with money, land, and honors, and appointing Indians to consultative assemblies. The methods had evolved since the first days of their presence, but the British strategy remained the same: India was controlled by dispensing prizes and protection to Indian collaborators. "The British have not taken India; we have given it to them," Gandhi wrote in 1906. "They are not in India because of their strength, but because we keep them."[24]

Nationalists

Some Indians had always resisted the raj, and in the late nineteenth century a few had come forward to give this resistance a national voice. These were mostly professionals, whose English-language education helped them traverse the bound-

India, 1930-1931

aries of India's myriad languages and dialects. As journalists, lawyers, or public servants, they were also mobile, circulating around the country on the fast, cheap railroads built by the raj. To them India became not only a mosaic of disparate pieces but also a fully rendered whole. And in the same way they used the raj's common tongue and trains, they began to absorb and apply the political ideas of nineteenth century Europe, with its new vocabulary of nationalism.[25]

The focal point for nationalist politics was the Indian National Congress, founded in 1885. Each December, delegates converged on one city or another for three days of meetings, speeches, and social events, at the end of which they passed resolutions, sent them to British officials, and retired until the next year. At first Congress was anything but a seditious body; it was dominated by moderates who wanted to reform, not overthrow, the government. They blamed the raj for aggravating poverty, and they sought to reduce the imperial drain on India's resources, but their methods were decorous—resolutions, petitions, and press campaigns—and they considered themselves a "loyal opposition." The British saw them as an irritant but never a threat.[26]

Politics was not the only outlet for nationalists. Others were less patient, more determined to end the raj altogether, and willing to take militant action. The first secret terrorist groups arose in the 1890s. Destroying the raj, they believed, was as simple as killing the British officials who directed it—an illusion about the power of violence shared by later, twentieth century revolutionaries. Although different from the moderates in their choice of sanctions, the radicals had the same strategic idea: transforming India from the top down.

Two other currents ran through the broad stream of Indian nationalism: One urged the "constructive work" of promoting native crafts and education; the other was political, led by extremists within Congress who wanted to mobilize the masses to stop cooperating with the British. "Though downtrodden and neglected, you must be conscious of your power of making the administration impossible if you but choose to make it so," said Bal Gangadhar Tilak, one of the extremist leaders, in 1902. "It is you who manage the railroad and the telegraph, it is you who make settlements and collect revenues . . . "[27]

Any leaders who tried to draw Indians into the nationalist movement had to make their way through the dense religious and linguistic jungle that was India. Most Congress leaders were Hindus, as were the majority of Indians. But roughly a quarter of all Indians in the late ninteenth century were Muslims, some the descendants of invaders from earlier centuries, some of Hindu converts. In parts of northern India and in Bengal, Muslims were either a majority or nearly so. A smaller number of Indians were Sikhs, most of whom lived in the Punjab on India's northern plains, where they formed a sizable minority.

While many Congressmen and educated Indians had mastered English, everyone else spoke native vernaculars. India had two major linguistic groups, each with a number of separate languages, which in turn had different dialects. Indo-Iranian languages (including Hindi, Urdu, Bengali, and Gujarati) predominated in northern India, while Dravidian languages (such as Tamil and Telugu) were found in the South. The result was a hodgepodge of linguistic areas that were distinctive arenas for politics and culture.

Overlaying these differences was another complication: People everywhere were born into particular castes, determining their rung on the social ladder and their roles in religious rituals as well as whom they could marry and what kind of work they could do. In most places those in the top castes, such as Brahmans, were barred from manual labor and became landholders, administrators, or businesspeople. At the bottom were "untouchables," who did jobs such as tanning hides or clearing human waste. While the system was not rigid—life choices were not absolutely fixed by the chance of birth—it walled off many Indians from each other.

The British did their best to reinforce the ways that Indians were divided. For example, when the East India Company annexed the Sikh-ruled Punjab in the mid-1840s, it used a mostly Bengali army to do the bloody work. A decade later, when Bengali soldiers in northern India rebelled, Sikh recruits were asked to return the favor and crush the mutiny. This divide-and-rule strategy, however, only bolstered already-existing tensions, and the greatest of these was religious. Animosity between Hindus and Muslims often boiled over into communal violence. A movement among Hindus to protect cows from slaughter in Muslim festivals, for example, led to a rash of deadly riots in 1893.[28]

How to knit together the fractious parts of India was just one of the quandaries facing nationalists as the twentieth century opened. Was their ultimate goal to reform the raj or to end it? How could they broaden the movement beyond the tight circle of educated, affluent men in Congress? Should they employ legal and nondisruptive methods, mass mobilization, or also violence? In 1914 there was no clear way to answer these questions—and no one to show the way. But that was about to change.

GANDHI AND HIS NATION

"A Real Awakening"

Gandhi arrived back in India after the beginning of World War I. Although the battlefields were in distant Europe, the British enlisted Indian men to fight and die on the empire's behalf, and they raised taxes on Indians at home. For Indian nationalists, who mostly supported the war, these sacrifices were a new reason to assert their rights. Because Indians were doing their share for an alliance of free nations, they argued, their own rights should be respected. In 1916 Congress and the Muslim League joined forces to propose full home rule through constitutional reform.[29]

For Gandhi, the country's constitutional status was not the prime issue. In South Africa he had come to believe that swaraj could not be won by political change at the top but necessitated reform at the roots of society and popular nonviolent action. Once back in India he went straight to these matters, though the projects he pursued were not what other all-India leaders thought important. Paradoxically, his work away from the spotlight would thrust Gandhi into the center of the nationalist movement.

For a year Gandhi traveled around the country by train, always going third class, and saw India from the bottom up—sharpening his sense of the far-reaching transformation his homeland would have to undergo to be capable of self-rule. Swaraj involved an "awakening in all departments of life," he said in 1917, and it had to begin in the consciousness of individuals. It would take unity among castes and religious communities, a love for all things Indian, and down-to-earth improvements in local administration, education, and public health and hygiene. "We may petition the Government, we may agitate . . . for our rights; but for a real awakening of the people, the more important thing is activities directed inwards."[30]

This agenda fired Gandhi for the rest of his life. He decried religious intolerance and appealed for unity among Hindus and Muslims. He lamented the mistreatment of women, shown by enforced seclusion (purdah) and the avoidance of contact with menstruating women. He beseeched landlords and employers to take responsibility for the poor (though he deflected calls for economic redistribution, such as land reform). Above all, Gandhi reviled the practice of untouchability, and—much as Abraham Lincoln had spoken of American slavery a half century before—said that "as long as this curse remains with us, so long I think we are bound to consider that every affliction that we labor under in this sacred land is a fit and proper punishment for this great and indelible crime that we are committing."[31]

Gandhi's "constructive program" was not just a skein of exhortations to others about how they should live. In his own life he also tore down the barriers that separated Indians by associating publicly with Muslims and untouchables and by mingling with the poor. Likewise, he always wore Indian hand-spun cloth (khadi), organizing an association to encourage spinning and making time for it in his daily routine, even when he was leading nationwide campaigns.[32]

Gandhi also founded communities of like-minded people who would live according to his concept of swaraj. The most famous of these was the Sabarmati ashram, in the Gujarat town of Ahmedabad, whose members vowed to adhere to truth and ahimsa—remaining celibate, leading simple lives focused on prayer and manual labor, and disregarding untouchability. The last vow was the hardest: The admission of an untouchable family just months after the ashram opened led many members to quit. (Gandhi managed to raise sufficient money from a local merchant to keep the community going.)[33]

For Gandhi, social regeneration was not an end in itself; it was the groundwork for nonviolent action, because the rancor between Muslims and Hindus, the exclusion of women and untouchables from public life, and the poverty and ignorance that beset huge parts of the population all were obstacles to a unified and disciplined nationalist movement.

His first satyagraha in India was an act of individual protest: He refused an order by local officials to leave the Champaran district of Bihar province, where he had gone in 1917 to look into charges that indigo planters were exploiting peasant laborers. In response, the government appointed a board to investigate conditions there. Early the next year he became embroiled in a labor dispute in Ahmedabad, where textile workers were protesting wage cuts. He first urged compromise, then organized a strike, and finally announced a fast (the first of many), which ultimately produced a settlement.

By intervening on behalf of peasants and workers, Gandhi broke from the mold of nationalist politicians. Swaraj was not just a fine word used by the high and mighty; it had something tangible to offer the downtrodden. In each locale he recruited volunteers to build schools, improve hygiene, and promote crafts, thereby making connections with teachers, lawyers, merchants, and landed peasants. In later years they would become his most loyal allies. Finally, publicity about these satyagrahas boosted Gandhi's growing fame throughout India as a man who might just invigorate the nationalist cause.[34]

"I Was . . . Shown the Bullet-Marks"

While Gandhi was crusading for social reform and taking local nonviolent action, Congress continued to agitate for home rule. But its leaders soon came to recognize that they needed his unmatched popularity and his abilities as an organizer and strategist, and Gandhi had a growing conviction that winning swaraj at the commanding heights would be, after all, an essential correlate of building swaraj at the grass roots. They were ready to join forces.

The British provided the catalyst. In 1919 the Rowlatt Act had extended restrictions introduced as emergency war measures, including administrative detentions and trials by judges rather than juries for seditious acts. Gandhi was appalled. "I feel I can no longer render peaceful obedience to the laws of a power that is capable of such a piece of legislation," he said. Now, for the first time, he thought about a satyagraha on an all-India scale.[35]

Gandhi first planned a limited campaign by disciplined activists, who would take an oath to disobey the laws and refrain from violence. He designated April 6, 1920 as a day of fasting and prayer, fashioned after the customary day of mourning known as a *hartal*; then the protest would be confined to open sale of prohibited literature. That way, Gandhi assured moderate politicians, opposition to the raj could be channeled away from violence. "The growing generation will not be satisfied with petitions, etc.," he wrote to a moderate leader. "Satyagraha is the only way, it seems to me, to stop terrorism."[36]

The hartal went off more or less as planned: All over the country people stopped work, closed their shops, and went to meetings. After the hartal, however, events spun out of Gandhi's control. Rumors that he had been arrested sparked a rampage of mill-hands in Ahmedabad, where more than fifty buildings were burned down and twenty-eight people were killed. In the Punjab, in the north of India, strikes and rallies turned into street fights between protestors and police. This was too much for General Reginald Dyer, sitting in the Punjab city of Amritsar, so he decided to quell the uprising— and also teach the population a lesson.

On the thirteenth, Dyer banned any public gathering of more than four men. Nationalists ignored him and called a meeting that afternoon at Jallian- wallabagh, a large open area surrounded by brick buildings, with just a few exits. Dyer did nothing to prevent thousands from gathering, but just after 4:00 P.M. he arrived with two armored cars and about fifty soldiers. Without warning, he ordered his men to open fire. Ten minutes later they marched off, leaving behind the bodies of the dead and wounded. (An official British commission counted 379 killed; Indian estimates ranged as high as 1,500.) Later the unrepentant Dyer admitted he could have ended the meeting without bloodshed but that he had used "the least amount of firing which would produce the necessary moral and widespread effect . . . from a military point of view, not only on those who were present, but more specially throughout the Punjab."[37]

In the next weeks the British drove home this "moral effect." Officers imposed curfews, prohibited meetings, held summary trials, tortured prison- ers, and flogged and executed people in public. Military airplanes bombed and machine-gunned Indians from above. In many towns Indians were ordered to salute or bow to British officers. Dyer demanded that any Indians who ventured onto a street where one British woman had been attacked would have to crawl on all fours.[38]

Amritsar and its aftermath were never forgotten by those who survived it. Shiva Dua, later a student activist at Lahore University, recalled being taken to Jallianwallabagh by her family when she was still a little girl. "I was literally picked up and shown the bullet-marks in the walls," she recalled. "We brought blood- stained, red earth back . . . and my sister said: 'This is a sacred thing. It has to be kept in a silver casket. And every day it will be your duty to put flowers on it. Early in the morning, this will be your first duty to do.'" The bloodbath in the Punjab had only intensified the thirst for self-rule.[39]

Gandhi was shocked by the violence that his anti-Rowlatt campaign had inadvertently produced. He fasted for three days in penitence, but his attitude toward British rule hardened. He called an official British report on Amritsar a "whitewash," and he was incensed to learn that General Dyer had become a hero to part of the British public. Having earlier held out hope that India could achieve swaraj within the British constitutional structure, he now viewed the raj as "satanic" and "dishonest." Indians, he argued, must stop tolerating such a government.[40]

Noncooperation

To rally Indians against the raj, Gandhi looked to Congress to provide organization, and he plunged into party affairs, helping to turn it into much more than an elite debating society. Congress expanded its network of provincial and local committees, absorbed new members, and took up the provocative work of mounting mass protest. Moderates had misgivings about extra-constitutional methods, but Gandhi's stature prevented them from standing in his way. Soon he had won the party's approval for noncooperation and also for a new constitution he had drafted, making it more efficient and more representative. The changes went to style as well as substance: No longer was a suit and tie the uniform of choice; now it was more likely to be the hand-spun cloth, or khadi, that Gandhi had popularized.[41]

Several different stages of noncooperation were planned: After fund raising and organization building, there would be a boycott of schools and courts; next would be a boycott of foreign cloth along with promoting the weaving of cloth from hand-spun yarn. Noncooperation would conclude with the resignation of Indian civil servants and carefully prepared civil disobedience in a few selected areas. By organizing well, by proceeding gradually, and by keeping a rein on deliberate lawbreaking, Gandhi hoped that the new campaign would not devolve into the violence that had flared in the Punjab.[42]

Although few lawyers boycotted the courts and not many civil servants quit their jobs, and while most students soon returned to classes, Congress for the first time brought the cause of national freedom to the Indian masses. Gandhi was in the vanguard: He caravanned around the country—on train carriages, on the back of carts, and by foot—spreading his message to multitudes. People everywhere, educated and uneducated, rich and poor, urban and rural, Hindu and Muslim, took up the call, picketed a merchant selling foreign cloth, joined a volunteer society, or found some other way to back the cause.[43]

But while Congress leaders proved they could spark popular protest, they found it hard to tame. Congress leaders in Assam were dismayed by strikes of migrant workers on tea plantations; leaders in Bengal and in the Andhra delta failed to prevent peasants from withholding rent and taxes and from violating rules on access to forests. Gandhi made it clear that the campaign was aimed at ending imperial rule, not at the long litany of local inequities, and he had ruled out strikes and anti-landlord actions. But that did not stop many from draping their personal causes in the colors of the larger movement.[44]

Worst of all, in Gandhi's view, there were riots. In the United Provinces (U.P., later Uttar Pradesh), peasants raided bazaars and landlords' homes. In Bombay, crowds attacked Europeans, Anglo-Indians, and Parsis. "I confess my inability to conduct a campaign of civil disobedience to a successful issue unless a completely nonviolent spirit is generated among the people," Gandhi said in reaction. "If I can have nothing to do with the organized violence of the Government, I can have less to do with the unorganized violence of the people." In February 1922, just as Congress was preparing a new round of civil disobedience, a massacre of twenty-two police constables in the U.P. led Gandhi to call off noncooperation altogether.[45]

Until this point, India's nationalist movement had exhibited a new maturity and vitality, animated by Gandhi's leadership, spurred by changes in Congress, and strengthened by a growing social base. But Gandhi's popularity was a mixed blessing. Everywhere he went, people flocked to hear him speak or just to glimpse this man they considered holy, this *mahatma*. "It is amazing what an influence this man is getting," wrote the governor of Madras, one of whose assistants "was tremendously impressed with the huge crowds at every station, their orderliness, and absolute devotion to their leader."[46]

His eminence, however, did not translate automatically into acceptance of Gandhi's ideas. While the number of his faithful followers was growing, they were few compared to those who made the persona of Gandhi an icon for their own goals or methods, which often had little in common with his. For peasants in one corner of the U.P., "Gandhiji's swaraj" came to mean the radical vision of a world free of landlords and rents, and his name was even invoked as a justification for looting.[47]

Moreover, while Gandhi had instilled a new sense among Indians of their own power, his campaign had not yet delivered swaraj. Neither the political autonomy sought by conventional politicians, nor the national unity and discipline that Gandhi saw as the backbone of self-rule, was in prospect. In the years after the noncooperation campaign, both Congress and Gandhi shifted away from mass nonviolent action to pursue their ends by other means. For many Congressmen, reforms by the British in 1919 offered them limited but real authority at the provincial level and opened up new personal opportunities. Perhaps working within the system would encourage the British to make further reforms—or so they hoped.

A few weeks after suspending noncooperation in 1922, Gandhi was arrested and spent almost two years in prison. It was a time of reading and intense reflection. After his release, he continued to work behind the scenes in Congress. But in the main he now directed his energies back toward the "constructive work" of his first years after returning to India, such as promoting spinning, easing tensions between Hindus and Muslims, and opposing untouchability. He had no intention of giving up political leadership and satyagraha, but at least for now he turned again to constructive work.[48]

CIVIL DISOBEDIENCE

"A National Call"

The mid-1920s were a time of flagging effort and disarray in the nationalist movement. With Gandhi largely off the scene, Congress politicians squabbled about how to deal with the raj. Those who stood for election to the provincial councils were rebuked by radicals who demanded a renewed drive for all-out independence, and local and provincial committees withered. Congress also suffered communal stresses, with Hindu fervency rising and Muslim membership plummeting.[49]

As before, it was an act by the British that reenergized Congress. In 1927 a commission to review the results of the 1919 reforms, headed by Sir John Simon, was unveiled, an apparent prelude to further change. But the commission did not include a single Indian, sending the message that the British were not willing to treat Indians as partners in shaping the country's constitutional future. The commission was, in Gandhi's words, an "organized insult to a whole people." Indian leaders boycotted its hearings, and as commissioners traveled around the country, they were greeted by hartals and demonstrations.[50]

Indian politicians now scrambled to put together a united front against the raj. Groups that had boycotted the commission sent delegates to an All-Parties Conference. Charged with drafting a constitution for a free India, it produced the Nehru Report (after Motilal Nehru, one of its drafters), envisioning India as an autonomous dominion within the British empire, with an executive and an all-India legislature elected by universal adult suffrage. But the report was rejected by most Muslim leaders, because it passed over their demands for decentralized states and reserved Muslim seats in provincial legislatures. Moreover, Jawaharlal Nehru, Motilal's son, and his fellow militant Congress members were furious that it stopped short of demanding full independence.

With divisions threatening to stall the revived movement, Gandhi was implored to come to the rescue. He responded that he would take on the mantle of leadership again only "when the nation comes to me to be led, when there is a national call." But he agreed to attend a Congress session in December 1928 in Calcutta, where he hammered out a deal acceptable to both moderates and militants. Congress would adopt the Nehru Report, and the British would have until the end of 1929 to accept it. If they refused, a nonviolent struggle for full independence would be launched. In the meantime, Gandhi insisted that Congress revitalize its organization and take up constructive work again—and since he threatened to withdraw again from Congress affairs if his terms were not accepted, they were.[51]

Now there was also renewed confidence in the potential of satyagraha, thanks to a campaign in the Bardoli area of Gujarat in 1928. Constructive work had put down deep roots in Bardoli, especially among the Patidars, a caste of fairly prosperous farmers. At Gandhi's urging, the Patidars had established a network of ashrams that promoted spinning, temperance, and general welfare. When the British ordered a 22 percent hike in land revenue assessments, the Patidars used this network to resist. They found a leader in Vallabhbhai Patel, a Patidar lawyer with strong ties to Gandhi, and resolved to withhold all revenue payments until they got satisfaction from the government.[52]

The campaign succeeded in rallying behind it the whole population of Bardoli. When the government auctioned land that was declared forfeit due to nonpayment, those who bought the land were boycotted. Patel consulted regularly with Gandhi, who spread news of the Bardoli satyagraha in the two journals that he edited. The provincial government considered sending in armed detachments, but the raj was concerned that the movement would spread and pressured provincial officials to negotiate with Patel, leading eventually to a big reduction in assessment levels.[53]

If the Bardoli action was a victory for the Patidars, it was a vindication for Gandhi. It demonstrated what nonviolent resistance could achieve when carried out by organized, disciplined, and united people, and it showed that the British could be made to bend. "It is indeed true that man forges his own fetters and he himself can break them," Gandhi said. Now he was once more prepared to try satyagraha on the vast, complex tapestry of India.[54]

"I Know . . . How to Lead"

The achievement of Bardoli would have to be duplicated on a gigantic scale. Only Congress could provide the necessary all-India framework. But many of its provincial committees existed in name only, without regular funding, record keeping, or even proper offices. Only in a few areas, such as Gujarat, was there a healthy structure of committees.[55]

So in 1929 Gandhi took steps to pump new life into the party apparatus, which produced a cascade of new members and signs of vigor in certain provinces. In U.P., for example, an old Congress stronghold that had become dormant, there was a shake-up at provincial headquarters, recruitment was stepped up, funds were raised to pay volunteers, and the message went out via the press and mass meetings. Tours of U.P. by Jawaharlal Nehru and by Gandhi kindled tremendous enthusiasm. But what happened there was not matched everywhere. What had to be done was simply too extensive, and Congress could not be rejuvenated in a single year.[56]

Compounding uneven strength at the grass roots was the party's persistent disunity at the top. Many old-timers were still reluctant to get involved in a disruptive mass struggle and wanted some accommodation with the British. Younger, more combative members objected to any compromise and were enticed by violent tactics; the Bengal Congress committee and its leader, Subhas Chandra Bose, even had close links with terrorists. Gandhi managed to prevent a rupture, in part by engineering the election of Jawaharlal Nehru as president of Congress, to keep the loyalty of radical members.[57]

Gandhi also faced the daunting challenge of bridging communal discord. In all of his previous satyagrahas, whether in South Africa or India, he had been able to strike alliances with Muslim leaders and persuade ordinary Muslims to take part. But now even Muslim politicians who had worked with Congress looked askance at a campaign to be led by the Hindu-dominated party. Gandhi tried to reassure them that Congress would not impose "Hindu raj" in place of British raj, but his own reliance on Hindu symbols may have undercut his credibility. The effort to enlist the Muslim political elite failed: Only a small number of so-called Nationalist Muslims were willing to see Congress as a partner.[58]

In a further sign that a new nonviolent campaign would not have smooth sailing, terrorists carried out attacks against British officials in 1929—including an attempt to assassinate the viceroy—and massive strikes in Bombay, Bengal, and elsewhere, led by militant communist-influenced labor unions, showed that industrial workers rallied as easily to the banner of class struggle as to that of national unity.[59]

While politics engrossed Gandhi in 1929, his constructive work never waned. He continued to lambaste untouchability and the mistreatment of women and to champion a boycott of foreign cloth, thereby expanding the scope of political action. Anyone—even the elderly, invalids, and women secluded in their homes—could join the campaign for a free India, by making simple changes in their lives. Aloo Dastur, a girl at the time of the great campaigns, saw people everywhere, even on trains, spinning on lightweight spindles. When her school adopted a uniform of white blouses and navy blue skirts, Dastur's mother had her buy blue dye and sewed her an outfit of khadi.[60]

Again Gandhi moved around the country making speeches and raising money. No other politician got to know India the way he did, but what he saw made him question whether the nation was ready for another nonviolent campaign. "I know well enough how to lead to civil disobedience a people who are prepared to embark upon it on my terms," he wrote. "I see no such sign on the horizon." There was one place where Gandhi could find a core of activists who would accept his terms: the Sabarmati ashram. So he began to look to the

Lord Irwin, British viceroy in India during Gandhi's salt satyagraha.
Credit: ©CORBIS/Michael Nicholson

ashram as an alternative base for launching a satyagraha, albeit on a limited scale. As for an all-India movement, he kept preparing for it, but he harbored doubts about whether it would work.[61]

Watching these developments from atop the raj was another man of renowned integrity and large intelligence. Edward Frederick Lindly Wood, Baron Irwin, had been the British viceroy in India since 1925, with long distinguished government service behind him and more ahead of him: He would replace Anthony Eden as Neville Chamberlain's foreign secretary. He was, as the later appointment suggests, a man who would sit down with anyone, even Hitler or Mussolini—a man who, in the face of threats even against himself, preferred negotiation to fighting.

Irwin had been born in Yorkshire, the son of the second Viscount Halifax, and his entire life had been colored by deep religious belief and a marked empathy for his fellow man—which was sometimes expressed in unexpected ways. In 1928 Irwin had written Gandhi a note of condolence on the death of his nephew, Maganlal. "I can guess what his loss must mean to you and to his family," Irwin wrote, "for all humanity meets on a common ground of experience, as sorrow and loss come to us all."[62]

As 1929 proved to be a year of incomplete progress for Gandhi, so too was it for Irwin. He had authored a new reform proposal envisioning dominion status for India, with details to be decided at a Roundtable conference in London including Indian as well as British representation—and he won backing for the policy from the new Labour government in London, despite bitter opposition from his own Tories. But the government's offer did not meet the demands Congress had made the previous December. Still, Irwin hoped that Congress moderates could welcome the proposal without losing face.[63]

They did press for a conciliatory reply, but others in Congress still opposed compromise. To Gandhi, the proper response to Irwin's gambit was not self-evident. At first he leaned toward striking a deal, but within a few weeks his doubts grew. He questioned the wisdom of staking constitutional reform on talks with a politically vulnerable Labour government, especially since the policy had drawn fire in London. And he knew that if he did accede to Irwin, Bose, Jawaharlal Nehru, and their impatient followers would rebel and leave Congress. Near the end of December Gandhi and other Indian leaders met with Irwin. He refused to meet their conditions for entering negotiations, and both sides steeled themselves for a collision.[64]

A few days later Congress opened its annual meeting, at Lahore. Gandhi's resolution—that Congress's goal should be full independence, through civil disobedience—passed by a huge majority. But his authority in Congress owed more to his skill at mediating between divided factions than to members' dedication to his program. Moderates resisted forcing members to resign from provincial councils, and they prevented Gandhi from adopting a boycott of courts, schools, and municipal boards as official policy. The enticements of the raj—the bait of its prestige and the carrot of gradual reform—were still sweet.

At the same time, Congress militants called for tactics such as general strikes that went beyond what Gandhi would endorse. A resolution condemning the assassination attempt on Irwin, moreover, passed by only a slim margin, revealing that a large minority was not decisively opposed to violence. Gandhi, once again, pleaded with the unruly wings of his party to fall into line: "If you want me to conduct the civil disobedience, I would conduct it," he told them. "But you must be soldiers of the battle."[65]

Strategy for Action

Gandhi left Lahore without a definite plan for the campaign, nor did he hurry to develop one in the new year. Instead, he spent much of his time at the Sabarmati ashram, often sitting on the shaded veranda of his modest home, talking with others, reflecting, and allowing time for a sensible strategy to become apparent. In the meantime, Congress took some preliminary steps.

On January 6 Jawaharlal Nehru went ahead and ordered all Congress members to resign from the provincial councils; members who refused would be removed from the party's elective bodies. The response was strong but uneven; many were still reluctant to forgo the rewards of cooperation. Especially troubling to Gandhi was that even most Muslims who had stuck with Congress after the storms of the previous year or two declined to obey the resignation order.[66]

Congress's Working Committee designated January 26 as Independence Day, when a declaration drafted by Gandhi and Nehru would be read aloud everywhere. Throngs of Indians gathered under groves of trees and in public squares across the subcontinent and heard words echoing Thomas Jefferson's trumpet call to liberty in the American Declaration of Independence: "We believe that it is the inalienable right of the Indian people, as of any other people, to have freedom . . . We believe also that if any government . . . oppresses them, the people have a further right to alter or abolish it . . . We believe, therefore, that India must sever the British connection and attain Purna Swaraj, or complete independence."[67]

Within a few weeks Gandhi and the Working Committee tackled the problem of what to do if there were violent outbreaks by radicals. In 1922 Gandhi had responded to a massacre of policemen by calling off civil disobedience. But if Gandhi took the same tack this time, Nehru argued, the British could abort the new campaign simply by provoking violence. Gandhi conceded the point, deciding that he would not be responsible for the disorder of those who rejected his strategy. He would not allow their violence to interrupt his movement.[68]

This was a critical moment, for if Gandhi had elevated his abhorrence of violence above all other interests, he would have handed his opponents leverage against the larger movement, which remained nonviolent. The force of nonviolent resistance was not, he realized, a faucet that could suddenly be turned on and off. Even if it were, he would not always have his hand on it. In mid-February the

Working Committee decided that Gandhi would supervise the first stage of civil disobedience—but after Gandhi's arrest, which everyone expected, Congress itself would assume leadership, especially the provincial committees. As more arrests were made, initiative would pass down and be closer to the people themselves.[69]

It was during this interval at his ashram that Gandhi fixed on the idea of starting civil disobedience with a satyagraha aimed at the salt tax. Since the nineteenth century, the government had monopolized the manufacture of salt—a vital dietary substance—and levied a tax on its sale. Now Gandhi planned to break this law by having Indians make their own salt. For some Indian leaders salt seemed like a paltry issue to make the object of a momentous fight with the British, a distraction from the more exalted goal of political freedom. But Gandhi had his reasons.

To begin with, the salt tax was plainly inequitable, hurting the poorest Indians the most, and British officials had a hard time justifying it. In effect, Gandhi argued, the government stole salt from the people and then made them pay heavily to buy it back. "The people, when they become conscious of their power, will have every right to take possession of what belongs to them," he declared. Because the tax embodied the injustice of colonial rule, breaking the monopoly would dramatize swaraj in a way that would have material meaning to the lowliest Indians. Swaraj, the salt campaign would show, was not just about glorious political goals but also about the control by Indians over their everyday lives.[70]

Not only would making salt attach the poor to the cause of self-rule, Gandhi hoped, it also would build unity among Hindus and Muslims. Fighting a wrong that touched all of them equally would strengthen their sense of common purpose. The salt campaign would have strategic value in the overall conflict with the British as well. Since it did not threaten vital interests of the raj (revenue from the tax was only a small part of total government income), it would be unlikely to stimulate a preemptive or harsh response. Instead it would give the movement time to grow and might draw in people who were sympathetic in general but hesitant about taking riskier action.[71]

Having picked his target, Gandhi now offered to call off the campaign if Irwin would meet eleven demands, including changing currency exchange rates, reducing land revenue assessments, cutting spending on the military, and imposing a tariff on foreign cloth, in addition to abolishing the salt tax. Although Irwin would not even consider these demands, they reached over the heads of the Hindu political elite to a larger constituency, especially business interests and peasants. Swaraj, Gandhi signaled, would have real economic value.[72]

On March 2, still at Sabarmati, Gandhi wrote an open letter to Irwin. He addressed the viceroy as a "friend," saying that he felt no ill-will toward the British people, only toward the institution of the raj. Stressing the economic burdens of imperial rule, he asked Irwin to help him avoid the impending conflict and told him that—if they could reach no agreement—civil disobedience would begin on March 11, with the salt satyagraha. All he got back, from Irwin's secretary, was an acknowledgment that the letter was received and a statement of regret about Gandhi's intentions. Gandhi made public both his letter and the reply: He had extended a hand to his adversary, and it had been refused.[73]

Irwin was not inclined to compromise. "At present the prospect of a salt campaign does not keep me awake at night," he wrote to London on February 20. His officials were confident they could withstand civil disobedience, just as they had the noncooperation campaign. What was at stake seemed clear enough: Gandhi and other Indian leaders believed that they could "reduce us to submission by making government impossible," wrote Lord Peel, the secretary of state, in a letter to Irwin in January 1929. "It will be our business to show conclusively that they cannot."[74]

Yet Irwin still wanted to hold a Roundtable conference on constitutional reform, even if Congress would not cooperate, and he realized that it would be a joke if Indian political groups outside of Congress did not take part. Especially important were Muslim leaders and more moderate Hindu nationalists. To enlist their help, the government would have to avoid overreacting to civil disobedience and would have to operate with at least a veneer of legality. Furthermore, interruption of ordinary civilian rule, warned William Wedgwood Benn, the secretary of state for India, might harm India's credit in international markets.

At the same time, the regime had to keep the loyalty of Indians who staffed the army, the civil service, and the police force, and that meant the authorities would have to show that they were firmly in control, no matter how intense the opposition. "We must remember that it will inevitably lead to disaster if we let the Police get the idea that the Government is impotent in upholding its position and authority," wrote the director of the Intelligence Bureau. Government policy needed to be tough enough to reassure its servants that they were working for a regime that was in India to stay, but not so harsh as to alienate moderates outside of Congress who were still inclined to live with the raj.[75]

"The restraining action of Government must be effective," read instructions to local governments, "but it should not exceed the actual requirements of the situation." It would also be crucial to arrest Gandhi as soon as he stepped outside the law; leaving him at large a moment longer than necessary would only encourage his supporters and dismay the government's forces.[76]

"There Will Be No Retreat"

During prayer on March 5, Gandhi called on his fellow ashram members to march with him, starting seven days later, to the sea, where they would make salt. Marching was a familiar tactic for Gandhi. In South Africa he had led a large ragtag group on a five-day march through unfriendly territory, under constant harassment from the authorities. This time the marchers would be a smaller, tight-knit group, they would go farther, and they would pass through the Gujarat countryside where Gandhi was idolized. He imagined the march as political theater, playing vividly to firsthand witnesses and, via the press, to the entire country.[77]

The seventy or so marchers were people Gandhi knew were devoted to his principles, unlike many in Congress. They had endured the manual toil and self-denial of ashram life, and their discipline would, he believed, shine forth as an example to other Indians. Drawn from different regions, religious communities, and castes, they would be a metaphor for the nation, cemented in a righteous cause. On Gandhi's instructions, however, the march would not include women. When some women activists objected, he explained that if women joined the march, the British would accuse Indian men of using them as shields to protect themselves from police attacks. He wanted women to contribute to swaraj, but in this case a pragmatic sense of how to confront the British took precedence.[78]

The week before the starting date was a time of intense preparation. With the help of Vallabhbhai Patel, his chief ally in Gujarat, Gandhi planned a 240-mile route southward from Ahmedabad to the coastal village of Dandi. Along the way marchers would stop in villages where constructive work and satyagrahas in recent years would generate a receptive spirit for the message. Students scouted the route and gathered information about those villages, and a schedule of stopping places was published in Gandhi's Gujarati-language weekly *Navajivan*. Every effort was made to publicize the march in Indian and even foreign media.[79]

The atmosphere at the ashram and in Ahmedabad grew electric as March 12 approached. "This is a battle to the finish," Gandhi intoned. "We shall face the bullets with our backs to the wall . . . there will be no retreat at any cost." The authorities helped to sharpen the tension: A local magistrate arrested Patel on March 7, setting off a hartal that closed textile mills, schools, shops, and municipal offices. On the evening of the twelfth, crowds stood vigil through the night, and in the morning there were prayers and devotional songs. Then Gandhi spoke: "This fight is no public show; it is the final struggle . . . I do ask you to return here only as dead men or as winners of swaraj." Gandhi's wife, Kasturbhai, garlanded him with khadi, and gave him a walking stick. As he strode out of the ashram, the Indian leader stirred fervid and somewhat contradictory feelings among his onlookers. For Mahadev Desai, his secretary, Gandhi conjured up visions of both the great warrior Lord Rama, "on his way to conquer Sri Lanka," and the Buddha, "inspired by the mission of relieving the grief-stricken and downtrodden."[80]

As the marchers entered each village, a crowd would assemble and make a commotion with cymbals, drums, and other instruments. Gandhi would give a brief address attacking the salt tax as "inhuman" and declaring that the salt satyagraha was a "poor man's battle." At each stop he also exhorted village officers to resign, and he gave instructions for personal boycotts against those who refused to quit: Villagers who wanted their headman to resign could refuse to attend weddings or other celebrations at his house, but they must not deny him necessary services. "The appeal must always be to the head and the heart, never to fear of force," he insisted.[81]

Gandhi wanted the march to the sea to bring ordinary villagers into the bigger movement for independence. He knew it was not enough to talk about solidarity with the poor; marchers had to confirm their words through personal simplicity and unselfish behavior. Each night, Gandhi ordained, they would sleep in the open and ask of villagers nothing besides raw food and a place to rest and wash. But the standards that Gandhi set were too demanding for some; he said he was humiliated that some marchers had milk and vegetables trucked in and received rides in automobiles. In the village of Bhatgan, he spoke about these extravagances. "Everyone was very still on hearing the grief in his voice," wrote one observer. "His words pierced our hearts. One by one, all the petromax lamps were extinguished, the meeting was in darkness except for a small lantern burning near Gandhi."[82]

The persistent fissures in Indian society were obvious along the route. Few Muslims attended the meetings in villages and towns, and the presence of untouchables among the marchers provoked disgust from some. Still, the droves who came to hear Gandhi swelled as the destination grew closer. Thirty thousand greeted them in Surat, not far from the scene of the Bardoli satyagraha, and at the railhead for Dandi more than 50,000 gathered. A wave of resignations by local officials also followed: By the first week of April, almost a third of all village headmen in Surat district had quit.[83]

The salt march made waves well beyond the Gujarat region. Gandhi wrote articles and gave interviews along the way, and Indian newspapers splashed news of the march across their front pages, spreading word of Gandhi's exploits far and wide. "And by god, even I who was only a school boy at that time, I tell you, my hair stood on end when I realized he was slowly approaching the goal," recalled the actor Alyque Padamsee. Three Bombay cinema companies sent crews along to shoot newsreel footage, and foreign journalists turned Gandhi into a household name in Europe and America. (At the end of 1930, *Time* magazine made him "Man of the Year.")[84]

After three weeks on the road, the marchers arrived in Dandi on the morning of April 5, a day ahead of schedule. By that evening over 12,000 people had

Mohandas Gandhi in a meeting with women during the Salt March, Gujarat, India, 1930.
Credit: ©Dinodia/The Image Works

congregated in the tiny village. Gandhi commended the government for not interfering with the march and ascribed this to concern for world opinion. To the international public he appealed for gestures of support for Indian independence, telling Indians that they were headed to "the temple of the goddess of swaraj" and that they must not let the government know any peace until they reached their destination. The beach at Dandi, he said, was "sacred ground."[85]

At dawn the next day, April 6, Gandhi stood on the shore, bent down, and picked up a clump of mud, a signal to begin breaking the salt monopoly. The marchers immediately started to fill pots with seawater. Deliberate, systematic civil disobedience was finally under way.[86]

"Gandhi Caps Fill the Streets"

The march from Ahmedabad to Dandi could hardly have been a greater triumph. Before the eyes of the nation, Gandhi had presented an object lesson in the use of nonviolent action against an unresponsive government. By his unambiguous words and brazen example, he had asked Indians to declare their independence from the laws and levies of the government. He told the British he would flout their authority, he marched through the land for weeks trumpeting the impending crime, and he told everyone that it was their duty to do the same.

For British officials, any course of action would play a role in Gandhi's drama. If they arrested the salt lawbreakers, they would create martyrs for the nationalist movement and confirm Gandhi's claims about their oppressive intent. If they let the salt resisters alone, they might sow doubt that they had the will to enforce their own laws in the face of Indian resistance. Either way they stood to lose something.

Joining the campaign was easy, because anyone with access to seawater could make salt: All it took was collecting water in a pot, boiling it down, and scraping up the residue that remained. There were reports of this happening in almost all parts of the country, though salt-making became a general activity only in the coastal regions of Bengal, Madras, and especially Bombay. In Bombay City, those who made salt in the open were protected from police by as many as a dozen concentric rings of volunteers with arms linked together. "It seemed as though a spring had been suddenly released," recalled Jawaharlal Nehru, who along with his father sold salt in the U. P. town of Allahabad. "It was really immaterial whether the stuff was good or bad; the main thing was to commit a breach of the obnoxious salt law . . . "[87]

In the weeks after the salt march, Gandhi looked for a way to goad the authorities to arrest him. So on April 24 he announced an especially provocative action: He would lead a raid on the salt works at Dharasana, which would surely be met with force. Wedgewood Benn understood the trap that Gandhi was laying. "They are deliberately attempting to present us with the alternative of using what they will represent to be unjustifiable and tyrannical repression or conceding their demands," he wrote. "They won't let us leave them alone."[88]

When the salt march had begun, Irwin had thought he had a plan: He would leave Gandhi alone until the moment he broke the law and then arrest him without delay. Yet when the bantam figure had stepped into the sea at Dandi, the viceroy had hesitated. It was clear by then that arresting Gandhi would set off a storm of protest and antagonize moderates whom Irwin wanted to recruit for the Roundtable.

Other officials were more concerned about keeping order. The governor of Bombay insisted that Gandhi's freedom discouraged the government's supporters as much as it encouraged its opponents. There was no way round the dilemma. "To arrest Gandhi is to set fire to the whole of India," a nationalist newspaper said. "Not to arrest him is to allow him to set the prairie on fire." Irwin finally made up his mind: He had Gandhi arrested on the night

Sarojini Naidu, Indian poet and member of the Congress working committee,
who led the nonviolent raid on the Dharasana salt works, May 1930.
Credit: ©CORBIS/Bettmann

of May 4, under an 1827 regulation obviating the need for a trial or a fixed
sentence.[89]

Gandhi's internment did not stall the action at Dharasana. Abbas Tybaji, a
seventy-six-year-old retired judge, came forward to lead 300 volunteers to the
salt works on May 12, with Gandhi's wife, Kasturbhai, at his side. They were
arrested before they reached the site and were sentenced to three months in
prison, but the Dharasana satyagraha still did not end. Sarojini Naidu, a poet
and Working Committee member, rushed to the coast and took over. Several
times she and volunteers approached the salt works. On each occasion their path
was blocked by police, so they simply sat down and waited, once for twenty-
eight hours. Hundreds more were jailed.[90]

Naidu knew that the raid courted violence, and she was anxious that it not come from the raiders: "You must not use any violence under any circumstances. You will be beaten but you must not resist: you must not even raise a hand to ward off blows." On May 21 the demonstrators tried to pull over the barbed wire enclosures around the salt pens. The police charged and began clubbing them with steel-tipped clubs called *lathis*. "Not one of the marchers even raised an arm to fend off the blows," a foreign journalist reported. "They went down like ten-pins . . . The survivors without breaking ranks silently and doggedly marched on until struck down." When the first column was felled, stretchers were brought up to carry off the injured—and more confrontations followed every day. Not until June 6 did the action at Dharasana end.[91]

During the march to Dandi, Gandhi had thought about the campaign's next phase. Civil disobedience should remain focused on the salt monopoly, he believed. Not paying taxes or breaking forest regulations were to be discouraged, because neither targeted an inherently unjust measure like the salt levy. But he felt the campaign should include boycotts of foreign cloth and liquor, acts that were not illegal but that did undermine the raj. The campaign should be unremitting but well regulated—though not by him. Gandhi and his colleagues knew they could not direct the movement in every city, town, and village, especially after they were arrested. They left it up to provincial committees to devise tactics that took advantage of local conditions, with one proviso: All action had to be strictly nonviolent.[92]

Congress organizers in the city of Lucknow, who had little luck with salt-making and a cloth boycott, turned to another sanction to force officials to choose between repression and retreat. After the 1857 mutiny, the raj had cut two boulevards through old Indian neighborhoods—demolishing houses and even cemeteries—to ensure quick access by troops. They also carved out a new British enclave and, running through its center, a shopping street known as the Hazratganj. Everyone understood that imperial control in Lucknow was symbolized by keeping order in what the British regarded as their part of town; Congress had long since been barred from leading processions on the Hazratganj. Now nationalist leaders decided to lay down a challenge: Indians would not be kept from any place in Lucknow.[93]

Twice, on May 14 and 22, Congress volunteers trying to march on the Hazratganj were blocked by police but after a standoff were allowed to enter. Thirteen leaders were arrested, but Congress was told it could march if it applied for a license. The British would allow the Indians within their citadel, but only if they first acknowledged the raj's supremacy. Congress leaders still at large would not let the British off the hook so easily. On May 25 an unlicensed procession of about 200 volunteers, led by a few dozen women, headed for the

Hazratganj, but police blocked their access. After a magistrate warned that force would be used to disperse them if they did not retreat, they waited a few minutes; then police hauled away the women at the front. When mounted police moved up, leaders ordered protestors to lie down, and foot police dragged them off. When some resisted, the police rained down lathi blows on marchers and onlookers alike. Over a hundred were injured, many seriously, and Congress claimed that some were killed.

The challenge to the sanctity of the Hazratganj had unfolded as a textbook satyagraha. Congress had identified an issue that had personal meaning to the people and was a symbol for the general injustice of British rule. Volunteers then persisted in defying British orders, eventually exciting an attack by police on unarmed people, while eschewing violence themselves. The physical suffering that protestors sustained was a badge of courage and a reminder of the violence that the raj had, characteristically, employed.

But the conflict did not stop there. The next day, when city officials heard that Congress planned to try again, about 400 police and soldiers descended on its headquarters, cleared the streets, and pulled down the Congress flag. Leaders then called off the march, and troops and police withdrew. Angry residents pursued the police back to their station—despite the pleas of Congress volunteers that they go home—and hurled bricks, stones, and bottles, eventually chanting for the station to be torched. After about a half hour, the police opened fire. Troops restored order but not before four people were killed.

Authorities imposed a curfew, banned large assemblies and marches, and arrested many. Civil disobedience in Lucknow did not win the right to march through the street that signified British power. But nationalists scored a larger victory: They forced the raj to abandon the fiction that imperial rule was anything other than government at gunpoint. Yet they also learned a difficult lesson: Many of those they wished to rouse against British rule did not understand the reason for nonviolent discipline, and its breakdown handed initiative back to the side that could be more violent.

Lucknow was not the only place where, in the wake of the salt march, the raj found itself cornered and obliged to choose between giving up control and using violent force. The telegrams and reports that arrived in Delhi from the provinces in the weeks and months after April 6 punctured British hopes that the campaign would fail to gather steam and pose no serious threat. Gandhi's call for civil disobedience engendered small and large convulsions in many spots around the country, unnerving the raj.

In Bombay City the salt satyagraha and cloth picketing were everywhere, and volunteers took over the streets to direct massive and well-organized marches. "The Congress House openly directs the movement of revolt," recorded H. G. Haig, the home secretary in New Delhi. "Gandhi caps fill the streets, volunteers in uniform are posted for picketing with the same regularity and orderliness as police constables." In the Midnapur region of Bengal presidency, a police attack on salt-making volunteers sparked a rural insurgency: Peasants turned villages into forts, built barricades out of bamboo and trees, and dug trenches through fields. "I feel very little hope of restoring any measure of peace until we have a few more shootings," the panicked district magistrate wrote in June.[94]

As events began to take on the feeling of an uprising, the contours of the movement that Gandhi had set in motion were sometimes warped beyond recognition. At Chittagong, also in Bengal, terrorists barged their way into a campaign begun in the spirit of ahimsa. On April 18 about sixty men sacked a local armory and seized a large supply of weapons. They celebrated with the triumphant cry "Gandhiji's Raj has come!" and issued an independence proclamation, before fighting it out with police and soldiers.[95]

Worse news for the government came from the rugged Northwest Frontier, populated mainly by Muslim Pathans. The key figure was Abdul Ghaffar Khan, a champion of ethnic pride and social reform who had become an adherent of nonviolent action. When his followers picketed liquor stores in Peshawar, leaders were arrested, and a great throng of people marched through the town in orderly protest. Soldiers opened fire and killed at least sixty-five; then two platoons of Hindu riflemen refused orders to subdue the mostly Muslim crowd, and officials withdrew all soldiers from the city. For ten days the British lost control in Peshawar, and the unrest spread to the countryside, where officials resigned and revenue collection and courts came to a halt. The province's chief commissioner, Irwin said, was in "a state of mental prostration." Bolts seemed to be popping from the rafters of the raj.[96]

Crackdown and Resilience

Before Gandhi was arrested, the government had no strategy for curbing civil disobedience, besides waiting for it to subside. Then local officials had been given special powers, and they had resorted to outright physical force to deal with civil disobedience. Gandhi had been allowed to walk unmolested for more than 200 miles to Dandi; other Indians who broke the laws of the raj learned they would not be treated so gently. By the end of May local officials were authorized to prosecute people who picketed, intimidated public servants, or instigated "no-tax" protests.[97]

On June 3 the Viceroy's Council permitted provincial governments to outlaw the "organizing bodies of the civil disobedience movement," and by the end of summer the Working Committee was declared illegal in most places. The jails began to fill with Congress leaders, including the Nehrus and Patel. Censorship of Congress correspondence was also imposed, and in October officials started seizing the buildings and property of banned organizations. The government also prepared a comprehensive Emergency Powers Ordinance, to be held in reserve for an acute crisis.[98]

The British strategy for putting down the campaign also had a more dignified face. The Roundtable Conference was to begin in October, and Irwin still wanted Congress to be there—hopes that were shared by Indian politicians remaining loyal to the raj, who knew that going to the Roundtable without Congress would leave them badly isolated. So two of them visited Gandhi and the Nehrus in prison and hashed out what it would take to pull Congress in. After much back-and-forth discussion, the prisoners agreed to give ground if, among other conditions, all civil disobedience prisoners were released, special ordinances were repealed, confiscated lands were returned, picketing and salt-making were permitted, and India's right to secede from the Empire was acknowledged. Irwin would have no part of these sweeping demands, and by the first week of September, both sides had given up on a deal.[99]

Irwin's strategy—combining repression and negotiation to return things to normal—was stalled. But the regime's measures—arrests, ordinances, violence against protestors—complicated civil disobedience. If Congress was going to keep the campaign alive and feed the momentum it had achieved, it would have to neutralize the regime's attempt to clamp down. To do that, it had to ensure that violence did not frighten off people who wanted to join the movement. Large concentrations of protestors, as at Dharasana or in Lucknow, made people vulnerable to attack. So Congress emphasized small-scale dispersed actions, such as making salt and boycotting cloth and liquor, that were less likely to expose people to lathis or bullets.

Congress also understood that the raj could be made to pay a price for repression. The arrest of Gandhi had sparked demonstrations and hartals in numerous cities and towns as well as the resignation from legislative councils of some moderates who, until then, had resisted calls to stop cooperating with the raj. Sympathetic journalists also reported in gruesome detail about how police had dealt with unarmed opponents, and Congress released photographs showing the injuries at Dharasana. Every act to crack down could be used by Congress to win stronger allegiance from Indians.[100]

Now seeing that they faced a determined adversary, the British knew that stopping civil disobedience required crippling the organization that drove it. When they tried to prevent nationalist journals and newspapers from communicating with the field, Congress responded by printing and distributing leaflets and—when the government confiscated printing presses—by sending out letters, telegrams, and couriers to local leaders. Still, in the face of repression, all-India coordination was limited. Detailed directions to provincial bodies were not issued, beyond calls for the salt satyagraha and cloth boycott or admonitions to remain nonviolent. "The strategy of the battle must . . . be determined by local circumstances and change with them from day to day," declared a writer in Gandhi's journal *Young India* in July. The government offensive, rather than stifling the campaign, simply splintered it, as first provincial leaders and—after they went to prison—local activists stepped into the breach.[101]

Pervasive Resistance

Gandhi's great feat as a movement leader was to marshal support for his cause by fusing national independence—an exalted goal cherished by a small elite—with down-to-earth demands that offered millions of Indians modest improvements and thus a stake in the outcome. In his vision, Indians would fight for self-rule first by freeing themselves from the government's unjust monopoly on salt, and in the months that followed, local leaders would identify similar issues around which to organize protests. Every point where the raj intruded into the lives (and livelihoods) of Indians was a potential target of resistance.

The most unyielding practitioners of civil disobedience were the Patidars, living on the fertile plains of Gujarat, just north of Bombay. Nowhere else in India did Congress, Gandhian activism, and popular sentiment meld more smoothly into a unified force. Along with Gandhi, Vallabhbhai Patel, the regional Congress leader, had turned Gujarat into a hotbed of constructive work in the 1920s; and they also had led a number of small-scale satyagrahas that won them the loyalty of the people.

The Patidars were widely respected for toughness, self-reliance, and solidarity. "They are capable of accomplishing anything on this earth whether good or bad," recorded an awestruck revenue collector in 1930: "their resourcefulness and tenacity of purpose are really very wonderful." Thus they were naturals for civil disobedience, and as soon as Gandhi reached the beach at Dandi, salt-making began in coastal Gujarat. Thousands braved arrests and beatings to make and sell salt.[102]

But for the Patidars, the vital issue was land revenue. The British viewed themselves as the ultimate owners of the land cultivated by the Patidars (and by other Indians), and they considered land assessments a kind of rent. Withholding payments—something Gujarati Patidars had done on previous occasions—was an avowal of independence, denying the legitimacy of the British claim to an essential resource. It was also a nonviolent sanction that could do real damage to government operations.[103]

Agitation for breaking the land revenue law had begun months before the official launch of civil disobedience. Patel, disappointed that Gandhi wanted at first to restrict the campaign to salt, met with peasants in Kheda district and pushed them to halt revenue payments. The district's revenue collector had Patel arrested in the village of Ras, and to challenge the arrest, villagers withheld their payments, enlisting Patidars from surrounding villages in the drive. When the salt marchers arrived in Ras on March 19, Gandhi wanted the Patidars to stand down, but in the end, he felt obliged to endorse the action, though he warned that the government would not react mildly.[104]

To prevent revenue collectors from confiscating their belongings in lieu of payments, the Patidars packed up their cooking vessels, jewelry, and other valuables and carted them across the border into the princely state of Baroda, where many had relatives. Baroda officials, mindful of the reaction of their own Patidars, refused to confiscate these goods. By mid-May the no-revenue effort had spread to other areas of Gujarat, linked to the demand that Patel and Gandhi—both then under arrest—be released from prison. The real battle, however, would not come for months, until the next round of payments was due in December. At the behest of Bombay authorities, the central government ordered that land forfeited due to revenue nonpayment would not be returned to its owners and that any officials who left their jobs would not get them back.

Congress organizers in Gujarat did their best to discourage violence by their sympathizers. In Kheda district, they avoided drawing landowners from the Baraiya caste into the no-revenue campaign, since the Baraiyas had a taste for violent reprisals. Village leaders in Od went so far as to call off revenue withholding after a crowd of Patidars and Baraiyas together attacked a widely hated police officer. These precautions kept the no-revenue drive nonviolent, but they also foreshortened its reach beyond villages dominated by Patidars.

In the fall the Patidars needed to harvest and sell their crops and get the proceeds over the border to Baroda before they could be intercepted. But the revenue collectors went after the year's payments early, while the crops were still in the fields. Truckloads of police officers appeared one morning, rounded up villagers, beat them, and stripped them of gold ornaments. Some were tied up and thrashed; others were forced to stand naked in the center of the village, as the police broke into homes and hauled away valuables. But the Patidars had one more card to play. More than 20,000 fled en masse into Baroda, where they set up camps. "Many villages were totally abandoned," a British journalist reported. "I could see through the windows that every stick of property had been removed. In the silent street, nothing moved till a monkey skipped from a roof across the lane . . ."[105]

Resistance to land revenue also took hold in U.P. Sharp declines in agricultural prices in the second half of 1930—a result of the worldwide depression—made the payments an unbearable burden for many peasants, and pressure for a no-revenue satyagraha rose during the summer. In October the U.P. Congress embraced the cause. Organizers held processions and meetings where people were asked to make written pledges to join the resistance. The police struck back hard, destroying crops and driving away livestock. In some areas peasants resorted to mass exodus to remain out of reach of tax collectors.[106]

In other parts of India the main target of tax resistance was the levy on villages to pay for watchmen, known as *chaukidaris,* who reported to police on local comings and goings. Peasants in the Midnapur region resented this intrusion into village life, made all the more bitter because they had to pay for it. Once the coming of the monsoon season put a damper on the salt satyagraha, the chaukidaris became the focus of civil disobedience. Village officers, including chaukidaris, were harassed and ostracized. About 1,000 chaukidaris resigned, and in some places as many as eight out of ten people refused to pay the tax.[107]

For the Gond and Korku tribal peoples of the landlocked Central Provinces (C.P.), making salt was not easy. They had a more pressing grievance: restrictions on access to state-owned forests and high fees for grazing livestock on these lands. In the summer, masses of people descended on the forests armed with lathis and axes, cut down wood and bamboo, and grazed their cattle. The raj was ready to use violence to stop the despoiling of state property. "I shall have to hit hard and may have to shoot a bit," reported the governor in late July. By the end of October, police action had largely suppressed the forest raids.[108]

In rural civil disobedience, Congress often found itself behind the curve of popular action and struggled mightily (and not always successfully) to impose some direction and check violence. The protests in cities, on the other hand, generally arose on Congress's initiative and were tied primarily to symbolic issues. Nonviolent action became quite inventive, nowhere more so than in Bombay. When the salt protests subsided, Congress assigned picketers to patrol the streets in front of cloth and liquor stores, distributed propaganda, lit up the nighttime sky with bonfires of foreign cloth, held meetings on the beach attended by tens of thousands, declared periodic hartals to protest arrests or police abuses, and led long marches through the streets.

The climax in Bombay came on December 12. When picketers lay down in the street to block trucks carrying foreign goods, a young volunteer was killed—crushed by a truck, according to Congress. The news coursed through the city, and by nightfall people were making pilgrimages to the spot of the tragedy. The next day Congress volunteers handed out bulletins about the incident and led a procession bearing the body toward Chowpatty Beach. The police blocked their way with bayonets and charged those who were watching on adjacent streets; all day there were clashes. Afterwards the site of the death became a flower-covered shrine, new bouquets arriving as quickly as police cleared away the ones already there. "You had to live in Bombay to feel the atmosphere of anger . . . against the British," recalled Aloo Dastur.[109]

Congress organizers in Madras City, Calcutta, and other places adopted similar tactics, openly defying the laws of the raj or seizing control of public spaces. Sometimes the police let them alone; other times they were scattered with lathis. Staged for the benefit of the hundreds or thousands of ordinary people who turned out to watch, these confrontations did little tangible damage to the raj, but the sight of police attacking nonviolent men and women won immense sympathy from the public. On the other hand, action that led to the sword was double-edged: It could draw in violent sympathizers, diffusing responsibility for violence, frightening bystanders, and risking a harsher crackdown, which might in turn slow the movement.[110]

Civil disobedience took the form of collective action, but the individuals who joined these struggles faced intensely personal decisions. University students in Lahore did their part by going from house to house collecting foreign cloth and heaping it on a giant bonfire. Shiva Dua's family had already gone over to khadi and given up most garments made from foreign cloth. All that was left was a sari that Dua had inherited from her dead mother. How could she let this be added to the inferno? But when she saw her neighbors tossing things to the students on the street below, she knew what she had to do. "Mother was Mother," she resolved, "but the Mother country was higher than Mother, and the sari must go, so I gave it . . ."[111]

Neither the British nor Congress leaders expected that women would participate so ardently in the campaign. Women carried pitchers to the shore and boiled water for salt. In villages they boycotted auctions of confiscated goods and harassed and shamed buyers. They were beaten by police, and perhaps 20,000 went to jail during 1930. Women also became provincial and all-India "dictators" of civil disobedience. "The British Government had been given a jolt by the women of India," wrote an organizer of student protests in Lahore. "We were not . . . meek, mild, illiterate Indian women, content to remain within the four walls of our homes . . ."[112]

Gandhi was in many ways a traditionalist about women, although he saw them as having greater moral purity and capacity to endure pain, which he thought made them ideal candidates for satyagraha. He first wanted to confine them to spinning and clothing their families in khadi, only later permitting them to picket cloth and liquor stores while saying that lawbreaking should be left to men. When women complained bitterly about this exclusion, Gandhi relented. He had no doubt inspired many women to take part in civil disobedience, but most did so on their own initiative, not his.[113]

Keeping Control, Losing Ground

Civil disobedience, despite relentless exertions by the British to stamp it out, erupted in practically every province of India during 1930. Time and again the raj had to rely on the police to reassert control. On occasion—briefly in Peshawar, for months in Gujarat—even lathis and jailings were not enough, and officials had to concede that they no longer governed in some places. The volley of sanctions on many fronts took a toll on the financial and psychological infrastructure of the raj.

The liquor boycott, withholding land revenue and chaukidari payments, and the forest raids all squeezed revenues in several provinces. Bihar and C.P., for example, depended heavily on liquor excise taxes, so liquor boycotts there had immediate impact. The cloth boycott reduced the customs fees accrued by the central government (and also struck a blow at industrial interests back in Britain); the value of cloth imports dropped by half in a year. The depression could have accounted for part of this, since it cut the purchasing power of Indian consumers; but the fall in cloth imports was larger than that in other commodities, and the boycott may well have been the difference.[114]

Budget strain induced by nonviolent sanctions was compounded by new direct outlays, since police work was costly. From the salt march through the struggle with the Patidars (still under way in early 1931), some 60,000 people were jailed at one time or another for civil disobedience. Bombay, Bengal, and the Central Provinces had to boost spending on jails, find makeshift solutions (such as temporary huts) to house prisoners, and assign extra police detachments to trouble spots. Restoring order was made all the more difficult by the avalanche of resignations by local officials.[115]

But the panjandrums of the raj were less worried about the financial toll of fighting civil disobedience than they were about the impact of the campaign on the morale of their Indian hirelings, especially the provincial police forces. After the Amritsar massacre, the British were reluctant to use soldiers to disperse or restrain Indian protestors, preferring to rely on the police. They were acutely aware that if nationalists could undermine the loyalty and discipline of Indians in the police forces, they would shake the foundation of continued British rule in India.[116]

Civil disobedience put a fearful burden on policemen. As a report on conditions in the U.P. admitted, "they were openly abused and vilified, and frequently assaulted; shopkeepers occasionally refused them supplies, and menial services were denied them; even their wives and families were frequently subjected to social boycott." The inspector general of police in Bombay reported that he was not certain his officers could be relied on to carry out the government's repression.[117]

In his memoirs, John Court Curry, a British police officer who had served in Bombay City, confessed that he had "strongly disliked the necessity of dispersing these nonviolent crowds and although the injuries inflicted on the lawbreakers were almost invariably very slight the idea of using force against such men was very different from the more cogent need for using it against violent rioters who were endangering other men's lives . . . my intense dislike of the whole procedure grew to such extent that on every occasion when the Congress staged a large demonstration I felt a severe physical nausea . . . "[118]

British officials gave unstinting support to those who bore the brunt of the campaign. The Madras government, for example, exempted police from pay cuts imposed on other civil servants and showered bonuses on officers who clashed with protestors. Policemen also were assured that higher-ups would stand by them against accusations of brutality. In contrast, the effort of Congress to subvert police loyalty was never consistent. At first Congress appealed to their patriotic sentiment; in Madras activists mailed postcards to officers, imploring them to refrain from violence against their "brothers." But police excesses turned Congress against them, and censuring the police helped rally popular support. Congress's goal of deflating the legitimacy of the raj conflicted with its goal of winning over those who defended it.[119]

By September 1930 the viceroy was able to report to London that Congress had "definitely failed" in shaking the morale of the police and that new recruits were easy to obtain. As a consequence, India as a whole was not made ungovernable by civil disobedience. As the months went by, Irwin and his colleagues became increasingly confident that they could withstand the offensive by Congress and divide the movement into a series of local problems. By the last months of 1930, the tide of the campaign seemed to have crested and receded. Although anti-tax actions were still going strong in a few areas, the authorities felt secure enough that they never enacted the Emergency Powers Ordinance that had been drafted in mid-summer.[120]

While Congress had mounted a national crusade against the raj, it had not been waged evenly across the country's breadth and was weakened by communal divisions that long predated Gandhi. He had known by the end of 1929 that Muslim leaders would not join formally with Congress. But he had hoped that by fastening nationalist demands and nonviolent sanctions on economic grievances, Congress might overcome the distrust between ordinary Hindus and

Muslims and that the fellowship that proved so elusive during normal times could be forged in the heat of battle. Congress also tried to reassure Muslim politicians by reiterating a promise not to accept any constitutional arrangement without their assent.

But good intentions and political gestures failed to arouse much Muslim spirit for civil disobedience. Most Muslim leaders persisted in denouncing Congress, and ordinary Muslims were disinclined to join protests devised by its local organizers. As a measure of national participation, just 1,152 out of more than 29,000 prisoners in jail for civil disobedience offenses in November 1930 were Muslims. Without strong Muslim enrollment, the geography of the campaign could only be patchy: The Punjab and the Sind, with Muslim majorities, gave the British little trouble in 1930, while Muslim apathy diluted the campaign in other places. The only exception was in the remote Northwest Frontier, where Abdul Ghaffar Khan had infused his volunteers with Gandhian principles.[121]

Class divisions also sapped the movement's strength. Congress had financial and institutional links to privileged groups, such as businessmen who helped underwrite the party and uphold the cloth boycott, and landlords who were key cadres in rural areas. Although Gandhi reached out to all strata of society, down to the very poorest, the party's ties to affluent, influential Indians muffled appeals to the lower classes. Even Gandhi refrained from proposing a general strike—which would have hurt Indian businesses as well as the raj—and working-class militance in industrial areas remained an untapped resource throughout 1930.[122]

Not all the constraints on the movement came from within; measures taken by the regime stung as well. Although the strategy of decentralized control and dispersed sanctions helped the campaign survive the repressive onslaught in the early days, the physical attrition produced by lathi charges, mass arrests, punitive police raids, curfews, and other forms of persecution curbed the spread of civil disobedience in some parts of the country and liquefied it in others.

Where the regime's violence failed to intimidate campaigners, the raj found other ways to punish defiant Indians. The attachment of land belonging to tax resisters was a devastating tactic. People who were prepared to go to jail and even stand up to physical assaults found it much harder to face the loss of their land, which might leave their families destitute. Land seizures pressured peasants in Bihar, for example, to resume payment of the chaukidari tax by the end of 1930.[123]

Economic fatigue also braked the movement. Cloth dealers, who had cooperated with the boycott at first, began to lose heart as their losses piled up. As early as July, Bombay merchants joined moderate politicians in trying to persuade Gandhi and the Nehrus to reach a compromise with the raj. Later in the year, collective discipline began to crumble almost everywhere outside of Bombay City, as dealers sold foreign cloth on the side.[124]

Congress itself was debilitated by the second half of 1930. Arrests forced the leadership to hand initiative to provincial committees, which repression disrupted, and the breakdown of both central and provincial control eroded nonviolent discipline. There were few places in India like Gujarat, where the Patidars had years of experience with satyagraha and were committed to remaining nonviolent. The tax resisters of Midnapur, the forest raiders of C.P., and the crowds of Bombay City and Calcutta showed little appreciation for the risks of violence, and attacks against police, forest guards, and other agents of the raj began to mount. Even in Gujarat, a local official who refused to resign his post was murdered. The more that civil disobedience sprang from local grievances rather than from strategic intent, the more it was likely to stray from the nonviolent standard.[125]

Truce

As Congress looked out over a campaign that was waning in many places and an organization that was in tatters, the British looked across the table at other Indian representatives at the Roundtable Conference in London. It ran from late October until mid-January and included British officials, delegates from the princely states, and Muslim, Hindu, and liberal leaders—but not any members of the one organization with the greatest claim to speak for the Indian people: Congress.

The talks produced a formula for constitutional change that both the non-Congress Indian conferees and the British could live with: a federation of the princely states with British India, in which executive power would answer to a legislature. During a transition period, the viceroy would hold certain "reserved" powers, such as defense and finance. For Indian liberals, the agreement was progress toward self-government. Muslims were reassured by the federated structure, which afforded protection from Hindu domination. Even the British Liberals and Tories, who had vehemently opposed Irwin's 1929 reform offer, could support dominion status under such arrangements. The influence of the undemocratic princely states in the legislature, and the powers reserved for executive control, seemed likely to safeguard the raj.[126]

But the process begun in London with this unrepresentative band of Indian delegates would have had little potential if Congress was kept away. Although Irwin was not confident that Congress could be persuaded to join the next phase of talks, he felt that the chance for lasting Indian consent to a settlement that was reasonably favorable to the raj would not come again soon. He also wanted to relieve the strains on his regime and the drain on its coffers from the vexation of civil disobedience. So the time was ripe for a gesture toward peace with

Congress, and he announced on January 24 that all Working Committee members would be released from jail unconditionally.[127]

Once free, Gandhi insisted that Congress would not suspend civil disobedience and enter the talks until the government met certain demands—such as allowing picketing and salt manufacture, returning property that had been confiscated from tax resisters, and repealing repressive ordinances. Behind the scenes, however, he was hearing from both inside and outside Congress that it was time to come to terms with the government. Moderates in Congress, always hesitant about civil disobedience, wanted to abandon it. The militants, who might have resisted a softer line, lost a champion when Motilal Nehru died on February 6.

Gandhi also canvassed the business community and found it keen for compromise. "It may not be amiss to suggest to Mahatma Gandhi and the Congress that the time has come when they should explore the possibilities of an honorable settlement," declared D. P. Khaitan, president of the Calcutta Indian Chamber of Commerce, on February 11. "We all want peace." Finally, Gandhi's own conviction that the suffering of those who practiced satyagraha could work a change of heart in their opponents led him to hope that face-to-face talks with the government might be the place for this to emerge. Accordingly, on February 14 he sent a letter to Irwin requesting a meeting. The viceroy accepted without hesitation.[128]

Irwin, known as a decent, reverent man, struck Gandhi as the ideal partner with whom to settle the conflict. And Irwin, who returned Gandhi's respect, took care to confirm this impression. He wrote to Wedgewood Benn that he would try to convince Gandhi of his sincerity, of his "sympathy" and "understanding of his hopes, suspicions and disappointments." He would take the advice of an Indian liberal and show up for the talks wearing his "deepest spiritual robes."[129]

On the afternoon of February 17, wearing a woolen shawl, Gandhi strode up the steps of the Viceroy's House in New Delhi, completed just a few years earlier. Sporting fountains and sculptured elephants, it was capped by a soaring dome and fairly radiated the spirit of empire. He climbed the colossal staircase and was taken to Irwin's study, where he sat down and warmed himself before the fireplace. Each day, after talking with Irwin, Gandhi went back to the home of a friend and chewed things over for hours with members of the Working Committee.

These were preliminary, non-binding discussions—to clarify issues and positions that would be the basis for a second round of talks. First, there were constitutional questions emerging from the recent Roundtable: Would Congress negotiate within the framework of a federated state, a responsible central government, and various powers temporarily reserved for the executive? Second, there was the question of what to do about civil disobedience. Irwin made it clear that if Congress suspended its campaign, he would release all civil disobedience prisoners, repeal related ordinances, and recall punitive police detachments. But Gandhi wanted more: restoring jobs of local officials who had resigned, returning land confiscated from tax resisters, allowing salt manufacture and picketing of liquor and cloth stores, and inquiring into police abuses.

The thorniest questions were not, after all, constitutional. Although the government's scheme for reform fell far short of independence, Gandhi got Irwin's guarantee that Congress could bring up India's right to secede from the empire at the next Roundtable. Besides, from Gandhi's personal vantage point, constitutional questions—whether India would win dominion status or full independence, and how the transition would proceed—were not critical to the kind of swaraj that he had in mind for India.

But it would not be so easy for Gandhi to back down on other issues. After all, his strategy for the campaign had been predicated on resisting the most tangible manifestations of British rule, such as the salt monopoly and cloth imports. If he gave in on these issues, civil disobedience could be seen as a failure by many Indians on the front lines. For Patidar farmers, constitutional change would be trifling besides the staggering defeat of losing their land. Likewise, the men and women who had spilled blood at Dharasana would hardly welcome a deal that preserved the object of their protest and exempted the police from any liability for violence. Compromise on these issues was no less hard for Irwin. His provincial officials made clear that any settlement punishing the police or making the campaign victorious on everyday issues would dishearten the very men on whom the raj depended for its force. "We have to judge any proposed course of action not so much by its possible effects on the Congress, but by its probable effects on our supporters and our officers and men," warned one of Irwin's ministers a few days before the talks at Delhi.[130]

Gandhi and Irwin began conferring again in Delhi on February 27. They quickly agreed on a formula for constitutional talks, based on the three points of federation, accountable government, and reserved powers. But on the question of how the campaign would end, it looked like things would fall apart. In the end Irwin gave a little, Gandhi gave a lot, and they struck a bargain: Civil disobedience would end; the government would repeal the repressive ordinances, withdraw the punitive police, free prisoners, and allow banned organizations to resume operations. Indian officials who had quit their jobs would get them back, so long as the jobs had not been permanently filled in the interim.

On the other hand, there would be no inquiry into police abuses. Farmers could not recover seized land that had been sold. Peaceful picketing of cloth and liquor shops could continue, but not as a political sanction. And although the salt laws would stay in place, the government would not interfere with small-scale manufacture for domestic use. Jawaharlal Nehru was bitterly disappointed, but Gandhi managed to secure the consent of the Working Committee, and the terms of the truce were made public on March 5.[131]

Gandhi gambled that Congress would gain more—or lose less—by calling off civil disobedience and joining the Roundtable process than by soldiering on. Although he saved face on several points, he could hardly claim a clear win on any of the bread-and-butter issues. Still, he seemed to have bought time in which to rebuild Congress's battered apparatus, and the leadership remained intact, although militants were disgruntled about Gandhi's conciliatory course. What kept them in line was believing that if no agreement came out of the new Roundtable, due to begin in August, they could always take up the cudgel and renew the campaign.

Four days after the "Delhi Pact" was signed, Irwin wrote to Wedgewood Benn in London, relieved that he had not needed to give ground on "quite a lot of points that were . . . worrying us both, such as conduct of police, methods of repression . . . " As ever, the viceroy was focused on his means of control, which the agreement did not impair. If the deal did not prevent Congress from regrouping, it also left the raj with its full panoply of power. "Looking over the whole thing," Irwin remarked, "I do regard it as a very astonishing thing that Gandhi should have been so far persuaded to come into line."[132]

Many Indians in the police force and civil service were less enthusiastic than Irwin about the agreement, and British officials decided that the police had to be shown that their hands would not be tied in a renewed conflict. "Nothing short of a declaration in the most unequivocal terms, followed by equally unequivocal ocular proof, that Government is determined to assert itself and crush the subversive movement" would guarantee the loyalty of the police, warned the provincial administration in Bengal. So officials drew up a new Emergency Powers Ordinance almost as soon as the ink was dry on the truce.[133]

With hard-liners on both sides ready for the truce to break down, events seemed to invite failure. The architect of accommodation, Lord Irwin, returned permanently to England in April, and his replacement as viceroy, Lord Willingdon, had a different set of instincts. For Congress, now commit-ted to peace, popular struggles over local issues became problematic. In parts of Gujarat and U.P., peasants continued to withhold land revenue payments, as much out of economic distress (agricultural prices had fallen in the depression) as in protest. In the Northwest Frontier, Abdul Ghaffar Khan's forces had become active again, picketing cloth stores and calling for a land revenue boycott. Gandhi found himself counseling local activists to show restraint while urging officials to compromise. Other Congress leaders, such as Patel and Nehru, began to wonder if the benefits of sticking to the truce were worth the loss of local support.[134]

Gandhi sailed for London in August as Congress's sole representative at the next Roundtable conference, where he faced the British along with delegates of other Indian parties and the princely states. The British insisted that any headway on India's final status was contingent on agreements about how different communal groups would be represented and about the precise layout of the country's federated structure. As they expected, the Indian delegates became hopelessly deadlocked on these issues, and Gandhi's attempts to bridge their differences were to no avail. When Prime Minister Ramsay MacDonald closed the conference on December 1, India was no closer to dominion status than when it started.[135]

With the Roundtable over and nothing to show for it, the only alternative to admitting defeat was reviving civil disobedience. By the time Gandhi returned to India, the government had already offered serious provocation. Provincial officials had reenacted repressive measures in Bengal, U.P., and the Northwest Frontier, while putting a number of Congress activists, including Nehru, back in jail. Gandhi's request to discuss all this in person with the new viceroy, Lord Willingdon, was peremptorily denied, and on the first day of 1932 Congress announced it would resume civil disobedience.

This time, however, the government knew what was coming and showed more confidence in foiling nonviolent action. A preemptive crackdown, planned months before, took shape through a wave of arrests and new ordinances. Gandhi himself was back in jail by January 4. In effect, the new British policy was martial law. At the same time, many key Congress supporters had been turned off by the campaign's earlier suspension and restraint of local action. Now they were unwilling to reverse course and put their lives and property on the line for another campaign. Although the new round of civil disobedience did not end formally for another two years, after the first six months it never seriously challenged the raj.

෴ ෴ ෴

The results of the civil disobedience campaign against the British in India in 1930-1931 were decidedly mixed. In terms of the stated goals of Congress, as well as the hopes of resolute nationalists such as Jawaharlal Nehru, the campaign miscarried. When the second phase finally sputtered out in 1934, Indians had made scant progress toward either dominion status within the empire or outright independence. Neither had they won any major concessions on the economic and mundane issues that Gandhi considered vital.

But even if the campaign did not produce constitutional change or material benefits, it demonstrated that ordinary Indians had the power to drive events. In several parts of India nationalists succeeded in weakening the structure that undergirded the raj. Tax resistance, product boycotts, and resignations stretched the twin sinews of government—money and personnel. On a few occasions—in Peshawar at the end of April, in parts of Gujarat for most of 1930—civil disobedience showed the British what it would be like if they could no longer take for granted the reliability of Indians who staffed colonial government and law enforcement. And the British could not be certain that brushfires that started in these areas would not jump to other parts of the subcontinent. The costs of containing the campaign were high enough to move Irwin to negotiate an end to the conflict, on terms that failed to satisfy all his colleagues.

Yet beneath the surface, the raj never faced a general crisis of governability. Nationalists did not undermine the loyalty of police forces, and repression, although often clumsy and always costly, was never foiled effectively. The campaign had been designed to deflect any single shattering blow—local activists hardly missed a beat when all-India leaders were arrested, and there were too many people involved, spread out over too much territory, for the authorities to stamp out all opposition. But beatings, imprisonment, land attachments, and other measures wore down resistance in many places. And whatever strategic adjustments Congress might have made to neutralize repression would not have altered the fact that there were large communities of Indians that did not join the campaign. Without solidarity from Muslims and industrial workers, civil disobedience by Gandhi's followers could accomplish only so much.

While Congress did not wreck the raj, it did succeed in shredding the legitimacy of British rule. For over a century the regime had represented itself as benign, standing for sound economy and gradual reform—and likely to bring home rule in the long run. As long as Indians went about their business and cooperated with its laws and institutions, the British could maintain this façade. But civil disobedience shattered it.

Time after time and in place after place, Indians disobeyed laws they saw as unjust, and their rulers beat them, jailed them, took their property, banned their publications, and outlawed their organizations. On the streets of Lucknow, at the salt works in Dharasana, in the villages of Gujarat, the regime demonstrated in broad daylight that colonial rule was a form of domination. The British were happy to have the consent of Indians wherever possible, but, in the absence of consent, they would rule by the club and the gun. Civil disobedience exposed this truth, and it resounded through British and Indian relations in years to come.

Nothing reveals the loss of authority suffered by the raj better than the change in what it meant for Indians to go to jail. Once a mark of shame, a term in prison became a badge of pride. Narayan Desai recalled shouting in delight, when he was a boy, "This time no less than two years!" as his father (Gandhi's secretary) was hauled off to prison in the back of a police van. Imprisonment still worked as a means of physical coercion, but it no longer carried any stigma in the eyes of most Indians.[136]

Congress leaders were out to do more than destroy the prestige of the raj; they also tried to become the one force that could speak in the name of the people. In this sense nonviolent mass action was a bid by Congress to seize political primacy from the British by offering overwhelming evidence that, while the British still ruled Indians, Congress *led* them. Congress declared and suspended the campaign, and Congress leaders and volunteers undertook the most well-publicized acts of civil disobedience and suffered the most visible brutalities. And during most of the conflict, Gandhi and his colleagues managed to retain the initiative.

But their position was never unchallenged, for reasons that had less to do with the British than with Indians. Congress saw itself as guiding the masses for disciplined nonviolent action, but its national and provincial leaders often ended up authorizing actions they did not inaugurate and could not control. Congress all too often found itself following rather than leading, restraining rather than mobilizing. Morever, the failure to bring most Muslims and Sikhs into the struggle meant that Congress did not speak for all India, foreshadowing the later division of India as well as bitter communal strife that far outlasted the British.

Yet the experience of civil disobedience transformed the people who went through it. Just a generation earlier a zealous sense of Indian nationhood was limited to a small number of mainly educated, urban Hindus, and allegiance to religious communities, castes, and linguistic groups overshadowed citizenship. But after Indians at all levels of society joined together in collective nonviolent action against forms of injustice that touched them all, a new civil spirit was operating in India.

The salt campaign gave people a joint calling and forged durable links among Indians from different classes and regions. The Bombay merchants who lost their shirts by sticking to the cloth boycott, the university students in Lahore who were thrown in jail for picketing, and the Congress volunteers who were battered at Dharasana—all these Indians now shared with each other, and with revered leaders like Gandhi and the Nehrus, a common history: They had put aside their personal interests to promote the nation's interest in evicting the British. India was no longer just a patchwork on a map—it was a fluent idea in the public mind.

The simple act of standing up to the authorities dispelled the sense of inferiority that colonial rule both fostered and required. Usha Mehta recalled how proud the old women in her family were to participate in the salt satyagraha. Her great-aunts and grandmothers would bring home salt water, boil it down, and "then they would shout at the top of their voices: 'We have broken the salt law.'" The campaign also changed the way their overlords were seen: The British were no longer invincible. Their viceroy had negotiated with Mohandas Gandhi, recognizing, if only fleetingly, a man whose authority derived from his ability to articulate his people's longings. The British, until they sat down with Gandhi, "were all sahibs and we were obeying them," said Narayan Desai. "No more after that."[137]

Gandhi's personal role in the civil disobedience campaign was towering. For millions of Indians he was the embodiment of national purpose. Inside Congress his stature gave him enormous leverage, which he used to keep quarreling factions together and to spur the party to turn itself into a mass political organization. Gandhi's ideas about satyagraha and swaraj, moreover, galvanized the thinking of Congress cadres, most of whom by 1930 were committed to pursuing independence by nonviolent action.

That the civil disobedience campaign flowed from Gandhi's leadership does not, however, mean that it was a simple projection of his ideals. The dynamic of satyagraha, as Gandhi originally conceived it, started with breaking the laws of the raj, then forcing the British to punish protestors. Their suffering would touch the hearts of the oppressors, expose the injustice of their rule, and create conditions in which the British would choose to leave. Naively, Gandhi even believed that Irwin's willingness to negotiate indicated a personal change of heart. But Gandhi and Irwin were not the same as India and Britain: Irwin was impressed by Gandhi, but his government was not ready to regard the Indian people as sovereign.

Apart from Irwin, the British naïveté was to see Gandhi as a kind of tribal witch doctor, whipping up the unwashed masses; Churchill had called him a "fakir." But for all his appearance as a saintly and unworldly figure, Gandhi understood the realpolitik of Indian liberation. He knew that civil disobedience had to strain imperial control sufficiently that the game for the British would not be worth the candle. And his "truth force" was adaptable to this very worldly goal: Most of his followers took part in nonviolent action not in order to seek some sort of moral transfiguration but to overcome their adversaries—by denying them the cooperation and revenue that made it possible to hold India. Demonstrating to the British that they were wrong was ultimately beside the point; the goal was to force the British out.[138]

Nonviolent action did not force out the British in 1930-1931, and it did not work the way that Gandhi had expected—but it worked. The suffering of protestors did not change the minds of the British, but it did change the minds of Indians about the British. For tens of millions of Indians, satyagraha and its results changed cooperation with the raj from a blessing into blasphemy. The old order, in which British control rested comfortably on Indian acquiescence, had been sundered. In the midst of civil disobedience, Sir Charles Innes, a provincial governor, circulated his analysis of events to his colleagues. "England can hold India only by consent," he conceded. "We can't rule it by the sword."[139]

The British lost that consent, and had civil disobedience been more disciplined, had Congress separated the raj from its means of coercion, and above all, had India been united, they might have lost their empire's brightest jewel long before they did.

Aftermath

By the middle of the 1930s, with civil disobedience suspended and the raj still in place, Indian nationalists charted a new course. Gandhi continued as a unifying symbol for the cause, and when the occasion demanded, he briefly stepped onto the political stage. But he devoted himself first and foremost to constructive work: liberating untouchables and women, promoting village industries, reforming education and sanitation. As if to symbolize this, he moved his home base to a new ashram in the village of Sevagram, in central India.

Congress kept its eyes on the prize of India's independence, but after reforms in 1935 expanding the electorate and enhancing the role of elected provincial legislatures, its leaders turned to working within the system. It parlayed its popular influence into votes, won the majority of seats in a number of provinces in the 1937 elections, and formed provincial governments.

World War II saw the end of this participation. Following the lead of the British Parliament, the colonial government declared war on Germany without consulting any representatives of Indian opinion and refused to meet nationalist demands as a reward for loyalty. In October 1939 Congress ordered the resignation of its provincial ministers and moved, once more, into all-out opposition. In 1942 a "Quit India" resolution triggered a mostly spontaneous and violent popular rebellion, in which almost 100,000 people were arrested and over 1,000 killed. Meanwhile, outside the country, Subhas Chandra Bose raised an "Indian National Army" and fought the British alongside the Japanese.

The raj overcame both these problems, but the British exited the war certain to face a new round of opposition from Congress and having to choose between crushing the movement or accepting nationalist demands. They had dealt with fierce resistance—both violent and nonviolent—many times before, but discipline and loyalty among the police had slipped badly during the war, and the reliability of Indian soldiers was also in doubt. Those who fought the British in the Indian National Army were being hailed as heroes; their example might tempt government soldiers to ask whether their loyalty belonged to the raj or to India.

What was more, any new repression in India would have been a heavy burden on Britain's depleted postwar economy. Although Churchill remained wedded to India as the gem of the empire, his nostalgia was not widely shared by the British public, and it was decidedly not a concern of Britain's powerful ally the United States. After the Labour Party swept to victory in July 1945 and promised to give priority to rebuilding Britain itself, the time was ripe for change.

By then any political settlement would have had to win the consent not just of Congress but also of the Muslim League, which had established itself as the main vehicle of Muslim aspirations. Now the question was no longer the nature of communal relationships in an independent India but rather the possible creation of a separate state, Pakistan, incorporating the Muslim-majority areas. No group was more threatened by all this than the Sikhs, whose homeland in the Punjab seemed likely to be partitioned between the two states. As Muslim resolve to separate from a Hindu-dominated India grew, tensions exploded into violence during 1946 and 1947, violence in which Hindus, Muslims, and Sikhs all took part and suffered.

With India seeming to crumble around them, the British became eager to get out. The plan arrived at in May 1947—and agreed to shortly thereafter by Congress, League, and Sikh leaders—called for granting dominion status to two states, India and Pakistan. The British Parliament and Crown ratified the India Independence Act in July, and two nations became free at midnight on August 14.

Gandhi made himself conspicuously absent from the celebrations in Delhi. India had won its independence, but only at the cost of dividing it in two, dashing his dream of unity. The new India also retained the class inequalities, caste discrimination, and sexual oppression that he viewed as the great stains on Indian civilization. The great sage lived to see the end of the raj, but he was assassinated by a Hindu communalist in 1948, believing until the last that India was still a long way from swaraj.

Gandhi may have been disappointed with the character of Indian nationhood, but he surely knew that the door to self-rule had first been opened by the mass nonviolent movement that he aroused and led. Systematic nonviolent opposition to an unrepresentative, entrenched government had never before been mustered on such a scale. Assembling and building that opposition had schooled Indian leaders in the political skills that would be crucial in operating a viable democracy. The movement that changed the country's history also laid the groundwork for sustaining a civil society. Three generations after Gandhi, India is still divided by faith, class, and caste, but it is also still free and democratic.

CHAPTER THREE

Poland:
Power from Solidarity

Saturday, August 16, 1980

THERE WAS A LIGHT BREEZE ON THE BALTIC COAST THAT NIGHT, as two dozen workers sat in a smoke-filled conference room, beneath the motionless cranes of the giant Lenin Shipyard. They debated until dawn and came up with a list of demands to present to the government on behalf of 50,000 striking workers, asking for everything from a pay raise to longer maternity leave. At the very top was the demand that turned Poland inside out over the next sixty-eight weeks: the right of workers to form their own self-governing trade unions.

As much was at stake in Poland in August 1980 as in India in April 1930 or in Russia in October 1905. Unlike the St. Petersburg Soviet or the Indian National Congress, however, the workers in Gdansk were not out to change the government. They knew that twice before—in Hungary in 1956 and in Czechoslovakia in 1968—Soviet tanks had crushed attempts by Eastern Europeans to create freer political systems, and they were not going to risk the same fate for Poland. They wanted industrial rather than political rights.

In the ensuing days, the men and women in that conference room would make a series of decisions that confounded the regime's every attempt to subdue the strike without accepting their chief demand. Their strategy was not improvised on the spur of the moment, because the August strike was not the first time Polish workers fought to have their own unions. Several in that room had already dedicated years of their lives to campaigning for just this goal. They had lost their jobs, endured long interrogations and beatings, spent time in jails, witnessed riots and massacres. But they had also learned how to plan shrewdly and act prudently in conflicts, and now they were ready to put that knowledge to work.

In Poland, in the next-to-last decade of the twentieth century, a great popular movement was about to rise up and use nonviolent action to change its nation's destiny.

SELF-ORGANIZATION

Promises, Promises

Harry Truman, Winston Churchill, and Joseph Stalin met in the German city of Potsdam at the close of World War II and redrew the map of Eastern Europe. They agreed that Poland would shift its borders to the west, ceding territory to the Soviet Union. As compensation, it would get lands that had belonged to Germany, including the Baltic seaport that the Germans called Danzig and the Poles Gdansk.

Gdansk's old medieval town and its modern industrial harbor had been reduced to rubble as the Soviets drove out the Germans in March 1945. Factories, apartment buildings, bridges, power plants, and pumping stations were leveled or badly damaged. The Germans who had been there for generations were deported, and in their place came hundreds of thousands of weary Poles, uprooted by the war and by the Soviet annexation of territory to the east. One of the people who came wandering into this devastated twilight zone was a teenage girl named Anna Walentynowicz.

The war had made Walentynowicz an orphan. Both her parents had been killed, and her brother had ended up in a Soviet labor camp. Arriving in the Gdansk area in 1945, she worked first as a farm servant, then at several other jobs, and in 1950 she became a welder at the Gdansk (later Lenin) Shipyard, which the new communist government had inherited from the Germans. The communists were a small faction, with little popular support. They had rigged elections, jailed opponents, and relied on the intimidation of the Soviet army to install a dictatorship. But while they used force and deception to seize power, they also promised the people something better than what they had known before. They would create a new Poland on top of the ruins of the old one—an egalitarian society, with good education and a prosperous economy. Those who were to build this new order and enjoy its benefits were the workers, like Anna Walentynowicz.

After Walentynowicz went to Gdansk, the workers and the communist party (known by its Polish initials, PZPR) did make a new Poland, and the outward evidence was imposing: the huge new industrial complexes of the Zeran automobile factory and Ursus tractor works around Warsaw, and the Nowa Huta steel mills outside of Krakow. Millions of peasants left the countryside to work in these factories, in the coal mines of Silesia, in the textile mills of Lodz, and in the shipyards of the Baltic coast. By the late 1960s, there were about 15,000 people at work at the Lenin Shipyard in Gdansk, another 8,000 at the Paris Commune Shipyard in Gdynia, a neighboring port city, and another 10,000 at the Warski Shipyard in Szczecin.

But life in Poland had not fulfilled communist promises. Resources went into industrial infrastructure: steel mills, chemical factories, power plants, and mines. Money from farm exports was reinvested in industry. Consumer goods, housing, and human services got what was left over, and so the products that Polish workers bought were scarce or shoddy. Meat was rarely on the dinner table. Years were spent on waiting lists for private apartments, and in the meantime families lived in cramped rooms or in factory dormitories. Most did without indoor running water or telephones.

While the party trumpeted that Poland was a "workers' state," workers noticed that not only were they poorer than their counterparts in Europe's capitalist countries, they were also less free. They could vote in elections, but the ballots meant nothing since the communists had banned all political competition. Besides, real decisions were made behind closed doors by PZPR committees, not by elected representatives. Only by joining the party and being promoted through the bureaucracy could individuals gain a voice.

Workers also had no right to organize and represent themselves with the state-owned enterprises that employed them. In 1945-1946, the communists nullified workers' attempts to form shop-floor councils and independent unions. Instead, they installed official unions, directed by appointees answerable to them, not to members. In principle, these unions would act on employees' complaints. In practice, they did not bargain on behalf of workers for higher wages, shorter hours, or better work conditions. "Under capitalism, the unions are to protect workers from capitalists," went one joke. "Under socialism, they exist to protect the socialists from the workers."[1]

Polish workers nonetheless found ways to press their grievances. Sometimes they went out on wildcat strikes, and some argued at factory party committee meetings for higher pay and better conditions. Anna Walentynowicz was one of these. She was a model worker, the kind who won medals and went to international youth congresses, and she took the communists at their word when they promised a better society. But because she believed in their egalitarian ideology, she could not hold her tongue as party functionaries became a new ruling class, while workers on the shop floor were powerless. Walentynowycz made herself such a nuisance that she was later fired, only to be rehired after dozens of workers signed a petition for her.

In 1956, objecting to wage rates, Polish workers took to the streets of Poznan, Gdansk, and Warsaw, and one party building was stormed. Shocked, the regime answered by shooting protestors, which inflamed the country. A new party leader was brought in and, with him, new reforms. Feeling a fresh breeze, workers tried to revive shop floor councils, but the councils' independence was crippled by harassment and co-opting of militant members. A precedent, however, had been set: Workers had refused to be silent cogs in the system and had claimed the right to organize. They had failed, but the desire to be free did not fade. It was to come back with a vengeance—not once, but twice.

"The Revolt Will Be Put Down"

In the late 1960s the Polish economy began to stall. Wladyslaw Gomulka, the PZPR's first secretary since 1956, was alarmed that Poland might lag behind its neighbors. "In life," Gomulka warned (echoing Stalin), "the weak everywhere and always . . . will be beaten." But rather than reforming the inefficient command economy, the communists decided to ratchet up the pressure on Poland's working people.[2]

In 1969 and 1970 the regime announced spending cuts in health and housing, a wage freeze for two years, and reductions in piecework rates— meaning that the same pay would require more work. Factory meetings were called and people were exhorted to work harder—sending the message that workers, rather than planners or politicians, were to blame for Poland's woes. For workers in Gdansk, the news was especially bad: Shipbuilding would be phased out in the long run and receive little investment in the meantime. The mood on the coast was bleak; soon it would turn angry.

On Saturday, December 12, 1970, the 3,000 PZPR members who worked at the Lenin Shipyard gathered for a special meeting at 4:00 P.M., and a letter from the party politburo was read aloud: Across-the-board increases in food prices would go into effect at midnight. Meat prices would go up 17.5 percent; fish, 11.7 percent. The party members were stunned. Some cried. They knew that workers spent close to half their wages on food. And they expected trouble.

The shipyard workers had all day Sunday to think about Gomulka's Christmas present. They arrived at work before dawn on Monday and grumbled in front of their lockers, as managers tried to hustle them off to the workshops. Some decided to strike, and Anna Walentynowicz was one of the instigators, as was a young electrician named Lech Walesa. They marched through the yard to the director's office, pulling more workers along. Miroslaw Marciniak was taking his breakfast break when he heard a group of shipfitters chanting as they marched by. "So partly out of curiosity I went," he said. "I didn't have the faintest idea there was going to be a strike. In fact, I didn't know what a strike was."[3]

Soon strikers were swarming in front of the director's building; they demanded not only repeal of the price hikes but also the resignations of those responsible, including Gomulka. The director offered a pay bonus and ordered them back to work. Someone shouted that they should march from the shipyard to the provincial party headquarters and force officials to hear their complaints. Around 11:00 A.M., a thousand or so filed out of the yard, carrying clubs and metal tools for self-defense, singing the socialist hymn, the "Internationale," and the Polish national anthem, and full of indignation but with few ideas about what to do.

Arriving at the party building, they chanted "We want bread! Down with Gomulka!" A few people scrawled graffiti on the walls while police looked on. After a party boss told the strikers he could do nothing, they wandered around Gdansk, asking workers from other shipyards and students from the Polytechnical Institute to join in. Upon returning to the party building, they faced a cordon of internal security police, known by the acronym ZOMO—but they tried to push through, fending off nightsticks, throwing rocks, picking up tear gas grenades and pitching them back at the police. As night fell the streets teemed with rioters.

On Tuesday morning workers arrived at the Lenin Shipyard and heard that strike leaders had been arrested in their homes during the night. Again they poured out of the shipyard toward the city center, where they were met by thousands of strikers from other state enterprises. First they charged the police station, trying to free the prisoners taken the night before. Next they marched to the trade union building, beat down the door, surged inside, and flung desks and chairs out the windows. By 10:00 A.M., over at the party building, strikers were hurling stones and Molotov cocktails. From inside came a volley of shots, but the crowd would not retreat. Soldiers disobeyed their orders to fire more rounds, throwing their weapons and truncheons out the windows; a few even threw down their pants. By then the building was ablaze.

The torching of the party headquarters was celebrated as a victory. But while the flames leapt high, two army divisions were en route to Gdansk, authorized, by decision of party leaders in Warsaw, to use live ammunition to suppress the strike. In the afternoon troop carriers rolled into downtown streets. Workers stuffed burning rags into their vents and jammed tire treads with steel pipes; one person was run over. That night a Politburo member went on television and labeled the strikers "gangs of criminals and blackguards." Another Politburo member flew into a rage at a meeting of the provincial party committee, saying it was a counter-revolution and swearing "Even if 300 workers die, the revolt will be put down."[4]

On Tuesday afternoon strikers had wandered back to the shipyard once the party building was incinerated; that night, while most workers went home, the strike leaders stayed put. Waking up before dawn, they saw that the shipyard was surrounded by troops and tanks. Warships in the gulf also had artillery trained on them. When a group of young workers walked out of Gate No. 2, they were caught in a hail of bullets. Fifteen were wounded, four killed. More strikers came out of the gate, picked up the bodies, and retreated back, singing the national anthem and later hoisting to half-mast a Polish flag trimmed with black crepe.

The shooting at Gate No. 2 was a catalytic moment. Inside, workers immediately elected a strike committee dominated by rank-and-file militants, including Walentynowicz and Walesa. Their demands went beyond bread-and-butter issues, insisting, for example, that union leaders not be party members. Strikers at the Gdansk repair shipyard demanded that the army be withdrawn, that special privileges enjoyed by party and military officials be scrapped, and that trade unions be independent of management and the party. Workers were determined to turn the space for self-organization, created in the chaos of the strike, into something institutional. The myth that party-controlled unions spoke for the workers had been swept away.

Now the question was how to put force and thus credibility behind workers' demands. Burning down the party headquarters had only brought the army down on their heads. And now, on Wednesday morning, the Lenin Shipyard was sealed off. Those inside had seen what would happen if they tried to venture back out onto the streets. So the strikers chose the only path open to them besides capitulation: They declared an occupation strike and vowed to remain in the shipyard night and day until their demands were met.

As night fell, strikers collected flammables and explosives and prepared to defend themselves in case troops attacked. But at 10:00 P.M. they heard that army commanders had issued a tough new ultimatum: If they were not out in four hours, the shipyard would be assaulted by troops on the ground and bombarded from the air. Having already seen enough violence, they voted to end the strike, and they walked out between lines of police and troops—with their heads down, Walentynowicz recalled, like captured prisoners.

Yet even in defeat they had begun to develop a strategy of nonviolent action that would succeed years later. They had rallied support by workers from other enterprises, found leaders in their ranks, built a short-lived organization, and pushed demands for meaningful change. And they had learned the hard way that taking on police and soldiers in the open was futile and dangerous. Staying in the shipyard, on the other hand, offered a measure of security from a regime quite capable of destroying property and killing people to quell protest. The next time, whenever it came, the shipyard workers would know what to do.

The results of a strike at the Paris Commune Shipyard in Gdynia showed even more clearly the danger of not controlling the workplace. On Wednesday night radio broadcasts warned strikers they had to return to work the next day. All night conscript troops flowed into the city and took up positions around key buildings. Before dawn trams heavy with workers started arriving in the shipyard station, but as they disembarked and moved down a narrow passage to the yard, they heard loudspeakers blaring that the yard was closed and they had to go home. As more trams pulled in, newly arrived workers blocked any retreat. The soldiers opened fire, and those in front were inadvertently pushed forward into the spray of bullets by those behind them.

More hopeful lessons came from Szczecin, several hundred miles west, where workers at the Warski Shipyard struck on Thursday morning. Events followed the Gdansk pattern. The Warski workers marched into the city center, where they were joined by workers from other factories. They burned down the party committee building, without much interference from soldiers. That night police showed up at the homes of activists and hauled them off to jail, while party leaders in Warsaw gave orders to mobilize the military, including tanks, helicopters, navy ships, and more than 60,000 soldiers. When the Warski workers showed up at the shipyard Friday morning, they had to pass through an armed cordon to get in.

Later that morning strikers launched an attack out of the shipyard against the troops, only to retreat back inside after shots were fired and two were killed. The workers were furious. After a technician found a microphone and called for occupying the factory, a strike committee was elected; it sent delegates to another shipyard, also gripped by an occupation strike. The two sets of strikers cooked up twenty-one demands, topped by a call to disband the Central Trade Union Council and form new independent unions. Messengers took the list to other factories, which sent their delegates to Warski Shipyard, creating a city-wide strike committee.

Their timing was fortuitous. On Friday night the Politburo, after receiving a note from the Soviet ambassador apparently rebuking them for using force against workers and advising negotiations, ousted Gomulka and replaced him with Edward Gierek, who said he would defuse the conflict. On Saturday morning officials in Szczecin proposed talks. The first round was in a school next to the shipyard, but the next two sessions were held in a government building elsewhere. That cut off the rank-and-file from their negotiators, several of whom were party members and had mixed loyalties. The eventual agreement was weak: Officials agreed to consider wage increases, cancel some price hikes, and dismiss some officials as well as compensate families of dead and injured workers—but no concession was made on the key issue, free trade unions.

In January 1971 new strikes broke out on the Baltic coast. This time the party invited workers to submit demands at officially sanctioned meetings. Once again trade union reform was high on the list. Then officials set up meetings at factories, where workers were asked to help solve the economic crisis. At the Warski Shipyard, most workers refused to take part in this charade. To hide an embarrassing turnout, authorities doctored television news footage, making it look like spirited throngs had shown up. The Warski workers struck in protest, returning only after meeting with Gierek himself. On January 25 the party boss held a meeting at the Lenin Shipyard. Explaining that he too had once been a worker like them, he begged them to join a patriotic effort to save the country. "Will you help me?" he asked. "We will help!" shouted Anna Walentynowicz, Lech Walesa, and others, who still wanted to believe.

There was one more act in the drama of 1970-1971. This time the center of action was the city of Lodz in central Poland, and the protagonists were poorly paid textile workers, most of them women. When they struck in February, the Politburo flew in high-ranking officials, including the prime minister, to sound the same public-spirited appeal as Gierek had before—but the 3,000 women who assembled would not even let them speak. "Your wife," one striker shouted at the prime minister, "loads ham on her sandwiches, while my children eat dry bread." When asked to help the party, they answered with a resounding "No!" The next day the regime backed down and announced a return to the old food prices.

That winter placed a heavy burden on Polish communism. The workers of Gdansk, Gdynia, and Szczecin would never forget the sight of soldiers and police gunning down their comrades. In the coming years the anniversaries of the massacres became unofficial days of mourning. A regime that used tanks, machine guns, and troops to deal with strikers, that labeled them counterrevolutionary hooligans, would have a hard time convincing those same workers that they were on their side.

For workers there was a new sense of collective strength. In Gdansk and Gdynia the PZPR had used force to overwhelm strikes. But new party leaders had chosen to avoid strife and reach settlements without violence. In Szczecin they bullied the strikers' negotiators but still negotiated, and that had never happened in communist Poland. Two months later they gave in altogether when they were stared down by thousands of adamant women in Lodz. From that point on, Polish workers were keenly aware that if they stuck together and took systematic action, they could make the regime bend.

Less apparent was another legacy: Workers on the Baltic coast had been schooled in conflict with the state. Burning down party buildings gratified militants but achieved nothing strategic and only gave the regime an excuse to start shooting. Workers found a better way to fight: They could take their shipyards and factories hostage and organize themselves, not only within an enterprise, but throughout a city. In Szczecin strikers overcame two decades of party rejection and forced talks on their issues. Above all, workers found a goal worth struggling for, something more than the sop of a pay raise but something less than a political threat: the right to speak for themselves, through unions that were really their own.

"Our Freedom Begins With Ourselves"

The demand for independent unions bucked the core imperative of the communist system: to concentrate all power in the party. When they took over Poland, the communists had emulated their Soviet sponsors by nationalizing industries, instituting central planning, and amalgamating peasant lands into large collective farms. They also had seized control of media and the arts, imposing a stern orthodoxy on what could be written, spoken, and even painted. They even invaded the domain of the Catholic Church, confiscating property, shutting down religious schools and periodicals, usurping the power to confirm ecclesiastical appointments, and putting the Church's Primate, Cardinal Stefan Wyszynski, under house arrest.

Yet all over Eastern Europe there was a gap between totalitarian intent and reality, and it was widest in Poland. Hesitant liberalization after Stalin's death had turned into a major retreat in 1956, when strikes and demonstrations forced the regime to compromise with workers. The prime mover behind this flexibility had been Wladyslaw Gomulka. He had eased censorship, permitted the Church to regain control over its people and newspapers, allowed independent discussion clubs, and recognized factory councils elected by workers. Social justice, self-determination, and even democracy had entered the official vocabulary.

But the Soviet bloc had been shocked by the Hungarian uprising, and the regime had suspended further relaxation, ending factory councils' autonomy and silencing scholars and writers who dissented from the official line. The regime "allowed one to think but not to speak, allowed one to hum but forbade singing," remarked the poet Adam Zagajewski. There was more leeway than elsewhere in Eastern Europe, but no one doubted who was in charge. It took until the late 1960s for Polish intellectuals to abandon hope that party reformers might regain the upper hand, and in 1967 Gomulka kicked out the Politburo's remaining reformers.[5]

In January 1968, when officials closed down production of a play by the venerated nineteenth century playwright and poet Adam Mickiewicz, saying it was provoking anti-Russian outbursts, a wave of protests ensued, with meetings and petitions by students and intellectuals demanding freedom of expression. When students demonstrated at Warsaw University on March 8, police stormed the campus and clubbed protestors. Thousands of students were expelled, professors were fired, and hundreds were jailed. Anti-Semitic rhetoric appeared in the media, and thousands of Jews, including party members, fled the country. The communists had identified themselves with the most reactionary elements in Poland.

One final blow leveled any hope for reform. On August 20 Polish troops joined the armies of the Warsaw Pact (the military alliance of the Soviet Union and its Eastern European allies) in invading Czechoslovakia, having been ordered by Moscow to smash the democratic changes introduced by communist reformers there. Now, even if Polish leaders wanted to grant demands for freedom, it was clear that Moscow would block the way. For Poles intent on a more open society, the outlook was bleak. But by the early 1970s a number of people who had worked in the opposition during the 1960s moved toward a new strategy of political action, one better adapted to life after 1968.

Among the architects of this strategy were Leszek Kolakowski, Jacek Kuron, and Adam Michnik. Each of these men had gone from faith in socialism to disillusionment with the party, then into stark opposition. Kolakowski, the oldest, was a political philosopher at Warsaw University who, by the mid-1950s, had renounced dogmatic Marxism. Remaining a party member, he became a thorn in the side of the regime, which he blasted for welshing on its promises of pluralism. He was dismissed from the party in 1966 and fired from the university in 1968—and then left the country, but not its affairs.

In 1956 Jacek Kuron had been a student protest leader at Warsaw University. He also had been a Marxist who believed that critically thinking people could work within the party—and he organized a scouting troop to imbue the next generation with communist values. But by the early 1960s he had become disaffected, and he and a colleague, Karol Modzelewski, drafted an "Open Letter to the Party," saying it could not be reformed, only overthrown by a workers' revolution. In 1964 Kuron was ejected from the party; the next year he was arrested and sentenced to prison. Kuron was out of jail in time to organize rallies in March 1968, only to find himself under lock and key again in just two days.

Michnik, the son of communist intellectuals, had joined Kuron's scouting troop at the age of eleven. "A Communist is a man who fights for social justice, for freedom and equality, for socialism," he later recalled having been taught. "He goes to prison for years because of his beliefs . . . and, once released, he again undertakes his revolutionary activities." Like his mentor, Michnik discovered that the party had no room for idealists. In high school he was arrested for distributing Kuron's and Modzelewski's "Open Letter." He led protests at Warsaw University in 1968; the next year he too was sitting in jail.[6]

In a series of articles in emigré and underground journals in the early and mid-1970s, these men diagnosed their own mistakes. They had assumed, Michnik wrote, "that the system of power could be humanized and democratized." They had bet on "reformists" in the communist elite—but 1968 broke "the umbilical cord" that tied them to the party. For Kolakowski, it was now clear that the intolerance and brutality of communist rule were not simply the mistakes of bad leaders, they were essential qualities of the regime.[7]

But if the party was hopeless, that did not mean all was hopeless. Believing that nothing could change, Kolakowski wrote, sanctioned "every act of cowardice, passivity and cooperation with evil." The question was how to oppose it. Trying to overthrow the regime, Michnik noted, was unrealistic. The Soviet Union could intervene, just as it had in Czechoslovakia and Hungary. Besides, a revolutionary underground would "only serve the police, making mass hysteria and police provocation more likely." The communists would be in their element demolishing a conspiratorial opposition. Even if successful, achieving power by raw force might only replace one dogma with another. "By using force to storm the existing Bastilles we shall unwittingly build new ones."[8]

Gradual reformism had turned out to be barren, and a frontal assault was also a dead end. But Kolakowski, Kuron, and Michnik believed something else could be done: Rather than trying to change the government, opponents of the regime could change Polish society—by resisting the party's propensity to control every corner of social life. Each independent initiative by citizens, each example of self-organization by people acting outside of party control, Kuron declared, "challenges the monopoly of the state and thereby challenges the basis upon which it exercises power." The immediate task of opposition intellectuals, Michnik wrote, was to build "a real, day-to-day community of free people."[9]

Paradoxically, the road to political change for Poles began with a dismissal of politics. "Our freedom begins with ourselves," Michnik proclaimed—and, in doing so, echoed the spirit of Gandhi's ideas sixty years before. "Self-rule" in the lives of Indians seeking independence from the British had to be achieved before the nation could rule itself. The patrons of the Polish opposition were borrowing two jewels from the crown of Gandhi's strategy:

Polish dissident Adam Michnik and Solidarity leader Lech Walesa, in 1985.
Credit: ©CORBIS/REUTERS

declining to use violent force and sparking private work to develop the habits of a self-responsible people.[10]

Independent self-organization did not, however, mean relinquishing the goal of reforming the state. Kuron and Michnik thought that the regime could be prodded to change. "Organized society is a power," Kuron wrote, "and a power every authority must reckon with." As Michnik put it, "Nothing instructs the authorities better than pressure from below." Democracy and civil liberties were the ultimate prizes; activating and organizing the Polish people were necessary first steps.[11]

To take them, intellectuals would need allies. The first accomplice had to be the Catholic Church, the one major institution in Poland with an independent voice, though it had not been on friendly terms with Poland's intelligentsia. Kolakowski had condemned the Church in the 1950s for its history of "clerical fanaticism," and Cardinal Wyszynski had lamented the "mental and moral relativism" of the intellectuals. But now conditions were ripe for a rapprochement. The Church had spoken out in favor of human rights for all Poles, not just Catholics, and many intellectuals—disillusioned not only with communism but also with its materialism and hyperrationalism—began to seek new sources of moral authority.[12]

Poland, 1980–1981

Kuron and Michnik also hoped to find partners in the industrial working class. They recognized that twice before, in 1956 and 1970, workers had rebelled and pried concessions from the regime. The party, Michnik wrote, feared workers more than any other group, and so they had to be part of any movement that would push Poland toward democracy. Intellectuals had done nothing in 1970 when workers on the coast had been repressed by the ZOMO and the army, a source of personal shame for Kuron. The next time they would have to show some solidarity.[13]

"The Responsibility of Society to Organize Itself"

Next time came in 1976. Once again food prices were the spark. On June 24 the prime minister announced the first increases in six years: The prices of some items—sugar, sausages—would double; others would rise by about 50 percent. The next day there were strikes all over Poland—in the textile factories of Lodz, shipyards on the coast, the machine works in Poznan, the mines of Silesia, and the steel mills of Nowa Huta. In Warsaw's suburbs, workers at the Ursus tractor plant tore up railroad tracks and halted the Warsaw–Paris train. In Radom, forty miles from the capital, the scene was reminiscent of Gdansk six years before, as workers burned down the party building. Even before the rioting subsided, the prime minister was back on the air saying the price hikes would be revoked.

As in 1970, the regime backed down, yet it also acted to discourage future protests: The rioters in Radom were denounced as "drunken hooligans and hysterical women," and a vindictive drive was launched to punish strikers there and elsewhere. Some were forced to run the gauntlet between truncheon-wielding police. More than 2,000 were arrested, and over 300 were imprisoned, some for up to ten years. Thousands more were fired—losing not only pay but also access to medical care in a country that provided almost no unemployment benefits.

This time, unlike 1970, intellectuals rallied to the workers' side. Within days Kuron, Michnik, and twelve others (including two priests) signed a "Declaration of Solidarity" with the strikers. In July, when the first trial of Ursus workers began, the court building was packed with defendants' families, foreign reporters, plainclothes security agents—and about a dozen dissidents from Warsaw, among them Jacek Kuron. They had come to help the workers' families, but it would not be easy—agents tailed them everywhere, snapping pictures, and the families were wary of the strangers. The ice was broken during a recess, when two women dissidents offered sympathy to a crying woman, a relative of a defendant.

The families proved to be dissatisfied with their court-assigned lawyers, and the dissidents recommended a lawyer, offered to pay the fees, and arranged baby-sitting for one worker's child so his wife could attend the trial. Warsaw intellectuals and students from other cities offered similar aid to the families of Radom workers facing trials. There surveillance was even tighter, and activists braved detentions and beatings; the regime removed Kuron from the scene by calling him up to active duty in the army reserves.

To sustain the drive to aid workers, some younger activists wanted to act more openly and recruit prominent people, believing a crackdown less likely if bad publicity were probable. Some older intellectuals feared that a formal group would be an easy target for repression. But a statement by the Polish episcopate on September 9 defending workers' rights heartened the young activists, who formed the Workers' Defense Committee. Known by its Polish acronym, KOR, the committee followed the strategy conceived by Kuron, Michnik, and others: It demanded amnesty for arrested workers and reinstatement of those fired.

"Society has no other means of defense against lawlessness than solidarity and mutual aid," KOR declared. "Wherever the repressed live . . . it is the responsibility of society to organize itself in order to defend them." They hoped their example would "stimulate new centers of autonomous activity," wrote one of the founders.[14]

KOR began with fourteen members and never exceeded thirty-three, mainly historians, sociologists, lawyers, writers, philosophers, and priests. A few well-known names were recruited: Jerzy Andrzejewski, a famous novelist; Edward Lipinski, a respected economic historian; Halina Mikolajska, an award-winning actress; and Leszek Kolakowski, by then a professor at Oxford. Other members had fought in the anti-German underground during World War II or were from the generation that rose against the regime in 1956 and 1968. Michnik, who was abroad in 1976, joined in 1977. Ideologically the group was diverse, including Catholic intellectuals, social democrats, and liberals. What they shared was opposition to the regime and a commitment to democracy and human rights.

The new organization focused on giving accused, beaten, and fired workers the services denied them by the regime. KOR found lawyers to defend them and doctors to write certificates attesting to the injuries they suffered (as evidence in trials). It raised money—from its members, the Church, the public at large, and abroad—to create an unofficial relief fund. Foreign writers such as Saul Bellow, Heinrich Böll, and Günter Grass donated the royalties from sales of their books in Poland. West European trade unions contributed. In all, KOR gave out about 3.25 million zloty (equivalent to the average annual income of sixty-five people) to several thousand people between September 1976 and September 1977.

KOR also orchestrated a publicity campaign to pressure the regime. Party chief Gierek had shown that he could be swayed by public opinion, so the group printed and distributed accounts of the protests, the subsequent repression, and workers' trials, and they also encouraged lawsuits against the Public Prosecutor's office for police mistreatment. Late in 1976 more than 1,000 workers from Ursus and Radom signed a protest letter to Gierek. Around the same time hundreds of scholars, priests, writers, and artists signed petitions to the Sejm (Poland's parliament) demanding an investigation of police abuses.

KOR knew that the party would give as much heed to foreign opinion as to what Poles were saying, since Gierek had cultivated a benign image abroad, knowing that financial credit from the West depended on the belief that Poland had a "liberal" communist regime. KOR attacked this vulnerability relentlessly: Kuron and Lipski gave interviews to German reporters in Warsaw, and Michnik, in Western Europe during 1976, talked with French and Italian journalists. He, Kolakowski, and Wlodzimierz Brus, another expatriate at Oxford, held a press conference in London and asked for financial help. Committees of solidarity with their cause formed in London, Paris, and New York.

These tactics worked. Between March and July 1977 all workers imprisoned since the previous June were released, and most who had been fired returned to their jobs. The regime apparently hoped that by meeting KOR's main demands, it could dissipate the pressure that was building at home and abroad and make the organization go away. Instead, when work for the Ursus and Radom workers ended, activists shifted to different priorities. "We will continue our activities," they declared, "as we are sure that the most effective weapon against the constraints enforced by the authorities is an active solidarity of all citizens."[15]

Publishing was the single most important weapon, since breaking the regime's monopoly of mass media and information was essential to breaking its grip on Polish life. No independent action could be coordinated unless people could communicate. Polish dissidents in the past had demanded that censorship be loosened, and occasionally the state-controlled media opened up a little. But limits remained, and these bred self-censorship in people who feared that by being outspoken they would forfeit the chance to publish anything at all. Now, after 1976, the dissidents simply ignored the official media and started publishing their own journals and books.

In September 1976 KOR had issued its first publication, *Komunikat* (communiqué), which appeared more or less each month. It ran the texts of KOR's declarations and appeals as well as news about trials of workers and reprisals against activists. The writing was terse and factual, aiming to be nothing more than a reliable source, unlike any official publication in Poland. At first members had to type up copies, then give them to others who typed new copies and passed them along; later, mimeograph machines were smuggled in from abroad. KOR also helped spawn other news and opinion journals, such as the journal for industrial workers, *Robotnik,* which carried advice about organizing, work safety, health care, and wages. By late 1978 about 20,000 copies of each issue were being printed and distributed.

With KOR's money and mimeograph machines, Miroslaw Chojecki, a chemist and KOR member, founded an underground publishing house called NOWA. The first book appeared in August 1977, and more than 100 books and pamphlets followed, including novels, memoirs, and essays on politics. Works came out that would never have cleared official channels, such as the poetry of Czeslaw Milosz, a Lithuanian-Polish emigré living in the United States (who later won the Nobel Prize for literature), and works by foreign writers such as George Orwell and the poets Osip Mandelstam and Josef Brodsky. NOWA had its own print shops, storehouses, and distribution network, and financed itself through sales and contributions.

As Polish dissidents combated censorship by turning their backs on it, they countered the party's control of higher education by sponsoring their own lectures. In the fall of 1977 KOR members joined with other scholars to create the Flying University. Unofficial student groups in university cities would announce a date and venue—usually a private apartment—for each lecture. Dozens of students and others would show up and cram inside, sprawling all over the furniture and floor as they listened to talks that would never have been heard in regular classrooms, such as "History of People's Poland" (delivered by Adam Michnik) and "Contemporary Political Ideologies." In Krakow the Cardinal, Karol Wojtyla, provided assembly halls on Church property, accommodating more people and deterring police harassment. By the end of its first year, the Flying University had held 120 lectures.

When KOR had appeared in 1976, it was the only functioning dissident group. Within a year or two, it had become a general model for self-organization. Student Solidarity Committees formed at six universities as alternatives to party-controlled student groups. In Gdansk, Szczecin, and Katowice, KOR-connected workers established free trade union groups to lead organizing drives in factories, and KOR activists helped start a few peasant self-defense committees. Separate dissident groups were begun by people who objected to the social democratic leanings of KOR figures like Kuron and Michnik.

The intellectuals, professionals, and students who helped workers and their families, or who printed journals and lectured underground, all were in defiance of a regime that wanted no encroachment on its control of public life. Police beat, arrested, and detained activists, spied on them and searched their homes. In May 1977 Stanislaw Pyjas, a student and KOR collaborator, turned up dead in a Krakow alley—the handiwork of the Security Service, most believed. Halina Mikolajska, an actress and KOR member, was the target of relentless abuse: She received insulting phone calls and letters, had her car vandalized, and one morning a dozen men barged into her apartment and screamed threats at her. Other activists were fired or accused of ordinary crimes. Student Solidarity Committee members were expelled from universities. Police raided publishing operations and confiscated equipment and books.

In early 1979 the Flying University came under steady attack. The authorities planted "discussants" to disrupt lectures, and people outside were hassled. Once Michnik and two students were beaten up while their assailants shouted, "You traitors, how much is the CIA paying you?" Kuron was thrown down a flight of stairs, and once a group of thugs showed up at his apartment, where a lecture was scheduled but had been postponed. They assaulted his wife and son and prevented him from calling for medical help for his father. All the while, police cars surrounded the building but refused to intervene.[16]

Despite this punishment, KOR and the groups in its orbit made openness their hallmark. Journals, for example, listed the names, telephone numbers, and addresses of editors. Rather than work in secret, they moved in broad daylight; it was the only way to inspire others to follow their example. While it made them targets—there was no mystery about who the main figures in the opposition were—it offered a certain protection. The regime was inhibited if it had to operate in the open. The more visible the dissidents were, the higher would be the political costs of hounding them. The strategy of public resistance was risky, but it worked.

The regime never tried to wipe out the opposition. It inflicted brutal penalties on a few people and milder sanctions on many more. Organizing a meeting, attending lectures, and circulating independent publications were difficult and sometimes hazardous. But people were not arrested *en masse* and locked up for years, because the party—afraid of the outrage at home and outcry abroad that a major crackdown would bring—did not want to jeopardize the domestic stability and foreign economic ties that had been cultivated since 1970. If tolerating the limited autonomy seized by KOR and other groups was the price for those conditions, it would be paid.

Still, dissidents led beleaguered lives. While this was not enough to deter hard-core activists, it was enough to dissuade even many sympathetic citizens from joining them. "Society hates the authorities, but it is weary," recorded the writer Kazimierz Brandys in his *Warsaw Diary* during March 1979. "It still has its own skin to lose—salary, apartments, children getting into the university, trips, daily life. That's enough to make people afraid."[17]

The dissidents had spurred a renewal of independent social and cultural life in Poland; they had forged links with workers and the Church. But the gains of self-organization would remain modest and vulnerable unless they constrained the power of the regime. And forcing the regime to accept limits was beyond the ability of KOR. It would take a more diverse movement, one with size and muscle, one that could strike at vital state interests, to engage the communists in a true contest for Poland's future.

"We Became Braver"

May Day was a major holiday in communist countries, an opportunity for regimes to celebrate their roots in nineteenth-century socialism and a chance for ordinary people to parade through the streets in pleasant weather. When the day arrived in 1978, in the city of Poznan, apartment buildings were festooned with flags and banners bearing the usual official slogans: "Long live the Polish United Workers' Party—the vanguard of the working class" and "Proletarians of all countries unite." Beneath these official trappings, visible from the streets, on the inside of almost every window, there was something else: a reproduction of a medieval icon, the Black Madonna of Czestochowa, the most beloved symbol of Polish Catholicism.[18]

The Madonnas of Poznan revealed a paradox of Polish life: Atheism was the official creed of the state, but each Sunday millions of Poles—including many party members—attended mass. There they entered a spiritual and cultural world outside the pull of communist teachings. "You would think the country was in the midst of a religious revival rather than living under Communism," wrote Radek Sikorski, remembering what it was like going to church in the town of Bydgoszcz. To the regime's consternation, the prestige of the Church only seemed to grow over the years, contesting the appeal of the party's dogmas.[19]

The Church's message was itself a display of doctrine. Sermons and pastoral letters came forth in hortatory language not unlike the party's rhetoric; both constructed worlds in which good and evil were locked in battle, and each appealed to believers from a posture of absolute authority. The Church, like the party, was hierarchical; initiative came from the top. Hence it did not appear, at first glance, to be a logical ally to Poles for whom free thought and democracy were sacred.[20]

Yet that was the role the Church came to embrace. While the communist regime was a ubiquitous and coercive presence in the life of every Pole, the Church depended on voluntary acceptance and participation. Being a devout Christian offered few public advantages for citizens living under a government that regarded religious belief as a reactionary influence. To survive and flourish in communist Poland, the Church had to meet real needs, connect with honored traditions, and express deeply held values—so the Catholic hierarchy looked beyond matters of faith and spoke out on the great national questions.

Stefan Wyszynski, the Church's Primate, and Karol Wojtyla, the bishop of the Krakow archdiocese, had been moving the Church toward cautious but unmistakable opposition in the 1970s. Wyszynski's sermons showed sympathy for the material demands of industrial workers and hailed the "courageous defense of freedoms and of the right to unite and organize for one's aims," words that virtually endorsed the work of groups like KOR. The tree of the Church thus gave welcome shade to Poland's harried dissidents, more than a few of whom were nonbelievers.[21]

If the Church already had unrivaled stature in Polish life, the 1978 election of Cardinal Wojtyla as the Bishop of Rome cemented its influence. "People ran through the streets of Warsaw shouting with joy," remembered Kazimierz Brandys of the October day when the election was announced. Old churchgoing women and sophisticated intellectuals alike spoke of a "miracle." Almost

Pope John Paul II celebrates mass in Victory Square, Warsaw, during his first trip as
Pope to his native Poland, June 2, 1979.
Credit: ©CORBIS/Bettmann

immediately the Vatican and Polish authorities began to negotiate about when
Wojtyla, now Pope John Paul II, would be allowed to return to Poland in his
new capacity as head of the worldwide Roman Catholic Church.[22]

On June 2, 1979, John Paul II touched down in Warsaw and spoke before
a gigantic crowd in Victory Square. Later he stopped at sites with great symbolic
resonance—Gniezno, the "cradle of Polish Catholicism," and the monastery at
Jasna Gora, where the Black Madonna of Czestochowa was kept—ending with
a triumphant return to his native Krakow. The Pope's words—uttered with an
articulate and honest grace, unlike the hackneyed drone of politicians—
challenged the regime on two levels: He affirmed Christian faith in opposition
to atheism, and he indirectly condemned violations of human rights and Soviet
domination of Poland. Poland's future, he predicted, "will depend on how many
people are mature enough to be nonconformists."

By 1979 these were no longer novel statements from Church leaders. What
made the new Pope's words extraordinary was his access to the airwaves: He was
heard by millions of listeners. He turned Victory Square, a spot identified with
formal doings of the regime, into a forum where a multitude of Poles chanted
"we want God" over and over. And he spoke as the supreme leader of Catholics

around the world, an authority so great that even the communist party remained mute before it.[23]

The pope's visit drew Poles into independent organizing on a greater scale than anything that KOR had dreamed of. The state stepped aside and allowed the Church to make most of the arrangements. In Krakow Jan Kubik, a student, and other volunteers were fed by nuns as they worked day and night making red-and-white Polish flags and yellow papal flags. On the eve of the pope's arrival, they were up on a scaffolding hanging the flags on a palace when the streetlights on the block mysteriously went out. Spontaneously people drove their cars up and turned on the headlights so the work could be finished. "There were no complaints about dead batteries," Kubik recalled. "We could do all kinds of things by ourselves," a Catholic intellectual explained to an American journalist. "We didn't need the authorities . . . "[24]

In the days before the Pope came, there were chilling rumors about what would supposedly happen: Millions of peasants would swamp the city, sleeping anywhere, leaving behind "disease, excrement, and corpses." Thousands would be crushed in the huge crowds. But when one writer ventured onto the streets, he found a "different way of walking, a change in style and rhythm . . . the crowd undulated slowly, people moved without bumping into each other, made way for each other . . . " Civilians kept order; there was not a policeman in sight. "A crowd of many thousands had beheld itself and been strengthened by feeling its own presence." Another who believed that thanks to the Pope's visit, "people got closer to each other," was Anna Walentynowicz. "We became braver."[25]

At his last appearance in Krakow, the pontiff said an outdoor mass for 3 million people, the largest public assembly in Poland's history. The nation had suddenly and briefly become the center of the world, and every Pole knew it. It was a moment when the state almost ceased to matter—a space had been created that was not delineated by its edicts. As Adam Michnik put it, people "who had been repressed for so long suddenly regained their ability to determine their own fate."[26]

SHOWDOWN IN GDANSK

"First Taste of . . . Solidarity"

In his diary entry for December 1978, Kazimierz Brandys described a long line of people standing in the dirty slush outside a fish store in Warsaw, having heard a rumor about a delivery of herring. The store would not open until 11:00 A.M., but the first people had started queuing up at 2:00 in the morning.

That evening he watched a government official on television hail the country's economic achievements. For ordinary Poles, the lines were a constant frustration. For the regime, they meant that sooner or later it would have to do the one thing that the upheavals of 1970 and 1976 had demonstrated should not be done: raise prices.[27]

Gierek's decision in 1971 to cancel his predecessor's price increases had changed the course of Poland's economy. Driving industrial growth by starving consumption—the old policy—had been politically explosive, so he discarded it. To finance industry, without consigning consumers to material hardship, credit was seen as the magic wand. The regime borrowed huge sums from the West, using hard-currency loans to get technology for industry as well as consumer goods for shoppers. Once industry became more productive, exports to the West would raise enough money to pay back the loans. The regime would reap industrial growth, rising standards of living and political peace. Or so went the theory.

For a few years it looked like Gierek was a magician. Thanks to the loans, investment shot up in the early 1970s, and the industrial growth rate was among the highest in the world. Store shelves, for a change, were packed with blue jeans, electronics, food, and other imports. Per capita consumption of meat rose by almost 50 percent between 1970 and 1975, and housing and health care were more available.

But Gierek's salad days were numbered. The regime made no real effort to reform the sclerotic system of centralized planning, and heavy industries like steel and shipbuilding, with poor export prospects but strong political clout, took the lion's share of investment. Money was also siphoned off by corrupt officials, who bought yachts and built lavish vacation homes. Workers' incomes rose fast, but farm productivity failed to keep pace, so more food had to be imported. As loans piled up while revenues from imports never materialized, foreign debt soared. New loans were mostly swallowed up by payments on old debt. Imports of food and other goods had to be curtailed. Ultimately there were shortages of everything, from meat to razor blades.

By 1980 the PZPR was boxed in by its own blunders. Reduced food imports required higher prices as a way of rationing limited supply. Officials announced price hikes at the beginning of July. They were under no illusions about how workers would respond, but they hoped at least to prevent turmoil. Local authorities were told to put out any fires by offering wage increases and sending loads of meat to appease workers in trouble spots. A few local concessions, the regime hoped, would be enough to defuse the anger.

Strikes began immediately in and around Warsaw. As they spread to other cities, officials scrambled frantically to tamp down the discontent. But this time

Anna Walentynowicz, Polish shipyard worker and Solidarity activist.
Credit: ©Erazm Ciolek

they had problems keeping Poles in the dark about what was happening. From his Warsaw apartment, Jacek Kuron called activists all over the country to gather and circulate information about the strikes. He reached Western journalists, who broadcast the news back into Poland over Radio Free Europe and the BBC. When workers in one city learned that workers elsewhere had struck and won a raise, they walked out themselves. In a few places, including Radom, officials offered preemptive raises to forestall unrest. One place where there was no strike was Gdansk. By the end of July it looked like wage hikes had done the trick and the storm had been weathered.

But then, at the beginning of August, just as party leaders were heaving a sigh of relief, officials at the Lenin Shipyard in Gdansk did something they would soon have reason to regret. On August 7 they fired Anna Walentynowicz, who had worked at the shipyard for almost three decades and in a few months would have qualified for her pension. After starting as a welder, Walentynowicz had worked as a crane driver, a job that made her known all over the sprawling complex. A grandmotherly figure in a floral print dress, she had earned a reputation as an honest, tireless advocate for her fellow workers, but she was more than merely popular. She was also a link between thousands of workers and the political opposition that had been building outside the shipyard gates in Gdansk.

In the summer of 1978, Walentyowicz had learned from a BBC radio broadcast that some activists in Gdansk wanted workers to have their own trade unions. She soon joined the group; it included Andrzej Gwiazda and Joanna Duda-Gwiazda, a husband and wife who were both shipbuilding engineers; a young historian, Bogdan Borusewicz, who was a veteran of the 1968 student demonstrations and the only KOR member in Gdansk; and Alina Pienkowska, a nurse in the Lenin Shipyard's medical clinic, who came to the group after reading Borusewicz's address in a KOR *Komunikat*. Lech Walesa, who like Walentynowicz had been a leader of the 1970 strike, joined around the same time, and they recruited a few young workers, including Jerzy Borowczak and Andrzej Kolodziej from the Lenin Shipyard and Bogdan Lis from the neighboring Elmor shipyard supply enterprise.

Through Borusewicz, the union activists had ties to opposition groups operating in the city. They distributed copies of the workers' journal *Robotnik* around local factories, and in August 1978 they started producing their own news sheet, *Robotnik Wybrzeza* (coastal worker). Much of the group's energy went into organizing a memorial ceremony each year in December to honor shipyard workers killed in 1970. In the weeks before each anniversary, Walentynowicz and her friends would plaster the city with posters and hand out leaflets on trams and outside factory gates; on the day itself people would gather outside Gate No. 2 of the shipyard, lay flowers, observe a minute of silence, sing the national anthem, and listen to speeches.

While force was not used to disperse those who went to the memorial, individual organizers paid a price. They were arrested and tried on phony charges, detained for brief periods, attacked by unknown assailants, and fired from their jobs. Tadeusz Szczepanski, a young worker from the Elektromontaz factory who helped out at the memorial ceremony in 1979, disappeared a few weeks later. In the spring his mutilated corpse was found floating in the river.

Taking action in the face of this kind of savagery demanded a wily determination, and no one had more of that than Lech Walesa. He had arrived in Gdansk in 1967, married another young newcomer, Danuta, and found work as a shipyard electrician. By the time of the 1970 strike, Walesa was already something of a leader. He was smart and not afraid to speak his mind, but he also had a good sense of humor. His reputation as a highly skilled, hard worker meant that shipyard officials had to give him a wide berth. In the years after 1970 he tried that patience repeatedly by helping to organize the memorial ceremonies and by blasting officials at union meetings. After a particularly long tirade in 1976, he finally got the sack.

Over the next several years Walesa was fired from one job after another. He and his growing family survived the intervals of unemployment with donations from the Church, KOR, other opposition groups, and collections taken up by workers. Although the authorities made his life difficult, they also spurred him to become a relentless organizer. Already well known at the city's biggest enterprise, he spread the message of independent unions to other factories as he bounced from job to job. In between, he was a full-time activist, often seen driving around town in a tiny car plastered with copies of Poland's democratic 1791 constitution. He also showed up at meetings of political groups in Gdansk, looking for allies among intellectuals and students; he seemed to know everyone and was likely to pop up anywhere.

Walesa and Walentynowicz had long known that the official unions were a sham and that workers had to organize and speak for themselves if they wanted their interests promoted. The 1970 strike had shown them what would fail and what would work when the time came to act again. Now, thanks to their contacts with the Gwiazdas, Borusewicz, and others, they realized that they were part of something that transcended the shipyard and Gdansk. Walentynowicz relied on material from KOR, she read dissident publications, and she went to Flying University lectures. And Walesa felt the experience of working together with other activists as his "first taste of genuine human solidarity."[28]

Until the summer of 1980, the free trade union group followed the model of opposition prescribed by Kuron and Michnik and pursued by KOR. Rather than protest as a way to plead for change, they defied the regime's pretense of controlling society. Instead of asking for freedom of expression and association, they acted as if they already had it, producing and distributing their own newspapers and holding their own events. In doing so, they kept workers informed, kept alive the memory of 1970, hammered home the need for independent trade unions, and developed ties between militant workers and dissident intellectuals in Gdansk.

Yet at heart the free trade union group was also aiming higher, at organizing all Polish workers. Its members were interested in forcing fundamental changes in the system itself, so that workers would have the right to organize and defend themselves. And when it came to changing the system, the methods pioneered by the Warsaw intellectuals would not suffice; it would take the mobilization of thousands upon thousands of people and intense conflict with the regime. In the summer of 1980 Walesa and his friends suddenly found themselves leading just such a movement. And the firing of Walentynowicz was the spark that lit the fuse.

"We Are Occupying the Shipyard!"

On the night Walentynowicz was dismissed, about half a dozen of the Gdansk activists met at the home of Piotr Dyk, a doctor and member of Young Poland, a nationalist opposition group. Walesa was there, along with Borusewicz, Pienkowska and Andrzej Gwiazda, and two young workers: Bogdan Felski, who worked at the Lenin Shipyard, and Andrzej Kolodziej, who had been fired for trying to instigate a strike and who was about to start work at the Paris Commune Shipyard. They feared that Dyk's apartment might be bugged, so they went outside into the courtyard behind the apartment block, where they talked about a strike.[29]

Over the next few days, Borusewicz and three young shipyard workers—Felski, Jerzy Borowczak, and Ludwig Pradzynski—made plans. When a strike had been tried in July, shipyard workers did not respond. This time they had an issue that hit closer to home: Walentynowicz. They cranked out thousands of leaflets explaining why she was fired and demanding her reinstatement, and they asked for a raise and for a monument honoring the workers killed in December 1970.

Inside the shipyard, Borowczak quietly sounded out a few workers to see if these issues would bring them out; the answer was yes. The four organizers kept their plans a secret, even from colleagues in the free trade union group who knew only that a strike was in the offing. But they knew they needed someone on their side with more experience, so they went to Walesa on Tuesday, August 12, and asked if he would help lead the strike the next morning. Walesa begged off—Danuta had just had her sixth baby; he was needed around the house. But by Thursday he could get free. So the strike was put off for a day.[30]

At 4:30 on Thursday morning, Borusewicz was at a tram stop on the line to the shipyard from Gdansk's northern outskirts, toting several thousand leaflets about Walentynowicz. At first light his leafleting partner showed up, and the two men boarded a southbound tram carrying the first load of workers for the morning shift. They passed out leaflets, stepped off the tram at the next stop, and got on the next one that passed through—while another team leafleted the trams on lines from the south. When his hands were empty, an exhausted Borusewicz went home.

When they reached the shipyard, thousands of workers knew the details of Walentynowicz's career and her firing. They had read about her three merit awards, her fights on behalf of other workers, and her work with the free trade union group. They knew how management had harassed her, until she was jettisoned on August 7. "Anna Walentynowicz has become unacceptable," the leaflet declared, "because she defended others and could organize her co-workers." And it warned, "If we are not able to resist this, there won't be anybody who will speak out against raising work quotas, breaking safety regulations, or forcing people to work overtime." Anna Walentynowicz had defended them; now it was their turn to defend her.[31]

When the 200 or so people who worked in the small K-5 hull assembly shop ambled into their locker room just before six, they saw posters calling for a strike. Borowczak, who had not slept all night, had hung them up just a little earlier. As they changed into their blue work clothes, Borowczak pressed a leaflet into each pair of hands. The same was happening in the much larger K-3 shop, where Pradzynski worked, and in the W-3 shop, where Felski and others were leafleting.

In locker rooms and workshops, Felski, Pradzynski, and Borowczak explained the strike and asked co-workers to come out into the open yard. Although many, especially older workers, were reluctant, some agreed. "Leave your machines, come with us," they called out as they passed ship hulls and workshops. By the time Borowczak's and Felski's groups linked up and reached Pradzynski's K-5 workshop at one end of the yard, 2,000 had formed up; then they marched back the other way, their numbers still swelling.

It was now a little after 9:00 A.M., and they approached the infamous Gate No. 2, where strikers had been gunned down in 1970. A few people started yelling that they should leave the shipyard and march to the party committee building. The leaders were prepared for this; they had no desire to relive the debacle of 1970 and create a new roster of martyrs. Borowczak and the others called for a moment of silence in memory of the 1970 victims and then led the crowd in singing the national anthem, afterward calming down the strikers and keeping them inside the shipyard.[32]

A little later the strikers congregated in the open square outside the administration building. Borowczak, just twenty-two years old, clambered on to the raised shovel of an excavator and turned it into a platform. He took a bullhorn and called on the strikers to elect a committee. "We need people we can trust, who have authority in the shops, in the work brigades." Workers from different shops and departments clustered into groups and chose delegates, twenty in all.[33]

Then the shipyard director, Klemens Gniech, appeared and climbed up on the shovel. Gniech was liked and respected by the workers. He had started over twenty years before as a hull-assembly worker. Like other party members, he had been part of the strike in December 1970, and he was considered a progressive. So when he said he would sit down and talk with the strike committee members as soon as strikers went back to work, many were ready to trust him. It looked like the strike might collapse after just a few hours.[34]

Suddenly Gniech found Lech Walesa standing next to him on the shovel. "Do you recognize me?" Walesa asked the director. He had spent the morning trying to ditch the security agents who habitually tailed him and just minutes before had climbed over the shipyard's perimeter fence. Now, in front of thousands of workers, he grilled Gniech. "Tell them why I was fired from the shipyard," he demanded. "Did I steal anything? Was I a thief? I worked in the shipyard for more than ten years, and I still consider myself to be a real shipyard worker. It's been four years already since I've had a regular job." As Borowczak was adding Walesa's name to the strike committee, making him the twenty-first member, Walesa boomed out: "We are occupying the shipyard!" The strikers erupted in applause, and he promised, "I'll be the last one to leave . . . "[35]

Walesa's appearance dashed Gniech's hope of ending the strike before talks could start—a stratagem that would have robbed the workers' delegates of any leverage. Now, as the two men stood uneasily together on the excavator shovel, the strikers shouted out a condition of their own: Anna Walentynowicz must be added to the strike committee and driven to the factory—in Gniech's own car. The strikers knew they had the upper hand, and they savored a chance for mild revenge on one of the bosses. Walesa added a second condition: that negotiations be broadcast throughout the shipyard by loudspeaker. That way the rank-and-file could follow what was going on and would know that the delegates were not selling them out. Then the strike committee left and bivouacked in the cafeteria of Walesa's old workshop.

Sitting around a table drinking tea, they devised demands that outstripped what the strike organizers were advocating just hours before. Walentynowicz and Walesa both had to be rehired. The workers had to get a raise along with a cost-of-living clause, and meat price increases had to be rolled back. Special allowances given to police and militia officers had to be removed. A monument to the 1970 martyrs had to be erected. The strikers needed a guarantee of no reprisals, and workers needed the right to organize independent trade unions, just as Walesa and his colleagues had been insisting for the last few years.

With these demands the committee went back to the administration building and sat down with Gniech. But the director had done nothing about the preconditions. The conference room was not hooked up to the public address system, he told them, so broadcasting the talks was impossible. And there was no point in bothering Walentynowicz, he said; she had not been feeling well and might be upset by all the excitement. But the committee could not be deflected so easily. Walesa announced that they would not negotiate until the preconditions were met, and the workers walked out.

Around noon, the strikers standing around in the yard learned they had won the first skirmish when a small gray car crawled into the yard through Gate No. 2 with Walentynowicz inside. As the strikers crowded around the car, Walentynowicz got out and climbed up on the excavator shovel. Presented with a bouquet of roses (cut that morning from bushes outside Gniech's office), she was nearly speechless and had to wipe tears from her eyes. Later Gniech gave in and permitted broadcasting the talks over the loudspeakers. The talks would begin the next day, Friday.[36]

On Thursday afternoon the strikers prepared for the contingency of having to stay in the shipyard. Pienkowska, who worked in the health clinic just outside the yard, spread the word to people in the Gdansk area to donate food and recruited a brigade of students to collect it door to door. Other strikers guarded the yard's entrances and enforced a ban on alcohol. Some set up an antenna so they could tune in Radio Free Europe and stowed away all explosives in the yard. Others laid hands on fresh water supplies, and those who lived close by went home and brought back mattresses and blankets. As daylight faded, a tent city made out of spare sheets of canvas went up.[37]

While the strikers were busy inside, Pienkowska started phoning Jacek Kuron as soon as she learned strike details. From Kuron word went out to foreign journalists and then back into Poland via Radio Free Europe. Bogdan Borusewicz went to the harbor to let dockworkers know what was happening and made the rounds of other factories. An outsider at these places, he could not convince many to take the risk of striking. The free trade union group, however, had close contacts with militant workers at several major enterprises in the Gdansk-Gdynia region, and on Friday morning these people made their move.

Friday was the second day of work for Andrzej Kolodziej at the Paris Commune Shipyard. On the bus that morning, this unknown twenty-year-old approached his new co-workers, told them of the strike at the Lenin Shipyard, and asked them to quit work. He kept this up in the locker room of the hull-assembly shop and then on the square where work teams huddled at the start of day. It looked like he and other young agitators had failed when the foremen and party officials hustled the teams off to the shops and ship hulls. But a little later a few dozen workers left their posts and returned to the square; soon thousands joined them, and a strike began.

At the Elmor factory, almost next door to the Lenin Shipyard, Andrzej Gwiazda and Bogdan Lis—a free trade union group collaborator who, remarkably, was also chairman of the factory's PZPR committee—led 2,000 workers out on strike. Henryka Krzywonos, another ally, convinced the municipal transport workers to leave. Workers at the Repair Shipyard and the Northern Shipyard in Gdansk also quit working, as did dockworkers at the Northern Port. By noon Friday about 50,000 workers had left their jobs. At each enterprise strikers stayed put, made ready to occupy the premises, elected strike committees, and sent delegates to the Lenin Shipyard, which looked to be the nerve center for the region.

Little more than twenty-four hours after the strike came alive at dawn on Thursday, a handful of young activists armed with nothing but leaflets and posters had managed to bring out a giant workforce. The next day the same happened all round the region. Everywhere, strikers held back from spilling out into the city and confronting police; instead, they stayed in the yards and factories—protected spaces where they could exercise control and organize democratically. By sending delegates to a central point, they started to build a single organization to unite and guide all strikers. And their demand for an independent union raised the stakes: Decision makers higher than workplace administrators would have to get involved.

These were the first steps in an unexpected escalation, launching a movement that surpassed anything the free trade union group could have predicted. Once the activists triggered the walkouts, they could not fully direct what happened next, because momentum came from the moves of thousands of individuals. But key decisions that first day—to occupy the factories, organize, and demand an independent union—were not spontaneous. They reflected lessons that workers who had gone through the trauma of 1970 had learned and passed on to younger workers; they also had been ventilated in publications by the free trade union group over months and years. "We didn't have to explain to them why they shouldn't go out into the street, why they should stay inside," Borusewicz recalled. On the Baltic coast, workers already knew what to do.[38]

"Who Wants to Strike?"

As workers across the region joined the cause, local authorities waited for instructions from Warsaw, where Gierek arrived Friday morning after cutting short a vacation in the Soviet Union. The regime decided to smother the strike by snuffing out the central flame in Gdansk. The first step was to seal off the city from the rest of Poland. On Friday all telephone and telex lines out of Gdansk were disconnected and roads out of the area were blockaded. At the Lenin Shipyard, Gniech's orders were to accept most of the workers' economic demands. "Do anything to stop the strike," he was told. Only the workers' "political demands"—above all, the call for independent unions—had to be rejected. Once the shipyard workers made a deal, officials believed, strikers elsewhere could be coaxed back to work.[39]

The problem with this scheme was that the strike committee elected at the Lenin Shipyard was made up mostly of militants—young stalwarts like Borowczak and hardened veterans like Walesa and Walentynowicz—who were unlikely to be bought off by a pay raise. But Gniech contrived a way to make the strike committee bend. When the talks opened Friday morning, workers listening to the loudspeakers heard him propose that since the committee had delegates from only a few of the shipyard's departments, each department should choose three delegates, to produce a more representative committee.

There was no way Walesa or anyone else could oppose this without appearing to disregard their own democratic principles within earshot of fellow strikers. But they feared that in many departments, official union and party people—who could grant privileges or get someone fired or transferred—would railroad workers and get themselves or other cautious employees elected. Their suspicions were justified: When the new, larger committee assembled later that day, strike organizers were a minority within a more conservative group.[40]

In the talks on Friday, Gniech gave the strikers much of what they wanted. Walentynowicz and Walesa could return to work. The regional party secretary would guarantee that strikers would not suffer reprisals. There would be a monument to the 1970 victims. The director also made vague promises about revoking food price increases and reforming the existing unions. By the end of the day, the one remaining issue was the size of a wage hike. As delegates from other factories arrived Friday afternoon and evening, they discovered that the strike was close to collapsing at the center, just as it was gaining strength across the region.

When talks began Saturday morning, Gniech stalled for a while and then offered a pay raise close to the original demand. Committee members now seemed eager to take the money and get back to work, but Walesa made a last pitch: They should hold out for the wages they wanted, for rescinding price increases, for strike pay, and, most of all, for the right to have free trade unions. Gniech promised that they might still get all those things if they ended the strike, and he prevailed. The majority voted to terminate the strike. Walesa felt he had no choice but to go along, take the microphone, and declare the strike over. Thousands of workers who had spent the last two nights in the shipyard got up and headed for the gates.

Key leaders of the strike at the Lenin Shipyard, Gdansk, August 1980;
from left: Bogdan Borusewicz (rear, in sweater), Andrzej Gwiazda, (at table,
bearded), Joanna Duda-Gwiazda, and Anna Pienkowska (standing).
Credit: ©Zbigniew Trybek

Outside the building there was chaos. When they emerged, Walesa and
other committee members were besieged by delegates from other enterprises.
"The Gdansk shipyard is betraying us!" yelled one of them. Henryka Krzywonos,
who knew Walesa well, told him face to face, "You can't do it, Lech. If you
abandon us, we'll be lost." Suddenly Walesa knew he could not refuse these
appeals. "We must respect democracy and therefore accept the compromise,
even if it is not brilliant," he told the crowd. "But we do not have the right to
abandon others. We must continue the strike out of solidarity until everyone
has won. I said I would be the last person to leave the shipyard. And I meant it.
If the workers who are gathered here want to continue to strike then it will be
continued. Now, who wants to strike?" "We do!" they all roared.[41]

Walentynowicz and Pienkowska rushed back to the conference room to
broadcast the decision to stay on strike, only to find that the microphones had
been cut off. Gniech was back in his office, telling workers over the loudspeakers
that the strike was over and they must go home—anyone found there after 6:00
P.M. would be prosecuted. Many workers had already left, and the rest would
soon follow, having heard only Gniech.

But the two women raced over to Gate No. 3. Pienkowska, ordinarily subdued, grabbed a bullhorn, had the gates locked, called for quiet, and declared, "In three minutes time, everybody will be able to leave, but I want to say a few words, and for three minutes you can wait." She stood on a barrel and told the workers that the director's words were a sham. The workers' demands had not been met, there would be no free trade unions. "If you go out, the same thing will happen as in 1976; the people who are left will be surrounded by the militia and crushed. They will be fired . . . Is that what you want?" She seemed to be winning them over. "The most important thing is the solidarity of everyone, all the factories, all the workers." By then the workers were cheering, and when the gates reopened just four people left. Then Pienkowska rode an electric cart to the other gates, where she made the same pleas.[42]

The shipyard's size prevented getting the word to everyone, and many strikers were tired and eager to go. So, despite Pienkowska's exertions, most strikers left by the end of the afternoon. How many remained is unclear: 400 or 500 by some accounts, 1,000 or so by others. This hard core would have to hold out over the weekend and hope that when their co-workers showed up on Monday morning, they would join the strike once more. In the meantime, messengers hurried to all the other striking factories to say that the strike was still on and nothing had been settled.

"For the Whole Nation"

The activists holed up in the shipyard had saved the strike and, with it, the campaign for an independent trade union. But to win the right to organize, the entire working class of the coast, and possibly of other parts of Poland as well, would have to be mobilized. Only a vast general strike could threaten enough economic damage to make the regime back down on such a fundamental issue. Now that they had stopped Gniech from dousing the fire before it could spread, there was a chance to rally a broader movement.

First they had to have a program—"a banner, a flag that everybody could follow," in Borusewicz's words. By Saturday evening delegates from twenty striking enterprises met in a conference room of the shipyard's Health and Safety Building—where the talks with Gniech had taken place—and declared themselves the Inter-factory Strike Committee (known by its Polish initials, MKS). Walesa, Walentynowicz, Gwiazda, and Krzywonos were at its heart. After years of handing out leaflets, holding memorials, and taking abuse from security agents, they now spoke for tens of thousands of striking workers. Also present were a number of dissident intellectuals who had long cooperated with the free trade union group. Together, they worked past midnight on Saturday and all through Sunday. When they were done, they had twenty-one demands.[43]

Number one was the right to form free trade unions, independent of the party. This was the pole star of the Gdansk activists, and it had been a dream of rank-and-file workers on the coast since 1970. Number two was immunity from reprisals, and then came demands for tangible benefits: strike pay, a 2,000-zloty raise, and a cost-of-living allowance. Like the petition to the Tsar that Georgi Gapon and his fellow Russians had carried on Bloody Sunday, the demands also sought basic rights and justice, including freedom of speech, press, and publication; reinstatement of people fired from jobs or expelled from universities because of their views; and an end to privileges for the security service and party apparatus. And their demands also included changes that would touch the life of every Pole, not just workers: reducing the retirement age, improving the health service, making day care more available and maternity leave longer, and Saturdays off.

Yet the demands stopped short of challenging the regime's hold on power. On Saturday night Tadeusz Szczudlowski, a passionate human rights activist, had proposed demanding a total ban on censorship. Borusewicz objected. They should not threaten the PZPR's political control, he insisted. "You know what happened when they abolished censorship in Czechoslovakia in 1968," he reminded them. They had to respect the reality that Poland was part of the Soviet bloc and had to stay under communist rule. For the same reason, a proposal to call for free elections was dropped. Just three days into the strike, its leaders were already observing a speed limit on their challenges to the regime.[44]

From the beginning, the MKS wanted the strike to be the mainspring for a popular movement. Its leaders realized that workers would not prevail in a long struggle unless they could count on the people's support. So they draped the strike in symbols that invoked widely shared values. On Sunday morning Father Henryk Jankowski arrived at Gate No. 2 to celebrate mass. Thousands came out from the city, carrying flowers in their arms and Polish flags over their heads. Someone stuck a picture of John Paul II to the gate. Workers inside and townspeople outside sang hymns, and the priest consecrated a wooden cross placed where workers had been killed in 1970. Later a ribbon with the red and white national colors and an image of the Black Madonna were attached to the cross. At the top was a piece of paper with a quote from Jozef Pilsudski, the hero of Poland's drive for independence from Russia after World War I: "To want to, is to be able to." The dreams of the strikers had been affixed to the Polish spirit.[45]

As the weekend waned, the MKS faced having to enlarge the strike beyond the twenty-two factories and shipyards already participating—to encompass hundreds of thousands of workers around Gdansk, and then to extend the strike to the coal fields of Silesia, to the industrial regions around Krakow and Warsaw, and to the other great Baltic port, Szczecin. But now the state-controlled media were in full cry against the strike. Newspapers in Gdansk insisted they would worsen the economy. The prime minister had gone on television to warn that Poland's "allies"—a code term for the Soviet Union—would be unhappy if the strikes were not settled soon. Strikers still in the shipyard were portrayed as a band of malcontents, interfering with the wishes of the majority to go back to work.

By Sunday night underground printers had run off the first leaflets about the MKS and its demands. On Monday a network of couriers went into action, running leaflets to factories on the coast. Truck drivers making deliveries at the Lenin Shipyard carried news back to supplying factories. Workers had a hard time getting past roadblocks thrown up to quarantine Gdansk, but sympathetic students, doctors, and engineers had more success getting through. All over Poland, listeners to Radio Free Europe learned a little of the MKS and its demands, courtesy of Kuron in Warsaw. Monday also brought thousands of workers, who had gone home on Saturday, back to the shipyard, rejoining those who stayed behind. Delegates from more than thirty new striking plants had shown up; all day, guards announced the arrival of even more delegates. By nightfall the MKS represented over 150 factories in the region.

With the wind of this new support at its back, the MKS was ready to negotiate, but now the tables were turned and the authorities stonewalled. On Monday Stanislaw Kania, a Politburo member, met with the provincial party committee, hatching a new plan to end the crisis. Earlier the regime had tried to break the strike at its center, by reaching a deal with shipyard workers. Now they tacked in the opposite direction, talking with strikers at a dozen or so enterprises not yet in the MKS, promising big raises—and also trying to peel away those who had joined the MKS by offering them separate deals. The underlying strategy, though, was the same: buy off workers and detach them from the goal of free trade unions. At the same time, they hoped to stanch the strike's outward flow by enforcing the telephone and road blockade of Gdansk, harassing strike couriers, and jailing opposition figures, including Kuron. One thing was paramount: Under no circumstances would they recognize the MKS.

On Tuesday party officials briefly considered one other option: breaking the strike by force. All weekend the Lenin Shipyard holdouts had feared an assault, imagining paratroopers descending from the skies. But both Kania and Tadeusz Fiszbach, the party boss in Gdansk, wanted a peaceful settlement; 1980 was not 1970, and Gierek was not Gomulka. The party chief had repeatedly shown that he would go to great lengths to avoid mayhem. And thanks to Kuron and, later, to foreign journalists who came to Gdansk, the drama at the shipyard was visible not only to many Poles but to much of the world. That the strikers were holding valuable ships and machinery hostage offered them some protection. Publicity offered them even more.[46]

So at least for the moment, the fate of the conflict would hang instead on whether the regime's bribes, misinformation, and intimidation could stem the mobilization that had bloomed the previous week and surged ahead on Monday. If that did not happen, and the strike spread far enough and lasted long enough, eventually the regime would face a distasteful choice: negotiate with the MKS or use the military to smash it.

In the meantime, sitting at three long tables in a shipyard assembly hall, under a statue of Lenin, the MKS listened to new strikers' delegates, argued with each other, and made plans. In the back of the room, technicians transmitted the proceedings live to the rest of the shipyard and made cassettes for strikers at other factories. Outside the hall, guards at the shipyard's gates kept out unwelcome types, especially security agents. Others watched the ships and machinery to prevent any damage. Translators helped foreign journalists and photographers. Butchers slaughtered live pigs and cattle, and meals were prepared from the meat and potatoes, cheese, bread, and produce that people brought in from all over.[47]

By midweek an MKS statement insisted that the strikers "are not fighting for a mere pittance for themselves, but for justice for the whole nation," and the nation seemed to agree. Every day a large crowd of well-wishers collected outside the gates. On Wednesday a delegation from the Gdansk Polytechnic Institute arrived and announced its support; the Gdansk Writers' Union and the University of Gdansk did the same the next day. Radio Free Europe broadcast an endorsement of the strikers, drafted by Tadeusz Mazowiecki, the editor of a Catholic weekly, and signed by sixty-four other Warsaw intellectuals.

After midnight Friday Mazowiecki and Bronislaw Geremek, a highly respected historian, arrived from Warsaw to talk with Walesa. Like many intellectuals, Kuron among them, they were concerned that the demand for free trade unions went too far and might provoke a confrontation. They failed to sway Walesa, but they decided to remain in the shipyard anyway and—at Walesa's invitation—serve as advisors.

All the while the strike kept barreling across the coast. By the end of Tuesday, 263 enterprises were represented on the MKS; another 40 or so joined the next day—and news of strikes elsewhere began to filter into Gdansk. Workers at the Warski Shipyard in Szczecin had quit work on Monday; soon other factories in that region formed their own inter-factory strike committee, as also happened in Elblag, on the border with the Soviet Union. On Thursday night the strikers from the Gdansk enterprises who had been negotiating separately with the government joined the MKS.

The regime's strategy of dividing to conquer had failed. Since the week began, the strikers had won over the people of Gdansk, inspired dissidents, and captivated a flock of foreign journalists. The strike now paralyzed the entire Gdansk-Gdynia region and was poised to jump to new areas. By Friday night the regime's leadership was ready to try something new. Perhaps they could deal with the MKS, which had repeatedly invited them to talk, and still not give up much; with that hope, they said they would come to the shipyard on Saturday.

After a week-long standoff, the movement had forced the regime to accept the MKS as the voice of striking workers. To pull that off, strike leaders went beyond the lessons of 1970. They called on new alliances that had evolved in the intervening years: Farmers and townspeople supplied the strikers; professionals and students ran word of the strike to enterprises up and down the coast; academics and dissidents translated for the foreign media and advised the MKS. This wider front had not started the strike, but it frustrated the regime's attempts to isolate and wear out the strikers. Unlike 1970, the workers were not on their own.

"We Have Achieved All We Could"

On Saturday evening the two sides met in the Health and Safety conference room, separated by a glass wall from the assembly hall where hundreds of MKS delegates looked on. Every word could be heard by thousands of strikers outside, through whom the government's men had to walk on their way in. Mieczyslaw Jagielski, the deputy prime minister, headed the regime's side. He had a reputation as a troubleshooter, earned in July when he managed an end to a general strike in Lublin. Walesa, Gwiazda, Krzywonos, Kolodziej, Pienkowska, and other strike instigators spoke for the MKS.

With hundreds of thousands of strikers in several hundred enterprises now fused to a single agenda, the MKS wanted to remove obstacles to an even wider mobilization. They refused to negotiate on the twenty-one demands until arrests and beatings of strike couriers stopped, news about the talks was aired over official media, and telephone lines to Warsaw were restored. Jagielski and his colleagues were taken aback. Knowing their position would grow weaker with each new factory joining the strike, they offered general assurances, pointed to "technical" difficulties, and tried to steer the discussion back to the core demands. One of them claimed that telephones could not be restored because a hurricane had hit Warsaw the night before, damaging much of the city, including the central telephone exchange. "May I point out that telephone links with Warsaw were cut off last Friday, a week ago," Pienkowska pointed out. "Nothing was said then of any hurricane." MKS leaders made it clear they would wait as

Polish government negotiators arrive at the Lenin Shipyard, Gdansk, August 1980.
Credit: ©Erazm Ciolek

long as it took for the preconditions to be met. They were dealing from a position of strength, and they were going to use it.[48]

The regime blinked first. It took until Monday night for the telephone connection between Gdansk and Warsaw to come back on line and for local and national television to start airing reports about the talks. Negotiations began again on Tuesday, as more publicity fed the strike wave. That day workers in Wroclaw struck and formed a committee, bringing the strike near the vital coal fields of Upper Silesia. By Wednesday 500 factories were on strike in the Gdansk region. Strikes broke out in two more industrial centers, Bydgoszcz and Torun, while workers at the giant Nowa Huta steel mill were preparing to walk out. By Friday 20,000 copper miners had joined the movement, and workers at the Cegielski machine works in Poznan warned that they would strike if no settlement was reached in Gdansk. The regime was now in a race against time, as each day brought the threat of even more injury to the economy.

Although they were losing control of communications and the deference of the country's workforce, top leaders still hoped to salvage something at the bargaining table. If they gave way on economic demands, they thought they might escape without fundamental changes, especially independent unions. The regime had faced workers' uprisings in 1956 and 1970 and both times it had calmed the waters through bread-and-butter concessions and promises to reform the existing unions. Even some intellectuals advising the MKS argued that democratizing the official unions was the best that could be hoped for and that obstinately refusing to accept that would wreck the chance of a settlement. But they were talking to people who had made independent unions the central cause of their lives and who were not about to give up after coming so far.

When talks resumed on Tuesday and Jagielski made his pledge to overhaul the official unions, the MKS delegates stood firm. "The fact is that our present unions do absolutely nothing and never have done anything," insisted the dockworkers' delegate. Bogdan Lis was more graphic: "We don't want an infusion of new blood, we want a completely new organism." After a break, Jagielski proposed that each side appoint "experts" to meet behind closed doors to draft the agreement's language, while the main negotiators continued the public talks. That would be a breach of the openness that strike leaders had required since August 14, but Walesa and the others agreed. They sensed, and it turned out they were right, that the regime was preparing to retreat and wanted to do so out of sight of the public and foreign press.[49]

The communists were finally ready to yield on what mattered most to the strikers, and a settlement was possible because the MKS was ready to return the favor. Presenting themselves as a loyal opposition rather than a threat to party rule may have been an illusion, but it greased the wheels of the talks. Walesa had opened the Tuesday meeting with the assurance that strikers were "not fighting against the socialist system." Later in the week, at a meeting of the "experts" group when a government negotiator insisted that the MKS recognize the "leading role" of the party, the workers' side agreed. It was hard to endorse the party's monopoly on power, but it would be dangerous to force-feed it with political humiliation.[50]

The MKS made one more concession. Although it had wanted to obtain the right of free trade unions for all workers in Poland, the regime refused; workers outside Gdansk would have to win that right for themselves. Some strikers wanted to stonewall on this, but Walesa, Gwiazda, and the advisors argued for yielding, and they carried the day.

By week's end an agreement was close at hand, and the PZPR faced a moment of truth. Meeting in Warsaw, the Politburo argued about whether to accept the deal or turn to armed suppression. Kania, head of the security services, and General Wojciech Jaruzelski, minister of defense, balked at repression, fearing that their forces might disobey orders to attack the shipyard and other enterprises. Later that day Jagielski received instructions to finalize the deal as soon as possible.

On Saturday and Sunday the full negotiating teams worked out the last details. The government would honor the right of workers to organize their own unions while binding the unions to recognize "the leading role of the

PZPR in the state" and "not to oppose the existing system of international alliances." This was the heart of it: The workers got their unions, but the unions would have to stay out of politics and not antagonize the Soviets. The strikers also won the right to strike, a new law on the press, investigations of political repression, economic pledges—and a promise of no reprisals against strikers or those who helped them.

At the final session on Sunday afternoon, Walesa knew that not all MKS delegates, strikers, and dissidents were happy with the agreement, especially the clause about the party's leading role. "Have we achieved everything we wanted?" he asked. "No, not everything, but we all know that we've achieved a lot. We have achieved all we could . . . We'll achieve the rest too, because we have the most important thing: our independent, self-governing trade unions. This is our guarantee for the future." Then he declared the strike over, and soon he and Jagielski signed the document. It was Sunday evening, August 31, and hundreds of thousands of workers would be back on the job the next morning.[51]

The pact recognized the MKS as the founding committee of a new union representing workers in the Gdansk-Gdynia region. Within days it set up shop in an old hotel on the outskirts of Gdansk. Walesa was the chairman, and he invited Jacek Kuron to be chief advisor. The strike organizers decided to name their new union Solidarity—the title of the strike bulletin published in the shipyard—capturing the spirit of common struggle that had animated the opposition in the 1970s. The strikers in Szczecin, who signed their own agreement with the government on August 30, chose the same name for the new union there.

As promised, the official media printed the agreement's text, and all Poles learned what the Gdansk workers had won. Within days workers in other regions demanded the same rights and then sought advice from Solidarity in Gdansk about how to occupy factories and form inter-factory committees. Inspired by the August strike on the coast, workers in every part of Poland seized the right to unionize. On September 17 delegates from all over met in Gdansk to create a nationwide structure—electing a National Coordinating Commission to give guidance to the regional unions. Nationally, Solidarity could count more than 3 million members by that date, and by the end of the year, almost 10 million Poles.

During the August days, Adam Michnik was sure that the strikers were demanding the "impossible" when they insisted on free trade unions. Like other dissidents, he was certain the regime would never accept such a breach in its wall of control. But the workers on the Baltic coast gave the regime no other choice, and the majority of Polish wage earners became part of a national organization not controlled by the party or the state. Nothing like it had ever happened before in any communist-ruled country.[52]

SIXTEEN MONTHS

"The Façade . . . Must Stay Intact"

When the dust settled after the August strike, Solidarity found itself in much the same place where the Tsar's opponents had been after the October Manifesto in 1905: The movement had just forced unprecedented changes but now faced a regime divided between moderates and hard-liners, and capable of reverting to its arbitrary ways. The conflict that arose from the shipyards and engrossed the nation was unlikely to subside.

In a narrow sense, Solidarity's objective was to make the government deliver on the twenty-one points in the Gdansk agreement, trade union rights above all. But while Solidarity had sprung from a strike and was still a union, it also had become the serrated edge of a movement that drew in millions—many of whom were not industrial workers—who were intent on creating space in which all Poles could organize independently. In effect, Solidarity was heir to the political hopes of the 1970 strikers and the intellectuals in KOR, whom the regime had appraised as a threat to communism. Those in the movement's forefront after August knew that leaning too hard on the regime might precipitate a crackdown or, even worse, military action by the Soviet Union. In speech after speech during the fall of 1980, Solidarity leaders insisted that they were not hostile to socialism, to the leading role of the party, or to the Warsaw Pact. Just as they had done during the August strike, they left genuine democracy off the agenda.

Within these constraints, the Catholic Church seemed to be a model for what Solidarity might become. For the most part the Church ran its own affairs and kept the loyalty of a mass following. In return it abjured frontal criticism of communist rule, although individual churchmen prodded the regime to respect human rights. Some thought Solidarity could be another separate and stable public realm, offering shelter to other kinds of believers—leaving the communist party to reign in name only, a sort of husk around an embryonic democracy and self-organized society as well as a prophylactic against Soviet intervention. "Poland was like an old house living under a preservation order," wrote Neal Ascherson, a British journalist. "The interior could be modernized, even gutted and replaced. But the façade and the roof must stay intact."[53]

Solidarity's project—to vie with the party for control of Poland's future without aiming for its perch atop the state—would take immense self-restraint as well as all the force of its popular base. For the endeavor to succeed, the union's supporters would have to remain united behind "self-limiting" goals, even though many chafed under them. During the strike only Walesa's personal standing and political skills had enabled him to quiet an uproar over the clause accepting the party's leading role. These same voices, determined to press for democracy regardless of the Damocles' sword of Soviet intervention, were bound to speak up again. And if the economy continued to weaken and the party failed to make good on promises of material gains, then Solidarity would either have to confront the regime on wages and prices or else risk losing the support of its rank-and-file.

Solidarity's ascendancy also would be contingent on the party accepting its waning influence. Days after the August pact was signed, Edward Gierek was felled by a heart attack, and Stanislaw Kania was chosen as first secretary— marking the advent of party pragmatists who, under the slogan "renewal," seemed ready to implement the deal with the strikers and avoid new confrontations. But many in the party and the security service were not so enlightened— and were likely to do all they could to block more concessions.

Everything Solidarity hoped to achieve, finally, depended on the USSR choosing to stay out of the picture. But even before the August accords were signed, Moscow had been alarmed. *Pravda* and *Izvestia* had denounced the strikes as "counter-revolutionary" and claimed that "anti-socialist" intellectuals were exploiting the workers. The orthodox regimes in Czechoslovakia and East Germany were even more strident, and other communist capitals in Eastern Europe let it be known that if Warsaw could not put Solidarity in its place, then "fraternal help" might come to the rescue, invited or not. The international, economic, and military costs of invading Poland would be inordinate, but not everyone thought the Soviets unwilling to pay the price. "We simply cannot and must not lose Poland," Andrei Gromyko, the Soviet foreign minister, is reported to have said at a Politburo meeting in Moscow on October 29.[54]

Maneuvers and Sirens

In the fall and winter of 1980-1981, a rhythm of crisis, relaxation, and renewed crisis took hold in Poland. Repeatedly the authorities either broke promises made in the August agreement or else acted in ways that violated its spirit—dragging their feet on raising wages, writing a new law on censorship, and harassing workers trying to create new unions. In November police raided the Warsaw region offices of Solidarity and arrested a young printer, Jan Narozniak, charging him with "disseminating state secrets." In January the government announced that Polish workers would have to be at their jobs two Saturdays a month, a breach of the promise of free Saturdays. Official media, especially television news, constantly attacked KOR and started investigating its "anti-state" activities. Jacek Kuron was arrested and held for six hours on March 5.

These affronts created a dilemma. If Solidarity did nothing, both friend and foe might see it as a paper tiger, lacking the resolve to back up the August pact. If it pushed too hard, it risked a hard-line reaction. The union found a middle way: It tailored its response each time to sustain the momentum of change without driving the regime to the brink—it would make demands, call or threaten a protest strike, but then meet with officials to work out a compromise. In this way it won a new promise of wage hikes, the release of Narozniak, only one working Saturday each month, television and radio access, and a newspaper. None of these half loaves left its supporters fully satisfied, and Walesa and other leaders had their hands full convincing workers to call off strikes once the deals were made. But tensions were calmed, offering brief respites before new disagreements.

The paradox of Solidarity's position—having power to constrain the regime but facing hazards in using that power—became obvious in March 1981. Since the fall farmers had been seeking recognition for their own union, to be called Rural Solidarity. They had strong backing from workers' Solidarity and the Church, but the state stubbornly refused to register the organization, contending that farmers were not wage earners and thus could not be unionized. After months of friction, the dispute erupted into a nationwide crisis.

On March 19 Rural Solidarity representatives along with Jan Rulewski, the leader of the regional Solidarity branch, went to a government council meeting in the city of Bydgoszcz. They were told they could speak in favor of registering the farmers' group, but the meeting was adjourned before they could take the floor. The activists and some council members then stayed to work on a joint statement. They were still there in the evening when 200 police officers twice came to the room and asked them to leave. They refused, linked arms, stood in a circle, and sang the national anthem, until police dragged them away and threw them out. Later some said they were forced to run the gauntlet, just like arrested workers in 1976. Three people, including Rulewski, ended up with bruises all over their bodies.

The news sparked outrage all over Poland. In Bydgoszcz crowds chanted "Gestapo." Solidarity demanded an inquiry, and its offices were hung with photos of the bloodied faces of victims. The next day delegates to the union's National Commission met in Bydgoszcz to decide what to do. Many wanted to threaten the ultimate sanction, a general strike. Tadeusz Mazowiecki and Bronislaw Geremek, advisors and veterans of the August talks, warned that a general strike would only give hard-liners an excuse for repression. The next day Walesa proposed a four-hour nationwide warning strike for that Friday, March 27. If, after four days, no agreement with the regime was reached, an unlimited general strike would be called. But delegates wanted an immediate general strike, and only when Walesa stormed out did they adopt his plan. It had five demands, including punishment of the perpetrators at Bydgoszcz and recognition of Rural Solidarity.

The mood over the next days was unbearably tense. Soviet leaders extended Warsaw Pact military maneuvers then taking place in Poland, and Soviet forces were within striking distance of the Polish capital. Both Washington and Western European governments warned that an invasion might be coming. Meanwhile Solidarity mobilized its members. The National Commission set up shop in the Lenin Shipyard, and the regional headquarters moved out of defenseless buildings and into factory strongholds. In Bydgoszcz the union operated from the railroad yard, where repair workshops and trains offered defensive positions. In case of a general strike, Solidarity members were to occupy factories and organize themselves on the model of the MKS and the Lenin Shipyard the previous August. If the regime declared a state of emergency, strikers were to form shadow committees that would take over once Solidarity leaders were arrested. If the Soviets invaded, civilians were to change street signs and refuse to supply the occupiers.

When Friday came, at 8:00 A.M., factory sirens sounded from one end of Poland to the other and workers put down their tools. More than a million party members defied orders from the Politburo and obeyed the strike call. Television screens went blank, except for the words "solidarity–strike." Only a few enterprises—essential services, steel mills, arms plants—were exempt. "It was an eerie sight," recalled Radek Sikorski, then a high school student. "Not a kiosk was open, not a streetcar or a bus moved." Buildings were draped with red and white flags, and people wore red and white armbands. Then, at noon, the sirens wailed again and the strike was over.[55]

Solidarity had flexed its muscles. But the Soviets displayed their brawn too: Tanks were still rumbling through the countryside, and TASS, the Soviet news service, issued a hysterical report that "subversive elements" were trying to seize power in Poland. While Solidarity prepared for a general strike to begin on Tuesday, Geremek and Mazowiecki urged Walesa to pull back from the brink. Cardinal Wyszynski, too, advised the union leader to find a way out of the crisis. From Rome, the Pope pleaded for compromise. Walesa shared this sense of caution, and while he knew that the rank-and-file were spoiling for a strike, he decided that "democracy must be limited" and that he and the union advisors alone would deal with the regime that weekend. While Walesa faced off with the government's negotiator, Mieczyslaw Rakowski, other Solidarity leaders were stuck in a Warsaw hotel room, left in the dark.[56]

At 7:30 Monday evening, after spending the weekend stashing food and sleeping bags at work to prepare for the strike, Poles turned on the television news. They saw Andrzej Gwiazda reading a statement: Solidarity and the government had signed an agreement. The authorities admitted that the police actions in Bydgoszcz had violated agreed-on principles about solving problems through negotiations and expressed "regret" about the beatings; the perpetrators would be punished. The government would not interfere with Rural Solidarity, pending approval of its registration. For its part, Solidarity would stand down from the strike. "In my opinion, the risk was too great," Walesa would say a little later, explaining his decision for another deal.[57]

The National Commission met Tuesday and Wednesday in Gdansk, and the delegates vented their fury at Walesa. He had been frightened by Soviet tanks, they fumed, and he had let the regime off the hook without getting much in return—and they were incensed by his "anti-democratic" methods. Gwiazda, who had been persuaded by Walesa to announce the strike's suspension, denounced his own complicity and offered to resign from the Commission's presidium. Anna Walentynowicz argued that Solidarity should go ahead with the strike anyway, and she was dismissed from her post as the Lenin Shipyard's delegate. The union's founding nucleus was in pieces.

Despite the recriminations over Bydgoszcz, the results achieved by Solidarity through the spring of 1981 seemed to justify the strategy of accepting less to avert a blow-up. The union's key sanction was the general occupation strike, pioneered by the coastal workers in August 1980 and then copied by workers all over Poland in the ensuing weeks. In the hands of a nationwide organization with roughly 10 million members, the strike could mangle the country's economy in a very short time. By brandishing this club but not using it, Solidarity staved off violent conflict even as it changed Poland nearly beyond recognition.

The most basic change was that a vast swath of the Polish workforce was now organized outside of party-controlled institutions. Solidarity members included not only industrial workers but also teachers, doctors and nurses, engineers and technicians, even police officers. Over a million farmers belonged to Rural Solidarity. University students had set up their own unions. The ideal of a self-organized society inside a communist state had become a reality in only a matter of months.

Equally exhilarating were changes in the tenor of public life. More than 100,000 people, including leaders of Solidarity, the PZPR, and the Church, congregated outside the Lenin Shipyard on December 16 at a new 140-foot-tall monument to commemorate the 1970 massacres. Everyone complied with the union's ban on alcohol throughout the event—a display of public sobriety that the regime had never succeeded in coaxing from a people not known for abstinence. The privately developed civil society advocated by Kolakowski, Kuron, and Michnik had materialized.

The state's control over the mass media also relaxed, as early as the fall of 1980. People waited in long lines at kiosks to get their hands on official newspapers, which carried lively coverage of political controversies and crusaded for causes such as environmental clean-ups. Every regional branch of Solidarity had its own newspaper. Censorship of television news remained stringent, but Solidarity had guaranteed air time on television and radio, and Sunday masses were broadcast nationwide over the radio. Poles were beginning to find out what it meant to be free.

Hard Words, Soft Hopes

The new liberties were born of the power of Solidarity to threaten the regime's control of the country with debilitating strikes. The resolve of workers underpinning this power encouraged other groups of Poles who sought to organize themselves—the Bydgoszcz crisis, after all, had been triggered by an attack on farmers trying to launch Rural Solidarity. But, as the months went by in 1981, the strategy that secured this power became harder to execute.

Solidarity's approach rested on a sanguine assumption about the prudence of its adversary. In the 1970s Michnik had written that the PZPR was made up of pragmatists and opportunists, not true believers in Marxism-Leninism. "A party 'pragmatist' has no reason to aim for democratic change—for pluralism and authentic self-government," Michnik asserted. "But he does have reason to understand the effectiveness of compromising with forces favoring plurality . . . For he knows very well that repression solves nothing and instead prepares the ground for the next explosion of social discontent, the consequences of which are impossible to foresee." If Michnik was right, then persistent but carefully regulated pressure by Solidarity might succeed in winning successive compromises, each one creating new openings for civil society to grow.[58]

The two top communists in the post-August period each seemed to fit Michnik's profile of a pragmatist. Stanislaw Kania, the first secretary, was a communist apparatchik cut from the same cloth as Edward Gierek, and like his predecessor, he came from a lower-class background and had worked his way up the party hierarchy by mastering the rules of the political game. He would go to great lengths to avoid open conflict. It was thanks largely to his influence that the party had signed the August agreement rather than resorting to repression, and he kept right on negotiating with the new union.

General Wojciech Jaruzelski, the minister of defense and, beginning in February 1981, the prime minister, displayed a different character altogether. By 1980 most of the party elite were men of limited education and little refinement, quite easy for opposition intellectuals to ridicule. In contrast, Jaruzelski was the scion of an old landed family, and it showed in his bearing; he had a reputation for self-discipline and honesty, standing apart from the corruption rampant among party bosses in the 1970s. It was widely though incorrectly believed that the general had refused to allow the army to shed workers' blood in the 1970 uprisings. When the general became prime minister, Walesa greeted him as a "good Pole," and during the Bydgoszcz crisis, he called him a "uniform we can trust."[59]

Kania and Jaruzelski seemed reasonable men who would accept a modus vivendi with Solidarity, not because they wanted to but because the alternative was worse. But there were other forces in the regime that did not share that flexibility—old union officials who had the rug pulled out from under them by the new union, party bureaucrats sure to lose privileges if the August agreement was honored, and industrial managers whose clout would be curtailed by democracy in workplaces. They were offended by uninhibited talk, over the airwaves and in newspapers, about the regime's crimes and blunders, and for them, Kania's willingness to bend to Solidarity's demands was a sellout, a retreat before "anarchy."

Kania and Jaruzelski had more to worry about than disgruntled party comrades. Soviet leaders had been unable to perceive Solidarity as anything other than a cover for enemies of socialism out to sever Poland's ties to the USSR. Any sign of anti-Russian feeling inflamed the Kremlin, which even complained about a cartoon of Leonid Brezhnev, the Soviet leader, in a Solidarity newsletter in the tiny village of Pulowy. Brezhnev himself began harassing Kania by telephone—calling sometimes three times a day, insisting that he impose martial law. Once the Kremlin chief suggested that the regime plant a weapons cache that the authorities could later "discover" and claim to be Solidarity's, as a pretext for cracking down. Both Kania and Jaruzelski were dragged to meetings with Soviet Politburo members several times, where they were browbeaten for hours and accused of coddling their opponents. Jaruzelski later said he spent more time during 1981 with Marshal Viktor Kulikov, a Soviet military commander, than with his own wife and daughter.[60]

There was also another source of volatility. The August strike had sparked a rebellion at the grass roots of the party. More than 200,000 members (out of little more than 3 million) had simply quit, and perhaps 1 million of those who stayed also joined Solidarity. For the most part, these were not mid-level bureaucrats but rank-and-file members, and they pushed for democratizing the party—abolishing privileges, allowing open debate in party meetings, and making elections to the hierarchy free and fair. Here was a threat to both the "hard" and "soft" factions in the party elite.

For a while it appeared that the reformers might succeed. In early 1981 provincial party conferences held competitive elections to choose delegates to a congress in July, which turned out to be free-wheeling and tumultuous. The delegates lambasted party leaders and reformed the party's internal workings. But many were no doubt intimidated by a Soviet Politburo letter labeling the democracy drive "an instrument for dismantling the Party." Going too far might prove to be dangerous, it implied. Although delegates refused to re-elect most Central Committee members and the Politburo, few reformers made it into the new leadership. A precarious balance between accommodationists and obstructionists still prevailed at the top.[61]

Solidarity showed little interest in the party's ferment. As far as most of its activists were concerned, the PZPR was a spent force. The most they expected from it was a dignified retreat, so its dead weight on top of the system would not hold down the free young society rising from below. If known players like Jaruzelski were ready to accept a reduced role for the party, why should Solidarity pin hopes on insurgents wanting to rejuvenate it?

But Polish communists were not masters of their own fate—they could not be deaf to the choleric noises coming from the Kremlin. Already the first contingency plans for martial law had been sent to Moscow over Jaruzelski's signature at the beginning of March, two weeks before Bydgoszcz. A month later Kania and Jaruzelski had found themselves in an abandoned railroad car hung with lace curtains, just inside the Soviet border, listening for six hours as two senior Soviet Politburo members—Yuri Andropov and Dmitrii Ustinov—demanded a date for a crackdown. The Polish leaders stalled, but the question was not whether but when. By mid-September final martial law plans were complete. On October 18 Kania was bounced out as party first secretary and Jaruzelski took his place.[62]

The moment when a military reckoning became inevitable cannot be pinpointed even in retrospect. The preparations for martial law took place out of sight of Solidarity, so the union had no clear signal it was time to prepare for the worst, although Lech Walesa warned his colleagues not to underestimate the regime. Even if they had been warned of the dangers that lay ahead, the union's leaders would have had difficulty shifting the course of their increasingly unruly movement. In late 1981 popular agitation, not calm strategic thinking, was driving Solidarity.

Darkening the conflict further were storm clouds from the economy. Goods were becoming scarcer and shop lines longer. Sugar, flour, and meat were now being rationed. Months of hardship began to grind down the hopeful mood born in Gdansk the previous year, and it was hard to enjoy the new freedoms when meeting basic needs was difficult. The shortages, people believed, were due to corruption, sabotage by recalcitrant bureaucrats, or Soviet exploitation of Poland's economy. In the summer and fall of 1981, wildcat strikes and food protests began to multiply. Spasmodic violence by crowds of hungry people did not seem far off.

Economic crisis complicated Solidarity's strategy. A trade union could not stand idle while its membership suffered. But expanding the space for a freer society would be imperiled by a fight with the regime over wages and prices, and strikes would only destabilize an economy already unable to service foreign debts. It seemed smarter to make another deal. If Solidarity restrained its members, defused wildcat strikes, convinced workers to give back some of their Saturdays—and even support price increases, which officials were again suggesting—the union could ask for a voice in the making of economic policy. Solidarity would deliver order in return for a share of power.[63]

But as the days grew shorter in 1981, Solidarity was pulled away from the self-imposed limits of August 1980. Since the first MKS meetings in the Lenin Shipyard, when political demands were set aside, Solidarity activists had censored themselves. Most of them bitterly resented Soviet domination, and most longed for real democracy. But something short of that was tolerable, if it denied their opponents cause to crush the movement. A year after the birth of the union, however, those inhibitions were fading. Intoxicated by the overwhelming popular support that Solidarity enjoyed and mirroring the country's acrimonious mood, the militant wing of the opposition turned up the volume.

The most uncompromising rhetoric came from a nationalist group, the Confederation for an Independent Poland (KPN), which demanded free elections, something that would spell the end of PZPR rule. As for what the Soviets might do if that happened, "it would be a mistake to take into account a real or an imaginary threat from the Soviet Union," declared Jan Rulewski, a victim of the Bydgoszcz beatings. And the leader of KPN insisted that "everything is possible if we have the will to act."[64]

Solidarity's leaders could not lag too far behind the movement's most aggressive voices and still remain in the vanguard. While not advocating an end to the party's political monopoly, and although bowing before "the system of powers that emerged in Europe after the Second World War," the union modified its position at the beginning of October and said that the only way to save Poland was "reforming the state and the economy on the basis of democracy and universal public initiative." Local government must be democratized. All citizens must be equal before the law, and judges should be independent.[65]

As Solidarity drafted manifestos and appealed for new compromises, Jaruzelski and his subalterns prepared for martial law—and weighed the reliability of their forces. The ordinary police would be of little use; more than a quarter of them belonged to Solidarity. Army soldiers, mostly conscripts, were kept apart and bombarded with anti-Solidarity propaganda—but a two-year term of service would expire in October, when 150,000 new conscripts, whose loyalties were anyone's guess, would be called up. To be on the safe side, the regime had tacked on two months to outgoing troops' service, but in any case the army was slated for a secondary role. The shock troops would be special paramilitary units, especially the 100,000 men of the Internal Defense Forces and the ZOMO riot police; they were well fed, isolated from their fellow Poles, and heavily indoctrinated. There was no reason to doubt that they would follow orders.

Although martial law was planned in secret, the turn in the regime's strategy was not invisible. Starting in late summer, official media began blasting away at the union. Talks with Solidarity continued, but its proposals for sharing authority on economic policy were rejected; the regime seemed content to let the economy slide, all the while blaming the union. There was also evidence that something was up with the military. In late October the government announced that army detachments would be sent to 2,000 villages to help with food supplies and law and order; a month later detachments were sent to large factories. At the end of November the party central committee asked Poland's parliament to give the government emergency powers, including the right to ban strikes. Finally, on December 2, the ZOMO showed what it could do, by carrying out a lightning raid—complete with helicopters landing on the roof—of a Warsaw firefighting academy that had been occupied by its students.

That the regime intended to shutter the windows of Polish society which Solidarity had opened seems obvious in hindsight. But this was not apparent to the union's leaders, who were preoccupied with day-to-day problems. Most saw that Jaruzelski was tightening up but did not imagine how heavy a blow was coming. Perhaps, having faced the regime's men across one negotiating table after another, Solidarity's leaders saw them as merely mortal, no longer quite so merciless. Or perhaps they were reassured that the head of government now wore a uniform and could be counted on to do the right thing, which, to a Pole, meant never shedding Polish blood. Like their Russian precursors in 1905, they certainly doubted that boys in the ranks would open fire on their own kind. Some may have believed that, if an attack did come, the union could call a general strike and bring the regime to its knees in a matter of days.

In any case, Solidarity's leaders made almost no advance preparations for martial law, besides caching some printing equipment. They had fielded the world's most powerful popular movement of the second half of the twentieth century, but they only knew how to operate in the sunshine. And darkness was fast approaching.

"State of War"

Solidarity's National Coordinating Commission met in Gdansk on Friday, December 11. The delegates were literally back where they started, in the Health and Safety conference room of the Lenin Shipyard. Walesa, as he had all year, counseled the other members to be careful and held out hope that compromise was still possible. "I declare with my full authority: we are for agreement," he said: " . . . we do not want any confrontation." Others, however, believed the union must do something to protest the party's legislative bid to assume emergency powers. So they endorsed a day of protest on December 17.

The Commission continued meeting the next day, amid rumors of unusual troop movements around the country. Rulewski, as before, went the farthest. He proposed that Solidarity hold a referendum early the next year in which the people would have a chance to vote "no confidence" in the regime, clearing the way for Solidarity to form a provisional government. The majority voted to adopt his plan. Walesa looked around the room, clearly vexed with his colleagues. Around 10:00 P.M., the delegates received reports that telex lines into Gdansk had been cut. When the meeting ended at midnight, the out-of-town delegates went back to their hotels, while those from Gdansk went home.

Zbigniew Bujak, a twenty-seven-year-old technician from the Ursus factory, decided not to return to the hotel. Instead, he and Zbigniew Janas, another Warsaw delegate, went to the train station and bought tickets home that night. From the platform, they noticed that ZOMO men had surrounded the Hotel Monopol, one of two hotels where delegates were staying. A cab driver told them the same thing was happening at the other hotel. An hour later the ZOMO unit left, and Bujak and Janas went over and learned that the entire Solidarity presidium had been hauled away. Security agents were searching room by room for other delegates. Back on the street they heard that Walesa's apartment block and the union's regional headquarters were surrounded. Agreeing to rendezvous the next day at a church, they split up.[66]

All over Poland the boom was being lowered. Police rounded up thousands of Solidarity leaders, intellectuals, and other activists. Major cities were sealed off, telephone and telex lines were cut, and troops set up roadblocks. The military seized television and radio stations. When Poles turned on their televisions the next morning, the announcers were in uniform. A twenty-three minute speech by Jaruzelski was broadcast over and over, interspersed with a pianist playing Chopin. The general claimed that Solidarity leaders had tried to take power the night before and that, to save Poland from disaster, a "state of war" had been declared. The country would now be run by a body called the Military Council of National Salvation, consisting of twenty-one high-ranking officers. The army would do its patriotic duty, end the "anarchy," and start the economy on the road to recovery.

Among the government's decrees: Public gatherings and strikes were banned, and Solidarity was "suspended." There would be a curfew from 10:00 P.M. to 6:00 A.M. Telephone calls and mail would be censored. People suspected of being threats to the state could be interned without trial for an indefinite period. The military would take over important enterprises. Workers would face criminal charges for absenteeism or disobedience.

If Solidarity was going to mount any resistance, it would be up to the activists who remained at large. The delegates from Wroclaw hopped a train out of Gdansk on Saturday night and jumped off before they reached the Wroclaw station, where police agents were waiting for them. Bujak and a few others escaped the dragnet and remained in Gdansk. Some of them went to the Lenin Shipyard on Sunday, formed a National Strike Committee, and printed an appeal for a general strike, saying they would begin negotiating only when the state of war was lifted and all detainees were released.

On Monday an occupation strike began at the shipyard, and in a day or two there were similar strikes around the country. But this time the regime showed no interest in talking. Instead, troops surrounded the factories, tanks smashed through walls and gates, and ZOMO men rushed in, shooting tear gas, ejecting the strikers, and arresting the leaders. Then they closed the shipyard so it would not be retaken. In Gdansk and Gdynia there were riots and hundreds were injured. The last holdouts were 1,000 miners who occupied their pit 1,000 feet below ground and remained there for two weeks until, starving and freezing, they gave up. Everywhere now the freshly pressed uniforms of Jaruzelski's regime were firmly in control.

Solidarity had been routed. In a matter of days a Polish military ruler— afraid of losing control to his Soviet overlords if not his Solidarity foes—moved to shatter the organizational basis of an independent civil society that had taken root and flourished in less than 500 days. Tens of thousands of opposition leaders and activists were swept away, and their 10-million-strong union vanished from the public stage.

Unwittingly improving the odds for martial law, the union had failed to adapt to the political changes it had set in motion. Between August 1980 and March 1981 Solidarity had mastered the art of waging nonviolent conflict against a regime that sought to keep control without resorting to violence. By organizing or threatening general strikes, the union repeatedly had presented the communists with three options: outlast the workers and wear them down, break the strike with force, or negotiate a deal. Economic weakness precluded the first option, and reluctance to relive 1970 foreclosed the second. Each time the regime settled, and these partial victories had allowed Solidarity to expand the boundaries around independent life in Poland.

In early 1981, however, the regime had started inching toward a less compliant posture, though secrecy in decision making and continuity in leadership provided camouflage. By the end of the year, bullied by the Soviets to subdue Solidarity, Jaruzelski became resigned to the battle he had wanted to avoid. When the blitz came, the union did what it had done before: It invoked a general strike. But the regime had learned valuable lessons from earlier engagements. The nighttime arrests on December 12 took almost all the union's leaders off the board before the game began. Blockaded roads and intercepted telecommunications confined strikers within their cities, while troops and tanks circling factories thwarted city-wide coordination. And this time strikers were not given time to improvise an organization. Troops overran striking factories, even at the risk of casualties. This was an adversary with more cunning than Solidarity had seen before.

In the kind of irony that the Cold War foisted on people caught between East and West, American officials in Washington knew in advance about Jaruzelski's plans to crack down but did nothing to alert Solidarity, even though it represented the most powerful initiative for freedom that had ever materialized in the communist bloc. A year before, President Jimmy Carter, through his national security advisor Zbigniew Brzezinzski (a native Pole), had warned Solidarity and the Pope of a possible Soviet invasion in December 1980, which never came. He was able to do so because Colonel Ryszard Kuklinksi, the deputy chief of operations for the Polish army, had been spying for the CIA. Although Kuklinski was in place until November 1981, no one in the new Reagan administration—not its Secretary of State, or its CIA director, or a White House working group on the Polish situation chaired by Vice President George Bush—saw fit to tell Solidarity about Jaruzelski's martial law plans; they were all transfixed with what the Soviets might do, rather than what the Polish regime could do.[67]

If Solidarity had known, what could it have done to deflect the blow? The most obvious precaution would have been to set up a network of safe houses, couriers, and underground transportation, available to use at the first sign of serious repression, and to spirit away as many leaders and activists as possible. Another would have been some provision for emergency financial aid (since the union's bank accounts would be closed by the state) as well as stashes of food and other supplies for striking workers in or near factories, to allow occupiers to hold out longer if troops did not attack.[68]

Had the union shielded its leaders and resources, it might have been able to transform itself into a well-coordinated underground movement once the initial onslaught was over. But Solidarity was from the beginning an open and democratic organization, and it was ill-suited to clandestine arrangements. Those few activists who tried in late 1981 to stow away money or printing equipment in the event of a crisis were ridiculed by union militants.

As with the Russian opposition in 1905, there was also no effort to subvert the reliability of the uniformed services, to boost the possibility that if the regime ordered repression, the men in ranks would balk. Jaruzelski himself thought this could happen. In October 1980 Soviet Foreign Minister Andrei Gromyko had told the Politburo that Jaruzelski feared "the army would not act against Polish workers." In fact, when the crackdown came, Bogdan Borusewicz believed that broken-down tanks lining the road to Gdansk were more likely the result of crews hoping to avoid fighting workers than of insurmountable technical problems, and he saw tears in the eyes of one of the tank crews that came to the Lenin Shipyard.[69]

Jaruzelski, however, had taken out some insurance against widespread disaffection in the ranks by immersing his soldiers in anti-Solidarity propaganda, and the union did nothing to offset this. Years later Zbigniew Bujak called this a mistake, noting that soldiers had been made to believe that the union was "preparing to murder politicians and their children." But regular army units were deployed mainly as a backup; the spear of the attack was the ZOMO and other elite forces, which were better immunized against potential alienation.[70]

For Solidarity, winning this showdown might have proven as dangerous as losing. Had the regime been unable to clamp down on its own, the outcome might not have been a new accord with Solidarity. A humiliating defeat for Poland's military rulers might instead have provoked an invasion by the Warsaw Pact. At no point in 1981 was Moscow likely to allow the state on its western border to surrender decisive ground to a movement that it correctly analyzed as a grave challenge to communist rule.

FROM RUIN TO THE ROUNDTABLE

"A Slow Disintegration"

In the days after December 13, 1981, the few Solidarity activists who were still on the loose dodged security agents and hid out in apartments of friends and sympathizers. Gradually they found each other and pieced together an underground network. In Gdansk the nucleus consisted of Bogdan Borusewicz, Bogdan Lis, and Aleksander Hall, editor of a journal put out by a nationalist organization. Bujak disguised himself as a railroad worker and returned to Warsaw; by early January he and other oppositionists were meeting. Similar cells of activists formed in Wroclaw and Krakow. In a matter of weeks Solidarity went from having 10 million partisans on the streets and factory floors to hundreds of believers in the catacombs.

By early 1982 these city-based groups were communicating via couriers and planning a full-blown national underground. In April Lis (from Gdansk), Bujak (from Warsaw), Wladyslaw Frasyniuk (from Wroclaw), and Wladyslaw Hardek (from Krakow) met and declared themselves the Interim Coordinating Commission (or TKK, by its Polish initials). Lis and Bujak opposed a centralized organization; they would not make the movement vulnerable to a second decapitation. The TKK would only set a general direction; the real organizing would be done from the ground up.[71]

The committees in Gdansk and Wroclaw decided to mount a counterattack against martial law by organizing in factories. Militant workers from the days aboveground were urged to form secret factory committees. If they could mobilize in enough places, Lis hoped, they could call a general strike and make the regime use the regular army to put it down, perhaps spurring a mutiny. In the meantime, to show that resistance was alive, monthly fifteen-minute work stoppages were staged, and a street rally was planned for the anniversary of the 1980 Gdansk agreement.[72]

But a wave of arrests took out key parts of the Wroclaw underground, and the work stoppages only got people thrown out of their jobs or into jail. Turnout for the Gdansk rally was low, and when the Lenin Shipyard went on strike in October after Solidarity was officially outlawed, underground leaders decided against a wider action, and the strike was soon over. Instead, the TKK planned a four-hour warning strike for November 10, but workers' response was weak. Forced by martial law to operate as a conspiracy, the opposition in 1982 could not gain legitimacy in workers' eyes, as Solidarity had as an openly functioning, democratic organization in 1980-1981. The underground had to reconsider its direction.[73]

Jacek Kuron, writing in an article smuggled out of prison in February 1982, wanted Solidarity to create a tight, centralized structure and build toward a national offensive, culminating in a general strike and a "simultaneous attack against all the centres of information and power." At that point, Kuron argued, the opposition should signal it was ready to compromise with the government and declare its "goodwill towards the USSR," to fend off an invasion.[74]

Bujak and fellow activist Wiktor Kulerski disagreed; they argued in the underground press that open confrontation would provoke more repression and perhaps Soviet intervention. A centralized resistance would be infiltrated and smashed. Rather than mobilizing for an early and decisive struggle, the underground ought to engage in "positional warfare" and expect "long, hard work." All opposition forces should join in devising "a mechanism of resistance against the monopolistic activities of the government in various spheres of life." Factory organizers should concentrate on defending workers' rights, by strikes and protests when necessary. Church parishes should create committees to help the poor and people fired for political reasons. In short, they should revive the methods of the pre-1980 opposition.[75]

Kulerski framed this in strategic terms: Since they could not take control by storm, they should seek a "a slow disintegration of the system." A decentralized movement could leave the authorities in control of "empty shops but not the market . . . state-owned mass media but not the circulation of information . . . the post and telephones but not communications, the schools but not education." If the regime lost control over society, then it would be obliged to introduce "gradual liberalization and democratization." As Bujak said, this strategy "shifted the responsibility for the strength and form of opposition from the leadership to society as a whole."[76]

The TKK did not renounce the tactic of a general strike but did rely heavily on the ideas of Bujak and Kulerski, and Polish citizens were already acting along these lines. Recapitulating KOR's aid to victims of repression in the 1970s, factory committees collected dues, and priests solicited contributions for fired workers. Support was lavished on those interned in December 1981 or arrested after that. "My family receives a lot of help," wrote one prisoner. "We are the focus of the most beautiful qualities of the nation." By such acts, Poles kept alive the spirit of Solidarity. One woman even halted divorce proceedings against her husband when she learned that he was arrested. It was "a matter of honor," she said.[77]

The independent press bounced back quickly, as writers, editors, printers and distributors revived their old methods. Underground committees published their own bulletins and newspapers; the Warsaw committee's paper put out between 15,000 and 40,000 copies per week. Bujak estimated in 1984 that the readership of all unofficial papers exceeded a million. NOWA, the underground publishing house, was still in business, with over 200 employees. The Flying University also reappeared.

Once again Poland's rulers faced an opposition that was organizing itself to resist oppression. By providing its own social services and information, the opposition did not so much beset the regime as ignore it; that, of course, was an old strategy. But during martial law Poles also turned to a new sanction, and that was the boycott. New unions that the regime formed when Solidarity was banned were a special target. The TKK urged a "front of refusal" (a term originally coined by official media to refer to Arab states refusing to recognize Israel): Workers should not join the new unions, and those who did should be ostracized. "Once they lose their anonymity," Bogdan Lis said, "only self-confessed traitors will join the ranks of the state unions."[78]

Official media were a second boycott target. Most of the country's best actors refused to appear on television, leaving talk shows and reruns to fill the screens. The producers of a radio soap opera had to contrive plot twists that explained why almost all the main characters had disappeared. As with the unions, those who defied the boycott were themselves boycotted. The media protest sometimes went beyond the supply side: The people of the town of Swidnik made a point of taking walks at just the time the evening news came on.

By the mid-1980s the conflict between the regime and the opposition had reached a stalemate. From the party's viewpoint, repression had been successful: Jailing thousands of people and suspending civil liberties had dispersed Solidarity and discouraged the underground from counterattacking with a general strike. The party had rid itself of an open opposition that had forced it so many times to compromise. But activists adjusted their strategy and brought to partial life Kulerski's vision of an "underground society." The state no longer had an overt, mobilized adversary, but everywhere there was small-scale resistance, as the regime's legitimacy bled from a thousand cuts.

Communist control in Poland had long ago lost the people's consent, and the military crackdown in December 1981 was a sign of this debility. The fragments of opposition active after 1981 could not accelerate the final breakdown, but they represented another future for Poland, one that already existed in the minds and lives of the people. And when the regime finally exhausted its options, they were there to step in and reconstruct the Polish nation on the basis of a different model.

Ironically, martial law had marked the end of the communist preeminence in Poland. Jaruzelski never tried to restore the old days. Instead, he kept control largely through security measures; one by one, underground leaders were ferreted out and put behind bars: Wroclaw's Frasyniuk in October 1982, then Lis in June 1984, then Borusewicz and Bujak in 1986. Jaruzelski also tried to curry popular favor by making many of the changes Solidarity had demanded, albeit in diluted form, claiming that the "state of war" had been imposed to save the post-August 1980 renewal. Workers were promised that the new unions would give them the right to strike. The official media published a wide range of voices, in the hopes that intellectuals would rally to Jaruzelski, just as they had to Gomulka in the 1950s. The Church was wooed, by permitting another papal visit in 1983 and by subsidizing new churches and broadcasting Easter services.

Jaruzelski's liberalization even extended to his old antagonists. Lech Walesa was released from prison in November 1982. Two years later amnesty was offered to underground leaders who turned themselves in. (Few did.) Finally, in the fall of 1986, all those detained under martial law received full amnesty. Most of these steps were intended mainly to regain favor abroad, especially with foreign governments that had slapped economic sanctions on the country after December 1981.

By the end of 1986 Jaruzelski's strategy was also being driven by another exigency: Incipient economic trouble required political anesthesia. Shortages and shopping lines were growing again, and austerity measures seemed imminent. But this time higher prices would be peddled as part of basic economic reform, including enlarging the scope of private enterprise. The regime started courting outspoken members of the opposition, and the terms of a deal took shape: The government would open up public life further and consult with opposition leaders, who in turn would lend cover to the new policies. The opposition, a party official said, was now recognized "as a lasting element on the country's political map."[79]

Seats of Victory

In 1986 it was not yet possible to foresee that the new leader of the Communist Party of the Soviet Union, having adopted bold domestic economic and political policies—perestroika and glasnost—would soon condone a parallel evolution in Eastern Europe. It was only just becoming evident that a new generation of Polish workers—men and women too young to have participated in the 1980 strikes and with little connection to surviving opposition networks—might be capable of new agitation that would force the government to go beyond a gradual thaw.

The actors of 1980-1981 were still on stage, but they began writing new roles for themselves. Jaruzelski saw himself as a kind of Polish Gorbachev—and the comparison was apt in one respect: He had started to pull the unraveling threads of communist control and would soon unwind his own base of power. As for Solidarity, by the late 1980s the name no longer referred to a strapping popular movement capable of leading millions of people. "Solidarity" now meant the leaders and advisors of the former union who had turned themselves into a small but still-prestigious political front. Even in this less commanding mold, Solidarity played a central role in the political transition that would soon create a multi-party democracy in Poland.

In April 1988, in the wake of fresh price increases, a new wave of strikes hit Poland, but Solidarity did not call them. "I am not on strike, although I am not against them," Lech Walesa said, and he made himself available to help end a nine-day work stoppage in Gdansk. Young activists who sparked the fire looked with disdain on "the senators" of the movement like Walesa, who in turn seemed more responsible to the regime. Four months later a new round of strikes broke out, and Jaruzelski decided the government needed help in dealing with events it could not regulate.[80]

On August 26 the General told the Politburo he wanted roundtable talks with the opposition, with no conditions. The hard-liners bitterly resisted, though five days later the minister of defense told Walesa privately that the regime would legalize Solidarity if he would help end the strikes. Walesa saw an opening, and he lent a hand. Weeks later he was invited to a television debate with the head of the communist trade unions, and in his affable, pleasant way he disarmed his opponent. For Jaruzelski it was a useful fiasco—how could the stiff necks in the party dismiss this man as a fanatic?

At a party plenum in January, when the general heard more denunciations of dealing with Solidarity, he threatened to resign if the party did not approve negotiations, and he walked out. Sobered up, the hard-liners gave way, and on February 6, 1989, at a polished round oak table over eight meters in diameter in Namiestnikowski Palace, twenty-nine delegates from the party joined twenty-six representatives from Solidarity plus Church observers to discuss the plight of Poland. One party delegate said later of the unionists, "the ones we had considered the wildest turned out to be the most sensible." (Jaruzelski later even read Adam Michnik's books and concluded he was "faithful to himself and his principles.")[81]

For Walesa, Michnik, Bujak, Lis, Kuron, and other pioneers of the opposition, their roundtable seats finally placed them at the center of decisions about the nation's future. On April 6 they reached the goal that had always fired their hearts: the right to free unions as well as expanded freedoms of the press and association, an independent judiciary and free parliamentary elections. Then on June 4, 1989, Solidarity turned its popular stature into votes and overwhelmed the communists at the polls. On August 24, the Sejm made Tadeusz Mazowiecki prime minister of a Solidarity-led coalition government and ended autocracy in Poland.

In 1999, on the tenth anniversary of the convening of the roundtable, when thousands of Poles lined up outside in the winter chill to walk into the palace and through the historic room, one man, a former railway worker, said, "This is where our freedom began." He was wrong. His freedom had begun in a thousand different places in Poland, wherever strikers demanded their own union in 1970, wherever food or money was given to the families of imprisoned workers in 1976, wherever strikers put down their tools and refused to work in 1980, or anywhere someone read an underground newspaper in the 1980s. Negotiations produce change when real power has already shifted, and when Jaruzelski turned over the keys to the house of Poland in 1989, its leadership had already been taken from him.[82]

The end of the communist dictatorship is not the only measure of what Poland's nonviolent opposition movement accomplished. Communist governments collapsed everywhere in Eastern Europe during 1989, even in countries where resistance was spontaneous and disorganized. The Polish party may not have lasted long in power after that even had there been no KOR, no August strike, no Solidarity, and also no Kuron, no Walentynowicz, no Walesa, and no Bujak. What marks these names as momentous is not just that they triggered the end of tyranny but that they reinvigorated Poland's spirit of self-rule even before the communists fell.

The first kilometers in this road were paved in the 1970s when Polish intellectuals took direct action—helping workers, publishing journals and books, teaching courses. But what KOR and other dissidents could not do was force the regime to accept institutional limits on its power and create a lawful sphere for a free society. That took massive nonviolent action—the August 1980 strike. Learning from the 1970 uprising and the experience of KOR, the Baltic workers organized themselves on a giant scale in a matter of weeks, roused the public, and outmaneuvered the party inside factories and across negotiating tables.

Solidarity then became a vehicle for all Poles. The dynamic new union used threats of a general strike to constrain the regime not only to accept its existence but to allow others to organize and speak out. If KOR had fought a nonviolent guerrilla war to liberate a beachhead of independent space, Solidarity seized a popular mandate for an entire coast of freedom. For a shining interval, communist Poland had a free, civil society. After the crackdown broke up the union, an opposition reemerged to contest control of Polish life. Even under martial law, the struggle for self-organization went on. Then, toward the end of the decade, as Jaruzelski looked for ways to save a sinking economy and stem a new tide of turmoil, he turned for help to the alternate power that Solidarity signified—and soon he was finished.

The rise of the movement that changed the history of Poland was the most momentous display of people power against arbitrary rule since Mohandas Gandhi shook the foundation of the British raj in India. For a century and a half, the British had controlled India by having Indians collaborate in running the country. Likewise for thirty years the communists in Poland kept the lid on discontent by co-opting reformers and isolating disruptive voices—until another way to oppose oppression was found, by disengaging from the state and engaging the people.

Zbigniew Bujak regarded Václav Havel's essay, "The Power of the Powerless," as the theory that explained his work. Havel saw the reliance of an authoritarian regime on the people's cooperation as a weakness, because it required them to live a lie—and those who found the space in which to "live in the truth" would open up "singular, explosive, incalculable political power." Those who remained "within the lie" could be "struck at any moment . . . by the force of truth," and as they changed, the truth would become visible—

through "a social movement, a sudden explosion of civil unrest, a sharp conflict inside an apparently monolithic power structure . . . "[83]

Eighty years before in South Africa, Gandhi had said this "truth force," or satyagraha, when employed by resisters, would eventually draw power away from oppressors. So it was in Poland. Lech Walesa creates independent space in a shipyard, and the regime comes to him to negotiate. Bujak goes underground, and eight years later Jaruzelski invites him, Walesa, and others to help remake the country. All the oppositionists at the roundtable in 1989 were there because they had first refused to cooperate with the state—they had stopped lying to themselves—and then they had made space in their lives and workplaces for the truth to be the basis for action.

As they did so, they refused to use violence in taking that action. Havel said real dissidence "is and must be fundamentally hostile toward the notion of violent change." Bujak rejected "any acts of violence." Even in the face of violence? The year after the events in Gdansk in 1981, a worker wrote in his diary, "We were ready to take the cross upon our own shoulders, the cross in the form of the caterpillar tracks of the tanks, if it came to an assault on us."[84]

In the twentieth century's armed liberation movements, portraits of gun-wielding martyrs—the Che Guevaras of the world—were often flaunted as symbols, but none of those struggles produced freedom. Throughout the years of Solidarity's ceremonies and marches, the only person whose picture was held aloft was the Pope, whose most inflammatory injunction to his fellow Poles was to be "nonconformists." And Solidarity's most common decoration, laid at factory gates and monuments, received by leaders and given to heroes, were garlands and wreaths of flowers. Hammers and sickles, fasces and clenched fists: Symbols of revolution all, and each one easily used as a weapon. Not so, flowers.

Disdain for dictators is easy. Disdain for violence, their favorite tool, is not so easy, especially when it threatens you. But renouncing it pays, in the coin of achieving power. Polish workers remembered how little progress they had made in 1970 and 1976 by burning down party buildings. And had Solidarity stowed away caches of weapons only to be discovered later, as Brezhnev told Kania to pretend it had, or if Bujak had organized hit squads to assassinate party bosses, would Jaruzelski have dismissed the party hard-liners when they denounced Bujak and other Solidarity chiefs in 1989 as political criminals? You reap exactly what you sow, as Gandhi told India.

If the ultimate reward of forswearing violence was not foreseeable in August 1980, the immediate risks were in plain view. Every striker in the Lenin Shipyard realized that the regime, the nation, and the world were watching every move they made. If, when the shipyard's administrator first outwitted them, they had beaten and thrown him into the street, would the regime have been likely to return to the talks? Later, if the union had inflamed the Bydgoszcz crowds and incited them to attack the police, would martial law have come sooner and been seen as a justifiable response to public disorder? Those who start the violence usually pay the cost of its dishonor. And if bloody revolt instead of nonviolent organizing had been the culminating action of the movement, would the regime have seemed so odious and Solidarity so worthy, all the long years of the "state of war"? Lech Walesa won the Nobel Peace Prize in 1983—the world's blessing on the Polish people's cause, and another mark of disrepute for those who held it back.

Those who sat in the chairs at the roundtable felt the weight of Poland's fate on their shoulders. But by then it was the people's leaders, not the officers of state, who had the wind of history at their backs. For twenty years its speed had gathered, then receded—then it rose again. The gale of power blowing communism out was not the weather of violence. It came out of the climate of a new civil society that Poles had built under the very awning of authoritarian will. It came up through the eaves and windowsills of every church where dissidents met, every factory occupied by strikers, and every house that harbored a member of the underground.

To plant the vine of freedom in the soil of communist Poland, the people's movement of the 1970s and 1980s challenged a regime that was part of the deadliest family of modern tyrants. From Stalin's elimination of the kulaks to Pol Pot's genocide in Cambodia, whole peoples had been sacrificed in the name of communism if not in the service of its original ideals. The Polish variety was not as demonic, but the prison cells that awaited those who challenged its control were no incentive for opposition. Yet against this citadel, the movement set clear goals, rallied massive popular support, enlisted the Church and foreign help, avoided tactics that would trigger quick repression, and brought the use of strikes and self-organization to their highest development in the history of nonviolent action. Its only serious lapse was not to prepare for a military crackdown.

For all his ignorance of what was really going on in Poland, Leonid Brezhnev was right when he saw Solidarity as a dagger pointed at the heart of his empire's control. It refused to respect the guidance of the party. It defied the orders of the state. It demanded that the consent of Poles, not the fiat of government, determine the conditions of life and labor. And it had the audacity to press its demands by threatening the state with economic chaos, political stalemate, and international disgrace. It did all that, and it turned the history of communism on its head—without having to take the head of a single Polish communist. Had it aimed at heads, its own might never have taken power.

PART TWO

RESISTANCE TO TERROR

The flight shall perish from the swift, and the strong shall not strengthen his force, neither shall the mighty deliver himself.

—Amos 2:14

CHAPTER FOUR

The Ruhrkampf, *1923:* Resisting Invaders

"Show the Germans Force"

One winter afternoon five years after the end of World War I, French and Belgian soldiers, with consummate precision, marched across the Belgian border and into Essen, one of Germany's largest cities. They occupied schools and hotels, to be used as command posts for their invasion. Detachments of cavalry and motorcyclists seized the telephone and telegraph offices. Most important, the offices of the Coal Syndicate and railroad director were taken. The city's capture seemed almost too easy to be true. "Show the Germans force and they always bow to it," a French soldier said later.[1]

Essen was the eye of a hurricane that had been gathering force over the Ruhr, Germany's industrial heartland, for some time before that Thursday in January 1923. France and Belgium had decided to enforce the terms of the treaty ending the war by entering and taking resources from the nation they had defeated. Germans had seen this coming and were angry at their leaders in Berlin for failing to resolve the crisis. Earlier that morning Esseners had gone to the city's main concert hall and were exhorted to resist the invasion, and then they had poured into the streets, breaking out into strains of "Deutschland, Deutschland, über alles!" But as the day progressed, patriotic songs gave way to gloom as the invasion loomed.[2]

As soldiers swarmed over Essen and took up positions, restaurant and pub owners had already shuttered their doors and windows. The square and streets around the central railroad station filled with people who were absolutely silent, giving no hint of a demonstration. By the end of the afternoon, Esseners had become the reluctant host to over 4,000 soldiers and more than a dozen armored vehicles—and they began to fear that their former enemies were there to do more than protect the French, Belgian, and Italian engineers sent to take over the coal mines of the Ruhr.[3]

An elderly man, a veteran of Prussia's decisive defeat of France in 1870 that resulted in the founding of the German Reich, was seen weeping softly into his handkerchief as he watched his city submit. When asked why he was crying, he responded simply, "We never truly thought they would do it."[4]

"The Heart of Germany"

Beyond the appalling losses sustained by the armies who fought it, the war that was called the Great War had ravaged some of France's most productive lands. The nation's northernmost areas were virtually leveled. When German generals still had high hopes of winning the war, they planned to annex the northern coal fields of France and seize Belgian mines. When it became clear that Germany would be defeated, General Eric Ludendorff ordered the mines blown up and flooded out. The only purpose: to cripple their rival's industry.[5]

Six months after the armistice, French Senator Paul Doumer had described the obliterated territory as "a desert, a zone of death, assassination and devastation. There are corpses of horses and corpses of trees covering the corpses of men." Before the war it had had some of the best cropland and most efficient manufacturing capacity in the country. Now it was clear that France itself could never recuperate until the northern lands were up and running again.[6]

One man with a personal sense of the north's agony was Raymond Poincaré, who had served as French premier during the war. He was from Lorraine, a region between France and Germany whose resources had made it a prize traded by a millennium of alternating invaders. When France was crushed by Prussia in 1870, Poincaré, only ten years old at the time, saw German troops on his native streets—an occupation that lasted until French war indemnities were paid. The premier would often justify his intractable position toward Germany by noting that "the Germans stayed in France until 1873 and were paid before evacuating our territory."[7]

When Poincaré's term ended shortly after the French ratified the Treaty of Versailles, he did not fade away like many wartime leaders. He was a hero and the public admired him greatly. On ceremonial visits to the war's battlefields in

France, he questioned German motives to abide by the treaty. "Who would allow the promises, signed by Germany, not to be kept by her?" he asked in a rousing speech at Verdun, where the German advance had been stopped in 1916.[8]

The treaty had ordered the evacuation of all conquered territories and withdrawal of all German troops west of the Rhine, along with Allied occupation of its left bank. The German army was reduced to 100,000 men, its navy to 15,000, and heavy artillery, tanks, and warplanes were forbidden; in the Ruhr, the police only had sidearms. Alsace and Lorraine were ceded to France. In the north, part of Schleswig was given to Denmark. In the east, various territories went to Poland. Surrendering this land meant a loss of 6.5 million citizens and a staggering forfeiture of resources and industry—little wonder that the Germans regarded the treaty as *diktat,* a dictate from the war's victors, devoid of fairness. In Berlin cabarets, performers on stage tore up copies.[9]

As the Germans tried to dodge each French demand for timely reparations payments, the French public complained about their leaders' patience. The new premier, Aristide Briand, was a career diplomat who wanted to negotiate with the Germans. But unable to balance British calls for lenience toward Germany with French popular agitation for action, Briand had been forced to resign in January 1922. His replacement: Poincaré, who became the first premier in French history to return to government.[10]

Once back in office, he had been advised that German industrialists were leading a propaganda campaign to absolve their country of guilt for the war. Led by the influential magnate Hugo Stinnes, they called the treaty's terms vindictive and said that Germany would never be able to satisfy French demands. One scholar later estimated that if the original schedule of reparations had been carried out, Germany would have been making payments well into the 1970s or 1980s. The burdens on Germany, one of Stinnes's newspapers argued, were "due to France's militarist and imperialist spirit."[11]

Besides the financial weight of reparations, and the loss of territory and population, much of Germany was initially occupied by Allied forces. Germans were denied the use of their own postal system as well as the use of radios. Perhaps most degrading was a food blockade, which persisted until June 1919. At one point, weekly rations included only four and one-half pounds of bread, five ounces of meat, two ounces of butter, and two-and-a-half ounces of coffee. German householders faced these hardships with a quiet decency. Families lived on the official ration and shunned the black market out of civic duty.[12]

By 1922 most of the postwar occupying forces had gone home, leaving only a few regiments deployed along the Rhine and French units in cities along the German frontier. If the world had not yet forgiven Germany for starting the Great War, it had begun to realize that, like the war's other belligerents, it needed time to heal. Thus, in mid-July of 1922, the Allied Reparations Commission considered granting a two-year moratorium without any future guarantee of payments. This was a red cape to the bull-like Poincaré. At an Allied conference in London in August, he threatened independent action, warning that "Germany's bad faith worsens everyday."[13]

On August 16 the Germans refused to comply with a French request that state mines in the Ruhr be used as pledges for coal deliveries owed to France. The only choice left, in Poincaré's mind, was to seize the mines and extract the coal, which the French badly needed to get its industries running again. Before the war, the area's mines had produced 90 billion tons a year at only 40 percent capacity—a rate second only to the coal fields of Pennsylvania. As Marshal Ferdinand Foch, another French war hero, once said, "March to Berlin? That would be a waste of time. The heart of Germany is in the Ruhr, which is much nearer."[14]

Without military protection, it was a tempting target, and the French may have had ulterior motives for what they were about to do. At a decisive cabinet meeting in late November, where the consequences of using force were discussed, Poincaré predicted that Germany would crumble, would fall apart—implying that France could pluck the Rhineland from the shards of invasion, something Germans feared. Whatever the motives, the French Chamber voted 452 to 72 in favor of going in. A few weeks later the Reparations Commission declared Germany in default on delivery of telephone poles and timber to France. On January 9, 1923, it declared a coal default. Two days later French and Belgian soldiers moved in.[15]

"A Mission of Control"

What the French had seen as the Germans' refusal to pay was seen in Berlin as the need to stay afloat financially. German administrations after the war actually had intended to keep up with reparations, but the government failed to raise the necessary taxes or expropriate property to produce enough revenues to meet the payment schedule—though it did resort to foreign loans, which exacerbated inflation.

By October 1922 failure to manage either reparations or inflation had forced out one chancellor. President Friedrich Ebert's surprising choice for successor was Wilhelm Cuno, head of the Hamburg-America Shipping Line, and someone with scant political experience. But Cuno, a handsome man, was a captain of industry, and Ebert understood that business support would be indispensable if Germany were to right its economy. The new chancellor also spoke English and had links to Britain and the United States, whose leverage with the French was viewed as vital if reparations were to be revised.[16]

In his maiden speech to the Reichstag on November 24, Cuno summarized his policy as "first bread, then reparations." He deplored French designs on the Ruhr. "We do not ignore the possibility of tendencies beyond our frontiers aiming at further encroachments." And he lauded Rhinelanders' "wonderful patience" with the Allies' occupation. Not a fiery orator, Cuno won cautious applause for this, but when he closed his speech by stoutly declaring "this government will never surrender any German territory," legislators rose to their feet and shouted agreement.[17]

Ovations in Berlin were not, however, the same as support for hard-headed policies. The government wanted major price and wage increases, while the industrialists wanted to prevent them. The government needed more revenue to pay reparations, but neither industry nor labor liked higher taxes. When France threatened occupation of the Ruhr, the industrialists assumed it was inevitable, since they doubted Germany could ever satisfy Allied demands—and thus they had little incentive to help Cuno.

On December 11, when the chancellor proposed another revised payments schedule, it was not only rejected out of hand by France, it was also attacked by Hugo Stinnes's newspaper, *Deutsche Allgemeine Zeitung.* The chancellor's final offer on January 2 promised a payment of 20 billion gold marks, to be funded by an international loan and contingent on French evacuation of Düsseldorf, Duisburg, and Ruhrort, which had been occupied in 1921 to quell communist uprisings. Poincaré did not even consider it.

On January 9 the French government described the forthcoming operation as "a mission of control composed of engineers." Disavowing any intention to mount "an operation of a military nature" or "an occupation of a political character," the French insisted it was sending only those troops that were "essential to safeguard the mission" and that there would be "no dislocation . . . in the normal life of the population, which can continue to work in order and peace."[18]

The Germans made few preparations for an occupation they thought unlikely to go on very long. Little coal or other raw materials were cached, and no organization existed to carry out whatever strategy the government might adopt. Until the last possible moment, Cuno hoped that his last reparations offer would be accepted and Poincaré would call off the invasion. Replying with force was not an option, since German troops were not permitted within 50 kilometers (31 miles) of the Rhine. Cuno and his cabinet could either acquiesce and watch the invasion from the sidelines, or show some kind of resistance while appealing to the world for support.

Any German strategy would have to concentrate on delaying the French from taking coal until Poincaré relented and agreed to renegotiate reparations. Cuno and Ebert recognized that invasion was France's last remaining option, with more detractors than supporters in London, Washington, and elsewhere. If Germany could resist in a way that stirred sympathy among the English and the Americans, the Anglo-Saxon powers might intercede, and economic stress in France might expedite an end to the crisis. Then reparations could be "de-politicized" (a word used at the time). To the extent the Germans had a strategy, that was it.[19]

On January 9, Chancellor Cuno asked President Ebert to release a manifesto to the local papers exhorting the Ruhr's citizens to remain calm despite "French injustice and force . . . committed against a disarmed and defenseless nation." Later that day and well into the night, Cuno met with his cabinet and with trade union officials in the Reichskabinettspaleis in Berlin to develop a plan of action supportable by different German interests. For the mine owners, aggressive resistance would be financially perilous, since their mines would then be occupied or production would be halted. The socialist unions tied to Ebert's political party were fearful that any belligerence could encourage a revolutionary uprising by right-wing nationalists or the communists, capsizing the Socialists' hold on power. The president felt that the unions would cooperate if the employers did, but neither Cuno nor Ebert could make the owners budge.[20]

Regardless of how much internal support they could rally, the president and the chancellor came to believe that Germany had to impose economic costs on the occupiers. The Ruhr and its coal were essential to Europe; any major stoppage of this mammoth industrial machine would complicate economic life everywhere. Cuno believed that the Allies would soon face up to this and pressure Poincaré into pulling out. He expected the occupation to last no more than a month before it became too expensive for France to continue.

From the outset, aversion to violence was embedded in the government's idea of resistance. For forty years the Socialists had been a nonrevolutionary party, unlike their Bolshevik cousins to the east, so violent action was anathema as a way of seeking advantage in any political situation. Even a general strike against the French seemed too provocative, especially to the unions; it might risk losing control of their workers. It was also obvious that using violence would damage the image of the resistance in the eyes of Britain and America. The cool-headed Prussians who set the tone in Berlin advised against anything rash.[21]

Accordingly, Cuno and Ebert told the trade unions to rally their members behind a policy of "passive resistance" to the occupation (using a term that Gandhi had coined seventeen years before). For his part, the chancellor pledged economic support of workers once he received a mandate from the Reichstag. The unionists were confident that the rank and file would quickly fall in line. While workers had reason to be skeptical that Berlin's support would be adequate—since the government always had put the industrialists first—the unions had organized a countrywide strike just two years before, virtually halting German commerce, to thwart a coup by former military officers. Moreover, workers had long displayed loyalty to the German state, and they had all gone to schools where hatred of the French had been taught for a hundred years. They would resist.

Yet Berlin remained concerned that workers' zeal could go too far. If the conflict brought "sanctions and violent measures," Cuno said, there could be "an uncontrollable swell of national pride." So the government had to be "careful not to let . . . national feeling become the kind used to support the swastika." If many workers were forced out of their jobs, then possibly "the protests against the French will turn against this government." To preclude that and bolster the resistance, Cuno felt that Berlin had no choice but to subsidize workers' wages as well as food supplies and law enforcement in the Ruhr. "However," he admitted, "the economic difficulties this entails could eventually lead to the dissolution of the Reich."[22]

Beyond a sense that hazards lay ahead, questions of strategy rarely came up during these initial meetings. Cuno and Ebert did little to chart a course of action for city and district governments in the Ruhr. In a meeting with local officials in Recklinghausen, the president conceded that there were "no plans for the method of organization of this resistance." What would strikes and demonstrations look like? Who would participate? How were the workers, their unions, and the mine owners to get directives from Berlin? How would Berlin be kept up to date on events in the Ruhr? No one knew.[23]

On January 13, two days after the invasion, Cuno appeared before a tense, late-afternoon emergency session of the Reichstag to present his plan, such as it was. Atop the building, flags flew at half-mast. He decried the invasion and threw down the gauntlet. "Two days ago, the French and Belgian troops entered free German territory . . . Cavalry detachments with drawn swords headed the column . . . These warlike actions were committed against a nation that had completely disarmed . . . I ask the whole world, was there ever a people that, having suffered unparalleled hardships and sacrifices, has worked harder and more zealously than the German nation despite its enervation and enfeeblement?" Every member, save the communists, stood up and shouted, "Never! Never!" Then the chancellor framed the German choice: "The German Government cannot forcibly resist, but is certainly not willing to cooperate with this violation of peace." The Reichstag voted 283 to 12 to commit the government to support the resistance.[24]

Sitting on Bayonets

Even before the German government acted, the people of the Ruhr already had made the French mission more difficult than Poincaré had anticipated. On

January 10, the day before troops arrived, a furious mob of 5,000 materialized in front of Essen's Hotel Kaiserhof—rumored to be housing members of the French engineering commission—to demand their expulsion from the Ruhr. Within an hour several hundred protestors broke through a line of police guarding the entrances. They were ready to charge upstairs to lay hands on the French, when Essen's mayor stood on a table and begged them to go home and save their energy for the French soldiers arriving the next day. After a round of patriotic songs, the crowd dispersed.[25]

Later that night the officials of the Rhenish-Westphalian Coal Syndicate packed up all their important files and put them on trucks for Hamburg, some 320 kilometers (199 miles) north of Essen; the rest were buried under floorboards of the building. The syndicate was the control center for the entire Ruhr coal basin. Without its records, the occupiers would have to take over all the mines instead of only the most productive ones, requiring more troops than initially planned. Moving the syndicate was the idea of Hugo Stinnes, who owned mines as well as newspapers, and who personified conservative interests. Later he noted proudly that without the files transfer, "the resistance against the external enemy" would have been slower to develop. Stinnes had a vested interest in any German action that might hold up reparations to France: Coal shipped west under reparations was sold at less than market price.[26]

Now the press began to champion resistance, claiming that France wanted to wrench the Ruhr away from Germany. One Socialist paper distributed among Ruhr workers editorialized that the occupation was "an historic event" and that to "oppose force with force is so impossible that no serious politician advocates armed resistance." Its solution: " A wise Frenchman once said that you can do anything with bayonets except sit on them. Now, we must show you that you cannot mine coal or ship coal with bayonets." The more conservative papers depicted an epic struggle, appealing to romantic notions of German nationhood. "The further they move in, the longer will be the way out," said *Deutsche Allgemeine Zeitung,* "for did not Arminius lure the Roman legions so deep into the Teutoburger forest that escape was no longer open to them?"[27]

Despite this bravado, there were still reluctant actors in the unfolding drama. At a meeting on January 10, the Reich Transport Ministry refused to endorse resistance, believing that the French would either compel German workers to man the trains or simply commandeer most of the system for troop transit and coal delivery to France. If that happened, they argued, life for people in the Ruhr would become intolerable. Reviving their initial reluctance, the mine owners saw no reason to resist if the railroad workers would not. Cuno averted a crisis by instructing the railroads to disobey French and Belgian orders.

Physical resistance on the ground was sparse in the first days. In Essen there were no strikes and only a few minor disturbances. Workers were bewildered; they had been aroused by cries to fight for the Ruhr but had not been told what to do. The only action taking place was hundreds of kilometers away in Münich, where a young nationalist leader named Adolf Hitler stirred up a crowd of 10,000 by lamenting Germany's plight. "We dishonored and disarmed ourselves and have become objects of contempt, a laughing-stock to the enemy and the world," the native Austrian declared.[28]

Getting workers and employers to collaborate was an enormous challenge. The industrialists viewed workers with contempt and even a bit of fear, for communism was attracting a following, particularly in the Ruhr. The workers viewed their bosses even less generously. "Some of our workers even say there is no difference whether we are robbed by the French or Germans," one Essener wrote. "But there is a difference, apart from sentiment. We are holding our own against Ruhr capitalism just because the German Government is weak and our bosses have no army to use against us." If ways could not be found to bridge these traditional animosities, the resistance would be unsustainable.[29]

Coming a few years after what had been the world's worst war, whose center of conflict was only kilometers from the Ruhr, these events transfixed the world. Some feared a new war; others felt that France was justified in forcing Germany to pay its debts. But the British and Americans tended to sympathize with the Germans, a reaction that Berlin strove to cultivate. It regarded the United States as the war's major winner but as now essentially neutral, since its Congress had rejected parts of the Versailles Treaty. Only America, it believed, had enough leverage to pull German irons out of the reparations fire, if the resistance won their hearts.

Some Americans fed this hope. The opinion journal *The Nation* approvingly cited a recent precedent half a world away. "What Germany needs in this hour is a Gandhi, an expression of the soul, not the fist," it proclaimed, "a prophet of that inward resistance which alone can avail nations today against the force of greater arms . . . If it could be accomplished, no answer to the French invasion would be more effective than the practice of non-cooperation. If the miners and technical men of the Ruhr were brave and united enough simply to refuse to work for the French . . . they would give the immediate and effective reply to the French attempt to win by force what is . . . economically impossible."[30]

Right after invading, the French engineering mission, led by Emile Coste, and the French military commander, General Joseph Degoutte, tried to win over the German mine owners by guaranteeing payment for any coal they delivered. By paying below-market prices to the Germans, the French could sell the coal to other countries and use the profit to help defray the occupation's costs—

racking up a profit of about 1 billion francs. At the same time, they would prevent the German government from collecting the 40 percent coal tax, which, surprisingly, had not been collected in the last three months. Reaction in Berlin was swift. If the mine owners went along, the resistance would collapse. Cuno forbade them from supplying coal to the invaders, but Coste met with the owners in Düsseldorf and ordered them to begin deliveries under penalty of immediate arrests. They refused, pledging their loyalty to Germany.[31]

Friedrich Thyssen, the young heir to the Thyssen industrial empire, served as spokesman for the mine owners, and in the days following the Düsseldorf meeting, the press and public made him a hero; "the native Ruhrite, be he mine owner or worker, is a man of stubborn mind and unbending will," he declared. But Thyssen's visibility boomeranged: Coste had him and five other coal magnates arrested on January 20 for refusing to deliver coal. The men were brought before a French military tribunal in Mainz, where they were treated as political prisoners.[32]

The arrest was a serious miscalculation. On January 22, 75,000 men and women at nine Thyssen coal mines and steel mills throughout the Ruhr went on strike. At Oberhausen, railway workers abandoned their posts and cut off electricity to all the signals. In Recklinghausen, miners left their jobs, and at Osterfeld, miners refused to work unless French troops withdrew. As the Thyssen trial date neared, crowds in Mainz protested, obliging the French to send more troops to maintain order, fearing that big demonstrations could deteriorate into rioting—and that if French soldiers used force against civilians, the British and Americans might turn decisively against the occupation.[33]

On the day of the trial, thousands gathered outside the courthouse; inside, the gallery was packed with anxious onlookers. Lieutenant Colonel Debugny, the presiding officer, warned that anyone who disrupted the trial would be court-martialed. When asked point blank by the French prosecutor if he had refused to obey the order to deliver coal, Thyssen replied, "It is my duty to obey the laws of my country. According to my government, the invasion of the Ruhr region by French troops was unjust." Thyssen admitted that the owners had originally agreed to furnish coal if the German government did not object. But since Berlin sent orders not to deliver any coal, he and his colleagues could not comply after all. His lawyer demanded Thyssen's acquittal because he had only been following orders. Quickly Debugny returned with his verdict: The government's order was an extenuating circumstance; the defendants were to be released but fined 307,000 francs.[34]

Demonstrators outside were jubilant, dancing and singing "Die Wacht am Rhein" (Watch on the Rhine) and "Deutschland, Deutschland, über alles." Thyssen made a short but triumphant journey to the train station. "It appeared

French soldier stands atop railcar full of coal bricks, the Ruhr, 1923.

Credit: ©Bundesarchiv, Germany

as if an overpowering force of nature had captured these people," his lawyer wrote later. "Now we understood the soul of the occupied territory." On the train ride back to Essen, "Flags waved everywhere. Each train station . . . filled with the sounds of the national anthem. All of this occurred despite the heavy presence of French soldiers, who were completely powerless against these outbreaks of patriotism."[35]

The trial punctuated a tumultuous week and a half. Because mine owners refused to hand over coal, Poincaré hoped to overwhelm the resistance by taking over more mines plus rail lines and canal junctions. But the French only faced more protests. "Reports of riots are coming in from all over the Ruhr," wrote an American reporter. "Here in Essen . . . There are 20,000 people in the street . . .

The Ruhr, 1923

the French have thrown a ring of bayonets around the hotel. The soldiers bring out a machine-gun. The crowd pushes forward; there is a mighty groan of anger; they threaten to attack with their bare hands, with the sheer force of thousands unless the gun is removed . . . The only way the French can defeat these mobs is to retreat."[36]

"Never Fear the Strength of Man"

The crux of the occupation strategy was getting coal out of Germany and back to France by rail. When the French invaded, they first went after coal already stacked up at the pit heads—some locations had an inventory of two or three months' production. So the real test of any resistance strategy was to hinder French rail shipments, and the Germans quickly pulled most coal wagons out of the Ruhr. While the French brought in their own rolling stock, rail workers were still needed on the ground. Wherever German rail workers went on strike, the French had to use their own engineers, but there were not enough for the whole Ruhr and few of them spoke German, and—since rail systems in Europe were each different—it took time to learn the equipment.[37]

When workers in Dortmund struck, a French troop train was immobilized on the tracks for hours before French engineers took control of the locomotive and powered it as far as Essen, where German workers had moved passenger cars onto the tracks, blocking the train's progress. In Bochum and Recklinghausen, spontaneous strikes broke out, and trains loaded with coal and coke bound for France were stuck behind rows of locomotives and other cars. Throughout the region German rail workers moved idle cars, loads of rocks, lumber, and coal onto the tracks to obstruct French-controlled trains. On other key stretches the workers removed single rails, causing numerous derailments.

In one city where the French had sent just one train out of the main station each day, a young French commander proposed a deal to get German workers back on the job. But among the union's conditions: No French soldiers could occupy signal stations, soldiers could not fix their bayonets near stations, and coal trains could not be escorted by French troops. The officer rejected these terms, and French engineers then tried to teach soldiers how to man the locomotives. Soldiers "sat in the cab beside a driver, learning the curves, signals, switches, and grades so they would be able to take over the lines if the strikes spread."[38]

The French were nothing if not persistent. To keep trains moving, they nailed down switches to avert sabotage, disregarded signals with no warning lights (caused by cuts in electricity), and placed guards along the right of way to keep resisters off the tracks. The French also tried to counter the strikes by expelling from the Ruhr any railway official who refused to obey their orders, expecting that this would create chaos within the railway ministry and unions—but it took time for this to happen. In the meantime, a coal-starved France had to purchase about 1 million tons from England, further straining the French economy and increasing pressure from the public and opposition politicians for an end to the Ruhr adventure.[39]

Miners in the region also refused to obey French orders. On January 19 the miners at the Bergmannsglück (miner's luck) Mine, just north of Essen, saw the glint of French bayonets for the first time. At 8:30 in the morning, a French colonel, Mayer by name, and a group of staff officers, engineers, and about a hundred soldiers pulled up in front of the mine's offices. A group of fifteen soldiers calmly marched through the main entrance and then to the director's office. They burst through the door with bayonets fixed and positioned themselves around the room, before Colonel Mayer and the engineers entered. The colonel demanded that all coke then in the ovens be loaded for shipment, but Oberbergrat Ahrens, the mine's director general, refused. He was arrested and driven to a nearby schoolhouse, where he was questioned and ordered to pack up and get out of the Ruhr. Mayer, the soldiers, and the engineers then questioned the shipping clerks and other functionaries. All refused to help. After almost every official had been arrested and driven away, Mayer ordered that no more coke be shipped anywhere other than France and that no coke was to be dumped from the ovens until his demands had been met.[40]

Since it was still early in the morning, the first shift's miners were still underground. But some senior workers connected to the union were above-ground manning the coke ovens. They convened spontaneously and scribbled out a list of demands—asking for the release of arrested officials and employees and the withdrawal of all French troops from the mine. If these conditions were not met, the miners would leave and begin a full strike. The colonel acquiesced and released most of the detained clerks but none of the mine's higher officials. He also removed most troops from the pit heads, leaving four soldiers to guard the coke ovens.[41]

But the miners still refused to dump the ovens and load their contents for France, creating a volatile impasse. If the coke ovens were not emptied within a few days, the coke would blow up and destroy the ovens. The workers pointed this out but were rebuffed by Mayer. "If you don't obey our orders," he snapped, "the coke will simply remain in the ovens, and if they go kaput the mine management will be responsible." But the miners still let the ovens run dangerously hot in a game of chicken with the colonel, who finally backed down. The coke was dumped on a train bound for northern Germany, not France.[42]

Similar standoffs occurred at mines all over the Ruhr. When French soldiers took mine directors into custody for refusing to deliver coal, workers laid down their tools, came up from the shafts, and protested until either the officials were released or the soldiers left. In some places miners sprayed the loaded coal with a mixture of water and sand, making it practically useless by the time it reached France's blast furnaces. All told, the French were seizing little coal and transferring even less to France. In the first few weeks, there was little they could do about this, for soldiers were no more skilled as miners than they were as locomotive engineers.

Out of frustration, the French began to harass mine personnel all across the Ruhr. At one point, the French met with the Ruhr district treasurer and demanded tax information on local mine owners. "I am a German and I do not accept orders from the French," he replied. A French finance official, momentarily taken aback, responded, "You have ten minutes to surrender the records." The district treasurer stood up and prepared to leave, pausing in front of the official to say, "Don't waste those valuable ten minutes. My answer is still no." He was arrested and taken away.[43]

Resistance was not limited to rail connections and mine locations. In many of the major cities—particularly Essen, Dortmund, and Bochum, which had become command centers for the Franco-Belgian mission—Germans cut telephone cables and power lines to the hotels where foreign engineers and officers were staying. French reaction to civilian resistance was often so disproportionate it could only have spurred further rebelliousness. In Essen, singing "Die Wacht am Rhein" or "Deutschland, Deutschland, über alles" brought a 200,000 mark fine or a six-month imprisonment. The same penalties were set for displaying any kind of flag or wearing symbolic pins.

In Gelsenkirchen, a German policeman stopped a French automobile whose lights were not working. French soldiers riding in the car fired on the officer, fatally wounding him in the neck. Observing the commotion, some German civilians rushed to the scene, overpowered the soldiers, and began beating them. In reprisal, the French sent armored tanks and machine guns into the city, demanding that the town pay an indemnity of 1 million marks. When the city's leaders refused, the French sent in more troops, surrounded city hall and the rail stations, and confiscated the city's entire supply of paper marks.[44]

All these confrontations required more troops, and the French were constrained to call up reservists, which stirred resentment among French civilians. Inside the Ruhr, some French soldiers also started to question their purpose as occupiers, realizing that hounding resisters would not deliver coal to France. Unlike the British in India, the French had no desire to stay in the Ruhr; they wanted what they were owed and then they wanted out. Repressing the population was not the object.[45]

But the object of resistance was to prevent the French from doing their work in the Ruhr, and that created a dilemma, which the Germans did not see: The more successful the resistance, the longer it would have to last, so long as the French refused to go. Sustaining nonviolent action over time is never easy, but until its costs mounted for the Germans, there was a consensus for just this kind of opposition. Having survived a horrific war, most Germans had no stomach for violence. "Passive resistance was just following the feeling, the atmosphere" of the time, recalled Theo Gaudig, a resistance activist. It was also reinforced by local work councillors who often calmed down resisters if attacks on the French seemed imminent.[46]

The inclination to be nonviolent was coupled at first with immense zest for resistance. It came from believing that what they were doing was right—

Germans were defending their homeland. At an Essen performance of Friedrich Schiller's opera *Wilhelm Tell,* the audience rose from their seats and nearly in unison repeated a few familiar lines: "We want to be free like our forefathers were, Better to die than to live in servitude . . . And never fear the strength of man." After this, the French prohibited performances of *Wilhelm Tell* throughout the Ruhr. In Bochum, the play's cancellation and the closing of the Bochum Opera House sparked a protest parade of 5,000 people.[47]

A tide of national pride rose throughout Germany. "In the expensive shops and cafes, there is loud talk against the French," reported an American writer in *The Nation.* "And everyone, of course, does his bit in the way of sabotage . . . children give to an inquiring soldier or stranger the wrong direction." Restaurants took French wines and pastries off their menus. If German girls were found romancing French soldiers, their hair was cut off. The League of German Actors urged the public to boycott all French productions, insisting that Germany was "simply inundated with smutty and valueless art imported from France."[48]

The French tried to silence the public voice of German resistance by censoring or shutting down local newspapers. Early on, papers that printed pro-resistance editorials or appeals by nationalist or labor groups were fined and temporarily suspended—but the papers moved their offices and kept on publishing. As more newspapers flouted French restrictions, soldiers turned to ransacking their offices and confiscating or destroying their typewriters, printing presses and paper supplies. Editors and reporters also were fined and either imprisoned or expelled.[49]

Both sides tried to curry public favor, inside and outside Germany. French pamphlets, leaflets, and posters put up on kiosks and walls portrayed the conflict as a showdown with German industrialists, alleged to have capitalized on postwar inflation by making investments at the expense of workers' wages. One eighteen-year-old Englishman named Graham Greene wrote the German embassy in London and offered his "services as a propagandist." After getting a stipend and a list of contacts, he perambulated the Ruhr. "There was a delightful sensation of being hated by everybody," he wrote his mother, explaining that foreigners were mistaken for French officials. "In the evening we went to a cabaret, and a rather fat naked woman did a symbolic dance of Germany in chains, ending up of course by breaking her fetters."[50]

The month-old occupation was costing the French government about $60,000 a day, aggravating the government's budget deficit and encouraging foreign speculation against the franc. Poincaré was compelled to ask the Chamber Committee of France for 45 million francs to pay for its extension through February. The engineers were not yet in full control of the mines and their leader, Emil Coste, abandoned his headquarters in Essen and returned to

France, where he told the Council of Ministers that they had a choice: Either give up trying to extract coal from the Ruhr, or bring the whole region under military rule.

Poincaré was especially baffled by the reaction of German workers. Although he had taken pains to portray the mission as aimed at helping workers rather than their employers, labor had rallied to defend German sovereignty. For Ruhrites, the conflict was a struggle over the fairness of burdens imposed on Germany after the war, and, for the time being, blood was thicker than money. The tough jobs of coal miners, steelworkers, and ironmongers had acclimated them to adversity. So while inflation was high and their lives were hard, they were not suddenly going to surrender, particularly to the French. They had nothing to lose, so why not resist?

From "Solidarity" to Stupor

Despite financial subsidies to resisters and some success in telling the world about French excesses, Berlin was slow to develop a centralized organizational network in the Ruhr to lend direction to those on the front lines. Instead, the initial steps were taken by local unions, work councils, police departments, and city and municipal governments. During the first week there were meetings in almost every city to discuss options and plan resistance action geared to the size of occupying forces, to the location of mines, railway stations, and canals, and to the size of each city. In Gladbeck, for example, a defense group met twice a week to coordinate resistance, and similar groups were established in Essen, Buer, and Recklinghausen.[51]

On January 17 a regional conference was held in Münster, attended by Ernst Mehlich, the Reich State Minister, Berlin's main intermediary in the Ruhr. Mehlich was impressed by the largely spontaneous local efforts but thought that if the resistance was to succeed, Berlin would have to do more directly. Cuno and Ebert, who had been getting only spotty information from their people in the region, agreed, and the Rhein–Ruhr Zentral was established, becoming Berlin's channel for orders to the press, municipalities, industrialists, and unions. Mehlich also organized labor-management defense committees, which planned action and paid out subsidized wages.[52]

But this elaborate dance of cooperation was a bit stilted; long-standing suspicions between workers and employers kept bubbling to the surface. Cuno's announcement that the government would reimburse mine owners for their losses incensed the Socialists, who thought the owners' 40 billion marks in back taxes should be collected first. When Berlin tried to set up a private relief fund drawn from a percentage of wages and employer contributions, unions refused;

they felt they could disburse emergency funds to their workers more efficiently. So the industrialists held back their share. Ultimately it was the government's relief organization that funneled billions of marks to strikers. Despite Berlin's generosity, the unions were sure that Cuno was a stooge of commercial interests. Cracks in the national front were hard to paper over.[53]

On January 22 the Ministry of Finance, on credit advanced by the Reichsbank, dispensed 30 million marks to the relief organization and the labor-management defense committees. This financed local propaganda, paid unemployment benefits, supported pensioners, and bought food for workers and their families. Mehlich reported to Cuno that the amount was insufficient, because the prices for basic necessities had risen so fast. So on February 1 the Reichstag passed a bill authorizing the minister of finance to open another credit line worth 500 billion marks to be distributed throughout the occupied area.[54]

The government had stepped into financial quicksand. It had committed to subsidizing 12 million Ruhr workers for an indefinite period of time, but to do that, the Reichsbank had no choice but to print new marks. By the time the money reached workers, it had already lost considerable value. Alternatives to this financial game were precluded by Germany's dismal fiscal condition. Months before, the Socialist Party had called for tax increases on the industrialists, in part to pare the inordinate inflation rate. Business leaders, however, reminded the politicians that their entrepreneurship had made Germany a world power and would be the basis for Germany's return to economic might, so the political parties aligned with the industrialists blocked new taxes. As for making sacrifices for the cause of resistance, the industrialists argued that accruing losses from reduced production was sacrifice enough.

In the cities there were signs of frayed nerves. A large part of the population was drunk each night, one American reporter noted. "'What else can we do?' was a common excuse. 'We are beaten and squeezed down and have no arms; but we feel better when we are drunk.'" (Not for Germans the abstinence of "self-rule" that Gandhi urged on his noncooperation movement half a world away.) "It is true that the cafes and places of amusement are still full," *The Nation* reported, "but, when a glass of beer or a seat at the movies costs about two cents, it is cheaper to spend the evening there than to burn a fire at home." To help people fend off the cold, miners would load bags and wheelbarrows of coal to take to their families and neighbors. At some pit heads, miners would leave coal piled up for locals. A few even dug their own makeshift shafts—a dangerous practice that caused cave-ins.[55]

Despite economic strain and social stress, the resistance continued to be ardent and pervasive throughout the month of January and into February. Moreover, Poincaré feared expanding the French operation because that might jeopardize relations with Britain and the United States as well as the support of moderate legislators at home. Surprisingly, he was also concerned not to alienate the Germans, for he believed that Europe's ultimate stability would be based on a Franco-German partnership. But such a vision was far ahead of its time, and Poincaré's public persona as a military hero and defender of French security ruled out any entente.

At the same time, Cuno and Ebert saw little incentive to compromise. Germany's nascent democracy was teetering on the brink of collapse, and they could not risk alienating either the nationalists on the right or the communists on the left. Resistance to the French, they thought, would resolve the contradiction by binding all elements together in a united cause. During the first weeks, the men in Berlin seemed to be right. But they ignored latent instabilities; and, being purely reactive, the resistance had no strategic path—it existed but was not steered. To sustain it, the government had to shut down the nation's economic heart and print money to cover lost income. It was buying time, hoping to outlast the occupiers' resolve, hoping that the Americans and British would intervene, hoping that the cost to the French would exceed the cost to themselves.

"Anybody May Be Arrested"

On February 4 Chancellor Cuno made a secret two-day tour of the Ruhr; by the time he returned to Berlin he was convinced that the people's will to resist was just as firm as when the French first entered Essen three weeks before. "I visited every section of the invaded territory," he wrote afterward, "conversed freely with the industrialists, and all classes of civilians and workers, and was everywhere assured of their unwavering resolve to further oppose the French encroachment with passive resistance." He attributed this to citizens being "fully conscious" of their "human rights" and their desire "not to bow down before hostile bayonets."[56]

The chancellor's visit helped jolt Poincaré into realizing that his approach was not working. Cuno's tour had produced "dangerous excitement, particularly among the industrials, functionaries, and agents of the government," the French leader believed, so he forbade further visits by members of the German government. Yet by two weeks later there were 22,000 German workers on strike. Under rising pressure from the French press and parliament, which expected speedy results from the invasion, members of the French engineering mission panicked and suggested the evacuation of troops. But Poincaré, soon to face an election, realized that pulling out would be tantamount to defeat.[57]

The premier's predicament was acute. The country was only getting 30 percent of the coal and coke it had received before the war. How to make

Germany produce? "You can punch a hole through the wall of a house with such violence that the wall, and perhaps the whole structure, will collapse," explained a German engineer in Essen. "Yet you can cut a hole carefully through a house in such a way that the wall and the building will remain firm." While the invaders had not been violent, they had not been well focused either. Forced to confront strikers who were snarling production and transport, they were sparring with the resistance instead of keeping the Ruhr running. Until the mines and rail lines were fully under control, the occupation would be futile.[58]

In late January Poincaré had decided to send General Maxime Weygand and the French minister of public works to go see for themselves and devise ways to neutralize the resistance. After three days they returned and said that France had to seize the railways and the postal and telegraph services, intimidate the mine owners to break up strikes and deliver reparations coal, and isolate the region from the rest of Germany with a strict customs zone. This report may have stiffened the premier. When it became clear that the Germans would miss a reparations payment of 500 million gold marks, he sent a stern order to not allow "one train, one car, one ton, or even one pound" of coal or coke to go to the unoccupied regions of Germany. More soldiers were sent in to man the region's borders and to thwart the smuggling of coal on canals and railroads.[59]

Since the initial acts of resistance, the French had started expelling German civil and industrial officials from the region. Now they began wholesale expulsions of almost anyone who refused French orders, including miners and rail workers who would not cooperate. In the first few weeks of February, 40 people a day were ejected from the Ruhr—over 140,000 people during the whole conflict. Many city governments and industrial organizations were left without any experienced people. Resistance cadres were hard hit, leaving workers and citizens to fend for themselves. In reaction, the pace of strikes and protests was intensified, but with fewer organizers, they lost tactical bite and control. Strikes turned violent and now were sometimes aimed at working conditions, not only the occupiers.[60]

The French also began to make headway at the mines. Unemployed French miners were shipped in to work in place of striking Germans, and Polish and Czech workers also gladly joined the effort, having suffered years of discrimination by German employers. But the resistance of German rail workers remained effective. At the Elberfeld Locomotive Works, for example, the French had requisitioned eleven locomotives that had been standing idle for weeks. As soon as French engineers, guarded by a contingent of soldiers, tried to man the engines and drive them out, German workers began removing the rails. In response, the French arrested the facility's three directors and imposed a daily fine of 1 million marks for every day the engines were held up.

"Of the 170 railway stations in the district of Essen," one British observer wrote, "66 were closed and 44 were taken by the French. Before the occupation 112 trains left Essen every day. Things are practically at a standstill today. On one of the French lines only 6 instead of 50 trains are running." So General Weygand and his ministerial colleague recommended a "Commission de reseau de chemins de fer des pays occupes." The Regie, as it was called, was charged with taking over as many key rail lines as possible and was free to employ whatever force was necessary to end the strikes.[61]

Because not enough French and Belgians could be imported to run the locomotives, the Regie tried to win over Germans who might be desperate enough to work for them. Posters were plastered everywhere, offering hot meals and guaranteed wages in French francs. For the most part, the Germans remained steadfast, not necessarily out of loyalty but out of fear. The local defense organizations countered with their own notices warning that anyone working for the French would be considered a traitor and subject to expulsion or worse. Cuno reiterated his earlier order that all railway employees were legally bound to refuse French and Belgian orders, no matter the threats.

But as February wore on, the stream of incoming foreign workers became a flood. Since it took time and effort to train them, and there were not enough skilled French engineers to do so, General Degoutte (now in charge of the French mission) summoned all German rail workers on March 20 to return to work under penalty of expulsion. When they did not, the French began a mass expulsion and imprisonment of workers and their families. Using payroll sheets for names and addresses, two or three soldiers would go to a worker's home and escort him to the local jail. By June 2, 17,837 railway workers had been either expelled or imprisoned, leaving the ranks of German rail men desperately thin and their spirits low.[62]

Most workers preferred expulsion to arrest, since the squalor in French-run jails was no secret. "The sanitary conditions are extremely bad," reported the German Red Cross on the prison in Germersheim. "On account of the overcrowding . . . the shower bath can be used by a given individual only at long weeks' intervals . . . the prisoners must attend to their evacuations within their cells, in pails with loose covers . . . " Railway workers were not the only ones liable to be locked up. "Anybody may be arrested any minute," wrote an American correspondent. "Hundreds of people are thrown out of their houses every day, allowed to take with them nothing but a toothbrush." In Hattingen, the most frequent offenses triggering arrest included possession of a carrier pigeon, not greeting a soldier, passing out flyers, tearing up French posters and selling bread without a license.[63]

Now every day saw more coal and coke heading west, and the mines were finally yielding what the allies had come for. By mid-April a French-imposed coal embargo and customs zone had virtually severed the Ruhr from the rest of Germany. Germans set up secret passages through the hills and forests along the border, and some coal and benzene were smuggled out, while food and other necessities were snuck in—quite literally now, the resistance was on the run.[64]

And it was also slowing down. A number of ordinances passed in March, April, and May severely curtailed civilians' mobility by limiting the use of automobiles and trucks to those with special permits. After June 10 autos could be driven only by those with French-issued driver's licenses, which the French authorities had to endorse before travel outside drivers' hometowns was possible. All this was intended to oblige the Germans to use the Regie-operated trains, since every other form of public transport, including buses and streetcars, was being used to carry food and other necessities within cities.[65]

Slowly but surely, the occupiers' tightened grip eroded German morale. Many workers, weary of life in perpetual crisis, did the unthinkable and returned to work. On May 6, after a French ultimatum, over 1,000 rail workers in the Mainz district resumed work. "The French authorities called on the men to present themselves for work before 5 P.M. yesterday afternoon or be discharged and expelled," *The New York Times* reported. "They were assured that if they resumed work all rights, pensions, and prerogatives formerly enjoyed would be restored . . . At a mass meeting of the striking workmen it was finally decided that all advantages lay in the resumption of work."[66]

By May 20 the occupation had at last started paying for itself. On that day, the French government released figures showing that the occupation had cost over 145 million francs and that receipts from the sale of coal and coke totaled 102 million francs, but receipts were accumulating faster than outlays. Poincaré could see light at the end of the tunnel.[67]

"A Fighting Front of Fanatics"

Where the French premier saw light, the workers of the Ruhr saw red. They called the occupation "Die Bajonette" (the bayonet) and many were primed to lash back. At the Krupp factory in Essen, they had already done so—and had shaken the whole nation.

While Krupp workers had not gone on strike, they were ready to leave at the first sight of French soldiers. Siren cords hung in every factory shop, to be pulled if troops entered the plant. On the morning of March 31, the day before Easter, French Lieutenant Durieux and eleven soldiers went for a scheduled inspection and inventory of the autos and trucks in the factory's garage. While they waited for the door to be opened, the sirens began to wail. Durieux was taken by surprise and asked the superintendent what it meant. "Down tools," he responded. The soldiers looked outside and saw hundreds of workers glaring at them and inching ever closer, pinning them in the garage. Meanwhile, two workers on the roof opened a steam valve, and the room filled with a thick mist. Durieux ordered his men to fire a number of warning shots, but the workers pressed closer. Practically blinded now, Durieux apparently ordered his troops to shoot at the men. By the end of it all, thirteen workers were dead and fifty-two others were wounded.[68]

While some Germans felt that the French soldiers had fired in self-defense, this "Bloody Easter on the Ruhr" outraged most of Germany. The funeral of those killed was a solemn and patriotic affair, the kind reserved for fallen dignitaries. A procession through the streets of Essen was followed by zealous speeches from civic leaders calling on the people of the Ruhr not only to avenge this cowardly act by stepping up their resistance but also to refrain from violent reprisals.[69]

The message was essentially the same as in January, but the context of events had changed dramatically. With the French bearing down more heavily, many could not resist hitting back. Fearing exactly this, the French commander in Essen had called in tanks and a platoon of machine gunners. But militant nationalists were determined to retaliate for the Krupp killings, and on the very same afternoon a Belgian soldier, a French police agent, and two French engineers had been attacked and beaten. Later hand grenades were thrown at French soldiers in Düsseldorf, and a sentry was murdered in Essen's main train station by a German gunman lurking in a ventilator shaft.[70]

The Krupp crisis accelerated both nationalist and communist violence, and, in the absence of any countervailing vision of how to respond to repression without violence, upset popular confidence in passive resistance. Already on March 1, General von François, a personal friend of Kaiser Wilhelm II, had tried to incite guerilla warfare. "Will a nation of 60,000,000 remain impassive while our brothers in the Ruhr are being strangled by white and black Frenchmen?" he asked. "I have no doubt that a well-organized guerilla war on our own soil would soon end with the enemy's destruction." The general was not the only German who noticed that the French had included African troops in units brought to the Ruhr, and leagues were formed to protect German women from the imagined threat of rape by black soldiers.[71]

Across the Ruhr young men, students, unemployed security policemen, and war veterans organized into bands of Free Corps with the help of former officers. At the same time the Reichswehr High Command decided secretly to enlarge the army. These new formations, known as the Black Reichswehr, consisted of soldiers who were sent into the Ruhr to blow up railway cars and try to assassinate French and Belgian soldiers. One future German chancellor who then worked

French soldier encounters German civilian during the occupation of the Ruhr, 1923.

Credit: ©Scherl Bilderdienst, Berlin/Bundesarchiv, Germany

for the army, Heinrich Bruning, went to the Ruhr with suitcases full of money to distribute to saboteurs.[72]

To combat this "active resistance," the French fined the cities in which violence occurred if no culprits could be found. In the city of Kettwig, where two French soldiers had been shot at, a fine of 1 million marks was imposed. When city officials refused to pay, the soldiers began going door to door to collect every resident's share. On March 11, on a country road near the town of Buer, a French patrol found the bodies of two French soldiers who had been shot in the back. In retaliation, French soldiers killed eight Germans in the city during a free-for-all.[73]

Violence was directed not only at occupying soldiers but also at French-controlled railways and canals. In mid-February German demolition teams had sunk coal barges to block vital points of the pivotal Rhine–Herne Canal, through which most barge traffic passed to France. French soldiers at the canal were told to shoot anyone on sight, but Germans went ahead and blew up a major branch, leaving the rest to run dry and stranding barges in the riverbed. In Duisburg, the main rail bridge into the city was blown up, and nine Belgian soldiers were killed. Retaliation took the form of fines and curfews as well as requiring Germans to ride in the middle cars of trains, as these were most likely to be attacked.[74]

One man behind the sabotage was Albert Schlageter, a former Prussian officer, who was captured, convicted, and executed in May. The French believed he had been a chief of the nationalist gangs assassinating their soldiers. In the ensuing weeks, the right-wing press anointed Schlageter as a kind of German Nathan Hale, hoping to use his execution to fan the flames of violent resistance. "Woe to the German nation if Schlageter's murder inspires no other feeling than passive submission, enduring and suffering, which were never Germanic qualities," cried one newspaper. "Schlageter's death must remind us that we do not live in peace and order but in the midst of Germany's mortal struggle," Adolf Hitler told 25,000 people at a memorial service. "What we need is not a united front of weakness, but a fighting front of fanatics."[75]

"Giving Up . . . "

Chancellor Cuno was not yet prepared to give up on nonviolent resistance. At Karlsruhe he argued that "the passive, defensive fight once begun must be carried through." But Cuno's plea fell on deaf ears. Sabotage was now the resistance method of choice, as even labor leaders—who had known that it brought harsh reprisals on workers—now appealed to Cuno to stop ignoring active resistance. But action that ceased to be nonviolent carried a price. Strict curfews were enforced and Germans throughout the Ruhr were subjected to even more humiliating affronts—citizens were pushed down, kicked off their bicycles, even robbed by French troops.[76]

Deepening the Ruhr's descent from civil discipline to social disorder was the collapse of the mark. On April 18 it dropped from 23,000 to 33,000 marks to the dollar, even though the Reichsbank had tried to stabilize the currency by buying marks on foreign exchanges with its gold reserves. But the central bank was impotent to check the plunge, which came as a shock to the Cuno government. The Socialists, who realized that resumption of reparations was inevitable, wanted the government to conserve its gold and foreign currency holdings rather than to squander them in hopeless attempts to support the mark. The nationalists believed that, to continue subsidizing the resistance, the mark had to be pegged to the dollar. "In this battle, the Reichsbank's gold is our gun powder, which we must shoot off," declared their spokesman in the Reichstag. Financial violence was to be the handmaiden of physical violence.[77]

Coping with inflation had been a daily chore since early postwar days, but now it became an ordeal. "Suddenly all the money that the people had saved for years, all the savings accounts were worth nothing," recalled Theo Gaudig. When wages were paid, workers' wives would come to factory gates, in order to get the money quickly and spend it, before its value dropped the following day. "The farmers could not be induced to go to the trouble of bringing their produce to market where they were forced to sell it for marks which depreciated in value before they returned home," wrote a British journalist.[78]

In March rationing had been introduced throughout the region. Fearing that world opinion would hold them responsible for German starvation, the French cached two weeks of food supplies in Antwerp and Rotterdam in case the Berlin government stopped bringing in food to the Ruhr. They also opened soup kitchens and served propaganda with a free meal. Germans stayed away in droves, for fear of reprisals and because industrialists had opened up their own kitchens.[79]

It was ironic that desperate Germans would accept charity from the industrialists, who had done so little to help the government stem inflation. Indeed, the industrialists even profited from it, using some of the credits they got from the Reichsbank to build new facilities, with the loans to be repaid later in depreciated money. Hugo Stinnes began building a huge new factory between Bochum and Essen, and the Thyssen plant purchased new coke ovens at cheaper prices.[80]

Because of rising unemployment, social disarray, and workers' renewed resentment of their bosses, many of those who had been on the front lines of resistance now joined the communists, whose strikes and protests came to a head on April 18 in Mülheim. A day after the mark's collapse against the dollar, a mob of 2,000 jobless Germans blockaded city hall and held about 300 officials hostage. The city's center was cut off, and all shops and offices were closed. The same day in Essen, 1,800 men marched to city hall and demanded an immediate cash indemnity for the work they had lost while resisting the French. Both actions had been planned two nights before in Bochum, in a meeting addressed by two Soviet emissaries.[81]

By May 22 the mark had plummeted to 57,000 to the dollar. Communist agitation spread rapidly, and on May 24 a riot broke out in Gelsenkirchen between communist workers and the citizens' defense forces. Eight people were killed and between seventy and eighty were injured. The communists then took over the police headquarters and set it on fire. Similar riots followed elsewhere in the Ruhr; in both Essen and Dortmund, stores and warehouses were looted and burned to the ground.[82]

By the end of May some 800,000 miners were on strike, though the line had blurred between those engaged in government-sponsored passive resistance and those fighting for their jobs. In many towns the passive resisters and communists feuded via propaganda, strikes, and counter-strikes, although in other cities both factions tried to work together. It was every city for itself, every worker for his own idea of security.[83]

The unions, which had poured so much energy into resisting the French, began to see their investment go up in the smoke of turmoil among Germans— without any progress in persuading the French that occupation was more costly than a new deal on reparations. As early as March 20 the Mine Workers' Association had called on the government to "leave no possibility unexhausted to end the Ruhr battle and settle the reparations crisis through negotiations." But the nationalists were inflexible, and Cuno was nearer them in his real sentiments. (Later, after resigning, he would hoist the kaiser's flag above the building where he worked in Hamburg and, before he died in 1933, strongly support Adolf Hitler.)[84]

Fervid defiance until the last possible moment was a high-risk strategy at best, and it promised no relief from the economic costs borne by the nation or the human costs imposed on the Ruhr. Had Cuno and Ebert sensed when the high-water mark of the resistance had been reached—when German unity was still potent, before the French were getting coal, but when the cost of the *Ruhrkampf* was not yet astronomical—they might have struck a deal worth having, had they given Poincaré a face-saving alternative to cracking down.

In the end game they actually faced, the resistance was hijacked by both ends of the political spectrum. On the right, the struggle had become a war by those who wanted to requite the loss in World War I and the "shameless" mandates of Versailles. On the left, inflation-drained workers were becoming so desperate that some were turning wholly to communism. In a matter of weeks, Cuno and his cabinet were faced with even worse inflation, escalating violence, plunging morale among the unions and defense committees, and, finally, the threat of a no-confidence vote in the Reichstag. They had no choice; they had to settle.

The chancellor and his men drafted a diplomatic note listing new demands and sent it on May 2 to the French and Belgian governments. It was a desperate offer to cut the Gordian knot of reparations and vitiate the purpose of the occupation, offering 30 billion marks in cash for total reparations, contingent on a four-year moratorium and a massive foreign loan. But in a piece of gall that proved fatal to his purpose, Cuno said that passive resistance would be continued until the occupied areas were evacuated. "The occupation . . . called forth the passive resistance of its population. The German Government shares the desire . . . that the daily increasing tension be relaxed and the wanton destruction of economic values be stopped . . . without, however, abandoning its legal standpoint or desisting from passive resistance."[85]

Cuno claimed the people had mobilized the resistance, but the government could call it off. Poincaré was not so credulous. "It was not the population, it was the German Government which desired and organized the resistance," he replied; "the German Government recognizes this implicitly, since it declares today that the resistance will cease only after a settlement. If the resistance was spontaneous, how could the German Government either halt it or prolong it? . . . The Belgian and French Governments cannot take under consideration any German proposition so long as the resistance is kept up." The French would not settle until the Germans gave up.[86]

After the British and the Americans also showed little interest in his new offer, Cuno was pressed by his foreign minister to resign. He refused and instead drafted a second note, which tried to pry Britain away from France. It requested the same terms but this time made no mention of passive resistance. Once again the French rejected it.

By the end of June it was clear to everyone in the German government that the resistance could not be sustained, for it was bankrupting the state. Compounding the chaos, the communists had instigated strikes not only in the Ruhr but throughout Germany. Merchant seamen in Hamburg, Bremen, and Emden went on strike, as did metal workers in Saxony, Brandenburg, and Mecklenburg. As far east as Berlin, 100,000 metal workers were idled. Something dangerously like a mass movement of hunger and desperation was gathering. The parties that had supported Cuno now felt threatened, and they turned against him.[87]

On August 8 the Reichstag held an emergency session. When Cuno took the floor, the communists rained insults on him. "Executive of Stinnes' Republic, deceiver, swindler, dirty crook, criminal, liar, and traitor" could be heard in the uproar. But Cuno had nothing new to offer. "Germany must and will continue passive resistance," he insisted. Fed up, the Socialist Party called for and got a vote of no-confidence in the Cuno government. On August 11 he was out.[88]

Dr. Gustav Stresemann, the leader of the nationalist Deutsche Volks Partei, succeeded him. At first he wanted to carry on the resistance while putting Germany's fiscal house in order with a series of draconian measures—forcing donations of $100,000 from the industrialists, pushing German industry to export more, and limiting imports to foodstuffs and raw materials. But when the economy did not respond, the Socialists told Stresemann either to halt the resistance or face a no-confidence vote himself. For nationalists, the resistance had become so invested with symbolic importance that to abandon it would be a betrayal. But Poincaré held firm: no negotiations until the resistance died.

With little choice left and with the support of President Ebert, Stresemann announced the official end of resistance in the Ruhr on September 26. "Giving up passive resistance is perhaps more patriotic than the phrases used to combat it," he noted in his diary. "I knew when I did it . . . that I was putting my own political position in my party—yes, and even my life—in jeopardy. But what is it we Germans lack? We lack the courage to take responsibility."[89]

❧ ❧ ❧

By October 1923 the people of the Ruhr were physically exhausted and psychologically spent. Victory, for them, would have meant just two things: getting the French out of their schools, hotels, and work places, and denying them access to coal and coke. If they refused to work for the enemy, they were told, the occupation would fail and the troops would be sent home. But the government in Berlin had had additional goals: to reopen the reparations question and end Germany's subordination to France's postwar exactions. Resisters never grasped the importance of those goals, because the government never fully explained them.

Unlike nonviolent actors in most other conflicts in the twentieth century involving popular resistance to military forces, the Germans had an entire government—their own—on their side. But Chancellor Cuno and his cabinet did little to organize a systematic movement against the occupiers. Instead, the infrastructure of resistance was developed mainly within the Ruhr itself. Because there was no theater-wide plan for identifying vulnerable points in the occupation or even for supplying resisters and keeping them mobile, the resistance remained local, stationary, and reactive.

Unlike oppressors or invaders in other twentieth century conflicts, the French always had a limited goal: to extract value from the Ruhr and leave, not to dominate indefinitely. That gave the Germans a narrower scope for interaction with the occupiers, and it meant that choosing to resist the French at full throttle from the outset would only encourage the invaders to perform their extractive work without local help, minimizing opportunities for the Germans to control the conflict. If the Germans had regulated the pace at which they withdrew cooperation from the French, the occupiers would have remained more dependent on German help, and less pressure would have been placed on the German economy.

German resistance on the ground was effective for several weeks thanks largely to the valor and sacrifice of workers all over the region. For months they held off what was then the strongest army in the world. But the resisters' local initiative and collective passion tempted the government to believe that the resistance eventually could win a physical victory, so it missed the moment when the French might have settled. When the cost of control exceeds the benefits of how much is extracted, an occupier has incentive to cut its losses. That point was reached, but the Germans failed to see it. Instead, the French cracked down harder, and, with no strategy to counter repression and ambivalence about violent reprisals, the resistance lost coherence.

Even as it flagged, the resistance became too expensive to sustain. The burden of supporting it had never been shared fairly by those who had been its loudest advocates—both the industrialists and the nationalists made Berlin pick up the tab. But the cost of subsidizing striking workers through nothing more than printing marks brought the country's economy to its knees. When the mark collapsed in April, the door was flung open to chaos: Workers paid with worthless paper were easy marks for those who were hawking extreme ways to fight the French, which in turn further undermined the resistance. Nonviolent discipline—an asset in every movement of nonviolent resistance in the century— disintegrated along with financial stability.

At the time, the valiance of the Germans in resisting the invaders had been likened abroad to the spirit of Gandhi's campaign of noncooperation with the British. The Germans enjoyed claiming the moral superiority that unarmed resistance was supposed to confer, but, unlike Gandhi, they did not develop a repertoire of nonviolent sanctions that could narrow their adversary's range of maneuver and impose costs for violent repression. Instead, the Germans' own apostles of violence, from Bolshevik agitators to right-wing chauvinists, pitched the Ruhr into disorder, and the workers and citizens who had carried the battle of opposing the French were abandoned. Less than sixteen years later another German government, led by the selfsame Adolf Hitler who hated the very idea of passive resistance, would start a war—and occupy France.

As for the problem that created the conflict—reparations—the outcome was ironic. In only a matter of weeks, the British and the Americans came to the rescue. Recognizing that the German economy was coming apart, they proposed a new framework for negotiations and made reparations an international issue. A committee headed by the American Charles Dawes proposed a five-year settlement funded by an international loan to Germany and a reduction in its debt—precisely the kind of solution that Cuno had thought was possible. By April 1924 Germany had relief.

Raymond Poincaré always maintained that the occupation of the Ruhr had been a success, because it forced the Germans to give up passive resistance. But that had not been his goal: The French wanted the full measure of what Versailles had promised and, along with it, hegemony in western Europe. Instead, J. P. Morgan & Company told the French it could not sell bonds to American investors to refinance German debt if the French remained in the Ruhr. The French went home, never got the coal they needed, and had to rebuild their devastated northern provinces with their own resources. Never again did France wield decisive power on the continent.[90]

The *Ruhrkampf* failed. The *Ruhrkampf* succeeded. Sometimes history can have it both ways.

CHAPTER FIVE

Denmark, the Netherlands, the Rosenstrasse: Resisting the Nazis

DENMARK: WAR BY OTHER MEANS

"They Had Occupied Denmark"

WHEN DAWN BROKE over the waterways and cities of Denmark on April 9, 1940, the Danes no longer controlled their country. During the night German forces had descended and quickly overwhelmed Danish military contingents on the islands of Zealand, Jutland, and Fyn. The seizure of the capital had occurred just as easily. The troopship *Hansestadt Danzig* had docked in the heart of the city, and by five o'clock German troops had swarmed the Citadel, an ancient fortress overlooking the harbor, capturing seventy Danish soldiers without firing a shot.[1]

As this was happening, German bombers flew so low over the capital that citizens could identify their Luftwaffe insignias. They dropped leaflets saying that the Germans were coming to "forestall a British invasion," but mainly their purpose was to frighten the populace into submitting quietly. Jytte Brunn, a shop clerk living in Copenhagen, remembers "German airplanes coming down . . . we got out of our beds and looked out the windows and there they were. Then suddenly we realized that it was something terrible, that they had occupied Denmark."[2]

In the months after Adolf Hitler's military juggernaut had overrun Poland in September 1939, triggering World War II, no military strategist or world leader had given Denmark the slightest chance of withstanding a German onslaught. "I could not reproach Denmark if she surrendered to Nazi attack," Winston Churchill had remarked in February 1940. "The other two Scandinavian countries, Norway and Sweden, have at least a ditch over which they can feed the tiger, but Denmark is so terribly near Germany that it would be impossible to bring help."[3]

Denmark's king, Christian X, and the Danish government had recognized the country's peril and had pinned their hopes on a nonaggression pact signed with Germany in May 1939. Hitler himself had reinforced the illusion of benign German intent in a speech before the Reichstag on October 6, saying that "a loyal and friendly partnership" had been constructed with the Danes. But as the world was to discover, the Nazis preferred their partners to be vassals.[4]

Few Danes saw that in 1939. When the war began, Denmark was the only European country to reduce its armed forces. On the day of invasion, Denmark's troops tallied less than 15,000, not much more than half of what they had been. Yet despite their military superiority, German strategists had prepared the attack meticulously, since they knew that concerted Danish resistance could jeopardize the German offensive timetable and throw off the simultaneous invasion of Norway. A massive strike had been imperative.[5]

Five days before, the German battalion commander responsible for capturing Copenhagen had arrived in the capital for some personal reconnaissance. Posing as an ordinary businessman, he surveyed the port and selected a suitable landing area for the main troopship. He moved on to the Citadel, then housing the Danish Army General Staff. Soldiers on guard duty cordially welcomed the curious tradesman and introduced him to their sergeant, who then showed the visitor the General Staff headquarters, the communications center, and the fortress's two main gates. He came away with no worries about the invasion's likely success.[6]

The night before German forces swooped down, General Kurt Himer, chief of staff of the invasion task force, called on Cecil Von Renthe-Fink, German minister to Denmark, to give him a note to take to the Danish government a few hours later. Von Renthe-Fink, a dignified diplomat with close ties to the Danes, was shocked. It was an ultimatum, telling the Danes to submit—and

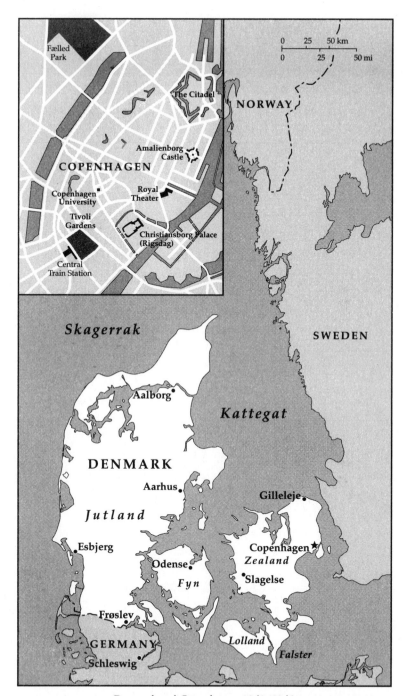

Denmark and Copenhagen, 1940–1945

saying that the Germans had arrived to protect them from supposed Allied plans to turn Scandinavia into a theater of war and that while Germany had no hostile plans, any resistance would be quashed. It offered another reassurance: The Germans would not interfere "with the territorial integrity of Denmark or her political independence."[7]

With shots echoing outside Amalienborg Palace, King Christian conferred with his ministers, including Prime Minister Thorvald Stauning and Foreign Minister Edward Munch, to decide what to do. Both argued for submission. The king agreed just a few minutes before 6:00 A.M. General Himer, who saw him later, reported that the monarch seemed "inwardly shattered" while preserving "outward appearances perfectly." The king said that he and his government "would do everything possible . . . to eliminate any friction between the German troops and the country. He wished to spare his country further misfortune."[8]

As the day wore on, Danes felt disbelief. In a message, Stauning urged them to remain law-abiding, acting "correctly" toward German forces. "Under protest the Danish Government has decided to arrange the conditions of the country, with regards to occupation," he explained. "The government has acted in the honest conviction that we have saved the country from an even worse fate . . . and we shall rely on the people's cooperation."[9]

This was compliance but not surrender—a policy that clung to the useful fiction that the country, although occupied, had not been conquered and remained a sovereign state. This *samarbejdspolitik* (policy of cooperation) was also a strategy to salvage as much room as possible for self-determining national life. "We could have committed a heroic suicide on April 9," Danish historian Palle Lauring said later. "'To survive' became the goal." Not every Dane agreed. In what was widely seen as the first act of resistance, Denmark's ambassador to the United States declared himself the "free" Danish ambassador.[10]

No one knew then that the war would escalate into a world conflict engulfing scores of nations and tens of millions of people. Danish leaders assumed that the war would be short and might well end in a unified, nation-less Europe under Hitler's control. If this were to occur, German recognition of Danish sovereignty could hold an umbrella over Danish society instead of submerging it in the German Reich. Cooperation would be the lesser evil. For their part, the Germans wanted to keep Denmark docile so its labor, agriculture, and natural resources could be exploited. To make Danish textiles, military equipment, and food flow to the Fatherland, going along with the government in Copenhagen rather than forcibly annexing the country seemed prudent.

The Germans were prepared to deviate noticeably from the way they treated most occupied peoples to buy peace in Denmark. Wehrmacht officials prohibited their soldiers from buying Danes' rationed goods and stopped the distribution of a German armed forces newspaper. A circular for soldiers admonished them to treat Danish women and girls with respect, avoid political arguments, and, above all, remember that the Danes were not the enemy and held a privileged position on the Nazi racial hierarchy. Berlin wanted Denmark to be a "model protectorate" that could be paraded before the world as proof of German civility. And if the Danes were obedient, fewer German troops would be needed to keep control.

Many Danes felt the invasion as something of a relief, since it meant the full fury of war would be kept at bay—and the king's advice to remain calm seemed sensible. While Denmark had fascist and nationalist parties, the nation's political decorum kept radicals on the fringes and also kept the streets free of the sharply ideological, often violent battles going on elsewhere in Europe as the Nazis took over. Since Danish institutions remained in place, at least as symbols of Danish authority, the impetus to resist did not feel as urgent—outright resistance would have been, in one sense, insubordination.

Yet many Danes felt humiliated that the country had not put up a fight; many believed their leaders had succumbed too quickly. For centuries the Danes and Germans had struggled over Schleswig (the southernmost Danish province or northernmost German state), culminating in the Danish-Prussian War of 1864, which the Danes had lost—and German mistreatment of Danes there in the following decades had heightened Danish hostility. So beneath the country's quiet exterior and official accommodation, there was anguish. "There was very little physical opposition," recalled Herbert Pundik, a thirteen-year-old student at the time, "but already . . . you felt that the Danes were not going to welcome the Germans."[11]

"What Is a Good Dane?"

When the Germans invaded, Arne Sejr was a seventeen-year-old schoolboy living with his parents in Slagelse, a small town in western Zealand. On his way to school on April 9, he was shocked by how friendly people were to the newly arrived soldiers and later how they applauded a German military band giving an open-air concert of Danish music. He picked up a copy of the local newspaper, which carried the king's message telling citizens to behave like good Danes. "What is a good Dane?" he asked himself. "How does a good Dane behave in a situation like this, when his country is occupied by an enemy?"

Sejr returned home and compiled his answers into what he called the *Danskerens 10 bud* (Ten Commandments for Danes). He typed out twenty-five copies, which read:

1. You must not go to work in Germany and Norway.
2. You shall do a bad job for the Germans.
3. You shall work slowly for the Germans.
4. You shall destroy important machines and tools.
5. You shall destroy everything which may be of benefit to the Germans.
6. You shall delay all transport.
7. You shall boycott German and Italian films and papers.
8. You must not shop at Nazis' stores.
9. You shall treat traitors for what they are worth.
10. You shall protect anyone chased by the Germans.
    Join the struggle for the freedom of Denmark!

Sejr then made a list of Slagelse's most influential citizens, including the mayor, bankers, doctors, and journalists. The next night he rode his bicycle to their homes and stuffed the Ten Commandments into their mailboxes. Soon he found that his fellow Danes' public courtesy to the Germans masked considerable spirit for resistance, which Sejr found new ways to express. He and his friends put sugar in the gas tanks of German cars and army vehicles and copied and mailed anti-German leaflets to high school students throughout the country. Before long his Ten Commandments would be passed from hand to hand and eventually become sacred to the Danes as they waged their national resistance.[12]

In May a number of youth groups met in Copenhagen and, under the guidance of theology professor Hal Koch, established the Danish Youth Association, dedicated to preserving Danish identity and democratic values. Koch also drew large audiences and newspaper coverage with lectures on Danish history that emphasized the need for national solidarity against the Germans and against Danish Nazis. The occupation of the Danish state, he argued, did not nullify the strength and legitimacy of the Danish nation.[13]

This rising wind of national spirit blew most publicly at community song festivals, which were often huge regional events. On July 4 about 1,500 people near the town of Alborg sang hymns about the war with Germany in 1864, soldiers' bravery, and the girls they left behind. Throughout August and September three-quarters of a million people sang in similar festivals. On the king's seventieth birthday on September 26, thousands crowded the streets of Copenhagen to sing birthday songs to the man who embodied the nation. "It was a provocation to the Germans for so many people to gather in the parks around Copenhagen and just sing," Jyette Brunn recalled.[14]

Frontally challenging the occupation would have breached the government's policy of cooperation, but cultural assertions of Danish honor and character could be offered at face value, as ostensibly nonpolitical. Implicitly, however, they contested the idea of German dominion, at a time when the popular mood might otherwise have been depressed. Although the resistance movement would not really take shape until 1941, the songfests and other daily acts of symbolic protest laid the psychological groundwork—not unlike, over thirty years later, the way in which the activity of labor militants and dissenting intellectuals in communist Poland would create social space for opposition that had not yet become a movement.

Danish journalists also played an early role in priming resistance. Shortly after the invasion, the German press attaché personally visited the press bureau of the Danish Foreign Ministry to set the ground rules for publication: All foreign news and editorials had to be cleared in advance, no criticism of the occupying forces would be allowed, and no military news of any kind could be printed without prior approval. But the Danish media, accustomed to total freedom, responded with thinly veiled contempt. The afternoon newspaper, *Ekstrabladet,* printed articles double-spaced, hinting to readers that they should read between the lines. Announcers for Radio Kalundborg and Radio Copenhagen often would read the standard opening for the censored war news, "Here is the latest German communiqué," and the standard closing, "That was the latest German communiqué," with a strong tinge of sarcasm.[15]

Hardly a corner of Denmark was left untouched by the impulse to embrace and dramatize Danish identity, if not confront the occupiers. The nation took responsibility for its own morale while its government went through the motions of cooperating with the invaders—who looked more and more invincible with every passing week. Less than six weeks after Denmark was taken, the Germans seized the Netherlands, Belgium, and France, leaving Britain as the main European holdout against the Nazi war machine.

"Down with the Traitors!"

Emboldened by German success on the battlefield, and heavily bankrolled by German Nazis, the Danish Nazi Party tried to stage a coup in Copenhagen in June 1940. It failed, but Danish leaders moved to immunize the government from any further attempt at nazification. On July 2 five parties formed a parliamentary group called the Committee of Nine, which would make the real decisions in government from then on. Ministers were purged, including Foreign Minister Munch, whose fingerprints were all over the policy of cooperation. But though Munch was ousted, his policy was not.[16]

The new foreign minister was Erik Scavenius, who had held the job before and been ambassador to Germany during World War I, when Denmark managed to stay neutral. Scavenius, although arrogant and unpopular, was thought pragmatic enough to deal with the beast in Berlin—and he went about executing the policy of cooperation with a rather more fatalistic attitude. While not pro-German, he was convinced that Germany would win the war, so his goal was saving the country from Nazi oppression.

Scavenius tilted noticeably toward Denmark's new masters, saying that the nation "should not under any circumstances come into conflict with its great neighbor to the south." He lauded German battlefield victories, asserted that "a new era in Europe" had begun, and called on Danes to engage in "mutual active cooperation" with Germany. This ingratiating approach was fodder for Danish Nazis, who asked the king to fire all his ministers save Scavenius and replace them with Nazis or others who "understood the new era." The king refused, but the government still paid homage to German sensitivities. In early 1941 public statements viewed as detrimental to Danish foreign relations were criminalized—even a private conversation could lead to a jail term. New laws authorized life imprisonment for "enemies of the occupying power."[17]

On June 22, 1941, German forces attacked the Soviet Union. The Germans asked Denmark to break off diplomatic relations with the Soviets and round up leading members of the Danish Communist Party (DKP). That put Danish leaders in a bind: Knuckling under to these demands would further breach Danish citizens' constitutional rights, but not doing so could prompt the Germans to arrest the communists. Members of the conservative People's Party admitted that the request "clashes with the usual Danish sense of justice" but also alleged that the communists were perpetrators of "terror and sabotage." In August Denmark's parliament, the Rigsdag, outlawed the DKP, and police arrested 300 party members, including three legislators. The space for Danish liberty was being squeezed.[18]

As fighting on the eastern front continued, Hitler decided that his battle against Bolshevism should involve all of Europe, and in November 1941 he "invited" Denmark to become a belligerent. In an emergency meeting, Danish ministers equivocated. Von Renthe-Fink renewed Berlin's invitation on November 23: "Denmark must immediately sign the Pact. If not . . . Denmark will be regarded as an enemy country and must face the unavoidable consequences." Scavenius went to Berlin and signed.

The next day students in Copenhagen massed in Amalienborg Square and marched to the office of the Danish Nazi newspaper and then on to the Rigsdag. "They swept the police aside and demonstrated in many parts of the town with cries of 'Down with Scavenius' and 'Down with the traitors,'" *The Times* of London reported. "The police used searchlights, charged the crowd with truncheons, and fired a number of blank shots, successfully barring the way to . . . where the German headquarters were established." When Scavenius came back from Berlin, he did so under the tightest security, lest his return touch off more demonstrations.[19]

All this surprised both the Germans and the Danish government, which now had to abandon the illusion that the policy of cooperation had any real public support. A few days later the government reprimanded the protestors, but the Danish cabinet quietly decided that if the Germans insisted on using Danish troops and military equipment on the eastern front, or asked for anti-Jewish legislation, it would refuse. But what little backbone that displayed was gone within weeks, as the government was coerced into delivering six new torpedo boats to the German navy. Little was also done to stop German enlistment of Danish soldiers. Soon all Danish men of military age were being recruited for the Frikorps Danmark. Options for how to respond to the occupiers no longer were limited to songfests or street marches—now it was whether to fight with them or against them.

"Action Is Required of Us All"

In early 1942 Danes began to challenge the Germans with physical force and even sabotage. One group was made up of schoolboys from Alborg, who called themselves the Churchill Club; their slogan was *"Vi maatte gore det, naar de voksne ikke ville"* (If the adults won't do something, we will). "We had an anti-Nazi sign, a swastika with an arrowhead at the tip of each arm, which we painted on walls, in stairways, and wherever we could," recalled one of their leaders. "Our best job was the burning of a freight train loaded with war materials."[20]

The most active sabotage group was led by communists who had gone underground after Germany's attack on the Soviet Union. Organized as KOPA (Communist Partisans), they raided small factories that produced war materiel. Within a few months, noncommunist members were allowed to join, and the group's name was changed to BOPA (Middle-Class Partisans). Scant damage came from these operations, but they complicated the policy of cooperation: If the government cracked down on saboteurs, it would weaken its already shrinking popular support; if it did nothing, it would antagonize its German overlords, on whose sufferance the government's existence depended.[21]

At the same time, a newly flourishing underground press started to promote action against the occupying forces. *De Frie Danske,* which had come out in the fall of 1941, was followed by the influential *Frit Danmark,* started by anti-German politicians, and by other papers. Many who got involved were young people with little experience in journalism and with only a few typewriters and old duplicating machines. Money, paper, ink, and trustworthy assistants were hard to find, as were places to operate without risk of detection. Yet the

King Christian X of Denmark on one of his daily rides on horseback through Copenhagen's streets,
during the German occupation.

Credit: The Museum of Danish Resistance 1940–1945

underground press matured quickly and was never effectively suppressed. In late 1942 Information, an illegal press agency, began to provide reports gathered from the BBC, Sweden, the Danish ministries, and uncensored news sources. In 1943 illegal publications reached a combined circulation of 2.6 million copies, and an illegal press coordinating committee and joint newsroom were set up.[22]

Arne Sejr and his friends, who had left Slagelse and enrolled at Copenhagen University, joined the publishing front. Procuring an old mimeograph machine, they set up the Studenternes Efterretniingstjeneste (students' information service). Soon they were publishing illegal books, binding them in cardboard and distributing them from their apartments and homes. *The Moon Is Down* by John Steinbeck was a best-seller, along with the Danish *White Book,* which reprinted government and army documents about meetings at the time of the German invasion. The government's conciliatory actions revealed in the book appalled many Danes; more than 20,000 copies were sold. Another book, entitled *Führerworte,* a collection of Hitler's speeches, had a cover humorously depicting him in knight's armor on a white horse, carrying a swastika banner.

Two thousand copies were mailed to German military post office addresses; the Nazis, who thought the image disrespectful, were infuriated.[23]

Whether in print or in public, resistance and not cooperation became the theme of Danish response to occupation. At the state funeral for Prime Minister Stauning in May 1942, more than 12,000 people packed Copenhagen's largest meeting hall to pay their respects. King Christian was expected to attend, and when the back of the hall began to stir, everyone rose to their feet thinking they would see the beloved leader. Instead, German Minister von Renthe-Fink entered. An observer reported that it was "impossible to describe with what speed the people got down again, and as the hall is large, the movement was like a ripple and became a unique demonstration of silence." When the king finally did arrive, he was warmly applauded.[24]

As the incarnation of the Danes' heritage, King Christian became a key social and spiritual figure. Before the war, he had ridden his horse daily through the streets of Copenhagen, and these rides continued during the occupation. As he rode unescorted, crowds would line up along the route and either applaud or come up and shake his hand. German soldiers would also snap to attention, but the king would invariably turn his gaze away from them. "He sustains us, he unites us, he guides us," the bishop of Copenhagen observed.

Another rallying point was John Christmas Moeller, an uncooperative member of parliament who, as minister of commerce, the Germans had pressured to resign in 1941. After he kept on criticizing German policy through underground newspapers and at mass meetings, von Renthe-Fink demanded that Moeller be expelled from his parliamentary seat and forbidden to make anti-German speeches. The Danes refused, so the Germans decided to arrest him. But he escaped to London where, throughout the resistance, he served as a clarion voice of defiance through rousing radio appeals.

In August 1942 the Germans tried to counter the mounting resistance by asking for expanded press censorship and the death penalty for resistance fighters. The government rejected these demands but also condemned the resistance. A few days later Moeller broadcast a different appeal to his country-men over the BBC, one much more characteristic of the spirit in his homeland: "Action is required of us all. It is our duty to have only one thing in view, that which hurts Germany the most . . . Do your duty—do your work."[25]

Insults, Badges, and Strikes

As Danish defiance intensified, Hitler became convinced that the country was on the verge of revolt. At this point, the British and Americans were readying final plans for the invasion of North Africa, and the Führer was concentrating on trying to stymie the Allies. Any potential diversions, as in Denmark, had to be preempted. So the German leader decided that a change in German-Danish relations was necessary—although he needed a provocation to justify his actions.

That came on September 26, 1942, King Christian's seventy-second birthday. Hitler sent up a telegram with his congratulations and best wishes for the king. The king responded coolly and tersely: "My utmost thanks. Christian Rex." Hitler interpreted this as a personal affront and a sign of Denmark's noncooperation. In response, he recalled von Renthe-Fink, demanded that Denmark provide 30,000 young men for the German armed forces, and called for the ouster of the Danish government. The London *Daily Telegraph*'s headline read: "Hitler Ready to Take Over Denmark. Gestapo Rule Threat to King Christian."[26]

The Germans sent two new henchmen to bear down on the Danish. General Hermann von Hanneken was dispatched to take over the army command. SS General Dr. Werner Best, a longtime Nazi bureaucrat, became the German plenipotentiary in Denmark; he was instructed by Hitler in a personal meeting to "rule with an iron hand." Berlin's final directive was to install Foreign Minister Scavenius, long favored by the Nazis, as prime minister. He promptly filled his cabinet with pro-German colleagues. The Danish public, whose contempt for him was already blatant, unleashed protests and demonstrations everywhere.

Werner Best, determined not to jeopardize the Danish *Lieferungsfreude* (willingness to supply), believed that the first priority was winning the war and that repressive measures would only spur the growth of resistance. This put him in direct conflict with von Hanneken, but Best had the last word until told otherwise by Berlin. He went about cultivating cordial relations with Danish legislators, and in a report covering his first months in charge, he noted that Danish citizens were "sick and tired" of the war, Danish imports to Germany were up, and industrial and agricultural production had climbed. Berlin applauded, but Best had whitewashed the situation: Beneath the surface strong currents were running against the occupiers.[27]

On March 23, 1943, Best—in one of his biggest blunders—permitted Denmark to hold parliamentary elections; Germany wanted to prove that it valued the autonomy of occupied countries. Although Danish communists urged voters to cast blank ballots in protest, other parties sought a big vote. Most resistance groups threw their weight behind a coalition of democratic parties. The Danish Youth Cooperation Movement distributed over 1 million voter's badges with the national flag and the caption "has voted." Sporting a badge was not only a symbolic gesture, it also shamed would-be abstainers. In the end, participation was 89.5 percent, the highest in the nation's history. The coalition parties received over 94 percent of the vote and won 141 out of 149 seats in the Rigsdag. The Danish Nazis barely held on to their 3 seats.[28]

Danish Prime Minister Erik Scavenius and SS General Dr. Werner Best,
German plenipotentiary in Denmark, during the German
occupation in World War II.

Credit: The Museum of Danish Resistance 1940–1945

Best blamed the Nazis' weak showing on the incompetence of the Danish party's leader, Fritz Clausen. He failed to grasp that the election, by reaffirming the people's clear preference for native democracy over foreign domination, had been a major setback. Rarely in the twentieth century did authoritarian regimes appreciate the subjective power—and the potential for strengthening the opposition—that holding an election could hand a popular movement.

The resistance now increasingly tied the rationale for its actions to Danes' opportunity to make a difference in the war. The BBC stepped up its propaganda campaign, urging Danes to break with Germany. Blacklists were drawn up and the names of Danes involved in pro-German actions were announced over the air—reminiscent of the disgrace poured on the heads of Indians who collaborated with the British raj. Allied victories, especially the resounding German defeat at Stalingrad, were well covered in the hope that Danes would be encouraged to resist.

All this helped foster more sabotage. In July there were 93 incidents, and in August, 220. Named after a legendary Danish hero who rose from his sleep whenever his country was in danger, the group Holger Danske was a major instigator. "I was sick and tired of looking at the Germans crowding the streets," explained Jens Lillulund, about why he helped start the group. "I was cycling along the Haraldsgade . . . and when a company of soldiers came trapping by, I exploded. I spat at them and a couple of policemen grabbed me and hauled me off to a police station . . . I decided that if I were ever arrested again it would be for something which had hurt the Germans." But what hurt the invaders more was something other than sabotage.[29]

Inspired by other signs of active resistance, workers began to go out on strike. The Danes were not new to this type of protest: In 1920, a nationwide general strike had been called by labor leaders who demanded constitutional changes (which led to more decision-making power for the cabinet and parliament). Now the target was an external enemy. In Odense shipyard workers walked off their jobs when the city's German commander sent troops into the yard after a sabotage attack on a German cruiser undergoing repairs. Much like German workers in the Ruhr, there was nothing more galling to the Danes than to be forced to work for foreigners. As word of this reached other factories in the city, workers walked out in solidarity.

From Odense, the strikes spread to Esbjerg, a port on the west coast of Jutland, where a walkout at a fish warehouse became a city-wide "folk strike." Everyone, including fishermen, police, firemen, office workers, and civil servants, stopped work, closed their doors, and came together in the city center. Furious, the Germans imposed a strict curfew, which was ignored. People crowded into the streets and refused to go back to work until the curfew was lifted. After five days the Germans relented. Two days later another strike broke out in Odense, and the resistance spread to larger cities, including Aalborg and Aarhus. In Odense ministry officials, the mayor, and even union leaders implored workers to return. But the workers had seen how the strike upset German soldiers and administrators. If Germany needed a functioning Danish economy, the workers were going to do what they could to bring it to a grinding halt.

The strikes in Odense turned violent. At one point a German soldier, challenged by an angry mob, drew his gun and fired a number of shots into the crowd, wounding four people including a young boy. Enraged, the crowd overwhelmed the soldier and beat him to death. After Hitler heard the news, he immediately levied a 1 million kroner fine on the city, to be paid to the German army. A curfew also was imposed, as theaters and movie houses were shut down, and arrests were threatened if those "guilty of maltreating the German officer" were not handed over.[30]

To Werner Best, the strikes were utterly embarrassing, and he made countless appeals to the Danish government to get them under control. A plea by the Danish cabinet and parliament for a return to "calm and order" was ignored, however, as workers cast their lot with resistance leaders. Best was summoned to Berlin to answer for what was happening. He advised continued moderation and argued that the strikes were merely one-time events. But he was trumped this time by General von Hanneken, who had long advocated a military solution. With strikes and sabotage spreading uncontrollably, and with the war taking a nasty turn, Hitler finally agreed with the general. Unless the Danes agreed to harsh new conditions, a military state of emergency would be declared and von Hanneken would take over the country.

"This Is a Turning Point"

On August 28, 1943, the Germans gave the Danish government an ultimatum: Proclaim a state of emergency and take eight specific measures—prohibit strikes, public meetings of more than five persons, and any private meetings in closed rooms or the open air; impose a night curfew; collect all weapons; turn censorship over to Germans; establish summary courts to deal with any infractions of these rules; and impose the death penalty for sabotage, defiance of the German military, or weapons possession. In short, Denmark was to be silenced and emasculated.

The ultimatum was rejected out of hand. "An implementation of the German demands will ruin the possibilities of the government to keep the population calm," the government replied. The policy of cooperation was finished. Scavenius and his cabinet resigned. The following day German troops occupied railroad stations, power plants, factories, and other key facilities. Soldiers went into residential areas and arrested influential university professors, newspaper editors, legislators, and businessmen. German sentries were posted at every major building and facility. Danes switched on their radios to hear the news and were greeted by von Hanneken's proclamation: "Civil servants should continue work, obeying instructions given by German authorities . . . all strikes are prohibited and punishable by death." One other thing too: All telephones had been rendered useless and mail service had been shut down.

The military takeover left Werner Best out in the cold and eager to blame someone for his downfall. Like other self-absorbed political losers in the twentieth century, he blamed the press, rebuking them for ignoring his warnings not to aggravate the Germans. "In this ridiculous little country, the press has implanted the belief that Germany is weak," he told a meeting of prominent newspapermen. "Last night, you got your reward." For the Danish resistance, that is exactly what it was. Repression clarified its mission. "Of course, this is a turning point," said the underground paper *Frit Danmark*. "But actually, it only means that a condition which has developed slowly . . . is now publicly confirmed." The August strikes had shown that Danes would confront the Germans; troops on the street were now a reminder that they were part of a larger war.[31]

For the Danish population as a whole, however, personal risk was becoming the concomitant of public resistance. For the past three years their government, despite its detested policy of cooperation, had served as a buffer between ordinary Danes and the Germans. Although ministerial departments still functioned after the cabinet resigned, in order to keep public and social services running, that shield was now largely gone, and there was no way of knowing what General von Hanneken would do.

For Denmark's 8,000 Jews, the fear of the unknown ran even higher. From the occupation's start, the Danish government had guaranteed them equal rights. The Germans, hoping to prevent unrest, had soft-pedaled the issue of Danish Jews. Just six days after the initial invasion, von Renthe-Fink warned Berlin that "if we do anything more in this respect than is strictly necessary, this will cause paralysis of, or serious disturbance in political and economic life. The importance of the problem should not be underestimated."[32]

When Werner Best was calling the shots, he continued this hands-off approach, and his superior, Foreign Secretary Joachim von Ribbentrop, never pressed him to change the policy despite pressure from both Adolf Eichmann and Heinrich Himmler. But as the strikes and sabotage came to a head in August 1943, Best, who always could sense the political winds shifting, changed his tack. He drafted a long telegram to Berlin on September 8, recommending a roundup of all Jews in Denmark, knowing that would please Eichmann, Himmler, and, most important, Hitler. He also requested police forces to carry out the arrests.

SS battalions and security officials began arriving in Copenhagen on September 15, and two days later Best received Hitler's official go-ahead. By this time Best was worried again that rounding up the Jews would cause too much disturbance. He shared his reservations with one of his closest confidants in Copenhagen, Georg Duckwitz. A German shipping attaché who had been involved with the Nazi Party as a teenager, Duckwitz opposed the roundup because it would poison German-Danish relations. On the night he saw Hitler's reply to Best, he wrote in his diary, "I know what I have to do."[33]

Best realized he still had to follow orders and execute the plan. With Rosh Hashanah beginning on Thursday, September 30, Jewish families would be at their homes celebrating on Thursday and on Friday, October 1. So he recommended that the arrests start at 10:00 on Friday night and continue into Saturday morning. If all went according to plan, the Jews would be surprised and captured in their homes with relatively little commotion. But no German, not even Werner Best, anticipated what Georg Duckwitz would do.

On Tuesday, September 28, after meeting with Best, Duckwitz telephoned Hans Hedtoft, a Danish politician and personal friend, asking to meet with him and his Social Democratic Party colleagues. When they got together that afternoon, Duckwitz minced no words as he told them of the German plan, and he urged them to start warning the Jews. Right away they contacted the most important men in the Jewish community, including Rabbi Marcus Melchior, the chief rabbi, and Julius Margolinsky, who organized a messenger service to tell Jews to go into hiding.

The news spread like lightning, thanks in part to many non-Jewish Danes. Ambulance driver Jorgen Knudsen searched through local phone books for the addresses of families with "Jewish-sounding names." He then drove his ambulance to go warn them and, if they had nowhere to hide, took them either to the hospital or to homes of doctors active in the resistance. Other Jews were approached on the streets by total strangers who offered them keys to their apartments or houses. "Here was something Eichmann and his men weren't accustomed to," as Leni Yahil, professor of modern Jewish history at the University of Haifa, put it. Denmark's Jews had slipped away "behind a living wall raised by the Danish people in the space of one night." One Dane wrote: " . . . we underwent a great experience, for we saw how that same population which had hitherto said to itself, in awe of the German power, 'What can we do?'—how this same population suddenly rose as one man against the Germans and rendered active help to their innocent brethren."[34]

The rescue of the Jews galvanized the country, pushing many Danes into forceful resistance. *Frit Danmark* declared that Danes could not bow to German threats even "when hard punishment and the probability of being taken to Germany await us if we help our fellow Jewish countrymen . . . and we shall go on helping them by all the means at our disposal. The episodes of the past two nights have to us become a part of Denmark's fate, and if we desert the Jews in this hour of their misery, we desert our native country."[35]

Organizations representing almost every facet of Danish society denounced the German action. The universities of Copenhagen and Aarhus closed for a week in protest. The Danish Ministry of Religion sent a protest letter to Werner Best and circulated it to clergymen for them to use in their sermons. (From this point forward churches helped formed underground networks, and churchgoers joined existing resistance groups in huge numbers.) Finally, the recently established Freedom Council, a group of seven men who represented various resistance groups, issued a proclamation condemning "the pogroms the Germans have set in motion."[36]

But the Jews were not safe yet. A German order on October 2 instructed all non-Jews to turn them over to the authorities—so there was no way they could continue to be hidden safely within the country. They would have to find a way to neutral Sweden. Dozens of groups sprang up to transport Jews from inland hideouts to the coast, where they could be loaded into fishing boats, dinghies, and even kayaks. The Holger Danske sabotage group now concentrated on saving Jews, concealing them in homes in Copenhagen's port district until dusk, when they were taken to Sweden on the group's twelve fishing vessels.

Arne Sejr and his colleagues at the Students' Information Service gathered information on German troop activities along Jewish escape routes—an invaluable contribution that came at a heavy cost: Five of the students were killed on one reconnaissance mission. Reporters at the *National Tidende* maintained contact with resistance groups and underground rescue teams, providing information on escape routes and German troop numbers. The code word "potatoes" was used for Jewish refugees. One journalist recalls reporting: "Eighteen sacks of potatoes have been sold today to Mrs. Ege . . . Twenty sacks were sold through the middleman at Lyngby . . . It would be a good idea for the potatoes to be transferred to another place."[37]

With every boatload of Jewish refugees that sailed to Sweden, the Danish resistance could savor another success, and each one helped to strengthen its resolve and swell its ranks. Although German soldiers continued to pursue Danish Jews for the next few months, their efforts were largely in vain as 7,220 Jews successfully escaped to Sweden. Only 472 were captured, during the raids on October 1 and 2. The national solidarity that made the operation possible brought Denmark into harder opposition to the Germans, and it proved to both the Allies and skeptical Danes that a well-organized resistance effort with tangible, realistic goals could subvert the power of the Third Reich.

"The Greatest Victory of the Danish People"

On the heels of this success, Danish resistance was further aroused by the murder of one of the country's most revered poets and playwrights, Kaj Munk. A clergyman by profession, Munk used his sermon on New Year's Eve to condemn the German occupation and exhort his audience to commit sabotage. Later he was dragged from his home by a German terrorist squad and shot. That same night the actor Kjeld Abell opened a performance at Copenhagen's Theater Royal by asking the audience to spare "a moment's thought for Denmark's greatest dramatist, who died today." The theater fell silent and watched Abell pick up his coat and walk out. Over the next few days, despite German prohibitions, there were many memorial services, and booksellers dressed their windows in black paper.[38]

To utilize and build on this kind of intensity, the underground Freedom Council won the agreement of the Danish army to recognize the Council as the nation's de facto government, until the king could freely organize a new one. The Council agreed that the first goal of resistance should be active opposition to German forces, and it set up a Command Committee to coordinate all resistance actions. Having sprouted in a hundred localities and grown like weeds, the Danish resistance now had a centralized command and a single voice.

In early 1944 Denmark was divided into six resistance regions, each independent of the others but all under the direction of the Command Committee. Underground militias were formed in each region and were trained with weapons smuggled in from Britain and Sweden. Within a month these groups were acting alongside other sabotage units to strike at a number of Danish facilities that produced small arms, tanks, airplanes, and artillery for the Germans. In June, saboteurs carried out nineteen attacks on railroad lines, three times the average for the preceding five months.

The Freedom Council had now pushed the resistance beyond its earlier mission of making room for asserting Danish autonomy toward dynamic action that could seriously diminish German exploitation of Denmark. But one of its founders believed that it first had to achieve another goal. In a letter to John Christmas Moeller in London, Frode Jakobsen argued that "the battle for our people's soul is for me the most essential . . . For me the problem must be: 'How is one to draw the great mass of people into the fight?' rather than 'How is one to injure the Germans the most?' I will wager the paradox that, if the effect is the same, it is better that 1,000 men have been involved in the work than 10."[39]

To that end, Jakobsen objected to the Danish army's desire for an underground military, because he believed the resistance should be accessible to all citizens, most of whom had to live aboveground. He wanted an entire society opposing the Germans, not merely a group of armed gunmen, just as Gandhi had understood that if a foreign occupier were to be opposed effectively, people from all walks of life had to enlist. When the greater part of the population turned against the foreign force—when they withdrew their consent—then it would have neither the cooperation it needed to govern nor the legitimacy to pretend to do so.

Addressing all Danes, the Council had given primacy to nonviolent resistance. "All of us must purposefully and untiringly . . . put obstacles in the way . . . deny, delay and diminish." Violent resistance was to be undertaken only by those "who have the courage and the means" and was to be aimed "against points of vital importance for the occupation power." But as sabotage increased,

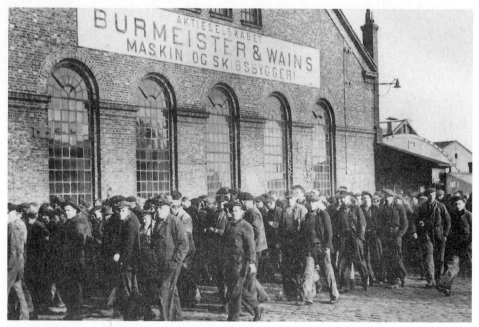

Workers at a Copenhagen shipyard walk off the job at mid-day, June 26, 1944, during the German occupation of Denmark, saying they have to tend their gardens.

Credit: The Museum of Danish Resistance 1940–1945

so did German reprisals. They were normally carried out by the Danish Schalburg Corps, veterans of the pro-Nazi Danish Frikorps. The Corps used counter-sabotage, which became known as *Schalburtage,* to attack national symbols and sites dear to all Danes. Two days after sabotage at a plant producing rifles for the Germans, for example, the Schalburg Corps set fire to the Royal Danish Porcelain Factory and placed bombs in Copenhagen's famous Tivoli Gardens.[40]

In mid–June, Best was ordered by Heinrich Himmler to crack down on the saboteurs. On the twenty-fifth, he decreed another state of emergency throughout the country, establishing a curfew between 8:00 P.M. and 5:00 A.M. In reaction, the next day 1,200 workers at the Burmeister & Wain shipyard in Copenhagen left work at 1:00 P.M. They assured their bosses they were not striking but simply leaving work early to cultivate their gardens, since the curfew did not give them enough time for that. Word of this ruse quickly reached other factories and became the excuse for stopping work.

Instead of watering their flowers, Danes converged on Copenhagen's streets, rallying and demonstrating against the Germans. The underground news service Information reported that "Copenhageners stood in groups of hundreds on street corners so they could escape down the by-streets when the German patrols came. To the Danish police they said, 'Don't interfere with this;' and the police did not . . . People closed the streets with barricades of paving stones, vans, bicycles, and threw things at the Germans, who fired around in wild fury." By the end of the day, six Danes had been killed and dozens more were wounded.[41]

The following morning workers from factories throughout the city joined the strike. The "go-home early" campaign had spread, and now parts of the city were in open revolt. Fearing the worst, Werner Best pushed back the curfew to 11:00 P.M., but to no avail; trams and buses were derailed and overturned, more barricades were built, and bonfires lit up the night sky. Incensed by the chaos, Best called an emergency meeting with Danish administrators and union leaders. The strikes had halted the manufacture and transport of weapons and vehicles to the German army, now heavily outnumbered throughout Europe. He threatened severe retribution if the strikes continued and warned Danish officials that they would be held personally accountable.

After thinking it over, Danish administrators appealed to the public. "The danger of measures with irreparable consequences is impending . . . Everybody is therefore earnestly requested to resume their daily work." But knowing that Danes would not take them seriously unless German repression was acknowledged, they also included a line blaming the Germans "for regrettably bringing about various measures." This inflamed Best, who ordered German troops to cut off all gas, electricity, and water to the city. In a final meeting with Danish officials, Best said that "German honor had been drawn into the mire, and this would have to be suffered for . . . The Copenhagen riff-raff would have to taste the whip."[42]

Late in the evening of June 30, the Freedom Council held an emergency meeting and decided that since the strikes had become the largest resistance action against the Germans thus far, it had to support them. "This is the greatest national demonstration ever to have taken place in Denmark," the Council declared the following morning. "The repeated attacks of the Schalburg Corps on lives and property and the systematic breaking down of law and civil rights by the German occupying forces have exhausted the patience of the people. The Freedom Council supports the continuation of the strike until the Schalburg Corps is removed and State of Emergency restrictions are lifted." Violence by the resistance had not seriously weakened the Germans, but violence against the people had roused the nation to take massive nonviolent action—and the resistance leaders hastened to catch up.[43]

The Germans next tried to cut off Copenhagen from the outside world. But since German troops were being pulled out of Denmark and transferred to the front, the blockade of Copenhagen was undermanned and thousands of citizens passed easily through it. Within the city strikes intensified, trenches were dug, and workers ripped up cobblestone streets and hurled rocks at German soldiers, inciting the troops to fire back. By Saturday night, July 2, 23 Danes had been killed and over 203 wounded. Strikes and protests spread to cities in Zealand and Jutland. The Germans retaliated: Tanks rolled into downtown Copenhagen, and rumors abounded that the capital would be bombed into subservience. With utilities disconnected, people fetched water from nearby lakes and collected wood to grill food on the streets. Underground groups coordinated secret deliveries of milk, eggs, and cheese, and store owners sold produce at reduced prices.

Despite this defiance, it was not clear how long the people could endure these conditions, and the threat of Luftwaffe bombing seemed dangerously real. So local authorities, union officials, and key legislators mediated between the Germans and the Freedom Council, to try to break the cycle of Danish provocations and German reprisals. Best agreed to withdraw the hated Schalburg Corps from the city, end the curfew, and order German troops not to fire on Danish citizens. He also promised to lift the state of emergency after the strike ended and resume gas, water, and electricity service.

For the Germans the "People's Strike" was a disturbing revelation: The Freedom Council, with its policy of noncooperation, now held sway over Denmark, and the strike had wrecked whatever credibility German control had previously enjoyed. The effect of these setbacks was compounded by battlefield losses throughout Europe, which demoralized the occupation forces and energized the Danes. On Monday evening, July 4, the Council distributed a "Victory Bulletin," listing German concessions and praising Danish citizens for their resilience in the face of German reprisals. It also concluded that "the total strike is a much more effective weapon than casual disturbances. The People's Strike was decisive—not the barricades or the unrest in the streets . . . The People's Strike in Copenhagen is the greatest victory of the Danish people so far during the occupation."

From that point, the Freedom Council de-emphasized sabotage and military measures in favor of nonviolent action. In August 1944 the Council stopped organizing underground militias and instead moved to coordinate strike efforts. One of its members wrote, "we can bring a general strike into force at very few hours' notice, from public offices and departments down to modest managers. The whole country will come to a standstill when we wish it, and not only that, we can order a general strike in branches of work in the population where it is expedient, and let other branches work normally." Limited, controlled, and selective nonviolent strikes would now be the sanction of choice.[44]

On July 12 there was a two-minute silence at noon throughout the nation in memory of those who died during the People's Strike, an action duplicated

on August 29. For the remainder of the occupation, these kinds of commemo-
rative demonstrations were frequent. On August 14, 1944, a strike broke out
among workers at the Burmeister & Wain shipyard in response to the execution
of eleven Danish teenagers for their roles in sabotage actions. The Freedom
Council stepped in and called for a twenty-four-hour strike the following day.
The Council also urged the workers to "avoid demonstrations. Stay calm and
dignified." The strike quickly spread throughout the country, and within ten
days, fifty-four towns had participated.[45]

Just a month later, on September 14, massive strikes broke out to protest
the deportation of Danish prisoners to Hamburg. A camp had been set up at
Fröslev as part of an agreement between Werner Best and the former Danish
government, so that Danish prisoners could remain on Danish soil. Now Best
reneged on this promise, and 200 prisoners were shipped to Germany. In
response, Danish railway workers along the German border walked off the job.
The strikes soon spread throughout Jutland, shutting down its rail network. The
Germans depended heavily on railways to get troops to the front; they responded
as the French did in the Ruhr, by occupying key stations. Strikers were
threatened with executions, and 500 more prisoners were scheduled to be
deported. Fearing the Germans would fulfill these threats, the director of the
state railways and union leaders tried to persuade workers to return to work—
but to no avail; general strikes broke out in Jutland. The Freedom Council
supported them and called for a nationwide strike, to end at noon on Monday.
That morning, life in cities came to a standstill, again halting production of
supplies for the German army.

The last and largest strike of the occupation came soon after. On September
19, under the cover of false air-raid sirens in Copenhagen, Aarhus, Aalborg, and
Odense, German soldiers in trucks pulled up outside police headquarters and
substations and began arresting Danish police officers. To the Germans, the
Danish police had become undependable by turning a blind eye to sabotage and
disorder. By the end of the day, close to 10,000 policemen had been arrested
and disarmed. At Amalienborg Castle, the king's police entourage was taken into
custody. When a German officer informed the king that he had orders to raise
the swastika over the castle, the king refused and exclaimed, "If this happens, a
Danish soldier will go and take it down." "That Danish soldier will be shot,"
the officer replied. "That Danish soldier will be myself," the king responded.
The swastika never flew over the castle.[46]

Responding to the police arrests, the Freedom Council called for another
nationwide general strike to end later that week. Citizens were urged to remain
calm and stay out of the streets to await "the right moment." Once again fifty-
eight towns and all of Jutland participated, with violent confrontations a rare

occurrence. But without police on the street, there was a marked increase in crime in the larger cities. On September 22 the Freedom Council called for maintaining discipline, maximum penalties for various crimes were raised, and underground militias began to serve as municipal guard corps.

Order was more or less restored in the fall, when Danes, along with much of occupied Europe, expected the war to end within weeks. As the war ground on and another winter loomed, there were shortages of coal, gas, water, electricity, and food in Denmark. Coupled with bare-bones police forces, this opened the door to more crime. At the same time, the Gestapo targeted resistance groups by infiltrating their ranks, torturing some and murdering others. The Schalburg Corps returned to Copenhagen, burning the hideouts of suspected saboteurs. Then whole resistance groups were arrested, along with prominent Freedom Council members. Retaliatory protests flared but, because of grim weather, had little impact. More effective was the continued refusal of the Danish administration to provide laborers for German factories in Jutland—and underground resistance groups saw a surge in enrollment; by the end of the war they had over 45,000 members.

Yet occupied Denmark remained at risk. If the Germans managed to eliminate the Freedom Council, there was no way of knowing how the remaining Danish administrators, who still saw themselves as a shield for Danes rather than a source of resistance, would deal with these new threats. In general, citizens still equated the administration with the conciliatory policies of Scavenius, and instead put their trust in the Freedom Council. To prevent the Germans from lashing out as their position eroded, the British Royal Air Force, at the request of resistance groups, bombed the three most important Gestapo headquarters, in Aarhus, Odense, and Copenhagen—an attack that probably saved the lives of thousands of resistance fighters.

In spring, peace finally came to Europe. On May 1, 1945 the news of Hitler's suicide was broadcast over the BBC, and three days later Europeans everywhere learned of Germany's surrender. The Danes rejoiced and jammed the streets of every town and city to celebrate. "All of a sudden, there were candles in all the windows," recalled Ninna Almdal, who was a student in Copenhagen at the time. "And then people flocked out into the streets and . . . down to the city center and . . . Amalienborg Castle. Suddenly, there were cars coming down the street filled with members of the underground movement. They were cheered and there was a terrific feeling of liberation and happiness."[47]

Resistance groups took responsibility for law and order, while underground militia groups arrested Danish collaborators. The Freedom Council joined with other resistance leaders and the recently returned John Christmas Moeller to form an interim coalition government. Shortly after the war Werner Best and

General von Hanneken were indicted for ordering acts of counter-sabotage and the deportation of Jews. Best was found guilty and sentenced to death, while General von Hanneken was sentenced to eight years in prison. Both men appealed and were brought before a regional court in Denmark, where Best's sentence was reduced to five years and General von Hanneken was set free. Resistance had not made the Danes incapable of leniency.

Thanks to the civic solidarity that had nourished the resistance, Denmark emerged from the war in good condition. Allied authorities found that Denmark could not only feed itself but had surplus food to export to the rest of Europe. The Danes had withstood German occupation without undergoing many of the rigors experienced by other Europeans held down by the Nazis—a dividend of having resisted without violently tearing their society apart in the process. Some Danes were disappointed that more of their countrymen did not, like many Norwegians, Greeks, or Serbs, pick up guns and fight their occupiers at every depot, pier, and airfield, but the watery lowlands of Denmark were not ideal maneuvering ground for armed partisans, and by the time the Germans were pressed on all fronts in Europe, the Danish resistance had imposed a different but discernible cost on Nazi capabilities.

The Danes proved that however dreadful the opponent faced by those using nonviolent action, if resistance is resilient and imaginative, military sanctions are not enough to stamp out a popular movement—and violent reprisals may only harden the opposition. Knowing the Germans wanted normalcy in Denmark, the Danish resistance worked to deny them that, and it refrained from magnifying any disruption to the point of prompting overwhelming repression or endangering the lives of many civilians. If the Nazis, the cruelest killing machine in the century's history, could be kept off balance by Danish schoolboys, amateur saboteurs, and underground clergymen, what other regime should ever be thought invulnerable to nonviolent resistance?

FROM ROTTERDAM TO THE ROSENSTRASSE: THE REICH DEFIED

"We Will Recapture Our Liberty"

One month and one day after German forces took possession of Denmark in April 1940, troops of the Wehrmacht crossed the border into the Netherlands while German planes bombed Dutch airfields. At the same time, Berlin's ambassador in The Hague delivered a note claiming that German forces were entering the country to protect Dutch neutrality and invited the government to place itself under the Reich's protection. Without hesitation Queen Wilhelmina and her ministers rejected the proposal.

As German bombers smashed Rotterdam and other Dutch cities, the royal family escaped to London, which the queen proclaimed the new seat of government, ensuring its legal existence. "I hereby issue a fiery protest against . . . the outrage done to the conduct customary between civilized nations," she declared. But five days later General H. G. Winkelman, the commander-in-chief of the Dutch armed forces, signed articles of surrender. On May 29 Dr. Arthur Seyss-Inquart, the Reichskommissar for the Netherlands, gave his inaugural address. He claimed the Dutch to be Germanic brothers and promised that all Dutch prisoners of war would be released by mid-June. But Nazi plans for the Netherlands were far more drastic: transforming Holland into a National Socialist state, exploiting the Dutch economy for the German war machine, deporting and exterminating over 100,000 Dutch Jews and Gypsies, and suppressing any form of resistance.[48]

The Dutch had a tradition of neutrality and no recent experience with resisting invaders. Like Denmark, the country's flat and open topography made paramilitary resistance problematic. But already on the day of invasion, groups of students and workers came together to offer some measure of defiance. One Amsterdam group, calling itself the Geuzen Action Committee, distributed a message promising that it would gradually develop an organization to fight for Dutch liberty: "one day we will recapture our liberty . . . Our country shall not become a part of Germany!"[49]

On June 29, the birthday of Prince Bernhard, people in Amsterdam rallied publicly against the Germans. The prince had adopted the habit of wearing a white carnation on all holidays and for every public ceremony. On his birthday, vases filled with carnations could be seen in the windows of every dwelling and storefront. Around midday people started appearing in front of the monument to Queen Wilhelmina's mother. Each person brought a carnation and placed it at the monument's base. By the end of the day, the monument was buried under a sea of blossoms. In response, the Germans arrested two of the demonstration's organizers—and even seized General Winkelman, who had nothing to do with it.

In the fall the Nazis began to go after Dutch Jews, at first firing all Jewish public officials and professors. At the University of Leiden, the dismissals led to a large demonstration that culminated in the singing of the national anthem. At the Technical University of Delft, the students went on strike, forcing the university to shut down. Leiden followed suit. As in Denmark, the Germans were to find that victimizing individual citizens, even Jews, would deepen the hatred of those who had been invaded.

On February 22, 1941, three days after a fierce showdown between Dutch Nazis and armed Jewish citizens in Amsterdam, 600 SS soldiers moved in, sealed off the Jewish quarter, and arrested 400 young Jewish men. They were beaten and then shipped to the Buchenwald concentration camp. News of this spread quickly. Communist workers met late one night and made preparations for a massive strike. With the help of underground printers, they distributed leaflets calling for every worker to join them. Two days later shipyard workers and streetcar drivers were the first to walk off their jobs; they were soon followed by industrial workers. Businesses, workshops, offices, and stores closed their doors, and workers massed in the city center, where they shouted and sang in protest. Over 300,000 out of a population of 800,000 took part in the strike.

The Germans, although stunned, were quick to crack down. Hundreds of German police and SS soldiers moved in with orders to fire without warning at troublemakers. A curfew was imposed, with violators subject to arrest. The threat of reprisals turned out to be too much for Amsterdam's mayor, who ordered city officials to return to work or risk dismissal. Unlike Denmark, the Netherlands had been conquered and its head of state had gone into exile, so Dutch administrators were left to their own devices—and, early in the war, many were constrained to carry out German decrees. This initial collaboration meant that strikers were acting on their own, and the February strike proved unsustainable.

But at the grass roots of Dutch society, resistance became an act of patriotism, and most of the population took part. Schoolteachers refused to submit their names for approval by the Germans. Artists refused to join the Nazi Kulturkammer (culture guild), even though this denied them income and public appearances. Over 160,000 farmers withheld required payments to the Nazis, and thousands of young men refused to report for the Arbeitsdienst, an occupation corps devoted to reclaiming the land.

The underground press, numbering about sixty papers, also thrived. (One of the most influential papers, *Het Parool*, still exists today and is one of the country's most respected dailies.) During the war everyday greetings and chores became imbued with symbolic pride. The "V" sign replaced the handshake and was painted on walls and kiosks in every major city. The simple greeting "'Hallo" became an acronym for "Hang alle landverraders op" (Hang all traitors). Citizens also wore coins bearing the portrait of Queen Wilhelmina.[50]

Seyss-Inquart came to realize that the Dutch were not going to become obedient National Socialists, so German repression intensified. By the end of 1942 over 800 resistance fighters had been arrested and deported to concentration camps in Germany. The country's largest Protestant political party was abolished, and its members were compelled to join a Nazi-controlled trade union. When the Dutch Catholic Church sent letters and telegrams to the

German administration protesting the deportation of Jews, some 700 Catholics of Jewish origin were arrested and sent to Auschwitz.

In less than three years, about 300,000 Dutch were relocated to Germany to work in the Ruhr—a threat to the livelihood of Dutch families that buttressed their will to resist. Around 100,000 deportees managed to escape back to Holland and found safe places to hide with farmers and householders. Vital to this operation was the Landelijke Organisatie (National Organization), comprising nearly 15,000 people, and the National Support Fund, established by a group of bankers who had escaped to England. The Fund also subsidized sabotage squads that damaged Dutch rail lines, stalled weapons transport, and raided German supply convoys.

Perhaps the greatest solidarity was displayed by Dutch doctors, who had been told that they had to join the Ärtztekammer (doctors guild) and follow Nazi medical guidelines, including screening patients for racial background and genetic defects. Over three-quarters of the country's doctors refused to join the organization and, in response, gave up their practices and removed their name plates from the fronts of their homes and offices. A group of doctors formed the Medisch Contact (Medical Contact) that worked closely with local physicians through eleven district representatives, to help hide doctors who came under attack from German police. By centralizing its direction, the Contact staved off a Nazi takeover of their profession.[51]

On April 29, 1943, the Germans announced that all former Dutch army soldiers, who had been captured and released in 1940, were to be recaptured and sent to labor camps in Germany. This startling order affected more than 300,000 men. Instantly workers in the town of Hengelo walked off their jobs. The strike quickly spread through the province of Overijssel and to the major city of Eindhoven, where every Philips factory ground to a halt. In the province of Limburg, over 10,000 miners came up from the pits and went on strike. By the next morning the number swelled to 40,000. Then German police and troops moved in and began shooting indiscriminately. Those arrested were given perfunctory hearings and sentenced to death. Thereafter the strikes diminished in intensity everywhere except in Limburg. A German police force was sent there and violent clashes broke out. On May 5 the Limburg miners finally gave up and returned to work. The strikes had cost over 180 deaths, 400 casualties, and 900 prisoners of war, who were sent to German concentration camps.

In the next months there were more incidents of resistance, but despite perseverance by groups like doctors and factory workers, whose lives had been directly affected by Nazi policies, the overall resistance lacked systematic guidance. As in Denmark, resistance groups had sprung up locally and communication was established slowly. It was not until later in the war that a group known as De Kern (The Core)—made up of union officials, resistance leaders, and editors of underground papers—tried to coordinate a national effort. They met weekly in Amsterdam but never achieved the stature of Denmark's Freedom Council and therefore could not speak for a majority of Dutch workers and resistance fighters. As a result, Dutch resistance never had clear national goals, and a strategic effort to challenge German control of the country never came to pass.

The last major act of resistance came in September 1944, when Dutch railway workers went on strike to obstruct the transport of Jews to concentration camps in the East and also to slow the movement of German troops back home to defend the Fatherland from Allied invasion. As the French had done in the Ruhr twenty years before, and as they had done in Denmark, the Germans imported their own railwaymen to keep the trains running. And in reprisal, the Germans shipped some 50,000 Dutch men from Rotterdam to Germany to help prepare defenses for German cities. In a bitter, unintended consequence of the rail strike, deliveries of coal, gas, and food were halted to Rotterdam and other Dutch cities, and the ensuing winter was unbearable for many. Allied victory the following spring delivered the Dutch from a harsher war than the Danes had seen.

In contrast to events in Denmark, the Nazis had made the Dutch authorities capitulate formally at the war's outset, and they dragooned a half million Dutch workers for service in the German war effort. Given this investment in Dutch submission, the Germans were willing to work much harder to maintain it than they ever did in Denmark, where the carrot-and-stick approach—the same strategy the French used initially against the Germans in 1923—brought mixed results. Morever, German sanctions depleted the ranks of potential resisters and narrowed the space in which they could operate. Able to offer only pockets of opposition, the Dutch were unable to prevent the Nazis from exploiting their labor and from wrenching nearly eight of ten Dutch Jews out of the country and into the Holocaust.

This frightful cost in lives and honor might have been reduced had resistance in the Netherlands been better organized. As it was, although hindered by the early collaboration of some Dutch officials and the lack of any real cohesion, the resistance still prevented Holland from being turned into a Nazi satellite state, which had been the Germans' original intent, and it turned the deportation process into a constant struggle that diverted the Germans' time and resources from other war activities. Having seized both Denmark and the Netherlands through offensive operations, the Nazis nevertheless were forced by nonviolent resistance in both countries to mount rearguard defensive actions to redeem the value of having occupied these countries in the first place. In Denmark, that value was seriously depreciated. In the Netherlands, it was at least diminished.

"Let Our Husbands Go!"

On February 27, 1943, SS soldiers and local Gestapo agents began seizing the Jews of Berlin in an operation called "the Final Roundup." They were loaded onto trucks and taken to the Jewish community's administration building at Rosenstrasse 2-4, in the heart of the city. The goal was finally to make the city *judenfrei* (free of Jews), necessitating the forcible collection of Jews with German spouses and their *Mischling* (mixed ancestry) children. For two years these Jews had escaped the jaws of the Holocaust because they or their German spouses were essential for the war effort, and the regime wanted no unpleasantness on the home front. But the stunning military defeat at Stalingrad earlier that month shattered German morale and led Hitler to call for "Total War," against Jews inside Germany as well as Allied armies.[52]

Word spread quickly about the abductions in Berlin, and before long a group of non-Jewish German women had gathered on the Rosenstrasse with food and other personal items for their Jewish husbands, whom they believed were being held inside. One of the women, Charlotte Israel, arrived and found 150 women already huddled outside. She asked one of the guards for her husband's potato ration cards, which he went to get. On the back of a card, her husband Julius wrote, "I'm fine." Other women began asking for personal effects to confirm that their husbands were inside and, soon after, began demanding their release. One woman's brother, a soldier on leave, approached an SS guard and said, "If my brother-in-law is not released, I will not return to the front." The crowds grew considerably despite the winter chill, and soon women waited outside day and night, holding hands, singing songs, and chanting "Let our husbands go!" By the second day of the protest, over 600 women were keeping a vigil on the Rosenstrasse.

This was not the first time many of these women had voiced dissent. For over a decade they and their families had challenged Nazi racial policies through letters and small demonstrations, insisting that the regime would be hurting fellow Germans by persecuting their Jewish spouses. Hitler and his circle had always tried to minimize unrest and avoid the kind of domestic opposition that German rightists saw as the "stab in the back" that had crippled the German effort during World War I. Until this point the regime had largely managed to keep the genocide against the Jews a secret. But when it affected a group who were unafraid to speak out against Nazi policies, that secrecy was jeopardized.

What gave further resonance to the wives' protest was that it was happening in the heart of Berlin, a city that had never been enthusiastic about Nazism. Cosmopolitan Berliners had always seen it as a crude Bavarian aberration. Moreover, Berlin was the German base for foreign news organizations that still operated during the war. If political malcontents or the wire services were to get wind of the protest, the myth of the omnipotent Nazi state could be exposed. In fact, London radio did report on the demonstrations.

By the third day SS troops were given orders to train their guns on the crowd but to fire only warning shots. They did so numerous times, scattering the women to nearby alleyways. But the wives always returned and held their ground. They knew the soldiers would never fire directly at them because they were of German blood. Also, arresting or jailing any of the women would have been the rankest hypocrisy: According to Nazi theories, women were intellectually incapable of political action. So women dissenters were the last thing the Nazis wanted to have Germans hear about, and turning them into martyrs would have ruined the Nazis' self-considered image as the protector of motherhood.

The campaign soon expanded to include women and men who were not in mixed marriages. The ranks of protestors bulged to a thousand, with people chanting to let the prisoners go and taunting the SS soldiers. Joseph Goebbels, seeking to stop more from arriving, closed down the nearest streetcar station, but women walked the extra mile from another station to reach Rosenstrasse 2-4. By the end of the week Goebbels saw no alternative but to release the prisoners. Some thirty-five Jewish male internees, who had already been sent to Auschwitz, were ordered to gather their belongings and board a passenger train back to Berlin.

Without fully realizing what they had done, the Rosenstrasse women had forced the Nazis to make a choice: They could accede to a limited demand and pay a finite cost—1,700 prisoners set free, if all the intermarried Jewish men were released. Or they could open a Pandora's box of heightened protest in the center of the capital and brutalize German women in the bargain. For the Nazis, maintaining social control was more important than making sure every last Jew made it to the gas chambers. The regime that terrorized the rest of Europe found itself unable to use violence against a challenge on its very doorstep. The Nazis were savage but they were not stupid.

As it happened, many more than thirty-five Jewish men were eventually set free. The protest confronted Nazis officials with an unresolved question: what to do with other intermarried Jews. Goebbels wanted them deported from Berlin so he could tell Hitler the city was *judenfrei*. Himmler prevented the deportations, but Goebbels lied and told Hitler that it had happened—and then tried to get Jews still in Berlin to stop wearing the Star of David. A month later Adolf Eichmann's deputy in Paris wanted to know what he should do about French intermarried Jews. On May 21 Himmler's deputy released them all, everywhere, from the camps. Five years earlier Gandhi had been asked about the Nazis. "Unarmed men, women and children offering nonviolent resistance," he predicted, "will be a novel experience for them."[53]

In February 1943 Ruth Gross was a ten-year-old girl who went down to the Rosenstrasse so she could catch a glimpse of her father, one of the Jewish men interned there before being shipped for a time to the camps. One day she saw him, and he waved back. "This thing with Rosenstrasse," she said years later, "that was always a bond between us, my father and me." When she would visit him in the hospital at the end of his life, each time she left he would stand up and wave at her. "I have always been convinced, that he too was always thinking about this scene there on Rosenstrasse. About how he stood there and waved." When love comes to rescue life, no one forgets.

৩ ৩ ৩

The occupation of a country subjects both the people and the invaders to a strange game of mutual suspicion: The occupier acts like a new owner and wants the tenants to behave and pay the rent on time, but those invaded feel violated—they know the country, by right, belongs to them, and while they cannot physically throw the occupiers out, they may well want to resist the invader's terms. Perhaps, if the invader finds the game is not worth the effort, he will leave. Or perhaps he will start killing uncooperative tenants. But the game gives one major advantage to those occupied: They will define the extent to which they are going to cooperate. And the offender, ironically, will have to defend his ill-gotten gains.

Both in Denmark and in the Netherlands, resistance movements took the offensive against occupying forces. Through symbolic and cultural protests, they asserted their right to govern their own lives, and that strengthened public morale—which inspired bolder resistance. Through strikes, defiance at work sites, and damage to physical property, nonviolent resisters attacked the economic interests of the invaders. In Denmark, through underground publishing, an alternate network of communication was established to counter the lies of the occupiers' propaganda. By involving so many civilians in strikes, demonstrations, and other forms of opposition, Danish resisters forced the Germans to stop violent reprisals and suspend curfews. They denied the Nazis their prime goal, on which other objectives depended: making the fact of occupation normal.

By definition, a successful military invasion gives the occupier superiority on the ground and in the air, in the ability to use physical force and violence. Despite that, when a military invader loses control of what the people read and believe, of when and if they work, of how they spend their money—when the occupiers are constantly on the defensive as they try to maintain their position—their ability to command events can be detached from their ability to use violence.

But when the resistance turns to violence, its capacity to direct the conflict also can be weakened. In the Ruhr in 1923, sabotage and violence by German militants triggered French reprisals which, combined with German economic blunders, exhausted the *Ruhrkampf.* In Denmark, though, the Freedom Council was often able to divert or discourage violent sabotage, and German repression had to be calibrated to avoid causing full revolt, as both sides realized that the price of violence can be too high.

On the Rosenstrasse in 1943, in the center of the century's greatest cyclone of killing, the violence that could have been visited on protesting German women and on almost 2,000 Jews was neutralized—by a few hundred wives who refused to go home. The Nazis' will to violence was notorious. But superiority of military force did not make them invulnerable: They were frightened of protest at the seat of their power, and the potential cost of suppressing it with violence—while trifling in blood and time—was politically too high to pay. So the evil they embodied was, in that place and at that moment, impotent.

War contorts the history of the nations it touches, but it also exhibits the greatness of their peoples. The Danes, the Dutch, and even dissident Germans challenged the most barbaric regime of the modern period and did so not with troops or tanks but with singing, leafleting, going home to garden, and standing in public squares. Yet the power they brought to bear in resisting the Nazis did not come only from these things. It came first from the essential decision that tens of thousands of them made, to refuse the terms they were offered by their tormentors—and it came from the movements they built and the strategy they used, to fling that decision in the face of their enemy and constrict his ability to fight.

The Danes learned how to separate the Germans from the spoils of taking Denmark. The Dutch would not be taken meekly off to Germany. The Rosenstrasse wives kept coming back until they got their husbands. The moment and the means of refusing to be overcome are never out of reach. King Christian knew that. And so did Ruth Gross.

CHAPTER SIX

El Salvador, 1944: Removing the General

House Calls

IN THE CITY OF SAN SALVADOR IN 1944, a thirty-three-year-old doctor named Arturo Romero started making house calls on Agustín Alfaro Moran. Most of the people who Dr. Romero treated were poor, and he often did not charge them. But Alfaro, who belonged to one of the country's elite families, was a wealthy coffee exporter. This unlikely pair were not, however, doctor and patient. During the previous year, the idealistic physician and the influential coffee magnate had joined in a plot to overthrow El Salvador's dictator, General Maximiliano Hernández Martínez. When they met, Romero gave Alfaro vitamin injections to allay suspicions from household members, but their real purpose was to plan an insurrection.[1]

The abhorrence they shared for General Martínez had different motives. Alfaro had been an official in the Martínez regime, but he quit his post in anger when the general started maneuvering to stay in office beyond the end of his second term in 1940. Alfaro's growing dismay with the president also reflected broad sentiment among the coffee elite. Romero, in contrast, saw himself as a spokesman for the country's poor, who had suffered while the general suppressed labor and peasant organizations.[2]

The two rebels were not alone in their antipathy for the dictator. Many respectable citizens were already languishing in prison for real or supposed subversive acts. Less than six months later, a new popular movement would emerge, drive the general out of the country, and give El Salvador another chance for democracy—a finale that neither Alfaro nor Romero could foresee when the "house calls" began.

The Republic of Coffee

For decades El Salvador had been dominated by a small circle of wealthy families. Descendants of Spanish conquerors and European immigrants, they controlled the country's most lucrative business: the growing, processing, and exporting of coffee—and they also dominated government. From 1898 until 1931 the Salvadoran presidency passed from one coffee producer to another. The coffee elite believed that freedom was the prerequisite for progress, and they disliked any institutions or customs—labor guilds, communal property rights, or clerical privileges—that they thought would stand in the way.[3]

Fondness for freedom did not stop the coffee lords from being eager beneficiaries of public spending on the roads, railways, and ports that coffee exports required, or from favoring action to suppress labor organizing and social discontent. The government ruled by decree, snuffed out dissent, and passed power from family to family via coups or rigged elections, even though the constitution promised rights and democracy. Those in control viewed the rural poor, especially Indians and mestizo peasants, as culturally backward and racially inferior—not ready for a voice in government.[4]

But the families' commercial success set in motion forces that would weaken their control of the country. Economic growth created an urban middle class of shopkeepers, civil servants, teachers, and professionals. The army, perhaps the best in Central America, acquired a measure of stature, developing an officer corps comprised mainly of young middle-class men. Less happily, the concentration of land ownership threw Indians and the poor off their ancestral grounds, making them dependent on wages from the coffee plantations. Many left the countryside altogether to find work in the small but growing industrial sector, which included some textile factories, a brewery, railroads, an electric power station, and a streetcar company.[5]

All these changes had political repercussions. For decades, a few dissenters had rallied around principles enshrined in the country's 1886 constitution, and free elections were among their goals. A growing educated class became a new constituency for these ideas. The first protests by students at the University of El Salvador came in 1890, and there were four more student strikes in the next two decades. Mutual aid societies sprang up to represent shoemakers, masons, carpenters, printers, and barbers. Protests by market women over a currency revaluation in 1922 forced a finance minister from office, and the first industrial unions appeared in the 1920s.[6]

El Salvador was coming of age as a political community. The problems of modernization—such as landless peasants streaming into cities and chronic government deficits—provoked criticism of the old order. Marxist ideas appealed to some students and had a greater impact on labor. Most influential were the ideas of the Salvadoran author Alberto Masferrer. A social reformer and newspaper editor, he insisted that all people be guaranteed steady work and basic necessities, which he called the "vital minimum." Masferrer even advocated breaking up the vast holdings of the oligarchy.[7]

Urbanization, student protests, labor organizing, Marxism and Masferrer: The Salvadoran elite could find any number of threats to its command of national life as the 1920s drew to a close. In the roller-coaster events of the next two years, it would be compelled to take desperate measures to defend its position. In the words of an American reporter on the scene, "El Salvador's propertied classes scare easily; the scene was ripening for a heavy-handed savior."[8]

"A Greater Crime to Kill an Ant than a Man"

Maximiliano Hernández Martínez was not a coffee baron. He was born in 1881 to a humble family of mostly Indian ancestry and received most of his formal education at a Guatemalan military academy. A sober, personally honest man, he was also intellectually curious, though his interests were unconventional: He studied Eastern religions and was a vegetarian and theosophist. As a young army officer, Martínez (who always used his maternal surname) reportedly composed a personal motto: "It is a greater crime to kill an ant than a man, for a man on dying becomes reincarnated, while an ant dies dead." As events would show, he took this perhaps too literally.[9]

Martínez's reputation as a disciplined and able officer propelled him steadily higher through the ranks. He became the first president of the Círculo Militar officers' club and seemed destined to spend his years as a career military man. Then something unexpected happened. Salvadoran presidents hand-picked their successors, but in 1930 President Pío Romero Bosque, piqued that none of his likely heirs was showing him enough deference, decided to throw the race open. The free-thinking Martínez, along with five wealthy landowners, entered the contest.[10]

The months leading up to the January 1931 election were turbulent. Profits from coffee exports had soared during the 1920s, but this did not

General Maximiliano Hernández Martínez, president of El Salvador, 1931–1944.
Credit: ©CORBIS/BETTMANN—UPI

translate into better lives for the *campesinos,* who lost even more land to the big producers. "In time," wrote the journalist William Krehm, "the mountainsides became a fairyland under snowy wisps of coffee blossoms, and the country a kettle of social unrest." With the onset of the worldwide depression, the price of coffee collapsed. Landowners left coffee berries to rot in the fields and left coffee pickers without work or wages. One union brought 80,000 protestors out into San Salvador's streets in April 1930 to demand guaranteed contracts and minimum pay.[11]

Arturo Araujo, a presidential contender, styled himself as an advocate for the lower classes. Although a large grower himself, his sense of social responsibility had made him something of an outsider among the elite: He paid his laborers twice the going wage and tried to start a Salvadoran version of Britain's Labour Party. Calling for modest reforms and hinting that he favored land redistribution, Araujo was endorsed by Masferrer, and then asked General Martínez to join him as his vice-presidential candidate in order to win military backing. Martínez accepted, and the ticket scored an upset victory.[12]

El Salvador's first democratically elected leader took power on the brink of national strife. Poor people hoped that Araujo would bring dramatic change, and the rich feared him for the same reason. But a limited land reform that he proposed was oversubscribed, Masferrer became a critic, and soon the communists were winning away the *campesinos.* Meanwhile coffee growers kept aloof from the administration, depriving it of the expertise concentrated in their families. The government's revenues started to dry up, and paying its employees, including military officers, became difficult. As the military's dissatisfaction peaked, a group of young officers ousted the new president in December 1931. Araujo left the country, with Vice President Martínez taking his place.[13]

The anointing of Martínez may have satisfied the military, but popular discontent kept bubbling and the government's enemies on the left kept agitating. Within weeks the communists, believing the country ready for a peasant rebellion, were plotting an insurrection. But officials got wind of it and hauled in most of the ringleaders. When actual fighting broke out in January, government troops needed only a few days to defeat the rebels, whose support was largely from Indians in the western part of the country. The rebels killed less than 100 but the military retaliated with indiscriminate terror in the countryside—killing between 8,000 and 30,000.[14]

In the aftermath, accounts of the uprising and massacre, known as *La Matanza,* were purged from libraries, replaced by the myth of Martínez as the savior of Salvadorans from vicious communists and barbaric Indians. "There have always been two essential classes in every society, the dominators and the dominated," wrote two coffee barons, Agustín Alfaro Morán and Enrique Alvarez, who tried to justify the outcome. Coffee growers looked out for the best interests of the "primitive" men and women who worked on the land, they explained, and so the uprising had not been due to real grievances, it had been inspired by the communists, who created "a dangerous lunacy in the simple minds of the peasants."[15]

Martínez, a social and economic outsider, had gained the respect of the elite by extinguishing the twin threats of communist and indigenous rebellion. On February 5, 1932, the National Legislative Assembly endorsed the general's claim to the presidency until the end of Araujo's term. Alfaro and even prominent liberals joined the administration. Then the general went on to extend his personal authority over the state: He centralized decision making, assumed the power to appoint mayors, and organized the only legally operating political party, the Partido Nacional Pro-Patria.

A state of siege declared at the time of the uprising remained in force for twelve years. New laws empowered the state to prosecute those who advocated, even privately, "doctrines contrary to the political, social and economic order." The press was restricted, and the university was put under direct control of the regime. Paid informants monitored private conversations, the president created a secret police force, and the communist party and peasant organizations were outlawed. Punishment of dissenters outside the official judicial system, including "disappearances," were not unknown.[16]

Among the regime's chief targets were labor activists. José Jesús Duarte, a tailor and former president of the Salvadoran Workers' Society, was one of the victims. A supporter of Araujo and advocate of Masferrer's ideas, he landed in jail when the general came to power. On nine occasions he was driven to a paupers' graveyard with other men slated for execution, but each time, for some unknown reason, his life was spared. His wife's efforts to get his wealthy clients to intercede on his behalf came to nothing. Then, after weeks in jail, Duarte was suddenly freed. But the policemen who constantly stood outside his shop scared his customers away, and he had to declare bankruptcy and sell his business.[17]

Notwithstanding all this, Martínez held onto a measure of public support during his first two terms. He paid public employees on time, practiced fiscal discipline, and was known to be incorruptible. He also did favors for the poor, stopping foreclosures on land mortgages and experimenting with social welfare projects. These initiatives were mild enough not to offend the coffee growers, who for some time remained grateful to the president for subduing the 1932 uprising. And the regime did favors for them too, setting up the Banco Hipotecario (Mortgage Bank), which underwrote agricultural projects, and a company that intervened in markets to stabilize coffee prices. "Chaos was substituted for a disciplined and efficient system," one supporter wrote about the great one's deeds.[18]

Making Enemies

In the summer of 1938, Martínez was already looking ahead to the end of his second term in 1940 when, according to the constitution, he would have to step down—but he decided that he would rather not. When he proposed changing the constitution, two of his advisors, the prominent lawyer Hermógenes Alvarado and the undersecretary of finance, Romeo Fortín Magaña, tried to convince him that was a mistake. Alvarado warned Martínez that his opponents would label the constitutional revision a crude grab for personal power, contrary to the "will of the people."[19]

Few Salvadoran leaders had been fastidious about following the particulars of the constitution, but the principle of term limits had held fast for more than half a century. Consequently, some erstwhile supporters of the president started to break away. Martínez sacked Colonel José Asencio Menéndez, undersecretary of defense, when his opposition to a third term became known. After that, a host of officials resigned: Agustín Alfonso Morán, by then auditor general; Alfonso Rochac, treasury auditor; as well as the undersecretary of public instruction, the chief of the treasury legal staff, the public works undersecretary, the finance undersecretary—and Hermógenes Alvarado. Martínez, unwittingly, had produced the nucleus of a new opposition.[20]

In January 1939 the rubber-stamp National Assembly approved a new constitution with a six-year presidential term, claimed the authority to elect presidents, and decreed a one-time suspension of the ban on consecutive terms. This enabled Martínez to qualify for a term lasting from March 1, 1939 to January 1, 1945, and the Assembly promptly awarded it to him.[21]

After losing the advice of independent-minded cabinet ministers and tampering with the constitution, Martínez surrounded himself with sycophants who told him what he wanted to hear. Ambitious men farther down the ladder found their upward path blocked by presidential cronies who monopolized the top positions. In the military, privileges and opportunities seemed concentrated in a shrinking clique of old-timers whom Martínez trusted, while poorly paid junior officers languished in the ranks.[22]

The president knew full well the dangers of a restive officer corps—he had, after all, been the legatee of a military putsch, and he had no intention of becoming a victim. That only intensified his drive to stock key positions with loyal men, and his spies compiled dossiers detailing financial improprieties of officers, giving the president leverage over them. At least five attempts to overthrow him from within the army between 1934 and 1939 were ferreted out; the last of these, led by the ousted Colonel Mendéndez, was supported by as many as twenty-eight officers.[23]

Other pockets of dissension existed as well. Students and university faculty chafed under the dictator's control of academic appointments and professional licensing. (Students had gone on strike in 1938 to protest the government's attack on university autonomy.) Newspaper editors had long been unhappy with restrictions on what they printed. Together with disenchanted liberals from the coffee elite and disgruntled junior officers, the pieces of a potentially formidable opposition were beginning to fall into place. With the onset of World War II, that opposition would soon coalesce.[24]

"Life Was Full of Ideals"

During the 1930s Martínez and some of his top military men had taken to courting the jack-booted regimes in Hitler's Germany and Mussolini's Italy. The affinities between El Salvador's rulers and Europe's rightists were strong: Both loathed the diverse and unruly aspects of a more open society, and both believed that the threat of communism demanded an iron-fisted response. In 1936 the Germans and Italians began to train Martínez's officers, and Italy traded war planes to El Salvador for coffee. Germans were brought in and given top positions in the military academy and the Mortgage Bank. El Salvador was also one of the first states to recognize General Francisco Franco's regime in Spain and Manchukuo, Japan's puppet state in Manchuria.[25]

Not all Salvadorans were happy with this fascist flirtation. People on the streets of San Salvador shouted insults when several hundred men in black shirts staged a march to celebrate Italy's entrance into the war in June 1940. When the Germans took Paris later that year, university students held a demonstration. Martínez, sensing that the protest was aimed just as much at his own rule, made it a crime to voice support for the Allied war effort.[26]

But romancing the Axis did not pay. The war cut off El Salvador's coffee trade with European countries, aggravating unemployment and interrupting military supplies. The president was forced to tilt toward the Allies. He issued a statement criticizing European totalitarianism, and he fired a number of Nazi sympathizers from government posts. When the United States entered the war in December 1941, El Salvador joined the other countries of Central America in declaring war on the fascist powers.[27]

The regime's new ties to the United States did pay off. The loss of coffee sales in Europe was offset by the stream of greenbacks flowing down from the North. American loans financed road-building and public health improvements; more than 10,000 Salvadorans went to work in the Panama Canal Zone and sent part of their wages back home. An Inter-American Coffee Agreement also raised coffee prices and wages.[28]

But if the war was an economic blessing for the regime, it was also a political nuisance. The newspapers were filled with news of the war and articles by British or North American columnists. An American observer wrote that the San Salvador's daily *El Diario Latino* was able "to conduct an anti-Martínez campaign for a whole year simply by quoting phrases of Roosevelt and Churchill . . . " Two thousand people in the town of San Vicente watched an American propaganda film and then heard an "eloquent pro-democratic speech" by a newspaper editor. The dictator himself felt obliged to mouth the democratic line, though his rhetoric somehow missed the point. Catchphrases like "democracy is highways plus well-being" amused more Salvadorans than they impressed.[29]

One group that soaked up the new democratic line was the officer corps. After a North American replaced a German officer as head of the Military Academy in 1941, democratic ideas started reaching officer candidates. Commissioned officers, already unhappy with the dictatorship, increasingly gravitated toward the U.S. example. Salvador Crespo Sánchez, a young officer who joined the opposition in 1944, remembered those days as a time when "life was full of ideals," when the "struggle of ideas between democracy and totalitarianism" was at high noon.[30]

To try to defuse pressure for reform, the president recast himself as a populist. He gave speeches lamenting the unequal distribution of wealth and said that he was on the side of the poor. Reconstrucción Social, a government-sponsored organization, tried to help shoemakers find work in Panama and held a meeting where workers discussed possible labor legislation. The regime went so far as to impose a new levy on coffee exports, a tax on excess profits, and tighter control over the Cattle Growers' Association, the Coffee Association, and the Mortgage Bank.[31]

None of this really helped Martínez. Labor activists largely ignored his overtures, and trade unions proliferated despite continued harassment. Coffee growers grew uneasy, and some began calling him "the crackpot little Indian"— the first part a reference to the president's eccentric personal practices. He was known, for example, to try to cure illnesses by having people drink water from colored bottles that had sat in the sun for long periods. His own son had died from peritonitis after Martínez insisted on treating him with these waters before permitting an operation—which reportedly provoked his wife to smash all his colored bottles.[32]

The clouds over the regime soon began to darken. Anti-Axis organizations, ostensibly meant to support the war effort, provided ideal cover for meetings of the president's foes. The most important was Acción Democrática Salvadoreña (ADS), which formed in September 1941. Its president was a retired lawyer who had also served as president of the Coffee Growers' Association, and its founding members included Hermógenes Alvarado, Romeo Fortín Magaña, and other former officials in the Martínez government as well as prominent professional men including the young doctor, Arturo Romero.[33]

ADS did not last long aboveground. By the end of September, the government had rammed through a law requiring anyone wanting to hold a political meeting to apply for a permit from the police. Unable to get the needed permission, ADS managed to hold only two public meetings. But members met privately and talked about how Martínez might be denied another term in power. An opposition had formed, and it had a goal: to get rid of the president.[34]

"Let Us Fight"

The new opposition decided to take on the government in plain sight as well as in secret. While some ADS members decided to prepare for military action against Martínez, some chose nonviolent action. Activists distributed a series of anonymous leaflets in the spring and summer of 1943, demanding Martínez's departure, calling for civil liberties, and asking citizens, soldiers, and government employees to stop cooperating with the regime. Workers were reminded of the 1932 massacre and told to resist the government's attempts to co-opt them with meager handouts and halfhearted promises of reform. The leaflets were signed by groups with names like the Democratic Revolutionary Committee and the Workers' Section of the Anti-Reelection Party, and they appeared on the streets until early 1944.[35]

Legal action was another weapon. In October 1943, 236 citizens, including most of the founders of ADS, signed a petition asking the Supreme Court to strike down a 1941 decree restricting political groups. The Court refused to consider the petition, but the public was electrified that the president had been challenged so boldly. According to a U.S. naval attaché, the petition marked the first time that "citizens of influence had come out in the open and said in effect . . . that they were opposed to the Administration." When the petition was printed in *El Diario Latino,* thousands of copies were snatched off newsstands before the police had a chance to confiscate them.[36]

The press added momentum to events by running veiled attacks on the dictatorship. Quotations condemning tyranny from famous names like John Milton and Simón Bolívar and articles blasting a hard-line regime in Argentina telegraphed disdain for the president without running afoul of the censors. Knowing they could not get away with criticizing the constitutional change that let Martínez serve an additional term, the newspapers did the next best thing— they ignored the matter altogether. After prior censorship was imposed in October 1943, editors found ways to keep jabbing at the government. In December *El Diario Latino* came out with a back page full of articles that mocked government propaganda, such as "Street-Cleaning in Capital Superb" and "Water So Plentiful in Villages That It Flows in Veritable Cascades."[37]

Then, late in 1943, a small number of Salvadorans took their opposition into the streets, again using the war as political cover. On December 11 about 400 students and professionals rallied to show support for the establishment of the United Nations, which the Allies had recently proposed. Despite the presence of police and National Guardsmen, the protestors shouted slogans aimed at Martínez: "Death to dictators" and "Down with *continuísmo*" (continuation in office). A speech given by a university student activist was equally transparent: "Let us fight so that governments will reflect the legitimate will of the people; only thus will we live in the democratic century which is now beginning."[38]

During this same period, the president's opponents started appealing for his North American ally to intercede. Alfonso Rochac, now a Mortgage Bank official, gave a letter to Washington's ambassador in El Salvador, Walter Thurston, asking the United States to press the general to respect the constitution, hold free elections, and observe the Atlantic Charter. In March 1944 Hector Herrera, president of the Mortgage Bank, made a proposal to Nelson Rockefeller, who was visiting the country as the U.S. State Department's coordinator of inter-American affairs. The United States, Mexico, and Colombia, Herrera suggested, should intercede with Martínez and urge him to accept a new, democratic constitution.[39]

Martínez fought back hard against the swelling opposition. The government clamped down on the press more tightly and stepped up surveillance of suspected enemies, keeping close watch over signers of the Supreme Court petition. On December 20 men with machine guns appeared on the streets, and forty or so people—including ADS leaders and the editor of *El Diario Latino*—were arrested, some charged with conspiracy to kill the president. One target, Ricardo Arbizú, holed up in his own house for more than a week before surrendering—and before he reportedly received a visit from Agustín Alfaro Morán, who walked away with names of opposition sympathizers in the army.[40]

Besides intimidating its opponents, the government also tried to drum up support for a new Constituent Assembly, to legitimize Martínez's bid to remain in office. A newspaper owned by the dictator claimed that more than 100,000 citizens had signed a petition calling for an Assembly, and noisy crowds at meetings organized by the regime made the same demand. When the Assembly convened in January 1944, it assumed the right to elect the president and voted Martínez back into office—just as everyone expected—for a new term to expire only in 1949. It also added language to the constitution further eroding civil liberties and giving the state sweeping powers over the economy. Salvadorans would have almost six more years of the dictator, and their rights were increasingly circumscribed.[41]

While the ADS and its allies secretly planned a violent move against the regime, an alternative strategy was also offered. Joaquín Castro Canizales, a Salvadoran journalist living in exile in Costa Rica, delivered a proposal to opposition leaders entitled "Toward Civil Disobedience: My Message to the Salvadoran People." He said there was "a decent way to achieve the overthrow of the government," and it was called "PASSIVE RESISTANCE or CIVIL DISOBEDIENCE." It simply required "every citizen" who was part of "the administrative and economic gearing of the country" to drop that role, noting that Gandhi, the "creator of this policy," had achieved "great conquests." To put this into effect, sanctions would be needed, such as winning over soldiers, police, and public employees, as well as precautions, such as stashing away money and essentials in case a prolonged strike was necessary. These ideas made some impression, since they cropped up in anti-Martínez leaflets. But the ADS was not diverted from believing that violence was required.[42]

The prime movers behind the coup were Agustín Alfaro Morán and Arturo Romero. Alfaro's participation was triggered by his outrage at the general's constitutional tricks, but Romero's opposition had different roots. As a student in Paris in the early 1930s, he had absorbed the popular-front spirit of the times, and back in El Salvador he called for a minimum wage and the right of workers to organize. This idealism endeared him to medical students, and his free treatments sanctified him among the poor.

After the coup plotters made contact with army officers who were hatching their own conspiracy, leaders of both the civilian and military groups convened at Alfaro's estate in February 1944 and made final arrangements. Among them were two officers with pro-German sympathies who had played a major part in the 1932 massacres of peasants, General Alfonso Marroquín and his half brother, Colonel Tito Calvo. They set April 2 as the date for the uprising, after army troops had come back from Easter maneuvers.[43]

"Hideously Staccato with Rifle Fire"

April 2, 1944, was Palm Sunday. It was a hazy, still day in San Salvador, which had been abandoned by many families seeking fresh breezes on the coast or at summer places outside the capital. The president was in the coastal town of La Libertad, and most other top officials were gone too. Those who stayed behind in the sweltering capital went to church in the morning to receive the palms that were believed to ward off common hazards like lightning. Around 3:30 in the afternoon, a rumbling noise brought people in the southeastern part of the city into the streets. Military planes were flying low, barely above their houses.[44]

The timing of the coup was shrewd. With Martínez and his key people scattered, their response would be slow. The rebels also had some firepower on their side, including the First Infantry and Second Artillery regiments of San Salvador. For a few hours it looked as if the operation might succeed. Insurgents quickly seized some valuable prizes: the air force, the state radio station, and telegraph offices. In Santa Ana, the largest town in the western part of the country, the garrison went over to the rebellion, while crowds held a demonstration and elected a new city council.[45]

But the insurgents made poor use of these assets. Rebel planes trying to bomb the police headquarters in San Salvador missed their targets and set nearby city blocks ablaze. After seizing the radio station, they went on the air and provided details of the fighting as well as the name of one of the leaders, Arturo Romero. But among the listeners was General Martínez, who gleaned crucial information about which of his units had not joined the rebellion and might stay loyal. The president then raced back to the capital, managing to evade the soldiers sent to take him prisoner, and ordered all electrical transformers disabled, extinguishing lights as darkness descended. Next he went to Fort Zapote, a citadel next to the presidential palace, where he made sure that soldiers there would back him. "If you are not with me, then go right ahead and shoot me," Martínez blustered. The next day the fortress blasted away at the rebel First Infantry, while the president's forces retook the airfield. By Tuesday morning the insurrection was over.[46]

Many rebel leaders were collared, but Romero and Alfaro both managed to escape. The two men were at the radio station Monday afternoon when they learned that the First Infantry had surrendered. They slipped out the back door and went their separate ways. Alfaro went to Santa Ana, which was full of drunken Salvadorans who had been prematurely celebrating the coup. The doctor hid out in the homes of patients for several days, before fleeing for the Honduran border on Friday.[47]

The president dispatched the coup easily enough, but the moves he made afterward showed that he was rattled. Meetings of clubs and unions were banned, and homes were searched without warning. In the capital, "nights were hideously staccato with rifle fire. Platoons of heavily armed police patrolled the city. Prisoners were rounded up and herded to the police station, from which grisly tales of torture emerged." Police and government agents snooped into bank transactions and made people leaving or entering the city show an official pass. Signers of the Supreme Court petition were unable to get permission to leave the city or take out the legal papers necessary to conduct business. The government, according to U.S. Ambassador Thurston, seemed to be on a crusade to "destroy the livelihood of many of the professional classes."[48]

Journalists were another group that paid a heavy price. Santa Ana's *Diario de Occidente* had too hastily printed an article on April 2 announcing the ouster of Martínez and his replacement by Romero, and its editor landed in jail. Jorge Pinto, editor of *El Diario Latino,* who was already in custody when the coup attempt began, was shot by guards on April 2 and later died. Several other journalists were either arrested or fled to safety, and all three of the capital's opposition papers stopped publication for several weeks.[49]

The repression went well beyond what was necessary to reestablish the president's authority. Leaning toward vindictiveness rather than sweetening his victory with magnanimity, he had more than 800 people from San Salvador hauled off to prison. An Extraordinary Council of War took just a few hours to sentence ten officers to death; the next morning rifle shots rang out from the cemetery as the men were executed. Twenty-five more officers and nine civilians received death sentences over the next two weeks. Martínez even had General Marroquín's son witness his father's execution.[50]

Victor Manuel Marín was one civilian who fell victim to the firing squad. In the insurrection he had coordinated the active fighters and civilian planners. After being caught, his captors—hoping to pry secrets about the conspiracy from him—broke his arms, smashed his knee, gouged out one of his eyes, and performed other gruesome acts. Later he had to be propped up at his own execution. When Father León Montoya, who performed the last rites, asked him, "Victor, are you afraid of death?" Marín said, "No, Father, it is my body and not my spirit that is shaking."[51]

All Latin America took notice of what was happening in El Salvador that April. Foreign diplomats called on the president on April 17 to ask for lenient treatment for the rebels; petitions urging the same thing came in from the Venezuelan Chamber of Deputies, from the Mexican labor leader, Vicente Lombardo Toledano, and from a group of Latin American doctors in Baltimore, Maryland. Newspapers in several countries lambasted the bloody crackdown, and it even drew a protest from the world-famous poet Pablo Neruda.[52]

The United States, too, could not ignore what had happened. The "Good Neighbor" policy espoused by President Roosevelt, and the natural disinclination to criticize an Allied government during wartime, dictated noninterference, but embassy staffers had personal contacts with opposition leaders and appreciated their democratic rhetoric. "The principal defect of a policy of nonintervention accompanied by propaganda on behalf of democratic doctrines," Ambassador Thurston wrote, "is that it simultaneously stimulates dictatorships and popular opposition to them." He rued inaction that implied accepting "dictators who seize or retain power unconstitutionally," saying it would "not only impair our moral leadership but foment the belief that our democratic professions are empty propaganda and that we are in fact simply guided by expediency." It would not be the last time in the twentieth century when this dilemma visited Washington.[53]

Thurston had to walk a fine line, and he was tested when Colonel Tito Calvo and one other officer who had joined the rebellion came to the embassy and requested asylum. Thurston allowed them in but refused asylum. That same evening he spoke with Martínez and agreed to turn the men over, getting the assurance that they would be given lawful treatment; later he asked Martínez to show clemency toward the men. But Calvo and his comrade were among those shot on April 10. That was the last straw for Thurston; Martínez had run out his string with the Americans.[54]

"A Movement Not of the Streets"

Within a fortnight of the insurrection, Martínez seemed unassailable once again, but the ambitious scope of the abortive coup revealed that leading Salvadorans— among them bank administrators, coffee magnates, and military officers—were willing to endanger their own lives to bring down the president. Morever, the president's brutal reaction alarmed other Salvadorans who before had only been onlookers. The U.S. military attaché noted that "market people, shop keepers and civilians" were decrying executions and torture.[55]

Even among government officials still associated with Martínez, doubts about his capacity to govern were growing. A U.S. Embassy staff member reported that the finance minister had criticized the postcoup blood-letting, and other ministers harbored misgivings. The diplomat concluded that "a feeling of apprehension, doubt and fear is developing among the ranks of the President's followers . . . not only because they feel the President's position is . . . vengeful and likely to prove ruinous to all interests, but also because these men . . . are beginning to think of their own personal and economic safety in the event that the Government is . . . overturned."[56]

If renewed resistance to the regime could be mounted, it might have fresh support in unexpected places. But first new leaders would have to be found, because the coup's instigators were dead, in jail, or on the lam. For years student groups had done political organizing, and students had been key players in anti-Martínez leafleting the previous year. When classes resumed after Easter break, news that Arturo Romero had been captured galvanized the students. The intrepid doctor had lain low in the capital for several days after the rebellion's collapse and then had tried to escape to Honduras. But his disguise as a laborer did not fool the National Guardsmen at the border. They set upon him with machetes and then brought him to a hospital in San Miguel, where his true identity was learned. There sympathetic doctors delayed pronouncing him fit to travel, knowing that he would be executed as soon as he recovered.[57]

As Romero lay recuperating, it took university students a week or more to work out a strategy to challenge the government. They realized it would be suicidal to confront the regime's armed units and that the dictator should not be given the chance to use violence. "The fundamental thesis," remembered Fabio Castillo, one of the student leaders, was that Martínez "was capable of defeating anyone militarily. Therefore, it was necessary to organize a popular movement that did not confront Martínez, so that he would not have anyone

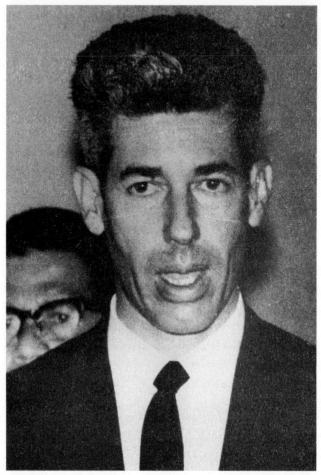

Fabio Castillo, one of the student leaders of the civic strike in El Salvador in 1944;
seen here in 1967 as a presidential candidate.

Credit: ©Bettmann/CORBIS

to shoot. This led to the conclusion that the movement should be a movement
not of the streets, but of hiding. And the *huelga de brazos caídos* [strike of fallen
arms] emerged. Nobody do anything. Simply stay [indoors] without going into
the streets, so that there would not be possibilities for repression."[58]

Medical students returned to school after April 17 wearing black ties, as a show
of mourning for those executed by the government and of concern for Romero,
whose own execution seemed likely. During those first days, some of the students
hit on the idea of a strike; the suggestion also came up at a meeting of law students
and began to circulate around other university departments. A number of leaders
emerged during these days: Castillo and Jorge Bustamente of the medical school;

Galindo Pohl and Jorge Mazzini of the law school; Raúl Castellanos from the engineering school; and Mario Colorado from school of pharmacy.[59]

Two different groups directed the student movement. One consisted of forty or so delegates, elected from the departments. The other was a smaller central committee, which circulated a public leaflet on April 19. "We are not in a position to provoke a revolution," it admitted, "but there are methods, which however unlawful they may be, could be considered honorable and praiseworthy ... We are fighting with an astute and sagacious man ... then to this astuteness and sagacity let us oppose ours, which because it is that of an entire people ... will now take by force that which has been usurped, ITS LIBERTIES."[60]

The students' secret organizing continued all that week. On Monday, April 24, a second wave of executions occurred—giving students a renewed sense of urgency. They assembled, voted to strike, and issued an anonymous statement declaring that they would not only suspend academic activities but also cease their work outside the university.

The strike leaders recognized that if they were serious about confronting the general, they would have to broaden the movement. A student strike in 1938-1939 had not accomplished much; "strikes of intellectuals were merely symbolic," Galindo Pohl remarked. What they needed, if they were going to force real change, was to build toward a general strike by all kinds of people. Castillo was the first to raise the idea, which was debated at central committee meetings during the week after April 24.[61]

The strategy was essentially what the exiled journalist Castro Canizales had suggested earlier to the ADS, only to have it ignored. To the students, who were familiar with the concept if not from Castro Canizales then from other sources, it made practical sense. First, they had no weapons so they knew they could not defeat Martínez that way. Second, they understood that the public could join them in nonviolent action, which might also win support from other interests. They went out of their way, for example, to inform the U.S. Embassy that they meant to lead a peaceful movement and would avoid bloodshed.[62]

May 5 was set as the day by which they hoped everyone would be on strike. Getting word of it to as many people as possible was complicated by constraints on the press and the atmosphere of fear that pervaded San Salvador in the weeks after the coup attempt. But medical students had close ties to doctors, law students to lawyers, and so forth, and they used those connections to propagate the idea of a general strike. They also typed up leaflets urging citizens to strike. Each bore a request that the reader make ten new copies and pass them along. Secretaries obliged, banging away on their typewriters, and children distributed the copied leaflets on the street—they "flaunted the seditious sheets before the police and dared them to make an arrest."[63]

Students also reached outside their professional circles to railroad workers, immigrant Palestinian shopkeepers, and other groups. Once the idea caught fire, the students received substantial help. Market women—described by Ambassador Thurston as "a formidable factor in the less polite strata of Salvadoran politics"—went around to shops and persuaded owners to close up. One banker approached a taxi driver and asked him to let other drivers know that money would be available to any who joined the strike.[64]

But organizers understood that individuals' enthusiasm alone had little chance of reaching enough people to shut down San Salvador, let alone the rest of the country. The strike would have to expand of its own accord, and for that to happen, the services and institutions on which people relied would have to be affected. If the strikers could shut down establishments like banks and drugstores, they could force every person to take notice and decide whether to side with the dictator or the people. A doctors' strike would have great impact, given their prestige. Transportation was also a critical target. Since the students were focusing on the capital, the only way that people elsewhere were likely to see the strike take hold was if trains failed to arrive in local stations (a tactic reminiscent of Moscow rail workers spreading their strike across Russia in October 1905).[65]

To do the hundred and one things that promoting the strike required, the students needed money, and when the strike began, they needed a way to get support to striking workers who might otherwise be unwilling to lay down their tools. Some initial funds came from the official student organization, and soon contributions were flowing in from off campus. Especially helpful was a finance committee that included Héctor Herrera, president of the Mortgage Bank, and Roberto Alvarez, a coffee magnate. Reportedly $20,000 was rounded up in thirty minutes at the affluent Club Salvadoreño.[66]

The movement picked up steam as soon as students started boycotting classes the last week of April, when students were also no-shows at jobs outside the university. Law students stayed away from courts where they had to attend sessions, while engineering students refused to report for work at the government agencies that employed them. Hospital interns also began to stay home, as did school teachers. After the strike began, secondary school students also walked out.[67]

One of the striking students was José Napoleón Duarte, a future president of El Salvador and the son of the labor organizer. "I became directly involved in the student movement against General Hernández Martínez," Duarte wrote later in his autobiography. When university students went to his high school and asked for delegates to a coordinating group, he became one, attending meetings that were raided by police. "To escape once, I raced down into a ravine, leaped a fence and landed on spiny thorns, tearing my clothes and my skin . . . The day of the general strike, our committee set out to create a disturbance at the school to force the suspension of classes . . . The strike was successful. No one went to school that day . . . "[68]

As the strike wave grew, the regime floundered. One official reported that none of his colleagues saw the strike coming, and they had no idea what to do. The president's top officials were now lined up against any violent repression. Although an order had come down before the end of April to arrest student organizers, the police had done nothing more than briefly detain a few people caught with leaflets. Some police officers went to private homes to try to force strikers to go to their jobs, but others were plainly ambivalent. Some even sympathized with the strike and did their best to help organizers avoid arrest.[69]

Even had the police been eager, crushing the strike immediately would have been difficult; it was simply expanding too fast. The regime seemed content to sit and wait until strikers had to go back to their jobs out of simple need. In the hope of defusing some of the underlying anger, the government announced it was releasing all the prisoners taken after the failed insurrection, and it tried to discredit the strike, via articles in regime-controlled newspapers, by describing it as a movement of rich and powerful people who neglected the needs of the poor.[70]

None of this stemmed the strike's momentum or erased the outrage inspired by the recent executions and the longer history of arbitrary rule by Martínez. The Salvadoran elite was now concerned that if the general was not stopped, the killings would go on. Trepidation about bucking the regime was outweighed by fear that anyone might meet a firing squad. And for many people outside the elite, the threat to the life of Arturo Romero, the gallant physician, had become a goad to action.[71]

Soon Romero's fellow doctors entered the vanguard of the movement, just as the student organizers hoped they would. They had their own grievances against Martínez, who had ordered the dismissal of several doctors suspected of subversive activities. Luís Macías, the director of the public hospital, called a staff meeting on May 2, and he and the doctors drafted demands. They would strike, they declared, unless all death sentences were commuted and an amnesty proclaimed, the fired doctors were reinstated, and "democratic principles" were honored by the government. Martínez received the demands personally and had them burned while Macías looked on.[72]

On May 5, 135 doctors (out of a total of 150 in San Salvador) walked off their jobs. Sixty of them had signed a new statement, a blunt demand that the president step down and that free elections be held. Emergency clinics remained open, and some doctors continued to see a few patients; "the rich paid through the nose," reported William Krehm, "the poor only nominally, and the proceeds went into the strike fund." Also walking out by May 5 were lawyers, pharmacists, and bank, railroad, and electric-utility employees. Hundreds of civil servants followed suit. The Sanitation Department announced it had to suspend all nonessential services. Already on strike were dentists, engineers, and technicians of the Public Health Service and theater employees.[73]

Not everyone who joined the strike did so with great fervor. Some Palestinian and Chinese shopkeepers, apparently, were reluctant to close their doors because they feared reprisals. One of the student activists, José Colorado, threw stones at stores whose owners wanted an excuse for closing down. Others kept their doors open but refused to sell goods. Many working people also held back, since the strike threatened to cut off desperately needed wages and expose them to retaliation. Railway engineers told Fabio Castillo that they would not join the movement unless they got their full salaries in advance and their families were hidden in safe houses. Yet enough San Salvadorans of all classes participated for the strike to be remembered, decades later, as a display of popular unity against the president. "Even the thieves were on strike," recalled one striker.[74]

For more than two weeks after their return to school, the university students who had spearheaded the strike had done their utmost to avoid any physical confrontation with the regime. While they had reason to believe that Martínez could not count on the loyalty of many police and soldiers, they held off from testing that belief at the possible cost of lives. Street demonstrations were therefore not part of the strategy. Students and widows of the executed officers did, however, organize a mass for the regime's victims on May 5, at the downtown Church of the Rosary. An overflow crowd showed up, and the church and the square outside were filled with women in black. When the mourners learned that the mass had been banned, they left and fanned out across the city, persuading more merchants to shutter their shops.[75]

This great civic strike, the most impressive of its kind in Latin American history, had been driven by a decentralized campaign, relying on a cascade of individuals contacting and recruiting one another. But now that it was a force to be reckoned with, some kind of executive organization, to speak for strikers and negotiate with the regime, was needed. On the night of May 5, at the home of Hermógenes Alvarado, people representing students, market women, banks, the professions, commercial employees, day laborers, and bus and taxi drivers met and elected a slightly less representative National Reconstruction Committee. It had five members: a student, a physician, a Mortgage Bank attorney, a commercial employee, and a retired general. The next day the Committee came up with a list of demands, while offering the president a guarantee of safety and suggesting that he leave El Salvador. The opposition was now organized and flexing its muscles.[76]

While the regime still had not done anything decisive to quell the resistance, neither did it show any signs of yielding. The general addressed the nation over the radio, hailing those who were still working and accusing strike leaders of trying to "sow panic in the different social classes." The next day a leaflet announced the formation of a "Workers Anti-Revolutionary Committee," and Martínez called on business owners to open their doors once again. The dictator, who had so recently aroused great fear, was now reduced to beseeching his people to do what he asked.[77]

Martínez seemed to be losing his appetite for intimidation, telling one official to "avoid trouble" with strikers. "In the first days of April, I defeated the insurrectionists with arms, but finally they provoked a strike," the general said in an interview shortly after the strike ended. "Then I no longer wanted to fight. At whom was I going to fire? At children and youths who did not completely realize what they were doing?" The general who had not blanched at the killing of thousands of peasants a decade before could not use his weapons when his moment of greatest peril arrived.

The moment also still appeared perilous to strikers. On May 6 the U.S. Embassy learned that groups of men were going around to striking stores and forcing them to open up. Some doctors received anonymous threats, and there were rumors that machete-wielding peasants were on their way to the city, to provoke violence that would legitimize a military crackdown. But when bloodshed did come, it was not fomented by the regime. It happened when a nervous police officer opened fire on youths who had gathered in the street on May 7. Seventeen-year-old José Wright, from a well-established Salvadoran family and a U.S. citizen thanks to his American father, was killed on the spot. Thousands showed up at his family's home to pay their respects and again the next morning at his funeral.[78]

The tragedy was an opportunity for the strike leaders. Still uncertain whether they could unhinge the regime before the strike began to simmer down, they had thought about bringing people out on the streets and forcing a moment of truth. The Wright killing did exactly that. Following the funeral, San Salvador-ans flooded into the Plaza Barrios, just outside the building where the National Assembly and government offices were housed. They were full of wrath, and student leaders had their hands full restraining people. But the Guardsmen patrolling the plaza did nothing to ruffle the crowd, and there was no violence.[79]

The murdered boy's citizenship was no doubt on the mind of the U.S. ambassador when he called on Martínez to see if those responsible could be found and punished, and many were convinced that Washington would have to intervene. That was not in the cards, but the shooting was a catalyst for change inside the regime. Most of the president's ministers met on the evening of May

7 and decided they had to resign. They were nervous that crowds in the streets would draw a new round of violence—and indeed the next morning, the army chief of staff informed Martínez that his forces were ready to clear the streets. One of the ministers objected and told the president, "We cannot join you in any violent measure." The president replied that "against the people, I am not going to take any violent measure. If the people now want me to retire, I am willing to do it without difficulty."[80]

Exit

By midmorning on May 8, Martínez knew that if he wanted to salvage anything, the time had come to talk to the opposition. It took no time to round up the five members of the National Reconstruction Committee, who sat down with government officials later that morning. That the president would step down was now assumed, but when, and under what circumstances? Martínez offered to leave at the end of the month, three weeks later. But the opposition was adamant about immediate resignation; they insisted the strike would go on for as long as he remained in power.[81]

Martínez proposed leaving the choice of his successor to the National Assembly, a body he had thoroughly dominated. The Committee members countered by presenting him with a list of four men from whom he could choose one. After another hour of talks with ministers, they added a fifth name— General Andrés Menéndez, the minister of war and a stalwart Martínez loyalist; in fact, he was probably the president's own choice. But as a mild-mannered man with a reputation for integrity and no real thirst for power, he doubtless looked appealing after years of a headstrong dictator. The Committee, one of its members later claimed, also managed to extract promises that the new president would lift the state of siege, declare an amnesty, and allow exiles to come home.[82]

Martínez refused the deal and kept insisting that he stay in office until the end of May. Out on the streets, there were rumors that the general was maneuvering to cling to power and might use force. Someone from a second committee claiming to speak for the strikers reportedly spoke with the president in the late afternoon and warned him that "there would be a great deal of bloodshed" if he did not resign on the spot. Cabinet officers continued to prod him to leave immediately. For whatever reason, he agreed and went on the radio at 7:00 P.M. to announce that he was resigning.[83]

The next morning the National Assembly passed the presidency to Menéndez, who promised constitutional reform and speedy elections; the Assembly also approved an amnesty for those accused of political crimes. Students and many others were not quite ready to end the strike, not until Martínez had actually left the country—and they were unhappy with the new cabinet, which included several Martínez appointees and only one person associated with the National Reconstruction Committee, Hermógenes Alvarado. But Menéndez dampened any remaining militance by promising that the dictator would be gone the next day. Realizing the country was exhausted, the students called off the strike. On May 11 buses and trains began running again, stores and offices reopened, and people returned to work. Just one thing was different: A little before noon Maximiliano Hernández Martínez crossed into Guatemala, and he never came back.[84]

El Salvador's triumph over tyranny proved to be ephemeral. There was a brief window of political openness, and Romero and Alfaro, the chief plotters of the insurrection, became the leading players in trying to consolidate civilian government before elections in January 1945. But the resolve of Romero and his supporters to achieve genuine reform split the coalition that had ousted Martínez. The military was unwilling to follow the general out of the corridors of power, and the coffee growers refused to expose their interests to the vagaries of democratic politics. In October 1944 a coup led by a colonel who was head of the National Police seized power from Menéndez. The opposition mounted nonviolent resistance over several weeks, but then discarded the lessons of the civic strike and tried an armed attack from Guatemala in December, only to be handily defeated.[85]

A new kind of military rule ensnared El Salvador in the decades after World War II: The intensely personal command of a single general was replaced by a collective, institutional control. But the government still wore a uniform—and the aroma of coffee fortunes still infused economic life.[86]

The political legacy of the civic strike was fleeting, yet it had been a formative moment for many young Salvadorans, who were heard from again. Fabio Castillo became a civilian member of a short-lived reformist junta in 1960, then served as rector of the University of El Salvador from 1963 to 1967 and was the 1967 presidential candidate of the Renovating Action Party. José Napoleón Duarte, the high school activist, went on to form El Salvador's moderate Christian Democratic Party and was elected president of the republic in 1984. Many would-be Salvadoran saviors vied for power in these long twilight decades of military dominance and civil conflict, but not until the 1990s were the voice and influence of the people ever expressed as clearly as they had been in the spring of 1944.[87]

૭ ૭ ૭

The combined breadth and speed of the Salvadoran people's nonviolent coup, to remove a president that violence had not dislodged, had no equal during the twentieth century. To be sure, the country is small, it had only one major city at the time, and the movement that arose against Martínez had willing accomplices in entrenched parts of Salvadoran society. But nothing as serious as taking down a dictator is a sure-fire thing. The sudden success of the civic strike did not mean that the astute strategic moves of its leaders were not important; in fact, they made it possible.

The contours of the coalition against Martínez had formed gradually as the autocrat's own actions alienated one group after another. Organized labor, political radicals, and disgruntled elements within the military had resented Martínez from the beginning. Many journalists had become hostile after their freedom was curbed. The antagonism of professionals, university students, and even many government ministers surfaced when Martínez refused to relinquish his office after two terms and became increasingly arbitrary and unpredictable. Finally, the big landowners were disillusioned by the president's shift to populism and marginalized by his concentration of authority in the hands of a tight coterie. All these divergent groups of Salvadorans became available to support a common objective—the dictator's dethronement.

But nonviolent resistance is not adventitious; it has to be planned and instigated. Opposition leaders emerged from the professions, the press, and the university student body, and they capitalized on the international political climate of World War II to rouse support for democracy, foster dissension within the military, and cultivate a network of sympathizers. Through ADS, financial institutions, university clubs, and newspaper offices, the movement developed support from the general public, diplomats, and influential citizens. The Supreme Court petition awoke the country to the fact that contending with Martínez was possible, even honorable. Without this sustained and patient work to challenge the regime, the civic strike would have been a game played in an empty arena.

The strike would also have been more difficult to organize had the president not overplayed his hand after the April 2 coup attempt. The armed insurrection had failed, and opposition leaders were on the run. When the general turned to violent retribution, many felt that they had to get him before he got them—and saving Romero and others from the firing squad became an object that brought working people into the movement and lent a sense of urgency to everything. The hanging sword of violence had kept people in line for years, but once death became promiscuous, the people's tolerance for the executioner was extinguished. Gandhi knew that as the soldiers of the raj responded to Indian resisters with deadly force, the repressive face of British rule would be revealed—and resistance would grow. Thus, in El Salvador, it would also prove to be.

When the opportunity to act decisively arose, the university students managed to improvise a strategy. They knew of nonviolent campaigns in India,

Chile, and Cuba in the 1930s, and they realized that Martínez's power rested on his ability to use violence to subdue opponents. So they chose not only to confront the regime without weapons, they avoided exposing people to the risk of attack. As Castillo explained, "it was necessary to organize a popular movement which did not confront Martínez, so that he would not have anyone to shoot"—a line echoed by the dictator himself, who later said ruefully, "There was no longer a target at which to fire." In the end, nonviolent action worked where violence had failed, because it marshaled a stronger opposition, it circumvented the regime's methods of coercion, and it discouraged the general's collaborators from opting for repression.[88]

A force more powerful than violence brought Martínez down, but it did not automatically create conditions for a stable civilian, democratic government. Removing the general at the top did not bridle the power of the military. The opposition had not had time to consolidate the basis for popular power in El Salvador—as Gandhi had tried to invigorate Indians with swaraj and constructive work in India, and as the dissident and trade union movements would later broaden the back of autonomous power in Poland. If it had been able to do so, the movement might have learned to be more resilient, or, in a contrary result, a more ambitious program might have alienated reformist army officers, former Martínez officials, and once-sympathetic coffee growers.

The Salvadoran strike was aimed at a leader, not a system. Once he was gone, those who yearned for true democracy found themselves with new opportunities but without old allies. Nonviolent action can force out rulers who have lost the consent of the people, but if the strategy behind it does not include changing the underlying structure of power that sustained those rulers, it may not propel the people's cause beyond the conflict. Still, in 1944 in El Salvador, the people prevailed, without violence. For that country, in that time, it was a new kind of victory.

CHAPTER SEVEN

Argentina and Chile: Resisting Repression

ARGENTINA—MOTHER COURAGE

"We Will Walk Until We Drop"

ON THE FIRST DAY, there were only fourteen in the resistance force—an improbable troop of women in their middle years, anonymous and ordinary, filled with anxiety, not knowing whether the gray hand of authority would crush them or merely brush them away. Through the equinoctial light of that autumn afternoon, this half-platoon filed across the stone paths of the city's most historic square, collecting near the obelisk erected to celebrate the nation's nineteenth century break with Spanish rule.

They had gone to the Plaza de Mayo, in the civic heart of Buenos Aires, in search of another kind of independence—freedom from an uncertainty more haunting than grief. They still hoped that what they had experienced was a cruel anomaly, perhaps beyond the doing or even knowledge of their leaders. It was to give voice to that loss, and to implore the government's help, that they had appeared on this last day of April 1977 on the plaza outside the Casa Rosada.

"We arrived separately," recalled one of the women, Maria del Rosario de Cerruti. "We wore flat shoes so we could make a run for it if they came after us. To demonstrate in front of Government House was very dangerous." But they were linked as securely as climbers on a rock cliff by the rope line of what they had in common: All were mothers; all had children who had disappeared.[1]

No one bothered them on that first day. It was a Saturday. Unaccustomed to the schedule of business, the mothers had inadvertently picked a time when the doors of the banks and government offices, of the pink presidential palace, would be closed. "We agreed to return . . . on a weekday and to prepare a letter together to send to Videla," the Argentine general then sitting as president. They settled on a time—half-past three the next Friday, when the streets would be crowded. Then one of the mothers reminded them that Friday was said to be the day of the witches, so they settled on Thursday.[2]

The women, whose number soon grew to several score, already sensed that they were testing a surface without knowing what was beneath. Many others elsewhere in the world who had lived under dictators could have told them what was below: the mendacity of authoritarian control. In the clear air, life in Argentina proceeded as it always had. Given the façade of normalcy, the regime seemed unassailable. No one appeared eager to penetrate it, except now for these desperate women.

Not until two months later, after weekly demonstrations, were three mothers allowed to see the minister of the interior, a general who said he had a file with the names of people who had disappeared, that it contained names from even his friends' families. But he did not know who had taken them; he said "that there were para-military groups out there who couldn't be controlled," Rosario recalled. "He passed the responsibility to other people. Then he said that perhaps our sons had run away with a woman, that perhaps our daughters were working as prostitutes somewhere."[3]

At that moment, it seems, the women's fear gave way to anger. "We told him that they were cowards, because even a cruel dictator like Franco had signed the death sentences with his own hand . . . We told him everything we felt and we told him that we would come back every week until they gave us an answer and that we would walk in the square every Thursday until we dropped." When the general told them public meetings were prohibited by the state of siege then in effect, they told him they would stay until he gave them an answer. Although they did not know it, these grieving women had declared war.

Coups, Kidnappings, and Chaos

The mothers' enemy was a military government whose tangled roots reached back half a century. Through much of the 1930s and 1940s, military dictatorships had waxed, declined, and revived the length and breadth of Latin America. Now and then, a long-sitting autocrat would be tossed out, as with El Salvador's

Maximiliano Hernández Martínez. Elsewhere military men rode high in the saddle, the stern alternative, many thought, to chaos.

Argentina saw eight military coups between 1930 and 1973, with only two free elections, in 1946 and 1951. Ironically, the man who voters elevated to the presidency was another general, Juan Domingo Peron. His blend of working-class populism and nightclub polish appealed to Argentines' flair for contradictions. Sporting a flashy wife, Evita, he was a new thing in Latin political culture: a matinee idol with epaulets—and he created, in his legions of Peronistas, a political movement so raucous and discontented as to render the country almost ungovernable. The style of power that he planted, watered by the polarities of the Cold War, would sprout into a vine of terror two decades later. In 1955, as his welcome expired, Peron was swept into Spanish exile by another general, soon toppled by another, and he by yet another.[4]

In 1966 a junta led by General Juan Carlos Onganía rode in, proscribing politics and parties, countering strikes with armed force, and ending the traditional autonomy of universities. All this invited riots and disturbances, and secret militias on the right were joined in the field by leftist counterparts: The Montoneros, spun off from the suppressed Peronistas, brought kidnappings and car bombs to the cities, and the People's Revolutionary Army (Ejército Revolucionario del Pueblo, or ERP), which described its philosophy as Guevarist, after Che, made trouble in the rural Tucumán province. In 1970, after the Montoneros kidnapped and murdered a former president, Onganía was evicted by another general, who in turn was replaced by another, Alejandro Agustin Lanusse. But none of the uniforms were able to produce economic stability or subdue the violent left. Lanusse was pressured to set elections, in effect opening the way for Juan Peron's return.

Chaos was Peron's natural habitat, and he stepped back into office in 1973, with his third wife, Maria Estela Martinez de Peron (called Isabel) as vice president. The new government turned like a lion on the left and tried to shore up the economy, but Argentina's extremists would not abandon their fratricidal war, and then Peron's body abandoned him. His heart failed in July 1974, leaving his inexperienced widow at the helm. The new president steered clumsily for the rocks, as the global skyrocketing of oil prices helped drive inflation to 3,000 percent per year by 1976.[5]

Meanwhile, a ruinous symbiosis had evolved between the hard-liners of left and right. The Montoneros stormed an army barracks in the city of Formosa, the ERP campaigned to seize Tucumán, and on the right, the Alianza Anticomunista Argentina murdered seventy intellectuals and lawyers during 1974 (and by 1975 had stepped up its killings to about fifty per week). Both sides bankrolled themselves by more kidnappings, robberies, and extortion. In late 1974 Isabel

Peron untied the army's hands. Five thousand troops marched on Tucumán to crush a hundred or so ERP rebels. With webs of spies and paramilitaries, the army fashioned a kind of clandestine armed service, licensed to do whatever was necessary. Within a few months the violence in Argentina had been quenched. But the army was slow to return to the garrison. In 1975-1976, when the nation tipped toward mayhem again, the military showed Isabel the exit. In her place stood a junta headed by General Jorge Rafael Videla, the army commander—and what was to come would be even more fearful.[6]

"The Country Was Feudalized"

With a flourish, Videla unveiled the Argentine Process of National Reorganization (the Proceso), promising to restore "the morality, competence, and efficiency" needed to reconstruct "the content and image of the nation." But to serve these high ends, the Proceso used low means: The congress, provincial governments, and Supreme Court were dissolved, political or trade union activity was forbidden, and civilians were made subject to trial by military courts.[7]

The prime directive of the Proceso was to obliterate subversion, and this meant all-out war—a dirty war, using any means. And who was the enemy? "A terrorist," President Videla explained, "isn't just someone with a gun or bomb." A subversive was "anyone who opposes the Argentine way of life." In every region the Proceso implanted covert detention centers and special task forces trained to capture and interrogate suspects. "First we will kill all the subversives," explained the military governor of Buenos Aires, "then we will kill their collaborators; then . . . their sympathizers, then . . . those who remain indifferent; and finally we will kill the timid."[8]

But killing was not enough. Guerrillas by definition move through the population like fish in the sea; to wipe them out, the ocean either had to be emptied or poisoned. The junta's poison of choice was a campaign of state-sponsored terror. It would employ the usual techniques of kidnappings, interrogation, torture, and secret detention. From the days of Onganía, making people disappear—into the forests, into the Rio de la Plata, into the ocean from helicopters—had been a favorite tool of both the left and the right. Disappearances had risen from only a handful in 1971 to a few hundred in 1975, then abruptly into four figures. In time, as many as 30,000 Argentines would disappear, and each disappearance was concealed and denied; survivors were left with only an empty place, as if the loved one had never existed.[9]

Typically, victims were taken by a squad of armed men in mufti, arriving in a fleet of blue Ford Falcons, which became their signature car. At first they worked only late at night, but as they smelled the fear rising around them, they began snatching people in broad daylight. The disappeared were driven to detention centers to extract information that few really had, as doctors stood by to ensure that torture did not produce death too soon; then followed weeks or months of further maltreatment and eventually execution. According to an Argentine report a decade later, victims endured the "meticulous and deliberate stripping of all human attributes . . ."[10]

As repression evolved, the apparatus of terror took on a life of its own. People were disappeared because they were only a few degrees of separation from another disappeared person. Each detention center was a law unto itself and used its own arbitrary criteria to identify its prey. "In those days," recalled a former political prisoner, "the country was feudalized; there were guys decorated by the First Corps, kidnapped in the Second, killed by the Third, and vindicated by the Fifth." The terror was also egalitarian: It might favor the taking of journalists, lawyers, academics, and politicians, but it also did not shrink from putting ordinary men, women, and children through its dehumanizing sieve.[11]

"The Military Have Taken Our Children"

At first the mothers of the disappeared felt only numb loss. Some were so shattered they could not eat, sleep, or rise from bed. But as they realized that no one else would solve the mystery of their missing children for them, they began a melancholy migration from the world of their families and homes out onto Argentina's cold plains of political lawlessness.

One by one they asked at first only where their children had been taken and when they might be seen again. Sometimes they had a writ of habeas corpus, a fundamental right of common law, which, they soon discovered, had disappeared along with their sons and daughters. As the epidemic of disappearances spread, families and friends distanced themselves from the survivors, who wandered as pariahs through the labyrinths of government. Yet the mothers knew that they were not alone: If they had no one else, they had each other.

Ironically, this realization came as they sat in a room in the Interior Ministry. There a sympathetic policewoman would take down their names, addresses, the names of their missing children, the names of their associates— names, the mothers realized too late, that would become grist for the mill of terror. Before they left the ministry, however, they had begun to shed their reticence and talk to each other, to share their unspeakable stories. Soon they were meeting in homes, as, almost without their knowing it, grief began to bind them into an association, a force.

Compelled to look behind the curtain of normalcy, the mothers glimpsed something that exceeded in horror even their personal losses: a national campaign of death carried out with the acquiescence of the judiciary, neighboring states, and even the Catholic Church. Short on political experience, they were nonetheless equipped with a fine maternal intuition. They understood immediately that this campaign was sustained less by the junta's physical might than by the frightened stillness of victims' families. So, searching for a weapon they might raise against this enemy, they resolved to deny the junta what it most needed: silence.

"Our first problem was how we were going to organize meetings if we didn't know each other," recalled Dora de Bazze. "There were so many police and security men everywhere that you never knew who was standing next to you. It was very dangerous. So we carried different things so we could identify each other. For example one would hold a twig in her hand, one might carry a small purse instead of a handbag, one would pin a leaf to her lapel, anything to let us know this was a Mother."[12]

The women also printed leaflets that told people where they were going to be, and signs that asked "Where are our disappeared children?" or declared "The military have taken our children." Dora de Bazze remembered that they "went out at night to stick them on the buses and underground trains . . . And we wrote messages on peso notes so that as many people as possible would see them . . . There was nothing in the newspapers; if a journalist reported us, he disappeared; the television and radio were completely under military control, so people weren't conscious."[13]

Azucena de Villaflor de De Vincente quickly emerged as the first leader of the mothers. She was not totally inexperienced—her parents had been trade union leaders and Peronistas. But, once married, she had become a homemaker, never looking outward—until 1976, when her Peronist son, Néstor and his wife, Raquel, were disappeared. From that moment on she was a whirlwind, rallying the mothers, offering her home as a meeting place, organizing letter-writing campaigns to Amnesty International and the Inter-American Commission on Human Rights. It was she who suggested that they take their grievance into the bright light of the Plaza de Mayo and, like a flock of ancient mariners, tell their story.

"At first we didn't march together in the square," remembered Maria del Rosario. "We sat on the benches with our knitting or stood in small groups . . . We had to speak to each other quickly, in low voices so it didn't look as if we were having a meeting. Then, when the police . . . began pointing their rifles at us and telling us to move on . . . we began to walk in twos around the edge of the square . . . There were so few of us we were hardly noticed and we had to make sure the public knew we existed. We wanted people to see us . . . so we began to walk in the center of the square, around the monument."[14]

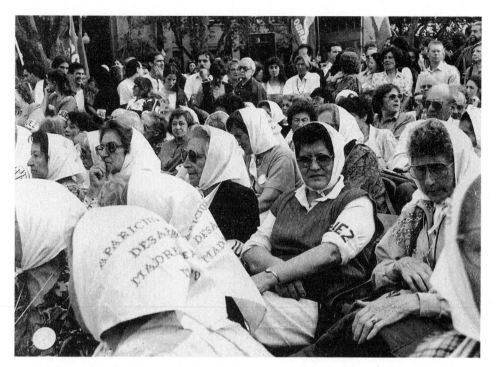

Members of the *Las Madres de la Plaza de Mayo*, the mothers of the disappeared in Argentina, seen here at a Buenos Aires demonstration in 1995.

Credit: ©Amy Mayer/Impact Visuals

As they eddied about the plaza, the mothers developed an instinct for political theater. Sometimes they piled up the personal effects of disappeared children, and often they carried carpenter's nails to show their solidarity with the Holy Mother, whose son had also been detained and tortured to death. In September 1977 they decided to join the annual pilgrimage to pay homage to the Virgin Mary at Luján, about thirty miles outside Buenos Aires—Azucena thought it would give them a chance to tell their stories to strangers during the long walk. But how to identify themselves among the thousands of pilgrims?

"Azucena's idea," said Aida de Suárez, "was to wear as a head scarf one of our children's nappies, because every mother keeps something like this, which belonged to your child as a baby. It was very easy to spot the head scarves in the crowds . . . so we decided to use the scarves at other meetings and then every time we went to Plaza de Mayo . . . and we embroidered on the names of our children. Afterwards we put on them '*Aparicion con Vida*''—literally, reappearance with life—"because we were no longer searching for just one child but for all the disappeared."[15]

"They Thought We Couldn't Do Anything"

By the last months of 1977, *las Madres de Plaza de Mayo,* as the women were now known, had grown from 14 reluctant housewives to about 150 protesting mothers, who were in touch with hundreds more, all intent on locating their children. "Many of us found out where they were held," said Hebe de Bonafini, "how they were tortured, what instruments they used, the names of the torturers, where they lived . . . All this changes you . . . We knew it was going to be hard but we knew we couldn't stop now that we were beginning to discover the truth."[16]

On October 5 of that first year, they managed to place a half-page Mother's Day advertisement in the newspaper *La Prensa,* addressed to the president of the Supreme Court, armed forces commanders, junta leaders, and the Church. "The most cruel torture for a mother is uncertainty about the destiny of her children. We ask for a legal process to determine their innocence or guilt," the ad demanded. A few weeks later they followed with a petition with 24,000 signatures, and the names of 537 *desparecidos.*

Around the world, news media and governments began to take notice. Tales of torture and disappearance circulated among human rights organizations. In the United States, the newly elected Carter administration sent down a plainspoken envoy, Patricia Derian, to look into stories of atrocities. But as the mothers became a beacon illuminating what was wrong in Argentina, they also became an easy target for the junta. When they had been forlorn, helpless women, the government had pulled its punches. Now and then a squad of police might rough up the mothers or detain them, but none had been taken away. That forbearance now evaporated.

"They started calling us '*las locas*'"—the madwomen—recalled Aida de Suárez. "When the foreign embassies began to ask questions . . . and the foreign journalists began to ask about us, they used to say, 'Don't take any notice of those old women, they're all mad.' Of course they called us mad. How could the armed forces admit they were worried by a group of middle-aged women? And anyway we were mad. When everyone was terrorized we didn't stay at home crying—we went to the streets to confront them directly. We were mad but it was the only way to stay sane."[17]

According to Marina de Curia, the government had waited too long to take them seriously. "They didn't destroy us immediately because they thought we couldn't do anything and when they wanted to, it was too late. We were already organized . . . At first they tried to trick and deceive us, then to frighten us by taking us prisoner and then by threatening us with death." But she knew her enemy. "The military were just trying to frighten us. They'd never have given us a warning if they were really going to do something."[18]

Chile and Argentina, 1980s

Among the volunteers who helped them was a young, blond man who claimed to have a disappeared brother. He called himself Gustavo Niño, with a countenance so angelic, according to Azucena, he could never hurt a fly. In the plaza, the mothers would flock around him to keep him from the police. One day when the mothers were at Santa Cruz Church, putting the final touches on their second advertisement, Niño dropped in with money collected for the ad, looked over the mothers, and quickly left. Moments later, men appeared as if from nowhere and began hitting mothers and hauling them away. "We never saw our friends again," said Maria del Rosario, who hid among people attending mass. Gustavo Niño never reappeared; only later they learned that he had been sent to France, to spy on Argentine exiles there, then to South Africa to do the same.[19]

Two days later Azucena was taken. In three days, said Maria del Rosario, "they'd taken fourteen . . . including the three most militant Mothers." The authorities thought that "by kidnapping the fourteen Mothers, they would destroy our movement," Aida de Suarez said. "They didn't realize this would only strengthen our determination. We said, no, they're not going to destroy us, we will continue, stronger than ever. They thought we would be too afraid to go back to the square. It was difficult to go back . . . but we went back."[20]

"We Want Them Returned Alive"

Returning to the Plaza de Mayo marked a crucial rite of passage; the mothers now understood that their campaign had a subversive effect, that their once-spontaneous protest had become a strategic thrust at the junta. Where the generals had thrown a cape of legitimacy over its crimes, the mothers lifted it. Despite threats and even the disappearance of some of their own, they refused to submit. They were now, in their way, as unassailable as the regime had been, having shown an audacious courage in the face of what was thought to be unopposable.

Argentina hosted the World Cup of soccer in 1978, and at first, the mothers were forgotten in the froth of excitement. But they soon realized they had a chance to speak to the world. Journalists who had come to cover soccer were drawn to the weekly promenade of the white-scarved mothers. Players from European teams came to the plaza to show solidarity. When Argentina won the World Cup, domestic television showed the generals in a throng of fans; on Dutch TV, there were *las madres*. When an international health conference was held that same year in Buenos Aires, the mothers were there too, along with a swarm of foreign media—who saw the mothers' new slogan, "They took them away alive, we want them returned alive."[21]

Having challenged the regime's legitimacy at home, they proceeded to lacerate it abroad, using their guise of naïveté like a blackjack. Three of the mothers embarked on an international tour heralded by the simple statement "We are the Mothers of the disappeared from Buenos Aires, Argentina, and we are coming to discuss human rights." They acquired a kind of celebrity, which tended to protect them: The famous, both they and the junta understood, are not easily disappeared.[22]

Other human rights organizations in Argentina—the Families of the Disappeared for Political Reasons, the Ecumenical Group for Human Rights, the Permanent Assembly on Human Rights—now sprang up in the mothers' wake. The Center for Legal and Social Studies stuck attorneys and lawsuits into the revolving spokes of state terror. Adolfo Pérez Esquivel, an advisor to *las madres,* pressed on with the work of his Christian Service for Peace and Justice, which later earned him a Nobel Peace Prize. And the grandmothers of the Plaza de Mayo appeared, searching for lost grandchildren.

In August 1979 the Association of the Mothers of the Plaza de Mayo was formally registered. By this time, the mothers were counted in the hundreds, with chapters linked across Argentina. That same year the Inter-American Commission on Human Rights was able to visit Argentina and explore the reports of illegal detention, torture, and disappearances. Its 374-page report, banned in Argentina, condemned the junta and may have helped reduce the disappearances—but it spurred little action elsewhere.[23]

Repression against the mothers then escalated so sharply that, after varying their days of protest randomly, hoping to slip past police cordons, they were forced to abandon the Plaza de Mayo temporarily. But in 1980 they were back, determined to retake their ground even if they died doing it. The first Thursday in February, they converged on the square, promenading slowly around the pyramid at its center. A week later police set upon the mothers with truncheons and dogs, and many were arrested and detained. But from that time on, they went to the Plaza every Thursday, a presence not even an army could disperse.

Finally seams became visible within the junta, as the air force split from the army and navy. The tensions borne of fighting the Dirty War and maintaining a fictitious normality took their toll, worsened now by symptoms of a collapsing economy. In March 1981 Videla was replaced as president, but the Argentine peso was in free fall, banks collapsed, and capital fled overseas. The military changed faces yet again, picking a hard-line anti-Peronista, General Leopoldo Galtieri.

His regime contrived what looked to be a splendid diversion. In March 1982 Argentine marines landed on the Falkland Islands, a British possession claimed by Argentines, who called them the Malvinas. The invasion was a ruinous miscalculation. Not four months later Argentine forces were unceremoniously routed by a British naval armada that Prime Minister Margaret Thatcher threw into the South Atlantic. Captain Alfredo Astiz, also known as Gustavo Niño, the mothers' erstwhile Judas, was among those who surrendered. The junta's last desperate act now brought it tumbling down. Before another year elapsed, the control of Argentina would pass to a constitutional, elected government—only the third in half a century.

For the mothers of the Plaza de Mayo, this might have meant the end of a long, often lonely struggle. In fact, it was only a point of new departure. During the political transition, they still drew hostile police attention. Instead of protesting disappearances, they now resisted the military's attempt to declare an amnesty for the malefactors of the Dirty War. Their goal, they explained, was not to mourn the dead as they turned up in mass graves but to bring their children's assassins to justice.

As the century ended, the survivors among the brave women who led the first wave of Argentina's nonviolent rebellion in 1977 were in their sixties, seventies, and eighties. Many still felt the effects of the days and nights of marching or queuing in government ministries, of beatings and detentions. But the force they had fashioned became a permanent feature of the Argentine political landscape, as Argentine women, and aggrieved women elsewhere in Latin America as well, put on white scarves. In the twentieth century there was no better emblem of the fact that replacing fear with truth is the first step toward freedom.

Germany, Argentina, Chile

Courage is part of the character of nonviolent action, especially when the ruler's authority is poised on the point of a bayonet. Thirty years before *las madres,* the non-Jewish wives of Jewish men being rounded up for the Holocaust stood for a week on the Rosenstrasse and demanded their husbands' release. Strutting with a self-conscious masculinity, the uniformed regimes of Germany and Argentina were confounded by unyielding groups of unpretentious women. There are perhaps no two stories in the long unfoldment of nonviolent conflicts involving a starker contrast of opponents: storm troopers using terror and women without weapons.

In Berlin in 1943, the Rosenstrasse wives jeopardized German acquiescence to Nazi terror, and the regime flinched from testing that threat. In Buenos Aires in 1977, *las madres* broke the silence about Argentine terror, awakening the world to what could not be tolerated. Both groups opened a small but living space in which the malice of a regime could be not only bemoaned but denounced and opposed.

When Videla took office in Argentina in 1976, one of his models had been the regime that had seized power in Chile three years before. But Videla's country had scarcely known democracy, while Chile had only rarely been under military sway. In Argentina, the disappeared were in the tens of thousands, an order of magnitude greater than those taken in Chile's chapter of slaughter. Yet it was in undemocratic Argentina, barely a year after the Dirty War began, that fourteen middle-age housewives walked into the Plaza de Mayo, ready to brave the devil himself. In contrast, once-democratic Chile endured its dictator in silence for a decade, and no white-scarved mothers appeared in the square outside Santiago's presidential palace—although, in 1983, there were signs that courage was reviving.

CHILE—RENOUNCING FEAR

May 11, 1983

The city of Santiago awakened listlessly that morning. Few people were out and about, and the squadrons of diesel buses that usually patrolled its boulevards had vanished. Many schools were closed, and in the afternoon office buildings began to empty as well. In its desultory way, the city was reacting to the call for a National Protest Day, to challenge the military government that had ruled Chile for ten years. By twilight there seemed to have been little protest, only a slowing of tempo and a certain ambient tension. At eight o'clock that evening, however, the city came to sudden life. In one neighborhood after another, a faint metallic clanking began, rising to a crescendo as people began to beat on pots and pans. In poorer parts of town, the young built bonfires and barricades, and the middle class drove around, horns wildly honking.[24]

"It was amazing . . . it went way beyond what anyone would have thought possible," said Lake Sagaris, a Canadian journalist who was there. "May 11 was an explosion of joy and excitement, because people were so amazed that they were raising their voices—that they were speaking out. It was like Chile had just won the World Cup." Soon the *carabineros* (national police) loosed their tear gas, trying to dampen the festive air. Two civilians were shot dead, apparently by plainclothes police agents. Drivers were dragged from their cars and beaten. More than 600 people were arrested, including Rodolfo Seguel, the head of the copper miners' union that started the protest, and reprisals multiplied in the days that followed.[25]

Insulated by his own confidence, Augusto Pinochet, Chile's military dictator, evidently took the protest to be an expression of pique, handily extinguished, especially among the poor. But the newspaper *El Mercurio,* which had backed the regime, heard a more unsettling message beneath the clamor.

The protest, it said, had been "the most serious challenge the government has faced in its almost ten years of existence."[26]

May 11 turned out to be a watershed, dividing the temporal landscape of Chile. On the far side was the coup of 1973, the violent rise and rule of General Pinochet; on the near side, nonviolent and violent landmarks sloped down until, for the regime, the terrain ran out. But on that day in May, "no one had much confidence that the protest would work," said Genaro Arriagado, a Christian Democratic leader. Yet it became "the birth of a massive, popular movement against the military regime." The spirit of Chile had taken its first step back toward democracy.[27]

"The Eleventh"

On September 11, 1973, the socialist government of President Salvador Allende Gossens was swept aside by a swift and brutal military coup, justified by its leaders as the only way of guiding Chile, one of Latin America's oldest and most stable democracies, away from the path taken by Fidel Castro's Cuba. Whether Allende's government was a well-intended experiment gone wrong or the carrier of Marxism, Chile had been brought to the brink of chaos and economic ruin. Many Chileans had come to regret giving Allende even the slim 36 percent of the vote he received in the election of 1971—enough, against badly divided opposition, to seat him in La Moneda, Chile's presidential palace. Hardly anyone believed he could survive the next election.

The military had not been prepared to wait. On the day that entered the Chilean idiom as "The Eleventh," strikes by a pair of Hawker Hunter aircraft and a barrage of artillery and small-arms fire turned La Moneda into a burning pyre. Allende was dead, evidently a suicide. By dusk the country lay under a twenty-four-hour curfew, and new rulers had anointed themselves: an air force general, a navy admiral, a general of the carabineros, and the man Allende himself had named army commander just a month earlier, General Augusto Pinochet Ugarte. He had come into the coup late, but as head of the largest military arm, he was made the junta's first leader.

This was not a coup d'état, the new government explained, but only a move to salvage the country. The rights of individuals, of enterprise, of labor, all would be respected, under the 1925 constitution. But the day after the coup, the junta declared the entire nation an emergency zone and imposed a state of siege, limiting citizens' rights and beefing up the military's powers. Still, there was a feeling of relief, now that men on horseback had galloped to the rescue. Since 1830 Chile had come under military rule for only thirteen months altogether; the armed forces had always been professional and incorruptible. Even the dour

Pinochet was reassuring. "As soon as the country recuperates," he said, "the junta will turn over the government to whomever the people desire." So most believed that when this latest conflict had cooled, they would dress in their Sunday best and parade to the voting tables. Anything else was unthinkable.[28]

But the unthinkable waited in the wings. As the armed forces, dressed for battle, found almost no one to fight, thousands of suspects were rounded up for interrogation, torture, execution, or exile. From the perspective of soldiers summoned to battle communism, disagreeable steps were necessary to cleanse society. Santiago's poorer neighborhoods were raided ruthlessly, and the agents of the newly created Direccion de Inteligencia Nacional (DINA) roamed the long, narrow land from Peru to Patagonia, inoculating the populace with fear. To muzzle exiled critics of the new regime, DINA used the outstretched arm of terror. A year after the coup Pinochet's predecessor under Allende, General Carlos Prats, and his wife were assassinated outside their home in Buenos Aires. In September 1976 Orlando Letelier, Allende's foreign minister and former ambassador to the United States, was murdered by a car bomb in Washington, D.C.

Within the nation, the army chief became the granite-faced arbiter of behavior and belief, a man absolutely certain of his own probity. In June 1974 he persuaded his junta to sign a decree naming him chief executive. From that it was just one notch up to the title of Supreme Chief of the Nation and another to President of the Republic. Within the junta, Pinochet divided and conquered. The air force junta member, for example, whose candor the president found offensive, was locked out of his Defense Ministry office and replaced by General Fernando Matthei, number nine on the list of possible successors.

With his fellow commanders marginalized, Pinochet had become the government. Chile's federal pockets were his pockets, and its enemies, his enemies. As one Chilean politician put it, "He is a man who needs to find a daily enemy in order to subsist. Without them, he wouldn't know who he is." His government closed three out of four of the country's newspapers, placed universities under military supervision, prohibited singing in public, and even outlawed guitars. One censor even ordered all books on cubism burned, believing that they were about Cuba.[29]

None of this found favor in the Catholic Church, once a supporter of Allende's overthrow. From the outset, it had offered sanctuary and clandestine help to those driven before the breaking wave of violence, and it also offered meeting venues for organizations that were, if not banned, officially "in recess." Four years into Pinchot's reign, Cardinal Raul Silva Henriquez and the Archdiocese of Santiago created the Vicaria de la Solidaridad (the vicariate of solidarity) to help victims of repression. It recorded disappearances and offered legal aid, shelter, and medicine to survivors.

"Officially, our mandate was human rights, not political activism, but that made us an opponent of the government," explained Father Christian Precht, who headed the Vicaria. "Defending human rights is practically the same thing as promoting democracy. They're different sides of the same coin. We helped in any way we could, and it was sometimes dangerous. Our priests and nuns were attacked by the government." With less drama than *las madres* in Argentina, the Vicariate set out to achieve the same goal: to make certain that the regime's crimes would be known far and wide. By itself, this could not push out the dictator, but without it, forceful opposition could not be roused.[30]

By December 1977 the United Nations had condemned Chile for human rights abuses, and the United States, which under President Nixon had promoted the ouster of Allende, pulled back from Pinochet after President Jimmy Carter took office. It abstained on votes for international loans and throttled the flow of American arms to the Chilean military. The dictator reacted by trying to sanitize the appearance of his government. The reviled DINA was formally dissolved, although its apparatus remained more or less in place. Erected in its stead was the Central Nacional de Informaciones (CNI).

In the meantime, Pinochet's so-called Chicago Boys—advisors who were followers of The University of Chicago's renowned economists Milton Friedman and Arnold Harberger—applied their free-market monetarist policies to Chile's ruptured economy but, betrayed by a global recession, saw it dive into a frightening tailspin. Later, as recession eased worldwide, Chile bounced back, leaner and more competitive. Then, basking under a warmer economic sun, Pinochet moved to relegitimize his claim to power.

Ignoring the outrage of colleagues, church leaders, and Chile's three living former presidents, he held a referendum in January 1978. Marking the symbol of the Chilean lone-star flag on the ballot said yes to a statement saying, in part: " . . . I support President Pinochet in the defense of the dignity of Chile and reaffirm the legitimacy of the government." Blank ballots counted as YES votes. No one thought it a fair process, but the dictator brandished his victory like a mace. "Mr. Politicians," Pinochet told his dispirited civilian enemies, "this is the end of you! Today there is a new Chile."[31]

A second referendum, on the coup's seventh anniversary, asked for a simple yes or no to a new constitution banning Marxist groups, reinforcing executive power, and making the congress partly appointive. Pinochet would remain in office another eight years; then a plebiscite would say yes or no to a candidate approved by the junta. The regime won the referendum, though perhaps not by the margin it claimed—in some places, voters outnumbered the population. Still, the regime used its victory as a license to continue repression. And there was other encouraging news. In Washington, the conservative administration of

President Ronald Reagan had just been installed and gave every sign that it would be indulgent with Chile's staunchly anti-communist regime.

Days of Protest

Pinochet had La Moneda restored, and, in 1981, he also built a private estate southeast of Santiago, El Melocotón, the Peach Tree. His roots of power seemed to grow deeper. But the two referenda, on his rule and his constitution, had a collateral effect that went largely unnoticed. Until the 1980s the opposition had been scattered, like the embers of a campfire. Now, provoked by the prospect of endless autocratic rule, the latent democratic fire in the country started to rekindle—just as the fluid of a good economy began to dry up. In 1982 the price of copper plummeted, the cost of imported oil soared, and a jump in the U.S. prime rate rippled south, driving Chilean interest rates over 16 percent. In a nation of 11 million, 5 million were jobless.

Organized labor had been neutralized by the 1973 coup, but to many, the end of agitation in the workplace was a welcome change. So not everyone was distressed that labor's ability to energize opposition to the regime was stunted. Still, a labor movement with the grand and radical credentials of Chile's could not shake the belief that it was a crucial force for change. Now and then, this force was roused.

In 1978, when the miners at Chuquicamata, the gigantic open-pit copper mine in the northern desert, had tried to boycott their mess halls after failing to win a wage increase, the government had quickly put them down. A sudden, localized state of siege ended with the demonstration's leaders being banished as communists. A few years later more radical labor activists created a national organization. But organizing was one thing, effective action quite another.

Goaded by threats of a boycott of Chilean goods from the AFL-CIO in the United States, the regime made some adjustments. In October 1978 it announced union elections, in which half a million workers would be able to choose plant leaders for the first time since The Eleventh. The candidates, however, had to be government approved and swear they would not join a political party. A few months later the government legalized strikes and the right to hold unapproved meetings. But there were strings attached: After thirty days a striking employee could be replaced, and striking longer than sixty days was tantamount to quitting. There was space for action but penalties if it went too far.

The action of two labor leaders came to symbolize the potential for using that space to interrupt the nation's lullaby with Pinochet and, also, the danger of doing so. Tucapel Jiménez, a humble bookkeeper, had long been active in the civil service unions. But after he began to attack Pinochet's policies, he was fired

Rodolfo Seguel, president of the Copper Mine Workers' Confederation of Chile,
who inspired the first national day of protest against the military dictatorship
of Gen. Augusto Pinochet, on May 11, 1983.

Credit: ©Marcelo Montecino

as a troublemaker. Unfazed, he kept blasting the government while urging labor
to shake off its lethargy. One morning in February 1982 Don Tuca vanished on
his way to a meeting with other labor leaders. Hours later, his body was found
alone in his car on an empty road, shot to death, with his throat cut. "I will stop
defending the rights of workers when I die," Don Tuca had said. The regime
had taken him at his word.[32]

The other unionist was a twenty-nine-year-old member of the Copper Mine
Workers' Confederation, Chile's largest union. Rodolfo Seguel was not even a
true miner but a payroll clerk at El Teniente, the huge copper mine that tunnels
under the Andes some 2,100 meters above sea level fifty miles southeast of
Santiago. Unbowed by the hardship of scooping cubic kilometers of ore from
pits carved from the northern desert, the *mineros* were generally the first to step
forward with a grievance. More often than not, their articulated moods were tied
to practical matters—pay, housing, health, or hours. But they were the elite
among all workers, and copper, after all, was Chile; so when these knights of
labor acted, the government paid attention.

In 1981 Seguel had led a fifty-nine-day strike at El Teniente, and this gave him enough of a reputation to become a compromise candidate in the February 1982 election to the union's presidency, which he won. Once in office, he became a Christian Democrat, effectively linking the country's largest union with its largest political party. In April 1983 he found himself at the head of the newly created Commando Nacional de Trabajadores (CNT), or National Workers Committee, and the proponent of a provocative idea: a strike not just of miners but a people's walk-out, a gauntlet to be thrown down before the government.

"When we announced the strike," Seguel said later, "we suddenly found our mines surrounded by tanks and troops. Military helicopters circled overhead. We realized there was going to be a bloodbath. I didn't want to be responsible for that, so just four days before the strike was scheduled we changed it into a National Protest Day. We tried to broaden it to the whole country, to protest not just the economic hardship, but human rights abuses, the whole system. Someone had to dare to tell the dictator that he was a dictator, that it was a dictatorship, that we needed a change."[33]

Now the opposition, with unions in the vanguard, fired a salvo of monthly protests against the regime. The second protest fell on Tuesday, June 14, and this time the demonstrations reverberated not just across Santiago but all along the shank of Chile. Citizens of all ages and classes joined in, and they were deliberately nonviolent. Then the opposition split. One faction viewed the protests as the prelude to rebellion, and the other insisted that if protests were going to work, they had to be nonviolent. "I and others argued that these protests are what force the government to sit at the negotiating table to agree on a transition to democracy," said Genaro Arriagada, who had organized one of the protest days.[34]

But three people had died in the June protest, and hundreds more were arrested, including Rodolfo Seguel. At around 1:30 A.M., Seguel recounted later, the authorities broke his door down, dragged him out of bed, and drove him away. He recalled thinking he was going to be either killed or deported. To challenge Seguel's arrest, the unions called for a general strike—and, effectively, threw in their hand, for the strike failed to materialize. In hard times, the reality of unemployment proved more persuasive than past threats of torture, prison, or exile. That, and visible military presence, kept the copper miners at work.[35]

"This failed strike represented the trade unions' first and last attempt to take a leading role in the protests," said Arriagada. "Although a national strike had been shown to be a practical impossibility, the idea of such a strike retained enormous power—to the point that belief in it became for some an emotional necessity rather than a rational conviction." At almost the same time, the same chimera was being chased by some in Poland's Solidarity after it had gone underground.[36]

A third protest day was called on July 12, to decry the arrest of prominent Christian Democrats, including their leader, Gabriel Valdés. What had begun with the discontent of copper miners had become broadly political, but without clear goals being spelled out. Many thought naively that the protests would grow so mighty that they alone would undo the dictatorship. But it became obvious that Pinochet's grip was too tight to be pried open by sanctions that were not more coercive than street protests. "I think that no one could believe that a movement backed by unemployed people that resorted to disruption in minor demonstrations, which had no doubt a great moral legitimacy, was going to be enough to overthrow the military regime," recalled Arriagada.[37]

There were long debates, especially in women's groups, about whether the struggle should use arms or be totally nonviolent. Many knew they would never be well-enough armed to prevail against the military. Patricia Verdugo, a journalist whose father had been executed soon after Pinochet took control, recalled that women protestors were told that when police appeared, they should kneel on the floor and raise their fists, so that blows would be absorbed while they were in a position of "peacefulness." It was meant to show that they were "different from those youths who were burning tires and building barricades in the streets or throwing stones." Even so, the threat of violence from both the government and the left was discouraging new adherents to the cause, curtailing the scope of the protests.[38]

To Organize or To Destroy

In early August 1983 a group assembled in Santiago representing most of Chile's political spectrum: Republicans from the right, Radical, Social, and Christian Democrats from the center, and some Socialist factions from the left. The communists had not been invited, given their penchant for violence. All these parties had been banned but remained alive underground. Now they formed a new group, Alianza Democratica (AD), led by Gabriel Valdés. Their objectives were reduced to a single sentence: "As individuals with differing political, philosophical, and religious positions, we unite in agreeing to respect and promote certain ethical principles and values that democracy upholds, without which a free, prosperous, just, and fraternal society is not possible." Like the Russian Liberationists at the century's dawn, the AD would strive to overcome class and ideological differences and build a broad-based opposition. It would not be easy.[39]

On August 10 the general went on national television to announce that he was replacing several cabinet ministers and authorizing the new interior minister—Sergio Onofre Jarpa, former leader of the right-wing National Party—to "begin a dialogue" with the opposition, but that he was also ordering 18,000 troops into the streets for the following day's scheduled protest. It was the proverbial iron fist in a velvet glove. The next morning army troops formed up along the concrete banks of the Mapocho River, which slices through one side of central Santiago. In the skirmishing that followed, twenty-six people died (seventeen according to the regime), including three children.

Having shown its mettle again, the government was ready to talk. With the mediation of the new cardinal in Santiago, Juan Francisco Fresno, contact was opened between Jarpa and the Alianza. In the first meeting, Valdés and his colleagues presented a list of demands, beginning with Pinochet's resignation. Jarpa refused even to accept the document. They met twice again, according to Jarpa, but there was no progress because, as he saw it, the opposition just wanted the government to step down. Still, the dialogue proceeded, and Jarpa agreed to three concessions: A number of exiles were allowed to return, some overt political activity was permitted, and book publishers were allowed to offer titles without prior approval.[40]

Many in the opposition thought that this progress meant Pinochet might eventually be brought down by more demonstrations, by more banging on pots and pans. But the real difference the protests had made was subtler. The opening after the Jarpa talks did not threaten the dictator, but it did widen the space in which the democratic opposition could operate and thus unfolded new opportunities for future action. Building a movement and struggling with a regime, as the democratic forces against Pinochet had not yet discovered, is not so much a succession of set-piece confrontations that are victories or failures as it is an interactive process that requires an opposition to alter its strategy as the action changes.

The Alianza Democratica was the nonviolent face of that opposition, reflecting the conviction of most Chileans that nothing was worse than civil war. But in Chile, as in earlier conflicts in the twentieth century in which nonviolent action had managed to rally popular support, the extremists of the left and the right refused to surrender their belief that achieving power meant killing those who stood in the way. Just as Bolsheviks had sparked the abortive December uprising in 1905, and German fascists sprang violent sabotage against French invaders in 1923, the radical left in Chile was devoted to proving that power came out of the barrel of a gun.

In 1980, as the dictator had pushed through his new constitution, the communists had spawned the Manuel Rodriguez Patriotic Front, or FPMR, named for a guerrilla hero of Chile's nineteenth-century struggle for independence. Exiled members of another group, the Revolutionary Left Movement, or

MIR—some of whom had been trained for guerrilla war in Nicaragua, Cuba, Algeria, and Eastern Europe—had drifted back into Chile early in the decade. Excluded from the dialogue with Jarpa, hard-line leftists formed an alternate alliance, the Popular Democratic Front, or MDP, combining Socialist elements with the MIR. The strategies of the Alianza and the MDP exhibited the basic split among Pinochet's opponents. The Alianza, Arriagada wrote, "viewed the protests as the social pressure that should bring the government to negotiations." But the MDP saw them as a springboard for mass insurrection. As the interior minister made concessions, the MDP sneered—and the MIR went to war.[41]

One morning in August, Santiago's military governor came under fire from shooters in a passing truck, killing him and two of his aides. The assassinations were attributed to the MIR, which had struck before—a guard at a monument celebrating the 1973 coup had been shot dead in 1980—but never so close to the center of power. The regime checked its impulse to impose martial law. A week later, however, squads from the CNI riddled two MIR safe houses with machine-gun fire, killing five occupants.

Opening a violent commerce, leftist guerrillas and government forces were happy to substitute combat for negotiations as the way to adumbrate change in Chile. Many younger dissidents gravitated toward the FPMR and MIR and away from what they took to be the docile maturity of the Alianza. "In the Communists' view," Arriagada recalled, "any kind of behavior was acceptable, from vandalism and pillage to unarmed men throwing rocks at security forces . . . What the Communist Party and the extreme left refused to understand was that such violence was not only completely ineffective in the struggle against the government, it was also the most effective way to destroy the protest movement." As violence seemed a likely new feature of the monthly protests, middle- and upper-class support flagged. What had once drawn a vertical cross-section of Chileans had now become mainly an outlet for the discontent of Chile's poor.[42]

The fifth protest was called for Thursday, September 8, only three days shy of the coup's tenth anniversary. Both parties had agreed that this demonstration should be peaceful; the colloquy between the Alianza and Jarpa was still evolving, after all. There would be no soldiers there, only carabineros to maintain order. But once the protest began, the police attacked with water cannons and tear gas. Arriagada was among those beaten with truncheons. A sixth protest on October 11 was staged not by the Democratic Alliance but by the MDP. The middle class failed to turn out for this one. Six people were killed, all in poor districts.

By the time of a November rally staged by the Alianza, that first protest on May 11 must have seemed very long ago, the price of modest progress very high, and the chance of achieving anything like democracy more remote than ever. Gabriel Valdés was "truly, truly afraid that this strategy of ours to create social mobilization of the politicians, professionals, teachers, social leaders, union leaders, intellectuals, and artists would be controlled by the extremists of the Communist Party." At all costs he wanted to avoid guerrilla warfare. "I realized we couldn't keep on this path because the violence was too extreme." But by downplaying open protest, the Alianza effectively ceded the field to those who were bent on murderous revolt.[43]

The protests that resumed in March 1984 were accompanied by such contrapuntal violence as subway bombings, attacks on the carabineros, and dynamiting of power pylons. An FPMR manifesto declared that a people's army had to be raised "to ready the blows that will demolish the forces of the dictatorship." The communists expected a national strike to immobilize all of Chile, followed by a rebellion of the entire population, including members of the armed forces (showing again the revolutionary left's enduring delusion that somehow soldiers would defect while being shot at). The MIRistas and other militias embarked on a campaign of terror that featured more than 700 bombings up and down Chile in 1984. In November Pinochet countered with a state of siege and began rounding up poor men by the thousands, as in the early days of the coup. Hundreds were sent into internal exile and 8,000 more were detained.[44]

Such exchanges between the violent left and a ruthless regime had achieved a kind of looking-glass symmetry, in which the action of one side was invariably mirrored by the reaction of the other. As one diplomat reportedly put it, "This government and the guerrillas have a nice, symbiotic relationship." Pinochet's tenure ensured terror from the far left, and violence gave him the excuse to enforce that tenure.[45]

New Momentum, New Violence

In August 1985, two years after the opposition's first summit meeting, key leaders convened again, at the posh Spanish Circle club in Santiago. Cardinal Fresno and a former minister from pre-Pinochet days, Sergio Molina, had spent months delicately poking the disparate players into place. Present were representatives of eleven parties, ranging from die-hard Allende-era Socialists to parties that had sprouted on the right—the Union Democratica Independiente (UDI), a group of young capitalists, and such moderates as the newly minted Union Nacional, created by Jarpa, who had resigned as interior minister. Everyone but the communists and the government was represented. Despite its diversity, the group agreed on a strategy, embodied in what they called the National Accord for Full Transition to Democracy (Acuerda Nacional).

The Acuerda Nacional framed a bold but reasonable challenge to Pinochet's supposed policy of a gradual—some might have said glacial—shift back to democracy. It avoided calling for the dictator's resignation, and, in a calculated move that risked everything, accepted the constitution of 1980—that is, the legal machinery that could keep Pinochet on top for the rest of his life. In return, the Accord proposed that the yes-no plebiscite set for 1988 be replaced by a free and competitive election, and it asked for an end to the state of emergency, a new electoral system, restored civil liberties, and no more exiling of people.[46]

By the time of the Accord, the prospects for forward movement had improved, thanks in part to the revival of open demonstrations; protest-hardened Chileans seemed willing again to run the gauntlet of carabineros and soldiers as they took their grievances into the streets. Even in Washington, the mood was different. "The sympathy shown toward Chile during the first years of the Reagan administration gave way to growing disapproval," Arriagada noted. The regime itself had kindled much of this internal and external disaffection, with a few well-reported outrages.[47]

On March 29, 1985, government security agents had snatched two men from the Catholic human rights office in Santiago, the leader of the teachers' union and a sociologist working with a church group. A fellow teacher who tried to intervene was shot twice in the stomach. The next day civilian agents drove away with a third person; all three abductees were communist activists. Their almost-decapitated bodies were found that weekend in a ditch along the same lonely road where Tucapel Jiménez had been murdered three years earlier.

Although Jiménez's slaying had brought mainly despair, the fate of these three *degollados* (slit-throated men) brought swift response from a public that began to shake off more of its fear. Notwithstanding the five-month-old state of siege, some 15,000 mourners followed the funeral procession from the cathedral to the cemetery. The judiciary also was not cowed. A four-month investigation led to the indictment of fourteen carabinero officials and the resignation of the head of the national police. His successor, General Rodolfo Stange, would turn out to be less of a Pinochet puppet, diluting the president's control of the junta.

Washington's patience with Latin American dictators now seemed visibly to be ebbing. In May, Langhorne Motley, a vocal backer of the Pinochet government, was replaced as Assistant Secretary of State for Inter-American Affairs by Elliott Abrams, the former Secretary of State for Human Rights and Humanitarian Affairs. Then another Pinochet apologist, the American ambassador in Santiago who had served since 1982, was replaced by Harry G. Barnes, Jr., a career diplomat. Presenting his credentials to the president, Barnes reportedly told him that "the ills of democracy can best be cured by more democracy."[48]

A springlike thaw seemed imminent. The state of siege had been lifted in June, and a protest on September 4, spreading from Arica in the north to Punta Arenas in the far south, had not prompted the usual large deployment of troops and carabineros. Some saw such restraint as a sign that Pinochet's junta partners were restless and might now replace him, or that he, seeing the future more clearly, would abandon the idea of a plebiscite in favor of full and free elections. To Pinochet, however, that was the kind of wishful thinking one expected from politicians. "We would be betraying the Chilean people if we were to retreat to the formal and hollow democracy that some politicians aspire to," he declared.[49]

The Chilean people begged to differ. The Church, already active through the Vicariate of Solidarity and the steady good offices of Cardinal Fresno, was the quiver for another arrow of opposition—a group of priests and nuns who staged sit-ins in front of known venues of official torture. At the same time, Rodolfo Seguel and his colleagues took new inspiration from a secular source. "I think it was the film, 'Gandhi,'" he recalled. "It was shown in the public cinemas in 1983, when we began, and we all saw it at least twice. We had to, to really get it in ourselves." Seguel saw parallels between Gandhi and Lech Walesa in Poland. "Both men took up struggles without violence that produced better results than armed confrontation."[50]

Protestors also found a new slogan: *Tenemos las manos limpias!*—"We have clean hands." In the streets of Chile's cities, students held up their hands, palms outward. Actors held out their palms to the audience after a play, and the audience, in silent acknowledgment, responded by showing their palms to the actors. The message was not simply that the opposition had not resorted to violence, it was also that democracy could not be restored by adopting the tactics of the regime: The people's sanctions had to be consistent with their goals. The opposition thus distanced itself not only from the regime but from violent insurrectionists on the left.

But out in the countryside, the guerrillas seemed deaf to such niceties, imitating and thus absolving the government of its odious methods. The funeral of the degollados had been followed by an explosion at Chile's main power plant, plunging more than three-quarters of the nation into darkness. For every indication that change might be at hand, there was another bit of proof that two opposing armies were in the field; if they finally faced off, Chile would go down in a maelstrom of internal war. Again the democratic opposition found itself trapped between these accomplices in violence. At year's end, hoping that the spirit of Christmas might soften the president, Cardinal Fresno made a personal appeal to Pinochet to negotiate with the signers of the National Accord. "It would be better," Pinochet replied, "if we just turned the page." But the new page would be written in fire, blood, and political despair.[51]

In January 1986 U.S. Senator Edward Kennedy visited Chile, and despite officially sponsored egg-throwing and personal slurs, he gave a badly needed morale boost to the opposition. February fairly boomed with adverse omens (for someone as superstitious as Pinochet): Two tyrants, Jean Claude Duvalier in Haiti and Ferdinand Marcos in the Philippines, were forced into exile. The ejection of Marcos even gave the world a new term for what was also clearly at work in Chile: people power. Not long after, when the American president's chief of staff, Donald Regan, was asked whether the United States was undermining the Pinochet regime, he replied, evidently without irony, "No, not at the moment," leaving the impression that it might later. The United Nations, with American backing, again condemned Chile for human rights violations.[52]

Yet even with the wind of world opinion at its back, the opposition found itself unable to make much headway. Faced with Pinochet's refusal to negotiate and the rising tempo of terror from the far left, the Acuerdistas felt sidelined, and then they split over tactics for further demonstrations: Socialists and some Christian Democrats argued for sustained protests, while conservatives, afraid of losing middle-class support, argued for moderation. Then a new group arose, the Asamblea de la Civilidad (assembly of civility), a coalition of truckers, retailers, and professionals, among others. In the Allende era, just such a coalition had had devastating effects; Chileans knew that a truckers' strike could strangle commerce, retailers could freeze the economy, and professionals could close hospitals, universities, and the courts. The Asamblea called for a series of national strike days, to begin on July 2. Some in the opposition cringed, knowing that the middle class would almost certainly stay home and that far-left firebrands would not. In the event, the moderately successful strike became lost in the glare of a terrible new atrocity.[53]

On July 2 nineteen-year-old Rodrigo Rojas de Negri was in the poor Los Nogales neighborhood, working as a freelance photographer for a magazine but without a journalist's credentials. He had grown up in the United States, the son of a Chilean mother exiled after being tortured in the wake of the coup. En route to where a street barricade was to be erected, he ran into two young men carrying discarded tires, a can of petrol (or perhaps paraffin), and some bottles for Molotov cocktails. Rojas took a few of the bottles. Soon they were joined by Carmen Gloria Quintana, an eighteen-year-old student trying to learn her way out of Los Nogales, and a quartet of young Chileans headed for the protest. Quintana and Rojas knew each other only casually, having met a few days earlier in a soup kitchen where she worked as a volunteer.[54]

Suddenly a truckload of soldiers in full battle dress and night-painted faces entered the street. As the troops spilled out of their vehicle, the youngsters ran off in all directions, and all but two got away. The patrol took their two captives, Rojas and Quintana, into a rutted side street and began interrogating them, the questions punctuated with blows from rifle butts. Then the soldiers doused the pair with gasoline and set them on fire. "The young people both tried to put out the fire on them," said Jorge Sanheuza, who watched in impotent horror from behind a utility pole, "but the girl was hit in the mouth with a gun by one of the soldiers, and the boy until he lost consciousness. After a while the soldiers wrapped up the bodies in blankets and threw them on the back of the truck like parcels."

The military truck turned toward the airport, finally stopped, and left their grim parcels by the empty road that had seen so much blood—Tucapel Jiménez and the three degollados had been found dead there. Quintana and Rojas were still alive, although their faces and bodies were charred by third-degree burns. They crawled out of the roadside culvert and stumbled along the track until a motorist stopped and gave them a ride. Four days later Rojas died in a hospital that was not well equipped to treat burns. Five thousand mourners followed his hearse to the cemetery, U.S. Ambassador Barnes among them, ignoring occasional volleys of tear gas from watchful police. Carmen Quintana was moved to the superior facilities of the Hospital del Trabajador, and, months later, to the Hospital Dieu in Montreal.

As Quintana fought her way back from the grave's edge, the government set about discrediting the story. Rojas and Quintana, it said, had accidentally torched themselves while readying acid-based Molotov cocktails to be thrown at carabineros. U.S. Senator Jesse Helms, on an unofficial swing through Chile, pronounced the burned victims "communist terrorists" and criticized the American press for its biased view of Pinochet's rule. The single eyewitness, Jorge Sanhueza, was kidnapped and threatened with death if he did not alter his story; he and his family took sanctuary in the Church and later received political asylum in Australia. Still, the regime could no more brush away the atrocity than the two teenagers had been able to brush away the flames—three officers, five noncoms, and seventeen draftees were detained as part of the ensuing investigation. The regime had acquired another face—not Pinochet's this time, but the scarred visage of Carmen Quintana.

It should have been enough to provoke the country. But fury is not reflexive, if people are insulated or preoccupied. Even as the regime's various masks of benevolence cracked, the Chilean economy was reviving. Its gross domestic product had regained considerable ground, and unemployment and inflation were coming under control. Its annual trade surplus was moving toward the billion-dollar mark, and, as other Latin American nations flirted with loan defaults, Chile emerged as a model of fiscal rectitude. Not many Chileans, and not many foreign trading partners, wished to see this bubble pricked by what might have been a misstep by authorities—a sad affair, but not the end of the world.

The Cold War, never far away in that period, again intruded, barely six weeks after the burnings. The U.S. Central Intelligence Agency detected from spy satellite images what appeared to be arms caches in Chile and passed the information to their counterparts in Santiago. It was an anti-communist's dream. Ten sites, three near Santiago and seven in the northern desert, yielded more than 3,000 M-16 rifles, hundreds of rocket launchers, and tons of explosives, grenades, and ammunition. As the government played to Chileans' latent fear of a communist insurrection, the opposition shuddered: The far left had again renewed Pinochet's lease on political life.

On Thursday, September 4, the MDP tried to stage another nationwide strike. Almost nothing happened beyond the usual cascades of water and tear gas, some arson, some robberies, two more deaths. "More than Pinochet's own strength," conceded the head of the MDP, "it's the weaknesses of the opposition that explain his durability." That durability would shortly seem almost supernatural.[55]

That Sunday the president's motorcade wound through the early evening haze of the Andes, a vanguard of two carabinero motorcyclists and a train of five sedans returning from El Melocotón to Santiago. As it threaded between a rising cliff and a precipice near the bridge across the Colorado River, it slowed for a trailer-towing station wagon parked athwart the road, as though stopped in the middle of a U-turn. Suddenly the group was swept by a fusillade from both sides of the road. A rocket turned the Opel leading the motorcade into a ball of flame, then another destroyed the beige Ford Granada in second place. The third car, an armor-plated Mercedes sedan, was raked by a hail of gun and rocket fire and destroyed; then the barrage moved down the line to the fourth and fifth vehicles, whose way was blocked by a second station wagon pulled up behind the motorcade.[56]

As the firing ranged up and down the stalled column, the fifth car's driver whipped his armored car backward, then turned and sped off to the safety of El Melocoton, about ten miles away. The sedan was riddled with bullets, its windows shattered, its flat-proof Michelins almost shot away; a rocket had caromed off its roof without exploding. The attackers faded into the countryside; some reports had them dressed as CNI agents, which got them past quickly erected barricades. For several hours no one knew the fate of the vanished car's occupants: the driver, an aide, a ten-year-old named Rodrigo, and the boy's grandfather, Augusto Pinochet.

That night the general appeared on national television and showed a bandaged left arm to his people, along with his bullet-pocked Mercedes. His first impulse, the dictator said, had been to abandon the car; then, realizing how vulnerable his grandson was, he had shielded the boy with his body as the sedan filled with ricocheting metal and glass. Whatever one might think of this seventy-year-old grandfather, no one could call him a coward.

Now Chile lay under yet another state of siege, another curfew, and the agents of darkness stepped into the Santiago night. Early on September 8 a group of men in mufti took a communist and two men who had MIR links from their homes; a fourth man was taken the following night. Their bullet-riddled bodies were later discovered in various neighborhoods. Eight opposition leaders were detained, several foreign priests were expelled from Chile, and dissident periodicals were shut down. In the wake of the general's amazing escape from death, an already-planned parade on September 9 went forward with particular gusto, the dictator waving merrily as his troops goose-stepped in review.

Seen as the work of communist guerillas—the FPMR described the twenty-five-man assault in a Buenos Aires press conference, and promised more of the same—the attack had the effect of confirming the autocrat's Cold War rhetoric. Worse, it gave him an aura of invincibility, and the opposition could see the chance for a negotiated return to democracy going up in the smoke of guns and rockets. Abruptly, they seemed to face two alternative disasters: Their democratizing dream either would crumple under an invigorated military rule or would be incinerated in a riotous reprise of the Allende years.

But the events on the road from El Melocotón had spawned illusions on all sides. His escape from death had confirmed Pinochet in his sense of destiny and led him to believe he would be an unbeatable candidate in the 1989 plebiscite mandated by the constitution. As for his nonviolent opponents, the ambush had reduced their options to the single one of participating in that plebiscite, which they found repugnant, and which they believed they would inevitably lose. And the leftist guerillas, having come within a whisker of getting their man, no doubt perceived the dawn of a cleansing civil war. These were all fantasies. Everyone was wrong.

Playing by the Rules

From the abortive assassination until the vote scheduled for 1989 (it would later change to October 1988), the guiding star in the government's sky was the approaching plebiscite, which it was determined to win. Given the up-or-down vote, requiring a choice between a government candidate put forward by the junta and no one, the scales were heavily tipped toward Pinochet. But in the improbable event that he lost, he would remain president for another seventeen months, until a full election. If his side lost again, he would still be the army's commander-in-chief for eight more years—and, after his military career, a senator for life.

Pinochet's new confidence took surprising forms. The state of siege and curfew imposed in August ended on New Year's Day, and political exiles were let back in. Conservatives were amiably disarmed by luncheons at La Moneda, and an April visit by Pope John Paul II became a glowing photo opportunity, despite the pontiff's embrace of Carmen Quintana, who had returned to Chile. Money was poured into poor neighborhoods—a tactic the regime in South Africa was using, at almost the same time, to undercut its opposition—and the entire government apparatus down to rural mayors and garrison commanders was mobilized behind the campaign for YES.

The rock-faced general also appeared to have grown gentler; the stern, familiar figure in full dress uniform softened into a kindly fellow in a suit. Voters saw him wearing a miner's helmet, holding babies, even smiling. Television, still largely government-controlled, hammered away at its captive audience with scenes of prosperity and stability. The campaign, with Pinochet teasing politicians with the possibility of his candidacy, unfolded with seamless continuity.

Against this juggernaut, the opposition seemed hopelessly wrong-footed. The National Accord was badly cracked as conservatives shifted sides and as oppositionists were forced to concede that protests, whatever else they might accomplish, would never bring down the government. Adding to their problems, the hard left kept up sporadic terrorism in Santiago and the countryside, reinforcing the view that the only alternative was killing and communism. Opposition leaders questioned whether they could achieve anything through negotiation, even as they felt strongly that elections and not a plebiscite should be held in 1989.

At first, that seemed achievable, even though a full election would require that the 1980 constitution be altered. Even the air force and navy junta members had said they would accept that change. Chasing the possibility, Sergio Molina had established the Campaign for Free and Fair Elections at the end of 1986 and asked Monica Jiménez, who had been with the Peace Commission of the Catholic Church for ten years, to head it. In time Jiménez was invited to the United States, under the auspices of the State Department, where she was advised that they needed to organize a movement; the Americans showed her examples of programs that relied on popular participation, such as the League of Women Voters and labor unions.[57]

The movement was called a Crusade for Citizen Participation—later, simply Participa—and soon attracted 7,000 volunteers to go out and register voters. Chile had 12 million people, more than three-quarters of them in urban areas. Eight million were eligible voters, but only 3 million were registered. "We began with a totally open campaign," explained Jiménez, "in which we targeted everybody. Then . . . we began focusing on the tough spots. We sponsored rock concerts, where prohibited music was played. We didn't charge admission, but to get in you had to bring your voter registration card. That motivated young people to get registered."[58]

The poor neighborhoods proved the hardest, Jiménez recalled, "because the Communist and Socialist identification was particularly strong in these areas and because the repression was much stronger there . . . There were rumors flying, don't vote, because my vote will be recorded by secret machines." The poor also were discouraged because the rules made them obtain an identity card, requiring time and money few could afford. "So we helped them with these obstacles." Before its work was over—registration would close two months before the plebiscite—Participa would add 4 million Chileans to the voting rolls.

But even as voter registration swelled, the chance of an open election was dissolving, until, by midyear, it was gone. There was no way, after all, to amend the 1980 constitution, and so no way to avert the yes-no plebiscite. The gambit had been a sink for time and effort, and now there were great obstacles to winning the vote. The opposition had to convince people it was possible to play by Pinochet's rules and prevail, that it was possible to have fair and honest balloting. And they would need access to television time.

Out of the public eye, the opposition sounded out the people's real feelings about the regime, something it could not do before. "We did a lot of public opinion polls," said Genaro Arriagada, one of its leaders. "Those who thought that the government of Pinochet was very good were . . . 20 percent to 30 percent of the population. Those who thought that the government of Pinochet was bad were 70 to 80 percent of the population. But . . . the surveys also told us that 80 percent of the people thought that Pinochet was invincible." The opposition had the public on its side, but it had to show them that it could win.[59]

To focus the campaign, the opposition launched the Commando Para El No, a fusion of sixteen parties headed by Arriagada. It had little in the way of funding, but it did have a cadre of people whose expertise as political activists had been on hold for fifteen years and who now began reviving their dormant networks—the circulatory system of Chilean people power. Soon, their theme song—"Chile, la alegría ya viene" (happiness is on its way)—was heard everywhere, and their logo, a rainbow with the single word NO, began soaking into public consciousness.

Meanwhile such respected figures as Socialist leader Ricardo Lagos went out among the voters. Their message: NO would win if people would only vote; it was in their power to bring Chile back to democracy. Patricio Aylwin, replacing Valdés at the head of the Christian Democrats, would act as a kind of imaginary candidate to fill the human vacuum on the NO side of the ballot. Perhaps most important, the squabbling among opposition parties at last subsided, as they

Demonstration for the "No" campaign, on October 1, 1988, before the plebiscite on permitting
Gen. Augusto Pinochet to be elected again to the presidency of Chile.

Credit: ©Ricky Flores/Impact Visuals

realized what they would lose if YES won. Even the radical Socialists renounced
violence to unite behind NO. Finally, even the communists threw in.

Television proved critical. During a June talk show, Ricardo Lagos stared
into the camera, pointed an accusing finger, and, speaking directly to Pinochet,
said "you promise the country eight more years, with torture, assassination, and
violation of human rights. To me it is unacceptable that a Chilean is so ambitious
for power as to pretend to hold it for 25 years." Then, as other panelists tried to
quiet him, Lagos ended, "You'll have to excuse me. I speak for 15 years of
silence." The incident made him a national celebrity. Later he said he had no
idea how powerful television could be. It was a platform for rallying popular
support that Gandhi could not have dreamed of.[60]

In August the junta set the date of the plebiscite—October 5, 1988—and,
some believed reluctantly, endorsed Pinochet as the YES candidate. For the first
time in Chilean memory, a vote was coming that was as plain as a coin:
Pinochet appeared on one side, a united opposition on the other. By then the
government's media broadsides sounded like the general himself, harsh and
paranoid, full of dire warnings that the only alternative was chaos. The
clanging propaganda contrasted sharply with the opposition's simpler, more

human messages—workers and businessmen, young and old, were shown coming together in amity.[61]

A final boost for NO came from action to ensure an honest vote count. The 1988 plebiscite was inherently more transparent, and so less likely to be rigged, than the 1980 vote had been, and a constitutional tribunal, to everyone's surprise, took its duties very seriously, arranging poll watchers at each voting table—and thereby rendering the process credible. The opposition added another layer of fraud-proofing by setting up its own parallel vote count. Because Chileans voted in the open, it was possible to station watchers at a 10 percent sample of Chile's more than 20,000 voting tables, to relay information to a computer center in Santiago. Models would then permit a reliable extrapolation to the actual result.

Still confident of victory, Pinochet also had reason to want a vote that indisputably endorsed his rule. His subordinates might harass the opposition and put up barriers where they could, but he clearly had no desire to follow the example of Ferdinand Marcos, whose exile from the Philippines had been set in motion by a fraudulent election. Still, some thought, Pinochet had plans to manipulate the vote to guarantee his own victory.

To preempt this, the movement turned to its foreign supporters. A month before the plebiscite, Monica Jiménez and a colleague went to see the city's security chief, to get permission for an international guest observer delegation. The officer said the police were hearing rumors of disorder and were preparing for the worst. "Essentially he was telling us that they were going to put a lot of troops in the streets who were going to find a pretext to take over by force and steal the election," Jiménez recalled. A Chilean political leader advised her to go right away and see the American ambassador. By then it was two o'clock in the morning, but Jiménez went anyway. Ambassador Barnes was awakened and, after he heard the story, sent a cable to the State Department—which sent a message to the Chilean foreign ministry the following morning. It said, Jiménez reported, that if all this happens, the United States will not recognize the results of the plebiscite.[62]

No to the Past

Fresh winds swept away the lavender pall of smog that typically blankets the Chilean capital, so that this Wednesday, dawn in the austral spring came up like thunder, the light exploding east of the *cordillera,* then filtering down through the warm, clear air to burnish and illuminate Santiago. It was October 5, 1988, Chile's day of reckoning.

"I went out and did the rounds," recalled Lake Sagaris. "Everyone was lined up, dressed in their Sunday best . . . waiting very quietly and very disciplined to vote. Huge lines in the morning, virtually no one around in the afternoon, because everyone was so afraid the thing was going to be called off or ruined at some point." Army trucks and carabinero black patrol wagons were everywhere around the city, along with crack troops in battle dress. Pinochet himself let reporters know he had 25,000 men at the ready. There was talk of ghostly figures in ski masks skulking through Santiago.[63]

As the day wore on, Sergio Molina fed his computers with information brought in by student couriers. By nine that evening, his count indicated that NO was well ahead, but the government continued to say that YES was winning. Two junta members, General Fernando Matthei and Admiral José Merino, followed both counts and soon sensed that NO would almost surely prevail. At the presidential palace, the carabineros were told to ease their grip on festivities downtown and create a pretext to extinguish the plebiscite—but they refused. Arriagada continued releasing the parallel count, but to little effect. The state's television station put the YES vote ahead, then switched away from election news to cartoons and American sitcoms. When no new results had been announced by midnight, two perennial rivals, Sergio Onofre Jarpa and Patricio Aylwin, appeared together on the Catholic University channel. NO, they said, appeared to be winning.

Not long afterward, Pinochet called in his cabinet and told them that they—that he—had lost the plebiscite and asked for their immediate resignations. Once the shell-shocked ministers had gone, he called in the three other junta commanders, who had crossed the plaza from the Ministry of Defense to La Moneda. On the way in, General Matthei stopped to speak to journalists and admitted the NO vote had won. As word of his comment percolated into the city, the opposition realized that, against all odds, they had a victory. The man waiting for the three commanders inside was enraged, pounding on his desk, ranting of betrayal.

When they got down to business, Pinochet said that he was counting on his colleagues to support him, implying that they were there to send out their forces to impose martial law. But then each of these proud senior career officers declined to go along. Disgusted, Pinochet said, "Okay, the Army will do it alone. We don't need your help." Then he asked them to sign a protocol. "What protocol?" they asked. His assistants brought in some papers. The officers read them over. It was a statement that the other members of the junta were transferring all their powers to Pinochet. One general tore it up right in front of the president and threw the pieces on the ground. Pinochet's opponents now included his colleagues. It was over.[64]

The "Commando de No" victory marked the end of the most strife-ridden period in Chile's history, although not quite the beginning of full democracy or the end of the country's agonizing relationship with Augusto Pinochet. When, over a year later, Patricio Aylwin swept to the presidency with more than 55 percent of almost 6 million votes, nearly twice that of the regime's candidate, he would command the nation but not its armed forces. Pinochet still perched like a condor above the new government. The other junta leaders, if they wanted to, could stay in place until 1997.

But in the immediate afterglow of victory, the people of Chile could have been forgiven for celebrating the end of the nation's political purgatory. On election night the streets of Santiago had been choked with Chileans waving flags and NO banners. As the National Police stood by stoically, demonstrators had blown their horns as they had on that night in May five years before, but this time they could cry aloud "Adíos, Pinochet" and know they would not be arrested—and know in their hearts they had triumphed.

⁊ ⁊ ⁊

The years following the plebiscite and subsequent election were marked by bursts of terror, from both right and left, and the re-democratizing of Chile was not smooth, as the country slowly metabolized the rancor of the Pinochet years. As for the general himself, he retired from the army in the 1990s and claimed his senatorial title. At century's end, he occupied center stage once more, but not as he intended. When a Spanish judge tried to extradite him from Britain (where he had gone for medical treatment) on charges of torture and genocide, he was widely seen not as having been Chile's stabilizing pilot but as an aging fugitive from an emerging global order that was determined to penalize violations of human rights wherever they might appear. Although the web of law and disrepute that threatened to entangle him at the end of his days was not half as convoluted as the path of his countrymen back to political liberty, Pinochet's eventual failure to secure the respect of history was foreshadowed by his failure to keep the consent of his people.

That consent was fractured the moment the people broke their decade of silence in 1983 and proved that it was possible for opposition to be expressed and take hold. But from the first day of protest to the last day of a dictator is rarely a swift or straight progression, and unlike the Salvadoran civic strikers of 1944, the Chilean opposition did not develop a unitary strategy against their ruler. Throughout the mid-1980s, the far left remained wedded to violent insurrection, which never stood a real chance of succeeding but did amplify the violence that Pinochet knew how to exploit.

Workers determined to reclaim their old strength, families and friends of people whom the regime had brutalized or killed, and the broad center of Chilean political life—these were the forces that gave up their fear and then never gave up the fight to restore democracy. By sustaining and not overplaying public protest, by not using violence that would heighten repression, and by inspiring the help of outside institutions and governments, this inchoate but resilient movement became the lever that dislodged the dictator. Pinochet managed to neutralize his violent enemies, but the movement that disavowed the violence he started became the catalyst for his downfall.

The Chileans who opposed Pinochet, like the mothers of the Plaza de Mayo in Argentina, did something very simple but absolutely essential if people are to bring down a despot: They withdrew their willingness to let the government pretend that it had any genuine popular support. With one sanction after another, they created doubts at home and abroad about the regime's control of events, and when the regime's hubris created a narrow opportunity for the movement to succeed at the polls, they used the dictator's own procedures to annul his claim to power. Then even the regime split, leaving the general stranded on the same island of history that Martínez and Marcos had reached before him. Bullets only scratched him. Ballots sacked him.

PART THREE

CAMPAIGNS FOR RIGHTS

For us to struggle, the forces being so unequal, must appear insane. But if we consider our opponent's means of strife and our own, it is not our intention to fight that will seem absurd, but that the thing we mean to fight will still exist. They have millions of money and millions of obedient soldiers; we have only one thing, but that is the most powerful thing in the world—Truth.

—Leo Tolstoy

CHAPTER EIGHT

The American South: Campaign for Civil Rights

"Invisible Forces"

IN MARCH 1936 Dr. Howard Thurman, an African American minister, went to see Mohandas Gandhi in India, to ask him about nonviolent action and what it could do to end racial injustice in the United States. The Indian leader's campaigns in the 1920s and 1930s had been reported carefully by leading American black journals and newspapers, and black political and intellectual leaders such as Marcus Garvey and W. E. B. DuBois had held up the Indian movement as a shining example to African Americans. So Dr. Thurman's visit was perhaps something of a pilgrimage.

When asked by the black minister if he regarded "non-violence" as "a form of direct action," Gandhi was emphatic: "It is the greatest and activist force in the world." And he compared its power to St. Paul's idea of love—revealing what made him a compelling figure for many black Americans, who had always looked to their religious faith for the strength with which to endure subordination. "Gandhi's power is a tribute to the life and teachings of the lowly Nazarene that we conquer not so much by power and might as by a certain bent of spirit," the black journalist Gordon Hancock wrote in *The Norfolk Journal and Guide* in 1932.[1]

But some black observers had been equally impressed by the practical lessons of Gandhi's work. At the time of the 1921-1922 noncooperation campaign in India, a journalist for *The Chicago Defender* foresaw public transit boycotts in America to protest segregation: "We believe that some empty . . . cars will some day worry our street car magnates in Southern cities when we get around to walking rather than suffer insult and injury to our wives and children."[2]

A year after his talk with Howard Thurman, Gandhi gave an audience to Dr. Channing Tobias and Dr. Benjamin Mays, two other prominent African Americans, and told them that nonviolent action "cannot be preached. It has to be practiced"—and not only by individuals, as if it were only a personal moral choice. "It can be practiced on a mass scale."[3]

As for resisting the use of violence, Gandhi conceded that Hitler, Mussolini, and Stalin were even then showing "the immediate effectiveness of violence," but he confidently predicted that "it will be as transitory as that of Ghenghis' slaughter," referring to the ancient Mongolian warlord whose empire had long ago returned to dust. Gandhi was certain that ultimately nonviolent action would cause "the whole world" to stand agape and call it a miracle, even though it was simply "the silent and effective working of invisible forces."[4]

What was visible in America as he spoke, and what remained blatant for another thirty years, was not a miracle but a monstrosity: the systematic and even violent denial of the rights of an entire race. The force of which Gandhi spoke, however, would change all that—on a mass scale.

SATYAGRAHA COMES TO THE SOUTH

Student of Ideas

In the fall of 1959 a young African American woman from the South Side of Chicago named Diane Nash arrived in the capital city of the state of Tennessee to enroll at Fisk University, a predominantly black institution. She had gone to college to "conquer the world," but in the city of Nashville she found a society that kept her behind an invisible wall. Every time she ventured into town, she came face to face with reminders that whites regarded her as inferior. It happened first when she went on a date to the Tennessee State Fair and discovered that she had to use a separate "colored" rest room—something she would not have encountered up north. When she went shopping downtown, she could not sit and eat lunch, even at a store like Woolworth's—"we don't serve niggers here," she was told. If she wanted a sandwich, she had to take it out and eat it on the curb, as she noticed other black people doing. "And it was humiliating. I grew to hate segregation."[5]

Nash asked other students at Fisk whether they knew of anyone or anything that was fighting segregation. "Be cool," they said. "You aren't going to be able to make any changes. You're just going to get yourself in trouble. Why don't you just go to class during the week and to the parties on the weekend?" Finally she asked Paul LaPrad, a white student at Fisk. He said he knew a minister who was looking for students to attend workshops on nonviolent action. Nash decided to give it a try.[6]

The workshops were held on Tuesday evenings at a small Methodist church. Most of those who attended were students enrolled at the area's black colleges, though a few white students also participated They learned about Mohandas Gandhi and satyagraha—that the anguish of people acting to end oppression was a form of truth that might change the minds and hearts of their oppressors. In role-playing exercises they practiced taking physical and verbal abuse without striking back, and they learned how to shield their bodies if attacked. Although no one outside their small group was paying much attention, the students were preparing for a frontal attack on what was called Jim Crow, the system of racial hierarchy in the American South.

James Lawson, a Methodist minister and graduate student at the Vanderbilt School of Divinity, was their teacher. This bespectacled, thoughtful young African American had been thirty years old when he went to Nashville in 1958, but his antipathy to violence and his dignity in the face of racism went back to his boyhood in Ohio, where he was raised by a gentle mother and a father who was a pistol-packing minister. As he grew up, these impulses had become defining facets of a worldview in which Christian commands to turn the other cheek were combined with a radical critique of racial oppression. His budding nonviolent militance had been reinforced by fascination with news of Gandhi's exploits in India, which Lawson devoured in the black newspapers.[7]

It was at Baldwin-Wallace College, a Methodist school in Ohio, that Lawson had first seriously studied Gandhi's ideas. On a visit to the campus, A. J. Muste of the Fellowship of Reconciliation (FOR)—an interfaith group dedicated to peace and justice—struck up a friendship with Lawson and introduced him to Gandhi's writings and the history of nonviolent action, including the Danes' resistance to the Germans in World War II. Muste also put Lawson in contact with other black leaders, such as Bayard Rustin and James Farmer, who were experimenting with Gandhian methods. Lawson subscribed to FOR's magazine and also learned about Howard Thurman, the minister who had met with Gandhi in 1936.

Even earlier, Lawson had experimented with direct action techniques that he would teach to the Nashville students. While still in high school, he and a friend had demanded to be served inside a hamburger joint that made black customers take their food out. In college when he traveled to youth meetings around the Midwest, he continued these personal raids against discrimination. In his boldest act of defiance, the target was war rather than racism. When U.S. forces were fighting in Korea—which Lawson believed was wrong—he refused to cooperate with his draft board rather than apply for a ministerial deferment or conscientious objector status. That refusal earned him a sentence of more than a year in federal prison.

After finishing his degree at Baldwin-Wallace, Lawson left for India, where he served as a missionary at a college in the city of Nagpur. Although his job was to teach, Lawson had gone to India to learn. In three years there, he undertook an intense investigation of Gandhi and met with several of the Mahatma's disciples—coming to believe, as had many other African Americans with far less knowledge of the Indian leader, that Gandhi's teachings and life mirrored the spirit of Christ. Being a Gandhian and being a Christian, for Lawson, became more or less the same thing.[8]

In December 1955, while he was still in India, Lawson picked up the *Nagpur Times* and read that black people in Montgomery, Alabama, were boycotting the city's segregated buses—hearing for the first time about a minister almost exactly his own age, Martin Luther King, Jr. Before going to India, Lawson had thought about putting Gandhian ideas to work fighting segregation in the South. Now, after Montgomery, it seemed that ordinary black people might be ready to join such a movement. Like India after World War I, the South appeared ripe for a nonviolent liberation struggle.[9]

Lawson returned to America in 1956, going to Ohio, where he studied for a master's degree at Oberlin College. His goal was a Ph.D. in theology, followed by work for racial equality. But a visit to Oberlin by Martin Luther King, Jr. in February 1957 pried Lawson away from his first priority. By then a recognized leader, King had gone to Oberlin to give speeches, but he also made time for a small luncheon with faculty and students. Lawson showed up, found King sitting by himself at a table, and sat down opposite him. He told King about his hitch in prison, his years in India, and his contacts with some of the activists who advised King—and how he expected to go down South after his studies. King asked him not to wait: The civil rights movement needed Lawson immediately—there were no other black leaders who really understood what was required in a nonviolent campaign. Unable to resist this plea, Lawson found himself agreeing to move South.[10]

Lawson had kept up his ties to FOR, and he soon heard that they were looking to place a field secretary in the South. The job was a good fit, and he eventually decided to base himself in Nashville, where he could study at Vanderbilt (which had just begun admitting black graduate students). In early 1958 he boarded a bus in his hometown of Massillon, Ohio, and headed down to lay nonviolent siege to the haunted edifice of American racism.

"Massive Resistance"

When James Lawson arrived in Nashville, the southern civil rights movement had lost momentum. The separation of the races and the exclusion of blacks from full citizenship—features of Southern life that had crystallized around the turn of the century—were coming under fire from all directions. But the overall structure was still intact in the late 1950s, and civil rights workers disagreed about how best to fight racist laws and customs. It was also not clear what role nonviolent action would play in the campaign.

For decades the preeminent civil rights organization had been the National Association for the Advancement of Colored People (NAACP). It was led by professionals and intellectuals whose pole stars were the Constitution's Fourteenth and Fifteenth amendments, passed right after the Civil War. They extended equal protection under the law and voting rights but were routinely ignored in the South. Through lobbying and lawsuits, the NAACP was trying to push the federal government to make good on these guarantees—a strategy that had scored some successes. President Harry Truman had desegregated the armed forces, and the NAACP's able lawyers had won a Supreme Court ruling (in the 1954 *Brown v. Board of Education* case) that held segregated public education to be a violation of the Fourteenth Amendment. For a time the NAACP's object, to trigger a broad federal assault on segregation, seemed within grasp.

But *Brown* engendered a backlash of "massive resistance" by white southerners, and although the effort to defend segregation often was cloaked in the rhetoric of protecting "states' rights" from intrusive federal power, its main targets were black people who asserted their individual rights. Black parents who signed petitions in order to file school desegregation lawsuits in federal courts were threatened with loss of their jobs or physical attacks. State governments also enacted a battery of measures designed to harass the NAACP; in Alabama it was shut down altogether in 1957. The organization lost hundreds of local branches and about 50,000 members in the South during the late 1950s.

While NAACP lawyers went on waging courtroom battles against "separate but equal" education, ordinary black people in southern cities took up economic warfare against segregation in public transportation. Black riders could sit only in designated seats at the back of city buses; if the seats were filled they had to stand, even if bench after bench of the seats designated for whites in the front were empty. For black passengers the system was demeaning, yet it was also a vulnerable target, since the bus lines depended on their fares. In three cities—Baton Rouge, Louisiana; Montgomery, Alabama; and Tallahassee, Florida—entire black communities boycotted the buses. They found leaders in black ministers who communicated instructions through their churches, boosted morale at mass meetings, raised funds, and set up car pools so that boycotters could get to and from work. In each city, the boycott lasted until a settlement was reached.

Although not the first of the bus boycotts, the one in Montgomery had been the most eventful. Martin Luther King, Jr. was only twenty-six and had lived there just two years when the boycott began. It was not his idea, nor was he instrumental in getting it started—the key instigators were Rosa Parks, the secretary of the Montgomery NAACP; E. D. Nixon, a labor organizer, and Jo Ann Robinson, a teacher at Alabama State College. Nixon and Robinson plotted the boycott after Parks was arrested for sitting in the white section of a bus, and they enlisted people through leaflets and other connections. But they realized that ministers could best rally the black community. Because his abilities were obvious and because older, established ministers shied away from taking charge, King inherited the leading role.

It did not take long for the young preacher to exhibit what would later make him a towering figure in the movement. King had the courage to keep going in the face of death threats and the bombing of his home, and he was an able organizer and a rousing speaker who filled his listeners with a sense of fighting not just for a seat on a bus but for a righteous cause. He was handsome, articulate, educated, and Christian—all qualities that would make him ideal to convey the meaning of black protest to white America in the still-early years of television. As the boycott continued into 1956 and showed no signs of letting up, journalists from around the country and the world converged on Montgomery and made its leader a famous man.[11]

Another of King's visitors was a black, bohemian, gay, middle-aged ex-communist from Greenwich Village named Bayard Rustin, who went down in February 1956. An experienced organizer who had worked for many years with labor and civil rights groups, he had endured beatings and jailings—and was a firm believer in nonviolent action. For that reason, he rushed to Montgomery when he heard about the boycott and briefed King and his colleagues about how to build and operate a nonviolent movement. When word of his radical associations threatened to taint the boycotters, Rustin left town, but not before getting Glenn Smiley of FOR to come and continue the work he had started.

Like other Americans who gravitated to nonviolent methods, King had found in the Christian gospels a strong religious injunction to eschew violence, but he also had studied the works of the theologian Reinhold Niebuhr, who offered a pragmatic rather than moral argument for nonviolent action. Most African Americans did not expect that equality would be won by violent force—if they tried that, severe repression from local southern authorities was likely, and the federal government's intervention on their side would be unlikely. What Rustin and Smiley did, besides providing useful tips and training, was open the door to a broader world of thought about conflict and alternatives to violence, the same door that was opened to James Lawson during his years at Baldwin-Wallace. Thanks to this and to his own experience in the boycott, King turned an inchoate aversion to violence into an explicit commitment to nonviolent action as the guiding principle of the civil rights movement he would soon dominate.[12]

For all the news it generated, the Montgomery boycott, like the ones in Baton Rouge and Tallahassee, was not a clear victory. The boycotters in all three cities had started out not to end segregation on buses but simply to modify it so that black people did not have to stand when there were empty seats up front. City officials in Baton Rouge managed to stop the boycott in a week by agreeing to first-come, first-serve seating, with black riders starting from the back of the bus and moving forward and white riders doing the opposite. The Montgomery boycotters would have accepted a similar deal, but white officials there held out for more than a year while the boycott continued. What finally ended it was a lawsuit, which resulted in the Supreme Court striking down the statutes that mandated segregation on the city's buses. The Tallahassee action forced the local bus line to suspend service altogether, but there too the boycott ended only after the Court's ruling.

Although the bus boycotts proved that nonviolent action was a force to be reckoned with, they failed to arouse a broader movement across the South. A number of southern cities integrated their buses to preempt boycotts and legal challenges, and in recalcitrant cities, including Atlanta, Memphis, and New Orleans, small-scale protests led to lawsuits that brought on court orders to desegregate. The boycotts, moreover, did not work well where blacks were a small part of the population with little collective purchasing power, or against businesses that relied little on black dollars. And since they needed near-universal participation to be effective, boycotts were unsuited to places without strong community-wide organizations. Before a nonviolent movement could pick up steam in the South, a new sanction would have to be found.[13]

In 1957 Martin Luther King, Jr. and other young black ministers, to rally local leaders and knit together black communities in the South, founded the Southern Christian Leadership Conference (SCLC). With King at the helm and northern strategists like Bayard Rustin giving advice, the SCLC announced it would mount a nonviolent crusade for civil rights. Hesitant about mobilizing people for bold action, it focused initially on a voter registration drive, with limited success. NAACP leaders, meanwhile, remained wedded to legal action, though many of its southern members were chafing under what seemed an elitist and gradualist strategy.

If the civil rights movement was not surging at the end of the 1950s, it was far from moribund. SCLC ministers were building organizations in cities such as Atlanta, Birmingham, and Nashville, and northern-based activists were helping to provide nonviolent training and to introduce a new tactic of direct action: sit-ins at the segregated lunch counters of department stores. They were tried in more than a dozen cities around the edges of the South, such as Miami, Kansas City, St. Louis, Louisville, and Oklahoma City. One of the people traveling around the region and initiating these actions was the young minister from Ohio, James Lawson.

THE NASHVILLE SIT-INS

The Athens of the South

When Jim Lawson had decided to go South in 1957, he leaned at first toward Atlanta, the region's fastest-growing metropolis. But Glenn Smiley persuaded him to go to Nashville instead. The smaller, less dynamic city in central Tennessee had a black elite that was unusually progressive and open to what the Ohioan had to say. The focal point was Kelly Miller Smith, a talented young Baptist minister and one of the founders of the SCLC and its local affiliate, the Nashville Christian Leadership Conference (NCLC). Nashville also had a large pool of potential activists in the thousands of students who attended the city's four predominately black colleges, ranging from the prestigious Fisk University and Meharry Medical College, to the less renowned Tennessee Agricultural and Industrial (A&I) College and the American Baptist Theological Seminary (ABT).

The racial atmosphere was also less intimidating for black people in Nashville than in such Deep South states as Georgia, Alabama, and Mississippi. The city's white establishment liked to think of itself as civilized and forward-looking, and the city called itself the Athens of the South. Black people were not shut out of the local political system: The poll tax, a traditional obstacle to black voting in the South, had been suspended several times in city elections, and black candidates had even won seats on Nashville's city council. The city's mayor, Ben West, was a moderate on racial issues, and *The Nashville Tennessean,* one of the city's leading newspapers, had a liberal editorial position on race—it had pushed hard to end the poll tax and generously covered the civil rights movement.

Yet for all its civility, Nashville was hardly less segregated than the most openly bigoted cities of the South. Black people could not eat in most restaurants. They had to use separate entrances off back alleys to get into movie theaters, and then they had to sit in the balconies. They were excluded from public swimming pools and golf courses and had to use a separate waiting room in the train station. Black employees of banks, department stores, and restaurants worked as janitors or dishwashers or in other jobs that kept them out of sight.

When a federal court ordered the city to integrate its schools in 1957, city officials devised a plan that became a model for other southern cities—it introduced meager change while still complying with the letter of the court ruling. One grade would be integrated each year, beginning with the first grade. Thanks to anonymous phone threats ("We'll beat your little girl to death and string her up by her toes") and rock-throwing and stick-wielding crowds, most black parents opted out of having their children take part that first year: Just 19 black first graders (out of about 1,400 in the city) entered previously white schools. This was the kind of racial progress that most white southerners could live with.

When James Lawson arrived, Nashville had a virtual caste system that determined where people of different races could live, eat, and play, what jobs they could hold, and how they should act toward one another when they met in a street or a store. But there were black leaders in town who were itching to challenge this, and there were white leaders whose support for it was halfhearted. Jim Crow was still standing on its two hind legs in Nashville, but Jim Lawson was about to cut those legs out from under it.

A Nonviolent Academy

After moving to Tennessee, Lawson traveled to southern cities for FOR, offering training and advice on nonviolent ways to combat segregation, and in Nashville he held workshops on nonviolent action. In 1959 Lawson decided the time had come to plan a civil rights action in that city, and he asked Kelly Smith and other black ministers to put out the word through their churches that he needed students to take part.[14]

The response was less than overwhelming. Local black campuses were not bubbling over with enthusiasm for the civil rights struggle; students were under pressure to conform and play by the rules, because young educated black people finally were being promised the kinds of job opportunities that earlier genera-tions could hardly imagine. The pressures were perhaps strongest of all on students from poor families. Rebelling against segregation could end up squandering all the sacrifices their parents had made to send them to college.[15]

The students who showed up in the fall of 1959 for Lawson's workshops at the Clark Memorial United Methodist Church were people who could not adapt to the status quo. Some of them, like Diane Nash, were northerners who abhorred the debasement of the southern system. Others were young southerners who, for one reason or another, had decided they were not going to keep quiet as their parents had. Marion Barry was a graduate student at Fisk who had almost been kicked out of LeMoyne College in Memphis for denouncing a racist statement by a college trustee. Two of the most committed workshop-goers were from ABT, the city's poorest, least distinguished school. Bernard Lafayette was born in the South and then moved north with his family before going to Nashville. He went to the workshops at the urging of another ABT student, John Lewis, a shy young man from a sharecropping family in Alabama's cotton country who had started going to the workshops the previous year. They were joined by a few idealistic white students, such as Paul LaPrad.

Lawson taught the students about the historical and philosophical underpinnings of nonviolent action—about the abolitionist movement, the Chicago sit-ins staged by the Congress of Racial Equality (CORE) in the 1940s, the Montgomery bus boycott, and the movements led by Gandhi in South Africa and India. The two central reference points were Gandhi and Christ. Lawson wanted the students to understand how satyagraha—"soul force," he called it— could work to fight injustice: The downtrodden did not defeat their oppressors but rather awakened in them a sense of common humanity by showing them the distress that their actions caused. Nonviolent action was more than a technique of social action for Lawson; it was a means of tapping more fundamental sources of power.[16]

His cool, clinical tone came as a surprise to his young acolytes—he offered himself as a teacher, not a leader. A few, including Lewis and Nash, were won over quickly. Others had a hard time accepting what Lawson was telling them. "You've got to be able to stand up and take your licks and fight back," they would say. By explaining how his methods were consistent with the religious faith in which they had been raised, Lawson was able to wear down some of their doubts. Others stayed involved because Lawson was planning to *do* something. "I thought nonviolence would not work," Diane Nash recalled, "but I stayed with the workshops for one reason . . . they were the only game in town."[17]

From the start Lawson was eyeing a campaign to end segregation in downtown Nashville's shopping district. Most of the students, like Lawson himself, were from out of town, so they had to pick a target that would win them backing from Nashville's black community—otherwise it would be easy for segregationists to isolate them and brand them as outside troublemakers. Some women from the Reverend Smith's church went to a workshop and explained that what bothered them the most were whites-only lunch counters in the downtown stores. Until the suburban dispersal of big department stores and the flourishing of fast food outlets in the 1970s, these downtown emporia and their diner-like lunch counters were standard features of most cities. In the South, black church women could shop at these stores for hours, but they could not sit down at the counters to rest their feet or use the stores' bathrooms. It was even worse when they had restless, hungry children with them. If the students decided to make an issue of the lunch counters, they could be pretty sure these women would be allies.[18]

As fall turned to winter, Lawson moved beyond theory and began training the students to prepare for what was to come. John Lewis said they "staged little sociodramas, taking turns playing demonstrators and antagonists. Several of us would sit in a row of folding chairs, acting out a sit-in, while the others played waitresses or angry bystanders, calling us niggers, cursing in our faces, pushing and shoving us to the floor. Always, Jim Lawson would be there, hovering over the action, pushing, prodding, teaching, cajoling." They learned how to defend themselves in case of attack: how to curl up to protect their vital organs and how to come to the aid of fellow protestors so that beatings were spread out over several people, rather than being concentrated on one victim. Lawson taught them to keep eye contact with their assailants at all times—experience showed that this could check an attacker's rage. And they learned how not to be provoked into striking back.[19]

The students in Lawson's workshops were training for nonviolent direct action, which was not yet a major part of the civil rights movement. It would be something far more confrontational than the bus boycotts: Black people who sat down at a whites-only lunch counter and asked for service would be physically violating the South's legal and social order; they risked getting hurt and going to jail. That was why Lawson had emphasized "the necessity of fierce discipline and training and strategizing and planning and recruiting and doing the kinds of things you do to have a movement. That can't happen spontaneously. It has to be done systematically." Anything less would dissolve under the force that opposed them.[20]

To become familiar with the lunch counters and the store employees, they made scouting forays on two consecutive Saturdays. Each time a group of neatly dressed black and white students from the workshops walked into the stores, bought something, took their seats at the counter, and waited to be served. When they were refused service, as they knew they would be, they asked politely to speak to the store manager and heard an explanation of the store's policy. Then they left, returned to the church and talked over what had happened with Lawson.[21]

Before the students left to go home for Christmas, the decision was made to begin the sit-ins in February 1960. When they got back to Nashville in January, they found that news of what they were planning was circulating on local black campuses, and more people were appearing at the workshops. So they met twice a week at the Clark Church; by that time, they were calling themselves the Nashville Student Movement. The most dedicated formed a central committee, reaching decisions by consensus and rotating leadership positions to keep from being overly reliant on any one person. They had become a tight-knit unit, bound together by the intensity of the workshops and the belief instilled by Lawson that they were going to make history. They were about to graduate from what Bernard Lafayette, an ABT student, later called "a nonviolent academy, equivalent to West Point."[22]

On February 3 John Lewis picked up a copy of the *Tennessean* in his dormitory and read that two days earlier four freshmen from North Carolina A&T had sat down at a Woolworth's lunch counter in Greensboro and refused to get up, even after being denied service. The same day Lawson's friend Douglas Moore, a North Carolina minister, called him to say that the sit-ins there were growing each day. He was trying to organize similar protests around his state, and he asked Lawson to help spread the word among activist ministers all around the South—and to act quickly in Nashville to keep the momentum going.

That night hundreds of students crammed into an auditorium at Fisk to hear Lawson announce that sit-ins would begin at Nashville's department stores on February 13 and that those who wanted to participate should volunteer. The next week, as sit-ins spread across North Carolina and into neighboring states, Lawson and the workshop veterans held daily sessions teaching the new recruits what they would have to do. "We were speeding up our schedule, yes, but we remained determined to do this right," Lewis later remembered. "We did not want to unleash hundreds of eager, emotional college students without properly preparing them in the ways of restraint." The trainers insisted over and over again to the newcomers that there must be no retaliation under any circumstances. They must dress well, talk quietly, and wait patiently for hours at the counters, and they must be willing to go to jail.[23]

The regulars at Lawson's workshops since the previous fall were now the nucleus of a much larger group. As final plans were made, they had to prepare for the chance that not everyone would remain nonviolent. There were some who balked at the risks involved: athletes who did not want to lose their scholarships, medical students who knew an arrest record could wreck their careers, or people who simply were afraid of getting beaten up or thrown in jail. Only people who knew they could control their impulse to strike back and were prepared to suffer for the cause would be sitting down at the lunch counters.[24]

Still, there would be plenty of work for everyone else to do. The students doing the actual sitting-in would have an entire logistical system behind them. There would be drivers to take participants from campuses to the First Baptist Church, which would be the staging area and control center. There would be people at the church keeping track of who was where and what was happening downtown, and there would be monitors and runners in the downtown streets, relaying information back to the church and instructions to the protestors in the stores. And there would be people assigned to deal with the press.[25]

The students in Nashville were about to go public and demand they be treated as equal citizens—just as workers in St. Petersburg had done fifty-five years earlier, in their march to the Winter Palace. Both the Nashville students and the St. Petersburg workers drew incentive from their religious faith, both were led by an unconventional clergyman—and both renounced the use of violence as a way to win social justice. But the similarities ended there. The Russian workers prepared in a state of feverish excitement, convinced that the Tsar would hear their pleas and make fundamental changes—and they had no idea what lay in store for them. The students in Nashville no doubt also felt excitement, but they kept their feelings in check and went about their business calmly and methodically. They had been thoroughly briefed on nonviolent action, and they had a good idea of what to expect.

This contrast was partly a reflection of the differences between Georgii Gapon and James Lawson. Gapon was impulsive, and he led others by inflaming their feelings. Lawson, on the other hand, was the most deliberate and cerebral of people, and he avoided whipping up his students. He wanted them to think about what they were doing, to assess what they confronted. But Lawson also had something that was not available to Gapon: the knowledge of how nonviolent action had worked and been developed over decades, throughout the world—and he applied that knowledge exhaustively. Although he was, no less than Gapon, a man of faith, he approached the tasks of nonviolent conflict like a man of science.[26]

"What Will We Do Now?"

Just three days before the sit-in was scheduled, there was a large meeting in the Reverend Smith's First Baptist Church. Smith and other members of the NCLC tried to get the protest postponed, until they could raise more money to pay bail in case the students were arrested (less than $100 had been raised). But Lawson's troops would not hear of waiting any longer, especially now that students in

Greensboro and other cities had acted. The moment of truth had arrived, whatever the peril.

On Saturday, February 13, the students woke to a half foot of fresh snow. They waited for their rides and were dropped off at the First Baptist Church, the men in coats and ties, the women wearing heels. When everyone had assembled, more than a hundred in all, they split up into groups of about twenty-five, each with at least one member of the students' central committee. Then they started walking two abreast past baffled onlookers toward downtown Nashville. After several blocks they reached Fifth Avenue, the city's main shopping street, and each group went into a store.

Lewis's group went into Woolworth's. Each person bought some small item, to establish credentials as a paying customer, and then headed upstairs to the second floor and took a seat at the lunch counter. The waitresses looked stunned. When Lewis tried to order, he was told that "niggers" were not served there. A crowd of shoppers gawked at them—as if, one person said, they were giant space grasshoppers that had invaded the city. A few young white men came up the stairs and shouted insults at them but left quickly when that drew no response. The students stayed put, even after other customers left and a waitress hastily scrawled a sign reading "Counter closed." After the lights were doused and the waitresses themselves left, the students remained behind, reading and doing schoolwork by natural light. Around six o'clock, a messenger from the First Baptist Church came to say that it was time to leave. They were elated when they got back to the church. "It was like New Year's eve—whooping, cheering, hugging, laughing, singing."[27]

Nashville's white establishment had no idea what was going on. Such was their self-containment, most whites had failed to notice the large public meetings over the previous week or two and the stir created by the Greensboro sit-in. All over downtown, store employees and managers were perplexed: They could not serve the students, as that would break longtime custom and, in some cases, explicit store policy. But the students would not leave, so all they could think of doing was to shut the counters down and leave the young people there.

There was no violence that day. But there was also no sign from the store owners that they were willing to reconsider and integrate the lunch counters. Some of them, such as John Sloan, simply believed that separation of the races was right and proper. Those who were not attached to segregation were sensitive to pressure from Sloan as well as from James Stahlman, the influential editor of *The Nashville Banner,* a staunchly segregationist newspaper. The owners also feared losing business from white customers if they let black customers eat at the counters. One sit-in, clearly, was not enough to make a dent in Jim Crow.[28]

African American college students in Nashville, Tennessee sit in at a downtown lunch counter to defy racial segregation, February 1960.

Credit: ©Jimmy Ellis/The Tennessean

The next two sit-ins, on the following Thursday and the Saturday after that, went much like the first, although there were more protestors. Bands of surly whites taunted the students but were kept in check by the presence of police. The students encountered no serious violence either time, but they could not get served at the counters. The city's merchants still apparently had no idea how to deal with the protests.

Saturday, February 27, was the date for the next sit-in. A day or two before that, the city's black leaders got word that different conditions could be expected that day. Will Campbell, a liberal white minister who was friendly with Lawson and Smith, told them he had heard that James Stahlman and other segregationist businessmen had been putting the screws to Mayor West. When the students took their seats Saturday, the police would pull out of the downtown and allow white thugs to go to work on the protestors. Then the police would move back in and arrest students still sitting-in.[29]

Nashville's segregationists finally had a strategy—physical intimidation. The thought of going to prison, even more than the prospect of getting beaten up, was terrifying to Nash, Lewis, and many others. Growing up, they had heard

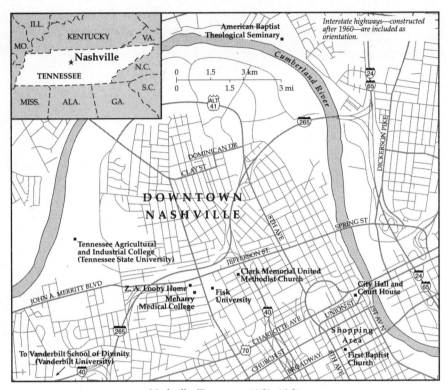

Nashville, Tennessee, 1960–1961

chilling stories about what happened to black people in southern jails and were lectured about the disgrace felt by their families. Still, Lawson had made sure they understood from the outset that what was coming would be dangerous. Now those hazards were at hand.[30]

On Saturday morning, as volunteers congregated at the First Baptist Church, Lawson and the central committee members met in the basement. They had to find a way to show segregationists and city officials that strong-arm tactics would not deter them. For every seat that opened up when a cop led away a protestor, another body would have to fill it. That would require good coordination and communication, so that new waves of demonstrators would be where they were needed. Most of all, it would take numbers: The leaders would just have to hope that prospective volunteers were not scared away by the rumors of arrests and impending violence floating around the campuses.

When the leaders went back upstairs, they discovered that more than 300 volunteers had materialized. It was now more important than ever to make sure that the protestors, especially inexperienced ones, kept their cool and avoided any scuffles that would only justify repression. Lawson and Lafayette had swiped some mimeograph paper from ABT the previous night and made copies of a list of "dos and don'ts" that were handed out to the new recruits:

DO NOT:

1. Strike back nor curse if abused.
2. Laugh out.
3. Hold conversations with floor walker.
4. Leave your seat until your leader has given you permission to do so.
5. Block entrances to stores nor the aisles inside.

DO:

1. Show yourself friendly and courteous at all times.
2. Sit straight; always face the counter.
3. Report all serious incidents to your leader.
4. Refer information seekers to your leader in a polite manner.
5. Remember the teachings of Jesus Christ, Mahatma Gandhi and Martin Luther King.

Love and nonviolence is the way.

MAY GOD BLESS EACH OF YOU[31]

The organizers made sure that anyone carrying a file or pocket knife turned it in, and they weeded out a few people from the new group; then they headed downtown.[32]

The students could tell things were going to be different even as they walked toward Fifth Avenue. White teenagers, as they had before, shouted insults, but this time there was also pushing and shoving, and the police did nothing to stop it. The real trouble began once the students were sitting at the counters. With the police nowhere to be seen, white toughs walked in and started swearing at the students, pulling them off the chairs, punching them and kicking those who went down. Lewis saw one of them stub out a lit cigarette on one student's back. Others were spat on or had mustard and ketchup poured over their heads and shirts. A television camera captured a group of white men and women attacking Paul LaPrad, as he lay on the ground of one store after being knocked off his chair. No student fought back.[33]

After a while the police arrived and began arresting the students, not their assailants. At that point, the plan worked out early in the morning went into effect. Monitors kept track of where the arrests were taking place and promptly dispatched new squads of protestors to take the vacated seats. Those taken into custody filed out of the stores into the paddy wagons through cheering crowds, their heads held high. The police were dumbfounded: These well-dressed, polite young black people—the kind who should have put distance between themselves and anything that might land them in jail—were actually courting arrest. The cops looked at each other, Diane Nash remembered, as if to say: "Do you see this. What will we do now?" After hauling away about eighty students, the police asked the managers to close the stores so no more arrests would be necessary. For most of the students, being arrested was not traumatic; they were buoyed up by what they had been taught. The "kind of power we felt," Bernard Lafayette recalled, "was more forceful than all of their police force . . . and all of their dogs or billy clubs or jails."[34]

"Big Saturday," as Lawson and the students started calling it, was a pivotal moment. The city fathers and police evidently hoped that one afternoon of turmoil would be enough to stop this nonsense, after which they could all heave a sigh of relief and go back to business as usual. White officials and business leaders, of course, had no clue about what had transpired in Lawson's workshops for months and how thoroughly prepared the students would be. They were stunned to find that the protestors were unfazed by beatings and arrests, and they realized they had only two options: They could either step up the violence and ride out the ensuing tumult, or they could try to buy off the students with some sort of concession.

Mayor West and a few business leaders chose the softer strategy. Bail for students arrested that Saturday was reduced to just five dollars—but they refused to pay. So later that night they were simply released without any bail at all. When a judge issued a fifty-dollar fine to each of the arrested students at their trial a couple of days later, they again refused to pay and were slapped with thirty-day sentences in the county workhouse. Two days later, however, West ordered their release. The protest telegrams coming in from around the country—from celebrities like singer Harry Belafonte and former First Lady Eleanor Roosevelt—had helped him realize that the students could hurt the city more behind bars than they could in downtown Nashville.[35]

The mayor then played his ace. He announced that he would appoint a biracial committee, including the presidents of both Fisk and Tennessee A&I, to look into segregation at the lunch counters and make a recommendation. He also asked the students to declare a moratorium on further sit-ins until the committee handed down its report. The students accepted West's offer, even though they were pretty sure it was nothing more than a stalling tactic. They held off from sitting-in for three straight Saturdays, starting March 5, while the committee deliberated. But when they learned that it would recommend

Rev. James Lawson being arrested on March 5, 1960 during his leadership of the
Nashville sit-in movement.

Credit: ©Bettmann/CORBIS

dividing the counters into two sections—one all-white, the other integrated—
they were back at the counters the next Saturday.

In the meantime, arch-segregationist James Stahlman was pushing in a
different direction. Unlike West and some of the store owners, he was devoted to
segregation as a bedrock principle of southern life, and he was not interested in
tampering with it just to restore calm in the business district. The reactionary editor
also had little understanding of the kind of adversary he faced—shown by the fact
that he armed himself and his staff for defense against violent attacks by the young
students. The way to end the sit-ins, Stahlman was convinced, was to go after
Lawson, the "outside agitator" who had stirred things up. Stahlman had influence
at Vanderbilt, where Lawson's assertiveness had already rubbed some of the faculty
members the wrong way. Under intense pressure, the university's divinity school
expelled Lawson on March 3; two days later he was arrested.

A Boycott, a Bombing, and a March

While white leaders cast about for ways to thwart the sit-ins, the nature of the
problem shifted. That, too, was a product of Big Saturday. For generations, both

blacks and whites in Nashville had accepted whites-only lunch counters along with the rest of segregation. But over the previous decade, the ice around the southern system had begun to melt: The NAACP's lawsuits, the bus boycotts, and desegregation court orders had cast doubt on the future of Jim Crow. The sit-ins, and the beatings and arrests they provoked, sowed more doubt among whites about whether the old order could be preserved safely. Black leaders schooled in nonviolent strategy believed that the kind of disturbing yet riveting public spectacle unfolding in Nashville would undermine segregation by changing the way it was seen and experienced by segregationists themselves.

Whatever change was occurring in the minds of white people was not yet apparent, but the impact on black Nashville was huge. Thanks to the coverage in the *Tennessean* and on local television, everyone in the city knew what had happened on February 27. Lawson's students, once seen by their peers as quixotic oddballs, were now treated like heroes on their campuses. Recruiting new volunteers to join the protests was now easier. The effect on black adults was just as dramatic. The week after Big Saturday, the First Baptist Church was jammed with people who came to show support.

A call then went out for all black people in Nashville to boycott the downtown stores until the owners agreed to desegregate. Ever since Montgomery the boycott had been a well-known weapon against segregation. So ministers talked it up from the pulpit, Nashville's black radio station publicized it, and women—the main shoppers and, hence, the key players in the boycott—relayed the news around town over the phone lines. Mass meetings held by Smith and the NCLC kept up the fervor. Monitors were posted in downtown streets so that any black person coming out of a store would be asked not to shop there again.[36]

The boycott's impact on retailers (an industry whose profits relied on sales volume) was significant. As Nashville's white residents had increasingly moved out to the suburbs, the stores had become more dependent on patronage from black customers. To make matters worse, many of those white customers who still shopped downtown had started to stay away because of the protests. "It was a ghost town down there," Bernard Lafayette recalled. Some days "the only people you saw . . . were the demonstrators."[37]

In the sit-ins' first weeks, the store owners had shown little interest in negotiating, even though not all of them were loyal segregationists. Greenfield Pitts, an executive at Harvey's department store, treated the students respectfully and let them know early on that he was not personally opposed to desegregating the counters. Close to one-third of his customers were black, and it made no sense to him that they could shop in one part of the store but not be served in another. Yet he was not prepared to buck the system. Once the boycott started sapping their profits, however, the merchants began singing a different tune. They now realized that this was no longer just a "student affair" but a campaign by all of black Nashville.[38]

The boycott's economic pressure on top of the public sensation of the sit-ins had shaken up the status quo. The store owners wanted out, but they did not want to take the first step. In a statement quoted in the *Tennessean* in early April, one of them explained that they wanted to avoid "the unenviable position of deciding on a social practice which would be a radical change in the customs of our community . . . it is most impractical for a small group of stores to assume the role of leading such a change." The catalyst would have to come from elsewhere. And when it came, it came from one of the system's custodians.[39]

Diane Nash was getting dressed in her dormitory around 5:30 in the morning on April 19, a Monday, when she heard a loud boom in the distance. By the time she reached the central committee meeting scheduled for six o'clock, she and the other students had learned that Z. Alexander Looby's home had been bombed. Looby was one of black Nashville's most eminent figures, a lawyer and city councilman. He had filed the lawsuit that led to Nashville's school desegregation, and he had been an early supporter of the student protestors and had defended them in court. As a proud, politically outspoken African American, he was a natural target for white supremacists. The blast was powerful—it practically wrecked the Loobys' home and shattered more than a hundred windows in a nearby building—but it somehow failed to injure anyone in the house.[40]

Nash and the other students were horrified, but they also saw an opportunity. The bombing was a serious escalation by Nashville's racists, going far beyond the punching and kicking at the lunch counters. It was also aimed not at college students from out of town but at a pillar of respectable black society. The students guessed that black adults would go further now in confronting the city's establishment and that many white leaders would be shocked by the bombing. It was time to turn up the heat: The students decided they would hold a march later that day.[41]

Immediately they scattered to let people know what had happened. Bernard Lafayette went to Tennessee A&I and commandeered the public address system, announcing that a march to protest the bombing would leave from the campus at noon that day. Then he went around to buildings not reached by loudspeakers, interrupting classroom lectures and exhorting students to join the march. By noon there were over 1,000 people on the campus ready to go. As they paraded in absolute silence down Jefferson Street, the main artery through black Nashville, students from Fisk and Meharry joined them, as did many adults. By the time they reached their destination at the courthouse, there were perhaps

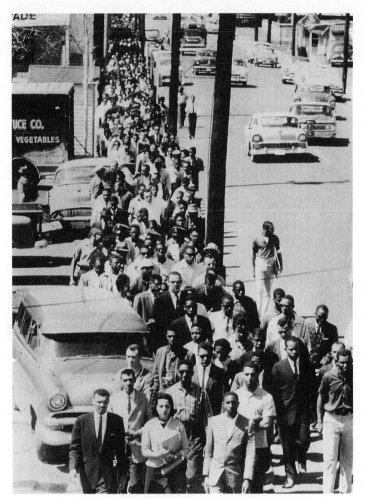

African Americans and others protesting segregation—including the student leader
Diane Nash (front row, center)—march to the Nashville City Hall on
April 19, 1960, to confront the mayor.

Credit: ©New York Times/Archive Photos

4,000. Nashville had never seen a civil rights demonstration on anything like
this scale before; no southern city had, in fact.[42]

   While the marchers were standing and singing in the courthouse square,
Mayor West was up on the steps talking to a delegation selected by the students.
C. T. Vivian, a fiery young black minister who had participated in the workshops
and sit-ins, excoriated the mayor for not speaking out against the violence and
said that his police force had not upheld the law. West was offended, got into a
heated argument with Vivian, and told the protestors about all the good things

he had done for black people. At that point, Diane Nash spoke up. Rather than attack West, she appealed to his sense of fairness (which he liked to think of as one of his virtues), asking the mayor if he felt "that it's wrong to discriminate against a person solely on the basis of his race or color." West tried "to answer it frankly and honestly," he said later; " . . . I could not agree that it was morally right for someone to sell them merchandise and refuse them service." Then she asked if he thought the lunch counters should be desegregated. First he hemmed and hawed, but Nash was not going to let him off the hook, and she asked again: "Then, Mayor, do you recommend that the lunch counters be desegregated?" West, finally, said "Yes." The crowd erupted in applause, and West and the protestors hugged each other.[43]

This scene was played out in full view of everyone at the base of the city hall's steps. The *Tennessean* made sure the message got through to the whole city the next morning, when its front-page headline blared, "INTEGRATE COUNTERS— MAYOR." The downtown merchants now had the political cover they needed to desegregate. Over the next three weeks, representatives of the protestors— including Nash and Smith—met several times with store owners and city officials and quietly worked out a plan to integrate the counters in the six stores that had been the main targets. May 10 was set as the date when stores would begin serving black customers. The students had an outright victory in their grasp, but they also understood that they had to shield merchants from the ire of the city's betrayed segregationists. So they agreed that initially only small numbers of black people would ask to be served and that the new policy would not be disclosed until it had been in effect for a week. That way, integration would be a fait accompli by the time any backlash came.[44]

James Lawson and his students had been targeting both the store owners, who had the power to change things at the lunch counters, and broader white opinion in Nashville that had created the climate in which the stores operated. Lawson had insisted that a change of heart among whites would come by students' sacrificing for the cause and awakening the sense of justice that he believed was latent in everyone. The sit-ins had been designed to disarm the superficial imagery of blacks that racists cherished: The students were polite, well dressed, and resolutely nonviolent—practically the picture, apart from darker skin color, of how Nashville's white establishment liked to view its own sons and daughters. The sight of them being bullied and hauled away in paddy wagons had been disquieting; the bombing of Looby's house had been appalling. The cumulative effect of all this on white consciousness seemed to break surface on April 19, when Ben West listened to Diane Nash on the courthouse steps and agreed that it was time for change. Whatever West's motive, this was the kind of transformative moment that Gandhian satyagraha was supposed to produce.

But there was more to the victory than the exemplary effect of nonviolent action. If the sit-ins helped change influential white people in Nashville, it was not solely by appealing to their sense of decency. The sit-ins had been terrible for business, they brought disorder to downtown streets, and they forced the managers to close down. Moreover, enduring beatings and arrests demonstrated the students' courage and selflessness in front of the very people—the city's black community—whom their sacrifice would benefit. Civil disobedience is not just for the purpose of unbalancing opponents; it also needs to galvanize potential supporters, just as Indian protestors in the 1930s used satyagrahas to draw fresh energy from their own people.

In the next several years in Nashville, there were sit-ins at hamburger joints and cafeterias, stand-ins at movie theaters, and sleep-ins in hotel lobbies. Stores were boycotted to protest racist hiring practices. In all of this, there were more beatings and more arrests of unarmed protestors. The 1960 sit-ins had not expunged the city's racism all at once, but they did give black students and activists a sense of momentum and a model of action that they applied in their relentless pursuit of equal rights. And while the struggle to desegregate Nashville went on, the young men and women trained by Lawson in 1960 were already laying plans for nonviolent action elsewhere in the South.

A National Crisis

Diane Nash remembered feeling vulnerable at times during the spring of 1960. Here she was just twenty-two, still a student, and she was "coming up against governors, judges, politicians, businessmen." One thing that boosted her morale was hearing radio reports about other students staging sit-ins in cities and towns all over the South. A mass nonviolent campaign was now a reality in much of the region.[45]

By the end of April there were sit-ins in seventy-eight cities, and students were in the vanguard. About 70,000 of them participated in some kind of protest during 1960, and well over 3,000 went to jail. Local NAACP or SCLC activists were often in the thick of the action, but the students were unwilling to let the established organizations call the shots. In April student leaders from around the South gathered for a conference in Raleigh, North Carolina, and they created a group of their own—the Student Nonviolent Coordinating Committee (SNCC). Lawson and the Nashville students were in it from the start, and Marion Barry (later to become mayor of Washington, D.C.) was elected chairman.

The sit-ins caught on fast because they worked, at least in places on the southern periphery, such as Tennessee, North Carolina, and Texas. By making audacious and highly visible demands for equal treatment, student activists inspired broader protests from black communities. By creating street disturbances and sometimes sparking consumer boycotts, they put economic pressure on merchants. And by provoking assaults from zealous segregationists, they upset the moral complacency of at least part of the white population. As a result business establishments in nearly 100 southern towns were integrated by the end of 1961.[46]

In the Deep South, however, there were not many sit-ins, and they met with less success. In Georgia, Alabama, Mississippi, and Louisiana, most white communities were determined to uphold segregation, and not many newspapers in these states would, as the *Tennessean* had done in Nashville, provide fair coverage. Retribution also tended to be sharp and swift: Besides mass arrests, the Ku Klux Klan was given rein to threaten or beat up demonstrators, and thousands of protesting students were thrown out of school. In this menacing atmosphere, black adults were less eager to rally round.[47]

Cities in the Deep South were also not as vulnerable to the Nashville strategy of producing a local crisis and exploiting divisions in the white community. Across the whole South, in fact, the movement's momentum waned by the second half of 1960. So civil rights activists were ready to try a new approach, one that modified the earlier strategy in one crucial respect: Although campaigns continued for the most part to be locally based, the activists were now intent on generating crises that reverberated around the nation. The Nashville students did not invent this strategy, but they were the perfect candidates to execute it.[48]

In the spring of 1961, John Lewis spotted an announcement in the SNCC bulletin soliciting volunteers for something called a Freedom Ride. The ad was placed by the Congress for Racial Equality (CORE), a mostly white and northern though long-standing civil rights group, which proposed to send an integrated team of activists rolling across the South on commercial bus lines, to have them test compliance with a recent Supreme Court ruling that required the desegregation of interstate buses and terminals. On May 4 Lewis and twelve other volunteers boarded two buses in Washington, D.C. Their plan was to ride through seven southern states and reach New Orleans, their destination, on May 17.[49]

The Freedom Riders had little trouble in North Carolina and Virginia, where sit-ins had already made inroads. But their first stop in South Carolina, at Rock Hill, was a different story. Lewis was attacked by two white men—slugged in the head and then kicked when he was on the floor—as soon as he stepped into the "White" waiting room at the bus station; two of the other riders were also roughed up. While Lewis went to Philadelphia for an interview, the other riders continued into Georgia, and after they crossed over into Alabama on May 14, one bus's tires were slashed, and it was forced off the road and firebombed. Riders on the other bus were beaten and clubbed at the Anniston bus station and, later, in Birmingham. The white mobs responsible clearly acted with the permission of local police.[50]

The bloodied Freedom Riders decided they would cut short the rides—they had established that the Court's ruling was not being implemented—and fly from Birmingham to New Orleans. But the Rock Hill incident had put the rides in newspapers around the country, photos of the burning bus outside Anniston had made it onto front pages, and journalists from around the country were descending on Birmingham, a city that had acquired a reputation as perhaps the most vocally racist in the South. In addition, federal officials in the Department of Justice were becoming alarmed.[51]

The violence in Alabama put the Kennedy administration on the horns of a dilemma. Like other postwar presidents, John Kennedy believed in civil rights, but he was reluctant to antagonize southern politicians in the Congress, who chaired key committees and could block his legislative agenda. Since the New Deal, the Democratic Party had been held together in part by a tacit understanding that southern Democrats would support liberal northerners at the top of the national ticket, so long as the party looked the other way when it came to race relations in the South. This arrangement was already under strain, due to the *Brown* decision and the conflict-ridden process of school desegregation. But by focusing national media attention on ruthlessness against protestors and on brutal characters like Birmingham's police chief, Eugene "Bull" Connor, the Freedom Rides forced the White House to choose between their higher ideals and white southern support.[52]

For Robert Kennedy, the U.S. Attorney General, the main goal after May 14 was simply to help the beleaguered riders make it out of Birmingham and end the rides without further incident. For that reason, he and other officials at Justice were hugely relieved when they managed to get the riders safely on a plane bound for New Orleans on the evening of May 15. The situation looked ready to simmer down, easing the pressure to act decisively. But they were stunned to learn a few hours later that a group of young people from Nashville was planning to go down to Birmingham to pick up where the original riders left off—and nothing they could say would dissuade them.

On May 20 twenty students who had made it to Birmingham boarded a bus for Montgomery. Thanks to the mediation of Robert Kennedy's aide, John Seigenthaler (a *Tennessean* editor before joining the administration), the students had a state police escort until they reached the Montgomery city limits. The city police were supposed to take over then, but they were nowhere in sight. Instead the bus was greeted by a flock of reporters and a pack of white supremacists, who assaulted the riders as they stepped off. Three students, including Lewis again, were badly beaten in full view of the press. So was Seigenthaler, who was knocked unconscious with a lead pipe while trying to rescue two of the students.[53]

Robert Kennedy could hardly tolerate the clubbing of his own deputy by a vicious gang acting with the acquiescence of local law enforcement—but the cauldron of these events also surely fired his sense of history. He sent federal marshals into Montgomery to assure that there was no further violence while the riders were in town, and federal officials worked out a deal with Mississippi authorities to guarantee that there would be no repeat there of the Alabama assaults. The state officials kept their word, and the Nashville students, now reinforced by more riders who had flown into Montgomery, rode safely into Jackson. There they were arrested, charged with violating state and local laws, and sentenced to sixty days in jail.[54]

The Freedom Riders served most of their sentence at Parchman Farm, a place that was infamous among black people as the most hellish of prisons. But thanks to media coverage, they not only had reaped enormous publicity for themselves and the movement, they also had exposed to the nation the snarling face of Jim Crow. At the end of May, the Attorney General petitioned the Interstate Commerce Commission to mandate the desegregation of all interstate bus terminals, which it did in September. The Supreme Court's ruling finally had teeth, and the integration of terminals was well under way, even in the Deep South, by the end of 1961.

Diane Nash, Bernard Lafayette, John Lewis (later elected to the U.S. Congress), and their fellow students had changed the course of American history by doing what James Lawson had taught them and what they had learned in the sit-ins. To those who condoned segregation, they demonstrated the cost to the community's honor of enforcing it, and they imposed tangible costs on all who upheld it. In Nashville this meant sitting down at lunch counters, in the full knowledge that they were likely to be beaten and jailed. In Alabama the next year, it meant endangering their very lives. The demonstrative value of nonviolent action had never been so evident in the thirty years since Gandhi's campaigns against the British in India. The Nashville students and Freedom Riders forced a crisis on the nation, and out of the crisis they wrested swift if unfinished changes in the system that withheld their rights.

When those who marched in Nashville on April 19, 1960, reached the base of the courthouse steps, a young white man named Guy Carawan started playing his guitar and singing. Carawan had met James Lawson and several of his students at the Highlander Folk School, a training center for labor and civil rights organizers in the Tennessee mountains. He was a collector of folk songs, and that day he chose to sing one of the songs that John Lewis and Bernard Lafayette had learned at Highlander, "We Shall Overcome." It had come out of black churches and been turned into a protest song by black women strikers in South Carolina some years earlier. Not too many others in the crowd that day knew it, but the lyrics were easy to pick up, and they started singing along.

"We Shall Overcome" went on to become a universal anthem of protest. It was sung at peaceful demonstrations in Cape Town, Prague, and Jakarta—the most easily noticed example of how African Americans, who studied and learned from the campaigns of Indian nationalists, themselves became examples for people using nonviolent action to secure human rights and justice. But for those who watched it from afar, the American civil rights movement yielded more than just a song. Thanks to its timing and location, the struggle to end racial segregation in the American South was the first popular nonviolent movement to unfold before the modern mass media. The media's presence created new strategic possibilities in waging nonviolent campaigns, especially the opportunity to involve third parties who do not have a direct stake in a conflict but who have the means to tip the balance toward one side or the other.

Since the 1960s, as technology and commerce have expanded the global reach of electronic media and communications, activists for rights and democracy have given careful attention to the images their movements project to decision makers in Washington and other key capitals, and to the people who keep them in power. Media-related tactics have the potential to be damaging if they foster false hope that intervention by external players can substitute for patient internal organization or good strategic choices in a conflict. But knowing that the world is watching has lifted the morale of many movements, and the coverage has helped channel material support from distant places to those on the front lines.

The American civil rights campaigners of the 1960s contributed one other thing to the power of nonviolent resistance in the final third of the twentieth century. Because they were conscious that nonviolent sanctions had been successful earlier in history, and because they were convinced that the use of these sanctions had intrinsic advantages in resisting oppression, their success conferred on nonviolent action a new aura of effectiveness that it had never before possessed. Not only did the mass media popularize the story of what was done in the American South—they universalized the impression that nonviolent force could be more powerful.

In the United States, that force transformed the social fabric and political direction of the nation. In Nashville and in other southern communities, the sit-ins separated white leaders who had no deep interest in preserving segregation from those who did; the most ambivalent elements of the old order were detached from the most intransigent. The Freedom Rides played out on a larger stage—the riders destabilized the balance of interests that kept the American system of apartheid in place, by provoking the national government to act against its institutions and practices. The quickest way for civil rights activists to make headway in the Deep South was to nationalize the struggle by igniting crises that would draw federal intervention. "The key to everything," Martin Luther King declared in the early 1960s, "is federal commitment."[55]

What made this possible was, again, the growing role of television in American life: Commotion on the streets was experienced vicariously by millions of people. Even if this did not guarantee immediate action, it did reframe the public interest. The Freedom Rides and the Birmingham demonstrations in the spring of 1963, (and the march from Selma to Montgomery two years later), created unforgettable images of conflict between local authorities and nonviolent protestors, transferring legitimacy and popular sympathy from one to the other—and changing the political environment in which national leaders had to operate.

The civil rights movement followed a simple logic: It mobilized black people behind nonviolent sanctions that compelled the nation to change. Martin Luther King's declaration on the steps of the Lincoln Memorial in 1963 that he had a dream of racial equality capped the largest nonviolent demonstration of the postwar period in America, the March on Washington. In the wake of President Kennedy's assassination later that year, a white southerner, Lyndon Johnson, moved into the White House and drove the Civil Rights Act of 1964 and the Voting Rights Act of 1965 into the annals of human liberation—as Dr. King and his legions drove their spirit outward to the world.

In 1936, when the African American leader Howard Thurman visited with Gandhi in India, his wife, who had accompanied him, sang two Negro spirituals for the great Indian sage. Dr. Thurman then explained that "striking things" in hundreds of spirituals reminded him of what Gandhi had told them and that black Americans needed to use his solutions to lift up their own people. "Well," Gandhi replied, "if it comes true, it may be through the Negroes that the unadulterated message of non-violence will be delivered to the world."[56]

CHAPTER NINE

South Africa: Campaign against Apartheid

Sophiatown

EARLY ON A WEDNESDAY MORNING IN 1955, thousands of police and a fleet of military trucks drove into the dusty streets of Sophiatown, a black neighborhood less than seven kilometers (four and a half miles) from the center of Johannesburg. Armed men stalked into the yards of homes, shouted at the people inside to come out, and ordered them to pile all their belongings into the trucks. Then they were driven away with their pots and pans, mattresses and old furniture, to the newly built township of Meadowlands, eight miles away. Within a few years everyone had been cleared out of Sophiatown, and all of their homes and dwellings had been torn down.

The first Africans had moved to Sophiatown around the turn of the century, when it was still some distance from the settled heart of Johannesburg. It was one of the few places in South Africa where nonwhites were allowed to own real estate, and it turned into a boom town for black Africans and the Indians and people of mixed descent called "Coloureds"—all of whom were legally barred from living in white areas. Sophiatown became a rollicking, diverse community, home to writers, jazz musicians, doctors, lawyers, clergymen, flashy gangsters, factory workers, and domestic servants. But by midcentury, while still a veritable brewery of rich African and Asian culture, it had also become overcrowded, crime-ridden, and mostly poor—offering a fertile medium for political ferment, where political opposition groups like the African National Congress (ANC) found strong support.

During the same decades, Johannesburg's white population surged out and around Sophiatown, and its coveted location doomed this vibrant enclave. When voices were heard calling for removing blacks and Coloureds from Sophiatown and other townships perched on the desirable northern rim of the city, South Africa's government started readying new towns for those about to be dispossessed, on less desirable ground to the southwest. By the end of the 1950s, all those made homeless by forced relocation had been installed in these Southwestern Townships (which became known by the acronym Soweto), and a new white suburb went up on top of their old town. It was called Triomf, the Afrikaans word for "triumph."

The new name was apt, for in those days most South Africans, white or black, could see no end to the domination of white reality over black and Coloured dreams. "Many of us believed in the righteousness of our cause," recalled Azhar Cachalia, an anti-government activist born after the emptying of Sophiatown. But he "was never persuaded that we were going to win." Yet Cachalia and others like him would soon turn South Africa upside down. Intellectuals and religious leaders, both black and white, would denounce the ideology behind the racial system. Miners and factory workers would use economic leverage to push for change. And guerrillas based outside the country would launch armed raids. But nothing would be more fateful than what ordinary people would do to challenge the state in their own neighborhoods and, as they transformed their townships with nonviolent resistance, to embrace a new strategy of seeking national power.[1]

WHITE SUPREMACY AND BLACK RESISTANCE

Fortress Apartheid

The razing of Sophiatown and the raising of Triomf were two of many landmarks along the rocky trail of South Africa's racial travail. Since Dutch colonists had first disembarked at the southern tip of Africa in the seventeenth century and then pushed aside the natives and taken their land, there had rarely been a moment when white rulers' belief in white supremacy had faltered. While a modern state evolved in the nineteenth and twentieth centuries, the racial attitudes of the governing minority did not. Africans and Coloureds, together with Indians who first arrived as indentured laborers, were barred from high-wage jobs and largely excluded from politics. During the 1920s an explicit policy of segregation was adopted, but it was not until the 1948 victory of the National Party that the nadir was reached. Its new policy was called "apartness"—in Afrikaans, *apartheid.*

Racism was made the organizing principle of South African life. The state assigned each individual to a racial category—European, Indian, Coloured, or African—and then saw to it that these "races" were separated from each other as much as possible. Eight (later ten) reservations were set aside, so-called Bantu Homelands, where each African "nation" was to develop its own society, eventually attaining independence. The rest, eighty percent of South Africa—including all major cities, ports, industrial areas, and prime farmland—became the homeland for Europeans, who accounted for 20 percent of the population.

The chief architect of this social zoology was Hendrik Verwoerd, who was born in the Netherlands and raised in South Africa. After attending German universities, where he and other young Afrikaaners swallowed a large dose of the racialism at the core of Nazi thinking, he decided that "separate development" was necessary to prevent conflict among South Africa's different peoples. He then became a teacher, worked as a newspaper editor, served as minister of native affairs in the government—and was made prime minister in 1958. "Our motto," this tall, domineering man declared, "is to maintain white supremacy for all time to come over our own people and our own country, by force if necessary." Stabbed to death on the floor of parliament in 1966, he had once said he did not "have the nagging doubt of ever wondering whether perhaps I am wrong."[2]

But Verwoerd had been wrong. As much as he and his political heirs might fantasize about racial separation, nothing could isolate the nonwhite majority from the national economy. South Africa's mining and manufacturing industries relied on black labor, white merchants depended on black spending, and white bungalows were tended by black domestics. While whites might not wish to live with blacks, it was clear they could not live without them. And there was no way that the parched homelands, bypassed by industrial investment and transportation, could employ or feed the hundreds of thousands of people dumped there. Blacks gravitated to the cities, because that was where they could work and that was where they were needed.

So the government had to find some way to run a multiracial society. Its solution was an intricate system of control over the comings and goings of non-Europeans: Africans needed permission from local authorities to live in cities, and they had to carry passbooks in which this permission was recorded. Moreover, Africans (along with Coloureds and Indians) could not live wherever they wished; they were confined to racially zoned townships, usually miles outside city limits, leaving white neighborhoods safely insulated. Others were forced into the homelands, which were soon populated mainly by women and children, whose husbands and fathers worked as migrant laborers.

The strictures of apartheid were applied in manifold ways. The state prohibited sexual relations and marriage across racial lines. It required segregation in every public facility and conveyance, from churches to movie theaters, from taxis to hearses. African students went to schools designed to teach them, in the words of one official, "to realize that equality with Europeans is not for them," and the government spent ten times more on white students than on African ones. Politics became an exclusively white realm, as Coloured and African voters were stripped of the franchise. The result was a system of white power, pure and simple.[3]

In defense of white supremacy, the regime erected a citadel of laws and rules giving itself arbitrary authority over civilians. Police could arrest people and hold them in solitary confinement and without trial for indefinite periods. Africans who protested or joined an opposition group could lose permission to live in a township, even if they had been born and raised there. And censorship was very tight, especially over radio and television broadcasts.

But this fortress state was not self-sufficient. The wealth and muscle of white South Africa depended, as with most modern nations, on fruitful ties with the rest of the world. South Africa's military was equipped with hardware produced in Europe, North America, Israel, and Taiwan. Its economy required foreign capital, technology, petroleum, and international export markets, especially for minerals. Only as long as key trading partners were willing to do business with a state committed to racial inequality could South Africa's economy and its white proprietors prosper.

There was another weak thread in the fabric of apartheid. White dominion could be maintained only with the cooperation of a critical number of blacks. Control over the homelands required compliant African leaders. The bureaucracy and the police employed many black people in subordinate staff jobs, and their control in the townships rested partly on black informers. Black soldiers were a substantial minority of the permanent ranks of the armed forces, though conscripts and reserves were all white. The mines, factories, and farms that kept white South Africa in material comfort could function only if millions of blacks did most of the grinding manual labor. If blacks could suspend their cooperation with the system in some or all of these ways, they could mount a challenge to white rule—as some had discovered decades before.

Early Resistance

At the century's outset, the European rulers of South Africa had faced resistance from African, Coloured, and Indian civilians, spurred by anger over forced population transfers, registration laws, and dismal conditions. Black people had launched petition drives and boycotts, held marches and demonstrations, organized strikes, established squatter settlements, and joined "vigilance associations" to voice grievances. But the most systematic campaign was waged by Indians, led by Mohandas Gandhi. Starting in 1907, thousands of Indians had protested discrimination for seven years, through strikes, burning registration cards, and mass illegal border crossings, until the government canceled some of the laws. Nonviolent action had prevailed, though only temporarily, against racial injustice.

In ensuing decades, prominent Africans, Coloureds, and Indians had established national organizations, including the African National Congress, to represent their interests. Much like the Indian National Congress before Gandhi's return to India, these were groups of educated professionals who often remained aloof from the struggles of ordinary people. They professed loyalty to the state and used legal, respectable means to protest—even as one brick after another was mortared onto the lengthening wall of white supremacy.

When the stridently racist National Party won the 1948 elections, hope had expired that gentle persuasion might alleviate the burden on black people. A generation of young militants, led by Nelson Mandela, Walter Sisulu, and Oliver Tambo, turned the ANC toward popular mobilization and declared a Defiance Campaign against newly enacted apartheid laws, modeled on Gandhi's nonviolent protests. Thousands violated curfews, segregation, and other ordinances and went to jail. But the campaign was strong only in a few regions and won little support from whites. The ANC called it off in early 1953 after violent riots broke out and repressive laws were passed that authorized, among other things, the whipping of protestors.[4]

The ANC then desisted from lawbreaking for several years, but it did call for school and consumer boycotts, and it became involved in local protests, from opposing the destruction of Sophiatown to challenging rents and bus fares. Meanwhile, beginning in 1955, women all over South Africa held demonstrations, meetings, and marches to denounce the law that made them carry passbooks. The Federation of South African Women, which was behind these campaigns, defied the racialist order simply by bringing white and black women leaders together to plan and carry out the protests.[5]

In 1959 dissidents in the ANC who rejected the organization's nonracial ideology and its goal of forging alliances with sympathetic whites created a rival group called the Pan-Africanist Congress (PAC). Early in 1960 the PAC called on Africans to go to police stations without their passes and let themselves be arrested. On March 21, 5,000 appeared at the police station in Sharpeville, an industrial city in the Transvaal, and waited to be taken into custody. After doing nothing for hours, the police finally fired into the crowd, killing almost seventy people. The Sharpeville massacre sparked weeks of mass protests all over the country, including strikes and riots. The state hit back hard. Over 10,000 people, almost all Africans, were arrested, and the PAC and the ANC were banned.

Forced to operate underground, African leaders debated how to confront a regime that answered nonviolent protest with bullets. Nelson Mandela had harbored doubts about a nonviolent strategy since the mid-1950s, and now he argued for armed action. At a meeting of the ANC Working Committee in June 1961, he quoted an old proverb: "The attacks of the wild beast cannot be averted with only bare hands." Mandela carried the day; the ANC formed an armed wing, *Umkhonto we Sizwe* (spear of the nation), and bombed government buildings, railroad lines, and power stations. But the state moved swiftly to round up the fighters; by the end of 1964 Mandela and other ANC leaders had gone to prison. Those who escaped arrest fled the country and set themselves up in exile. Armed struggle had not brought black people any closer to liberation than the nonviolent campaigns of the 1950s.[6]

"To Hell with Afrikaans"

Popo Simon Molefe had been just three years old when he watched the police herd his family into trucks and haul them from Sophiatown to Soweto, and he had been only seven at the time of the massacre at Sharpeville. He had come of age in the 1960s, when popular civilian protest against the regime seemed dormant. Yet through it all, humiliating lesson by humiliating lesson, he and his generation of young black people were gradually being motivated to act.

Because Molefe's parents could not afford to raise all their eight children, he had been taken in by his aunt, who worked as a live-in domestic servant. Molefe sold apples at railroad stations and football matches and worked as a caddy at Johannesburg's golf courses. Only when he was ten did he begin school; some days he walked there barefoot, some days hungry. Although he was a bright student, he was twenty-four when he finished high school, which was not unusual for someone from the townships.[7]

As Molefe inched his way through school, more Africans seeking jobs and deserting the homelands had flooded into Soweto, but housing and municipal services were not ready for them. By the mid-1970s about seventeen people lived in a typical four-room house, while many put up shacks on whatever open space they could find. Most houses had no running water. When Molefe went to work at the golf courses or visited his aunt at her employer, he discovered the difference between white and black Johannesburg. In the white neighborhoods there were paved roads, big houses, and everybody had electricity. Molefe also found out he was not welcome there. One day he was taunted by a white boy his own age, who called him *kaffir* (a near equivalent of "nigger") and slapped him. Molefe hit him back. "There was an adult white woman coming from the opposite direction. She threatened to assault me for doing what I did to this white boy. I felt very angry, perturbed and terrified."

Molefe came to know the law and the police as capricious and intrusive. Police officers known as Black Jacks would descend on Soweto houses in the night, roust everyone from bed, and demand to see passes proving they had permission to live in the township. One time Molefe was standing outside his house when a policeman came up and asked him to produce his pass. He explained that it was inside and offered to go get it. The officer refused, handcuffed him, and hauled him away by foot. After they had gone several kilometers Molefe was suddenly released and left to walk home. Like other black South Africans he learned that his ability to be at a certain place at a particular time depended on getting permission from the authorities.

In the early 1970s Molefe gravitated toward a new force in African society, Black Consciousness. Steve Biko, its most prominent advocate, contended that white rule had divided the oppressed peoples of South Africa and instilled a psychology of acquiescence. Biko proposed that Coloureds, Indians, and Africans should acknowledge a common identity as "black" people and build a united front. He believed, as Gandhi did, that emancipation had to originate in the minds of individuals. They had to reject the message, hammered home in schools, history books, and the white media, that their lives and customs had lesser value; they would have to liberate themselves, not look to whites for help.

Molefe came to believe that black people "were capable of doing anything that any other human being was able to do"—a self-confidence that was bound sooner or later to collide with the myriad barriers of apartheid. For young blacks growing up in cramped and fetid townships, marking time in schools designed to prepare them for obedient service to white employers, the message of Black Consciousness could only be a call to rebellion.

In May 1976 Molefe and other members of a Black Consciousness group— rankled by the government's new policy of teaching some subjects to Soweto students in Afrikaans, the language of their oppressors—decided to protest. One June morning students dressed in their school uniforms marched toward the center of town, singing songs and carrying signs overhead with messages like "To Hell with Afrikaans." Then they ran into a police detachment, which shot

Popo Molefe, national secretary of the United Democratic Front, at a rally
in Soweto, South Africa, in February 1985.

Credit: ©Reuters/Archive Photos

off tear gas. The students held their ground, and some threw stones. The police
opened fire, killing a thirteen-year-old boy. Packs of young people smashed
windows and set fire to municipal vehicles, schools, and government buildings.
The police kept shooting at students wherever they could find them. For three
days there was rioting and rifle fire in Soweto. When it was over, more than sixty
Africans were dead, and the rioters had killed two white men.

During the months that followed, the uprising spread to African and
Coloured townships in practically every part of South Africa. Everywhere

students were the nucleus—they marched, clashed with police, rioted, and died by the scores. By the time the violence subsided ten months later, the death toll had reached 1,149 people, just 5 of whom were white.

Fighting police in the streets was a fierce but futile way to resist white rule. Students had only stones and other crude weapons—and piling up casualties was not a way to build a movement. Absorbing the lesson, they experimented with other sanctions. They created a Soweto Students' Representative Council to coordinate new protests, which included refusing to go to school, organizing work "stay-aways" for a few days, and asking township residents to boycott liquor and Christmas spending as a sign of mourning for those who had been killed. But enlisting other people had only mixed success, and by the following year student organizations had been decimated by killings, mass arrests, and the flight of many leaders. A crushing blow came in September 1977, when Steve Biko died after brutal treatment at the hands of police. The greatest wave of popular resistance to apartheid that the country had ever known was over.

The Black Consciousness movement had also run its course. Liberating blacks from a sense of inferiority had been its foremost goal, and that had been widely accomplished. But the movement had no plan for organizing a broad campaign against the regime or any strategy for overcoming white political control. The students who had moved from consciousness-raising to active opposition had had to improvise. Although they had been checked by repression, some now began to form a new movement based on the lessons they learned. At the same time that workers and intellectuals in Poland were taking steps to operate independently of the regime they faced, instead of fighting in the streets with security forces, opponents of apartheid in South Africa were moving in the same direction.[8]

THE CIVIC MOVEMENT

Rents, Bus Fares, and Electricity

In June of 1977 a group of Soweto's leading citizens—people from Black Consciousness, the YWCA, YMCA, and the Black Parents' Association—met to talk about the future. They elected a "Committee of Ten" led by a doctor active in earlier ANC campaigns and then drew up a "blueprint" for Soweto, with ideas for better local services and democratic self-government. But its members were not very representative, and the police put all of them behind bars. It took another two years for a true grass-roots organization, the Soweto Civic Association, to spring up and give ordinary people a way to deal with

South Africa, 1985–1986

everyday problems. Using a lawsuit, a work stay-away, and a rent boycott, it contested a rent increase—and delayed it for a year.

The Soweto organizing reflected the desire of local black activists around the country to tap into the militant energy shown in 1976 but also make the movement more inclusive and disciplined. Some tried to learn from history, by reading works of foreign revolutionaries or political theorists, including Leon Trotsky's history of the 1905 revolution in Russia. Especially influential was a manual written by Filipino activists in 1974 and later published in English by a Japanese organization under the title *Organizing People for Power*. While Black Consciousness had insisted that thinking independently was a precondition for change, the Filipino activists said success would come from helping people win modest but real improvements in their lives. From making decisions together and struggling for real gains would come self-assurance, and also tools and sanctions for new campaigns.[9]

This made sense to activists. Since the 1977 crackdown, many Africans had been afraid of getting involved in political groups, which looked like a sure ticket to jail. By disavowing subversive claims and focusing on complaints about housing, sanitation, and other problems, organizers hoped to build a sturdier movement. Popo Molefe, who would join the Soweto Civic Association in 1982, was one of those who felt this way. Opposition groups, he wrote, should identify those issues that are "essential, real and vital" in the townships and that give the people "the confidence that through their united mass action they can intervene and change their lives on no matter how small a scale."[10]

There was a precedent for this in the South African labor movement. In the 1970s African workers had gone on strikes and fought for the right to form their own trade unions—which, once established, had largely steered clear of political protest, so as not to invite repression and jeopardize the chance to improve conditions in factories and mines. They even had convinced state officials that allowing workers to unionize was better than driving them into the arms of revolutionaries. The unions had not attacked apartheid, but they had given Africans the opportunity to develop power in the workplace.

The strategy of organizing communities around tangible grievances dove-tailed with new conditions facing the townships. The regime's goals had become contradictory: To secure political stability, it wanted now to improve various services—but it also wanted to make the townships pay for them. Black South Africans, carrying the millstone of apartheid, also would have to bear the cost of rehabilitating their dismal neighborhoods. Anticipating unrest, the government tried to insulate itself by having administrative boards (which had supervised townships) surrender powers to councils elected by local voters. Now black council members would have to evict squatters, collect rents (almost all township housing was municipally owned), and raise fees for services. Unwittingly, the government had handed local activists a new, accessible target against which to mobilize people.

In townships all over Transvaal province, rent hikes and the destruction of squatter settlements spurred people to organize and resist. There were public demonstrations, rent boycotts, and picketing of community council meetings. In the township of Duduza, where the council announced that rent and service charges would double over three years to pay for the installation of sewer lines, women carried "night buckets" full of waste to the township's administrative offices, so the bosses there "would feel the smell."[11]

In Port Elizabeth, an automobile manufacturing center on the Eastern Cape, the regime's tough new way of running townships meant additional hardships. Not only was the community council going to hike rents and service fees, but the government announced that all the residents of one small township, Walmer, would have to relocate so that the "buffer" zone adjacent to the white neighborhood of Walmer Estates could be expanded. Alarmed, 6,000 people gathered in October 1979 and decided to form the Port Elizabeth Black Civic Organization (PEBCO), to represent all the city's townships.

PEBCO succeeded in getting rent hikes canceled and preventing metered water charges for one township, and it also helped people evicted for arrears on rent to break the locks on their homes and move back in. Next it threatened a boycott of buses and white-owned businesses if the government went ahead and leveled Walmer, winning a reprieve for the condemned township. When its chairman was fired from his job, PEBCO helped coordinate a two-month strike wave at a number of Port Elizabeth factories, demanding township improvements as well as better working conditions.

In just a few months PEBCO had united Port Elizabeth's black community and forced local authorities to bend, but its success was short-lived. Arrests of leaders in January 1980 left it in disarray. The new leadership drifted away from bread-and-butter issues and was caught up in bigger political themes. Older, cautious people who came to mass meetings heard inflammatory rhetoric and songs. They were told, one organizer acknowledged, "that PEBCO was there to liberate them," and they were scared off.[12]

The black townships around Durban, a port city on the Indian Ocean, were the site of another productive campaign. People in Indian-designated areas organized a women's march on city hall to protest higher service fees. In the African township of Lamontville, a bus fare increase by the monopoly controlling the route to Durban—the only way for most people to get to work—sparked an eighteen-month bus boycott. A fleet of minibuses driven by township people shuttled workers to their jobs, and the bus company eventually backed down. In place after place, township people undertook the most disciplined of nonviolent actions to put pressure on local councils. "Due to constant pressure the Divisional Council has finally woken up," reported a newsletter put out by the Lotus River-Grassy Park Association (Western Cape) in 1982. "More roads are being built, street lights erected, sewerage pipes laid and a new civic hall is to be built soon." Passive acceptance or violent rebellion manifestly were not the only choices open to black people.[13]

The civic movement in townships proved it was possible to mobilize older, more conservative Africans whom Black Consciousness had not reached—so long as action was based on local issues. Since it did not present a political menace, the civic movement did not attract the kind of crackdown that had curbed the ANC in the early 1960s and Black Consciousness in the late 1970s. The authorities in Pretoria decided to treat orderly action by those who had an economic or community agenda in a more accommodating way, thinking it might distract them from their political impotence or co-opt blacks who might otherwise become militant. Just as the state had recognized black trade unions in the late 1970s, it now appeared willing to tolerate civic organizations.[14]

Township organizing in South Africa in the early 1980s succeeded in doing what Polish dissidents had done in the 1970s. Instead of directly defying a regime steeped in its own orthodoxy and capable of repression, they opened up room for independent action beneath the roof of the state, in which they could organize people to help themselves. The civic movement was in this sense "self-limiting"—it strove to create the basis for wider resistance before presuming to challenge the existing political structure.

Yet the civics' leaders still had their sights set on that higher goal. For activists like Popo Molefe—politicized veterans of Black Consciousness and 1976—lower rents and better sewers were not the point. "Are we fighting for lower rents to stretch our poverty wages a bit further?," asked Cape Town activist Wilfred Rhodes. "We must see the increasing rents, bus fares and electricity charges as being only the smoke. Our work must be geared to extinguishing the fire which causes the smoke." The fire, of course, was apartheid.[15]

"We Want All Our Rights"

Retaining the tactical advantage of organizing around local grievances without sacrificing the goal of political change was the strategic challenge now facing civic activists. Their response: Civics would stick to campaigning on local matters, as new "second-level" organizations channeled grass-roots energy into the broader battle against white power. "From that base of first-level grassroots organization," Molefe wrote, "we can start to build progressively more political forms of organization—a process which would culminate in the development of a national democratic struggle . . . "[16]

In 1982 the regime made constitutional changes that sharpened the need for a stronger movement. Prime Minister P. W. Botha's government proposed a new parliament, composed of three separate chambers, one each for white, Coloured, and Indian representatives. Africans would be denied any role, but African townships were given full autonomy. Intended to soften the regime's image abroad and boost its legitimacy at home, the reforms rearranged the furniture of apartheid without changing the floor plan of white power. Africans would gain more say over townships but still would be unable to live and work where they wished.

These changes were hazardous to the opposition, because, by giving Indians and Coloureds even partial rights that were denied to Africans, the regime might divide their interests and thwart the movement's unity, just as the Tsar's October

Manifesto was supposed to do to the Russian opposition in 1905. But the constitutional reforms were also an opportunity, because the ratification and election process permitted political debate, especially among Coloureds and Indians—and this debate could add another dimension to resistance.[17]

Resisting the reforms also might be a cause that could link civics with other groups, in a new coalition against the regime. Allan Boesak, a Coloured minister in the Dutch Reformed Church, proposed just that in January 1983. "There is no reason why," Boesak told a Johannesburg conference, "the churches, civic associations, trade unions, student organizations and sports bodies should not unite on this issue." That very night serious planning began for a new national opposition, an organization that would appeal to voters to boycott elections to the new chambers of parliament and elections to the new municipal councils.[18]

On August 20, 1983, people from more than 500 organizations rallied in a community center in Mitchells Plain, a Coloured township outside Cape Town, to launch the United Democratic Front (UDF). The hall was so packed that some people hung from the rafters; others listened from under a tent pitched nearby, while more sat outside as a light rain fell. The delegates—whites, Coloureds, Africans, and Indians—included veterans of ANC campaigns in the 1950s and young people who had watched as police shot down their schoolmates on Soweto's streets in 1976. Civics, churches, women, students, and labor unions were represented. The new group's structure was decentralized, but it had a single goal, and Allan Boesak made no bones about what it was: "We want all our rights, and we want them here and we want them now."[19]

This new, multiracial organization necessarily discarded the notion that liberation was a job for blacks alone. For Popo Molefe, who became UDF national secretary (he left his job as a machine operator for Kodak in order to take up the post), it was simply "morally indefensible" for those who condemned racism to exclude any group on account of race—but there were also strategic reasons not to do so. As long as white people were willing to contribute talent and money, excluding them would deny additional strength to the cause. In Molefe's words, "Uniting the largest section of South Africans committed to a peaceful and just future" was the keystone.[20]

Among the movement's most visible figures were a number of churchmen, white as well as black, who went about blasting the moral defensibility of white supremacy. Apartheid's builders had claimed that since God created different peoples, He must have meant to keep them separate. But Desmond Tutu, a black Anglican prelate, argued that the Tower of Babel story taught that breaking the human community into separate pieces was a sin, and since Christ had come to take away sins, apartheid was wrong. The clergy also joined the fight in practical ways: The South African Council of Churches (with funding from abroad) defended political prisoners and supported their families, and churches served as meeting places when other venues were off limits. Clergymen doubled as community organizers and public speakers, especially at funerals. Archbishop Tutu was especially active. Articulate and genial, he was an accessible figure to many white South Africans, and when he won the Nobel Peace Prize in 1984, he became essentially untouchable by the regime.

Secular white South Africans also joined the UDF. The mostly white National Union of South African Students was represented at the founding conference, and UDF "patrons" included Helen Joseph, an organizer of women's protests against the pass laws in the 1950s, and Dennis Goldberg, a communist and veteran of the ANC's armed campaigns in the 1960s. The white presence in the UDF, while limited, was enough to lend credibility to its commitment to a nonracial future.

Through that commitment, the UDF claimed kinship with the legacy of the ANC, whose Freedom Charter in 1955 had called for a nonracial and democratic South Africa. This was vital, as fervor for the ANC among black South Africans was rising—albeit due more to sensational raids into South Africa launched by the ANC's Umkhonto we Sizwe (familiarly, the MK). These sorties, while heartening to Africans, did not harm the regime. "The armed struggle," explained Lourence DuPlessis, chief of police intelligence in the Eastern Cape in the 1980s, "was never really a threat to us . . . they weren't effective at all. And I saw . . . ANC documents that were leaked . . . in which the ANC admitted that the MK was completely neutralized" by the regime.[21]

What could not be neutralized, however, was the iconic status of ANC leaders held in the prison on Robben Island or their influence on young opponents of apartheid. The "first generation" of Islanders, such as Nelson Mandela, were symbols of endurance, and the "second generation," who had received short-term sentences in the mid-1970s, had experience in local resistance. The Island became "an institution of politicians," in the words of Mike Xego, a former Islander. "You eat politics, you sleep politics, and then you are taught politics across the globe." Young rebels were thrust together with "very talented old people" who imparted "information and discipline and skill." Listening to them, young activists "came to realize that it's not color that counts—it's . . . how do you come together and work for an objective." When they were let out, they were different men. "Here was this cream of young guys who were prepared to go and say to South Africa, we're ready."[22]

One test of the UDF's readiness was its call to boycott the upcoming elections for a racially segregated parliament. In elections to the new African municipal authorities, held during November and December 1983, turnout was only 21 percent, down almost a third from an election a few years earlier, and in Soweto, the UDF claimed, only one in twenty eligible voters bothered to go to the polls. In elections for the Indian and Coloured parliamentary chambers held the next year, less than 20 percent of those eligible in each group voted. The UDF's call for a "politics of refusal" had been answered.

"Spontaneous Waves of Militancy"

Since the late 1970s, the strategy for stifling the opposition, pursued by the South African government in Pretoria, had been to temper the most blatant aspects of apartheid, in hopes of undercutting black rage. Putting down rebellion by armed force, as the government did in 1976, cost money and generated ill will around the world. If dulling the sharp edges of the system could tranquilize the defiant impulse, then reforms—allowing black trade unions, granting Coloureds and Indians further political rights, and giving Africans more say over township life— were expedient. White dominance would be more assured if it earned the consent of at least some of the nonwhite population.[23]

But the UDF's election boycotts complicated this strategy, and those who turned away from the polls turned down this sweeter-smelling apartheid. As a different model for achieving change, the civic movement had taught township people that their own organized, nonviolent action could force the government to yield. Yet by 1984 the market for gradual progress was weakening. A tougher economy had brought new hardships, and young people were boycotting schools again and injecting new volatility into the struggle. The election stay-away had denied legitimacy to black councillors, who were seen as agents of white power, so township politics were polarized. And the civics were run increasingly by those who wanted to rupture, not just pressure, local authority. A combustion point was nearing.

It was reached first in the Vaal Triangle south of Johannesburg, one of South Africa's centers of heavy industry, where small African townships had been created to house factory workers. One was Sharpeville, the site of the 1960 massacre. The state had long starved the township of much in the way of public amenities or adequate housing. But still people came to look for work, and the result was overcrowding. In recent years the regime had made a few improve-ments: Sewer lines had been laid, and at night the streets were bathed in the glare of stadium-style high-mast light towers. But the costs were passed on to the residents. Monthly charges for rent and services were the highest in the country.[24]

People who felt squeezed blamed the Lekoa Town Council, which the 1982 reforms had placed in charge of Sharpeville. The councillors delivered services and levied fees, and they were widely believed to abuse their power. If you were living in a shack and wanted to move your family into a permanent house, you went to Kuzwayo Jacob Dlamini, a Sharpeville councillor, paid him a bribe, and he would take care of it by evicting a current tenant. He and his wife tooled around town in a Toyota Cressida—"they thought they were like God," one resident remembered. Dlamini knew he was despised and armed himself for protection.

In August 1984 Dlamini announced a rate increase. On September 3, several hundred people—carrying placards reading "puppet councillors resign"—marched toward the administration offices to pay their fees. As they came alongside Dlamini's house, some threw stones. Police appeared and scattered them with tear gas and rubber bullets, but when they left, a mob regrouped outside the house and stone-throwing resumed. Dlamini took a shot from a window, hitting a person. Then someone set fire to his house, and when he ran out the back, he was showered with stones, knocked out, dragged into the street, doused with gasoline, and set ablaze. When the police returned, the councillor was dead.

Elsewhere in the Vaal Triangle that day, marches turned into riots after police opened fire. Young people built roadblocks to seal off townships, looted stores, and torched buildings. Councillors were the main targets: One was hacked to death, and others fled after their homes were destroyed. The police did their share of killing too. As township councillors resigned and local government disintegrated, soldiers were sent in to keep order, first as auxiliaries to police, then as an occupying force. In October, 7,000 troops sealed off the townships, conducted house-to-house searches, and arrested hundreds. Activists responded by recruiting a trade union federation to call a two-day protest strike in early November, demanding the withdrawal of troops, school reform, and freezes on rents and service charges. The stay-away did not sway the regime, but the strong turnout foreshadowed the availability of rank-and-file workers for political action.

The strife that had ignited in the Vaal Triangle in September 1984 swept inexorably across South Africa. In one township after another, conflict over local issues escaped from the control of civics and other organizations and turned violent. There were riots, arson, police massacres, and hundreds of horrific killings perpetrated by both sides. The initiative in opposing authority seemed to pass from nonviolent groups to the clenched fists of young African men—the *Amabutho,* or "comrades." Their "day-to-day sport was playing chicken with police vehicles," while the police—mostly "young white boys with too much testosterone"—selected black people to beat up "as part of life's daily sport."[25]

Yet beneath this mayhem and repression, there was still a political struggle going on, to challenge civilian government in the townships and overturn the old order. This was evident in the Eastern Cape, the next region to explode. Events began there with a school boycott in October 1984. In the following months, stone-throwing and arson in townships close to Port Elizabeth became common. Joint patrols of police and soldiers riding around in armored cars drew resentment. One soldier told of how his patrol grabbed young people, stuffed them into a metal box attached to their vehicle, and dragged them around. Meanwhile, vigilantes, working in cahoots with police, were firebombing the homes of student activists and union leaders.[26]

On March 21, 1985—the twenty-fifth anniversary of the Sharpeville massacre—a column of marchers filed through the streets of Langa, a township outside the white city of Uitenhage, not far from Port Elizabeth. At one point they came upon two armored cars, bristling with shotguns and rifles; the police surmised that the marchers were Amabutho on their way to wreak havoc in Uitenhage. In fact, the people were mourners, walking to a funeral on the other side of the city. The marchers were singing in Xhosa, a language that the white officers could not understand. When they came near, the officers opened fire with everything they had, killing twenty people, most of whom were shot in the back.[27]

"The Langa shooting was the last straw," said a journalist on the scene. "The people couldn't accept it. They attacked . . . every house belonging to a known informer." One target was Tamsanqa Benjamin Kinikini, a widely hated councillor—he and his family were believed to be helping the police to identify and abduct Amabutho. Two days after Langa, a crowd burned Kinikini's house and set upon him, his son, and two nephews. Someone stabbed Kinikini, and then people stacked tires around his shoulders and head, set them on fire, and watched as he burned to death inside of them.[28]

Kinikini was one of the first victims of the "necklace," a sadistic expression of the wrath that wracked township life in the mid-1980s. In the ensuing eighteen months, hundreds more black councillors, police officers and suspected informers met the same gruesome end. So fearsome was the violence directed at apartheid collaborators that councillors and police in some townships fled altogether and took refuge in guarded, barbed-wire enclosed compounds. By mid-1985 a few areas in Eastern Cape townships were designated as "no-go" zones, where police were not allowed unless they were in convoys of armored vehicles.

By May, 257 councillors had resigned, and authority in the townships collapsed entirely. By the end of that year just four of thirty-eight Black Local Authorities created by the 1982 reforms were still operating. With civilian administration and policing in disarray, keeping order was increasingly left to soldiers. Military commanders referred to operations in the townships as the "fourth front," in addition to their expeditionary operations in foreign countries. On July 21, 1985, the government in Pretoria declared a state of emergency covering areas where the uprising was most acute. The State Security Council essentially delegated martial law powers to police and soldiers. The regime's strategy to govern the townships with black collaborators was dead. The only alternative, besides dismantling white supremacy, was naked repression.

This imposed enormous costs on the regime, but the price paid by the populace was even higher. Killing councillors and driving out police, rather than bringing liberation, only turned neighborhoods into war zones, with curfews, roadblocks, house-to-house searches, and thousands of soldiers rumbling through in armored carriers at all hours. Even respectable, middle-class black people were targets of soldiers' harassment. Activists paid the heaviest price. In the eight months after the state of emergency was declared, at least 8,000 people were detained without any charges, most of them leaders of the UDF or its local affiliates.

The violence of the township rebellion created a dilemma for the opposition. If the UDF endorsed any violent acts, it could lose its status as a legal organization. One UDF leader warned his colleagues to not "confuse coercion, the use of force *against* the community, with people's power, the collective strength of the community"—the latter was qualitatively different. Echoing Gandhi, Desmond Tutu insisted that the struggle's methods had to be consistent with its ends, so it could withstand the "harsh scrutiny of history." Both he and Allan Boesak intervened personally to protect people from crowd violence. Even among ANC leaders, there were worries about events in the townships, and there was nervous talk of "Khmer Rouge" elements.[29]

But insistence on nonviolent conduct was not absolute. The 1985 Kairos Declaration (signed by 150 religious leaders) stated that it was wrong to equate the violent actions of an oppressive regime with "acts of resistance and self-defense." Some even insisted that violence served a purpose, since the threat of necklacings and arson had scared many collaborators and police out of the townships. For some activists, keeping their influence on the streets meant keeping their misgivings about the comrades to themselves—controlling violence was not regarded as important as controlling those who used it.[30]

Even if violence appeared to have tactical uses, it was still clear that township anarchy would only lead to more repression, not the end of apartheid. Although a statement from the exiled ANC in January 1985 had called for people in the townships to "render South Africa ungovernable" and the UDF had responded to the call, its leaders came to realize that they were "unable to respond effectively to the spontaneous waves of militancy around the country," as a confidential UDF paper admitted in May of that year. "One thing is clear, the process of mobilization has far outstripped that of organization." So a new slogan was coined, "From Mobilization to Organization," and Popo Molefe, speaking at a UDF conference, called for activists in townships to start setting up "alternative structures."[31]

"People's Power"

New models for organization already had taken root in townships of the Eastern Cape, where a handful of activists, some of them Robben Island alumni, had begun to experiment again with nonviolent opposition. For the region's towns, 1984 had been the first of three years of such experimentation—and dangerous living.

In March of that year, in Lingelihle, a township outside the Eastern Cape city of Cradock, on a dry plateau known as the Karoo, students boycotted schools to protest the firing of Matthew Goniwe, a school principal and leader of CRADORA, the local civic organization. Within a week police and students were fighting in the streets; within two weeks Goniwe and other civic leaders were behind bars and all public meetings had been banned. Attacks on councillors and counterattacks on CRADORA activists roiled the township for most of 1984. Until that point, events in Lingelihle had been no different from those in many other townships.[32]

Then Goniwe was released in October and went back to Lingelihle. A peculiar combination of political subversive and moral traditionalist, he had earlier spent four years in prison for taking part in a Marxist study group and also had been point man in Cradock for the banned ANC. But later, as a civic leader and school principal, he had crusaded for sexual chastity, abstaining from marijuana, and respect for elders. He enforced the school uniform code and punished students who came late or failed to do work. His credentials as a radical gave him credibility among the comrades, while his reputation as a disciplinarian won him points with older people. He was ideally positioned to restore the community's unity, which had vanished in the violence.

Goniwe's inspiration was to revitalize the civic organization by democratizing it. CRADORA activists went into township neighborhoods to get people on each street to form committees. The street committees, in turn, elected delegates to serve on area committees, which selected chief organizers to work with CRADORA. The committees were a way for older people to assert their authority and steer the township in a new direction. Stepping into the breach created by the disintegration of the old council, the committees assigned street patrols to discourage hooligans and public drinking. With its new mass base, CRADORA also seized public functions, supervising payment of pensions and setting up adult literacy courses.

It was, of course, too good to last. In early 1985, as Goniwe traveled around the Karoo, spreading the street committee system to a number of towns, his reputation spread across South Africa, especially in UDF circles. Others also took notice of what he was doing. On June 7 the Eastern Cape security police requested permission from Pretoria to arrange for the "permanent removal from society" of Goniwe. Three weeks later Goniwe and three colleagues were abducted on their way home from a UDF meeting in Port Elizabeth, and their bodies were found shot, stabbed, mutilated, and burned. Street violence in Lingelihle detonated at once. But by then what Matthew Goniwe had achieved in his remote township had become known to civic leaders across South Africa, and they were soon to blaze similar trails.

Port Elizabeth

The trail that Mkhuseli Jack took from the farm where he was raised about 70 kilometers (43 miles) outside Port Elizabeth, to the pinnacle of a mass boycott campaign against apartheid, was blazed entirely by his own determination. Pass laws restricting blacks' movement had prevented him from enrolling in school. After migrating to the city to seek an education, and without ever having heard the word "politics," he led demonstrations on behalf of admitting rural boys and girls to city schools and formed the Port Elizabeth Youth Congress—and succeeded in getting an education himself.

Influenced by Black Consciousness, Jack at first believed that his people's problem "was just whites." But after advocating that view in a school debate, he heard the story of Brown Fisher, a white lawyer from a privileged family who died in prison while serving a life term for opposing apartheid—and then he realized that "you couldn't judge people by their color." Jack was "a natural leader," wrote a local journalist. "For one thing, he was not arrogant. He would listen to the other man's point of view, but would convince him." Yet his methods were not merely verbal. "He was an extreme troublemaker," said Lourence DuPlessis, the police intelligence chief, "an activist in the true sense of the word."[33]

Jack had noticed that during previous uprisings, only small organizations had worked to rouse the people. Spontaneous eruptions, once quelled, left no structure in their wake to sustain action against the regime. For the next phase of the struggle, he realized, he and other activists had to build an organization outward, through many cadres. As it broadened, "it became extremely difficult for the security forces to crush," because "big centers of resistance within the community" had been created.

The young agitator, nicknamed "Khusta"—only twenty-seven years old when he came to national attention—was resolved to keep the next rebellion

Mkhuseli Jack, leader of the consumer boycott campaign against apartheid in Port Elizabeth,
South Africa, speaking at a funeral on May 10, 1986.
Credit: ©Reuters/Archive Photos

nonviolent. "It wasn't going to suit me to . . . carry guns," he later admitted.
Nonviolent action also had an advantage in building the movement: "there was
no excuse for anybody, old or young, disabled or not" to avoid joining. But the
chief reason to remain nonviolent was to win the "high ground in the community
. . . the majority of older people." The Amabutho "were committed to violent
strategies of direct action," and the bedlam they spawned had alienated the wage
earners, women, and ordinary citizens whom the movement would need to
sustain mass action against the regime long enough to prevail.[34]

As clashes with police turned streets into free-fire zones, Jack and his
colleagues realized that if the struggle was confined to the townships, it would
always be bottled up by repression and never confront those who allowed
apartheid to survive, namely the white community. So they said to each other,
"Let us take this fight in the townships away, and bring it right to their homes.
And that is what led to the boycott."

In May 1985 several middle-aged women had gone to PEBCO with the
idea of boycotting white businesses in Port Elizabeth. Khusta Jack became the

boycott committee's spokesman. In the first round, their demands were modest, including opening public facilities to all races, removing troops from the townships, and ending workplace discrimination. In July, two days before the boycott was to begin, Jack addressed a huge crowd at a funeral (the only kind of public gathering that the government still permitted). "We won't buy in town on Monday," he shouted. "We won't buy even a box of matches on Monday!" And on Monday, the North End retail district in Port Elizabeth, normally jammed with black shoppers, was virtually empty.

The boycott had immediate bite, but it was only five days later that Pretoria declared a state of emergency for a number of magisterial districts, with Port Elizabeth at the head of the list. Curfews and travel restrictions took hold, and soldiers in the streets were given the power to make peremptory searches and arrests. Khusta Jack went into hiding to avoid being picked up. Now the boycott committee added to their demands: The state of emergency would have to be withdrawn, and political prisoners—including Nelson Mandela—would have to be released before the boycott would be ended.

White-owned stores in Port Elizabeth lost, on average, 30 percent of their business. Economic pressure drove a wedge between business and government. Store owners rained telegrams on government officials, telling them to meet the boycotters' demands. A white member of parliament called the boycott "one of the most effective weapons that . . . the blacks have found for some considerable time," noting that he had received more phone calls from constituents on the issue than he ever had before. And the boycott could not be halted by repression. "If they don't want to buy, what sort of crime is it?" DuPlessis recalled. "It's mass action, and what do you do? You can't shoot all these people. You can't lock them all up."[35]

But the regime went after a few. On August 2 it located and arrested Mkhuseli Jack and other boycott leaders. "The police were very delighted to get us," remembered Tango Lamani. They told him the consumer boycott would be over in three weeks, "and you leaders, you will be rotting in jail." But the movement had put down deeper roots than the regime realized, and the boycott stayed in place like a tourniquet—and, like a tourniquet, it was loosened when it started doing more harm than good. White shop-owning families had been left prostrate. "Please, we are not the government," they pleaded with one black leader. Jack recalled telling the boycott committee, "we cannot be as bad as this government . . . let's not destroy them." In November a deal was reached: The boycott would be suspended until March if the businessmen arranged for black leaders to be released. Since the upcoming Christmas shopping season would have strained the black community's adherence to the boycott, suspending it also served to keep the movement unified.[36]

To make clear to the people that mass action had been effective, to "demonstrate the tangible benefits of negotiating, of making demands," explained Mark Swilling, a political scientist who often rode with Jack around Port Elizabeth, "Mkhuseli Jack masterminded a great symbolic entry of the released detainees into the township." The lesson that boycotts taught to South African business was equally large. "We were saying to business: you are part of this country," recalled Popo Molefe. "If the majority of South Africans are not treated like human beings, [if] their human rights are not respected, there cannot be stability in the country, and your business cannot thrive under conditions of instability."[37]

Feeding this instability itself, the regime succumbed again to the temptation of repression. On March 11, 1986, Pretoria banned Khusta Jack and one other civic leader. (Banning was equivalent to house arrest.) This drew protest as far away as Washington, D.C., where Assistant Secretary of State Chester Crocker told a congressional committee that the United States "condemned in the strongest terms" the banning of the two Port Elizabeth activists. Eleven days later a Supreme Court justice in South Africa lifted the ban on Jack, who tore up his banning orders at a giant rally where people were mobilized to resume the boycott nine days later.

The renewed boycott was even better disciplined than the 1985 effort. The boycott committee issued a price list to keep black merchants from gouging customers, and it issued licenses to street vendors who were allowed to buy goods from white wholesalers and resell them. A network of street and area committees helped activists communicate with citizens and filtered responsibility downward, at a time when top leaders were liable to be arrested. The committees also helped people cope with the collapse of local government, organizing street cleaning and penalizing those who threw garbage into the streets. They even helped settle domestic quarrels: Wife battering reportedly declined in Kwazakele after the committees sprang up.[38]

Nine weeks into the boycott, South Africa's president declared another, surprise state of emergency, intended to head off disturbances on the tenth anniversary of the Soweto uprising. He accused black "revolutionaries" of being interested "only in a violent takeover of power." But in fact it had been nonviolent action in places like Port Elizabeth that had confounded the government. The distributed wisdom of the Robben Islanders, the mass organizing of the UDF, and tireless warriors such as Khusta Jack had managed to harness the hearts of black youth and the sober heads of older citizens to a common cause. "People's consent and active participation on a very big scale" was the force behind that cause, and repression could only postpone the day when it would force the government itself to change.[39]

Alexandra

In the northern suburbs of Johannesburg, the dirty, unpaved precincts of Alexandra were an impoverished black island surrounded by an affluent white sea. Like Sophiatown, it had been earmarked for extinction but was saved from the bulldozers by years of protests—and then was neglected by the government. Some 200,000 people were crammed into 10,000 tin and plywood shacks on a treeless square mile. Water came from communal taps. Alexandra was a powder keg waiting for a match.

The police provided one in February 1986 by attacking a funeral procession. Over the next six days, the town was consumed by street warfare; security forces killed seventeen people, and Amabutho went after black councillors. On one of these violent days, a twenty-two-year old youth organizer named Mzwanele Mayekiso came across a squad of comrades preparing to necklace a black policeman. Mayekiso was new to Alexandra but not to this kind of scene. He told the comrades to listen to him: "[A]partheid and unemployment force people to become policemen," he pointed out. It was the system, not the man, that should be destroyed, so they should let the officer resign and turn over his police kit. They agreed, let their frightened prize flee, and burned his uniform.[40]

After the fighting ended, the house where Mayekiso lived became the headquarters of the Alexandra Action Committee (AAC), which tried to turn the uprising into a nonviolent campaign. It helped organize a mass funeral for those killed, and speakers implored young people to find another way to combat apartheid. AAC activists had started organizing yard, street, and block committees back in early February, consciously emulating what had already been done in the Eastern Cape.[41]

With the committees in place and the AAC gaining stature, over a hundred people representing all kinds of local organizations—from the chamber of commerce to the Alexandra Women's Organization—met and mapped out a strategy to undercut the local council. A rent strike had already dried up some of its funds: Monthly rent receipts had dropped from 156,000 rands to just 44,000. Now the AAC added a selective consumer boycott, targeting stores belonging to councillors and other collaborators. Stores and taxis refused to serve councillors, and police officers even were dumped by their girlfriends. The parishioners at the church where the mayor was a priest refused to hear him preach. Under this barrage, all council members resigned.[42]

The AAC now acted as the supreme authority, letting the committees elect a township-wide executive; in turn, the committees established their own courts and criminal justice system. Alexandra, ungovernable by white Pretoria, had been wrested away by its own people. The peasants who set up their own republic in Guriia, in the midst of Tsarist repression, would have understood why they did it.

Soweto

One day in June 1986 Nomavenda Mathiane peered out her window and became nervous when she saw some teenage boys coming to her door. A journalist who had lived in Soweto eight years, she had seen firsthand how young comrades could intimidate people—once she had to hide her daughter in a cupboard, so they would not take her (as a trophy) to a funeral. While she resented the bullying, she also had become convinced that their kind of struggle was doomed. Armed with stones and Molotov cocktails, they were no match for the formidable South African Defense Forces. And while they were getting shot in the streets, they were also boycotting school and sacrificing even the meager benefit that township education, second rate as it was, might have provided.[43]

But when she answered the door that day, the boys politely asked her to come to a meeting at a neighbor's house. They were trying to organize a committee on her street, an effort sponsored by the Soweto Civic Association. The next night, she and her neighbors waited until three boys, all under eighteen, walked into the house. The youths got cold looks from everybody—no adults were eager to take instructions from these young comrades. But much to their surprise, the boys said they wanted to work with the adults, so they could rein in ordinary thugs. They promised they would no longer come for girls to go with them to funerals and would no longer hijack cars. The adults started to see the committee as a chance to regain some control. They elected an executive, chaired by a man over fifty years old. He accepted the post with one condition—that he would never be told to necklace anyone or torch anyone's house. "If I am asked to do that, I want to tell you here and now that I will stop being chairman of this committee."

Mathiane noticed an immediate change on her street after that: Residents acted like neighbors to each other. When boys came to her house wanting to take her daughter to a vigil, she told them they had to clear it with the street committee. For people like Mathiane, it was a new way to help rule their own communities. Through the committees in Soweto, people made vacant lots into parks, patrolled the streets, and punished wrongdoers—easing the effects of the disappearance of central authority.

All across South Africa, civic organizations built networks of local committees, in conscious imitation of what Matthew Goniwe had done in Cradock and what Mkhuseli Jack and his colleagues did in Port Elizabeth. Taking hold most strongly in the Eastern Cape and the Transvaal but also in parts of the Western

Cape and Natal, these committees were bulwarks against wild rebellion and made the movement more resilient in the face of state violence. By applying sanctions such as consumer and rent boycotts, they brought ordinary people into the movement against apartheid without battling security forces. Like the Indian civil disobedience campaign, the committees integrated the mundane action of individuals into collective, large-scale nonviolent action.

As early as the end of 1985, UDF leaders had spoken of the committees as organs of "people's power." Having made townships ungovernable, the people "have broken the shackles of direct government rule," explained Zwelakhe Sisulu, the son of jailed ANC leader Walter Sisulu in March 1986. But at that point, the people had not yet "managed to control and direct the situation." There was "a power vacuum." By organizing democratically, people in the townships were filling this vacuum. Sisulu saw that power was not something black people would be awarded after they won an ultimate victory over white power; it was possible to create "people's power now, in the process of struggle, before actual liberation." People were "beginning to exert control over their own lives . . . beginning to govern themselves, despite being under racist rule."[44]

Township activists thought as much too. "We are already taking over, and that's no boast but fact," said a street committee president in Langa. "The community council has been brought down, the police have been forced to leave . . . Political power is shifting to the hands of the people's own organizations, and we can begin to think about forming our own people's government." In Kwazakele, outside Port Elizabeth, a local activist reported with pride: "We have built our own democratic government."[45]

"There Was Really Nothing That We Could Do"

The advent of consumer boycotts and street committees jarred Pretoria. Either as vehicles for nonviolent organizing or as embryonic forms of self-rule, they challenged its power. Fond of justifying racial tyranny by invoking the demons of the Cold War, the government saw Bolsheviks behind the organizing. "From backyards in Alexandra," government prosecutors said ominously, " . . . comrades usurped the functions of the police with anti-crime campaigns, and from local authorities by re-naming streets and schools and by setting up alternative structures of self-government, and the judiciary by operating 'democratic people's courts.'"[46]

The regime's answer was more repression. In the year after President Botha declared a second state of emergency in June 1986, more than 25,000 people were arrested and imprisoned without trial. Censorship regulations barred the media from covering "unrest" in the country, besides reprinting official bulletins.

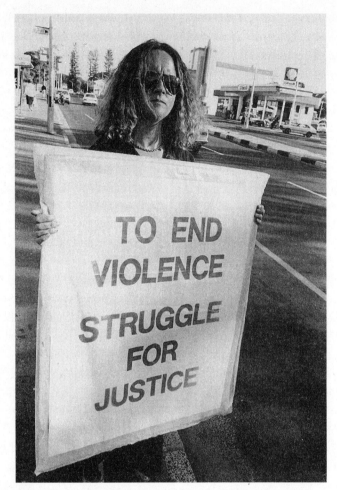

Demonstrator against apartheid, Cape Town, South Africa, 1986.
Credit: ©Dave Hartman/Impact Visuals

The regime forbade any of the major nonviolent sanctions used in previous years, including work stay-aways and consumer, rent, or school boycotts. All would now be punishable as subversion, as would street committees. In 1988 came more rules effectively prohibiting the UDF and local affiliates from taking any action at all.

Under cover of a virtual military occupation and equipped with expanded police forces, the councillors returned to the townships and took up the powers they had abdicated. Covert operations were mounted against opposition leaders, including break-ins, bombings, and assassinations. Vigilante mobs, supported by the police or military, rampaged through neighborhoods thought to be UDF strongholds. The regime also tried to inflame the tension between rival black organizations, printing fake pamphlets and using paid agents to sow trouble.

Against this onslaught, the civic organizations atrophied. The 1985 state of emergency had skimmed off big names, but the new detentions trawled much deeper. So great was the number of people arrested in the Port Elizabeth area that new prison cells were built to make room for them all. Street committees also wilted, and the consumer boycott lost steam. All over the Eastern Cape, the government dashed around pulling out the roots of "people's power."

Nowhere had those roots become more tenacious than in Soweto. In its sprawling maze of townships, security forces had a hard time hunting down activists. By adopting an all-or-nothing payment policy, the Soweto Council unwittingly helped sustain the rent boycott, since as arrears mounted, the incentive to pay and break ranks with fellow boycotters flagged. The council turned off water and electricity to non-payers' homes, but workers who belonged to a UDF-affiliated union turned them back on again. Police and soldiers evicted residents; the committees mobilized stay-aways to protest. Only in 1990, after major changes at the national level, would the Soweto boycott end.

The regime's attempt to "annihilate the enemy" was just one part of a multifaceted counter-insurgency strategy. Even as they jailed tens of thousands and shrank the space in which the opposition could maneuver, the authorities also tried to palliate black rage. Services and infrastructure were improved in the poorest townships. In Alexandra, new houses, apartment blocks, and school buildings went up, while a few roads were paved and sewers laid. The idea was to give reinstated councils a chance to regain legitimacy. Civic activists had been put behind bars, but the regime—which before had been unwilling to provide even the simplest modern amenities to black communities—was trying to pacify those it held down.[47]

Yet however soft-soled, repression was still a boot—and it came down clumsily. "We cordoned off the black areas with razor wire," recalled Lourence DuPlessis, but "it had no effect, because the people had to be let out every morning to go to work; some of them come in late, some of them come in early . . . So it served no purpose . . . There was really nothing that we could do." Using military measures against defiant civilians was no way to enlist their cooperation. The authorities "looked at various reasons for dissatisfaction and tried to sort that out," DuPlessis said, "but that's not what the whole thing was about . . . People just didn't want apartheid anymore. That's what it boils down to. They were not prepared to be suppressed any longer."[48]

FROM STALEMATE TO DEMOCRACY

The stalemate in the townships reflected a broader standoff in South Africa in the late 1980s. Popular mobilization could not overwhelm apartheid, but Pretoria's repression rechanneled opposition into new streams. The center of resistance after 1986 shifted to the black labor movement, especially the labor union federation COSATU, formed in November 1985. African unions established in the 1970s had been pushed by rank-and-file militants into cooperating with civics and students. In the mid-1980s the unions had coordinated protest strikes, and union leaders had been active in township organizing. Now, with troops patrolling township streets and opposition groups out of commission due to the crackdown, factories and union halls became major venues for resistance, and strikes became the prime vehicle for popular opposition.

Unable to stifle all resistance, the regime also made limited progress against the armed offensive. The ANC was accelerating the guerrilla campaign with each passing year. There were 281 reported attacks in 1989, compared to just 13 a decade earlier, and the guerrillas were going after more "soft" (civilian) targets than ever before. But even though the cost of containing these attacks was a great burden on the white government, black violence could never really overpower the armed forces.

Defending apartheid also imposed indirect costs, especially the consequences of international isolation. Although an arms embargo and United Nations-sponsored sports and cultural boycotts had been in effect for some time, many Western governments and corporations had earlier balked at serious economic measures against South Africa. In the early 1980s—before the township uprisings, police massacres, and states of emergency—the threat of tough sanctions seemed remote. Conservative governments in Washington and London clutched Pretoria as a talisman against communism in Africa and naively believed that the ruling National Party could be coaxed into reforming apartheid through "constructive engagement."

Now all that had changed. Images of South African police beating protestors and armored troop carriers rolling through townships had become staples of Western news coverage (until the state banned all media coverage of unrest in 1986). For the opposition, these damning scenes set the stage for petitioning foreign governments to escalate sanctions. "We face a catastrophe in this land," Archbishop Tutu declared, "and only the action of the international community by applying pressure can save us."[49]

In Washington, civil rights leaders and famous entertainers were arrested marching outside the South African embassy. Campus protests helped persuade universities to pull endowment money out of stocks of corporations that did business in South Africa, and city and state governments did the same with their pension funds. So strong had this campaign grown, that by 1985 even President Ronald Reagan—who was given to remind people that South Africa had been America's ally in World War II—had issued an executive order imposing limited sanctions. The next year Congress enacted a tougher law (overriding Reagan's veto) banning new investments, loans, and imports of certain South African products, and cutting off military aid to foreign countries that broke the arms embargo. The European Community imposed its own sanctions the same year, dozens of U.S. firms pulled out of the country, and banks refused to roll over short-term loans to South African corporate borrowers.

The magnitude of the impact of international sanctions is disputed, and there is no doubt that Pretoria and South African businesses found a multitude of ways to evade them. But their political effect was not a simple function of their economic results. By the end of the 1980s, South Africa had experienced almost a decade of slow growth and high inflation, and there was widespread pessimism that the government could turn this around. Sanctions only deepened this doubt.[50]

In this suffocating atmosphere, a rising number of influential white South Africans concluded that, since apartheid required repression and repression brought unacceptable economic damage, apartheid would have to go, sooner or later. Prominent opposition leaders—inside the country, on Robben Island, and in exile—also understood that no combination of brute force, whether armed raids or popular insurrection, could bring down the regime without devastating the nation. Both sides recognized that a violent showdown would be unthinkable—that a political way out must be found.

As early as 1985, they had begun to talk to each other; a group of white industrialists flew to Zambia to meet with exiled ANC officials. Over the next several years, white clergy, intellectuals, journalists, and others had more meetings with the ANC, and the regime held secret meetings with Nelson Mandela, still locked up on Robben Island. Mandela was both firm and flexible: Black South Africans, he insisted, would settle for nothing less than majority rule, but the end of white domination would not mean black supremacy, and whites would find a secure place in a democratic South Africa. All these contacts showed that there were white leaders who could imagine a future without apartheid, and there were black leaders who were committed to nonracialism. The years of intransigence had not extinguished either side's intelligence.

At the end of the decade, distant events gave further impetus to the end game for apartheid. In 1989 people surged through the streets of Eastern European cities, and, one by one, the communist regimes in those countries melted from the heat of nonviolent force. In Moscow, Mikhail Gorbachev was red-lining subsidies to would-be revolutionaries around the world who had long survived with Soviet stipends. Almost in the blink of an eye, the Cold War was over and with it, the idea of a "communist threat." The South African government would no longer be able to call itself the last barrier to a Moscow-directed takeover fronted by the ANC.[51]

Frederick Wilhelm de Klerk, who became the leader of the National Party in February 1989 and the president of South Africa in August, recognized that nothing would really change as long as apartheid remained and that the government's position would not improve with time. Moreover, if he waited too long, he might lose the opportunity to deal with Mandela and the older generation of ANC leaders who seemed to be more conciliatory than their junior associates. In the last months of 1989, the authorities began to allow the opposition breathing space and refrained from breaking up nonviolent protests. In October, seven ANC leaders, including Walter Sisulu, were released from prison. And on December 13, de Klerk met with Mandela.

Two months later the new president opened the South African parliament by stating that "the time for negotiation has arrived." The government would lift the ban on major opposition groups, including the ANC and the UDF; it would release political prisoners and permit exiles to return; and it would end the state of emergency and restrictions on the press. Apartheid laws were acknowledged to be "obstacles" to a peaceful settlement. On February 11, Nelson Mandela walked out of prison, finally free after twenty-seven years.[52]

Not long afterward, the government eliminated the key apartheid laws that still remained on the books, while the ANC set up shop inside South Africa and converted itself from an underground organization to a mass political party. Formal negotiations on South Africa's future began at the end of 1991, although it was two years before the parties reached a deal. Democratic elections were scheduled for April 1994, and a new, nonracial parliament would be charged with writing a new constitution. Until that was ratified, South Africa would be governed by an interim constitution, mandating that the homelands be integrated into the rest of the country, that individual rights be guaranteed, and that minority parties be given seats in the central cabinet. Thanks to this deal, the white minority would not be shut out of power altogether with the advent of majority rule.

This extraordinary agreement, this mutual accommodation by old enemies, exemplified what could be done without recourse to violence. But in one of South Africa's many sad ironies, it was hammered out against a backdrop of savagery—fomented mainly by those who figured to lose out in the transition to democracy. Right-wing whites carried out bombings and assassinations against opposition leaders. Chief Mangosuthu Buthelezi and his Inkatha

Freedom Party, determined to resist the incorporation of the KwaZulu homeland into a unitary South African state, battled ANC loyalists in Natal and the
Witwatersrand. Thousands were killed. It was as if violence itself would not give
way to democracy without a fight.

De Klerk and Mandela let none of this impede their progress. When the
elections were held April 26 to 29, 1994, the ANC won more than 60 percent
of the vote, but both the National Party and Inkatha (which agreed to participate
only at the last minute) won enough votes to be represented in the government.
The parliament elected Nelson Mandela as South Africa's president, and he was
sworn in on May 10, vowing that "never, never, and never again shall it be that
this beautiful land will again experience the oppression of one by another." The
last state bastion of racism had passed from the earth.[53]

℣ ℣ ℣

The political rapprochement that brought genuine democracy to South Africa
was not the fruit of a unilateral victory by the black opposition. It sprang from
the understanding by both opposition and government leaders that victory
through belligerent force was not possible. The opposition came to realize it
could not smash the regime, certainly not with any violence at its disposal, and
the regime knew it could not annihilate the opposition, not after years of
contending with protestors, civic organizers, and committees on every other
street corner of the townships.

Nonviolent sanctions were an indispensable link in the chain of events that
ended the old order. Stay-aways, strikes, and boycotts put pressure on white
business owners and employers, and they undermined white attachment to the
status quo. Rent boycotts defunded local councils, and street committees
usurped their functions. Faced with this variegated challenge, the regime reacted
with open force. Repression subdued the civics and committees, but it also cost
the regime any chance of avoiding economic punishment by the international
community. Nonviolent power did not by itself bring down the curtain on white
rule, but it discredited the regime's authority and undermined its strategy for
shielding apartheid from the many forces arrayed against it.

In his trial in April 1964, before he was imprisoned by the apartheid regime,
Nelson Mandela had argued that fifty years of nonviolent action by black South
Africans had not secured their rights but had only, it seemed, worsened the
repression. He said that his followers were losing confidence in the policy of
nonviolence and were turning, disturbingly, to terrorism. Since the government
was not flinching from brutality, he concluded that "as violence in this country

was inevitable, it would be unrealistic and wrong for African leaders to continue preaching peace and nonviolence at a time when the Government met our peaceful demands with force."[54]

Mandela was right: Preaching peace is not a strategy for winning a conflict. But if Mandela believed that nonviolent action is the opposite of force, he was not right—it is in fact another form of force. Principled preference for nonviolent methods does not, by itself, give such methods force, and taking nonviolent action in order to avoid using violence does not make it successful. What does work, and what worked in South Africa twenty years after Nelson Mandela delivered his valedictory on the first half century of the struggle, is mobilizing a movement that makes it impossible for arbitrary rulers to control life in the communities where people live and alienating those rulers from the support they need at home and abroad. "Despite all of the rhetoric of the ANC about the armed struggle," explained Janet Cherry, herself an underground member of the ANC, "it was, in fact, the activities of the UDF, in mass organization, which brought about the change in South Africa."[55]

The nonviolent legacy of the twentieth century is embedded in the histories of a score of nations, but many of the ideas and strategies that were its substance first germinated in South Africa, in the thoughts and actions of an Indian lawyer who felt the strop of bigotry laid on his own back as the century was dawning. So it is altogether fitting that before the century ended, the conflict that Gandhi began to fight in South Africa before he rallied to his own country's cause was finally won for all people of color in that land—and was won in part through strikes, boycotts, and other methods of resistance that he had pioneered.

"I suppose that human beings looking at it would say that arms are the most dangerous things that a dictator, a tyrant needs to fear," concluded Desmond Tutu. "But in fact, no—it is when people decide they want to be free. Once they have made up their minds to that, there is nothing that will stop them."[56]

CHAPTER TEN

The Philippines: Restoring Democracy

"Ninoy, You Are Not Alone!"

THE VIP LOUNGE WAS PACKED with his family and friends—his seventy-three-year old mother, his sisters and brothers, his in-laws and a few close friends—and 20,000 Filipinos waited outside Manila's airport. Nearly 1,200 armed soldiers and national police also swarmed around the terminal as the jetliner carrying Benigno ("Ninoy") Aquino taxied down the runway after landing. It was early on a Sunday morning in August 1983, and after three years in the United States, the leading opponent of the Philippines' authoritarian government was coming home from foreign exile.

Before boarding the last leg of his journey, an hour-long flight from Taipei to Manila, he telephoned his wife, Corazon, in Massachusetts. Cory Aquino had heard that her husband's nemesis, Major General Fabian Ver, Philippine army chief of staff, would try to block Aquino's entry and force the airline to fly him back to Taiwan. The regime of President Ferdinand Marcos had reason to dislike Aquino. As a member of the Philippine Senate, he had been the leading figure of the opposition before Marcos imposed martial law in 1973. Jailed for seven years before being flown to America for medical care, Aquino had come to symbolize Filipinos' longing for fairness and justice, to which Marcos paid elaborate lip service but little serious attention.

Shortly before landing that day in Manila, Aquino went to a bathroom on the plane and donned a bulletproof vest under his white shirt and safari-style jacket. He had been warned that he was putting his life at risk, and he even seemed to invite martyrdom, when he told people at a farewell party the night before his departure that "according to Gandhi the willing sacrifice of the innocent is the most powerful answer to insolent tyranny." On a layover in Los Angeles, he had visited the Ambassador Hotel and told an acquaintance that he might be shot and killed just as Robert Kennedy had been assassinated in the kitchen of that hotel.[1]

When the jet came to a stop at the gate, soldiers emerged from an aviation security van and surrounded it, high-powered rifles at the ready. Three police boarded the jet, spotted Aquino, and escorted him to the door. After they stepped onto the enclosed exit ramp, one policemen blocked the door, stopping a TV cameraman and news reporters. Aquino was hustled through a side door and down a stairway leading to the airport tarmac. Within seconds a gunshot was heard, followed by a volley of shots. When the other passengers emerged, Ninoy Aquino lay face down on the cement pavement, mortally wounded, arms spread wide. Nearby lay another bullet-riddled body later identified as that of Ronaldo Galman, who was accused of the crime.

News of the killing was transmitted across the world, but not in the Philippines. Marcos-controlled press, radio, and television carried nothing at all. Only Radio Veritas (Truth), a local Roman Catholic station, somberly reported Aquino's murder. Repeated many times over the air, it let loose an avalanche of public grief and spontaneous demonstrations. For two days streams of mourners filed through the living room of the Aquino residence in Quezon City, Metro Manila, to pay their respects. Aurora Aquino had ordered her son's body laid out without burial cosmetics and in his bloodstained clothes.

One morning Aquino's mother awakened before dawn to find several men moving slowly by the casket in the living room. "I went up to the men and remarked, 'You're here so early.' They replied that they were taxi drivers. They had to report for work at 6 A.M. and this was the only time they could line up and pay their respects. Later, women toting big baskets came in—they were fish vendors . . . In the afternoon I saw the Zobels [a wealthy family] and the Makati businessmen . . . The rich and the poor came to see Ninoy." A national assemblyman who saw the long line of mourners waiting on Times Street remarked: "All the cover-up—the lack of mention on the radio, when the world press was full of the news of what had happened—to me, this was a big reason why Metro Manila turned out in full force . . . They were being denied the news, so they went to see for themselves . . . They felt real outrage, indignation, and anger."[2]

Archbishop Cardinal Jaime Sin said a solemn funeral mass in Santo Domingo Church, eulogizing Aquino as having fallen in the cause of democracy. After the service, pall bearers placed the bier on a flatbed truck, which moved through thousands of people onto Epifanio de los Santos Avenue (EDSA), the widest and longest thoroughfare in Manila. Throngs swelled to nearly 2 million, many waiting for hours to glimpse the procession wending its way the eighteen kilometers (eleven miles) to a burial site in Memorial Park. Banners spanned the streets: "Justice for All Victims of Political Repression and Military Terrorism!!" "Fight Political Repression."

One of the largest demonstrations was staged at a park overlooking Manila Bay, the site of a statue memorializing José Rizal, a nineteenth-century fighter for Philippine independence from Spain. "If they shoot me, they'll make me a hero," Ninoy Aquino had said. "What would Rizal have been if the Spaniards had not brought him back and shot him? Just another exile like me to the end of his life." Now hundreds of thousands of Manilienos stood in the rain before the Rizal statue and the bier of Ninoy Aquino, fists held high, holding thumb and forefinger in the shape of an L to symbolize Aquino's political party, Laban (meaning "fight"). Some of the mourners called out in native Tagalog: *"Ninoy, hindi ka nag-iisa"* (Ninoy, you are not alone).[3]

None of this was carried on local television, and broadcast coverage was limited to Radio Veritas. The newspapers were also mute, except for one that carried a picture of a mourner who was fatally struck by lightning during the funeral procession. That was all.

"A Pharaoh, a Shah, an Emperor, a King, a Duce"

Filipinos first voted in elections just two years after Russians marched to the Winter Palace in St. Petersburg in 1905 and at about the same time that Mohandas Gandhi was organizing Indians in South Africa. These elections had been held under the auspices of the United States, which acquired the Philippines after war with Spain in 1898. A degree of self-rule was granted to Filipinos but not full democracy; only a small fraction of the population was eligible to vote. The first elected president did not take office until 1935, when the country received commonwealth status. Full independence, and rapid expansion of suffrage, came after the end of World War II, in 1947.

Two years later young Ferdinand Marcos, the son of a legislator, launched his political career. Though only in his early thirties, he had already made headlines, having been charged with and later acquitted of the murder of a political rival of his father. He quickly emerged as a national figure in the 1950s, helped partly by tales of heroic deeds as a wartime resistance leader and partly by his mastery of the patronage and alliance-building that were characteristic of Filipino politics.[4]

After earning a reputation as something of a reformer, Marcos won election as president in 1965, vowing to fight the corruption that was rife in public life and to carry out land reform to reduce the country's vast disparities of wealth. But he threw most of his energy and the state's resources into building roads, bridges, and ports, running up a gigantic deficit in the process. He managed to win reelection in 1969—the first Filipino president to do so— but only after spending huge sums of public money to buy votes. Election-related killings also climbed dramatically. "No election since 1949 has touched off louder cries of fraud and terrorism than the last one," declared the *Philippines Free Press* after Marcos's victory.[5]

Outraged by election improprieties and Marcos's ardent support for the U.S. war effort in Vietnam, students took to the streets in Manila in large and sometimes violent demonstrations. Meanwhile communist insurgency in the hinterlands was heightening the sense of instability. The president was also the target of sharp criticism from moderate opponents. Rather than answer his critics, Marcos moved to silence them. In September 1972, less than a year before Augusto Pinochet overthrew a democratically elected government in another former Spanish colony in the southern hemisphere, Marcos imposed martial law. Operating by decree, he nullified the country's constitution limiting the president to two terms, eliminated the office of vice president, shut down newspapers, took over commercial radio and television stations, set aside the right of public assembly, suspended habeas corpus, and started arresting political enemies on trumped-up charges of sedition. A constitutionally elected president had turned himself into a dictator.[6]

The defenders of democracy, a small minority of elected politicians, watched helplessly as Marcos replaced the bicameral Congress with a puppet unicameral national assembly that was dominated by his political party, the New Society Movement, or KBL. Little of this cheered the people of a country that had been learning about democracy for decades in schools modeled on those in America, and the way that Marcos capitalized on the power he had consolidated also alienated many.

For President Marcos and his wife Imelda, a former beauty queen whom he appointed governor of Metro Manila in 1975 and later a cabinet minister, locking up political control seemed to be the means to a further end: glorifying themselves as a world power couple that outshone, if rather gaudily, anything that Juan and Evita Peron could have imagined. The president insisted on a cut of every major business transaction in the Philippines, and the duo's personal wealth swelled to at least $5 billion. Imelda had their images incorporated into a giant mural in the presidential palace, depicting them as a Malay version of Adam and Eve, and she spent time and effort on such projects as booking the Muhammad Ali–Joe Frazier championship boxing match and the Miss Universe Pageant into Manila. Marcos had an enormous bust of himself set up overlooking a golf course and highway, both also named after him. Self-aggrandizement became the leitmotif of presidential action.[7]

When martial law descended, Benigno Aquino had been serving as an outspoken Liberal Party leader in the Philippine Senate, and he was soon arrested for allegedly exploding a bomb that killed several people at a rally. Aquino had an alibi—he was at a prenuptial party for his god daughter—but he was charged with murder and jailed, spending months in solitary confinement without trial. Writing from a prison cell in Fort Boniface, Aquino declared that the regime had reinstated "the oldest society recorded by history—a society of absolute rule by one man who in various epochs was called a pharaoh, a shah, an emperor, a king, a duce, a caudillo, a fuhrer, a chairman or a president."[8]

Civilian opposition to Marcos continued, but the headlines were taken over by the regime's violent enemies. The communists, who had led a peasant insurgency against the Japanese during World War II and against Philippine landowners in the postwar years, had renewed their guerrilla offensive against the state in the late 1960s. Their New People's Army (NPA) gained strength after martial law was imposed and at one point was thought to control nearly three-quarters of the nation's rural provinces. In addition, the regime faced an armed challenge in the south from Muslim separatists. Faced with pressure from Arab oil-producing nations, Marcos tried to negotiate an end to the conflict by agreeing to local autonomy but never delivered on his promise and failed to quash the rebellion.[9]

Challenges from communists and Muslim militants were the kind of threats that made it easy for Cold War–haunted policymakers in the United States to look the other way as Marcos strangled democracy. Moreover, a huge U.S. naval base at Subic Bay in western Luzon and a large bomber fleet at Clark Field, an hour's drive north of Manila, were anchors of American power in the Pacific and thus reasons for Washington to want stability in the Philippines. By embellishing the threat of a communist takeover in the early 1970s, Marcos had won solid backing from President Richard Nixon for martial law; over the ensuing four years, American military aid had more than doubled.[10]

American business also saw Marcos as a friend. The Philippines had attracted considerable U.S. investment, and the American Chamber of Commerce congratulated Marcos for overturning Supreme Court decisions that endangered property rights of foreign businesses. The country sat astride the South China Sea through which oil tankers passed to Japan from Indonesia and other oil-producing countries, so its strategic position was highly valued—and foreign money kept pouring in. Debt generated by loans from the International Monetary Fund and the World Bank, plus sizable infusions from American banks, expanded during martial law from $2.7 billion in 1972 to $10.7 billion in 1977.[11]

Meanwhile a legion of Filipino dissidents languished in prison. According to an Amnesty International Report in 1977, 60,000 political arrests were made between September 1972 and February 1977, and torture was a common method of treating suspects. At one point, after Jimmy Carter moved into the White House, Marcos released 3,000 prisoners. But the best known inmate, Ninoy Aquino, remained behind bars.

"A Force that Fosters Civil Disobedience"

In 1978 Marcos held an election to help maintain a democratic façade, and Benigno Aquino founded the Laban Party from his jail cell and stood for election to the national assembly in absentia. Knowing that the election would be fixed to favor KBL candidates, Laban circulated a chain letter calling for a noise-barrage protest on election eve. At the appointed time, *Manilienos* honked horns, banged on pots, and shouted, creating bedlam well into the night—as Chileans would do five years later, on their first national protest day against the Pinochet regime. But the election results showed Marcos's ability to control the polling process. Seven of the thirteen provinces reported 100 percent KBL victories. Only one province, the Central Visayas, recorded a majority for the opposition. In Metro Manila where Laban was strongest, the opposition vote percentage supposedly totaled just 31 percent to the KBL's 69 percent.[12]

Frustrated, the noncommunist opposition turned to confrontation. Businessman Eduardo Olaguer, with the assistance of exiled oppositionists, founded Project Public Justice as "a force that fosters civil disobedience, a force that destabilizes the dictatorship, and a force that organizes the people for the final drive to freedom"—seeming to endorse a nonviolent strategy. But impressed by the 1978 noise barrage, Olaguer's group believed that people who banged pots and pans could be persuaded to revolt. The group inspired acts of arson that destroyed a government building, several hotels, and a floating casino ship in Manila Bay. (The government controlled all casinos, which Marcos used as a lucrative source of funds for patronage and bribery.) But the torchings failed to get any coverage in the Marcos-controlled press, and members of the "force that fosters civil disobedience" were arrested.[13]

After seven years' detention, Ninoy Aquino was convicted of murder and sentenced to death by a Marcos-appointed tribunal. But when Aquino was diagnosed with a heart condition in 1980, the U.S. State Department intervened. Marcos suspended the death sentence and allowed him to leave the country for surgery in Houston, Texas. When he recovered, Aquino and his family remained in America, where he was awarded fellowships for study at Harvard University and the Massachusetts Institute of Technology.

From abroad Aquino affiliated with the radical April 6th Liberation Movement (A6LM), a Manila-centered group named for the date of the noise barrage. "I have been told of plans for the launching of a massive urban guerrilla warfare where buildings will be blown up, and corrupt presidential cronies and cabinet members assassinated," he disclosed in a speech at the Asia Society in New York. Within three weeks of Aquino's speech, nine explosions rocked Manila, causing minor damage and injuring two people.[14]

The A6LM had more in store. A few months later, in October, it sent letters to delegates going to a convention of the American Society of Travel Agents in Manila, warning that "the Filipino revolution has begun" and foreigners "might get caught in the crossfire." After Marcos promised to increase security, the group proceeded with plans to meet in the city's convention center. The president himself welcomed the delegates, assuring them they were safe, but an A6LM activist who had infiltrated the Ministry of Tourism planted a bomb that exploded minutes after Marcos finished speaking. He escaped injury but eleven delegates, a Filipino singer, and six others were injured.[15]

The bombings failed to incite a popular revolt, although Marcos opened discussions with Aquino, using his wife as an intermediary. At a four-hour meeting with Imelda Marcos in New York near the end of 1980, Aquino demanded the lifting of martial law and clean elections. Marcos seemed to accept these demands when, in January 1981, he lifted martial law and scheduled a presidential contest. But there was less to this than met the eye. The end of martial law turned out to be a formality, the president's executive powers remained largely intact, and the minimum age limit for candidates was set at fifty, thus barring Aquino, who was forty-eight. Certain it would be rigged, a coalition of opposition groups decided to boycott the June 1981 election, which Marcos claimed to win with 88 percent of the votes.[16]

Aquino kept speaking out against Marcos, but seeing the Richard Attenborough film *Gandhi* made him rethink his strategy. (He had already become familiar with Gandhi's writings while in prison.) Before leaving Boston on his way back to the Philippines, he told a reporter that he was returning to "join the ranks of those struggling to restore our rights and freedoms through nonviolence." Aquino even showed his willingness to reconcile with Marcos if democracy was restored. He said he hoped to appeal to the "good side" of the president, a one-time fraternity brother, and propose a caretaker government to oversee "free and honest elections." But first, Aquino insisted, Marcos must step down.[17]

Several friends cautioned Aquino to remain in the United States, but when Minister of Defense Juan Ponce Enrile warned of a possible assassination attempt, Aquino merely postponed his arrival by two weeks. By the summer of 1983, people were calling Ninoy "a steak commando" who was having a good time in the States while his countrymen were suffering, recalled former Senator Francisco Rodrigo. "We needed him for the cause," since the democratic opposition seemed to be weakening. "People were falling by the wayside, they were becoming radicalized," Rodrigo said. "Marcos wanted to radicalize us so that he can tell the Americans, 'You don't like me? What's your alternative? Communism. I may be a bastard, but I'm your only bastard.' And the communists also wanted that. They knew that people were angry with Marcos. They wanted to make it seem as if only the NPA could succeed in driving Marcos out. We were trying to give them a viable alternative . . . I felt that Ninoy had to return."[18]

Confetti, Capital, and the Trial

The airport murder of Benigno Aquino enraged the public, energized the opposition, and unsettled Marcos's relations with Washington. The funeral itself marked the beginning of prolonged civil disobedience against the dictatorship, as countless demonstrations were staged in Metro Manila. Week after week in the fall and winter of 1983, yellow confetti streamed from the windows of skyscraper office buildings along Ayala Avenue in the heart of Makati, the Philippines' modern financial center. (Yellow had been adopted as the symbolic color of Aquino's cause.)

The business community sensed uncertainty, and corporations and wealthy Filipinos withdrew an estimated $500 million from major banks, depositing their funds in the United States, Switzerland, and Hong Kong. This, in turn, forced a devaluation of the Philippine peso and a further increase in foreign debt, up $6 billion in October 1983 alone. Marcos's minister of information, who left the regime in 1980, said that "the government complained that the marches and showers of confetti were causing capital flight and scaring the IMF, the World Bank, and the country's creditor banks. Business had ground to a standstill . . ."[19]

Formerly complacent business leaders now demanded a speedy, impartial investigation of the Aquino murder, a clear line of presidential succession, clean and honest elections, a reformed election board, and a free press. Marcos responded by restoring the office of vice president and reducing the minimum age for presidential and vice presidential candidates from fifty to forty years, appointing new board members to the government-controlled Commission on Elections (COMELEC), and accrediting the National Movement of Citizens for a Free Election (NAMFREL).

Many of the post-assassination demonstrations had been organized by former Senator Jose Diokno, who had been arrested in 1972 with Ninoy Aquino and kept in solitary confinement for much of his two-year prison term. Diokno now organized Justice for Aquino, Justice for All (JAJA), and recruited the slain senator's younger brother, actor Agapito ("Butz") Aquino, and wealthy businessmen to help finance it.

Most of the public demonstrations were peaceful, but the one on September 21, 1983, on the eleventh anniversary of the declaration of martial law, triggered a major riot. Corazon Aquino opened the rally near Malacanang Palace (a walled complex of plantation-like buildings that had been the seat of government in Manila for more than a century). A crowd of 15,000 broke away and marched to the Mendiola Bridge over the Pasig River, only to face a solid wall of armed marines, riot police, and firemen. Suddenly an explosion in the government ranks killed two firemen. Marines charged, firing on the demonstrators. The ensuing riot left eleven dead and hundreds wounded and set off clashes and looting throughout Metro Manila.[20]

Some months later the opposition managed a greater measure of nonviolent discipline. In July 1984 Butz Aquino and a veteran Liberal Party leader rallied 20,000 demonstrators who occupied half of Mendiola Bridge. Two months later on a "National Day of Sorrow," thousands marched toward the bridge, now barricaded with barbed-wire fences. Some 3,000 demonstrators staged a candlelight vigil and stayed overnight. On the following morning when they refused to move, police dispersed them with tear gas and water cannons.

To try to dam the tide of protest, Marcos named Corazon Juliano Agrava, a retired Supreme Court justice, and a blue-ribbon citizens' panel to undertake a formal investigation into Aquino's murder. The probe lasted nearly a year, and the investigators agreed that Aquino had been shot from behind as he descended the stairway, but not by Ronaldo Galman, who turned out to be a member of an army-organized anti-communist terrorist squad. Investigators said Galman's killing was part of a cover-up.

In late 1984 Agrava told Marcos that the former head of the Aviation Security Command and six of his men had plotted the assassination, but the majority report, submitted a day later by the other board members, said Major General Ver, the army chief of staff, plus several generals, colonels, captains and lesser officers, had conspired to have Aquino killed and had staged cover-ups both before and after the shooting. Ver had already been replaced as army chief of staff (under pressure from Washington, unhappy with progress against the communist insurgency), and Marcos now had him placed him on trial, along with twenty-four military officers and one civilian.

Besides the effort to bring Aquino's killers to justice, the opposition focused on the 1984 National Assembly elections as an opportunity to weaken the government. The Kongresong Mamamayang Pilipino (congress of the Filipino people)—a group of 150 politicians, business leaders, church officials, and communists—convened to develop a common strategy. Using their sharper organizational skills and larger number of delegates, the communist NPA forced through a resolution calling for opposition parties to boycott the election unless the regime freed all political prisoners, granted full powers to the national assembly, guaranteed free and open elections, and lifted the Preventive Detention Act, which allowed arbitrary and prolonged imprisonment.[21]

No one expected Marcos to go along with these conditions, and not everyone was willing to forgo the chance to confront the regime at the polls. There was every reason to expect that Marcos would employ his usual combination of intimidation, vote buying, and fraud. But there were compelling reasons not to sit out the election. A boycott would make things easier for Marcos, by allowing him to win a big victory without much blatant vote-rigging. If his opponents could put up a strong fight, they could at least force the dictator to show his true colors and take actions that would further erode his legitimacy. In the end, it was just this strategy that would bring Marcos down.[22]

Salvador Laurel, head of the United Democratic Action Organization (UNIDO), a coalition of several moderate parties, announced they would not boycott the election, and Cory Aquino and her brother's party, the PDP-LABAN, followed suit. So the battle was joined, and perhaps its most vital combatant was NAMFREL. What Marcos had approved as procedural window-dressing became a lever for the opposition to make the elections into a viable method of challenging his rule.

NAMFREL had been conceived originally in 1951 as a Central Intelligence Agency-backed effort to clean up the electoral process. It was revived in 1983 by a group of businessmen, religious leaders, housewives, and professionals, headed by a flour-mill owner with ties to Cardinal Sin. They were convinced that the president would never voluntarily leave office, and they were concerned that as long as he stayed, the communist NPA would keep attracting followers, and violent revolution might upstage the nonviolent movement. Only by restoring some integrity to elections could they offer an alternative to armed rebellion—and now Marcos had provided them with exactly that kind of opening.[23]

NAMFREL's 200,000 volunteers, many of them nuns (who soon earned the nickname NAMFREL Marines), got the job of overseeing the voting. NAMFREL and COMELEC were to receive the same tally sheets from the voting precincts but develop their own vote counts. Although the communists, JAJA, and one wing of another party ignored the election, the 90 percent voter turnout was exceptionally high. Overall, the KBL claimed victory in more than 70 percent of the races. But in NAMFREL-manned Bicol province, Marcos opponents gained more than 65 percent; in Southern Tagalog, over 60 percent. In provinces with insignificant or nonexistent NAMFREL presence, the KBL won all of the races, a crucial lesson for the opposition. Yet the 1984 contest netted some real gains: Before the election, the KBL had controlled about 90 percent of the seats in the assembly; afterward, about 70 percent.[24]

"Joan of Arc"

The next presidential election would have been held in December 1987, but sensing erosion in American support, Marcos—appearing on David Brinkley's weekly public affairs television program in the United States in November 1985—announced plans to hold a snap election. Confident that he would win handily and so prove his democratic bona fides to skeptical Americans, he set the date for only three months later. Marcos also realized that the opposition was divided and would likely put forward more than one candidate, thus splitting the vote against him. Still, the announcement quickened the spirits of the opposition. Corazon Aquino agreed to run at the head of a united front, if a million signatures could be collected. Volunteers throughout the country quickly amassed 1.2 million. Actually unifying the opposition was another story.

Salvador Laurel of UNIDO had indicated five months earlier that he would run. As the December 11 deadline for filing approached, Cardinal Sin interceded. "I think you are going to win," he told Cory Aquino. "First of all, you are a woman, and it is humiliating for Marcos to lose. But that is the way God works—to confound the strong. You are the Joan of Arc." A day later Sin approached Laurel. "Well, you are not very attractive," he said candidly. "Cory is more attractive than you are, and if you run, you will lose. First of all, you should unite." Laurel finally agreed and, within hours of the deadline, Corazon Aquino and Salvador Laurel filed to run for president and vice president on a ticket that coupled her legions of street followers with his traditional political organizers and party activists.[25]

The campaign cast a spotlight on a sometimes shy, deeply religious widow, whose main appeal lay in her charisma and sincerity. But Corazon Aquino was not quite the simple, politically inexperienced housewife she seemed to be. Born

Corazon Aquino, widow of assassinated Filipino opposition leader Benigno Aquino,
addresses a rally on September 21, 1983.

Credit: ©Erwin Elloso, *People Power, An Eyewitness History*
The Philippine Revolution of 1986, Writers and Readers Publishing, Inc.

into one of the country's great landholding families, she had been educated at
Catholic schools in Manila and in America. Her marriage to Aquino had
cemented an alliance between two of the Philippines' most influential clans,
undergirding Ninoy's political career. After her husband's arrest in 1973, Cory
had taken over as treasurer of her family's real estate and financial empire. In her
own campaign, she avoided policy issues, such as the failing economy and
agrarian reform, and instead spoke personally about how she wanted to open
Malacanang Palace to the people and about Ninoy Aquino's years of imprisonment and his brutal assassination. Audiences hung on her words and many wept,
and she was soon called the "Nora Aunor of Philippine politics," after the
country's most popular movie star.[26]

Meanwhile, after a contentious seven-month proceeding, all twenty-five
defendants in the trial of Ninoy Aquino's killers, including General Ver, were
acquitted on December 2, 1985, just two months prior to the election. Marcos
promptly reinstated Ver as army chief of staff. Almost immediately Manila's
streets erupted with demonstrations. This time general strikes also broke out,

mainly in rural provinces. Popular anger at the regime was redoubled, giving further impetus to the opposition.[27]

The Aquino-Laurel campaign was run by an experienced former senator, whose zealous campaign council—including Butz Aquino and opposition figures who had been Ninoy's friends and supporters—organized immense, exuberant rallies for the ticket, which Cory attended by flying around the archipelago in a private plane donated by a major businessman. By mid-campaign in January 1986, Agence France Presse estimated that rallies in twenty-four provinces and cities had drawn 355,000 spectators. The opposition's campaign climaxed on February 4, three days before the election, at a rally in Luneta Park, Manila. There, a million men, women, and children cheered Cory Aquino's call for change.

In contrast, the Marcos campaign was ragged and dispiriting. First he chose an older, shop-worn politician for his running mate, the antithesis of the strong successor his Washington allies had expected. On the campaign trail, he seemed tired and weak, and spoke to just over 88,000 Filipinos in eight provinces. Then, within weeks of the election, the foreign media—uninhibited by domestic press constraints—published several exposés about the president, which two Filipino newspapers carried. An exiled businessman was quoted by the *Wall Street Journal* as saying that he and others "acted as front men" for Marcos in multimillion-dollar deals. *The New York Times* reported that the U.S. Army had branded as "absurd" Marcos's claim that he led the preeminent guerrilla force against the Japanese on Luzon. Going further, the *Washington Post* reported that Marcos had collaborated with the Japanese.[28]

But alleged fraud about his war record was not half as damaging to Marcos's hold on power as the fraud he was about to orchestrate at the polls.

The Election

What became the most fateful presidential election in Philippine history drew most of the country's 26 million registered voters to 85,938 voting centers on Friday, February 7, 1986. Even before the polls opened, the regime had tampered with the process. One opposition leader called the campaign in Tarlac "the dirtiest ever, full of vote buying . . . Ruling party goons were terrorizing the barrios . . . They told Cory supporters that they knew where they lived and where their children went to school and what time they left the house. A man might be willing to die for the cause, but he is not ready to risk the lives of his children."[29]

Voting irregularities were reported as soon as the polls opened. One of every 10 voters complained that his or her name had been removed from the voting list, while other names were mysteriously added: One reporter found a list with

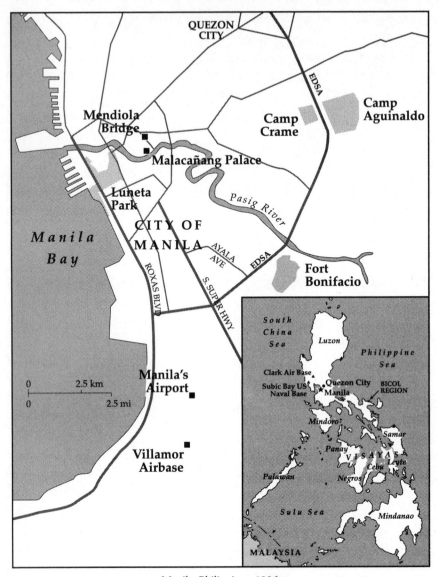

Manila, Philippines, 1986

200 voters supposedly living in one small house. The NAMFREL chairman for Metro Manila estimated that 15 percent of the voters in that area were disenfranchised. NAMFREL volunteer Benjamin Rieza was assigned to an elementary school to check the vote tallies in three precincts. When the polls closed, Aquino was leading in all three. After a while, said Rieza, "gunshots were heard. I took cover. People were running everywhere in panic. I saw the armed men poking their weapons at a NAMFREL volunteer and telling everybody to

go outside . . . Then a masked man came in, wielding a hand grenade. I took the opportunity to run away."[30]

The credibility of the government vote count was undermined two days after the election, when thirty-one technicians walked out of COMELEC headquarters in Manila after one was told that figures on the tally board did not match those in the computer printouts. The technicians, after being taken to safety in a church, issued a statement emphasizing they were nonpartisan and decided to walk out "when we realized that something wrong was going on."[31]

An American delegation, headed by U.S. Senator Richard Lugar, chairman of the Senate Foreign Relations Committee, visited COMELEC as observers and were maneuvered through pristine polling places, where they seldom found anything wrong. Lugar was suspicious, and back in Washington he told President Reagan that he thought Marcos was "cooking the results." Senator John Kerry, another observer, said there was a "total breakdown and slow-down" in vote counting. But Reagan told a press conference he thought there may have been fraud and violence "on both sides," and that Lugar and his team had returned with no hard evidence "beyond the general appearance of wrongdoing." Aquino cautioned the American president against supporting Marcos as the winner. "I would wonder at the motives of a friend of democracy," she said, "who chose to conspire with Mr. Marcos to cheat the Filipino people of their liberation."[32]

To respond to the threat of another stolen election, the Catholic Church stepped in. When Ricardo Cardinal Vidal of Cebu convened the Catholic Bishops Conference of the Philippines, he asked each bishop to describe his own election experiences and reports he had received from priests and laymen. "The reports showed a general trend," Vidal said. "We saw the same patterns of fraud." The bishops issued a thunderous statement: "In our considered judgment, the polls were unparalleled in the fraudulence of their conduct." They condemned "the deliberate tampering of the election returns" and objected to intimidation, harassment, terrorism, and murder that "made naked fear the decisive factor in people not participating in the polls . . . These and many other irregularities point to a criminal use of power to thwart the sovereign will of the people."[33]

The bishops then urged Filipinos to use nonviolent action to protest. "This means active resistance of evil by peaceful means . . . Now is the time to repair the wrong. The wrong was systematically organized. So must the correction be. But as in the election itself, that depends fully on the people, on what they are willing and ready to do . . . But we insist. Our acting must always be according to the Gospel of Christ, that is, in a peaceful, nonviolent way." Yet as the bishops spoke against violence, the country was shaken once again by another cold-blooded murder, this time of Evelio Javier, a passionate Aquino supporter and former provincial governor who was struck down by six hooded killers hired by a Marcos warlord. His death brought the total of election campaign-related murders to 264.[34]

Notwithstanding the general furor about election results, the National Assembly went right ahead and completed its official vote count by February 15, claiming Marcos received 10,807,197 votes to Aquino's 9,292,761. Led by the minority speaker, opposition assembly members walked out at midnight. "It's obvious the majority in this chamber would like to railroad through the proclamation of President Marcos," the speaker declared. Within minutes of the walkout, KBL loyalist legislators proclaimed Marcos president again, for a six-year term.

NAMFREL countered by posting victory results for Corazon Aquino and Salvador Laurel in a statement published in the *Manila Times*. According to NAMFREL, Mrs. Aquino had received 7,835,070 votes to 7,053,068 for Marcos, based on returns from 70 percent of the precincts. NAMFREL's volunteers had been unable to organize or had been prevented from doing their work in the remaining 30 percent. "NAMFREL believes," it concluded, "that this tabulation is a fairer representation of the real vote."[35]

Allegations of vote fraud were buttressed in Washington by university professor Allen Weinstein, a political advisor to the Lugar delegation, who said his own investigation had confirmed that the Philippine government had committed fraud and other abuses. José Concepcion, NAMFREL's chairman, told Weinstein that "never before has a more vigilant population witnessed a more pervasive travesty upon the sanctity of the ballot in our history."[36]

"The Way of Nonviolent Struggle"

Undaunted by the proclamation of a Marcos victory, an estimated 1.5 million Aquino-Laurel supporters massed in Luneta Park in Manila the next day for a Triumph of the People Rally. "I feel like the young boy, David, prepared to face the giant Goliath," Aquino told the crowd. "If Goliath refuses to yield, we shall escalate. I'm not asking for violent revolution. This is not the time for that. I always indicated that now is the way of nonviolent struggle for justice. This means active resistance of evil by peaceful means."[37]

Aquino chose a nationwide boycott of banks, newspapers, beverages, and movies as a way to escalate the struggle. She asked depositors to withdraw their funds from large banks with close ties to Marcos. Schools nationwide should shut down. Readers should boycott the Marcos-controlled press. Popular San Miguel beer and Coca-Cola products should be left on the shelves. Theaters showing films starring pro-Marcos actors should be empty. She asked people to delay paying utility bills until the electric and phone companies threatened to cut off service. Taking up the call, depositors in droves took out money from all of the Marcos-related banks. Less than a week into the boycott, sales of San Miguel beer were down 30 percent and the share price of San Miguel Corporation on the Manila Stock Exchange had slumped more than 18 percent.[38]

Mainly to mollify American opinion, Marcos sacked General Ver and replaced him with Lieutenant General Fidel Ramos, a graduate of the U.S. Military Academy at West Point and a career soldier. The president said officers beyond retirement age would be let go, although the very next day he promoted one of them. These and other changes were part of a campaign to portray a "new Marcos" who would be willing to let Corazon Aquino serve on a new council of state. One Marcos aide predicted that the leader would now be reform-minded.

But this was too little, too late, and now events were breaking against the man in Malacanang. Seven members of the President's Productivity Council resigned. On the Monday after the Aquino-Laurel victory rally, the Philippines Central Bank announced an increase from 19 to 30 percent in the interest rate it would pay on treasury bills, in an effort to pull back billions of pesos the government had shelled out for vote-buying during the campaign. The former president of the Philippine Chamber of Commerce and Industries concluded that "a majority of Filipinos now doubt that Mr. Marcos has the mandate of the people."[39]

Although the opposition was still not sanguine about their chances of toppling Marcos, especially as long as Washington was prepared to tolerate him, Corazon Aquino was willing to mount a long nonviolent siege. But President Ronald Reagan, who appreciated the Filipino president's long loyalty, was reluctant to give up on him. As long as Reagan held onto Ferdinand Marcos and vice versa, something stronger than boycotts seemed necessary. As it happened, crucial support came from an unexpected quarter: the dictator's own divided military establishment.

After martial law was imposed, Marcos had made personal loyalty to him rather than military professionalism the first priority in promotion to top echelons, and General Ver had put his own sons and aging cronies in key posts. Reform-minded officers had complained that troops were given inadequate supplies and poor training in their effort to counter guerrilla warfare. All this had fed a reform movement within the army, and by the time of the Aquino assassination in 1983, disgruntled junior officers, with ties to Defense Minister Juan Ponce Enrile, had organized a secret opposition movement, known as RAM (Reform the Armed Forces of the Philippines Movement).

Enrile, a graduate of Harvard Law School and chairman of the United Coconut Planters Bank, had spent many years as a political lieutenant of Marcos, delivering votes for the KBL as a demonstration of his loyalty. But after martial law arrived, Marcos bypassed his defense minister and concentrated power in Ver.

So Enrile secretly recruited forces loyal to himself, using foreign mercenaries to train them, and in 1984 he began to reach out beyond the military to find allies.[40]

In early 1985 RAM had begun to plan a military coup to be sprung the following December. The Marcos announcement of a presidential election in November made RAM cancel those plans; perhaps the election, they thought, would dislodge the president. RAM members had told their fellow soldiers to remain neutral in the election, but they also persuaded 747 cadets of the Philippine Military Academy to send out ten letters each to provincial officials pleading for honest and fair elections, and when election day came, they helped to prevent ballot manipulation in several precincts.

The day after the Aquino-Laurel victory rally, Enrile confided to his law partner, Rene Cayetano, that he had been targeted for assassination along with other RAM members, and that Marcos and Ver planned to arrest a number of opposition leaders. Enrile said he would resign. "I have served him for twenty years. I must now serve my country." The following Friday Enrile told Cayetano that his arrest might be imminent. His fears were well founded: Marcos and Ver had beefed up forces at Malacanang by bringing in loyalist troops from rural provinces, and they had already arrested four RAM officers and forced them to disclose the coup plans.[41]

On Saturday, February 22 two RAM leaders went to Enrile's home and warned him that his arrest could come at any moment. After debating about whether to disperse or consolidate his forces, Enrile ordered his 400 troops to convene at Camp Aguinaldo, the defense ministry headquarters, in Metro Manila. He then contacted General Ramos, who immediately pledged his support and said he and two battalions would make their stand at Camp Crame, the national police headquarters directly across EDSA from Camp Aguinaldo.

By evening, the camps were teeming with rebel soldiers and national police plus members of the local and international press corps. When Colonel Tirgo Gador heard that Enrile was on the list to be arrested, he commandeered a bus and brought his men to Aguinaldo, flying in their weapons. "We can no longer continue to pretend that Marcos has the mandate of the people," he said. "I would rather fight for my convictions than for an administration I do not believe in any more."[42]

Enrile and Ramos held a press conference in Aguinaldo's ceremonial hall. "As of now, I cannot in conscience recognize the president as the commander in chief of the armed forces," Enrile declared. "I believe that the mandate of the people does not belong to the present regime . . . I searched my conscience, and I felt that I could not serve a government that is not expressive of the sovereign will." Enrile appealed for support from "all decent elements in the cabinet, decent elements in the government, decent Filipinos, and . . . decent soldiers and officers . . ." Ramos then said he was directing the troops under his command and others who were "dedicated to the military service in the sense of being the protector of the people" to join him and Enrile. "We are committed to support Corazon Aquino," Ramos revealed. "I think, deep in my heart, that she is the real president of the Philippines."[43]

As Enrile and Ramos had to know, these were fighting words to Marcos, and they realized they could not withstand a frontal attack from loyalist troops. But now they felt that other types of forces might be available. Enrile and Ramos each called Cardinal Sin and asked for help. "All right, Fidel. Just wait," Sin said. "In fifteen minutes, your place will be filled with people." Then over Radio Veritas, referring to Ramos and Enrile, the cardinal said that he was "calling on our people to support our two good friends at the camp. Go to Camp Aguinaldo and show your solidarity with them in the crucial period . . . I wish that bloodshed will be avoided."[44]

Butz Aquino was the first civilian leader to join the rebel soldiers. Arriving at the camp, he met with a beleaguered Enrile, who was wearing a bulletproof vest and sweating visibly. "I am here at Camp Aguinaldo," Butz announced on Radio Veritas. "I have just spoken to Minister Enrile. He and his men are bracing themselves against an attack. We are here to try and prevent bloodshed . . . I am calling on all concerned citizens . . . to meet me at Isetan [a department store] in Cuybao. " By midnight Butz had a crowd of several thousand lined up to march to Aguinaldo.[45]

Manila, a tropical city, is vibrant at night, and EDSA and other major streets are normally congested until two o'clock in the morning. So word of the military revolt and the Cardinal's appeal spread like wildfire through streets and neighborhoods. A group of seminarians clad in white and carrying flags and a cross were among the first arrivals, and they began to form a human barrier around Camp Crame. Another crowd gathered at Luneta Park.

Hermino Astorga, former vice mayor of Manila, heard a request on Radio Veritas for help to drive people from Luneta Park to the camps. He turned to his wife and said, "Let's go." When they reached Luneta, they were "aghast to see the enormous crowd." As Astorga called his house for other cars to be sent, he was approached by drivers who offered their cars; they were followed by a big truck and by utility vehicles, all of which were filled with people and sent off to Aguinaldo. When Astorga saw three taxicabs, "I asked the drivers to take the rest of the people at my expense. When I asked them how much it would cost, their answer took me by surprise. 'You don't have to pay,' they said. 'Fill up our cabs and we will take everybody to EDSA for free.'"[46]

Anticipating an attack, civilians on EDSA created barricades at key points. In one place they aligned six empty buses across the multilane avenue. Young people climbed on top of the buses, waving flags and yelling "Cory, Cory" as more people kept arriving. Others ferried food and coffee to Aquinaldo for the rebel soldiers. A joyous but tense mood took hold of all these ordinary Filipinos, who stood guard over the rebel soldiers through the night.

Despite her husband's plea to stay home, housewife Teresa Pardo went to EDSA. She said later "it was for the children that I was going to risk life and limb—so that they could hope for a better future . . . I couldn't stay put in my comfortable house while thousands from the depressed areas were doing their share to fight for me. With towels and lemon juice to lessen the sting of tear gas, I walked into the early dawn alone, out of the house into the street . . . into independence and into freedom."[47]

A newspaper report later estimated the chanting, dancing, horn-blowing crowd at 50,000. "It was funny," Enrile said. "We in the defense and military organization who should be protecting the people were being protected by them."[48]

"I Saw No One Yield to Fear"

The rebels and Marcos traded threats and ultimatums via television and radio throughout Saturday night and Sunday morning. Enrile and Ramos declared Aquino the election victor and repeatedly called on Marcos to resign. In a televised press conference, Marcos ordered the rebel soldiers to "stop this stupidity and surrender." Appearing with a coterie of loyal general officers, he hinted at a possible artillery strike against the rebels and named officers suspected of plotting a coup. For his part Enrile decided to consolidate his forces and led his soldiers across EDSA to Camp Crame.[49]

Early on Sunday afternoon, two loyalist armored marine battalions moved toward the camps. Some of the advancing soldiers halted as civilians with nuns in front pushed forward, greeting them with hugs and sharing food and cigarettes. They tied yellow ribbons on soldiers' rifles, and some civilians knelt in prayer. At one point, as the giant crowd was being entertained by comedians from a platform in the middle of EDSA, someone announced that government tanks were headed toward the camps. "It is necessary for a large crowd to meet the tanks and to immobilize them," the crowd was told. A Jesuit priest later said that when he got to the line of defense in front of the tanks, he saw "a low wall of sandbags stretched across EDSA." Standing on them were "young people in their late teens, early twenties, with their entire lives stretched before them . . . a young mother with a baby in her arms and another in her womb, with toddlers, pre-teens, teenagers . . . I saw one doctor there who was beyond seventy . . . I saw no one leave. I saw no one yield to fear."[50]

Thousands of Filipinos surround government tanks headed for military rebels at Camp Crame, during the "people power" revolution in the Philippines, February 23, 1986.

Credit: ©Corbis/Reuters

Lulu Castaneda, a wife and mother, was there with her daughter Leia. "We were told to link arms," she recalled. "I looked at the faces of the people around me and especially at the man to my right who was holding on tightly to my arm. My big concern was, I am going to die with this man and I don't know his name. I wanted to ask his name, but then I did not want him to think I was fresh. I did not ask his name. As utter strangers, we faced what seemed like imminent death together."

The government's marines looked "tough and deadly" to screenwriter Amado Lacuesta. They were led by Brigadier General Artemio Tadiar, who was short and slightly stocky but, like his men, very hard-looking. Tadiar wanted the people to let armored personnel carriers (APCs) through to the rear of Fort Aguinaldo. "I have my orders," Tadiar shouted into a megaphone. Then Butz Aquino materialized, climbed onto the armored car, grabbed a megaphone, and told the people to hold fast, exclaiming "this is what people power is all about." Soldiers prodded Aquino off the armored car and started the engine, putting up a cloud of black smoke. Lacuesta raised his hands and shouted, "Go on, kill us!" The crowd booed the soldiers; cameras clicked all around. Then the armored car advanced. There were "defiant, nervous shouts" and praying voices became louder. The APC lurched forward again—and the engine stopped. After a moment of silence, "the crowd erupts into wild cheers and applause. General Tadiar looks at us, turns and shakes his head."

But the threat was not over. A belligerent marine stood on top of the armored car and signaled the driver to move forward again. The vehicle jerked toward a line of praying nuns. "I wonder how many will be crushed before they realize we mean to stay," Lacuesta recalled himself thinking. "All around us the horde of people that stretches far back to the intersection a block away begins to chant angrily, 'Coree! Coree!' as if the name alone and the Laban [L] sign had the power to stop arrogant men and metal. Just as I am ready to hear the first shriek of agony, a miracle—the APC stops, its engine winds down. Cheers and wild applause. We have won again. The soldiers glare down at us. Again the thousands gathered chant Cory's name."

Throughout all this, Radio Veritas was the communications nexus of the rebellion. Early Sunday morning, armed goons destroyed the Veritas equipment, but by 3:00 A.M. the voice of June Keithley, the main announcer, was back on the air, from a secret broadcasting station she named Radyo Bandido. At one point Veritas aired a personal appeal to General Tadiar: "Artemio, this is your Uncle Fred speaking," a voice said. "Your Aunt Florence and I and all your cousins are here in Crame. Now, boy, please listen to me . . . "[51]

One Veritas listener, Colonel Antonio Sotelo, commanded a helicopter strike wing based in Cavite, the province immediately south of Manila. Early on Monday morning Keithley "was giving a blow-by-blow account of what was going on," Sotelo said. "It made me sad." Following orders, Sotelo started to prepare an attack on the rebels, alerting his crews and ordering extra guns and ammunition. But instead of flying to Fort Bonifacio as ordered, the colonel and sixteen pilots flew the unit's helicopters to Camp Crame. "We circled Camp Crame once; on the second turn, my pilot dropped the wheels, slowed down and proceeded to land," he recalled. "Pandemonium broke loose. The rotor blades were still turning but people were swarming all over us. They were shouting and jumping and hugging. Reporters shoved microphones into my face. All I wanted to say was we followed our conscience. I have not really done much in my life and for once I wanted to make a decision for my country."[52]

The Sotelo defection gave the rebel soldiers the firepower they needed to defend the camps. The helicopters were busy all day Monday, firing warnings into the Malacanang Palace grounds, destroying three presidential helicopters at Villamor air base, and providing air cover to rebel troops who captured the government-controlled television station, Channel 4. Another contingent of rebels commandeered government-operated Channel 9, cutting off a Marcos broadcast from the palace. When several platoons of loyalist Scout Rangers approached the station from the rear, they were blocked by a priest in a white cassock leading a group of citizens in prayer. A schoolteacher in the group shook hands with troops, and others handed them doughnuts, orange juice, and hamburgers.

By Monday afternoon, February 24, Corazon Aquino had returned to Manila from Cebu and decided, over her security guards' objections, to visit the demonstrators on EDSA. "Look, this is my doing," she told them. "If you do not take me there, I am going by myself." What she saw was the reality of the nonviolent commitment she had summoned. "The people of EDSA amazed me," she said later. "It was a different thing altogether from rallies or political meetings. Life was on the line."[53]

"He's Had It"

The Reagan administration was watching these events with some ambivalence. It had already sent a respected diplomat, Philip Habib, on a fact-finding visit to evaluate the viability of the Marcos government. He had come back convinced that the dictator was through, but he also told Secretary of State George Shultz and Defense Secretary Caspar Weinberger that if the United States gave Marcos any encouragement to stay, "he'll hang on." They felt Marcos, pushed into a corner, could call for an attack on the military rebels that would precipitate a bloody conflict, and they feared the rebels might turn to violence.

It became obvious that a decision from President Reagan would be critical in signaling Marcos what course of action that Washington would support. The president and his wife, Nancy, had first met the Marcoses during a visit to the Philippines when Reagan was governor of California. Entertained lavishly and impressed with Marcos's strong anti-communism, Reagan had become a friend. Marcos would listen to him.

At a critical White House meeting with the president on Sunday, Chief of Staff Donald Regan sided with the faithful ally, arguing that an Aquino presidency "would open the door to communism." Habib was dismissive. "The Marcos era has ended," he said. Shultz was even more emphatic: "Nobody believes that Marcos can remain in power. He's had it." At that, the White House issued a statement warning Marcos to avoid bloodshed or risk an immediate cutoff of all aid. Privately, the State Department initiated talks with the palace through its ambassador in Manila, suggesting that Marcos's "time was up" and assuring him of safe passage out of the Philippines. By telephone, Nancy Reagan assured Imelda Marcos that she and her husband would be welcome in America.

But the stubborn dictator rejected these overtures and went on television to deny rumors that he had fled, insisting he was still in control of the government.

At a rally, Filipino mother and her daughter, who makes the "L" sign, standing
for the Laban party and the newly elected president Corazon Aquino, 1986.
Credit: ©Joey Manalang, *People Power, an Eyewitness History,*
The Philippine Revolution of 1986, Writers and Readers Publishing, Inc.

"I will fight to the last breath," Marcos pledged. Even as he spoke, Channel 9
went off the air. Then Marcos called Enrile to propose a coalition government
that would exclude Corazon Aquino, but Enrile refused.

That Monday, February 24, President Reagan released a public statement
urging Marcos to step down: "Attempts to prolong the life of the present regime
by violence are futile." But not until the middle of that night, when Marcos
called Senator Paul Laxalt, a Reagan confidant, to confirm the statement, did
the dictator really believe he had lost U. S. support. "I think you should cut and
cut cleanly," Laxalt told Marcos. "I think the time has come."[54]

That same Monday, confident of victory—through physical action in the
streets if necessary—leaders of the opposition gathered in Club Filipino and

adopted a resolution annulling the National Assembly's proclamation declaring Marcos president. The new document, "A People's Resolution," formally proclaimed Corazon Aquino and Salvador Laurel winners of the election. It was signed by 150 citizens, including 8 opposition members of the National Assembly and General Ramos.

On Tuesday, February 25, with one hand on a Bible held by Aurora Aquino, mother of her slain husband, Corazon Aquino was sworn in as president. She named Enrile defense minister and Ramos as armed forces chief of staff. One hour later, in front of several thousand flag-waving supporters, Ferdinand Marcos took his own oath of office, as previously scheduled, in a ceremony at Malacanang Palace. His supporters chanted "Martial law, martial law," as if repression were still feasible. The event, carried live by government-controlled television, went off the air as the oath was administered to Marcos. His last lamp of power, a single television signal, had been extinguished.

The end came quickly. Corazon Aquino denied a Marcos request to remain in the Philippines and take refuge in northern Luzon. In the evening, the now-powerless dictator, his wife, family, and close staff, were airlifted by U.S. helicopters to Clark Field. Early the next morning Marcos boarded a U.S. military transport plane which flew him off to exile in Hawaii.

Eight years later, a new American president, Bill Clinton, was welcomed by President Fidel Ramos to Malacanang Palace, and Clinton saluted the Philippines as having "led the world in the sweeping resurgence of democracy," which he noted had begun when Ramos and others "exposed yourselves to considerable risks to stand up for freedom . . . following through with the remarkable People Power Movement of President Aquino." Two years after that, 10,000 Filipinos marched in downtown Manila and rallied at a statue of Ninoy Aquino to celebrate the anniversary of "the EDSA rebellion." Three days later, in a vacant lot on Manila's bayfront, 400 "diehard Marcos loyalists" were addressed by Imelda Marcos, who asked the Lord to enlighten Swiss bankers who were still holding $475 million that she wanted back.[55]

Days of liberation are remembered by many. The loot of dictators is not.

෧ ෧ ෧

During eighteen days in February 1986, Filipino civilians climaxed three years of struggle against a corrupt ruler by seizing the public heart of their capital and facing down his loyal forces without firing a shot. The immediate counterforce they brought to bear was simply the courage and alacrity of ordinary citizens, richly earning the sobriquet of "people power."

Most popular movements that toppled authoritarian governments in the twentieth century were given openings to vie for power, but not all took advantage of those opportunities. In the Philippines, after eighteen years in power, Ferdinand Marcos overreached himself in 1983, when he or his subordinates conspired to kill his chief political opponent. Instead of eliminating a potential threat, they created a martyr whose murder touched the nerve of the nation. The killing of Aquino alienated the Catholic Church, the Manila business community, and liberal, moderate, and leftist politicians, thus supplying unity to a movement that surely would have taken longer to coalesce on its own.

Bending to demands from business leaders and from Washington for fair elections, Marcos then overcompensated by allowing the creation of a poll-watching agency that later compromised the regime's ability to rig the results. In the ensuing political warfare, the words and identity of the opposition candidate—the assassinated leader's widow—evoked a choice between the murder of democracy and its revival, between violence done to people and victory by the people. The tactics of the regime were turned into its shame.

The anti-Marcos movement was, after the U.S. civil rights revolution, and the rise of Solidarity in Poland, the third major nonviolent campaign in the century to be conducted in the full glare of the international broadcast media, which helped to export the Philippine people's alienation to viewers and listeners around the world. But the media's influence also had a domestic meaning. Unlike General Jaruzelski or even General Pinochet, Ferdinand Marcos had long used television to pose and preen for his people. So when in the pitch of battle he lost his ability to monopolize political imagery, his authority was instantly diminished.

Two respected institutions were available to transfer that authority to those opposing Marcos. In a country where more than eight of ten people are Catholic, the Church explicitly endorsed the nonviolent strategy of the movement and encouraged people to commit themselves on the streets. And in the century's most dramatic instance of soldiers abandoning a dictator to side with a popular movement, the timely defection of fighting troops and the government's own defense minister splintered Marcos's ability to use violence. Soon, only his friends in Washington were left, and they would not oppose the clamor of his own people for him to go.

The events of 1986 in Manila were not unlike those in San Salvador forty-two years before: The students, doctors, and merchant people who turned against General Martínez and took control of public life through a general strike, demonstrated to the army and his own ministers that he no longer had the ability to stabilize and govern the country. The housewives, priests, workers, and business people who turned against President Marcos and refused to accept a fraudulent election demonstrated to the army and his foreign supporters that he could no longer control events. Whether military strongmen or venal politicians, rulers who lose their capacity for repression and the people's consent cannot hold their positions.

The Philippine outcome was like that in El Salvador in one more way: Almost until the last moment, most Filipinos and foreign observers thought it would be impossible to remove Marcos through any kind of popular revolt. An authoritarian ruler's special vulnerabilities to nonviolent resistance are rarely visible to those who do not understand the mechanics and chemistry of that force. Once that force has prevailed, the assumption that the ruler was impregnable often is replaced by another, equally false belief: that he was so weak that even nonviolent action brought him down. The power of nonviolent sanctions may not be as strong as the power of denial, but it was great enough to send Ferdinand Marcos through the exit door of history.

From Russians marching to the Winter Palace in 1905, to Gandhi's march to the sea in 1931, to Poles' massing in Victory Square in Warsaw, to people power in Manila in 1986, there was a clear line of tactical descent. The Philippine people had an advantage in their struggle, however, that Russians, Indians, Poles, and other nonviolent resisters lacked: They had democratic memories to draw upon. While revolt against tyranny or foreign rule was a primal impulse of popular movements seeking self-determination earlier in the century, the cause worldwide that drew millions into the streets nearer the century's end was about more than ending something evil—it was about seizing or defending democracy. Filipinos already had a civil society. They simply used it. They already knew what was right. They simply did it.

CHAPTER ELEVEN

The Intifada: *Campaign for a Homeland*

"A Shaking Off"

THE RAIN FELL STEADILY as Hanan Aruri and other Palestinian students came together in the fog and chill on the campus of Bir Zeit University one morning in December 1987. Joined by people from the surrounding area of the Israeli-occupied West Bank, dozens soon grew to hundreds, and then hundreds became a thousand. By midday demonstrators thronged the campus and adjoining streets of Bir Zeit Village. The protest had been hastily called amid news from the Gaza Strip, the smaller occupied territory on the Mediterranean coast, that four Palestinians had been killed when an Israeli truck driver crashed into their vans at a military checkpoint. Rumors spread that it was not an accident but rather an act of vengeance for the recent slaying of an Israeli by a Palestinian.

What seemed strange to Aruri was not that so many people, most under the age of thirty, had shown up on such a gloomy day, but that the Israeli Defense Forces (IDF), in charge of policing the West Bank, had not yet come to disperse them. The soldiers were never far from Bir Zeit or the nearby town of Ramallah where Aruri lived, and such an assembly was illegal under the regulations of the Civil Administration that ran Palestinian-populated territories occupied by Israel. Waiting in the wet, surreal calm, Aruri and her friends felt a confrontation coming on.

It was not until shortly after dark, about five or six o'clock, that troops filtered into the village through a warren of streets and alleys. Clad in their green commando uniforms and black desert boots, and brandishing Galilee automatic rifles, they started clearing the crowds by firing rubber bullets (metallic slugs coated with rubber and intended to injure and not kill, but potentially lethal when fired at close range). Past demonstrations always had been dissipated with a rapid, conclusive show of force. Never during twenty years of occupation had Palestinians not eventually backed down.

As the protestors scattered, soldiers closed off the town's exit roads. Dozens of Palestinians were rounded up and arrested, but more stood their ground and hurled stones. Scuffling went on until almost eleven o'clock, as the remaining demonstrators ran off into the hills, eventually to find their way home. Aruri was not arrested or hurt, but the day was seared in her memory. It was one of the first episodes in what was soon to become the *intifada,* the Arabic word for "a shaking off"—the largest uprising of Palestinians ever in the Occupied Territories.[1]

Forty-eight kilometers (30 miles) to the southeast of Bir Zeit in the poorer, run-down Gaza Strip, Palestinians there were reacting to the tragedy at the military checkpoint. Riots broke out in refugee camps and villages and soon spread to the West Bank. Without the guidance of any well-known leaders, Palestinian youngsters, boys and girls alike, confronted IDF soldiers in the streets. Some were too young to have thrown stones in anger before, let alone understand what it meant. But with every rock let loose went some of the frustration that Palestinians had long felt about the Israeli occupation.

The images of Palestinian teenagers in street clashes with one of the most sophisticated armies in the world were irresistible to television news shows around the world. It was called a "shepherd's war" in which a modern army was squaring off against civilians using only the weapons at hand—rocks, tires, and jeering taunts. The foreign press flocked to Jerusalem and Tel Aviv, and in the three months after the outbreak of the *intifada,* more time was given to the story by the three major nightly U.S. television news programs than any other, including a summit meeting between Ronald Reagan and Mikhail Gorbachev.[2]

Most of this coverage highlighted graphic scenes of the violence that spilled out during the uprising. Less well reported was a transformation in the outlook of hundreds of thousands of Palestinians for whom the occupation had felt degrading. Beneath the roiling surface, away from stereotyped scenes of rocks heaved at soldiers who struck back with tear gas, was the steadier action of Palestinians who worked against the occupation without using violence, by trying to make the Palestinian community less dependent on Israel. The *intifada* was a pivotal point in the struggle of Palestinians to achieve self-rule, and violence often intruded on those who sought to make a movement from it. Yet the *intifada*'s impact on events stemmed more from the work of Palestinians who never raised a fist.

Hanan Aruri's day in the rain was one moment in what became a crusade of self-organization and civil disobedience as well as militant opposition, as Palestinian civilians refused to cooperate further with an occupation they regarded as not legitimate. While young toughs burned tires, erected roadblocks, and created havoc in the streets, other Palestinians used the tasks and tools of daily life to create a new direction for their cause. They shook off the stalemate of the past by breaching the dam of an occupying force and pouring out a new river of power that flowed directly from their own initiative.

One Land, Two Homelands

When Mohandas Gandhi was establishing himself as a lawyer in South Africa, Palestine was home to half a million Muslim Arabs, a smaller number of Christians, and approximately 50,000 Jews, most of whom lived in or close to Jerusalem. Under the suzerainty of the Ottoman sultan, the land was mainly agrarian and cut off from the West. But eight years before Father Georgii Gapon marched on the Winter Palace, the first Zionist Congress, held in Basel, Switzerland, had declared that Palestine would one day be the site of a Jewish homeland, regathering Jews from the diaspora and offering final haven from a millennium of persecution.[3]

Over the next two decades Jewish leaders in Europe raised money for the Zionist cause, and a trickle of Jewish immigration to Palestine ensued. Soon there were skirmishes with local Palestinian Arabs, some of whom were aware of the goal of a Jewish state. As World War I ground down the Ottoman Empire, Britain took control of Palestine in 1917 and issued the Balfour Declaration, encouraging Jewish settlement in Palestine and embracing the ultimate goal of a Jewish homeland—even though the British already had promised the guardian of Mecca, Sharif Husayn, that an Arab state would be created in Palestine in exchange for his help in defeating the Ottomans.[4]

Over the next thirty years, Jewish immigration continued, and with Adolf Hitler's ascendance in Central Europe in the 1930s, it became a steady stream. By 1937 the Jewish population had grown to 400,000, and the superiority of Palestinian numbers was gone. After World War II, the revelations of the Holocaust galvanized world support for a Jewish state, and in 1947 Britain ended its control of Palestine and the new United Nations proposed partitioning it into two states—one for Palestinians and one for Jews. Jewish leaders accepted the offer, but the Palestinians refused.

In 1948 Jews in the region climaxed their nation building by declaring the state of Israel in existence on May 14—and immediately war broke out with neighboring Arab states, which banded together to support Palestinian claims. Victorious, the Israelis obtained control of far more land than the UN plan would have furnished. About 120,000 Palestinians remained in Israeli territory, and the rest left for refugee camps and villages in Egypt, Syria, Lebanon, and the newly formed state of Jordan. Israel found itself surrounded by hostile neighbors and harboring a sizeable Palestinian minority within its borders.[5]

During the next two decades, Israel made no move without its security in mind. In 1967 its Arab neighbors made surreptitious preparations to go to war. Israel launched a preemptive blitzkrieg and defeated them all—a triumph of arms that won the Golan Heights from Syria, the West Bank from Jordan, and the Gaza Strip from Egypt, along with several hundred thousand Palestinians. While some of them moved into neighboring states, most stayed in what were now called the Occupied Territories, confident that the land was rightfully theirs. Now it was only Israel that stood in the way of their own state, a single but mighty barrier.

Playing to that foil, Palestinian nationalism thrived, and the Palestine Liberation Organization (PLO), established in 1964 by the Arab states as a way of both promoting and controlling the Palestinian cause, gained influence in the occupied lands. In 1969 the PLO acquired an unlikely chief in the person of the grizzled, diminutive Yasir Arafat, previously the leader of al-Fatah, a guerrilla organization. Under Arafat, the PLO presented itself as a Palestinian government-in-exile. With a payroll of 23,000 activists, teachers, physicians, and others, it raised money that kept it in business and popular support that gave it staying power, even as factions affiliated with the PLO launched military-style raids against Israeli targets and also mounted or countenanced terrorist attacks. Despite perpetual exile and little telegenic appeal, Arafat succeeded in keeping the Palestinian cause on the world's mind.[6]

"A Real Humiliation"

After 1967, the lives of Palestinians had become ever more closely intertwined with the Jewish state. By the 1980s some Palestinians even were receiving retirement pensions from Israel, despite the fact that the PLO refused to recognize Israel's right to exist. Each day about 150,000 Palestinian residents of the West Bank and Gaza left home before dawn and crossed the "Green line" separating the territories from nearby Israeli towns. Often speaking both Hebrew and Arabic, they earned their living in and paid taxes to the Jewish state, and back across the line they were subject to the rules of the Civil Administration.

About 1,200 IDF troops kept the peace in the territories on any given day, operating numerous checkpoints along the Green line and inspecting Palestinians' identification cards.[7]

Israel's population had swelled with new immigrants, and the Occupied Territories were seen as land for new settlements, since they were part of what many Jews regarded as their ancient, rightful inheritance. So property and underground water on the West Bank were appropriated for Jewish settlers. In business terms, the territories were inexpensive to administer, required only a small contingent of troops to control, and proved to be an excellent return on investment. At the same time, Palestinian labor and civil compliance were necessary to keep that return flowing—but the *intifada* would put that in jeopardy.

Palestinians in the West Bank and Gaza lived in hundreds of refugee camps and villages as well as several larger cities, such as Gaza City and Nablus. Another large group inhabited the eastern, or Muslim, quarter of Jerusalem. Unpaved roads and a shortage of arable land made life harsh for tens of thousands. Unemployment was high, especially among educated Palestinians, and only one in eight Palestinian college graduates could find work in his or her chosen occupations. In Gaza, life was especially trying: 1,730 people shared each square kilometer of land, making it one of the most crowded places on earth. When the *intifada* was touched off, it was no coincidence that it was ignited in Gaza and then spread to the West Bank.[8]

Material hardship was compounded by the psychological strain of living in circumstances the Palestinians could not seem to change. Of the thousands of Palestinians who went to work in Israel each morning, a few hundred lined up before dawn in the Old City of Jerusalem in what one journalist termed a "meat market." Israeli contractors who needed workers would drive by the line, and after telling the men about the work—often bricklaying, digging, or asphalting—they offered an hourly wage. If the terms were agreeable, the Palestinian laborers would be off to the site, often a Jewish settlement. "Don't you think we know we are helping them build their state?" one Palestinian worker told a journalist. "It is a real humiliation. Neither side is happy with you, and you know you are doing something against your own people, but you need the food."[9]

In fact, many Palestinians were helping to subsidize the occupation, the very thing they felt was the source of their economic disadvantage and legal subordination. In general, Palestinians received lower wages than Israelis for the same work but paid higher tax rates. They especially resented the value-added tax of 15 percent imposed on goods and services bought in the territories. While commerce was costly, at least it moved relatively freely. Not so physical traffic. The Erez checkpoint at the northern tip of Gaza, for example, was the site of

Israel and the Occupied Territories, 1987-1988

daily aggravation as Palestinians routinely waited in long lines and had their cars searched and ID cards confiscated by guards. "We are treated like animals" was a common refrain.[10]

The occupation also constrained public and civil life. A daily cat-and-mouse game was played by Palestinian youth, who would hang out black, green, and red Palestinian flags and spray walls with political graffiti, only to have the IDF tear down the flags and force people to repaint the walls. Anyone arrested could be detained for six months without being formally charged. The Occupied Territories met the qualifications to be covered by international law set at The Hague in 1907 and the Fourth Geneva Convention in 1944, which prevented deportations and destruction of property, but Israeli adherence to these standards was inconsistent.

Prior to 1977, many Palestinians and members of Israel's Labor Party expected the occupation to be temporary. But when Menachem Begin's Likud Party took over the Knesset, Israel's parliament, that year, the Israeli government signaled that the occupation might be permanent. Not all Israelis favored that, and peace groups began to protest IDF tactics in the territories. But Israeli politics had stalemated. While Labor Party leaders such as Yitzhak Rabin and Shimon Peres were open to territorial compromise, Likud leaders including Yitzhak Shamir and Ariel Sharon were not. In elections in 1984, neither side won a clear plurality, and the two parties were forced into a coalition government. Proposals for talks that might lead to a bargain of land for peace were tabled indefinitely.

In the early 1980s Palestinian resentment led to sporadic flare-ups in which IDF troops were pelted with rocks or an occasional Molotov cocktail was tossed. Defense Minister Sharon penalized turbulent communities with coercive measures such as curfews, destruction of homes, and the uprooting of trees. In 1985 the new defense minister, Yitzhak Rabin, reaffirmed this "iron fist" policy, and the military administration was authorized to use roadblocks, searches, arrests, deportations, and refusals of family reunification permits. Israeli settlements, especially in the West Bank, continued apace, and by the mid-1980s had incorporated almost half its real estate, a creeping de facto annexation that embittered Palestinians.

Meanwhile the PLO, then headquartered in Beirut, fulminated and flexed its paramilitary muscles. In 1982 Israel invaded Lebanon and laid siege to the city, where Arab radical groups such as Hezbollah and Islamic Jihad were also ensconced. The PLO was forced out altogether, alighting in Tunis, 4,000 kilometers (almost 2500 miles) away from the struggle it sought to direct. Ironically, this more distant exile would facilitate a new kind of movement against the occupation.[11]

Some Palestinians had dreamed of a civilian rather than military struggle to force the Israelis to accept Palestinian rights. In 1968 Feisal Husseini, who had been associated with al-Fatah and had learned Hebrew while sitting in Israeli jails, started giving lectures in Israel asserting that nonviolent methods were the only way to peace in the Middle East. Thirteen years later his organizing work in the territories led to the Committee Confronting the Iron Fist, which together with Israeli sympathizers campaigned to help imprisoned Palestinians—reminiscent of KOR in Poland, which helped families of workers being tried or jailed by that country's regime.[12]

In 1983 a Palestinian American clinical psychologist, Mubarak Awad, had established the Palestinian Center for the Study of Nonviolence and for three years had ridden his motor scooter around the West Bank, instructing any who would listen on nonviolent methods of opposing the occupation. Awad had studied the life of Abdul Ghaffar Khan, the Muslim Pathan on India's Northwest Frontier who had diligently taken up Gandhi's civil disobedience against the raj, and he had translated major works on nonviolent theory into Arabic. He knew that in all the wars fought ostensibly on their behalf and during the years of terrorism, Palestinians had been the losers. Violence would only produce failure.[13]

But the alternative to violence was not submission. "I felt strongly that we, as Palestinians, are under occupation because we choose to be under occupation," Awad argued, "and if our choice is not to be under occupation, we have to resist." Resistance, however, was not so much physical—at least at first—as it was mental. It required a decision from each individual. "We tried to tell them that if they want really to liberate themselves . . . their liberation is within themselves," he recalled. "If they choose that idea to be free, then everything becomes easy."[14]

On the ground in the Occupied Territories, things were becoming more difficult. By late 1987 tensions had sharpened, and events conspired to push Palestinians closer to a breaking point. At a three-day Arab summit, Jordan's King Hussein snubbed Yasir Arafat by refusing to greet him at the airport and then left the Palestinian question off the agenda entirely. That same month the Palestinian issue was also missing from the agenda at a Reagan-Gorbachev summit. Finally, Ariel Sharon, then Israel's housing minister, rented an apartment in Jerusalem's Muslim quarter, an act taken as an overt sign that further Jewish settlement in historically Muslim portions of Jerusalem was imminent. So too was the end of Palestinian submission.

Demons and Davids

After twenty years, the Palestinian community in the Gaza Strip and the West Bank had mushroomed to almost 1.7 million people, and East Jerusalem had 136,000 more. Despite a narrow layer of middle- and upper-class merchants and professionals, the vast majority was working class, and they were young. In 1988,

59 percent of Gaza's population was under the age of nineteen, and 77 percent was under twenty-nine. Most of this generation had known only occupation and saw Israelis solely as overlords. Yasir Arafat had bragged of a "population bomb" in the wombs of Palestinian women that would soon overwhelm the Israelis in their own land. But something explosive was closer at hand: a restive mass of people with a deepening sense of impotence.[15]

Many felt that if the crash at the military checkpoint had not occurred, it would have been only a matter of time before something else sparked the uprising. The incident had taken place near Jabalya, a refugee camp in northern Gaza described by one Israeli reporter as a place of "appalling poverty, overcrowding, and filth." When the funerals of those killed were held, the mood was tense. As crowds returned, they cast stones at the local army compound. The IDF could not restore order, and riots broke out, continuing past eleven at night. At dawn the next morning rioting began again. IDF Jeeps rolled in and soon were targets for Molotov cocktails and rocks. Word of the mayhem rocketed through the territories and protests broke out everywhere, including Bir Zeit.[16]

Perhaps most surprised was the PLO, which never had much hope that a movement from within the territories could propel the Palestinian cause. As a strategy for conflict, the PLO's unwavering commitment to armed struggle was not much help in Gaza and the West Bank, where the well-trained and equipped IDF was sure to put down a violent revolt. Besides, the PLO's leadership—comprised mainly of middle-aged politicians, religious radicals, and ideologues—knew little about organizing action in the streets. The only ideas and images about conflict they had propagated to their people over the years involved raids, bombs, and bloodshed.

So it would have been surprising if the *intifada* had not been violent in its opening moments. Indeed, the demonic fury of rioting youth was the uprising's first emblem, and extreme action always spawns attention-hungry copycats. Even though a few groups, such as Awad's Center for the Study of Nonviolence and Israel's Peace Now, had tried to point out the risks of disorder, what they knew was not yet appreciated by those who were acting spontaneously in the streets. The earliest days were an improvisation, loosely steered by an amorphous group of leaders who had no real strategy.

For those who read history or had eyes to see, however, there were precedents and portents that suggested nonviolent action could be effective. In 1936 Palestinians had staged a general strike against the British, which lasted for seven months and immobilized government, transportation, and business. In the 1980s students had joined together to thwart an Israeli attempt to put university curricula and the professoriate under the Civil Administration. Moreover, the prevailing attitude among Palestinians since 1967 had been one of *sumud,* or steadfastness, an attitude well attuned to the discipline under pressure that any movement requires. And since nonviolent action involves withholding cooperation from a regime, there were plenty of opportunities for that: Palestinian philosopher Sari Nusseibeh estimated that only 5 percent of the Israeli occupation's goals were achieved by force; the other 95 percent, he said, were reached because Palestinians complied with orders from the military government.[17]

The uprising shredded both sumud and the Palestinians' tendency to submit to their occupiers. In its opening days the Arabic word *intifada* was deliberately chosen (instead of the Arabic word for revolt, *thawra*); it connoted shaking off one's laziness. From the beginning it seemed clear that this would be more than a one-time eruption—but if the goal was to sustain a campaign against the occupation, going full throttle from the start would be reckless. Mubarak Awad's calls for a nonviolent movement had been shouts in the dark before, but he would attract more listeners as Palestinians began to see the benefits of being nonviolent.[18]

Almost as soon as the first rock was thrown, an informal set of ground rules began to circulate. It was understood that violence against the Israeli forces should be confined to throwing rocks and Molotov cocktails, though protestors also flung the IDF's own tear gas canisters back at them, along with pipes and bottles. The *intifada*'s budding leaders had strategic reasons for these limits: Because few Palestinians owned guns or other lethal weapons, armed action would minimize popular participation, and using firearms would give the IDF an excuse to use tanks and other heavy weapons. Morever, nonviolent action might turn the tables of world opinion against Israel, spotlighting the expected brutality of the Israeli reaction. Palestinians would be unarmed underdogs— Davids against the Jewish Goliath.[19]

At the same time, most were unwilling to proscribe violence. Palestinian activists had used it for over forty years, and they were not alone in assuming violence to be the sine qua non of a struggle against oppression. Throughout the post-colonial period in the developing world, the mystique of the liberator had been wrapped in combat fatigues, and for many Palestinians the very idea of nonviolent action seemed too Western. (Some distrusted Awad because he was a Christian with an American passport.) Failing to use violence felt to many like capitulation to armed force, and the ideology of militant Palestinians outside the Occupied Territories was geared to military action. "They tried to militarize the *intifada*," said Tayseer Arouri, from early on a leader of the uprising.[20]

Six months after the rebellion began, the nonviolent theorist and practitioner Gene Sharp argued that Palestinians did not have the best preparation to undertake disciplined nonviolent action, "given the severity of Israeli repression in the form of beatings, shootings, killings, house demolitions, uprooting of trees, deportations, extended imprisonments, and detentions without trial." Nevertheless, he argued that even limited violence would be counterproductive: It would hamper the fracturing of Israeli support for the occupation and enable the United States to hold back from condemning Israel. His words were prophetic.[21]

After the first riots following December 9, no one was sure what would happen next. The PLO and Israel were both caught off guard by the speed and ferocity of popular action, and neither had a strategy for responding. The one thing that was clear to everyone was that the occupation as they knew it was over. This would be no brief tantrum that the IDF could put down quickly. "It was not a revolt," remarked Ziyad Abu-Zayyad, a Palestinian organizer, "it was a new way of life."[22]

Leaflets and Leaders

After the initial student protests, Hanan Aruri wanted to be more involved in the uprising, so she volunteered to distribute leaflets, which had become a key part of coordinating action in the West Bank. Angering her family, she would sneak out of the house at three in the morning to go to a prearranged meeting spot and pick up leaflets from a stranger who had sent instructions through an intermediary. Aruri was to safeguard the handbills until she felt the time was right and distribute them quietly in her neighborhood. Her fear of arrest was salved by the pride she took in supporting the struggle.[23]

One week into the new year, the first leaflet, signed "The Palestinian Forces," had circulated surreptitiously in the Occupied Territories. A few days later on January 10, another leaflet appeared with the number "2" at the top; it was signed by the United National Command for the Escalation of the Uprising in the Occupied Territories. The public face of the *intifada* now had a name.[24]

On January 18 a third serially numbered handbill hit the streets bearing the signatures of the Unified National Command (UNC) and the PLO. It enjoined the Palestinian "masses" and "working class" to halt the "wheels of industry" in Israel. The PLO had been scornful at first of putting any stock in nonviolent action; for years it had fought to have Palestine recognized as a legitimate political entity, and it did not want the uprising to be cast as an economic protest. But as popular support zoomed ahead, the PLO was forced to either climb aboard or remain aloof. One Israeli journalist commented that in just a few weeks' time, youth protests and organizing had accomplished more for the Palestinian cause than the PLO had accomplished in three decades.[25]

Even with its name on the leaflets, the PLO never became the prime force behind the *intifada*. The UNC's ranks were filled by young Palestinians, most of whom were under the age of thirty. Many felt that the older Palestinian "notables" had grown complacent while conditions in the territories had steadily worsened. The pool of candidates for UNC membership was ample: There were at least 100,000 politically conscious high school and college age students in the territories and some 30,000 former detainees who had served jail time for security offenses against Israel. UNC members kept their identities secret for fear of arrest, and the fact that leaders were drawn from this new legion of unknown Palestinians meant that they were replaceable when arrests were made. There would be no famous avatar of the *intifada*.

The UNC also did not represent a common ideological viewpoint. Instead, it was a coalition of young men having a variety of affiliations with political and religious organizations that had been under the PLO umbrella, including the al-Fatah, the Marxist Democratic Front, the Popular Front, and the Communist Party. Two religious groups, the Muslim Brothers, part of the larger Hamas organization, and Islamic Jihad, also participated. (Hamas even issued its own leaflets, but its calls for a religious holy war were at odds with the secular mainstream.)

The language of the UNC's leaflets had a leftist bent, but the flavor of its ideas was largely nationalist: Like so many popular campaigns in the twentieth century, the *intifada* had self-determination at its heart. No radical alteration in the structure of society was on offer, and, in fact, the whole period was marked not by radical politics but by a revival of traditional Palestinian mores. From the hanging of flags to a renewed interest in Palestinian theater, poetry, and clothing, cultural insignia were a rallying force, especially among the young.[26]

The leadership was focused on "the need to think strategically in the long term, how to keep the *intifada* sustained and prolonged, to insure . . . the potential of victory," in the words of Tayseer Arouri. At their meetings they discussed the methodology of resistance, including steps to counter reactive moves by the Israelis; "making Palestinian daily life run as much as possible in a reasonable way"; how to undertake mass popular action, such as strikes, across the entire Occupied Territories; and how to maintain the struggle's relationship with the global mass media—selling the cause as a struggle for freedom.[27]

Cumulatively the leaflets became a kind of guidebook for civilians. They appeared every week to ten days and were passed around for about three years, despite the best efforts of the Israeli intelligence agency, Shin Bet, to break up production and distribution. The printing of political leaflets was illegal in the territories, so to get the first numbers out on the street without detection, UNC leaders used a large printing plant in East Jerusalem just opposite a Jewish neighborhood. From there copies of the handbills, sometimes 30,000 to 40,000, followed a circuitous route by car and then by hand to a corps of volunteers like Hanan Aruri.[28]

Occasionally the leaflets would reflect confusion or disagreement among the various UNC factions. It was not unknown for a leaflet with one set of directives to appear, only to be contradicted by a new leaflet just days later. But their inconsistencies notwithstanding, those who wrote and produced them were surprised at what Tayseer Arouri called the "magic influence" they had on Palestinians. He compared it to the effect of quoting the Koran, as if the power of proclaiming and invoking the written word were somehow embedded in the "psychological structure" of people in the Middle East.[29]

Given that impact, the leaflets represented one of the most ambitious mass education efforts in nonviolent action in the twentieth century. The first seventeen included appeals for flag-raising, church-bell ringing, symbolic funerals, demonstrations, marches, and strikes. Calling for a "white revolution," the leaflets recommended twenty-seven different methods of struggle, of which twenty-six were nonviolent. A content-analysis study by a peace institute in Jerusalem found that just 5 to 10 percent of the leaflets included directives for violence (although about half of all *intifada* stories in the *Jerusalem Post* were about violence).[30]

But some of the leaflets did call for "limited violence." Edy Kaufman, the director of the peace institute, noted that even though limited violence—defined as "the use of objects which are primarily intended to intimidate, aggravate, and cause minor injuries without causing great bodily harm"—led to the killing of fewer Jews than in other episodes in prior years, it was still counterproductive. Most Israeli soldiers saw rocks and Molotov cocktails as violent weapons, and Mubarak Awad noted that after teenagers threw stones, they fled—precisely the opposite move psychologically of what was needed for effective resistance. He had been "pushing hard for the kids not to run away, not to fear the Israelis." Moreover, "limited" violence also distracted the public from the real work of not cooperating with the Civil Administration and building alternative Palestinian institutions, which did more to develop the semblance of self-rule.[31]

In mid-January a systematic plan for nonviolent action was put forth at two press conferences by Hanna Siniora, a respected Palestinian intellectual and editor of the Jerusalem newspaper *al-Fajr.* The plan—whose architect was Mubarak Awad—had four stages: It would begin with the symbolic gesture of giving up Israeli cigarettes; two weeks later the purchase of Israeli soft drinks would cease. Then Palestinians would withhold tax payments to all Israeli authorities, and finally Palestinian workers would stop going to their jobs in Israel. The plan's goals included the release of political prisoners, an end to Israeli water drilling and settlements, and an end to the "iron fist" of Israeli control of the territories.

All these steps were designed to amplify the spirit of resistance and make it impossible for the Israelis to conduct business as usual. "The point is power," Awad explained. "The point is that we are challenging the power of the Israelis, and we will say when . . . the stores will open and when they will close." Awad recalled that when some Palestinians tried to keep time at a different hour than the Israelis had imposed, in effect to create a different time zone, soldiers would break people's watches if they noticed they were set to that time. They could not tolerate someone challenging their control. But that was the essence of the uprising.[32]

Comparing the *intifada* to other nonviolent movements, Siniora hoped that it could achieve what "the Gandhi movement did in India and the black civil rights movement did in the U.S." Like blacks in the American South, it was claimed, Palestinians were subordinated in their own homeland and denied full political rights. Siniora and Awad knew that the shocking images of police brutality toward American civil rights demonstrators had turned public sympathy against an unjust system, and they hoped that something similar would happen with Israeli public and world opinion.[33]

By the end of January, UNC leaders met to coordinate action for the *intifada,* and Awad was there to explain the Siniora plan and his ideas. He envisioned Palestinians refusing to produce their identity cards when requested, ignoring summonses from the police, ostracizing collaborators—in short, nullifying the infrastructure of Israeli control in the West Bank and Gaza. Six weeks later the tenth leaflet called for the resignation of all Palestinian policemen employed by the Civil Administration; mass resignations soon followed, despite the offer of a substantial raise. The Palestinians were finally doing what the Indians had done to the British raj and what resistance movements in wartime Europe had plotted: They were going after the symbols and props of the regime that they believed had held them down.

Committees and Cows

For the first half of 1988, the leaflets steered the actions of hundreds of thousands of Palestinians who lent their energies to the uprising. Even though scant attention was paid to the Sinoria plan when it was announced, many of the directives in the ongoing leaflet stream owed much to Mubarak Awad's original concept of destabilizing the occupation while developing all those institutions and practices that Palestinians would need to be truly autonomous.

Awad had offered a list of 120 nonviolent actions that could be used by Palestinians to weaken the occupying force. The list included acts of civil disobedience and noncooperation that were tailored to weakening everyday forms of control exercised by the Israelis and that virtually any Palestinian could undertake. The *intifada* had begun as a protest of the young, a "children's crusade," but it became a campaign of resistance by everyone. The backbone of the scheme was a network of "popular committees"—groups that saw a need in society and organized to meet it. Embedded in every village and refugee camp, they would work independently to procure the food and provide the social services necessary to exist. Yet they would all be united by one cause: ending dependence on the occupiers.

Popular committees had been in existence, more or less formally, since the occupation began. The byzantine system of taxes, permits, and regulations enforced by the Civil Administration often hampered ordinary tasks such as starting a business or cultivating land. Popular committees had sprung up to help with these problems but also to help support the poorest and most remote of Palestinian outposts. In 1988 existing committees, such as the Union of Women's Work Committees, were put on alert, and new ones were created by the hundreds to respond to crisis conditions when the IDF blockaded villages to restrict the flow of goods and services.

In May the UNC issued a "Civil Disobedience Statement" that formally identified committee functions, which included services (e.g., health, food, and education), direct action (e.g., closing roads and holding protest marches), and support. The high point of committees came in June, when the nineteenth leaflet instructed all citizens to consider the popular committees the government of the people, instead of the Civil Administration.[34]

One of the most successful committee organizations was the Union of Palestinian Medical Relief Committees. Founded in 1979, and including Palestinian physicians, nurses, pharmacists, laboratory technicians, and other health workers, the Union built several traditional clinics where Palestinians could come for at-cost health care, although it was more well-known for mobile clinics. Groups of five to ten volunteer health care professionals took medical care to Palestinians in rural areas and refugee camps; by 1987, several hundred mobile clinics were in operation.[35]

The demands on medical relief committees intensified in 1988. The IDF had become adept at riot control and increased its presence in the territories seven fold. Israeli Defense Minister Rabin, who wanted to crush the *intifada* quickly but was not willing to order the killing of protestors, opted for a policy of more force but less shooting. On one occasion, off the record but on camera, reporters picked up Rabin's suggestion that the soldiers begin "breaking their bones" in order to soften protestors' enthusiasm. Many IDF soldiers frustrated by their assignment took this remark literally. Blunt force trauma injuries began showing up in Palestinian clinics, hospitals, and private homes by the hundreds.[36]

Medical relief committees were soon overwhelmed by the scope of the conflict, and many injuries went untreated. Apart from fatalities, the Associated Press reported that approximately 20,000 Palestinians were wounded or injured in the first year of the *intifada,* and one-fifth in the first three months were women and girls. (A total of 402 Israeli civilians and a total of 730 soldiers were wounded, almost all by stones.) Responding to this emergency, medical relief volunteers drove mobile clinics to the increasing number of villages that were under blockade, often defying the IDF, which sometimes detained medical personnel.[37]

The medical committees represented the kind of self-reliance that gave even the most law-abiding citizens a chance to join in the movement. The spirit of solidarity that this cultivated among Palestinians even seemed to diminish ordinary friction in daily life. Tayseer Arouri recalls the *intifada* as a time when it was easy to resolve disputes between people—even traffic altercations were fewer, and "each neighbor was very caring" toward one another. Ten years after Poles noticed that they were drinking and arguing less with each other as they took public action in support of the Pope or Solidarity, Palestinians found the same sort of grace in a movement that was also new in their experience.[38]

Some committees chose more brazen methods of defiance. About a week into the revolt, merchants in Gaza padlocked the shutters on their stores to protest the treatment of demonstrators. The IDF was ordered to smash the padlocks and force shopkeepers to stand inside their stores. After ad hoc committees of Palestinian locksmiths made the rounds of shops to replace locks, IDF soldiers would break them again in hopes that looting would force the shopkeepers to tend to their stores. Palestinians responded with neighborhood watch committees that protected stores from looters. When the IDF changed tactics by welding shutters and doors shut, Palestinian metal workers volunteered to open them up. After four months of back and forth, the IDF simply gave up on attempting to punish commercial strikers.

Palestinian shopkeepers who ignored the leaflets' dictates and tried to profit by staying open were often punished harshly. In Gaza City alone, fourteen Palestinian businesses were torched for violating the posted hours for strikes. This use of violence may have convinced wayward merchants of the need for solidarity, but it also undoubtedly reinforced the view of some outsiders that the *intifada* was full of menace and not an orderly way of seeking change.[39]

Even more brutal was the treatment of "collaborators." Palestinian leaders aggressively sought to ferret out Palestinian police officers on the Israeli payroll who may also have been agents recruited by Shin Bet and the IDF. In the first sixteen months of the *intifada,* Palestinians murdered over 190 collaborators, dashing the early perception that it was mainly the IDF that used egregious tactics. For every ten instances of civil disobedience, it took only one act of viciousness to diminish the sympathy within Israel and around the world that Palestinians hoped to cultivate.[40]

Hanna Siniora's call in January 1988 for nonviolent measures against the occupation may not have been heeded methodically, but one of Awad's ideas— a call for a boycott of Israeli-made products, replacing them with home-grown and homemade goods—fell on receptive ears. Palestinian women and girls took the lead in creating an alternative home economy. Hanan Aruri and other women in her neighborhood were among the many who plowed uncultivated land to prepare it for planting vegetables. Their first crop of tomatoes and cucumbers was large enough to distribute to local households. For Aruri it was not the harvest's size that was important but the sense of self-sufficiency it gave the women. And men followed their example.[41]

In one antic episode, several Beit Sahour villagers bought eighteen milk cows from an Israeli kibbutz and set up a dairy farm near Bethlehem. The Israelis heard about it, and Shin Bet, civil administration officers, and the military governor himself visited the farm. They pronounced the cows a security threat, photographed each one, and ordered the farm closed within twenty-four hours. When the Palestinians moved the cows to a secret location and the governor returned the next morning and found them gone, he was incensed. "It seemed like he had lost eighteen terrorists," recalled Jalal Qumsiyah, a local teacher. Helicopters and hundreds of soldiers searched for the cows and found them with a butcher, who said he would slaughter them. The governor was satisfied, but when the Israelis came back in a week to check, there were twenty-three cows, because five had given birth. The Israelis blamed the butcher, and the Palestinians managed to move the cows again, but this time they were never found.[42]

Milk was not the only liquid Palestinians managed to politicize. When an Israel-based Coca-Cola distributor saw its business in the territories take a nosedive as Palestinians boycotted its products, an RC Cola plant in the West Bank eagerly welcomed the new business that came its way. The drive to reduce reliance on Israeli goods and services also extended to education. When the Israelis, in an effort to remove one perceived hotbed of dissent, closed 900 schools and sent 300,000 students home by February, Palestinian committees opened makeshift classrooms, to try to keep school-age children off the street.[43]

In the first few months of the uprising, Palestinians proved themselves adept at demonstrating, organizing, and insulating their communities from the costs of not cooperating with the Israelis. But for the *intifada* to cripple the occupation, a far more extensive campaign of civil disobedience would be

Illegal, open-air classroom for Palestinian children, during the *intifada*.
Credit: ©David Rubinger/CORBIS

needed. Over the next several months, leaflets urged all Palestinians to join in a larger campaign of merchant strikes, boycotts, nonpayment of taxes, and resignations from agencies connected to the occupation. Responding in that spirit, many Palestinians refused to produce identity cards when asked, others burned their cards altogether, and merchants ignored permit laws. Leaflet #5 called on Palestinians to refuse to work on farms or in factories owned by Israelis. By June leaflets were urging that Palestinians sever all ties with the Israeli civil administration.[44]

But a complete break with the occupiers was almost impossible to execute. Palestinians were linked to the Civil Administration, and thus to Israel, in many ways that were not easily suspended. The roads, pipes, and wires that carried people, water, and electricity interwove Israel and the territories in an intricate system. Twenty years of economic and civil connections could not be unbundled overnight. Nevertheless, most Palestinians hoped that the uprising's disruption would be sufficient to force Israelis to open a political dialogue with Palestinian autonomy on the agenda.

Curfews and Crisis

As self-organization and non-cooperation became pervasive, Israel intensified its campaign to break the *intifada*. In February Shin Bet agents had shown what they could do by arresting a courier transporting 35,000 copies of leaflet #6. Movement leaders found alternate printing presses and hastily created a new distribution network for the handbills, but then all but one of the leaders were rounded up. Thanks to its failure to copy the hierarchical leadership model of the PLO, the UNC was able to replace these leaders with others from the ranks, who distributed five more communiqués until they in turn were arrested in March. A third set of leaders survived until April, and still the leaflets came.

Yet Yitzhak Rabin's crackdown began to take a toll on both sides. By February the evening news was regularly showing Palestinian protestors being beaten with truncheons, and the IDF was dropping tear gas and CN gas (mace) from helicopters into public areas near schools and shops. A spokesman from Maquassed Hospital said that 1,800 of 4,500 *intifada*-related casualties that the hospital saw in the first eleven months were due to the use of gas. Every night pictures of Israeli soldiers clubbing Palestinian demonstrators or bulldozing their homes were beamed to television sets in Western countries whose support Israel needed. Israeli groups like Peace Now and the newer 21st Year came out against the use of violent force.[45]

The sense of pride and purpose felt by IDF soldiers who had to take repressive action began to flag. A corps of Israeli military men called Yesh Gvul even refused to serve in the territories. During the summer of 1988, a delegation of soldiers who had served there reported to Israeli President Chaim Herzog their feelings of demoralization. The IDF's General Nehmia Dagan felt the government had put his men in a no-win situation that brutalized both Israelis and Palestinians, reinforcing the mutual expectation of violence. He compared it to jumping repeatedly into a swimming pool without water, knowing that you will get hurt. The crackdown in the territories made him hate Arabs, he said, not because he had hated them personally but because using violence against them seemed to generate such feelings.

This reaction, widespread in Israel, was not incidental; it had been sought by nonviolent activists. Mubarak Awad recalled "bringing a lot of Israelis to the hospitals, to see what . . . the Israeli soldiers are doing to the kids." When these Israelis saw children with broken arms and legs, they got "shaky" because they were asking themselves, "are we becoming like people who did . . . something wrong to us"? Awad saw the *intifada* instill doubt in the occupiers about what they were doing and a sense of higher purpose in those who resisted. Confidence in the cause, or the lack of it, can affect the quality of choices that one side makes in the course of a conflict—the Danes never wavered during World War II, and neither did the students in Nashville.[46]

The discomfort with Israeli tactics that surfaced within the IDF itself might have been intensified even further had the Palestinians reacted with less violence, showing—as Indians had done at Dharasana in the face of the blows of the British raj—that no degree of force would break their determination to achieve self-rule. As it happened, *intifada* leaders may have come close to achieving a split between the military and official government policy on handling the uprising, when Dan Shomron, commander of the IDF, told Israeli political leaders in April that force could not resolve the crisis. But these words, which were exactly what UNC leaders were hoping to hear from a prominent Israeli, fell on deaf ears in the Israeli cabinet.

The nonviolent strategy promoted by Awad had assumed that Palestinians could exploit the condemnation that would befall Israel for the eventual crackdown. UNC leaders hoped that if Israel was criticized harshly enough by its allies, it would be forced to reevaluate the occupation. But responsibility for the turbulence of conflict was hard to assign only to Israel, and while the U.S. State Department's indirect condemnation of Israel's actions was the strongest it had issued since the invasion of Lebanon in 1982, no favor was shown toward the *intifada*. The United States did abstain from two UN votes condemning Israel, and stronger rebukes came from Western Europe, but the Israeli government was not swayed.

Greater than the political fallout for Israel was the economic damage. Profits of approximately $1 billion from taxes, low-cost Palestinian labor, and the sale of goods in the territories were wiped out in the first year of the uprising. The increased troop deployment from 12,000 to 80,000 raised defense expenditures by approximately $600 million. For their part, the Palestinians who refused to work on Israeli payrolls also paid a price, and so recruiting more people to resign and sacrifice their very subsistence would not have been realistic. But if other sanctions, such as commercial strikes and nonpayment of taxes, had been broadened, Israeli economic losses would surely have been even greater.

Whatever the full cost, the Israelis did not crack. Instead, they went forward with a strategy of "collective punishment" for the uprising that was especially hard on the popular committees. Most effective were curfews imposed on villages and camps; anyone in violation was subject to arrest. In the first month, some 200,000 Palestinians were affected, and over 1,600 curfews were enforced the first year, sometimes limiting activity for weeks at a time. The Jebalya Camp, where the uprising began, was under curfew intermittently for over 120 days. By the end of the second year, 1 million Palestinians were under curfew. In some ways this aided the resistance, since if everyone were at home, leaflets could reach people easily. But the mobility necessary for many committees to carry on with their work was seriously hampered.[47]

Since the occupation had first begun, the threat of imprisonment had been an effective sanction against Palestinian troublemakers. Mubarak Awad remembered that before the *intifada,* Palestinians had an image of the Israeli "superman" who had beaten all the Arabs in wars, who could come and put you in jail—where you would be alone, with nobody supporting your family. This feeling was an enormous disincentive to flout Israeli authority. But the *intifada* changed that; it taught people that Israelis could be resisted—they were not supermen. During the uprising, the jailing of a family member became a source of pride, because it showed that he had been resisting. Whole communities would visit mothers to congratulate them that their sons had been arrested—in the same spirit shown by the son of Gandhi's secretary, who had run after the police van in which his father was carried off, delightedly shouting that he hoped he would be gone at least two years.[48]

The Israelis, however, went right on giving the Palestinians this honor. Membership on a popular committee was made punishable by ten years in prison. Over 29,000 people were jailed in the first year of the *intifada,* and charges were pressed against 8,000. The right to judicial review of sentences was rescinded. Courts and jails were full to the point of chaos. But resistance continued behind bars. Awad remembers that when he was in prison, he and his fellow inmates had been trying to negotiate for more hours outside rather than being kept indoors. When they were told that the Red Cross was coming to visit, Awad told their jailers that unless they did not get more hours outside, he and all the other prisoners would take off their clothes and be completely naked when the Red Cross arrived. "And they said, okay, how many hours do you want?"[49]

As the scale of the crackdown expanded, dissent in Israel grew. Its most public display came from a coalition of groups known as the Women in Black. Once a week groups of a dozen or more women clad only in black appeared at busy intersections in a number of Israeli cities, including Jerusalem, Tel Aviv, and Haifa. While they stood silently, they were ridiculed by pedestrians and drivers who accused them variously of being anti-Israel, foreign agents, or heretics. Israeli officials ignored all the protests and pressed on with collective punishment. Curfews were accompanied by cuts in telephone and electric service, as penalties for failure to pay taxes or rent. Hundreds of homes were demolished.

In one severe episode, the IDF laid siege to the al-Bourej refugee camp in retaliation for the resignation of its local council. Electricity was cut off and food supplies to the 18,000 residents were restricted. No one was allowed to leave without a special permit and proof of tax payment. High school students seen

Nonviolent action advocate Mubarak Awad leaving Israel's Supreme Court
building after his deportation from Israel was approved, June 5, 1988.
Credit: ©Reuters/Jim Hollander/Archive Photos

at demonstrations were barred from taking graduation exams. Despite all this,
protests in the camp were held almost every day, with participants sleeping in
the countryside to avoid arrest.

The uprising reached a crisis in the summer of 1988, when the Civil
Administration began to order wholesale deportations of suspected *intifada*
leaders and agitators. Against the objections of the United States, Israel deported
Mubarak Awad, calling him a threat to state security. The IDF switched from
rubber to plastic bullets and started the mass arrest of popular committee
members.

With many *intifada* leaders in jail, the Palestinians left on the streets had no
strategy to sustain the campaign. That left the old Palestinian leadership back
in the driver's seat, and while there was a period when gains might have been
consolidated through an accord, Palestinian radicals—who did not fully recognize that institution building and the threat of nonviolent sanctions gave them

leverage—felt that negotiating was the same thing as throwing in the towel. So the moment for a different outcome came and went, and another four years passed before Yitzhak Rabin, who more than anyone else had taken the measure of Palestinian determination, entered into secret talks with the PLO in Oslo.

Looking back on the tumult in her homeland, Hanan Aruri remembered the hectic months after December 1987 as "a unique kind of revolution." Palestinian resisters did not achieve a physical victory on the ground, and most knew that the co-dependency of Israeli and Palestinian life meant that self-rule would come only when both sides realized that belligerent force would not produce a victory—the same realization that helped usher out apartheid in South Africa. But Aruri was right; the *intifada* had been a watershed. No one in the world doubted any more that the Palestinians would be satisfied with nothing less than their own homeland.[50]

In March 1989 Mubarak Awad took a delegation of Western advocates of nonviolent action (including Gene Sharp) to meet with the exiled PLO leadership in Tunis. "It was a very productive week," he recalled. The military minds in the PLO understood nonviolent action better than the political leaders—they saw that it worked. Not long after, Awad said, there was a shift in language from the PLO; "armed struggle" was no longer the single theme of how to wage the fight for self-rule. The Palestinians had discovered that the road to liberation was not necessarily paved with stones thrown in anger.[51]

ઝ   ઝ   ઝ

Like other campaigns for rights in the twentieth century, the *intifada* was a struggle about governing: Palestinians withdrew their consent from Israeli administration of the West Bank and Gaza more vigorously and systematically than ever before, even as they sought to extend their capacity to govern themselves. The Israeli authorities who tried to subdue the uprising faced the same choice that white South African authorities did in black townships in the same decade: Either they could keep suppressing the demands of a people who had lost their fear of intimidation, or they had to find a way to give those people a greater say in their own destiny.

In ways not unlike the Indians who had withdrawn their cooperation from the British raj by making salt without paying taxes and making their own cloth, Palestinians curtailed their cooperation with Israeli rule in the Occupied Territories by withholding their taxes, fees, and identification cards. Like the Indians who followed Gandhi, they multiplied the ways in which they severed their compliance with the state, pressuring the regime in too many places for control to be maintained everywhere. Palestinians from every walk of life were willing to protest, strike, and improvise in home economy if it meant plowing the ground of their own society.

But the mixture of violence with nonviolent sanctions, while perhaps impossible to prevent given the zeal on the streets, undermined Palestinian strength. Israeli soldiers felt justified in striking back when they themselves were put in harm's way, just as the French in the Ruhr more than sixty years before reacted with greater repression when German nationalists used sabotage against their troops. For Palestinians to lash out with violence against the IDF was to fall into "the trap of shifting to fight with the opponents' chosen weaponry," in the words of Gene Sharp. That was not a fight the Palestinians could win. And Western sympathy for Palestinian underdogs—which could have been translated into pressure on Israel—was undercut when violence came from both sides.[52]

The *intifada* did not drive the Israelis out of the Occupied Territories, but it did break the stalemate that had immobilized the Middle East for a generation. It transferred the motive power behind the Palestinian cause from militants and guerrillas to the Palestinian people themselves, and thereby endowed that cause with a legitimacy and urgency it did not have before. And it helped persuade a working majority of the Israeli people that only a political solution that involved the Palestinians, and not military constraints imposed on them, offered real hope for stability in the sacred land that both peoples shared.

CHAPTER TWELVE

China,
Eastern Europe, Mongolia:
The Democratic Tide

CHINA—DEMOCRACY ARRESTED

Rallying Cry

IN THE SPRINGTIME OF 1989, less than four months after Palestinians had shaken off their acquiescence to Israeli occupation and launched the *intifada,* the students of Beijing shook off a long winter of complacency, moved suddenly to the center of the world's attention, and demanded democracy for China.

It began on April 17 when students from the city's universities flocked to Tiananmen, the colossal esplanade in the center of the capital, and placed wreaths at the Monument to the Martyrs of the People, in memory of Hu Yaobang, a former general secretary of the Communist Party who had tolerated student dissent and who had just died. For five days, until Hu's funeral, there were demonstrations and wall posters calling for democracy and an end to government corruption. In that brief interval, a gesture of grief became a challenge to state power.

Tiananmen Square was a natural magnet for students with a yen to protest, because the Great Hall of the People, the Museum of Chinese History, the

Museum of the Chinese Revolution, and Mao Zedong's Mausoleum are all found there. A month later, as spring was in full flower, tens of thousands of students and other citizens would march back to the square, past police and barricades, and crowd around twenty-one-year-old Wu'er Kaixi, a charismatic student leader. They would hear him demand faster political reform, guarantees of rights to the people, a free press, an end to corruption, and real democracy.[1]

In the ensuing seven weeks, warming to what would be a year of liberation from communist rule in Eastern Europe and neighboring Mongolia, millions from across the wide mantle of the Chinese nation would join the students in a cascade of marches and demonstrations, culminating in a people's takeover of Tiananmen. And then this fresh, unexpected new movement would be engulfed by a military crackdown, and a square for the rallying cry of democracy would give way to the square space of prison cells. Where others would follow, China would not lead.

Students and Rulers

The seeds of democratic yearning in communist China were sown in the wake of one of the most hysterically destructive acts of twentieth century communism: the Cultural Revolution launched by Mao Zedong, which devastated Chinese institutions ranging from universities to collective farms. After it finally ended in 1976, the government had to rebuild the economy, which led to greater openness toward the world. That, on the surface at least, dislodged a narrow chink in the wall separating the Chinese people from freedom.

Not long thereafter, on a wall just west of Tiananmen Square, young dissidents took to posting signs and slogans urging more freedom. In 1979 Wei Jingsheng posted several essays on "Democracy Wall," criticizing the Communist Party and the supreme leader, Deng Xiaoping. That was too much for the authorities, and Wei was arrested and sentenced to prison for fifteen years. But dissent still bubbled underground, and essays demanding change were circulated extensively. When the authors went too far, however, they were silenced. In 1986 and 1987 Fang Lizhi, a prominent physicist, and Liu Binyan, a well-known journalist, were expelled from the Communist Party for expressing "bourgeois views" regarding China's future development.[2]

It was not surprising that intellectuals and students were those who came forward first to defy the regime. Chinese students had a long history of political action: Students had sparked a revolt against the Tang dynasty in the ninth century and also the Taiping Rebellion in the nineteenth century. Traditionally esteemed in China, students fell on hard times after the Cultural Revolution. University funding declined, classrooms and laboratories deteriorated, and dormitories were jammed to overflowing. Resentment of all this was sharpened as students noticed profiteering and nepotism among officials. One popular poem about bureaucrats was explicit: "A Japanese limo that costs big bucks, from the blood and sweat of the people is sucked, and inside a fat son-of-a-bitch is tucked."[3]

But the students chafed even more at the regime's restrictions on basic rights. Not only was dissent limited, the government often determined where students could work and live—imbuing personal grievances with political significance. Students knew what workers had done in Poland through Solidarity, to force the government to make changes, and they were keenly aware of how Mikhail Gorbachev was loosening the reins of control in the Soviet Union. So when Hu Yaobang died—perhaps the most reformist official in recent years—the tinder box of student alienation was ready to be lit.

When the five days of demonstrations following the wreath-laying in Tiananmen Square were over, the government faced the prospect of strikes at the city's universities starting on April 24, and party leaders were nervous about the potential for wider unrest. A blizzard of pamphlets critical of the regime had hit the streets, demanding a dialogue with Premier Li Peng, and the authorities began to feel besieged, fearing the same kind of chaos that overtook China in the late 1960s. Unwilling to concede that any part of society other than the party had the prerogative to spur political action, they labeled the demonstrations a "disturbance" and "a planned conspiracy" in an editorial on April 26 in the official newspaper *The People's Daily*.[4]

This threw fuel on the students' fire, who replied the next day with the largest demonstration yet. Over 100,000 students, joined by 400,000 other citizens, marched to Tiananmen in protest. Impressed by this support, many students thought they might succeed in bringing about change. They knew that the regime was divided about how to respond, and they sincerely thought that opposing corruption and advocating freedom would reinforce those inside government who wanted reform. Indeed, Zhao Ziyang, the general secretary of the Communist Party, was a reformer and soon would signal his sympathy for the students.

A quartet of students had emerged as leaders of the movement: Wu'er Kaixi, a cocky boy wonder who was often arrogant with officials; Chai Ling, an emotional twenty-three-year-old graduate student in psychology; Wang Dan, a twenty-four-year-old graduate student in history; and Li Lu, a student from the provinces, whom some thought was opportunistic. Backbiting among them seemed to be a problem. At a critical juncture in the occupation of Tiananmen, Chai said, in a taped interview, that she was "irritated at Wu'er Kaixi all along; he has at times used his own influence and position in ways that have caused

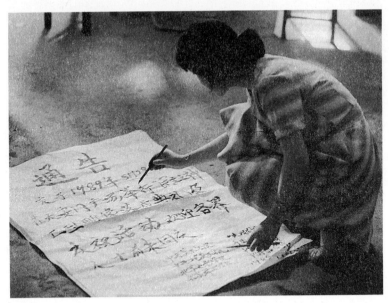

Young Chinese woman paints a sign for mass protests in
Tiananmen Square, April–June 1989.

Credit: ©David Turnley/CORBIS

great damage." Their lack of cohesion was apparently one reason that the
demands they put to the regime changed frequently.[5]

But the students' oratory was sensational. Wu'er, an ethnic Uyghur, stood
out easily, and in that first speech in Tiananmen Square, he proclaimed a "New
May Fourth Manifesto"—shrewdly invoking Chinese nationalism by linking his
protest to famous demonstrations in May 1919 that had assailed Japan's
annexation of part of China. When a movement can claim a higher legitimacy
antedating the regime it opposes—as Solidarity did in Poland by associating
itself with the Pope, and as the Danes did by reaffirming affection for their king
during the German invasion—it can tap wellsprings of popular support
unavailable to its opponents.

Animated by their own rhetoric, student leaders fired off a barrage of protest.
They drew 10,000 bicyclists into Tiananmen Square on May 10, demanded
meetings with the premier, and issued manifestoes that addressed the highest
officials as if they were secretaries taking dictation. Aware that Mikhail Gorbachev was due to visit Beijing on May 15, along with a swarm of foreign
journalists, they raised the stakes. On May 13 some 3,000 students started a
hunger strike in Tiananmen, again demanding a meeting with Li Peng and
presenting a menu of democratic reforms. Soon students in Shanghai, Harbin,

Tianjin, and other cities joined the action, and the Beijing Autonomous Union of Workers threatened a general work stoppage. One million people stood with the hunger strikers in the square on May 17 and 18.

Outwardly the regime seemed calm through most of this. Since Tiananmen Square was occupied, the leadership had to receive Gorbachev formally at the airport; this was embarrassing but it was endured. On May 18 the Standing Committee of the Politburo went to a hospital to visit hunger strikers who had been evacuated after showing signs of illness. The following day Li Peng met with students for a nationally televised discussion. In its own eyes, the regime was meeting the students halfway.

In the students' eyes, it had much more to do. In the televised meeting, Wu'er Kaixi angered the premier by cutting him off and chiding him for lecturing students instead of talking with them. It was a terrible error. The next day Li Peng declared martial law. Student leaders objected, arguing that they had not resorted to violence, and they demanded that the April 26 editorial in *The People's Daily* be retracted. Radical students called for Li Peng's resignation. It was all too much for the regime, which apparently gave up on negotiations. Off stage, Zhao Ziyang was pilloried for his conciliatory attitude toward students and shortly was replaced by Jiang Zemin, Shanghai Communist Party secretary. The hard-liners were poised to bring down the curtain.

The movement's response was ambivalent. On May 27 Wu'er Kaixi and Wang Dan, now wary of repression, called on the students to abandon their occupation of the square. Chai Ling, styling herself the general commander of the "Tiananmen Command Center," at first agreed—but, after getting complaints from radicals, broke with the others and supported staying. Later, in a temperamental interview that may have been videotaped without her knowledge, she confessed that they were waiting for "the spilling of blood, for only when the government descends to the depths of depravity and decides to deal with us by slaughtering us, only when the rivers of blood flow in the Square, will the eyes of our country's people truly be opened . . . "[6]

Having passed the point of no return, both sides prepared for the finale. Using the pretext that hooligans had injured troops and killed one, the regime sent 30,000 unarmed soldiers toward Tiananmen on June 3, but rings of citizens prevented them from advancing. In the early morning hours of June 4, a much larger force attacked and broke through with tanks and troops firing live ammunition. (Most of the soldiers were peasants from units in distant provinces and thus less likely to be sympathetic to city-dwelling protestors.) They reached the square and ordered the students to evacuate. Most complied, and tanks rolled in, crushing the tents and other pieces of shelter that had been put up.[7]

Because many students had left on their own, the government could claim that only one person died in Tiananmen Square, but many had perished trying to keep the army out. The government later reported that the overall death count numbered 300, many of them soldiers. Unbiased sources offered estimates of 2,600; others put the figure as high as 10,000. With their blood, into the sewers of Beijing, ran hopes for reform and democracy .[8]

❧ ❧ ❧

The communist regime's overweening use of force against the democracy movement of 1989 was very likely a tribute to the latent power that the government saw on display in Tiananmen Square: If the movement was allowed to salvage any space in which to operate, the regime could not be sure it would not resurrect itself. The gerontocracy that had ruled China for a half century had gone through the Sino-Japanese war, the civil war between the Nationalists and the communists, the Great Leap Forward, and the Cultural Revolution. Their fathers had told them about the Revolution of 1911 and the warlord era. With such a century to look back on, they craved stability. There was no threat too small to risk accommodating.[9]

But the defeat of the student movement cannot fully be explained by the violence used to send it underground or into exile, for many other nonviolent movements in the twentieth century deflected repression and endured to fight another day. Erratic and divided leadership, which believed more in the power of the moment than seeing the right moment to apply power, was at least as great a problem. This overconfidence diverted student leaders from the necessary work of organization and strategy. Had they seen the value of recruiting support from other parts of society—workers in transport and communication, civil servants, and, most important, the police and the military—they might have consolidated their gains and opted to develop a broader challenge not confined to Tiananmen, a convenient venue for repression.

Failing to appreciate or plan for the possibility of repression was an error in itself, but it also freed the students to indulge in whatever provocative action seemed enticing. Inflammatory gestures such as erecting, opposite Mao's Mausoleum, a "Goddess of Democracy," a replica of America's Statue of Liberty, doubtless antagonized the regime while not changing any facts on the ground. In short, while the students were familiar with the most ostentatious forms of nonviolent action—occupying public spaces, hunger strikes, and playing to the international media—their decisions in using these sanctions did not reflect "any significant degree of strategic thinking . . . "[10]

The failure of strategy at the moment of crisis kept echoing throughout the aftermath. The government's use of repression taught the wrong lesson to many about how rights and democracy should be pursued. In 1999 one former protestor called himself "a victim of June 4," since he was fired and prevented from getting another job; he had decided that "the only path for China was . . . cautious, progressive liberalization." Even the flammable Wu'er Kaixi, who fled China and later had to pump gas and wait on tables in California, succumbed to lower expectations. Explaining why he hoped that Beijing would not be forced to acknowledge its Tiananmen savagery, he said that doing so might only set back gradual reforms. And he wanted to return home. "I think if everything goes okay, I'll be able to go home in five years. If something happens, if there are demonstrations and another crackdown, it will take longer."[11]

But that view genuflected to the regime's version of history: that the use of nonviolent action risks violent upheaval, that popular action to seek human rights and democracy is the enemy of unspecified gradual change. Gandhi in India thought otherwise; if he had not, his followers would never have learned how to undermine the basis of British domination. At exactly the moment when the revolutionary potential of nonviolent power seems hopeless, there are always a determined few who will not be persuaded by repression to give up—and in the long run it takes only a few to reignite the motives and means of change.

At the end of the century Ding Zilin was a professor in Beijing engaged in a one-woman campaign to have China's state prosecutors investigate Li Peng for his role in the Tiananmen massacre. In June of 1989, she had pleaded with her son not to join the demonstrations. On June 4 he was shot by government troops. "The government's view about Tiananmen is inhumane," Ding declared in 1999. "They violated these people's rights to life and they are still insulting them to this day." Like *las madres de la Plaza de Mayo,* she refused to be silent. And the history of nonviolent resistance in the twentieth century does not augur well for those who try to enforce silence.[12]

EASTERN EUROPE—DEMOCRACY SEIZED

Parting the Red Sea

One month after China's communists rejected demands for democracy, the Soviet communist leader, Mikhail Gorbachev, in Strasbourg, France, told the Council of Europe that "any attempts to limit the sovereignty of states—both friends and allies or anybody else—are inadmissible," adducing why Moscow had not interfered while Poland's communists negotiated away their monopoly on power.

The Brezhnev doctrine—that Moscow would not allow communist control anywhere in Eastern Europe to be reversed—was dead. Only seven months before, hailed with chants of "Gorby!" on the streets of New York, the Soviet president had stunned an audience at the United Nations by announcing that tens of thousands of Soviet troops would be pulled out of Warsaw Pact countries. In Europe if not in Asia, the basis for communist control was shifting.[13]

For decades, the menace of Soviet invasion—made real in Hungary in 1956 and in Czechoslovakia in 1968—had stunted the region's democratic impulse. Where there was opposition, it was usually vented through labor strikes, underground literature, rock concerts, art exhibits, or environmental protest; political dissent was rare. Even Poland's Solidarity at first had avoided any bid for political power. Ironically, the subordination to Moscow that explained this timidity ended up weakening the communist grip on Eastern Europe once a new tune began playing in the Kremlin. As Gorbachev reformed the Soviet Union—opening the news media to critical views, expanding the scope of private enterprise, and injecting competition into politics in the late 1980s—his policies of glasnost and perestroika found immediate disciples elsewhere in the Warsaw Pact.

In Poland and Hungary, the foundations for change had already been laid. Solidarity had opened up a vibrant alternative to communist rule, and when General Jaruzelski invited its help in stabilizing the country, he heard no objections from Moscow. In Hungary, the regime had moved toward a market-oriented economy long before Gorbachev had shown tolerance for dissidents. So when opposition burst into the open in 1987 and 1988, bringing thousands of protestors into the streets, it responded calmly. The reformers who then took over the party tried to co-opt this process rather than repress it. In early 1989 the regime legalized opposition parties, and in June communist leaders worked out a deal with them for free elections. Hungary made it to the Sinai of democracy with popular pressure, dialogue, and accommodation, without crossing a sea of conflict.

Elsewhere in Eastern Europe, people knew that Polish and Hungarian communists had bowed to demands for free elections. It was obvious that the only obstacles to change were the indigenous regimes, now very much on their own. And obstacles are what they were.

East Germany's Erich Honecker, party chief since 1971, made no bones about his rejection of Gorbachev-like policies and banned Soviet books about perestroika. In Bulgaria Todor Zhivkov, in charge for even longer than Honecker, chatted about reform but did nothing of substance. Czechoslovakia was still ruled by the clique of leaders who conducted the brutal "normaliza-tion" of society after the Warsaw Pact invasion in 1968. And in Romania,

Nicolae Ceausescu, with the help of his Securitate political police, clung tenaciously to personal tyranny. These were rigid, unimaginative men who believed they could hold back the flood with the usual dike of repression, even without Soviet backing.

One sign of this intransigence was their tight control of public spaces in cities, hindering any political movement that might want to demonstrate to the people that change was possible. The regimes could not stop people from meeting in apartments or churches to share unorthodox ideas, and they could not (except, perhaps, in Romania) prevent such sessions from developing into human rights or other opposition groups. But when dissidents ventured out into city streets and public squares, they met with instant repression. Along with command over the mass media, control over the physical arena was a primary means by which communist rulers made sure that opposition was confined to intellectuals and activists, cut off from the larger public.

Leipzig: "We Are the People"

Since the early 1980s, a few dozen activists had been meeting on Monday nights for "peace prayer" services at St. Nicholas Church in the East German city of Leipzig. Communist officials in East Berlin took little notice, as the meetings were safely inside the building and under the auspices of cautious church leaders. But in1988 protestors demanding the right to leave the country began to join the prayer services and then went out to march silently through the streets of their crumbling, polluted city. In the spring of 1989 they broke their silence. "*Wir wollen aus,*" they chanted as they marched, "We want out."[14]

Before long, these "exit" protestors got their wish. On September 11 Hungary announced that it would open its borders with Austria, creating an escape valve from the formerly sealed communist bloc. Soon tens of thousands of East Germans were surging through on their way to West Germany. Thousands more crammed into West German embassies in Prague and other East European cities. But not all East Germans believed their only choice was between knuckling under or fleeing, and now the protests at St. Nicholas Church were taken over by opposition groups and turned directly against the authorities. As some of the 1,500 protestors who came on Monday, September 4, chanted "Wir wollen aus," others shouted back, "*Wir bleiben*" (we are staying). Despite more than 100 arrests at the protest two weeks later, the ranks of dissenters grew. Perhaps 8,000 turned out for the September 25 protest, demanding the rights of free travel and free expression.[15]

Mikhail Gorbachev was to be on hand two weeks later, on the fortieth anniversary of the founding of the East German state, and officials were determined not to have any embarrassing disruptions. Just days before the event, as many as 25,000 people sang and marched with lighted candles in Leipzig, and police set dogs on them and beat them. There were more assaults and arrests on October 7, in Leipzig, East Berlin, Dresden, and Potsdam. If the regime could not stop people from emigrating, at least it would make sure that those who stayed behind understood who ruled the streets. As the next Monday protest in Leipzig loomed, there were rumors that tanks ringed the city. Violence seemed likely if the demonstrations went ahead; people feared a "Chinese solution," referring to the slaughter in Tiananmen Square a few months before.[16]

One of those concerned was Kurt Masur, the conductor of Leipzig's renowned orchestra. He and his musicians, who were recording Beethoven's *Eroica* Symphony, could look down from the concert hall and observe the protestors each Monday as they passed through the Karl-Marx-Platz. On October 7 they had seen water cannons lined up to greet the marchers. Two days later, with the march just hours away, Masur arranged for several of the city's communist bosses as well as a popular cabaret singer and a clergyman to meet at his apartment. There they worked out an appeal for peaceful conduct and dialogue, which was read over the radio and from the pulpit of St. Nicholas Church that afternoon. By the time protestors arrived at the church, the joint appeal had reached Berlin, and someone—it is not clear who—ordered the troops to withdraw just as the demonstration began. That evening some 50,000 people marched unimpeded through the town and chanted "*Wir sind das Volk*" (we are the people).[17]

Through the first week of October, the regime responded with the usual repressive measures, but this time people were not scared off. They had learned from West German television about Gorbachev's reforms, about the changes in Hungary and Poland, and about the flight of their fellow citizens to the West. They knew that the government was isolated and vulnerable as never before, and they came out for the Monday protests in greater numbers. It was now a broad-based movement that could be restrained only by massive force. At the last minute, the authorities balked at repression, leaving the marchers alone on October 9.[18]

That was the turning point. In Leipzig protests swelled to more than 100,000 on October 16 and 300,000 a week later. In other cities tens of thousands came out. Unwilling or unable to crack down, the party leadership buckled. Honecker resigned in mid-October, and other hard-line Politburo members were forced out in weeks. New party leaders promised reforms but still lagged behind mounting popular demands. November 4 saw the largest rallies yet: more than a half million in East Berlin, and for once, state television provided live coverage. Even more mammoth street demonstrations followed, and more personnel shake-ups.

Finally, on the evening of November 9, a government press official announced that East Germans would no longer need special permission to travel outside the country. Within hours hundreds of thousands massed at the Berlin Wall and streamed past dazed border guards into West Berlin. More emigration, more protests, new convulsions in the party, and new reforms would follow, until March 1990, when voters rejected the communists in free elections. Reunification with West Germany was then on everyone's lips. The German Democratic Republic, a Marxist creation, was headed for what Leon Trotsky called the dustbin of history.

Sofia: Abandoning the Throne

Even under Todor Zhivkov's heavy hand, Bulgaria had grown restive in the 1980s. The Russians, who a century earlier had liberated Bulgarians from what was called "the Yoke of Turkish Oppression," could no longer prop up their satellite, and its economy was stuttering. Perhaps as a distraction, Zhivkov had initiated a mad scheme to assimilate ethnic Turks who lived in Bulgaria. Mosques were closed and Turks were given the choice of taking Bulgarian names, being detained in camps, or leaving for Turkey. Some 300,000 chose to stream southward, draining the nation's labor force—and the regime became an international pariah, drying up foreign investment.

Dissent still only simmered beneath the surface, limited to intellectuals in Sofia, the capital. Then on April 26, 1986, Krassen Stanchev, a young philosopher interested in the environment, learned about the nuclear accident at Chernobyl, in the Ukraine, from the BBC and the Voice of America. He was appalled that the Soviet bloc would try to keep it a secret. Bulgaria had similar reactors at Kozloduy on the Danube, but only in an open society, Stanchev realized, where people freely debated problems and proposed solutions, could the environment be protected. He and other like-minded Bulgarians formed Ecoglasnost and began demonstrating in Ruse, a city whose air was contaminated by chlorine gas from factories across the river in Romania.[19]

When an international environmental conference was scheduled for Sofia in October 1989, Ecoglasnost's organizers saw a chance to reach a broader audience. Demonstrators planted themselves in the same spot in central Sofia each day, holding up placards condemning the regime's environmental record and collecting signatures on a petition demanding public discussion of a river diversion scheme. Zhivkov gave them a week and then, on October 26, sent in the police, who beat up the protestors in full view of foreign diplomats and journalists; forty were arrested.[20]

While this might have scissored off dissent in the past, Ecoglasnost was not deterred. Activists had been watching Soviet television and knew that Moscow was way ahead of the hollow talk of reform that had dribbled out of Zhivkov, and they knew about the protests that were rocking East Germany. While few thought that Bulgaria's bosses were not capable of suppressing opposition on their own, there had never been a better chance to test the regime. Ecoglasnost returned in strength and brought 5,000 people into the streets of Sofia on November 3.[21]

But just as it seemed that popular opposition might be ignited, a faction within the party leadership seized the initiative. Zhivkov had antagonized many of his colleagues with policy blunders and nepotistic appointments and, perhaps most damaging, the disastrous campaign against ethnic Turks. The blatant assault on public demonstrators had given the regime another black eye. That was enough for Politburo malcontents, who decided to make their move against Zhivkov before the people could make a move against them.[22]

Zhivkov stepped down under pressure on November 10, supplanted as party head by Petur Mladenov, the foreign minister. Four days later opposition groups banded together in the Union of Democratic Forces and soon brought out vast crowds to push for reforms. The communists changed their name to the Bulgarian Socialist Party, negotiated with the opposition, dismantled the apparatus of party control, and held free elections in June 1990. Winning a majority, they formed a government that would hold power for more than a year, surviving by surfing the popular wave of democracy. Bulgaria's communists had abandoned the authoritarian throne before they could be thrown from it.

Prague: Space for Outrage

In the summer and fall of 1989, the people of Prague could feel the tremors shaking the lands just across Czechoslovakia's borders. Many had visited Poland and tasted the exhilaration in the air in Eastern Europe's first post-communist state. In Prague, they had seen East Germans pack into the West German embassy in a desperate lunge to freedom. And, though their newspapers censored Gorbachev's speeches and provided sparse or negative coverage of changes in the region, they managed to get news from the BBC, Voice of America, and other foreign sources. Inside the country, however, the regime seemed as immovable as ever.[23]

After the 1968 Warsaw Pact invasion, the opposition had been reduced to an elite group of intellectuals who decried human rights abuses and tried to shape an independent civil society, through underground publishing, alternative education, theater, and music. In 1988 they were joined by legions of students, and the opposition's face gained a younger complexion. The new converts were

Eastern Europe, 1989

not intimidated by memories of the post-1968 crackdown and, encouraged by the news from elsewhere in Eastern Europe, made bold forays into the streets of Prague. At least seven times beginning in August 1988, thousands of students and dissidents marched through the city in the most brazen protests seen in decades, but were turned back all but once by water cannons, tear gas, and phalanxes of police.[24]

The main prize in these battles was Wenceslas Square, a magnificent old boulevard running several blocks through the heart of Prague. The venue had vital importance: It could give activists commanding visibility for speaking directly to tens or even hundreds of thousands of people, and it was one of the most symbolically charged sites in the country. At one end sits a monument to St. Wenceslas, a tenth-century Bohemian king and martyr who believed in putting his faith into action. It had been the prime location for protests against Nazi occupiers during World War II, and it was there that a student had burned himself to death in January 1969 to protest the reversal of the Prague Spring.

Letting protestors occupy the square would allow them to invoke those potent memories of national resistance.[25]

On November 17, a week after the fall of the Berlin Wall, students tried again to take the square. About 15,000 people met at a university late in the afternoon for an officially approved rally in honor of a student killed by the Nazis. Once it turned dark and the ceremony ended, students lit candles, unfurled flags and banners calling for a new government and free elections, and then set out for Vysehrad hill, where medieval kings and cultural heroes, such as the great composer Antonin Dvorak, were buried. From there, after singing the Czech and Slovak national anthems, the marchers walked down the embankment of the Vlatva River, shouting for onlookers to join them, and then headed toward the square a few blocks away.

When their way was blocked by a cordon of police in riot gear, some yelled for everyone to sit down. As a cameraman got up on an aluminum contraption and started filming, students in front laid the country's flag on the ground, in the few meters that separated them from the police, and placed candles around it. Then everyone chanted for the police to leave and let them go to the square. After two hours or so, a voice on a loudspeaker warned that they had to turn back immediately. But for a few thousand people in front, retreat was blocked by a second line of police that had come up from behind. Pincered in, they had no escape when police from fore and aft waded in and proceeded to club and stomp on them, children and elderly people included.

"Soldiers in red berets forced us against the walls of the houses so as to make room for them to beat up defenseless students," Lenka Schwammenhoterova recalled. As the police pressed forward, protestors were crushed together. "I have never experienced such terrible fear because if anyone had fallen, the crowd would have trampled him to death." Eventually she found a route of escape: a narrow arcade, lined by police with German shepherds, letting out onto another street. She and others made their way through, while the police buffeted them with blows, but special forces troops waited for them on the other end. When it was over, more than 200 were hurt.[26]

The students were kept out of Wenceslas Square that night, but, though they were bloodied and bruised, they were not defeated. The brutal assault had provided a way to rouse people against the regime. Yet the official media were still tightly controlled, so getting the word out was critical. Through the weekend, students made the rounds of homes, campus meetings, and theaters and told their stories to the people of Prague. They showed videotapes of the demonstration and the police violence, and they pasted fliers on walls denouncing the brutality and calling for a strike. Western radio broadcasts also gave accounts of what had happened.[27]

Tens of thousands of Czechs jam Wenceslas Square in Prague, in opposition to the communist regime of Czechoslovakia, November 1989.

Credit: ©David Turnley/CORBIS

Mobilizing more people to join the next protest complicated the regime's task of maintaining public control. On Monday, November 20, more than 100,000 squeezed into Wenceslas Square. They jangled key chains, chanting that bells were tolling for the regime, and waved banners demanding political freedom—and the police did nothing to stop them. The next day, when even more gathered, the rally was better organized. A public address system was rigged up, and now leaders of a new opposition group, Civic Forum, such as longtime dissident Václav Havel, had a vast audience to appeal to. With each passing day, the protests enlarged and jumped to new cities, and the outcry for change grew louder. It was as if the public itself was holding an immense national, open-air convention and getting away with it. Fear of reprisals, always a major deterrent, was fading—and when that happened, the old reliable levers of communist rule started to jam.[28]

Newspapers and then television began reporting on the upheaval. The regime's monopolies over public space and mass communication had been broken, and cracks soon appeared in the party itself. Reformers booted out hard-

liners, proposed reforms, and opened a "dialogue" with the opposition, but as
in East Germany, it was too little, too late. A two-hour nationwide protest strike
on November 27 proved the opposition was not just a movement of Prague
students and intellectuals. Only the naming of a coalition government led by
noncommunists, on December 10, satisfied the clamor for change. The rulers
who had yielded possession of Wenceslas Square ended by surrendering
command of the state.[29]

Timisoara and Bucharest: Blood and Failure

By the last month of 1989, movements from below or reformists from above had
transformed all the former Soviet partners in Eastern Europe save one: Romania.
Within the communist litter, it had been the most feral, because its ruler, Nicolae
Ceausescu, had sacrificed every civility to his own aggrandizement. He had torn
down a wide swath of historic Bucharest and erected a vast plaza in his own honor
as well as palaces for his relatives and hideous concrete apartment blocks for the
masses. His secret police had kept a sample page from each typewriter in Romania,
so that any unorthodox writing could be traced to its source. He had made women
submit to random gynecological exams so the state could force all pregnancies to
be carried to term, to boost population. And his obsession with heavy industry
and foreign debt repayment had the side effects of "power shortages, food shortages
. . . ghastly pollution, galloping infant and maternal mortality, and general decay."
Some called it "the Ethiopia of Europe."[30]

Ceausescu's nouveau Stalinism was insulated from foreign sanctions by skillful
manipulation of the Soviet-American rivalry. He had courted and stroked
President Richard Nixon, kept Moscow at bay, and dealt severely with domestic
protest. When strikes broke out in Poland in 1970, he preempted Romanian labor
strife by encouraging workers to discuss the official trade unions. But when a
petrochemical worker wrote a letter proposing independent unions, he was forcibly
incarcerated in a psychiatric clinic. In 1977 when coal miners went on strike and
demanded to see Ceausescu personally, he did so and then promised to grant all
their demands. A month later the strike leaders had been disappeared and later the
concessions were withdrawn. There was labor unrest eight more times in the next
nine years, and in 1986 a strike to protest reduced bread rations in Transylvania
led to concessions, followed by twenty-five disappearances, and the concessions'
cancellation. In 1987 over 20,000 workers demonstrated in Brasov and trashed a
local party headquarters; troops were needed to restore order.[31]

Ceausescu had turned his country into a slum and its workforce into a
rebellious if repressed force for discontent, but Romania entered 1989 without any
coherent opposition—all room to organize had been flattened. Yet while the

dictator felt no need to be alarmed by Gorbachev's reforms next door, his capriciousness and self-indulgence had alienated military officers and convinced others in the regime that they might be better off without him. What they needed was an opening.

That opening came in December, in Timisoara, a city on the western edge of the country with a mixed population of Romanians, Hungarians, Germans, Gypsies, and Serbs. At the center was Laszlo Tokes, a minister in the Reformed Church, which served the large Hungarian minority. Tokes had risked punishment by speaking out against officials' abuses—he even had appeared on Hungarian television and denounced the government's plan to destroy old village homes and replace them with "rational" housing. That earned him an order to clear out of Timisoara by Friday, December 15. He refused and went on conducting services.

"Dear brothers and sisters in Christ, I have been issued with a summons of eviction," he told his parishioners the Sunday before the deadline. "I will not accept it, so I will be taken from you by force . . . Please, come next Friday and be witnesses of what will happen. Come, be peaceful, but be witnesses." He did not expect many to come, but by Friday afternoon about a thousand people materialized; some were Hungarians and others were Romanians for whom defending the minister was a means of protest. They formed a human chain around the church that night and the next day, warding off police and troops.[32]

As the crowd grew, their demands became political and the scene became chaotic. Cries of "Down with Ceausescu" were heard, and fighting flared, allegedly incited by the regime's agents trying to provoke violence. A group stormed the party headquarters; others threw rocks at soldiers, who answered with water cannons, tear gas, and clubs. On Sunday, troops occupied the entire city, took Tokes captive, and, on Ceausescu's orders, fired on demonstrators, killing close to a hundred.[33]

Unlike leaders in Sofia, Prague, and East Berlin, Ceausescu had no qualms about a bloodbath. But the massacre in Timisoara backfired. In the days following, the city's people continued to protest and also began a general strike. By the third day after the massacre, something had changed: Army troops were openly fraternizing with the protestors. By week's end the army had withdrawn altogether and a revolutionary committee had taken over the city. People around the country heard foreign radio reports about Timisoara, featuring inflated death counts, and unrest was spreading to new cities.

Unbeknownst to the protestors, a clique of high-ranking party members secretly had formed an opposition group, the Council of National Salvation, a few months before. When demonstrators besieged Bucharest, Ceausescu ordered his defense minister to fire on them. The minister refused and shot himself instead. The suicide helped inspire the army to turn on Ceausescu, and fighting between rival forces broke out in the capital. On December 22 a mob stormed Central Committee headquarters and chased Ceausescu out. On Christmas Day the dictator and his wife were summarily tried and executed, their bodies later displayed on television. A new cohort, the "National Salvation Front," took over, but its leader was a longtime communist.[34]

In Romania, as in the Philippines, people acting spontaneously in the streets had been the engine powering change, and the military had proven unwilling to defend the dictator. But with no popular movement to lend direction to events, new authoritarians stepped into the breach and, under cover of the prevailing violence, grabbed the state's reins. The protestors in Timisoara detonated a crisis that disposed of a tyrannical ruler, but in 1989 Romania was the one country in Eastern Europe where the fall of communism was not soon followed by stable democracy.

ه‌ه‌ه   ه‌ه‌ه   ه‌ه‌ه

Across most of Eastern Europe, the key inflection point in the anti-communist revolutions of 1989 came when nonviolent demonstrators confronted security forces as they tried to occupy city streets and squares. These locations were strategic assets, because they were places where people could be mobilized and galvanized, where movements could take off—which is why regimes had always placed them off-limits to dissidents. But by convincing thousands of ordinary citizens to join them, opposition groups defied attempts to bottle them up. Instead of being frightened by brutality, people were outraged and then emboldened to put their own lives on the line. State violence provoked the very resistance it was intended to quash.

When the protests grew large enough, they triggered public crises. Regimes had to choose between massive repression or compromise. In East Germany and Czechoslovakia, when it became clear that crowd control no longer worked, the regimes opted for a deal. Hard-liners knew that the Soviets would not cover their bets, and they also wondered about the reliability of their armies. In Bulgaria and Romania, communist factions used the disturbances as leverage against their rivals and grabbed power before the opposition could build momentum. In all the countries, the use of nonviolent sanctions in public empowered those in private who wanted some form of change.

All the "captive nations" of Eastern Europe, assumed for decades to be manacled to tyrants or ruling parties, shook off their subjugators in weeks. Although Soviet troops would no longer march west to enforce membership in the communist fraternity, every regime had its own repressive capacity. "All dominating elites and rulers depend for their sources of power," according to Gene Sharp, "upon the cooperation of the population and of the institutions of the society they would rule."[35] If the communist rulers of Eastern Europe had thought that their real power derived from their police and armies, they would have used that power to remain in their palaces. They knew better. When popular movements robbed them of their legitimacy and conquered the realm of public authority, most went as peacefully as their challengers had come.

MONGOLIA—DEMOCRACY GRANTED

Il Tod and Khonkh

A light December snow was falling outside, and Hashbat Hulan was working in her office at the Oriental Institute when she heard of a public demonstration going on nearby. Nothing like that had ever happened before, and she and her sister Minjin rushed over and were thrilled to see about 200 people and a band of fervent leaders proclaiming a new democratic movement. It was International Human Rights Day in 1989, and the authoritarian regime that had governed Mongolia for sixty-eight years had planned a carefully orchestrated celebration. But instead of military parades, long-winded speeches by party officials, and traditional songs and dances, the regime was upstaged by an unprecedented display of political protest.

Like most capital cities built in communist times, Ulaanbaatar had been designed with public ceremonies in mind. At its center lay a great square named for Damdiny Sukhbaatar, the Lenin of Mongolia, who had driven out the White Russians in 1921 and declared his country's independence. A huge equestrian statue of the great man dominated one end of the mostly empty plaza, flanked by Government House, a massive structure housing the Khural, or parliament, and the Palace of Culture, which held the Gallery of Modern Art, the State Opera, and the Ballet Theater. In a land nearly three times the size of France, with a population smaller than Panama's, all lines converged on Ulaanbaatar, and the square was its heart.

From the windows of Government House that day, party officials saw protestors carrying banners and placards demanding an end to "bureaucratic oppression" and a commitment to *orchlon bajguulat* and *il tod,* the Mongolian equivalents of Gorbachev's perestroika and glasnost. They were not disorderly, and security guards left the crowd alone. But the party's leaders could hear their chanting as well as music played by a rock band called *Khonkh* (bell). Slogans demanding change, now shouted under their very noses, recalled the wave of protest that had swept the communist world all that year. When the demonstrators quietly filed out of the square at the day's end, the chill left in Government House was not from the Mongolian winter.[36]

The Magpie and the Diplomat's Daughter

The regime's leaders would have taken cold comfort had they known that some of the demonstrators that morning were their own sons and daughters—men and women in their twenties or early thirties, the offspring of elite families, who were well educated and had traveled extensively outside Mongolia. Several had gone to schools or universities in the Soviet Union, where they had breathed the air of reform. All were fluent in Russian and a few in English and German, offering greater access to the West's media and publications.

Sanjaasuregiin Zorig, who would become known as the Golden Magpie of Democracy, epitomized this group. Born in Ulaanbaatar into the family of a prominent official, he was atypical in one way: His mother was half Russian and half Mongol, and his grandfather, a Buryat herdsman, had been "purged," most likely on Soviet orders. Ironically, it was at Moscow State University where Zorig was exposed to the zephyrs of change and a measure of relief from a stifling communist orthodoxy.[37]

Finding few echoes of Moscow's interest in political pluralism back home, he had broached these ideas himself with students and faculty at the Mongolian State University, where he had landed a position as a lecturer in 1986. He became friends with other young people tired of the oppressive state bureaucracy, and he joined a group that surreptitiously put up posters throughout the city calling for change and democracy. Zorig—a bespectacled, mild-mannered man—gained in academic stature, and his apartment became a center for the group's activity. He was also a staunch advocate of nonviolent change. "I get discouraged when an issue is resolved without any real discussion or forethought," he told Mongolian Radio in 1998. "Rash decisions occur too often." Never a rabble-rouser, he had helped calm the excited crowd at the December 10 protest.

Hashbat Hulan, one of those excited onlookers, also was from an elite family. Fluent in English as well as Russian, she was the daughter of a career diplomat, having lived in the Soviet Union, where she was educated from kindergarten through university. When she returned home, she "was amazed at the ignorance and seclusion in [her] homeland." She took a position at the Mongolian Academy of Sciences, later transferring to the Oriental Institute, and met others who had studied abroad and were interested in reform. By September 1989 Hulan was participating in secret meetings that sought to jump-start the process

Mongolia, 1989

of change in Mongolia (though she was not involved in planning the December 10 protest).[38]

Hulan and Zorig represented a common pattern among the regime's youthful opponents. Of the thirteen Mongols later known as the original reformers, eleven had studied in the Soviet Union, where they picked up on perestroika and glasnost—a great irony, since the Soviet Union had been despised by many Mongolian intellectuals. A surprising number of the reform leaders were not Khalkha Mongols, the country's dominant ethnic group, and the presence of many "half castes" as leaders in the early movement may have encouraged a less cautious attitude among the reformers.

Few of them were naive enough to believe that a small group of intellectuals in Ulaanbaatar could launch a democratic revolution by themselves. Support from workers, herdsmen, and others in small towns and the countryside was essential. Yet the fact that they could muster a contingent brave enough to march in Sukhbbaatar Square, which resonated with the legacy of communist domination, was significant. Physical control of the square could be vital in the relatively compact capital city, and supremacy in the capital—home to one-quarter of Mongolia's thinly dispersed population—would likely spell victory.

Yet no call went out from Government House to break up this challenge to one-party rule—perhaps because it was not clear how many dissenters there were and whether a crackdown would hand them more notoriety than they deserved. The regime also may have counted on the customary disunity that had always plagued Mongolians and that had famously delivered a once-great empire into Chinese and Manchu rule more than 300 years before. The December 10 demonstrators would have to overcome this belief and exhibit an exceptional solidarity to challenge a regime that still looked as monolithic as ever.[39]

"To Restructure People's Old Way of Thinking"

The Mongolian People's Revolutionary Party (MPRP) was built on the Soviet model. From the moment it took power, Soviet influence had overshadowed the country, and government policies often bore Moscow's stamp. In the 1930s herders whom the government tried to collectivize showed the same stout resistance that the kulaks gave Stalin—and were dealt with almost as harshly. MPRP leaders had not hesitated to unleash purges against former party chiefs, the military, and, in particular, Buddhist monks who had earlier controlled much of the country's wealth. Of 100,000 monks in the pre-communist era, only a few hundred remained by the early 1950s; at least 1 out of 5 had been killed.[40]

Sukhbaatar had been succeeded by a Stalinist-style leader, Choibalsan; the latter's death in 1952 had softened but not altered the system. The one-party monopoly remained, human rights were ignored, and purges persisted—although prison or exile now became the methods of disposal. Not until the early 1980s did the regime begin to lose its balance. Party chief Yumjaagiin Tsedenbal chose to ignore the more flexible line then coming from the Kremlin as well as the Soviets' rapprochement with Beijing, and his stewardship of the economy also lost touch with events. Bad management as well as bad winters reduced livestock production, and shortages of energy, foodstuffs, and consumer goods fed discontent. Party cadres also tired of periodic purges.[41]

When the dictator was told by the Soviets that he needed medical treatment and was taken to Russia to get it, his enemies replaced him with Jambyn Batmunkh. Although part of the old regime, Batmunkh had no choice but to try something new. He and his clique tackled economic troubles by de-emphasizing central planning, and Mongolia's leading newspaper printed the transcript of Gorbachev's speech to the 1986 Soviet Communist Party Congress, calling for greater freedom for local enterprises. In 1987 Batmunkh remarked that "a great deal of work will . . . have to be done to restructure people's old way of thinking," and he called for greater "transparency." Newspapers printed letters from readers who decried the highhandedness of government functionaries. Although the Mongolian leader did little to replace the old apparat, his own rhetoric tended to legitimize criticism and opened up space for public dialogue—space that dissidents would soon exploit.[42]

Nagged by the words of its own leader, the regime was also feeling outside pressure. The Soviet economy was not responding to Gorbachev's resuscitation—goods were in short supply and the government occasionally defaulted on wages. This reverberated in Mongolia, which conducted 90 percent of its trade with the Soviet bloc and drew 30 percent of its gross domestic product from Soviet aid, while thousands of Russian and East European managers, engineers, and advisors occupied key posts in the Mongolian economy. Moreover, a Soviet military contingent of about 60,000 troops, a relic of the Sino-Soviet conflict, was stationed in Mongolia, although now Moscow sought better relations with China.

In April 1987 Gorbachev ordered the withdrawal of a motorized rifle division, representing a quarter of the Soviet garrison in Mongolia. Sensing the new sweetness toward Beijing, Mongolia followed suit. In June, it signed agreements with China on technical cooperation and border disputes. As Gorbachev also eased tensions with the United States, Mongolia established its first formal relations with Washington. The regime was now fully engaged with the world, offering exposure to ideas that had long been taboo.[43]

In 1988 influential figures began to espouse views never previously entertained in Mongolia. One Politburo member praised democracy as the only way to combat the evils of bureaucracy, and several scholars and officials condemned secrecy, which had thwarted an honest appraisal of economic problems. One scholar even had the temerity to propose that the MPRP permit more than one candidate to run for each government position. In 1989, in the months before the demonstration of December 10, the government and the party issued one astonishing pronouncement after another. A commission conducted the first comprehensive investigation of the terror and purges of the 1930s and 1940s and concluded that the reputations of at least 20,000 people who had been executed should be rehabilitated. Batmunkh accused Tsedenbal of having developed a cult of personality and of having imprisoned innocent people.[44]

Meanwhile the Soviets withdrew an additional 8,000 troops from Mongolia and planned to remove all but 25 percent of the remaining forces by 1990. Mongolia's foreign minister asserted that the nation ought to cultivate its links with Western countries, and radio and television broadcasts from the West, including CNN and MTV, reached Mongolia.[45]

By late 1989 it was clear that some officials were sympathetic to political reform—but nothing tangible had been done. The only legal party was the MPRP, the government had not endorsed basic human rights, and the command economy remained in place. The secret police, the security service, and the army—the praetorian guard of the authoritarian system—also were still suppressing dissent. (People who posted placards demanding change in the economy and the one-party system were routinely arrested.) In short, the regime was ambivalent about change. This stoked the fire of impatience among young reformers, and it also gave them an advantage: If the regime's divisions prevented it from making decisions, time as well as space would be available in which to push the movement forward.[46]

Building Up, Taking Down

After December 10, the first hurdle facing the new reform campaign was to counter the belief that unity would be hard to come by. If the government were divided, unity would be a weapon in itself. The first step would be a commonly accepted statement of the changes the reformers proposed, and the banners they waved on December 10 reflected their general goals: "a multiparty system is essential," "honor human rights above all," and "freedom of the press." Within a week of the demonstration, the new Mongolian Democratic Union (MDU) had hammered out a program, and, after a rally that drew 2,000 people, it delivered a petition to top party figures outlining what it wanted—the first such citizens' manifesto.[47]

The reformers' chief political objective was a new election for the Khural in the first half of 1990, along with new electoral rules: Parties other than the MPRP should be allowed to field candidates, voters had to be free to choose candidates without intimidation, and the newly elected body should be free of domination by the Politburo. Its operations should be transparent, and its decisions should be the law of the land. They also demanded economic changes—a free market system, privatization of state enterprises, and a guarantee of the right of private property, and they wanted an affirmation of human rights, including freedoms of the press, speech, and travel, plus the end of special privileges for influential figures. Finally, the government had to acknowledge and publicize crimes against citizens and monks during Choibalsan's terror. And the reformers insisted that all these rights be incorporated into a newly amended constitution.

At a scheduled meeting of the party congress on December 11 and 12, MPRP officials had reaffirmed the principles of glasnost and perestroika and had, in theory at least, welcomed calls for reform. They knew that the Soviets were not going to back a violent suppression of the reformers—Gorbachev had frowned on the

Thousands of Mongolians at pro-democracy rally in Sukhbaatar Square,
Ulaanbaatar, Mongolia, January 21, 1990.
Credit: ©Richard Ellis/CORBIS/REUTERS

Chinese crackdown in Tiananmen Square six months earlier. Moreover, the hard
line from Beijing worried the Mongolians, who were traditionally fearful of giving
China (which had ruled and exploited their country in the past) any pretext for
insinuating themselves into Mongolian affairs. To avoid instability, they decided
to compromise rather than clash with the reformers.[48]

The government proceeded to give lip service to proposals for a multiparty
system, free elections, and protection of civil liberties but showed no sense of
urgency—the premier suggested a gradual phasing in of changes over five years.
While the young reformers had been impressed that opponents of reform in the
government had been demoted after the December 10 demonstration, and while
they were gratified that they had succeeded in shaping a program on which they
all agreed, they had no interest in waiting years for meaningful results.[49]

To force such results, they first had to expand their base outside their own
circle of intellectuals. Reaching beyond Ulaanbaatar, they targeted workers and
engineers at the copper mine in Erdenet. A joint Soviet-Mongolian venture, the
mine employed many Russian engineers and workers, who received higher wages.
Erdenet employees, unhappy with this disparity, already had held a protest meeting
early in December. Now the reformers helped channel workers' animosity toward

the government. On December 22 the MDU sent the scientist Erdenii Bat-Uul to negotiate with them. He argued that the workers' interests would be served only by a mass movement that fought for major changes and that the new movement needed backing outside Ulaanbaatar to impress the government. Bat-Uul carried the day, and after he returned to the capital, he encouraged the MDU to send people to other parts of the country to rally more support.[50]

By year's end, the reformers had both a clear program and diverse allies. They still needed a coherent strategy and an organization capable of more than ad hoc demonstrations. Since the MDU was too large to make decisions, they set up a coordinating committee, which began to tailor the movement's action for maximum impact. To offer a symbolic alternative to the Khural, which usually rubber-stamped decisions by top party leaders, the MDU drew 1,000 people to a full meeting in January, at the Lenin Museum less than two kilometers (a little over a mile) away from Sukhbaatar Square.[51]

To accelerate events, the coordinating committee called for a major demonstration for January 21 in the square. While the December 10 protest had been largely spontaneous and brought out a small if energetic crowd, the new event was well planned and attracted thousands, despite extraordinarily cold weather. (The temperature hovered around -30 degrees C.) Not only intellectuals came, but also people from Erdenet and the countryside—and their new demands were much more specific than the slogans of December 10. The date for the new demonstration had not been picked at random; it was the anniversary of Lenin's death. A famous actor helped lead the crowd in singing traditional folk songs, some of which praised Chinggis Khan, the ancient Mongol conqueror—a radical act, because the government, in deference to Russia (a land the great khan invaded), had previously reviled him as a barbarian plunderer.[52]

Sustaining the pressure on the government, demonstrations were held every weekend throughout January and February. As the campaign steamed up in the streets, the government vacillated. Khural members had been meeting regularly since the first protests while feeling growing dismay at events, but the parliament and the party could not agree on what to do. Since neither hard-liners nor compromisers could gain the upper hand, they temporized, issuing bland pronouncements favoring gradual change while trying to spread rumors about reform leaders, saying they were self-serving, corrupt, or alcoholics. The slander fell on deaf ears, since it failed to match anyone's image of the movement's main figures.[53]

Facing gossip rather than guns, reform groups began to take on the look of true opposition forces. On February 16, under the guidance of the economist Davaadorjiin Ganbold, the National Progressive Party was formed, advocating democracy, privatization of industries, and the restructuring of the banking system. On February 18 Bat-Uul convened 611 representatives and established the Mongolian Democratic Party. Now the country's constitution, which mandated only one party, had been flouted twice. Perhaps just as startling to the regime, a group of journalists put out without permission a newspaper called *Shin Tol* (new mirror), the first unofficial publication in decades. Equipped with new methods of disputing the regime's control, the reformers next appealed to hearts as well as heads.[54]

Some of them decided to target a visible symbol of the old order. Mongolian cities were cluttered with statues and busts of communist heroes, but cannily resisting the temptation to tear down icons of Mongolian figures, such as Sukhbaatar, they instead went after a mammoth statue of Joseph Stalin in front of the State Library. The reformers had been appalled at having the brutish Soviet dictator stand guard at a repository of Mongolian culture, and they had rallied popular support for taking him down. On the night of February 22, an anonymous crew spirited away the offending effigy, to parts unknown. (It was never found, nor its purloiners ever apprehended.)[55]

Two days later the movement's attention shifted back from icons to ideas. Despite the presence of spies from the security ministry, the official Mongolian Youth Union, meeting at the state university, enthusiastically endorsed the MDU's program, including a multiparty political system, human rights, independence for enterprises, and privatization of factories, banks, and retail stores. With determined leadership, support from workers and students, and sensational incursions into the public arena, the democracy movement had created the first opening for independent political power in Mongolia.

Striking for Victory

The reformers had put themselves on the government's front doorstep, but the regime had not altered the constitution to legalize new parties, and it had not committed itself to freedoms of speech, press, or religion. Submitting petitions, holding demonstrations, and challenging the party's legacy had earned the movement no more than tolerance. The reformers needed new sanctions to make more progress.

The sanction they chose was a hunger strike, something that Mongolia had never before witnessed. The reformers probably knew about the hunger strikes of Gandhi in India and of IRA prisoners in Britain, and they knew about the one that happened in Tiananmen Square. "I read everything I could about events in China during that time," recalled one reformer, "and I knew what the Chinese students were doing." That meant also knowing that hunger strikes did not always work.[56]

On Wednesday, March 7, at 2:00 P.M., with the temperature at -15 degrees C., ten men, including the ubiquitous Bat-Uul, took their positions in Sukhbaatar Square to begin their fast. By wearing their *dels,* or traditional robes, they signaled a break with the values of the regime, which had denigrated the remnants of the feudal past. The strikers' demands went beyond democratic reforms and a market economy, to challenge the very legitimacy of the government. They sent a manifesto to a concurrent meeting of the Politburo, arguing that because it was appointed and not elected, it was illegitimate. They also questioned the legality of the Khural because its delegates ran unopposed and were effectively appointed. Disregarding the effrontery, the Politburo insisted that the Khural was elected and had full sovereignty. This response hardened the strikers' resolve, and the MDU took the fateful step of demanding that the Politburo resign and that a new, truly representative Khural be elected. It was asking the regime, in effect, to consider suicide.[57]

When the hunger strike began, it had attracted curious onlookers, but many who came realized that it was a daring act of opposition, and some had marched around the square to indicate their support. By nightfall thousands had gathered and a few others joined the strike. The Mongolian students' union called on its members to back the hunger strikers in any way possible. Monks from Gandan, the only monastery still functioning in the country, came to offer their support. While the head of Gandan said later that "monks should not be involved in politics" and that the blessing of the strikers was merely a humanitarian gesture, they had made their presence felt.[58]

Responding to nationwide pre-strike appeals by the coordinating committee, 500 workers at Erdenet staged a one-hour work stoppage to show their support. "We crippled the mine totally for one hour," their leader reported. "That was an unreal feeling." He insisted that it was merely the beginning and that workers were ready for an indefinite strike to bolster the MDU. Simultaneously, workers in Darkhan, Moron, and other towns followed Erdenet and engaged in work stoppages. Never before had anything like this happened in Mongolia.[59]

The Politburo continued to meet, and members could see and hear the agitation from their perch in Government House. As their agents outside kept an eye on the strikers and their expanding troupe of sympathizers, reports of incidents around the country rolled in. Knowing they were facing the most serious challenge in their history, some Politburo members who had survived forty years of purges would have been quite comfortable with repression. A tough figure such as Demchigiin Molomjamts, who had filled a variety of senior positions, would not have flinched at the use of force. (As late as 1998, he would refuse to repudiate Tsedenbal, saying that the former leader had been underrated.) And there were enough like him still serving in the Politburo to prevent any quick surrender to the reformers.[60]

While the hard-liners wanted to summon the army to clear the square, others, perhaps thinking about Tiananmen Square and fearful of subjecting the country to disgrace, were not so sure. So the Politburo deadlocked on the first day of the hunger strike. Two of its members went down to plead with the strikers to stop, claiming to be concerned about their health, but they were politely turned down; the original ten strikers and at least three others who had joined them by evening were determined to bring down what they considered to be an unlawful government.[61]

The impasse continued through the next day, until the government took a tentative step toward accommodation. Dashiin Byambasuren, the first deputy chair of the Council of Ministers, recalled that "some older members of the Politburo opposed any discussions with the young people as long as they continued their policy of civil disobedience." He and other moderates overrode the objections, and Byambasuren—who was related to Bat-Uul and another reform leader—left Government House around 4:00 P.M. to meet with the reformers. Both sides presented their views, which were broadcast on radio and television, but the dialogue had no result, and the hunger strike continued.[62]

March 8 was International Women's Day, an important occasion in socialist Mongolia, and the holiday prompted more curiosity seekers to head for the square, including troublemakers. A few were inebriated, and they hijacked taxis and city buses and headed first for the Soviet embassy and then for Batmunkh's official residence. Tooting their horns, they made a tremendous racket and chanted anti-Soviet and anti-MPRP slogans. Over the next two days, scuffling broke out around the square and elsewhere in Ulaanbaatar. About seventy people were injured, and one was stabbed to death. Events were getting out of hand, and MDU leaders, who had faithfully stuck to nonviolent action, appeared to be losing control. They had hoped to unsettle the regime but had not foreseen that hooligans might try to join in—and had not taken security precautions to deflect the potential for violence.[63]

As it happened, the turbulence, as well as the size of the demonstrations, may have made the Politburo think twice. Estimates of the crowds varied from "tens of thousands" to "ninety thousand," but whatever the tally, the regime was alarmed. There is evidence that the minister of public security ruled out the use of the army to quell the disturbances—the implication was that the army might not follow orders. Simultaneously, the Soviets advised Mongolian leaders to prevent the crisis from escalating and arrange a settlement. The hard-liners knew that communist governments in Eastern Europe had been toppled in climactic confrontations and were surely looking for a way to salvage their position.[64]

With pressure mounting from the strikers, from moderates within the government, and from the Kremlin, the hard-liners finally relented on the afternoon of March 9. Party leaders knew that they still would have the upper hand in a free election—they had an infrastructure reaching to every *aimag* and *sum* in the country, while the reformers were political novices. Taking one step backward by making concessions could ultimately result in two steps forward by winning undisputed power. With these or similar thoughts probably in mind, Batmunkh drafted a statement released on Friday evening, March 9, announcing his retirement as secretary of the Politburo and the resignation of all the other members. The hunger strike ended, and MDU leaders told the demonstrators they could go.[65]

On Monday, 370 delegates from all over Mongolia convened for a meeting of the Khural, only meters from the spot where the hunger strikers had sat down five days earlier. After a fierce debate, they revoked Article 82 of the constitution, which guaranteed a monopoly to the MPRP. Over the next few days they were hit with an astonishing torrent of pleas from groups that would have been inconceivable before—the Mongolian Green Party, the Union of Mongolian Believers, the Mongolian Free Labor Committee—all contributing ideas about how to run the country. At the same time, the party began to transform itself, sending forward new and younger leaders more sympathetic to change. Finally the Khural approved new election procedures: The old single list of communist candidates would be scrapped, and each registered political party could list nominees on the ballot.[66]

Despite these concessions, the reformers were wary. They knew the MPRP had more money and still controlled the mass media. To protest these monopolies, they staged new demonstrations, which drew tens of thousands to Sukhbaatar Square and elsewhere by late April. While demonstrators were urged to remain nonviolent, protests often got out of hand. In one well-publicized incident, the diminutive "golden magpie" Zorig climbed on the shoulders of a sympathizer and spoke to an angry crowd, emphasizing the importance of averting violence. (Tragically, this proponent of nonviolent action was murdered eight years later, in a crime that remains unsolved.)[67]

Continuing tensions between demonstrators and security forces prompted the government to call out the military, and reformers returned to civil disobedience. In Hovsgol *aimag,* they convened a meeting in early April without seeking approval from local authorities, who arrested four people and mistreated them in jail—triggering a hunger strike by thirteen reformers. On April 30 the two sides, both of which had a stake in avoiding bloodshed, met to discuss constitutional and electoral changes that would level the playing field for all parties. On May 7 they agreed that meetings could be convened lawfully without government approval, and the hunger strike came to an end. Then all demonstrations ended when, on May 10, the Khural sanctioned a free and fair election in July. Now the movement focused on the battle for the ballot box.[68]

Victory by a Different Name

In less than half a year, a pro-democracy movement in Mongolia had staggered a regime that had lasted more than half a century, and had done so with nonviolent action. But the process itself, in comparison with other nonviolent struggles in the century, had required less of those who led it, so the movement had not had time to deepen its popular base. Moreover, because the regime had relinquished control without violent reprisals, it had not aroused wider hostility. In fact, the communists moved quickly to curry favor with specific constituencies, lowering the cost of heat in state-owned housing, increasing wages, and providing more benefits to students. A test at the polls would not, as in the Philippines or Poland, automatically favor the opposition.[69]

Already holding a poor hand, the reformers did not play it skillfully. Having elicited from the government the crucial concessions of free elections and protection of basic rights, the movement fragmented. Bat-Uul had already established the Mongolian Democratic Party, and Ganbold had set up the National Progressive Party. Zorig, who had been president of the MDU, initially stood for election as an independent, although the following year he founded another party, the Republicans. A fourth, the Mongolian Social Democratic Party, also advocated democracy but, unlike the other reformers, did not propose jettisoning the social welfare state.[70]

None of these parties actively recruited among the 35 to 40 percent of the population who were herders; at the first congress of the Mongolian Democratic Party, 53 percent were intellectuals, 40 percent were workers, and only 7 percent were herders. As urban intellectuals and technocrats, the reformers did not really know how to appeal to rural people. Moreover, the governor of every *aimag* was a member of the MPRP, and the herders, accustomed to treating officials with deference, would more than likely vote for candidates whom the governors endorsed.[71]

None of the leading reformers was a politician, and they found themselves unable to field sufficient candidates. The MPRP had a candidate for each seat in the Khural, but the three leading reform parties combined came up with only 346 candidates for 430 seats. Despite knowing about their shared weaknesses, the reform parties did not collaborate in any way, and—unlike the campaign against Pinochet in Chile, which also faced determined opponents—their

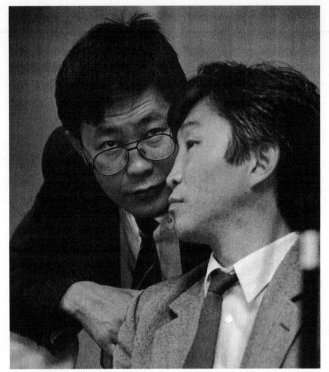

Sanjaasuregiin Zorig, the "Golden Magpie of Democracy," and scientist
Erdenii Bat-Uul—key leaders of the democracy movement in Mongolia—
confer on July 25, 1990, prior to the country's first free election.

Credit: ©AP/Wide World Photos

campaigns were lackluster, since they simply assumed that most Mongols shared
their animosity toward the MPRP.[72]

The July elections were their Waterloo. The MPRP won 357 seats while
the Mongolian Democratic Party wound up with 16, the National Progressive
Party with 6, and the Mongolian Social Democratic Party with 4. The popular
vote was actually less lopsided—60 to 40 percent. While the democracy
movement had forced Mongolia into a new political era, the first free election
in the country's history had confirmed the communists in power. Within the
ruling party, however, reform-minded leaders had replaced many of the hard-
liners. A moderate became president, and Dashiin Byambasuren, who had
negotiated with the reformers during the hunger strike, became prime
minister. Within a month Byambasuren reached out to the reformers by
appointing Ganbold, one of their leaders, first deputy premier, the second
most important position in the cabinet. The two men then embarked on a

two-year period of economic reform while adopting democratic changes as well. The spirit and text of reform were victorious, even though the reformers were held in opposition.

The reform parties eventually would coalesce in the Democratic Union and defeat the MPRP in elections in 1996. Bereft of Russian assistance after the collapse of the Soviet Union, they would turn to the West for help, but during the ensuing economic "shock therapy," industrial production would plunge, urban unemployment would top 20 percent, and almost four out of ten people would drop below the poverty line. As in Russia, corruption would become rampant, and some of the original reformers would find themselves caught up in shady deals and profiteering. Establishing a viable free economy and a stable political order would remain, for Mongolia as for other new democracies at the end of the century, a work in progress.

ॐ   ॐ   ॐ

The demise of Mongolia's authoritarian system was the outcome of a nonviolent uprising. The young dissident sons and daughters of the elite developed a mass organization in a matter of weeks, captured and used public space to create new political opportunities, and defied the old regime on its very doorstep. Something very like it had happened before, in El Salvador, in the Philippines, and elsewhere, but this time it was not merely a solitary dictator who had to go—it was an entire system, in a land that had known nothing else.

The movement that the Mongolian reformers built and the strategy they followed had several earmarks of successful nonviolent conflict: They drew in workers, youth, religious leaders, and others beyond the intellectual and professional classes; they developed simple goals that could be communicated in a few words; and they used a progression of changing sanctions that surprised a complacent regime. With no support from their Soviet patrons for a crackdown, the regime's hard-liners were also pressed by moderates in their own ranks—and both were apprehensive about Chinese intentions if instability continued. Then the reformers capitalized on the government's indecisiveness to drive the movement toward victory.

A nonviolent movement has at least two pedals to push if it decides to accelerate the conflict and force a regime to give ground: It can use new sanctions that squeeze the regime's room for maneuvering as the conflict proceeds, or it can multiply its political demands, risking an early crackdown or prompting a split in the regime's ranks. Sensing that repression was unlikely, the Mongolian democratic movement did both of these things, when it opted for a hunger strike in March 1990. Just as the students in Tiananmen Square had done in China the year before, the Mongolian movement sharpened the conflict, and with the same sanction. But instead of outrunning the underlying momentum of events, as happened in China, the movement kept its traction. Like the people's movements in Eastern Europe that also took the public space of their countries by storm, it took the top off an archaic and equivocal regime.

Yet in the aftermath of crisis, the sheer speed of achieving victory undid the Mongolian movement. Unlike the Poles, who had spent years developing alternate civil strength in their society to be ready for the moment of potential change, the Mongolian reformers freelanced a revolution but had few social or institutional levers with which to move the country. And unlike the South Africans, who were to wrest control from rulers whom the people reviled, the Mongolians overturned a regime that avoided the use of violence and thereby helped preserve its political fortunes. Without violence, democracy came to Mongolia. Without the lessons and experience of a demanding struggle, the movement did not know how to keep the popular allegiance that it had summoned to open up that society.

The communist regimes in the old Soviet sphere converted rapidly to democracy after Moscow's attitude toward reform changed from antagonism to encouragement. But the events that enforced that conversion were wholly domestic, and each of the old regimes was contested by a new force that rose up to make change happen. Without the initiative of political reformers using nonviolent resistance, the old order would have remained, decaying quietly into the century's twilight. Without the weight of a force more powerful, the hammer of history would not have bent back the iron curtain.

PART FOUR

VIOLENCE
AND POWER

Violence does even justice unjustly.

—Thomas Carlyle

CHAPTER THIRTEEN

The Mythology
of Violence

It is only small groups, who know that they cannot get sufficient popular support, that resort to methods of violence, imagining in their folly that they can gain their ends this way.

—Jawaharlal Nehru

TWELVE YEARS AFTER WORKERS IN ST. PETERSBURG MARCHED on the Winter Palace, in the century's opening act of nonviolent resistance, the Bolsheviks took control of that storied edifice in the midst of their bloody revolution. But they could not control the armed guards they put in charge of the wine cellar, and the men helped themselves to the Château d'Yquem 1847 (the Tsar's favorite vintage) and sold off bottles of vodka to crowds outside, who became drunk and took part in vandalizing the neighborhood. At length the wine was poured into the streets, and people drank it from the gutters.

The Russian writer Maxim Gorkii rued this "anarchic wave of plebeian violence and revenge," saying that instead of a social revolution, Lenin and his party had caused a "zoological" outburst of violence. "This is no longer a capital. It is a cesspit," he wrote his wife. Even justice had been perverted: Mobs tried criminals in the streets—when one thief's face was smashed and his eye was torn out, a group of children cheered. "These are our children, the future builders of our life," Gorkii wrote. A revolution unleashing this violence was "incapable of changing our lives but can only lead to bitterness and evil."[1]

Gorkii saw firsthand what many others in the century refused to acknowledge. But in his day, the European model for liberation from the ancien régime was the French Revolution—and the national anthem it gave to France celebrated "raising the bloody standard." The Bolshevik Revolution effectively internationalized this model, with the auto-da-fé of violence serving as a radical cleanser, sweeping the old order away. Even if the Soviet system afforded no genuine rights or democracy, political change certainly had occurred. So a pernicious if persuasive belief was fostered: that convulsive violence was the handmaiden of removing oppressors.

When Mao Zedong led an army of communist irregulars to victory over China's ruling Nationalists in 1949, that model was embellished further. If violent revolution could establish a "people's republic" in the most populous nation on earth, where would it not work? As Europe's colonies in Africa and Asia were pried loose from imperial control in the 1950s and 1960s, with the Soviet bloc supplying a revolutionary rationale as well as arms to insurgents, a generation of guerrilla warfare ensued. Violence, already seen as an exhilarating hallmark of liberation, was now embraced as a superior strategy for achieving it.

Propagating this paradigm were radical thinkers like Frantz Fanon, a Martinique-born psychiatrist and author, who argued in *The Wretched of the Earth* that "the naked truth of decolonization evokes for us the searing bullets and bloodstained knives which emanate from it," with liberation coming "after a murderous and decisive struggle." The style of this struggle would be nothing less than crime itself—"gangsters will light the way for the people," Fanon blared. This so beguiled French philosopher Jean-Paul Sartre that he bubbled, in a preface to Fanon's book, that only through the "mad fury" of "irrepressible violence" could downtrodden people "become men." It was now a Promethean feat as well as a method of taking political power.[2]

Seizing that power would be rebels in fatigues coming out of the jungle or down from the hills, and when Fidel Castro did precisely that in Cuba in 1959, only ninety miles from the United States, the cult of the guerrilla was lent further credibility. Then when North Vietnam and the Viet Cong held America at bay for ten years and toppled the U.S.-sponsored regime in Saigon in 1975, victory with violence—even over the most powerful military force in the world—seemed ineluctable. Never mind that violent victors had not always won because they used violence. The revolutionary propaganda of half a century and exciting imagery of violent insurrections transmitted by the modern media were irresistible to many latter-day nationalist movements. The Irish Republican Army, the Palestine Liberation Army, the Tamil Tigers in Sri Lanka, the Basque ETA, and other paramilitary crusades embraced violence as if it were a calling as well as a means of conflict.

But calls to arms leave little time for thought. Unlike Gandhi and later leaders of nonviolent campaigns, the twentieth century's avatars of violence never developed a systematic understanding of how their chosen sanctions— firefights, bombing, street battles, or terror—were supposed to replace old forms of authority with new opportunities for freedom. Instead, they wove a vague but seductive mythology around the putative power of violence: After violent insurrection was credited with having succeeded in a few prominent cases, it could be advertised as necessary to overthrow any offensive ruler. Once violence was seen as imperative, its destructive costs could be ignored.

Because violence became so widely accepted as a medication for injustice or tyranny, there was no incentive to consider less damaging—but also less sensational—alternatives for taking power, however effective they had been in the past. The work of nonviolent movements in the twentieth century led to independence for India, equal rights for African Americans and South Africans, democracy in Poland, and the removal of dictators in the Philippines, Chile, and a litany of other countries. In each of those conflicts, a relationship existed between the means of struggle and the political outcome. But never in the postwar period did a military insurrection or violent coup extend freedom to the people in whose name power was taken.

Power eluded entirely the grasp of many violent movements, and while the mythology of violence often obscured those failures in the world media, they were not overlooked by many popular movements that turned instead to nonviolent sanctions. The collapse of earlier violent uprisings convinced Solidarity to swear off extreme measures in Poland, and the futility of street fighting in South African townships persuaded the United Democratic Front and other activists to use boycotts and strikes to attack apartheid. Armed raids against the white regime may have made more news, but nonviolent action by black civilians made history.

History is ultimately a harsh judge of those who insist on substituting violence by a few for participation by all. The Bolshevik model always gave primacy to a revolutionary vanguard: The people were vital as an emblem of the cause, and once victory was in hand, they could loot the palaces of the old regime. But they were not to be the agent of change, and their empowerment was not its result.

It is not a myth that violence can alter events. It is a myth that it gives power to the people.

SRI LANKA: ORDEAL BY ARMS

"Sinhala Only"

In 1948, a year after they left India, the British withdrew from Ceylon (since renamed Sri Lanka), a lovely green island about the size of West Virginia lying just off India's southeastern coast. Both these two states in South Asia were now independent, and both shared an enormous political problem: how to maintain majority rule and minority rights in their contentious, multi-ethnic societies and redeem the promise of democracy for all their peoples.

The majority of Sri Lankans are Sinhalese, and most Sinhalese are Buddhists. But one in five people on the island is a Tamil, and most Tamils are Hindus (and are concentrated along the northern and eastern coasts, especially on the Jaffna peninsula). Early in the colonial period, the British drew the Sinhalese and the Tamils into a unitary state and recruited from both an English-educated elite. Wanting more say about running the colony, the Sinhalese and Tamil elites created the Ceylon National Congress in 1919 to press their agenda. But the ambitions of their leaders soon diverged, and by the time of independence, the Tamils were on the defensive: The British constitution for Ceylon rejected their demand that minorities be guaranteed half the seats in parliament. Instead, representation would be on a territorial basis, virtually ensuring Sinhalese supremacy.[3]

After independence, the parliament passed laws effectively disenfranchising the Tamil descendants of nineteenth-century laborers, brought from India to work on tea and rubber plantations (so-called Indian Tamils). This increased tensions, as did an effort to relocate Sinhalese to thinly settled areas that the Tamils viewed as theirs. Symbolic issues, such as the design of the flag (prominently featuring a lion, a symbol of the precolonial Sinhalese kingdom), only added to the sense among even educated Tamils that they would be relegated to a subordinate place in the new state.

No issue, however, was more explosive than language. It was clear that English would have to be replaced as the language of administration and education, since the great majority of the population—both Tamils and Sinhalese—could not understand it. Tamil leaders argued that the two main indigenous languages be given parity. But a strong "Sinhala only" movement gained momentum, driven by Sinhalese groups such as rural teachers, traders, and Buddhist monks, who believed that Sri Lanka ought to be a state of the Sinhalese "race," the Sinhalese language, and the Buddhist religion. In 1956 the Sri Lanka Freedom Party swept into power by tapping this nationalism and enacted a "Sinhala only" law. For Tamils, this was more than a slap in the face, since they had come to see English fluency and white-collar work as aids to advancement. Their ambitious young men would now have to forgo administrative careers or learn another language.[4]

Tamils did not suffer this in silence. During the 1950s, the dominant Tamil voice became the Federal Party (FP), led by S. J. V. Chelvanayakam, whose solution was constitutional change; he argued that Sri Lanka had to become a federation, in which the Tamil-majority areas would enjoy broad latitude for self-government. In order to fight for Tamil autonomy and protect Tamil rights, the FP tried its hand at parliamentary politics and, when that fell short, nonviolent direct action.

Weapons of Will

The FP's first use of nonviolent sanctions came in 1956, when Tamil members of parliament and volunteers held a sit-in at a park in Colombo, the capital, during parliamentary debates over the Sinhala-only bill. More protests followed: a "pilgrimage" in which Tamils marched to the town of Trincomalee, which the FP had designated as the capital of a future autonomous province, and a campaign to tar over Sinhalese lettering on buses running through Tamil-speaking areas. Actions like these drew massive government repression and triggered bloody anti-Tamil riots in places where they were a minority. The FP's largest mobilization, beginning in 1961, saw volunteers blockade entrances to government buildings and Tamil administrators refuse to conduct business in Sinhalese. The FP also created its own postal service and made plans for a Tamil police force. On rubber and tea plantations, "Indian" Tamils joined the cause by going on strike.[5]

The FP's strategy for nonviolent action had little more effect than had lobbying in parliament. The FP did negotiate agreements with the party in power to safeguard Tamil interests, but each time Sinhalese chauvinists inside and outside the government leaned on authorities to abrogate the deal. In fact, new laws and constitutional reforms during the 1960s and 1970s placed Tamils at an even greater disadvantage. Educational reform in the early 1970s, for example, imposed a kind of affirmative action on behalf of the Sinhalese majority in university admissions.

From the outset, Chelvanayakam, known among Tamils as "the trousered Gandhi," had insisted that Tamils' goals could be achieved by "weapons which call for strength of will and honesty of purpose," telling his people that "India's freedom was obtained by this righteous power." But calling his campaigns satyagrahas would not be enough, if Gandhian methods were not adapted to different conditions. The Tamils faced a different kind of adversary: The Sri

Lankan rulers were not agents of a foreign power, attempting to prolong their hold over a restive nation. They had been elected by the Sinhalese majority, to whom they were quite responsive. It was ethnic chauvinism, not an authoritarian hand, that circumscribed the Tamils. Had the Tamil nonviolent effort been more imaginative, it might have looked for inspiration to the civil rights movement in the United States, which had learned how to impose tangible costs and universal disgrace on an oppressive majority.[6]

By the early 1970s, Chelvanayakam and his party were losing prestige. Young Tamils, hit hard by unemployment and the government's education policies, had grown impatient with nonviolent shuffling. They knew that in 1971 an insurrection in East Pakistan had won the Indian army's backing and led to creation of an independent state, Bangladesh. Some Tamil activists had also spent time in jail with leaders of a mostly Sinhalese leftist uprising, which the Sri Lankan government had smashed. In an era when the attraction of guerrilla movements was still intense, militant young Tamils readily succumbed to the example, and armed bands were mustered out to fight for an independent Tamil state.[7]

The Tamil rebellion began slowly. For several years a successor party to the FP pressed the cause through parliamentary channels. But then bombings, bank robberies, and assassinations carried out by small armed groups began a vicious cycle of violence and counter-violence. There were anti-Tamil riots in 1977, 1981, and 1983—the last of which claimed at least 1,000 lives and produced more than 100,000 refugees. During the same period, the government took on an authoritarian tint, citing Tamil violence to justify curtailing civil rights and postponing elections. With constitutional remedies off the table and anti-Tamil violence on the rise, Tamils in the north and east began to close ranks behind the extremists. Soon after the 1983 massacres, Sri Lanka had a full-scale civil war on its hands.[8]

One group of Tamil fighters, the Liberation Tigers of Tamil Eelam (LTTE)—whose leader made his name by murdering a mayor—won a wide following as well as a reputation as one of the toughest guerrilla armies in the world, fielding up to 10,000 troops and at times almost winning control of the Tamil heartland. After 1987 the Tigers faced a counter-force of 100,000 Indian soldiers, sent in to subdue the rebellion and enforce a peace treaty in which the government conceded regional autonomy. Refusing to settle for anything short of independence, the LTTE stayed in the field and thwarted all efforts to stamp it out. The Indians pulled out in 1990, but the war went on, still continuing at the century's close.[9]

In a country of 18 million people, perhaps 50,000 Tamils and Sinhalese had been killed in the war by 1999, and another 30,000 or so "disappeared."

One-third of the Sri Lankan budget went to military needs, professionals fled the country, and large parts of the north were devastated. The violence also generated deep human problems. Fifteen thousand children, for example, who were separated from their parents in the northern war zones were shipped to Colombo and the southern beaches, where they were forced to sell sex to foreign tourists. The country's social equilibrium and political stability were fractured, with Tamil and Sinhalese extremists as the only beneficiaries, living off the hatred that the fighting perpetuated.[10]

The strife in Sri Lanka will end one day, and the outcome likely will be some form of compromise involving regional autonomy for the Tamils. If the LTTE is a party to that agreement it will doubtless claim some victory for its long adherence to armed resistance. But whether or not a fresh strategy for nonviolent resistance could have opened up a different road to Tamil goals, the cumulative costs of the ensuing violence—in sheer mortality and in civil disarray—will have been colossal. As a strategy to realize the dream of Tamil independence, the guerrilla paradigm was a rhapsody in blood.

THE BASQUES—FUTILITY IN TERROR

"Neither Slave Nor Tyrant"

In the fifth century after Christ, the Visigoths, a ferocious tribe of German barbarians, swept over the Pyrenees and conquered the Iberian provinces of the Roman empire. In 710 A.D., their king, Roderick, made the mistake of ravaging the daughter of the count of Ceuta, a Byzantine outpost across from the peninsula's southern tip. The following year, the count—hearing that Roderick was away in the north, putting down a revolt of the Basques—decided to wave through an invasion of 18,000 Berbers and Arabs who were interested in replacing the Visigoths atop the Spanish heap. A few weeks later, the king was killed at a battle east of Cádiz, where Visigoth power was staggered by the Moors—who stayed in Spain for eight centuries.[11]

The Basques outlasted them, as they have every other conqueror in the region, and they still inhabit a thick slice of land sandwiched into the area rimming the southwest part of the Bay of Biscay where France meets Spain high in the Pyrenees. The four largest and most populous of their provinces—Vizcaya, Alava, Guipuzcoa, and Navarra—lie in Spain and are home to 2.5 million people. One sign of their stubborn originality is their language; completely unlike any of those around it, Euskara is the only tongue remaining in continuous use since Roman times. If the Basques have Europe's oldest claim to self-determination, rarely has it been fully honored—although the Spanish Empire usually let them observe their *fueros,* or medieval laws, with elected leaders and local autonomy. But those who would be "neither slave nor tyrant," in a common Basque motto, never entirely reconciled themselves to life under the monarchs of Madrid.[12]

A century ago, as parts of Spain including Vizcaya underwent rapid industrialization, poor laborers from the south began to relocate to northern cities, a process that seemed to renew the threat of Spanish assimilation of Basque lands. In part to protect the Basque Country from the incursion of "inferior" migrants, the Basque Nationalist Party was established. When the Spanish Civil War began in 1936, the Basques established a separate republic, but it disappeared when Francisco Franco cemented his control over Spain. As ardent anti-Francoists, the Basques came in for harsh treatment by the regime: The Basque language was outlawed, Basque cultural expressions were forbidden, and political centralization sought to bring the region under Madrid's heel.[13]

Yet Franco's long tenure only strengthened Basque resolve. A separatist movement sprang up in the 1950s, and radicals opted now for seeking full independence. In 1959 they established Euskadi Ta Askatasuna (Basque homeland and freedom), or ETA, with the stated goal of combating Franco's oppression. Nothing was said about using violence. That changed in 1963 with the publication of *Vasconia,* a book by a German industrialist who was won over to the Basque cause while living in the country. Becoming something of a Bible for Basque nationalism, it called for direct action to achieve liberation. Inspired by the Algerian and Cuban revolutions (and the rhetoric of Frantz Fanon and Che Guevara), the book insisted on guerrilla war as the path to liberation.[14]

In June 1968 an ETA member was pulled from his car and killed by members of Spain's Civil Guard. Two months later ETA retaliated by murdering a hated police commissioner. That began a spiral of terror in which slain ETA members became martyrs while crackdowns by Spanish authorities poured yet more fuel onto the fire of Basque separatism. ETA membership grew rapidly, and not a few Basques began to see the guerrillas as courageous heroes defending their age-old rights. ETA hoped to incite a general uprising that would lead to civil war, but their infatuation with violence obscured the reality that the government always had more guns and that only a small minority of Basques had more than a romantic interest in armed struggle. Most felt that before long Franco would be gone, to be replaced by a friendlier government.[15]

"We Need Peace"

That expectation was fulfilled after Franco's death in 1975. King Juan Carlos and the new prime minister agreed to write expanded Basque autonomy into the new constitution: Basques would not have to pay federal taxes; they would have their own parliament that elected a president; and schools, police, and courts would be controlled locally. Even though the constitution prohibited any vote on dismembering the country, Spain's newly decentralized system offered hope for even more autonomy in the future. Among Basques, the Nationalist Party assumed the upper hand in politics and agreed to operate within the constitution.

Yet at this crucial point of departure with Spain's fascist past, ETA refused to abandon its devotion to armed struggle, arguing that Basque independence and not more democracy within Spain was the only correct goal. Unwilling to disarm unilaterally, and unable to envision any strategy that did not rely on threatening or taking lives, ETA escalated the violence. During the 1980s a "dirty war" ensued between ETA and Spanish paramilitary forces, which killed some thirty Basque nationalists. Eventually, instead of just targeting Spanish officials and local police offers, ETA members began extorting a "revolutionary tax" from wealthy Basque businessmen. Later, stores and cultural attractions were bombed in hopes that ruining tourism in Spain would force the government's hand. All this turmoil soured many Spaniards on the Basque agenda, and at length ETA alienated most of the Basque Country as well.[16]

By 1992 the pent-up yearning for a different approach led to the founding of *elkarri*, a "social, plural, and independent movement" that rejected armed conflict: "all manifestations of violence meet our disapproval, because all of them are located in a deadlock process of confrontation, which is precisely what *elkarri* tries to surmount by dialogue and agreement." Meetings and workshops were held in virtually every Basque town and village, and over a quarter million signatures were gathered in support of its plan.[17]

While appealing for dialogue did not stop the violence, public tolerance for twenty years of sporadic terrorism seemed to snap in July 1997 with the kidnapping and murder of Miguel Angel Blanco, a popular councillor from the ruling People's Party. Half a million Basques marched in Bilbao to protest, and 6 million took to the streets around Spain, their raised hands painted white, shouting, "*Basta! Basta!*" (Enough! Enough!). Roughly 300,000 returned to the streets in October, marching behind the banner "We Need Peace," after a Basque policeman was killed while foiling an ETA grenade attack during the king's visit to the Guggenheim Museum of Modern Art in Bilbao. The Basques and the Spanish did not agree on the right scope for autonomy, but they did agree that the violence had to end.[18]

A year later the ETA declared a unilateral cease-fire, and a younger core of leaders in Herri Batasuna, its political wing, began to distance the party from its violent past. The next month, who should appear on the tarmac of Bilbao airport but none other than Gerry Adams, the head of Sinn Fein, the political wing of the Irish Republican Army (IRA), addressing a throng of Basque nationalists waving Irish and Basque flags. Just months after the IRA agreed to negotiate peace in Northern Ireland, Adams appeared as an apostle of nonviolent solutions: "It isn't about guns or about explosives or other armaments of war," he observed, saluting the Basques for "taking the opportunity to get away from conflict and move towards justice and peace."[19]

While nonviolent movements often made progress in the twentieth century by instigating conflict rather than seeking peace, the addition of violence to a movement's sanctions can discredit any kind of cause. Terror as a weapon of insurgency frightens and eventually antagonizes the population whose support is needed for achieving legitimacy and attracting outside help; it can change the issue in the conflict from the substantive goal at stake to the means chosen to pursue that goal. In the Basque Country, violence on behalf of independence vitiated the possibility of independence.

Independence for the Basques also faced another barrier in the last two decades of the century. When Spanish dictatorship gave way to democracy, and the new constitution restored the status quo ante of traditional Basque autonomy, the movement's unity was gone for good: Only the more militant nationalists refused any compromise with the Spanish state. They ceased to be protagonists of a glorious cause and became antagonists of the people's hunger for a normal society. Those who turned to violence ultimately were broken by it.

જી   જી   જી

The choice of violence as the means of struggle by the Tamil Tigers in Sri Lanka and the ETA in the Basque Country was fatal to the ends they sought, if for no other reason than this: They could never match the firepower of the governments they confronted. As the political philosopher Hannah Arendt noted, "in a contest of violence against violence the superiority of the government has always been absolute." Arms alone are rarely the means of change. When Castro shot his way through the last perimeter of Batista's power, the Cuban people already had soured on the old regime. But in Ireland, the IRA never mobilized the bulk of the Irish people—north or south—behind its goals. No extremity of violence can substitute for the people's support.[20]

Even when violence seems certain to produce change, nonviolent action may be as or more effective. And the repeated success of nonviolent sanctions in the twentieth century at least should earn them equal consideration with the option of violence, by measuring potential gains in taking power and delivering justice against likely losses in lives, property, and human dislocation. Failure in nonviolent resistance can risk repression, as can failure when using violence, but the record shows that it does not jeopardize as greatly the flower of generations and the fate of movements on which freedom, human rights, and democracy may depend.

The liabilities of violence in the twentieth century are clearer in hindsight than they were in the midst of conflicts, but then leaders who invest so much in violent force have a stake in justifying its choice at the time. Their perspective is prejudiced by the tendency of news and contemporary history to amplify stories of violence: We remember successful insurrections—we remember the Bolsheviks, Mao, and Fidel—but many will not recall the Tamil Tigers, the Basque ETA, or the Chechen freedom fighters. Chechens have fought Russians for almost two centuries; a Russian novelist once said of them, "their law is war." Choosing that "law" as the path to autonomy from Russia in 1999, they were given back a devastated land and a ruined society. That a choice is habitual does not make it intelligent, and many who have chosen to use violence to seek power did not understand that every sanction chosen in a conflict not only promises rewards, it also levies costs. Strategies that do not measure one against the other are blindly chosen.[21]

Rational appraisal has not been the forte of those who adopt violence. The Bolsheviks, on whom so much was modeled, elevated violence from the level of what was instrumental to something sacramental: The ritual of revolution had to be violent or it would not be purgative. When I. N. Steinberg, the commissar for justice in Lenin's new Bolshevik government, objected to the regime's order to shoot "on the spot" all "profiteers, hooligans and counter-revolutionaries," he went to Lenin and asked sarcastically, "Then why do we bother with a Commissariat of Justice at all? Let's call it frankly the 'Commissariat for Social Extermination' and be done with it!" Lenin brightened and replied, "Well put, that's exactly what it should be; but we can't say that"—showing as succinctly as he ever did that terror was not only his means, it was also his motive.[22]

If killing, for the sake of sport or power, is the supreme assertion of the self over the other, then the exhilaration commonly felt by many hardened killers is, psychologically, a perverse antidote to the fear of failure—which is to say, to the fear of death. When Hannah Arendt heard Frantz Fanon extol violence as a "great organism" that linked men together, she saw it as a form of intoxication. In such a drunken state, death was not to be feared but embraced as a kind of apotheosis. But Arendt noted that death "is perhaps the most anti-political experience there is," signifying "an extreme of loneliness and impotence." Therefore "every decrease in power is an open invitation to violence."[23]

When S. J. V. Chelvanayakam in 1949 confidently promised his fellow Tamils independence through transferring Gandhi's style of nonviolent action from across the Indian Ocean, he raised the highest possible expectations. When, twenty or more years later, he still had nothing to deliver, the door to violence in Sri Lanka was flung wide open. Not promising what you cannot be sure of delivering is as much an axiom of nonviolent strategy as it is of democratic power. The next twenty years of deliberate violence were equally fruitless but far more ruinous.

Even if violent rebellion appears to be effective in changing power at the top, the culture of violence may destroy the opportunity to achieve a stable political order. Stone Sizani, a key leader in South Africa's anti-apartheid movement, remarked that "there are many countries in southern Africa that attained their freedom through the barrel of the gun," and they found after they did away with the colonialists that they "had to fight their own brothers and sisters who did not like the system which was put into place to supplant the colonial system."[24]

Violence may have coaxed colonial masters to leave, but military action to assume control is not the same as civilian action that develops the ability to govern. Nonviolent movements in India, Poland, and elsewhere were incubators of democracy. They taught individuals how to assume responsibility for their own action and make consensual decisions about the substance of goals and the process of reaching them. Violence is not a learning tool, and military force is intrinsically negative: It can deter or diminish an enemy, but it cannot force people to embrace its agenda. Shooting your way to power may destroy the old order, but you cannot free your people until they give you their consent.

CHAPTER FOURTEEN

The New World of Power

BURMA—THE GLOBAL MOVEMENT

New York and Thailand

IN THE SUMMER OF 1997, in his apartment near the stately halls of Cornell University amid the rolling green hills of upstate New York, Htun Aung Gyaw spent much of his time campaigning against the military junta that had taken over Burma in 1988. Although he was half a world away from a regime that had sentenced him to death in absentia for his role in the All Burma Students Union, Htun was a key player in an international movement, by student protestors, dissidents, political organizations, and even U.S. state legislators, to bring down Burma's military government.

Htun's weapon of choice was a personal computer connected to the Internet, and every morning he scrolled through dozens of e-mails from Bangkok, Los Angeles, Australia, and elsewhere in the world, and then logged on to the Internet site for a group he had established, the Civil Society for Burma. "We organize conferences over the Internet," Htun said. "We have a chat room where we meet to discuss strategy." In the all-enveloping realm of chat and group conferencing, the isolation of exile was replaced with a sense of ongoing, instant community.

After a night of several hours on-line, Htun would sometimes wake in the morning surprised to find that he was, after all, in Ithaca, New York.[1]

While using the Internet to take on undemocratic regimes was an innovation of the late 1990s, Htun had battled the generals in Burma for over a quarter century. In Rangoon, the capital, Htun had been arrested and severely beaten several times, and then after five years in prison, he was granted amnesty. But even in the tranquil retreat of an American university, Htun still saw himself as a freedom fighter. "I never thought of giving up politics," he said. "My best friend was sentenced to death and hanged in prison. I owe it to him."[2]

The same dedication spurred another Burmese dissident as he would sit in a straw and mud hut in a mosquito-infested jungle near the Thai border, typing furiously into a grimy, generator-powered computer. Win Min—a top leader in the All-Burma Students Democratic Front—was often on-line with Htun Aung, in global on-line strategy sessions with a worldwide network of Burmese leaders and non-Burmese activists who were fighting the regime in Rangoon. "Before, Burmese expatriates remained isolated from one another," a leading Burmese activist remarked. "The Internet has not only enabled us to share information, advise one another and coordinate action, but also has been a shot in the arm psychologically. No feeling is more powerful than to know that you are not alone in your fight for justice."[3]

"It's Our Task!"

In April 1947 General Aung San, the hero of Burma's struggle for independence from British colonial rule, had led his Anti-Fascist People's Freedom League to an election victory, winning a large majority of seats in the new national assembly. The general was poised to assume power when he was assassinated, along with six of his ministers, by a political rival. A colleague, U Nu, took over the government, and then Burma settled down to several election cycles, yielding only once to a military government.

In 1962 General Ne Win, claiming command of 100,000 troops, staged a coup against U Nu and abolished Burma's constitution, eradicating any traces of democracy. For twenty-six years he operated as a virtual dictator, replacing independent media with his *Working People's Daily* and replacing the free market with his "Burmese Way to Socialism." But ethnic insurrections, peasant relocations, and food riots periodically marred the placid image of the country that the military wished to advertise. In 1974, at the funeral of U Thant, a former United Nations Secretary General who was Burmese, student protestors at Rangoon University were machine-gunned. But even had it faced no repression, opposition would not have been easy. Burma has at least twenty different ethnic

Burmese monks and citizens march in Rangoon against the government, September 1988.
Credit: ©AP/ Wide World Photos

groups and a hundred or more languages, and Ne Win was adept at pitting one group against another.

In the 1980s the regime had to open up the country in order to court foreign investment, and by 1987, anti-government protestors had taken to the streets, and "people's committees" of monks, students, and workers were operating just under the surface. In 1988 General Ne Win stunned the Burmese people by announcing both his retirement and a referendum on holding multiparty elections. Newspapers, previously under government control, printed the demands of dissidents who were back on the streets. In early August thousands of demonstrators were rounded up, but the arrests only sparked more disarray. The ruling political party neared collapse, and there was looting, rioting, and police violence.[4]

Suddenly from within this chaos, a leader emerged to give focus to a popular struggle that had been largely disorganized. On August 26, 1988, Aung San Suu Kyi appeared at a pro-democracy rally at Rangoon's Shwedagon Pagoda. In a driving rain, this daughter of General Aung San, the revered hero of the Burmese independence movement, delivered her first public speech to a half-million Burmese who were standing in ankle-deep mud. Educated at Oxford and married to an Englishman, Suu Kyi had returned to Burma to care for her ailing mother.

Her impassioned calls for unity and nonviolent action enthralled the students, monks, and others who had been the reserve army of anti-government action.

Within days hundreds of thousands of protestors were parading through the streets of Rangoon shouting "*Doh ayei! Doh ayei!*" (It's our task!). Wearing slogan-labeled headbands, their faces covered with bandannas, the demonstrators carried sticks with Burmese flags hung upside down. On one occasion a group of 5,000 protestors held a demonstration outside the U.S. Embassy; on another, actors performed anti-government skits. In Mandalay, monks and teachers banged on pots and pans in the streets, and monks infuriated soldiers by turning over their alms bowls, preventing the men from making donations. (Refusing a donation was a monk's ultimate sign of disapproval, since, according to tradition, such donations counted toward saving the donor's soul in the afterlife.)

On September 10, in emergency session, Burma's parliament announced the end to twenty-six years of one-party rule and promised open elections. The new civilian president delivered a humble speech admitting that the party had committed major errors. "Power corrupts, and absolute power corrupts absolutely," he said, quoting the British historian Lord Acton. Across the street from Burma's parliament building, Buddhist monks and children bared their chests and dared soldiers to shoot them. Elsewhere in the city, motorcycle officers rode in a slow formation, and a military band played a stiff, staccato march, leading a thousand uniformed police officers and hundreds of soldiers who had defected and joined the ranks of the dissidents. Entire government departments were shut down as civil servants left their jobs to join in.

Excitement overtook Burma, but it would not last. After decades of strict control, some generals saw any protests as dangerous. On the afternoon of September 18, radios vibrated with martial music. "Because of the deteriorating situation in the country, the armed forces have assumed all powers," the announcer proclaimed. Soon parliament was dissolved, all government councils and ministers were dismissed, and a curfew was imposed. The new military government relieved the president of his duties, and all civilian functions of government were abolished. The defense minister declared himself president and created the State Law and Order Restoration Council (SLORC), the formal name for the junta that assumed control.

Over the next few days, soldiers hunted down suspected dissidents and executed them in the streets. Independent newspapers were shut down, schools were closed, meetings of more than five people were forbidden, and demonstrations were banned. An estimated 10,000 students fled to the Thai-Burma border, opting for armed resistance, and over the next two years the death toll from repression matched that number.[5]

In the next months, responding in a different way, Aung San Suu Kyi traveled to virtually every corner of Burma, insisting on Gandhian-style

Burmese pro-demoncracy movement leader Aung San Suu Kyi addresses a crowd
of supporters in Rangoon, July 7, 1989.
Credit: ©Jonathan Karp/REUTERS/CORBIS-BETTMANN

nonviolent resistance, which she demonstrated personally. The following April,
for example, a car in which she and a few supporters were riding was ordered off
the road by soldiers. She got out and began walking toward them. Troops were
ordered to raise their rifles and shoot, but she continued walking. At the last
second, a major ran forward to prevent the shooting, perhaps realizing that
killing a woman who embodied the opposition could reap a world of trouble.

Despite nonviolent and also violent opposition, SLORC felt sufficiently
confident of its control to rename the country Myanmar and call for elections
to be held in May 1990. Soon ninety-three political parties emerged to vie for
elected offices, the most potent of which was the National League for Democracy
(NLD), led by a former general and Aung San Suu Kyi. Two weeks after she
spoke at an illegal rally of 10,000 people, troops surrounded her compound and
placed her under house arrest—and her candidacy for office was invalidated.

Unintimidated, hundreds of thousands turned out on May 27 to cast their
ballots. SLORC was stunned when NLD opposition candidates won 80 percent
of the seats and 60 percent of the votes. Pro-democracy supporters ran through
the streets of Rangoon, waving opposition flags in celebration. But SLORC was
not done yet. After a new round of arrests, it ordered that a new constitution be
written before anyone elected could be seated. Even after Aung San Suu Kyi was
awarded the Nobel Peace Prize in 1991, the regime refused to honor the elections

Nonviolent theoretician and practitioner Gene Sharp gives seminar in the jungle
for members of the All Burma Students' Democratic Front,
Mannerplaw, Burma, October 1992.
Credit: ©The Albert Einstein Institution

and instead arrested nearly all NLD leaders. When a constitutional convention finally convened in 1993, the military was given the central role in government. While Aung San Suu Kyi was formally released from house arrest in 1995, her home was ringed by police barricades, and only rarely was she allowed to meet with supporters, make speeches, or speak with reporters. Democracy remained stillborn.

Jungle Schools and Global Sanctions

In February 1996 heavy rains had turned the land around Htee Ka Phalal into a bog, and after getting a late start on the morning of the twenty-first, a party of American scholars and instructors, including Gene Sharp and Robert Helvey of the Albert Einstein Institution, slogged through the muck and dense jungle near this outpost just across the Thai border from Burma. They were on their way to convene ten days of classes for an unusual group of students, who came from half a dozen different Burmese groups and outlawed parties that had promised to use political defiance—their term for nonviolent action—as a means of toppling SLORC. Despite the weather and armed battles that had been raging nearby, three dozen students made it to "school."

Sharp and Helvey had tailored their syllabus to both the students' needs and prior experience; early classes covered political and military writers like Machiavelli and von Clausewitz, before moving on to the dynamics of nonviolent action and practical tasks of organizing. This particular session ended four days early when Thai intelligence officers found the camp; the students were dismissed and filtered back into the jungle, since it was only a matter of time before SLORC would be notified of the meetings. The February 1996 field classes were one of at least eight educational missions made by Sharp and the Einstein group between 1992 and 1998. "The only thing I have done is to expose them to the potential of nonviolent sanctions," said Helvey, a retired U.S. army colonel, "and showed them that nonviolent sanctions can be planned and executed like any other kind of warfare." In 1996, when the junta put nineteen political prisoners on trial, among the evidence they used was the protestors' possession of writings by Gene Sharp.[6]

In the ensuing three years, while Aung San Suu Kyi and nonviolent resisters within Burma continued to be harassed, jailed, or silenced, exiled Burmese such as Htun Aung Gyaw intensified their use of the Internet's capabilities to keep one another informed, recruit new support, and push for international sanctions. But the effort was not simply driven by individuals. On most days in 1999, in a Manhattan office space cluttered by cubicles, copiers, and file cabinets, program assistants and Burma experts busily answered phones, responded to a crush of correspondence, and attended meetings of the Burma Project, affiliated with the Open Society Institute, a nongovernmental organization (NGO) intent on promoting support for democracy in Burma. E-mail from chat rooms and news updates from listservs streamed in from everywhere, dozens by the day. As the project's webmaster posted links to Burma-related Web pages on the organization's own site, they were accessible within ten minutes from any Internet-connected computer in the world.[7]

Around the world, several thousand Burma watchers, including many non-Burmese, used Internet sites maintained by groups like Burma.net and the Free Burma Coalition to keep informed. In 1994 members of Burma.net had to decide whether to allow representatives of SLORC to participate in their on-line community. They ultimately decided to permit "official" postings from Rangoon, believing that obvious government propaganda might backfire. Pro-democracy Internet users also understood that just as beneficial information could be disseminated quickly, so too could faulty information, and its providers could be spied on. SLORC eventually decided to put up its own Internet site, trumpeting the "Golden Land" of Myanmar and minimizing its past repression. By 1997 it also had offered its own listserv, but postings were strictly moderated and displayed only those views that the regime approved.

One nonviolent sanction against the Burmese junta that was pioneered by NGOs and promoted on-line was "selective purchasing." City, state, and national legislators in the United States were lobbied to support legislation prohibiting any business dealings with the regime. A boycott by another name, selective purchasing had been used in the campaign against South African apartheid in the 1980s. The Commonwealth of Massachusetts and the city of Los Angeles were at the forefront of adopting this sanction, and laws also were passed in New York City, Portland, Berkeley, and twenty-one other American cities.

In some cases, entire campaigns against corporations that did business with Burma were run mainly via e-mail chains. In 1995 a handful of Harvard undergraduates banded together and, using the on-line Burma dialogue as a starting point, launched a campaign against the university's plan to sign a dining services contract with Pepsi, which did business in Burma with SLORC's approval. The grass-roots cyber movement spread quickly and ultimately was successful in convincing the school to reject Pepsi's bid. "This would not have happened without the Internet," said one of the student leaders."[8]

In January 1997 PepsiCo announced that it was pulling its remaining business operations out of Burma, capping a two-year battle by hundreds of electronically connected activists. Three months later President Clinton signed federal legislation outlawing any new investments by American companies in Burma. This fell short of forcing the pullout of all U.S. capital, but the threat of boycotts and selective purchasing laws, plus the sting of bad publicity, pushed other companies, such as Walt Disney, Eddie Bauer, and Liz Claiborne to quit Burma. "The Internet—*by its very nature*—lends itself as a potent tool for advocates engaging in nonviolent direct action," one study declared about this campaign.[9]

Within Burma, using the Internet or fax machines without a license was illegal, and getting a license was out of the question for all but a small cadre of approved military and business people. Punishment for violation of technology-related laws was severe, and in 1996 a supporter of Aung San Suu Kyi died in prison while serving a three-year sentence for using a fax machine without a license. "In this country, only the SLORC owns communication rights," said an NLD leader. "[W]e can't use our machines to print, we don't own fax machines, we don't own mobile phones, our telephones have been cut continuously . . . " A small number of "fixers" who made connections to the Internet for a fee operated in bigger cities, such as Rangoon and Mandalay, but most civilian Internet usage took place either abroad or in the zone along the Thai-Burma border.[10]

The Burmese junta was aware that it could not be disconnected from the rapidly proliferating international communications network and still survive economically, so in 1997 it contracted for a digital link with a firm in Thailand.

But given the culture of open access permeating the global network, strict gate-keeping on electronic access was naive—and unlikely to convince new investors that the country could take proper advantage of the new technologies. In Burma, the regime's economic future depends on connections that its opponents can obstruct or influence. In May 1999 Htun Aung Gyaw remarked that every authoritarian regime believes that introducing a market economy can help it hang on to political power. "But most of them never succeed. Look at Poland, Hungary and Czechoslovakia." As for the significance of nonviolent sanctions in undermining that power, Htun concluded: "Without sanctions, we will not win the battle."[11]

That seemed increasingly clear within Burma. After years of living in squalid and dangerous conditions in the jungle, training with rebel soldiers, and learning to handle machine guns—but also after nonviolent training—students in the All-Burma Students Democratic Front decided to abandon armed struggle in mid-1997 and joined Aung San Suu Kyi in her commitment to nonviolent direct action. Inside the country, the pro-democracy movement began to try new tactics: lightning-quick street protests, sit-ins, and opposition leaflet distribution in the moments before troops could arrive. In 1995 Radio Free Asia had beamed into Burma a series of interviews featuring former Polish communist leader General Jaruzelski and Solidarity leaders Lech Walesa and Adam Michnik. Their consensus, which the Burmese listeners were able to hear, was that eventually the military rulers would have to negotiate with the opposition.[12]

But talking with the opposition is usually a regime's last resort. When crisis threatens, the reaction is typically defensive. In 1998 the Asian financial crisis halved foreign investment in Burma. By 1999 inflation of the kyat reached 70 percent, and homes and businesses were going without electricity for half of each day. At the same time, human rights groups condemned new outrages by the regime—death squads used against certain ethnic villagers and rape used as a form of terror by special army troops. Economic disability and political disrepute were closing in on the junta.[13]

That pressure is doubtless why the regime began a new crackdown, putting 150 senior members of the NLD in detention centers, including Suu Kyi. In a videotaped message in April 1999 to the United Nations Commission on Human Rights, she said that the country's oppression had "worsened greatly." Two months later there were reports that the junta was plotting to assassinate expatriate dissidents. In the century's last year, the regime in Burma was on a global stage, visible everywhere. Technology has internationalized the struggle for rights and democracy, and in doing so, it has opened up new avenues for nonviolent action against violent regimes. The dream of every dictator is to hang on forever. But as Htun Aung Gyaw said of Burma's junta in 1999, "Their dreams are evaporating."[14]

SERBIA, 1996–2000—
FROM WORDS, POWER

"We Have Whistles Instead of Guns"

On November 17, 1996, hundreds of thousands of Serbs, Montenegrins, Bosnians, and ethnic Albanians went to the polls in Yugoslavia to choose candidates for local public offices. After four decades of communist rule in which voting was limited to the party's handpicked nominees, these elections had been opened to other parties. As the returns came in that night, noncommunist candidates, affiliated with a political coalition called Zajedno (Together) were winning race after race, including those in the capital, Belgrade, and thirteen other cities.

Zajedno's victory was a repudiation of President Slobodan Milosevic, the leader of Serbia, the largest Yugoslav republic. A communist party apparatchik, Milosevic had assumed the title of president in 1989 and held on to it during Yugoslavia's bloody breakup by deftly shedding the image of communist autocrat for the new cloak of a Serb patriot. As he was not about to allow local elections to challenge that power now, his regime simply annulled the vote because of "irregularities" and refused to acknowledge the results.

What happened then was unprecedented in Yugoslavia. Two days after the election and for the next three months, marchers filled the streets of Belgrade and other Serbian cities in protest. Not unlike Salvadoran medical and professional students who spearheaded the 1944 civic strike, Belgrade university students in engineering, computer science, and mathematics organized the initial marches, in which professors and staff joined in—all singing "The Hymn of Saint Sava," a paean to the patron saint of education. When students elsewhere heard of the marches, they took to the streets too, in thirty cities and towns.[15]

Separate from the student marches were rallies led by Zajedno leaders Vuk Draskovic, Vesna Pesic, and Zoran Djindic, calling for greater democracy. Students blew whistles in disdain for the regime, and so did civilians; a mother of teenage sons said, "We have whistles instead of guns." One day marchers covered the Electoral Commission building in rolls of toilet paper. When authorities postponed parliament's opening, blaming a mosquito infestation, demonstrators sprayed the building with insecticide. After six weeks of this kind of thing, one marcher, Miroslav Pavlovic, noticed that fear of the regime was subsiding. "For the first time, people have started to think for themselves," he said.[16]

Despite provocations from police, the student and Zajedno marches remained largely nonviolent. Organizers videotaped marches to document any violent attacks, to prove their people were not responsible. Early stone throwing gave way to more evocative gestures; the walls and windows of many ministries, for example, were spattered with eggs. One feminist group called Women in Black handed out fliers to marchers containing suggestions for nonviolent action from Gene Sharp. Their message was simple: " . . . we are convinced that only a network of civil society and nonviolent resistance can change the logic of war and stop war machinery. It is a long-term strategy that requires patience."[17]

"Where Is that Internet?"

Had all these events taken place a decade earlier, the opposition's room for maneuver would have been limited by the regime's control of communications. Milosevic had stifled opposition media through arrests, intimidation, and property destruction. But by 1996 the hardware for communicating had become cheaper and more accessible. Fax machines had become vital, and mobile phones were used to direct marches. The Serb ruler was also outflanked by the 3,000 users of Sezam Pro, an Internet service provider. Only hours after the elections were annulled, strategies for response were being discussed via e-mail. Some calls for marches went out on Sezam Pro's politics forum. And for perhaps the first time anywhere, one reaction to a regime's use of arbitrary power was the creation of a pro-democracy Internet site.[18]

Unlike Burma, where access was difficult, Yugoslavia had a fairly open computer culture, and student Internet users with access to the computer science faculty's resources probably were ahead of the government in cyber knowledge. "Most of the authorities don't even know what e-mail is," said Vuk Micovic, a student leader. "During the student protests our web page was popular, and the police broke in and said, 'Where is that Internet?' as if they could confiscate it."[19]

Although they had shuttered the independent press, the authorities neglected to notice that new technology had increased the velocity of information. "They understand computers as a calculating tool, not as a communications tool," said Milan Bozic, a member of a Zajedno-affiliated political party. "The people in the street know that they must get Western media attention . . . That the media is here is one of our best successes. The Internet has helped get them here, and bring us more attention."[20]

The Internet also carried foreign media reports about the opposition's views (banned from print and the airwaves). When Milosevic's men raided independent Radio B92 on December 3, editors were able to divert their broadcasts away from the airwaves and onto the Internet, where they were broadcast globally to anyone with Real Audio software. The authorities could do little to prevent the Voice of America and the BBC from picking up Internet carriage of the broadcasts and beaming them back into Serbia via shortwave radio.[21]

Popular backlash against regime violence was also sharpened by use of the

Internet. In December Milosevic bused in 20,000 paid "supporters" to disrupt the marches. Fights broke out after one of them fired a gun and injured a protestor. Student Internet users relayed information about the injuries to friends and family in other countries. An American journalist blasted an e-mail about the beatings to his personal address book of 3,700 names, urging them to spread the word. Within thirty-six hours the message had reached 15,000 people.[22]

In seeking to feed indignation abroad, the opposition was targeting a vulnerability of Milosevic: Having gotten the West to lift sanctions against Yugoslavia for its actions in the war in Bosnia, he needed foreign trade to help the economy recover. Opposition groups knew that as long as they remained conspicuous, Milosevic would be reluctant to crack down hard and risk renewed Western censure. In addition, the protests succeeded in wringing some sympathy from the police, the military, government workers, and judges.

In their public action, opposition groups chose not to multiply their demands but to stay focused on a simple goal: having the election results honored. By late winter Milosevic began to look more and more isolated, and under the daily onslaught of angry civilians taking over the boulevards and sidewalks of Belgrade, he chose to relent. In late February he allowed the election winners to be seated. After 88 days, the campaign had prevailed.

Yet from that point forward, the movement failed to follow up its victory with renewed organizing linked to fresh goals. The students and Zajedno, which had conducted separate marches, proved unable to transcend their differences; the students wanted more democracy, but some Zajedno leaders were, like Milosevic, not much more than expedient nationalists. Many of the newly elected local officials turned out to be nearly as corrupt as their predecessors, and when Milosevic's term as Serbian president ended, he assumed the presidency of Yugoslavia, hitherto a figurehead post, and retained the same powers.[23]

"A Pretext to Kill More Innocents"

Slobodan Milosevic had risen to power during the disarray following the death of Josip Tito, the socialist strongman who ruled Yugoslavia from its inception in 1945 until 1980. An ambitious but not especially gifted party official, Milosevic had followed a communist party colleague, Ivan Stambolic, through a series of directorships in the nationalized gas and banking industries. In 1986 he became head of the Serbian Central Committee, one step behind Stambolic, then the Serb president. In only three years he would take his mentor's office, and his portrait would replace Tito's in public places.[24]

A crisis in Kosovo provided the spark for Milosevic's transformation from party hack to Serb champion. In 1987 Milosevic visited the province as tensions flared between majority Albanians and minority Serbs. Near Kosovo Polje, site of the "Field of Blackbirds" where Serbs had slain an Ottoman ruler in 1389, Milosevic gave an impassioned speech to irate Serbs who had battled with Kosovar police, saying that no one should dare beat them. Their acclamation convinced him of the political payoff from appeals to Serb nationalism.

Kosovo's status had long been an issue for politicians in Belgrade. Tito, the suave manipulator who had kept the country intact for half a century, had agreed to more autonomy for Kosovars and allowed them to fly the Albanian black eagle flag underneath the Yugoslav tricolor. In 1989 Milosevic rescinded that autonomy, and ethnic Albanians could no longer teach schoolchildren in their own language. The next year Milosevic dismantled their parliament, and Kosovar leaders exiled themselves or went underground.[25]

Until 1995, Milosevic kept Kosovo on the back burner while Belgrade fought successive wars in breakaway Croatia and in Bosnia. In three-way conflicts among Bosnians, Serbs, and Croats, a quarter million people, most of them Bosnian Muslims, were killed. An equal number were wounded, and some 2.3 million people were left homeless. Europe was appalled. After international intervention ended the war and the Dayton Accords created a Serbian entity within Bosnia, Milosevic's attention soon returned to Kosovo.

Among Kosovars, two rival ideas had emerged about how to regain autonomy or even achieve independence. One belonged to Ibrahim Rugova, who in underground elections in May 1992 was voted "President of the Republic." This somewhat disheveled literature professor, fascinated by Gandhi, wanted his people to win self-rule through nonviolent means. He and his Democratic League of Kosovo (LDK) exhorted Kosovars to achieve de facto autonomy by building up their own society from within, and there were some successes: 18,000 Kosovar schoolteachers reportedly taught in the Albanian vernacular, and 92 clinics provided basic health care and free medicine to the population.[26]

While the emphasis on self-reliance did echo Gandhi as well as Polish dissidents in the 1970s, Rugova did little directly to defy Serb hegemony. He seldom traveled, keeping to his office in the city of Pristina, seemingly out of touch with life in the streets and villages. Unwilling to communicate in English, he also failed to rouse much outside support, and his insistence that Kosovo achieve statehood was a nonstarter for Serbs, given Kosovo's role in the Serbian historical narrative. It also found no support among Western powers, who feared it would give false hope to every stateless ethnic group in Eastern Europe and the Middle East, from the Ruthenians to the Kurds. And there were Kosovar leaders who were willing to settle for less. Adem Demaci, whose term in prison won him the title "the Albanian Mandela," favored autonomy within Yugoslavia and advocated protest—comparable to the marches in Belgrade—as the way to get it.[27]

The combination of Rugova's cloistered style, his intransigent goals, and his passivity in the face of Serbian repression cost the nonviolent path credibility among Kosovars looking for a way forward. When the Dayton Accords contained nothing for Kosovo, the family clans that make up ethnic Albanian society leaned toward the Popular Movement for Kosovo (LPK), a radical group formerly tied to the Albanian communists, and the Kosovo Liberation Army (KLA). Since the Croatians and Bosnian Serbs had fought for independance, many Kosovars felt they should too. "It was a sign for Kosovars that only those who engaged in armed struggle in Yugoslavia get anywhere," said Ylber Hysa, executive director of Kosovo Action for Civic Initiatives. "We are through with these Albanian intellectuals in Pristina, with journalists, diplomats," said one rebel. They knew Rugova had failed, but many did not know that dozens of other nonviolent movements in the century had succeeded.[28]

Since 1993, the KLA had been recruiting in villages, and when neighboring Albania teetered on the brink of collapse in 1997, some of its armories were looted, and guns found their way into Kosovo. By March 1998, Serb police had cracked down on ethnic Albanian fighters, killing eighty people, including women and children. "These armed groups, or individuals who use violence, will only give the Serbs a pretext to kill more innocents," Rugova had foreseen. "In any conflict the lucky ones would be driven over the borders as refugees."[29]

But few were listening to Rugova any longer. When peace talks began at Rambouillet, France, in February 1999 to put an end to the Serb-KLA fighting, he was only a bit player, and the Kosovars were badly divided. Diplomats patched together a "provisional government," but the choices for Kosovo had been reduced to internecine violence or outside intervention. When Milosevic refused to sign an agreement that included concessions for Kosovar autonomy, NATO threatened military action unless he changed his mind. He did not.[30]

"Keeping that Creature in Power"

As Milosevic's wars had whittled down Yugoslavia to a rump state of only Serbia, Montenegro, Kosovo, and the province of Vojvodina, he lavished spending on his military and special police, many of whose officers were later named as war criminals. The regime became what one journalist called a "kleptocracy" in which top officials used their positions to enrich themselves, while unemployment reached 50 percent and per capita income dropped by more than two-thirds since 1989. All this fueled forceful if divided opposition that first showed its muscle in the 1996-1997 protests. People who saw Milosevic as a rapacious autocrat were as numerous in Belgrade as in Brussels.[31]

If, at the century's end, Milosevic was the cause of Balkan instability in general and "ethnic cleansing" in particular, the question was how to bring him to heel. To engage him violently would be to play a game he knew. What he would not have expected, well before NATO's options were narrowed to bombing or capitulating to genocide in Kosovo, was a systematic program to support the Serbian democratic opposition and preoccupy him at home. But that had never been high on the list of possibilities in the White House or Whitehall.

Instead, the drive to pacify the Balkans through diplomacy, which reached its first climax in Dayton, subordinated all other options. Once a treaty became the object, then Milosevic's signature was necessary—and that meant wooing rather than undermining the sponsor of the region's miseries. Desko Nikitovic of the Serbian Unity Congress in the United States claimed that the West "elevated Milosevic to royalty" when Assistant Secretary of State Richard Holbrooke refused to deal with other Serb leaders in the run-up to Dayton. Nebojsa Covic, a Serb opposition leader, told the Helsinki Commission that the very source of Milosevic's power in the ensuing period was "the legitimacy given de facto to him by the international community."[32]

Even Richard Holbrooke, who negotiated the Dayton Accords, eventually regretted the West's failure to give timely support to Milosevic's opposition, concluding in his memoir on Dayton that "Washington missed a chance to affect events" by showing support for the 1996-1997 protests. The Clinton administration had sent no senior officials to Belgrade at that time, Holbrooke explained, because it was feared that visits would be misused by Milosevic to pretend he had its support. It was more concerned about what Milosevic might do than what his opponents could do, if they had possessed the means to do it.[33]

Although Zajedno fell apart from infighting in 1997, the elements for a strong movement against Milosevic still existed: The president was unpopular, the opposition had not yet been silenced, international human rights groups were on the ground observing events, and scrappy independent media outlets like the *Daily Telegraph* were kicking. Moreover, if the opposition had devised or been shown a strategy for taking power through nonviolent action—how to separate Milosevic from his means of coercion, and how to deny him the civilian cooperation needed to rule—it would have had more incentive to remain united.

But Western governments had been giving short shrift to Serb democrats for some time. Veran Matic, the editor of Radio B92, told the Helsinki Commission that there were "numerous pro-democracy and antiwar demonstrations in 1991 and 1992 and 1993. All these movements and the media survived with minimal or even without any support from the West."[34] What they might have done with such support to shorten Milosevic's grip on power, even earlier as he spurred the killing in Bosnia, will never be known.

In mid-1998, hopes were raised for a stronger front against Milosevic when the Alliance for Change was formed. Headed by a respected former banker, it tried to restore the movement's unity, but time was running short as many feared that Milosevic would use trouble in Kosovo to distract attention from Serbia's domestic problems. For Milosevic, it was never about the Kosovars; it was always about himself. Former Prime Minister Milan Panic urged the West in December 1998 to stop dealing with Milosevic and impose sanctions until democratic reforms and press freedom were granted. But two months later the diplomats were talking to him again at Rambouillet, and when the deadline passed for him to act on the deal negotiated there, NATO made good on its threat of military action, in March 1999.

"If the Serbian democratic opposition groups had been helped with the cost of a few American missiles, the situation might be different today," said Desko Nikitovic during the NATO bombing. "I believe Milosevic would have been history already." What movements can always use are the credibility accompanying international backers, the funds to help civilians survive as they go on strike, equipment for underground publishing, and other resources. The U.S. State Department noted that it gave $15 million to independent media in Serbia in 1998. In the spring of 1999, the U.S. Defense Department donated over $1 billion to Serbia, in the form of cruise missiles and ordnance.[35]

Negotiating with rulers who behave as warlords is often futile, and upping the ante of violence on them will surely raise the general level of chaos and take innocent lives in the bargain. But the people who have the deepest interest in removing them are the people they rule, and timely, substantial help to the Serbian opposition in 1997-1998—well before the crisis in early 1999—might have helped it divert Milosevic from his crimes in Kosovo and thus avert the human losses and massive costs of NATO military intervention.

Just days after the air campaign began, policemen again raided Radio B92's offices, and its editor was arrested. Then, Slavko Curuvija, the editor of the *Daily Telegraph,* was assassinated by hired Serb shooters outside his Belgrade apartment as he was walking with his wife. The regime also took care to disconnect 30,000 to 40,000 students from the Internet, to limit independent information. "It is not only Albanian human rights at stake, it's mine as well," explained Vesna Kostic, a journalist and former police target. "Milosevic is already moving ahead against the independent press and the opposition. This bombing will mean keeping that creature in power another 100 years . . . " Her prediction was exaggerated, but her sense of his intentions was exact.[36]

For other Serbs, who—under other circumstances—might have been drawn into a movement to bring down Milosevic, having their nation ravaged by the very alliance many of them had thought they should join was a form of betrayal. Young people spoke openly not of one day rebuilding their country but of emigrating. "He's ruined our lives, the best years of our lives," said one. "We just can't take it any more."[37]

"He's Finished"

The despair and alienation of the young, which the violent cauldron of Milosevic's Serbia had brewed, was to prove critical to the dictator's undoing. On October 10, 1998, a handful of student veterans of the 1996-97 protests had founded Otpor ("Resistance") as a vehicle for a new kind of defiance—choosing as their symbol a black clenched fist, a deliberate parody of the bloody fist that was an old Bolshevik symbol and a favorite image of Milosevic. Unlike the communists, however, they formed no centralized or hierarchical leadership but instead focused on grass roots organizing. They turned their back on the dictator's power as the first move in a struggle to take it from him.[38]

After the NATO bombing, which had helped the regime suppress opposition, Otpor's organizing took hold with a quiet vengeance. It was built in some places around clubhouses where young people could go and hang out, excercise, and party on the weekends, or more often it was run out of dining rooms and bedrooms in activists' homes. These were "boys and girls 18 and 19 years old" who had lived "in absolute poverty compared to other teenagers around the world," according to Stanko Lazendic, an Otpor activist in Novi Sad. "Otpor offered these kids a place to gather, a place where they could express their creative ideas." In a word, it showed them how to empower themselves.[39]

It also offered them a new philosophy of how to seize political power. The organization's leaders knew that they "couldn't use force on someone who . . . had three times more force and weapons that we did," in the words of Lazendic. "We knew what had happened in . . . Tiananmen, where the army plowed over students with tanks." So violence wouldn't work—and besides, it was the trademark of Milosevic, and Otpor had to stand for something different. Serbia "was a country in which violence was used too many times in daily politics," noted Srdja Popovic, a 27 year-old who called himself Otpor's "ideological commissar." The young activists had to use nonviolent methods "to show how superior, how advanced, how civilized" they were.[40]

This relatively sophisticated knowledge of how to develop nonviolent power was not intuitive. Miljenko Dereta, the director of a private group in Belgrade called Civic Initiatives, got funding from Freedom House in the U.S. to print and distribute 5,000 copies of Gene Sharp's book, *From Dictatorship to Democracy: A Conceptual Framework for Liberation.* Otpor got hold of Sharp's main three-volume work, *The Politics of Nonviolent Action,* freely adapting sections of it into a Serbian-language notebook they dubbed the "Otpor User

Manual." Consciously using this "ideology of nonviolent individual resistance," in Popovic's words, activists also received direct training from Col. Robert Helvey, a colleague of Sharp, at the Budapest Hilton in March 2000.

Helvey emphasized how to break the people's habits of subservience to authority, and also how to subvert the regime's "pillars of support," including the police and armed forces. Crucially, he warned them against "contaminants to a nonviolent struggle," especially violent action, which would deter ordinary people from joining the movement and alienate the international community, from which material and financial assistance could be drawn. As Popovic put it: "Stay nonviolent and you will get the support of the third party."[41]

That support, largely denied to the Serbian opposition before, now began to flow. Otpor and other dissident groups received funding from the National Endowment for Democracy, affiliated with the U.S. government, and Otpor leaders sat down with Daniel Serwer, the program director for the Balkans at the U.S. Institute for Peace, whose story of having been tear-gassed during an anti–Vietnam War demonstration gave him special credibility in their eyes. The International Republican Institute, also financed by the U.S. government, channeled funding to the opposition and met with Otpor leaders several times. The U.S. Agency for International Development, the wellspring for most of this financing, was also the source of money that went for materials like t-shirts and stickers.

Stickers were far from trivial; in fact, they represented both the cheerful insolence and ubiquity of Otpor's effort to undermine Milosevic. Popovic called stickers "the key medium," in part because putting up posters made people more noticeable to the police, but "you can count on everyone" to get involved "when it comes to a sticker." Near the climax of the struggle, Otpor went into sticker overdrive, slapping 1.8 million stickers that said, "He's Finished," on flat surfaces everywhere. But it was also the content and not merely the abundance of opposition symbols that mattered. After the regime began making spurious claims that Otpor members were terrorists and drug-dealers, many began wearing t-shirts that said, "Otpor, Drug Addict," lampooning the government's propaganda. "Each of our actions was full of humor," Popovic recalled, because it draped on nonviolent activists the mantle of confidence.[42]

The audacity of tactics like this seemed to unnerve the regime. Srdjan Milivojevic, an Otpor activist in Krusevac, remembers spray-painting a big graffiti of a fist on police headquarters there, along with the line, "Infidels, you betrayed Kosovo," and Otpor's name. The next morning, security people came out and photographed the fist. "They stayed for a long time," Milivojevic said. "I noticed their fear of it." Emboldened, he climbed on the roof of the building that night and destroyed police satellite antennas with a hammer. But no one noticed the damage, and it seemed to have no impact. "I understood," he said of the spray-painting, "that through these small deeds I could do much more than by any violent actions." And such deeds were happening all over Serbia; at the crest of its wave, Otpor had 70,000 members in 130 branches.[43]

The psychological pressure of people power, when it proliferates in all directions—as Corazon Aquino's yellow-kerchiefed followers in the Philippines discovered—has two strategic benefits: It transfers anxiety about what's coming next from those who are challenging the regime to the regime itself (whose consequent repression often backfires), and it plants doubt in the minds of police and military cadres about how long the rulers whom they serve can last. Milosevic could "resist only with support from police and [the] army," opposition leader (later Serbian prime minister) Zoran Djindjic observed. "We knew if we can affect police and army around him, and bring them to think, 'should they support Milosevic or not' . . . that he cannot survive."[44]

To do that, Otpor and other oppositionists realized, meant that the police had to be persuaded that they were not viewed as enemies of the movement, but in fact were natural allies. "Our message was: There is no war between police and us," Srdja Popovic recalled. "Our message was that we together are the victims of the system. And there is no reason . . . to have war between victims and victims. One [kind of] victims are in blue uniforms, other victims are in blue jeans." Serb national soccer teams wore blue uniforms, and crowds had often chanted in support, "Blue Guys! Blue Guys!" So that's what anti-Milosevic crowds sometimes chanted exuberantly at the police.[45]

The events that converged to split Milosevic from the police and his other "pillars of support" were set in motion by the dictator's ramming through a constitutional amendment in June 2000, allowing him to run for re-election as president. On July 27, he set the election date for just two months later, confident that he could win or at least rig the vote count. As with Pinochet who went ahead with a plebiscite in Chile, Milosevic "wanted a legitimacy," in the words of Teofil Pancic, a reporter for *Vreme* (Time), a Belgrade magazine.[46]

At workplaces all over Serbia, official pressure to vote for Milosevic was fierce. But so was the campaign against him. Otpor pressured opposition parties to unify behind a single presidential candidate, Vojislav Kostunica, who was, in the words of the journalist Zoran Sekulic, "a man who was not compromised"— not a politician, but a scholar. Kostunica was hit with "attacks . . . slanders . . . defamations" from the controlled press, but that "homogenized" his support, he said later, so deep was contempt for the state media.[47]

The persistent example of the Otpor kids was bearing fruit. "One of the opposition's final messages before the election was: We are not asking you to vote for us, but before going to cast your vote," Sekulic said, "you ask your children for whom you should vote, and then do just as your children tell you." Inherent in this was a larger choice about the future of Serbia; everyone knew that young Serbs were emigrating in record numbers, and Djindjic said the choice was simple: "We will be part of the world"—Serbia would reject the wars and isolation caused by Milosevic—or "your children, without you, will be part of the world."[48]

With foreign support, some 30,000 poll-watchers were trained, mobilized, and fanned out to cover 10,000 polling places, to help prevent Milosevic from stealing the September 24 election. In Cacak, the opposition went further: on the night the votes were counted, 20,000 Serbs assembled outside the building to intimidate any would-be vote-stealers.[49]

Two days after results showed a clear plurality if not majority for Kostunica, Milosevic conceded he had run second but held out for a run-off—and crowds poured into the streets of Belgrade, waving baby rattles to ridicule Milosevic for not conceding. The opposition claimed an outright victory in the September 24 vote; to have entered a run-off, Kostunica later said, would have been to "accept something that was falsification and a lie," echoing Vaclev Havel's conviction that liberation demanded an end to "living in the lie."[50]

A general strike was called for October 2, and citizens blocked bridges and roads, high school students boycotted classes, and 7,500 miners joined the strike, along with textile workers. The opposition was opting for nationwide civil disobedience, to seal its victory and obstruct a run-off. What followed were daily rallies and traffic blockades in 50 cities, and "the police were very, very confused," remembered Djindjic. But it was more than confusion. "We had secret talks with the army and police," said Zoran Zivkovic, the mayor of Nis and an Otpor ally. "And the deal was that they would not disobey [their orders], but neither would they execute . . . So they said yes when Milosevic asked for action—and they did nothing."[51]

The steady drumbeat of Otpor, the hopeful verve of the opposition's presidential campaign, and the exhausting, poisonous work of "confrontations with people, beatings, cordons" that the police were ordered to undertake had weakened the last stanchion of the regime. "One of the top people in the police," recalled Velimir Ilic, "told me . . . please defeat Milosevic already, even I feel sick of him." For months Ilic, the mayor of Cacak and an opposition leader, had slowly made lists of key people in the army and police, and went to talk to them, to determine who might fail to back the regime when the moment of truth came.[52]

That moment arrived on October 4, when a quarter-million Serbs rallied to support striking miners at the pit at Tamnava, and on October 5 when the police pulled out of the Kolubara mine complex where workers had been striking. And it happened when Velimir Ilic led a convoy of bull-dozers, along with thousands of cars, trucks, and buses from all over Serbia carrying 200,000 people into Belgrade—as the police and army largely stood aside. It was a provincial uprising, and when protestors arrived at the seat of official power, the people's refusal to stand down until Milosevic was gone became obvious to the world. But no one fired a shot: "We had the nation trained not to attack the police, not to use violence, to be organized," said Srdja Popovic. "As Gandhi said . . . you must train the nonviolent army for so long that the battle becomes unnecessary."[53]

Unfortunately the smoke that billowed out from the parliament and state television buildings when rooms were set afire encouraged CNN and other networks to use seemingly violent images as the visual emblems of their coverage, even though only two people were killed in unrelated incidents in Serbia that day. As usual, the world media focused on the final frenzy, not the patient movement that really produced change. The revolution was "imprinted to the end with Otpor's nonviolent ethos," according to Roger Cohen of *The New York Times.* When he had been arrested back in December 1998, Popovic remembered a line from Jorge Luis Borges: "Violence is the last sanctuary of the weak." Ultimately, he knew, repression would fail and a different, more powerful force would prevail.[54]

In just days after October 5, Kostunica was installed as president, and on April 1, 2001, Slobodan Milosevic—whom the West had first appeased and then mercilessly bombed, without either stopping his destructiveness or dislodging him from power—was arrested by Serb police for his crimes while in office. He and his regime were "preachers of death," said Srdja Popovic. "You know, their language smelled like death. And we won because we loved life more"—and converted that belief into power, at the polling booths, on the police lines, and on the streets of Europe's last, now-vanished dictatorship.[55]

NONVIOLENT POWER IN THE TWENTY-FIRST CENTURY

In all of the major conflicts in this book, arbitrary rulers were challenged by movements, with little or no military force at their disposal, using nonviolent sanctions. Almost all of these self-absorbed and heedless leaders, however intoxicated with power at their zenith, were thwarted by people who had no formal standing and no standing forces. They were overcome by those who were operating with a different paradigm of action, based not on fear or taking lives but on reclaiming power taken away without their consent.

The relevance of these stories for a new century is robust, for we are not yet rid of rulers who resist democracy. But the world in which they try to survive is far different from the one in which Tsar Nicholas, Lord Irwin, or even Wojciech Jaruzelski held power. Commerce, communications, and transportation are evolving into a single world system for exchanging ideas, talent, money, and resources—and that is why decisions in London or Los Angeles, and markets in

New York or New Delhi, can constrain governments elsewhere. To keep up, tightly governed societies are pushed to open up, and doing so puts stress on rigid structures of control. In the fissures of civil space that regimes can be forced to open, in global networks of political exiles, and through the new transnational community of advisors and practitioners in nonviolent sanctions, better strategies for taking power are finding new adherents.

These are hazardous developments if you are a dictator trying to outlast your welcome. The security of a government cannot be dissociated from the vitality of its civil society, but control-minded regimes are nervous about embracing the free exchange of ideas that fuels the global system. Walling a country off from world contact is self-depriving; as the case of North Korea attests, the more complete the control exerted over a nation by its government, the poorer it is likely to become. No system can last long in self-quarantine, and if it opens the sluice gates of information even slightly, forces for change will not be far behind.

The conflicts of the new century will continue to involve political, ethnic, or national groups that want to throw out unwanted rulers, achieve self-government, or win various rights—and it is these kinds of conflicts, in which nonviolent sanctions often have proved to be decisive, for which the last century provides well-developed models. The new global system also may hand opposition movements two advantages. First, as information and economic influence become more widely distributed in a society, an authoritarian's structure of control becomes more complex and costly to maintain; opportunities for nonviolent disruption and noncooperation are thus more plentiful. Second, because nongovernmental organizations and the international media have become more aggressive in rallying support for human rights, and because governments cannot afford to lose international legitimacy and related privileges such as loans, credit, and access to other markets, authoritarian regimes may be less hasty in using repressive measures—so long as world opinion and the great democracies respond.

These conditions should offer civilian movements more latitude in opposing a regime, as the Indonesian crisis in 1998 revealed. After that country's currency and stock market collapsed, the streets of Jakarta became the stage for demonstrators demanding not only reforms but also President Suharto's resignation. Corruption had ended people's patience, and instability had broken the tolerance of the international business community. In an earlier era, civilian unrest might not have been enough to force out such a ruler, but the Indonesian debacle was a global event, and faced with dismay abroad as well as domestic turmoil, Suharto's own military turned against him, which was the coup de grâce.

As people's movements have forced out dictators on five continents, and as police states have given way to fledgling democracies, other reasons for using nonviolent power have developed. Minorities seeking rights still often find themselves unable to influence governments that serve established interests. Political corruption—vote-buying, favoritism, bribery—and a restricted or flaccid media can limit the civil dynamism that genuine democracy requires. Nonviolent sanctions, such as boycotts and strikes, are likely to be used increasingly against these "little tyrannies" that often persist once the big tyranny of political autocracy is gone. Building free societies is not a finished task when political power changes hands.

New reasons for using nonviolent power may also develop as new democracies assess how to defend themselves from external threats. Shortly before the Soviet collapse, Mikhail Gorbachev sent more Soviet troops into the Baltics, ostensibly to protect Soviet interests when the republics moved toward independence. Armed defense had a bad precedent in the Baltics: In the 1950s a guerrilla movement called the Forest Brotherhood failed to resist forced deportations ordered by Stalin. During the crisis of 1991 all three republics deliberately considered how to integrate civilian-based resistance into national defense, as they planned how to respond to potential Soviet threats.

Sweden also has studied civilian-based defense, and Slovenians and Macedonians have shown interest. None of these peoples is interested in martyrdom; all want to maintain freedom and independence. That their governments have been willing to consider nonviolent force to defend their sovereignty may suggest that the idea of power based on the threat or use of violence is finally losing its grip on those who want to succeed when history is on the line.

But the world's leading democracies, which now are often expected to resolve deadly conflicts, have largely failed to see the preventive benefits of rooting out renegade regimes through nonviolent action, before their political or humanitarian crimes spawn war or mass violence. In 1998-1999 Kosovo was a violent collision waiting to happen, and Slobodan Milosevic was behind the wheel—but the West then paid little attention to those in Serbia who later drove events in another direction.

As nonviolent action has become more commonplace, it also has been studied more extensively. Looking back, political scientists and historians have seen a relationship between the way a nation overcomes authoritarian or outside rule and its ability to sustain civil society and democracy. When nonviolent action is used to achieve power, the people have to develop abilities and exemplify the spirit that are later critical in governing: empowering individuals to take public action, building consensus on behalf of common objectives, and insisting that laws and leaders derive from the people's consent. Nonviolent power becomes not only the means of achieving change; it becomes the first line of defense for a society's most sacred values.[56]

In the life of a democracy, nonviolent sanctions are frequently in use, albeit usually to press demands on elected parliaments and presidents. Every national issue of any emotional significance in the United States seems eventually to inspire a "march on Washington" aimed mainly at the media. From demonstrations against world trade meetings to boycotts of beef or energy producers, protest has become a public rite in the developed democracies."

While dealing first with civil rights and antiwar demonstrations in the 1960s and 1970s, and then with other causes marked by protest, U.S. police agencies acquired expertise in accommodating nonviolent action without losing control or cracking down. Most agencies now work closely with groups sponsoring protests, through "Public Order Management Systems" that have since been copied widely, for example, in post-apartheid South Africa and even China. The Chinese had a protest-permitting system in place at the time of the Tiananmen Square events that was patterned on the American model, but unlike the latter, it reserved the right to prohibit protests if they advocated positions the government disliked.[57]

As the events in Tiananmen Square demonstrated, however, it is not the magnitude or intensity of a single event that enables a movement to succeed. Physical protest does not persuade or even coerce a government to change its policies, much less surrender power. Movements have to challenge the legitimacy of the laws or the regime itself and undermine the means of its control, by disrupting public life and destabilizing the economy—and by sequencing that action over time and dispersing it in space, so that repression becomes difficult. At times during their occupation of Denmark, the Germans were hardly able to deal with one strike before another one broke out, and sixty years later the Burmese junta could not murder every dissident who used a computer somewhere in the world.

Every time a popular movement confronts a government, a struggle is taking place. Nonviolent action is rarely passive; each engagement can intensify the conflict. The movement's cause is unlikely to be quenched by outside interveners or negotiators who try to end a conflict, however laudable the goal of stopping violence. In fact, the object of nonviolent conflict is not to avoid violence, except insofar as violence damages the cause or the movement, as it so often does. The purpose of nonviolent power is to end oppression, check invaders, secure rights, or establish democracy. To its abundant credit, that was its record, throughout the twentieth century. In the conflicts of the new century, it will do so again—in ways we cannot yet foresee.

Victory without Violence

Violence can never destroy what is accepted by public opinion. On the contrary, public opinion need only be diametrically opposed to violence to destroy its every action.

—Leo Tolstoy

ON A NOVEMBER AFTERNOON IN 1989, many Czech actors, writers, and theater people in Prague went to meet at the Realistic Theater. The night before, government security forces had assaulted nonviolent demonstrators trying to get to Wenceslas Square. Students at the theater academy decided to strike in protest. Now they wanted others in the theatrical community to join them. But many who sat nervously in their seats at the Realistic were not sure they should strike— the regime could punish them badly, and the public might not support them.

Just as people started to leave, Arnošt Goldflan, a theater director, spoke up. "Sitting here, we have no power to direct anybody," he said. "We cannot decide for our colleagues from those theaters who couldn't get here . . . The inescapable fact is that every one of us will have to decide for himself. Take a risk and believe that everything will work out, and if it doesn't, then reconcile yourself to the fact that you are in for it." Goldflan said that his theater company would strike—and then others followed his lead. That very afternoon audiences throughout the city arrived at theaters to see plays but instead heard actors read political statements.[1]

Ten years earlier the Czech playwright who later became his country's president, Václav Havel, wrote a seminal essay, widely disseminated underground, called "The Power of the Powerless." Havel argued that the confrontation between an authoritarian regime and its opposition took place first not on a material but on an existential level—and on that level, the power of the opposition was "the strength of a potential, which is hidden throughout the whole of society." This potential did not rely on "soldiers of its own" but on "everyone who is living within the lie and who may be struck at any moment . . . by the force of truth."[2]

Two years before Havel wrote his essay, the mothers of sons who had been kidnapped by shadowy forces in the chaos of military-ruled Argentina decided they wanted the truth about their children, and they started marching every week at the plaza facing the presidential palace. Eventually they awakened a movement to bring down the regime that had "disappeared" thousands. A half century before the Argentine mothers marched, Gandhi explained that in a popular movement based on satyagraha—exposing the truth about an evil—"no one has to look expectantly at another . . . all are leaders and all are followers."[3]

Once the truth about oppression is circulating in the public mind, it cannot be evaded, and when acts of opposition—personal at first, then collective, and finally strategic—are seized upon and multiply, the people's acquiescence begins to come apart, and with it, their cooperation with oppressors. For over a hundred years, the British ruled their colonies in North America through local authorities and by American consent, much as they did later in India. Once that consent was withdrawn, they could keep control only by using military force.

In the twentieth century, that kind of force was overcome repeatedly by people's movements that sought self-determination, liberation from invaders, basic human rights, and democracy. None of these movements possessed any military advantages over the regimes they confronted, which is often why nonviolent methods were used. Often their progress was delayed or complicated by their adversaries' use of violence, but in none of these conflicts did that ordain the final outcome. Not only did a voice in a theater or individuals at factory gates have power to rouse people against injustice, the nonviolent action they took had strategic value in overcoming the violence that usually was the last resort of the governments they stood against.

But nonviolent action is like violent combat in at least two ways: It does not succeed automatically, and it does not operate mysteriously—it works by identifying an opponent's vulnerabilities and taking away his ability to maintain control. If a regime intends to remain in power indefinitely, it will require extensive, long-term interaction with those it rules—and that creates a dilemma: The broader the regime's system of control, the more vulnerable it is, because it depends on too many actors to ensure that violence against resisters will always work. Once an opposition shows its followers that this weakness exists, it can begin to pry loose the support that the regime requires—its revenue, its foreign investors, or even its military. But doing so requires a strategy for action, without which movements rarely prevail. Victory is not a function of fate; it is earned.

In many twentieth century nonviolent conflicts, that victory was fully earned: East Germans and Mongolians in 1989 displaced communist regimes without using violence, Filipinos defenestrated Ferdinand Marcos in 1989 without any deadly force, and African Americans desegregated public and commercial space in southern states in the 1950s and 1960s without picking up a single gun. In other conflicts, partial victories were achieved, and when nonviolent resistance was mixed with violent tactics, resistance was undermined: When Danish groups used sabotage to slow Nazi exploitation of their country, harsh reprisals came down on many citizens, and Palestinians' claim to autonomy in the *intifada* was compromised by those who threw stones and Molotov cocktails.

In some conflicts, success in defying abusive force was not sustained: The Germans who valiantly resisted French invaders in 1923 were exhausted by the cost of their strategy and by a crackdown triggered in part by their own violence; the Indians who staggered the British raj with civil disobedience in 1930-1931 gave ground at the negotiating table and waited another fifteen years for independence; and the Serbian opposition whose protests compelled Milosevic to honor local elections in 1997 was internally divided and externally not supported, enabling the president to prolong the nation's misery.

Still other movements used nonviolent action to lend momentum to long-running struggles for rights or liberty: Strikes and demonstrations in Chile in the 1980s laid the foundation for a broad opposition that changed the country through an election; and without boycotts, strikes, and other nonviolent sanctions in South Africa, apartheid would not have collapsed in 1991.

No one of the century's nonviolent campaigns offers an ideal prototype for achieving victory. But despite differences in time, place, and political milieu, they each entailed a sequence of choices about what to do and when to do it, and the skill with which those choices were made shaped the outcome. Throughout the century, taking power without using violence was often said to be impossible, until it happened—and then it was said to have been inevitable. But it was neither, not in any conflict. It was always the product of sensible decisions by shrewd leaders, on behalf of unified and persistent people—which is the everyday basis of heroism.

THE WAY TO PREVAIL

Shaping the Movement

Popular movements against established authority are as old as the modern nation-state, and in the twentieth century their use of nonviolent sanctions generated an alternative to violent rebellion as a way to overturn an unjust order. Nonviolent action is taken by individuals, but its impact is in the cumulative force of a series of sanctions—and so it requires an organization: a movement that develops and communicates clear goals to its followers and that is reasonably unified and broadly representative of the people in whose name it speaks.[4]

In December 1929, people from all over British India went to Lahore for the annual meeting of the Indian National Congress. A year before, Congress had called for India to be made an autonomous dominion within the British empire by the end of 1929. With that deadline soon to expire, Congress leaders declared that nothing less than full independence would be accepted—the first time that this popular dream was decreed as the movement's official goal. With this new, greater mission, Congress fired the imagination of those who were asked to endure the hardships of civil disobedience, which was proclaimed as the way to fight.

In Poland in August 1980, the Inter-factory Strike Committee representing workers from the Gdansk area met in a room at the Lenin Shipyard. They discussed the demands they would present to government negotiators, and all agreed that independent trade unions should be a top goal. Some wanted more: free elections and a ban on censorship. But the majority decided not to reach too far politically and to stick to goals that were worth the sacrifice of workers but also less likely to precipitate a crackdown.

Movements that set towering aims—a democratic republic in Russia in 1905, full independence in India in 1929, the ejection of the Israeli presence in the Occupied Territories—may elicit keen enthusiasm from those who join the fight. But not budging from lofty plans also may foreclose partial victories and harden adversaries, making repression more likely. Other movements in the century were self-limiting—they set goals that were short of their ultimate purpose, in order to use existing space to organize for later, further success. Thus it was in Poland in 1980. Ambitious goals, modest goals: The choice has to be realistic, for a movement must make progress before it can make history.

In September 1940 in Copenhagen, masses of people streamed into the streets of the German-occupied city to celebrate the birthday of Denmark's King Christian X. All summer hundreds of thousands had joined in songfests and other festivals, in which Danish deeds in the war against Germany eighty years before were extolled. The people were caught up in affirming their nationhood just at the moment when it came under the boot of a military invader—and without this sense of unity, the saving of Danish Jews or any later success in the Danes' wartime resistance would have been harder to achieve.

In 1989 the Mongolian Democratic Union, formed by students and intellectuals, was trying to mobilize support for its program of democratic reform. One of its leaders traveled to Erdenet, a copper mining center, and met with miners and engineers, convincing them that only political change at the top would open the way for economic gains. The next month the ranks of protestors in the capital were enlarged with workers and rural dwellers—showing the regime that the movement was attracting a popular following beyond its student leaders.

Most popular movements begin with a core of activists—the Indian National Congress, university students in San Salvador, the free trade union group in Gdansk—who rally support from other walks of life and go on to capture broad consent for their goals. That requires finding out whose support is likely and what divisions have to be bridged in order to forge a cohesive and expansive force for change. No task for a movement is more difficult. Russian lawyers and professors who made beautiful speeches in their private societies at the turn of the century, and Hindu politicians who headed the Indian National Congress twenty years later, discovered that not everyone was eager to follow them: Russian workers kept listening to militants like Trotsky who led them straight into the Tsar's crackdown, and India's Muslims and Sikhs kept largely aloof from Gandhi's campaigns. But if political cleavages could have been overcome in Russia in 1905, and if the entire subcontinent had been mobilized for civil disobedience in 1930-1931, the victories of democracy in Russia and independence in India might not have taken decades.

Controlling the Contest

Once a popular movement is in the streets and at the factory gates, once it starts to shut down business and public life—in whatever way the conflict with unjust rule is fully joined—the decisions that are taken to apply force and regulate the pace of action will dictate its effectiveness, because what is afoot is a competition based on skill, with an uncertain outcome. To shift the momentum of conflict toward its goals, a nonviolent movement has to diversify the scope and variety of its sanctions, keep the regime off balance with alert offensive moves, defend its popular base against repression, exploit any concessions, undermine the regime's claim to legitimacy, and diminish its means of retaining control. A movement has to punish the opponent for his refusal to grant its demands and minimize the punishment that it absorbs in return.

When it confronted the township revolt in 1984, the South African regime still wrongly saw apartheid's opponents as guerrilla warriors and its own action as counter-revolutionary, so the blunderbuss of repression was its method. But when township activists organized rent strikes, work stay-aways, and consumer boycotts, when African township councillors and police were condemned for cooperating with the government, and when street committees took over public functions such as sanitation and criminal justice, the movement was in too many places doing too many things for Pretoria's strategy of "taking out" key militants to work.[5]

On the West Bank and in Gaza in 1988, when the Israeli Defense Force tried to squash the *intifada,* many Palestinians did not invite physical confrontation as much as they suspended their cooperation with the Israeli administration: They withheld taxes, ignored police summonses, stayed away from jobs in Israel, refused to show identity papers, boycotted Israeli consumer products, and induced Palestinian police officers to resign. This scattered pattern of opposition partly diffused the impact of the Israeli response, and the recruitment of all kinds of Palestinians to engage in noncooperation also made it difficult for the *intifada* to be dismissed as a rebellion of hotheads.

In 1978 when Pope John Paul II returned for the first time as pontiff to his native country, the Polish people organized independently to take part in the visit, and the communist regime was pushed for the first time to the margins of a major story. Suddenly here was a new but traditional symbol of Polish singularity, an alternative emblem of national identity, and the Polish opposition rallied instinctively to its side. From then on, Solidarity members often carried the papal flag or the image of the Black Madonna of Czestochowa on marches and in strikes, borrowing a source of authority seen as higher and older than that of communism.

In February 1986, just before Ferdinand Marcos tried to rig another election to keep himself in power, 200,000 poll-watching volunteers conducted their own vote count, and the dictator's falsified returns were exposed—unraveling his last threads of legality as a political leader. In Poland and the Philippines, the rupturing of the regime's legitimacy was a turning point in the struggle to dislodge a government already disliked by the people. No longer could the state pretend that it had a popular mandate; thenceforth it would have to rely on the exhibition or use of force to work its will.

In every major twentieth century conflict in which nonviolent action made a crucial difference, the old order was known for its willingness to use repressive force to curb threats to its power. The slaughter at the Winter Palace in 1905, the Amritsar massacre in 1919, the firing squads in San Salvador in 1944, the vigilante and police brutality against blacks in the American South in the 1950s and 1960s, the Sharpeville massacre in 1960, the shooting of workers in Gdansk in 1970, the disappearances in Argentina and Chile in the 1970s, and the assassination of Benigno Aquino in 1983: These notorious incidents typified the character of rulers who were faced by the century's great nonviolent campaigns. Each movement's leaders knew, before they chose sanctions to force change, that they would very likely face violence, and how they responded played a crucial part in each conflict's outcome.

On a warm spring night in 1944 in San Salvador, student activists met to debate how to compel the country's military president to leave office. Less than a month before, General Martínez had foiled an armed insurrection and executed the ringleaders. Fabio Castillo, a medical student, argued that it would be suicide to use violence against the president—all he would do is shoot them. So they agreed to call a general strike, in which people could stay home, "so that there would not be possibilities for repression." Less than a month later, Martínez was out.[6]

In October 1905, a general strike paralyzed the railroads, utilities, and economy of Russia, offering few useful targets for rifles of the Tsar's troops. In Denmark during World War II, workers slowed down factories that produced goods for the Germans by simply leaving. In India and South Africa, rent boycotts transferred the cost of injustice to those who condoned it. In the American South and Israeli-occupied territories, businesses were boycotted to impose an economic cost for discriminatory laws or customs. And in these and other conflicts, taxes were withheld, collaborators were forced to resign their jobs, and banks that supported the regime were denied deposits.

All of these sanctions, spread across the calendar or the length of a country, can throw the weight of the people against a regime without exposing many of them to violence. Distributing nonviolent action over time and space can overstretch a regime's capacity to restrain events, limiting the reach of repression. In contrast, spontaneous or brushfire uprisings against autocratic regimes—such as the people power movement against Marcos in 1986, or the movements against the Chinese, East European, and Mongolian regimes in 1989—typically reach a single climactic showdown. Pitting the people directly against potential military action is a high-risk strategy: It can pay off in spectacular victory, as in the Philippines, or produce a devastating defeat when the regime cannot resist the opportunity to wipe out a huge concentration of its opponents, as in Tiananmen Square.

Another strategy for challenging a regime without exposing the movement to its full repressive force was seen at Dharasana and Lucknow in India and at the lunch counter sit-ins in Nashville. By training a select corps of volunteers to create high-profile protests that invite the presence of police or army units, and by deliberately committing acts that trigger the use of force, a movement can expose and dramatize the will to violence that underpins oppression, severing the regime from its remaining popular support. At the same time, such movements can also use less risky methods to confront authorities, in order to enlist the larger part of their followers in the action and widen the pressure for change.

When a regime is on the ropes, it may hold out a carrot instead of a stick—a freshet of concessions meant to damp the fire of the movement and steer it toward rapprochement rather than revolution—because in that way, it may reestablish control. In 1982, South Africa's prime minister proposed constitutional reforms to give limited voting rights to Indians and Coloureds and allow Africans more say in local affairs. But the following year, when hundreds of opposition activists met to launch the United Democratic Front, the delegates denounced the government's measures as a fraud and chanted, "We want all our rights . . . and we want them now!" The movement's leaders sensed that the people's heart for resisting the regime would not tolerate only half a loaf. The time had not yet come to talk.[7]

Sometimes rulers will open a legal process that can lead to their own undoing. In 1988 in Chile, General Pinochet went ahead with a plebiscite on whether he should be the sole candidate in an election the following year. After surviving an assassination attempt and holding off a leftist insurrection, he looked unbeatable. But the democratic opposition organized painstakingly, a constitutional tribunal took poll-watching seriously, and the general lost. The movement, divided and uncertain though it was, risked lending credibility to the dictator's own procedures to have the chance of building momentum for the continued struggle. Nullifying the people's cooperation with a dictator is a prerequisite for victory, but making practical use of new room to operate, when it is handed to the movement, does not compromise that strategy.

When the last leaf of a regime's legitimacy drops to the ground, when its concessions fail to soften the conflict or co-opt its opponents, and when repression can no longer disable the nonviolent force arrayed against it, the government's power to coerce begins to ebb. Then the conflict that may have begun as a skirmish with a few annoying dissidents becomes a battle for its very life.

Forcing the Outcome

Renato Chavez was a Filipino mason who joined the people power revolt against Ferdinand Marcos in 1986. The night after the dictator fled the country, he was among the first who burst through the doors of Malacanang Palace, the president's residence, where he wandered from one chandeliered room to another. When Chavez entered the library, there was a bowl of fresh grapes on a table, so recently had the palace been abandoned. He ate every one. Marcos had not left on his own schedule; he had been pushed from power.[8]

A mass nonviolent movement can force a favorable outcome in one of three ways: by coercing a ruler to surrender power or leave; by inducing a regime to compromise and make concessions; or by converting the regime's view of the conflict, so that it believes it should no longer dictate the result. The vulnerabilities of the movement's opponent are different in each case, presenting different opportunities—giving the movement a chance to control the mental contest before it takes control of the physical fight. Martínez and Marcos were given no quarter; they were driven out by movements that used nonviolent sanctions to end their dominance of public life and to alienate the crucial support of their military high commands and foreign friends.

In 1931, aware that he could not expect all his adherents to sustain civil disobedience indefinitely, and persuaded that his campaign might already have converted the viceroy to a larger wisdom about Indian demands, Gandhi agreed to negotiate with Lord Irwin to end the campaign. But Gandhi accepted terms that disappointed many, the movement was riven along ethnic lines, and energy drained from his followers. Moreover, the world was not yet a closely knit economic and media community: Pictures of repression in Calcutta did not deter the buyers of British coal—the raj had a bigger margin for error. Only years later, when the British empire lost its cadence at the center, did India break away.

But unwillingness to compromise also can derail the ride to power. In Russia in 1905, when the October general strike forced the Tsar to issue a manifesto promising a parliament and other reforms, it was rejected by the less moderate elements of the movement opposing him. By the end of the year, when an insurrection was fomented in the streets, it was pulverized by the Tsar's troops. Had those who fought for the people taken what the Tsar had offered and used it to reinforce the zone of opposition to autocracy, they would not have ceded the initiative back to Nicholas and his men in the long-term struggle for power in Russia.

When Bulgarian and Mongolian communists saw the streets and squares of their capital cities filling with people demanding democracy, and their colleagues in the Soviet bloc falling like dominoes, they decided that professing democracy was not such a bad idea: They converted to the process of change, so as not to be consumed by it. However impersonal an autocratic regime may seem, its decision makers can be demoralized, and they do not neglect their own survival as they choose their options. In Poland in 1988, faced with a new cycle of economic decline and labor strife, General Jaruzelski turned to Solidarity to help restore political stability. But the roundtable talks that followed led to an election that collapsed communist power. For movements that are flexible, the finale is no less glorious even if it does not come explosively.

There is no single straw that breaks the back of an authoritarian regime, but as the twentieth century wound down, the vise of change closed more often on rulers who suppressed the people's rights. Between the hard fact that a country is becoming ungovernable and the hard conditions imposed by international pressure geared to favor democratic change, arbitrary rulers are presented with a dilemma: As they are reduced to the sole option of repression, it becomes less effective in constraining the opposition. Disorder within and disaffection abroad are a lethal cocktail. Azhar Cachalia, a political activist in the South African Indian community, said that the power of the movement against apartheid was very simple: "They can't govern without us."[9]

Nonviolent resistance becomes a force more powerful than the hand of an oppressor to the extent that it takes away his capacity for control. Embracing nonviolence for its own sake does not produce this force. A strategy for action is needed, and that strategy has to involve attainable goals, movement unity, and robust sanctions that restrict the opponent. To shift the momentum of conflict in its favor, the nonviolent movement has to expand the scope and variety of its offensive action, defend its popular base against repression, pierce the legitimacy of its adversary, and exploit his weaknesses and concessions. When all this happens, an oppressor inevitably loses support inside and outside his country, and his means of repression or terror can be unfastened. When the regime realizes that it can no longer dictate the outcome, the premise and means of its power implode. Then the end is only a matter of time.

DEMOCRACY AND POWER

On the first morning of the strike in the Lenin Shipyard in Gdansk, in August 1980, twenty-two-year old Jerzy Borowczak and his fellow strike leaders convinced workers in several shops to lay down their tools. At one point they approached Gate No. 2, and some people shouted that they should march out into the city, to the communist party headquarters, as strikers had done ten years before. Borowczak asked them to wait first and observe a moment of silence for the workers who had been killed in 1970 when they marched downtown. After they sang the national anthem, he pleaded with them not to repeat that tragic history but stay and help occupy the shipyard. Few of them knew who Borowczak was, but nobody left the shipyard.

Popular movements are not armies, and their leaders are not generals who issue orders and expect obedient battalions to carry them out. Movements are participatory, not hierarchical—their ranks are full of those who join on their own volition, because they believe in what the movement stands for. Jerzy Borowczak, thrust into the center of events, could not demand that people follow him. He could only try to persuade them to do what he thought was best and then rely on their own emerging sense that his direction was sound. Once the great general strikes of October 1905 in Russia and May 1944 in El Salvador began, their accelerating force was not eloquent speeches from remote leaders but the commonplace words and strenuous work of tens of thousands of ordinary people.

Of course leadership is vital. Civil disobedience in India without Gandhi would have been inconceivable—but even Gandhi was not slavishly obeyed. In Gujarat in March 1930, Gandhi argued with Ashabhai Patel, a local leader who had convinced villagers to withhold rent payments—going against Gandhi's desire that civil disobedience be limited to breaking the salt law. Yet Patel would not be dissuaded, and a long struggle against state rent collectors went forward and rallied thousands to the larger cause.

If the cost of a movement based on persuasion rather than coercion is occasional freelance action by impetuous followers, the larger benefit is a movement that distributes initiative to its farthest outpost. Movements that expect people to take the personal risks inherent in nonviolent action have no alternative; they have to become what they want their country to become: open in form and democratic in function. Authoritarian governments can breed apathy in all but those who have acute grievances or an unquenchable thirst to speak the truth. When this truth is out, and when a nonviolent movement devolves authority to ordinary people, it can summon far more devotion than any dictator or armed minority.

Just as a free economy tends to reward entrepreneurs, the freewheeling community of a nonviolent movement and the civilian society in which it breathes can open up space in which imaginative action against the state is rewarded by a surprising ability to withstand repression. When Adam Michnik and Jacek Kuron realized they could not mount a frontal attack on the monolithic communist state, they and their colleagues in the Polish opposition in the 1970s opted to resist the state by ignoring it—by taking private action to help dissident workers and publish underground newspapers and books. This kind of action may not bring down a government in a year or even a decade, but it plants freedom right inside the hothouse of autocratic power—it does the work of democracy before democracy can open for business.

One school of thought believes that newly liberated countries with little democratic experience will have a hard time holding to that course; thus, supposedly, the political turbulence in Russia in the 1990s. It may be that if an earlier government was democratic—as in the Philippines—the aftermath of authoritarian rule can be easier. But Poland's stability after the failure of communism hardly suggests that dictatorship enervates the readiness for democracy. And other cases suggest that if the channel to democracy has been navigated with the pilot of a nonviolent movement at its helm, the nation's ability to sustain democracy will be greater than if no strategy for popular resistance has led the way.

India's independence was thirty years in the making, and violence was never part of Gandhi's strategy to achieve it. In the land of the Czechs, a generation of nonviolent dissidence set the stage for popular ferment demanding democracy. The movement that removed a military junta from power in Chile used democratic tools to do it. At the century's end, all of these countries were vibrant democracies. In the nonviolent movements that delivered change there and elsewhere, the elements of democratic skill could easily be discerned: building coalitions, leading by persuasion rather than fiat, and creating civic space through private action regardless of state approval. When the control of public life moves from the palace to the people, the location of a nation's sovereignty moves with it.

In the twentieth century, those who reclaimed that sovereignty, the men and women who marched and boycotted and occupied factories and streets—through the great nonviolent conflicts on every continent, against every kind of adversary—retrieved their consent from rulers who had disdained their rights. Henry David Thoreau, in his celebrated manifesto in 1848, "On Civil Disobedience," rebuked Americans for cooperating with a government that protected slavery. He hailed "the right to refuse allegiance to and to resist the government" when it sponsored tyranny, and he argued that if 1,000 people refused to pay their tax bills to restrain the state from violence, that would be "the definition of a peaceable revolution."[10]

A half century later Leo Tolstoy wrote that Thoreau had "specially influenced" him, and in 1909 Gandhi wrote to Tolstoy as "an utter stranger," asking his permission to republish one of his essays. In his preface to that reprint, Gandhi restated Tolstoy's message: "An oppressor's efforts will be in vain if we refuse to submit to his tyranny." The next year Gandhi again wrote Tolstoy, who replied that nonviolent resistance "is a question of the greatest importance not only for India but for the whole [of] humanity." In a final letter to Gandhi in September 1910, as Tolstoy felt himself "approaching death," he showed that he sensed in Gandhi's words and actions something that might be large enough to redeem his own hopes, blasted in Russia but burning brightly still in his heart, for a decisive shift away from violent conflict in human affairs: "your work in Transvaal, which seems to be far away from the centre of the world, is yet the most fundamental and the most important to us, supplying the most weighty practical proof in which the world can now share."[11]

In the century only then beginning, the world shared fully in that proof; but as the century ended, violence was undeniably the great remaining, dramatic evil in the affairs of nations and mass societies, in the form of terrorism, genocide, sectarian strife, and episodic acts by haters and extremists. Its use continues to be promiscuous, even as its record in effecting change is so dismal—suggesting that an old assumption about power is ready to expire.

In her peerless essay, "On Violence," Hannah Arendt argued that violence is "utterly incapable" of creating power—that it "does not promote causes, neither history nor revolution, neither progress nor reaction." In this she chose to refute the favorite nostrum of many would-be revolutionaries, distilled by Mao Zedong in his famous aphorism, "power grows out of the barrel of a gun," which could as easily have been a line from Hitler's *Mein Kampf.* But the same century that saw so much violence also saw the collapse of the authoritarian idea; absolute violence, or the threat of its use, did not guarantee absolute power.[12]

Violence is a tool of the state or of armed bands, Arendt taught, able for a time to instill fear, invite submission, or destroy lives and property but not able to endow its users with the legitimacy and consent they would require to keep their authority and position. In the stability and endurance of democracies she saw a superior idea of power, quite ancient in its derivation: "When . . . the Romans spoke of the *civitas* as their form of government, they had in mind a concept of power and law whose essence did not rely on the command-obedience relationship." The men of the great eighteenth century political revolutions resurrected this idea in constituting republics, "where the rule of law, resting on the power of the people, would put an end to the rule of man over man."[13]

People power in the twentieth century did not grow out of the barrel of a gun. It removed rulers who believed that violence was power, by acting to dissolve their real source of power: the consent or acquiescence of the people they had tried to subordinate. When unjust laws were no longer obeyed, when commerce stopped because people no longer worked, when public services could no longer function, and when armies were no longer feared, the violence that governments could use no longer mattered—their power to make people comply had disappeared.

One hundred years ago the map of the world was dominated by empires and monarchies. At the beginning of the twenty-first century, the continents are filled with republics. It is said that the Emperor Claudius yearned to revive the Roman republic but knew that his enemies would never let him try it. Today the spirit of the old Roman *civitas* has become the universal standard—and, with a few exceptions, its enemies are gone. Gone, too, will soon be their ideas about power.

NOTES

ACKNOWLEDGMENTS

1. V. S. Pritchett, *The Pritchett Century* (New York: The Modern Library, 1997), p. 649.

INTRODUCTION

1. Lech Walesa, videotaped interview by Tom Weidlinger for the documentary television series, *A Force More Powerful,* Gdansk, September 28,1998.
2. Peter Ackerman and Christopher Kruegler, *Strategic Nonviolent Conflict: The Dynamics of People Power in the Twentieth Century* (Westport, CT: Praeger Publishers, 1994), p. 6.
3. *The Gandhi Reader,* ed. Homer Jack (New York: Grove Press, 1994), pp. 313-316.
4. Gene Sharp, "The Role of Power in Nonviolent Struggle," Monograph Series, No. 3, The Albert Einstein Institution, 1990, p. 18.

CHAPTER ONE

1. *V Avguste 91-go: Rossiia Glazami Ochevidtsev* (Moscow: Limbus-Press, 1993), p. 14.
2. Victoria Bonnell, Ann Cooper, et al., *Russia at the Barricades: Eyewitness Accounts of the August 1991 Coup* (Armonk, NY: M. E. Sharpe, 1994); these and other details of the abortive coup attempt in the following paragraphs are drawn from this source.
3. David Remnick, *Lenin's Tomb: The Last Days of the Soviet Empire* (New York: Random House, 1993), p. 467.
4. *V Avguste,* p. 14-15.
5. Quote from Walter Sablinsky, *The Road to Bloody Sunday: Father Gapon and the St. Petersburg Massacre of 1905* (Princeton, NJ: Princeton University Press, 1976), p. 239; *Nachalo Pervoi Russkoi Revoliutsii* (Moscow: Izdatel'stvo AN SSSR, 1955), No. 62.
6. Sablinsky, *Road to Bloody Sunday,* pp. 346-349.
7. Orlando Figes, *A People's Tragedy: The Russian Revolution, 1891-1924* (London: Jonathan Cape, 1996), pp. 6- 7.
8. Jeremiah Schneiderman, *Sergei Zubatov and Revolutionary Marxism: The Struggle for the Working Class in Tsarist Russia* (Ithaca, NY: Cornell University Press, 1976), pp. 78-82, 191-192; Victoria Bonnell, *Roots of Rebellion: Workers' Politics and Organizations in St. Petersburg and Moscow, 1900-1914* (Berkeley: University of California Press, 1983), pp. 80-85.
9. Gerald D. Surh, *1905 in St. Petersburg: Labor, Society and Revolution* (Stanford, CA: Stanford University Press, 1989), pp. 10-18, 24.
10. N. M. Varnashev, "Ot Nachala do Kontsa s Gaponovskoi Organizatsiei (Vospominaniia)," in *Istoriko-revoliutsionnyi Sbornik,* ed. V. I. Nevskii (Leningrad: Gos. Izdatel'stvo, 1924), pp. 177-180.
11. Ibid.
12. Schneiderman, *Sergei Zubatov,* pp. 49-68.
13. Quote from Sablinsky, *Road to Bloody Sunday,* p. 47; Surh, *1905 in St. Petersburg,* p. 115.
14. Surh, *1905 in St. Petersburg,* pp. 110-111.
15. "They got to" quote from ibid., p. 109; "Essentially the basic" quote from Sablinsky, *Road to Bloody Sunday,* p. 85.
16. Varnashev, "Ot Nachala do Kontsa," pp. 191, 193-4, 200; Surh, *1905 in St. Petersburg,* p. 111.

17. Quote from Varnashev, "Ot Nachala do Kontsa," p. 195; Surh, *1905 in St. Petersburg*, pp. 116-117; Abraham Ascher, *The Revolution of 1905 in Russia*, Vol. 1 (Stanford, CA: Stanford University Press, 1988), pp. 80-81.
18. Varnashev, "Ot Nachala do Kontsa," pp. 196-197; Surh, *1905 in St. Petersburg*, p. 118.
19. Quote from Surh, *1905 in St. Petersburg*, p. 121; Varnashev, "Ot Nachala do Kontsa," p. 198.
20. Surh, *1905 in St. Petersburg*, pp. 102-103.
21. Shmuel Galai, *The Liberation Movement in Russia, 1900-1915* (Cambridge: Cambridge University Press, 1973), p. 190.
22. Andrew M. Verner, *The Crisis of Russian Autocracy: Nicholas II and the 1905 Revolution* (Princeton, NJ: Princeton University Press, 1990), p. 109.
23. Surh, *1905 in St. Petersburg*, pp. 125-127.
24. In Figes, *People's Tragedy*, p. 172.
25. Surh, *1905 in St. Petersburg*, pp. 127-131.
26. Verner, *Crisis of Russian Autocracy*, pp. 110-111, 117-119, 122, 128-129.
27. Ibid., pp. 139-140, 143.
28. Quote from Varnashev, "Ot Nachala do Kontsa," pp. 198, 200; Surh, *1905 in St. Petersburg*, pp. 139-142; Sablinsky, *Road to Bloody Sunday*, p. 110.
29. Quote is translated in Sablinsky, *Road to Bloody Sunday*, p. 135; Varnashev, "Ot Nachala do Kontsa," pp. 201-202.
30. Surh, *1905 in St. Petersburg*, pp. 147-151.
31. Ibid., pp. 155-157.
32. Ibid., pp. 148, 158-159.
33. Sablinsky, *Road to Bloody Sunday*, pp. 346-348.
34. Varnashev, "Ot Nachala do Kontsa," pp. 204-205.
35. Surh, *1905 in St. Petersburg*, pp. 161-162.
36. Quote from Sablinsky, *Road to Bloody Sunday*, p. 205; Verner, *Crisis of Russian Autocracy*, pp. 149-152; Surh, *1905 in St. Petersburg*, pp. 159-160.
37. Varnashev, "Ot Nachala do Kontsa," pp. 206-207.
38. Quote from Varnashev, "Ot Nachala do Kontsa," p. 206; Sablinsky, *Road to Bloody Sunday*," pp. 221-222.
39. Varnashev, "Ot Nachala do Kontsa,", pp. 207-208.
40. Sablinsky, *Road to Bloody Sunday*, pp. 241-242.
41. Ibid., pp. 249-252.
42. Figes, *People's Tragedy*, p. 178.
43. Ibid., p. 278.
44. Surh, *1905 in St. Petersburg*, pp. 177, 198-199.
45. Verner, *Crisis of Russian Autocracy*, pp. 159-161, 163-164.
46. Vladimir Andrle, *A Social History of Twentieth-Century Russia* (London: Edward Arnold, 1994), p. 107; Surh, *1905 in St. Petersburg*, pp. 181, 183-184,
47. Ascher, *Revolution of 1905*, p. 169; John Bushnell, *Mutiny Amid Repression* (Bloomington: Indiana University Press, 1985), pp. 54-56.
48. Ascher, *Revolution of 1905*, pp. 168-169.
49. Teodor Shanin, *Russia, 1905-07: Revolution as a Moment of Truth* (Basingstoke: Macmillan, 1986), pp. 89-92.
50. Ibid., pp. 104-106; Ascher, *Revolution of 1905*, pp. 153-154.
51. From Ascher, *Revolution of 1905*, p. 165.
52. Ibid., pp. 146-149.
53. Ibid., pp. 170-173.
54. Bonnell, *Roots of Rebellion*, p. 122, 128-130; Surh, *1905 in St. Petersburg*, pp. 275-277.
55. Ascher, *Revolution of 1905*, pp. 142-144; 166-167.
56. Surh, *1905 in St. Petersburg*, pp. 225-226, 261-262, 266.
57. Ibid., p. 258.
58. Verner, *Crisis of Russian Autocracy*, pp. 213-214.
59. Mark D. Steinberg, *Moral Communities: The Culture of Class in the Russian Printing Industry* (Berkeley: University of California Press, 1992), p. 178.
60. "Our peaceful economic" quote from Laura Engelstein, *Moscow, 1905; Working-Class Organization and Political Conflict* (Stanford, CA: Stanford University Press, 1982), p. 95; "only when the entire people" quote from Steinberg, *Moral Communities*, p. 179.
61. Sergei Witte, *The Memoirs of Count Witte*, trans. and ed. Sidney Harcave (Armonk, NY: M.E. Sharpe, 1990), p. 404.

62. Ascher, *Revolution of 1905*, pp. 196-201, 203-204; Surh, *1905 in St. Petersburg*, pp. 295-303.
63. Surh, *1905 in St. Peterburg*, pp. 310-311.
64. Ascher, *Revolution of 1905*, pp. 212-213; Henry Reichman, *Railwaymen and Revolution: Russia, 1905* (Berkeley: University of California Press, 1987), pp. 194-196.
65. Reichman, *Railwaymen and Revolution*, pp. 197-201, 217-218.
66. Surh, *1905 in St. Petersburg*, pp. 319-320; Reichman, *Railwaymen and Revolution*, pp. 205-206, 210-211.
67. Engelstein, *Moscow, 1905*, pp. 112, 116-122.
68. Ascher, *Revolution of 1905*, p. 215.
69. Engelstein, *Moscow, 1905*, pp. 130-131.
70. Ascher, *Revolution of 1905*, pp. 215-218; Verner, *Crisis of Russian Autocracy*, p. 226.
71. Quote from N. M. Nemtsov, "Na Metallicheskom Zavode Rasteriaeva," in *Istoriia Soveta Rabochikh-deputatov v S-Peterburge* (St. Petersburg: Izdatelstvo N. Glagoleva, nd.), pp. 271-272; Surh, *1905 in St. Petersburg*, pp. 319-323.
72. Surh, *1905 in St. Petersburg*, pp. 322-323.
73. D. Sverchkov, *Na Zare Revoliutsii*, Moscow, 1921, pp. 96-98.
74. Ascher, *Revolution of 1905*, pp. 220-221; Surh, *1905 in St. Petersburg*, pp. 328-329.
75. Sverchkov, *Na Zare Revoliutsii*, pp. 100-101.
76. G. Khrustalev-Nosar', "Istoriia Soveta Rabochikh," in *Istoriia Soveta Rabochikh-deputatov v S-Peterburge*, pp. 73-74.
77. Surh, *1905 in St. Petersburg*, pp. 332-334, 342-343; Leon Trotsky, *1905*, trans. Anya Bostock (New York: Random House, 1971), pp. 140-143.
78. Henry Nevinson, *The Dawn in Russia* (London: Harper and Brothers, 1906), pp. 25-29.
79. Verner, *Crisis of Russian Autocracy*, pp. 226-234.
80. "[I]n an utter fool's paradise" quote from ibid., p. 227; "I have ordered" quote from Surh, *1905 in St. Petersburg*, p. 323.
81. Ascher, *Revolution of 1905*, p. 223; Engelstein, *Moscow, 1905*, pp. 126-127, 131-132.
82. Verner, *Crisis of Russian Autocracy*, pp. 228-232.
83. Ibid., p. 240.
84. Quote from Verner, *Crisis of Russian Autocracy*, p. 240; Witte, *Memoirs*, pp. 485-486.
85. Ascher, *Revolution of 1905*, pp. 228-229.
86. Ibid., pp. 229-231.
87. Trotsky, *1905*, pp. 116-117.
88. Ascher, *Revolution of 1905*, pp. 253-256, 262; Engelstein, *Moscow, 1905*, pp. 139-141; Surh, *1905 in St. Petersburg*, p. 340.
89. Trotsky, *1905*, p. 123.
90. Nemtsov, "Na Metallicheskom," p. 273; Surh, *1905 in St. Petersburg*, p. 396; Nevinson, *Dawn in Russia*, p. 62.
91. Shanin, *Russia, 1905-07*, pp. 110-111.
92. Bushnell, *Mutiny*, pp. 76, 83-85, 92-93, 108.
93. Ascher, *Revolution of 1905*, p. 275.
94. Ibid., pp. 239-241.
95. Verner, *Crisis of Russian Autocracy*, pp. 260-264.
96. Witte, *Memoirs*, p. 404.
97. Surh, *1905 in St. Petersburg*, p. 347.
98. Ibid., pp. 368-369.
99. Ibid., pp. 350-351, 371-372.
100. W. S. Woytinsky, *Stormy Passage* (New York: Vanguard Press, 1961), pp. 15-16.
101. Quote from V. I. Lenin, *Collected Works*, vol. 8 (Moscow: Progress Publishers, 1977), p. 99; Bushnell, *Mutiny*, p. 63.
102. Quote from Ascher, *Revolution of 1905*, p. 84; Surh, *1905 in St. Petersburg*, pp. 264, 294, 327-328.
103. Quotes from Surh, *1905 in St. Petersburg*, pp. 342-343; Ascher, *Revolution of 1905*, pp. 285-286.
104. Nemtsov, "Na Metallicheskom," p. 275; Surh, *1905 in St. Petersburg*, p. 354.
105. Verner, *Crisis of Russian Autocracy*, p. 270-271; Surh, *1905 in St. Petersburg*, pp. 398-401; Engelstein, *Moscow, 1905*, p. 179.
106. Ascher, *Revolution of 1905*, pp. 299-300.
107. Trotsky, *1905*, pp. 231-233.
108. Ascher, *Revolution of 1905*, pp. 307, 313.
109. Engelstein, *Moscow, 1905*, pp. 191-193; Ascher, *Revolution of 1905*, pp. 307-314.
110. Engelstein, *Moscow, 1905*, pp. 202-208.

111. Quote from Ascher, *Revolution of 1905*, p. 320; ibid., pp. 219-220.

112. Engelstein, *Moscow, 1905*, pp. 220-221; Ascher, *Revolution of 1905*, pp. 322-324.

113. "Terror must be" quote from Verner, *Crisis of Russian Autocracy*, p. 275; "decisively" quote and "insurgents be annihilated" quote from Ascher, *1905 in St. Petersburg*, pp. 328, 334.

114. *Tolstoy's Letters*, vol. 2, ed. R. F. Christian (New York: Charles Scribner's Sons, 1978), p. 659.

115. Leo Tolstoy, *The Kingdom of God Is Within You* (New York: Farrar, Straus and Giroux, 1961), p. 265.

CHAPTER TWO

1. Gene Sharp, *Gandhi as a Political Strategist* (Boston: P. Sargent Publishers, 1979), p. 29.

2. Ibid., pp. 26-32.

3. Ibid., pp. 29, 38.

4. Judith Brown, *Gandhi: Prisoner of Hope* (New Haven, CT: Yale University Press, 1989), pp. 22-28; Antony Copley, *Gandhi Against the Tide* (Oxford: Blackwell, 1987), pp. 3-9, 15-16.

5. Brown, *Gandhi: Prisoner of Hope*, p. 31; Copley, *Gandhi Against the Tide*, pp. 17-19.

6. Brown, *Gandhi: Prisoner of Hope*, pp. 31-32; B. R. Nanda, *Mahatma Gandhi* (Bombay: Allied Publishers, 1968), pp. 48-50.

7. Quote from Brown, *Gandhi: Prisoner of Hope*, p. 32; Copley, *Gandhi Against the Tide*, p. 21; Nanda, *Mahatma Gandhi*, pp. 37-38.

8. Brown, *Gandhi: Prisoner of Hope*, pp. 36, 44-45; Copley, *Gandhi Against the Tide*, pp. 22-23.

9. Brown, *Gandhi: Prisoner of Hope* pp. 56-57; Copley, *Gandhi Against the Tide*, pp. 25-27; Dennis Dalton, *Mahatma Gandhi: Nonviolent Power in Action* (New York: Columbia University Press, 1993), p. 14; Nanda, *Mahatma Gandhi*, pp. 93-119.

10. Brown, *Gandhi: Prisoner of Hope*, pp. 17-18, 76-77, 81.

11. Quote from *The Gandhi Reader*, ed. Homer Jack (New York: Grove Press, 1994), p. 37; Brown, *Gandhi: Prisoner of Hope*, pp. 78-89, 84; Dalton, *Mahatma Gandhi*, pp. 10-11; Bhikhu Parekh, *Colonialism, Tradition, and Reform: An Analysis of Gandhi's Political Discourse* (New Delhi: Sage, 1989), p. 156.

12. Dalton, *Mahatma Gandhi*, p. 9.

13. Brown, *Gandhi: Prisoner of Hope*, pp. 55-57; Dalton, *Mahatma Gandhi*, pp. 9, 14-16; Bhikhu Parekh, *Gandhi's Political Philosophy* (Basingstoke: Macmillan, 1989), pp. 55-57.

14. Parekh, *Gandhi's Political Philosophy*, p. 153.

15. Ibid., pp. 153-158.

16. Parekh, *Colonialism*, pp. 134-136.

17. Gandhi, M.K., *Hind Swaraj and Other Writings* (Cambridge: Cambridge University Press, 1986), pp. xiv, xxvii.

18. Ibid., p. 73.

19. Ibid., pp. 28-32, 66-71, 74; Parekh, *Gandhi's Political Philosophy*, pp. 45-55.

20. Brown, *Gandhi: Prisoner of Hope*, pp. 40-42, 82-86.

21. Judith Brown, *Modern India: The Origins of an Asian Democracy*, 2nd ed. (Oxford: Oxford University Press, 1994), pp. 44, 47.

22. Ibid., pp. 67-70.

23. Ibid., pp. 93, 139.

24. Ibid., pp. 139, 148-150; quote from Sharp, *Gandhi as a Political Strategist*, p. 45.

25. Sumit Sarkar, *Modern India* (Basingstoke: Macmillan, 1989), p. 66.

26. Jim Masselos, *Indian Nationalism: An History* (New Delhi: Sterling Publishers, 1985), pp. 84-98; Sarkar, *Modern India*, pp. 88-92.

27. Sarkar, *Modern India*, p. 100.

28. Zareer Masani, *Indian Tales of the Raj* (Berkeley: University of California Press, 1987), pp. 23-24.

29. Judith Brown, *Modern India: The Origins of an Asian Democracy*, pp. 195-207; Sarkar, *Modern India*, pp. 149-153, 169-171.

30. *The Collected Works of Mahatma Gandhi*, vol. 14 (New Delhi: Publications Division, Ministry of Information and Broadcasting, 1971), pp. 56-61.

31. Quote from Dalton, *Mahatma Gandhi*, p. 54; Brown, *Gandhi: Prisoner of Hope*, pp. 210-212.

32. Brown, *Gandhi: Prisoner of Hope*, pp. 203-204, 206.

33. Ibid., pp. 100, 106, 199.

34. Ibid., pp. 109-112, 114-121; Dalton, *Mahatma Gandhi*, pp. 27-28; Sarkar, *Modern India*, pp. 183-187.

35. Brown, *Gandhi: Prisoner of Hope,* p. 129.
36. Ibid.
37. Stanley Wolpert, *A New History of India,* 5th ed. (New York: Oxford University Press, 1997), p. 299; Helen Fein, *Imperial Crime and Punishment: The Massacre at Jallianwala Bagh and British Judgement, 1919-1920* (Honolulu: University of Hawaii Press, 1977), p. 20.
38. Helen Fein, *Imperial Crime and Punishment,* pp. 35-36, 40-43.
39. Masani, *Indian Tales,* p. 112.
40. "[W]hitewash" quote from Brown, *Gandhi: Prisoner of Hope,* p. 144; "satanic" quote from ibid., p. 140; "dishonest" quote from Brown, *Modern India,* p. 221.
41. Brown, *Gandhi: Prisoner of Hope,* p. 162; Sarkar, *Modern India,* p. 226.
42. Brown, *Gandhi: Prisoner of Hope,* p. 163.
43. Judith Brown, *Gandhi and Civil Disobedience* (Cambridge: Cambridge University Press, 1977), pp. 160-164; Sarkar, *Modern India,* pp. 204-205.
44. Sarkar, *Modern India,* pp. 208-221.
45. Quotes from Brown, *Gandhi: Prisoner of Hope,* p. 166; Sarkar, *Modern India,* pp. 216-217, 223.
46. Brown, *Gandhi: Prisoner of Hope,* p. 168.
47. Shahid Amin, "Gandhi as Mahatma: Gorakhpur District, Eastern U.P. , 1921-2." In *Selected Subaltern Studies,* ed. Ranajit Guha and Gayatri Chakravarty Spivak (New York: Oxford University Press, 1988), pp. 294, 339-341; Brown, *Gandhi: Prisoner of Hope,* pp. 167-169.
48. Brown, *Gandhi: Prisoner of Hope,* pp. 182-184.
49. Brown, *Modern India,* p. 231.
50. Quote from Brown, *Gandhi: Prisoner of Hope,* p. 217; Sarkar, *Modern India,* pp. 265-266.
51. Brown, *Gandhi: Prisoner of Hope,* pp. 214, 218-219, 222-223.
52. Ibid., p. 214.
53. Brown, *Gandhi: Prisoner of Hope,* pp. 219-220; Dhangare, D.N. *Peasant Movements in India, 1920-1950* (Delhi: Oxford University Press, 1983), pp. 90, 93-101; Sarkar, *Modern India,* pp. 277-278.
54. Brown, *Gandhi: Prisoner of Hope,* p. 221.
55. Brown, *Gandhi and Civil Disobedience,* pp. 49-51; Tanika Sarkar, *Bengal 1928-1934* (Delhi: Oxford University Press, 1987), p. 21.
56. Brown, *Gandhi and Civil Disobedience,* pp. 51-53; Gyanendra Pandey, *The Ascendancy of Congress in Uttar Pradesh, 1926-1934* (Princeton, NJ: Princeton University Press, 1984), pp. 39-40, 76-84.
57. Brown, *Gandhi and Civil Disobedience,* pp. 53-57, 59; Sarkar, *Bengal,* pp. 20-26.
58. Brown, *Gandhi and Civil Disobedience,* pp. 47-48; Dalton, *Mahatma Gandhi,* pp. 119-121; Pandey, *Ascendancy of Congress,* pp. 117-144; Sarkar, *Modern India,* p. 235.
59. Sarkar, *Modern India,* pp. 267-274.
60. Brown, *Gandhi and Civil Disobedience,* pp. 43-47; Aloo Dastur, videotaped interview by Steve York for the documentary television series *A Force More Powerful,* Bombay, September 1, 1998.
61. Brown, *Gandhi and Civil Disobedience,* p. 58.
62. Dalton, *Mahatma Gandhi,* p. 105.
63. Brown, *Gandhi and Civil Disobedience,* pp. 61-63.
64. Ibid., pp. 64-73.
65. Ibid., p. 76.
66. Ibid., pp. 81-83; Sarkar, *Modern India,* p. 284.
67. Quote from Peter Ackerman and Christopher Kruegler. *Strategic Nonviolent Conflict: The Dynamics of People Power in the Twentieth* Century (Westport, CT: Praeger, 1994), p. 169; Brown, *Gandhi and Civil Disobedience,* pp. 90-91.
68. Brown, *Gandhi and Civil Disobedience,* pp. 88-89.
69. Ibid.
70. Dalton, *Mahatma Gandhi,* p. 100.
71. Brown, *Gandhi and Civil Disobedience,* pp. 94-96; Dalton, *Mahatma Gandhi,* pp. 99-101.
72. Brown, *Gandhi and Civil Disobedience,* pp. 92-93; Sarkar, *Modern India,* pp. 284-285.
73. Ackerman and Kruegler, *Strategic Nonviolent Conflict,* pp. 171-172; Dalton, *Mahatma Gandhi,* pp. 105-107.
74. "At present" quote from Sarkar, *Modern India,* p. 284; "Reduce us" quote from Brown, *Gandhi and Civil Disobedience,* p. 60.
75. Brown, *Gandhi and Civil Disobedience,* pp. 60, 97; quote from D. A. Low, "Civil Martial Law: The Government of India and the Civil Disobedience Movements, 1930-1934," in *Congress and the Raj,* ed. D. A. Low (London: Arnold-Heinemann, 1977), p. 167.
76. Brown, *Gandhi and Civil Disobedience,* p. 97; quote from Low, "Civil Martial Law," p. 168.
77. Brown, *Gandhi and Civil Disobedience,* p. 97; Dalton, *Mahatma Gandhi,* p. 101-102.

78. Dalton, *Mahatma Gandhi,* pp. 103-104; Geraldine Forbes, *Women in Modern India* (Cambridge: Cambridge University Press, 1996), p. 132.

79. Dalton, *Mahatma Gandhi,* pp. 104-105, 107-108.

80. "This is a battle" quote in Dalton, *Mahatma Gandhi,* p. 108; "This fight" quote from *Collected Works of Mahatma Gandhi,* vol. 43, p. 60; Desai quote in Dalton, *Mahatma Gandhi,* p. 109.

81. "Poor man's battle" quote from Brown, *Gandhi and Civil Disobedience,* p. 101; "The appeal" quote from *Collected Works of Mahatma Gandhi,* vol. 43, pp. 150-153, 312-313; "inhuman" quote from Dalton, *Mahatma Gandhi,* p. 112.

82. Brown, *Gandhi and Civil Disobedience,* p. 101; quote from Dalton, *Mahatma Gandhi,* p. 111.

83. Brown, *Gandhi and Civil Disobedience,* pp. 104-105; Dalton, *Mahatma Gandhi,* p. 113.

84. Padamsee quote from Alyque Padamsee, videotaped interview by Steve York for the documentary television series *A Force More Powerful,* Bombay, September 2, 1998; Brown, *Gandhi and Civil Disobedience,* pp. 103, 105; Dalton, *Mahatma Gandhi,* pp. 107-108.

85. Dalton, *Mahatma Gandhi,* p. 114.

86. Brown, *Gandhi and Civil Disobedience,* p. 106; Dalton, *Mahatma Gandhi,* p. 115.

87. Quote from Ackerman and Kruegler, *Strategic Nonviolent Conflict,* p. 173; Brown, *Gandhi and Civil Disobedience,* pp. 112-113, 115.

88. Ackerman and Kruegler, *Strategic Nonviolent Conflict,* p. 180.

89. Dalton, *Mahatma Gandhi,* p. 112.

90. Ackerman and Kruegler, *Strategic Nonviolent Conflict,* pp. 180-181.

91. Ibid., pp. 181-183.

92. *Collected Works of Mahatma Gandhi,* vol. 43, pp. 135-137.

93. Veena Taiwar Oldenburg, *The Making of Colonial Lucknow, 1856-1877* (Princeton, NJ: Princeton University Press, 1984), pp. 23-26, 34, 44, 52-56; account of Lucknow events drawn from D. A. Low, *Britain and Indian Nationalism: The Imprint of Ambiguity 1929-1942* (Cambridge: Cambridge University Press, 1997), pp. 72-118.

94. Haig quote from Brown, *Gandhi and Civil Disobedience,* p. 135; "I feel very little" quote from Sarkar, *Bengal,* pp. 94-95.

95. Quote from Sarkar, *Modern India,* p. 287

96. Ackerman and Kruegler, *Strategic Nonviolent Conflict,* pp. 176-177; Stephen Alan Rittenberg. *Ethnicity, Nationalism and the Pakhtuns* (Durham, NC: Carolina Academic Press, 1988), pp. 78-80; quote from Sarkar, *Modern India,* p. 288.

97. David Hardiman, *Peasant Nationalists of Gujarat: Kheda District 1917-1934* (Delhi: Oxford University Press, 1981), pp. 197-198.

98. Brown, *Gandhi and Civil Disobedience,* pp. 121-122; Low, "Civil Martial Law," pp. 169-170.

99. Brown, *Gandhi and Civil Disobedience,* pp. 147, 155-167; Ackerman and Kruegler, *Strategic Nonviolent Conflict,* pp. 188, 189.

100. Brown, *Gandhi and Civil Disobedience,* pp. 111, 114; Sarkar, *Modern India,* pp. 288-289.

101. Brown, *Gandhi and Civil Disobedience,* p. 117.

102. Hardiman, *Peasant Nationalists,* p. 201.

103. Ibid., p. 54.

104. Ibid., pp. 191-193, 195-196.

105. B. Krishna, *Sardar Vallabhabi Patel: India's Man of Iron* (New Delhi: HarperCollins Publishers India, 1996), p. 145.

106. Pandey, *Ascendancy of Congress,* pp. 172-174.

107. Brown, *Gandhi and Civil Disobedience,* p. 144; Chakrabarty, *Local Politics,* pp. 104-107; T. Sarkar, *Bengal,* p. 87.

108. Quote from Brown, *Gandhi and Civil Disobedience,* p. 142; Sarkar, *Modern India,* pp. 298-299.

109. Dastur, York interview.

110. David Arnold, *The Congress in Tamilnad: Nationalist Policies in South India, 1919-1937* (Canberra: Australian National University Press, 1977), pp. 124-125; Masselos, *Indian Nationalism,* pp. 71-83; T. Sarkar, *Bengal,* p. 95.

111. Masani, *Indian Tales,* p. 91.

112. Brown, *Gandhi and Civil Disobedience,* p. 146; Forbes, *Women in Modern India,* pp. 132, 134-135, 137; Radha Kumar, *The History of Doing: An Illustrated Account of Movements for Women's Rights and Feminism in India, 1800-1900* (London: Verso, 1993), pp. 74, 78, 80-81; quote from Manmohini Zutshi Sahgal, *An Indian Freedom Fighter Recalls Her Life* (Armonk, NY: M.E. Sharpe, 1994), p. 88.

113. Forbes, *Women in Modern India,* pp. 124-129, 132; Kumar, *History of Doing,* pp. 74, 82-83; T. Sarkar, *Bengal,* pp. 88-89.

114. Brown, *Gandhi and Civil Disobedience,* pp. 128-130, 144; Sarkar, *Modern India,* pp. 292-293.

115.   Brown, *Gandhi and Civil Disobedience,* pp. 124-125.
116.   Low, "Civil Martial Law," pp. 165-167.
117.   Brown, *Gandhi and Civil Disobedience,* p. 125; quote from *India in 1930-31* (Calcutta: Central Publication Branch, 1932), p. 574.
118.   Dalton, *Mahatma Gandhi,* p. 133.
119.   David Arnold, *Police Power and Colonial Rule: Madras, 1859-1947* (Delhi: Oxford University Press, 1986), p. 202.
120.   Brown, *Gandhi and Civil Disobedience,* p. 123.
121.   Brown, *Gandhi and Civil Disobedience,* p. 78; Pandey, *Ascendancy of Congress,* pp. 149-151; Sarkar, *Modern India,* p. 302, 303, 305-306.
122.   David Arnold, *The Congress in Tamilnad: Nationalist Politics in South India, 1919-1937* (Canberra: Australian National University Press, 1977), p. 129; Brown, *Gandhi and Civil Disobedience,* pp. 77-78, 136, 143, 144; T. Sarkar, *Bengal,* pp. 96-97; Sarkar, *Modern India,* pp. 274, 304.
123.   Arnold, *Police Power,* pp. 195-197; David Hardiman, "The Crisis of the Lesser Patidars: Peasant Agitations in Kheda District, Gujarat, 1917-1934," in *Congress and the Raj,* ed. D. A. Low. (London: Arnold- Heinemann, 1977), pp. 66-67; Low, *Britain and Indian Nationalism,* pp. 110, 115.
124.   Brown, *Gandhi and Civil Disobedience,* pp. 130, 161, 164, 165; Sarkar, *Modern India,* pp. 293, 295.
125.   Brown, *Gandhi and Civil Disobedience,* p. 121; Chakrabarty, *Local Politics,* p. 106; Sarkar, *Modern India,* pp. 296, 297, 298, 305, 307.
126.   Brown, *Gandhi and Civil Disobedience,* pp. 170-171; Sarkar, *Modern India,* pp. 308-309
127.   Brown, *Gandhi and Civil Disobedience,* pp. 170-172.
128.   Arnold, *Congress in Tamilnad,* p. 134; Brown, *Gandhi and Civil Disobedience,* pp. 174-175; quote from Sarkar, *Modern India,* p. 311.
129.   Quote from Brown, *Gandhi: Prisoner of Hope,* p. 248; *Collected Works of Mahatma Gandhi,* vol. 45, p. 189; Dalton, *Mahatma Gandhi,* p. 105; Anthony Read and David Fischer. *The Proudest Day: India's Long Road to Independence* (London: Jonathan Cape, 1997), pp. 204-205.
130.   Quote from Brown, *Gandhi and Civil Disobedience,* pp. 173; Low, "Civil Martial Law," p. 171.
131.   Brown, *Gandhi and Civil Disobedience,* pp. 181-186.
132.   "Conversations between the Viceroy Lord Irwin, and the Secretary of State for India, Governors of the Indian Province," The Viceroy's Family, quoted in Peter Ackerman, "Strategic Aspects of Nonviolent Resistance," Ph.D. diss., Fletcher School of Law & Diplomacy, 1976.
133.   Quote from Low, "Civil Martial Law," pp. 172-173.
134.   Brown, *Gandhi and Civil Disobedience,* pp. 209-212, 215-220, 229-230; Low, "Civil Martial Law," pp. 172-173.
135.   Ackerman and Kruegler, *Strategic Nonviolent Conflict,* pp. 196-198; Sarkar, *Modern India,* pp. 319-320.
136.   Narayan Desai, videotaped interview by Steve York for the documentary television series *A Force More Powerful,* Vedchhi, India, September 2, 1998.
137.   Desai quote from Desai, York interview; Masani, *Indian Tales,* pp. 109-111.
138.   Dalton, *Mahatma Gandhi,* p. 64.
139.   Ackerman, "Strategic Aspects of Nonviolent Resistance," p. 505.

CHAPTER THREE

1.   Roman Laba, *The Roots of Solidarity: A Political Sociology of Poland's Working-Class Democratization* (Princeton, NJ: Princeton University Press, 1991), p. 158.
2.   The account of the December 1970 strikes, in this and subsequent paragraphs, is drawn from Laba, *Roots of Solidarity,* pp. 15-82.
3.   Jean-Yves Potel, *The Promise of Solidarity: Inside the Polish Workers' Struggle, 1980-82* (New York: Praeger, 1981), pp. 16-17.
4.   Luba Fajfer, "December 1970: A Prelude to Solidarity," in *Poland's Permanent Revolution: People vs. Elites, 1956 to the Present,* ed. Jane Curry and Luba Fajfer (Washington, DC: American University Press, 1996), pp. 75-76.
5.   Adam Zagajewski, *Solidarity, Solitude* (New York: The Ecco Press, 1990), p. 26.
6.   Peter Raina, *Political Opposition in Poland, 1954-1977* (London: Poets' and Painters' Press, 1978), p. 179.

7. Quotes from Adam Michnik, *Letters from Prison and Other Essays* (Berkeley: University of California Press, 1985), pp. 135, 138; David Ost, *Solidarity and the Politics of Anti-Politics: Opposition and Reform in Poland since 1968* (Philadelphia: Temple University Press, 1990), pp. 58-60.

8. "[E]very act of cowardice" quote from Gale Stokes, *The Walls Came Tumbling Down: The Collapse of Communism in Eastern Europe* (New York: Oxford University Press, 1993), p. 22; "only serve the police" quote from Michnik, *Letters*, pp. 142-143; "By using force" quote from Stokes, *The Walls Came Tumbling Down*, p. 22.

9. "[C]hallenges the monopoly" quote from Ost, *Solidarity*, p. 69; "a real" quote from Michnik, *Letters*, p. 148.

10. Quote from Stokes, *The Walls Came Tumbling Down*, p. 22; Jan Kubik, *The Power of Symbols Against the Symbols of Power: the Rise of Solidarity and the Fall of Socialism in Poland* (University Park, PA: Penn State University Press, 1994), p. 256.

11. "Organized society" quote from Robert Zuzowski, *Political Dissent and Opposition in Poland: The Workers' Defense Committee "KOR"* (Westport, CT: Praeger, 1992), pp. 67-68; "Nothing instructs" quote from Michnik, *Letters*, p. 144.

12. Michnik, *Letters*, p. 145; quotes from Zuzowski, *Political Dissent*, pp. 129, 132.

13. Lawrence Goodwyn, *Breaking the Barrier: The Rise of Solidarity in Poland* (New York: Oxford University Press, 1991), p. 194; Michnik, *Letters*, pp. 144-145.

14. Jan Jozef Lipski, *KOR: A History of the Workers' Defense Committee in Poland, 1976-1981* (Berkeley: University of California Press, 1985), pp. 46-51, 64, 467-468.

15. Raina, *Political Opposition*, p. 344.

16. Quote from Kazimierz Brandys, *A Warsaw Diary, 1978-1981* (New York: Random House, 1983), p. 56; quote from Lipski, *KOR*, pp. 266-268.

17. Brandys, *Warsaw Diary*, pp. 58-59.

18. Kubik, *Power of Symbols*, p. 104.

19. Radek Sikorski, *Full Circle: A Homecoming to Free Poland* (New York: Simon and Schuster, 1997), p. 62.

20. Kubik, *Power of Symbols*, pp. 125-126.

21. Ibid., pp. 121-123.

22. Brandys, *Warsaw Diary*, p. 67.

23. Quote from Timothy Garton Ash, *The Polish Revolution: Solidarity* (New York: Charles Scribners' Sons, 1984), pp. 28-29; Kubik, *Power of Symbols*, pp. 139, 142-144; Stokes, *Walls Came Tumbling Down*, p. 34.

24. Kubik quote from Kubik, *Power of Symbols*, p. 138; "We could do" quote from Lawrence Weschler, *The Passion of Poland: From Solidarity Through the State of War* (New York: Pantheon, 1984), p. 15.

25. Crowd-related quotes from Brandys, *Warsaw Diary*, pp. 79-81; Walentynowicz quote from Jacqueline Hayden, *Poles Apart: Solidarity and the New Poland* (Dublin: Irish Academic Press, 1994), p. 38.

26. Michnik, *Letters*, p. 160.

27. Brandys, *Warsaw Diary*, pp. 32, 156.

28. Goodwyn, *Breaking the Barrier*, p. 141.

29. The account of the Lenin Shipyard strike in 1980, in this and subsequent paragraphs, draws heavily on: Stan Persky, *At the Lenin Shipyard: Poland and the Rise of the Solidarity Trade Union* (Vancouver: New Star Books, 1981).

30. Jerzy Borowczak, videotaped interview by Tom Weidlinger for the documentary television series *A Force More Powerful*, Gdansk, September 26, 1998.

31. Persky, *At the Lenin Shipyard*, pp. 9-10.

32. Bogdan Borusewicz, videotaped interview by Tom Weidlinger for the documentary television series *A Force More Powerful*, Warsaw, September 22, 1998, Borowczak, Weidlinger interview.

33. Persky, *At the Lenin Shipyard*, p. 22.

34. Borowczak, Weidlinger interview.

35. Persky, *At the Lenin Shipyard*, p. 23.

36. Klemens Gniech, videotaped interview by Tom Weidlinger for the documentary television series *A Force More Powerful*, Gdansk, September 27, 1998; Anna Walentynowicz, videotaped interview by Tom Weidlinger for the documentary television series *A Force More Powerful*, Gdansk, September 26, 1998.

37. Alina Pienkowska, videotaped interview by Tom Weidlinger for the documentary television series *A Force More Powerful*, Gdansk, September 28, 1998.

38. Borusewicz, Weidlinger interview.

39. Gniech, Weidlinger interview.

40. Borowczak, Weidlinger interview.

41. Goodwyn, *Breaking the Barrier,* p. 165; Persky, *At the Lenin Shipyard,* pp. 76-77
42. Gniech; Weidlinger interview.; Persky, *At the Lenin Shipyard,* pp. 77-78; Pienkowska, Weidlinger interview.
43. Borusewicz, Weidlinger interview.
44. Ash, *Polish Revolution,* p. 44.
45. Kubik, *Power of Symbols,* pp. 186-187.
46. Borowczak, Weidlinger interview; Pienkowska, Weidlinger interview.
47. Borowczak, Weidlinger interview; Borusewicz, Weidlinger interview; Walentynowicz, Weidlinger interview.
48. Goodwyn, *Breaking the Barrier,* pp. 9-21, 178-179; quotes from *The Birth of Solidarity: The Gdansk Negotiations, 1980,* translated and introduced by A. Kemp-Welch (New York : St. Martin's Press, 1983), p. 54.
49. *Birth of Solidarity,* pp. 81, 84.
50. "[N]ot fighting" quote from ibid., p. 70; Persky, *At the Lenin Shipyard,* pp. 124-125.
51. Persky, *At the Lenin Shipyard,* pp. 134-135.
52. Ost, *Solidarity,* p. 77.
53. Neil Ascherson, *The Polish August* (Hammondsworth, UK: Penguin, 1982), p. 19.
54. Gromyko quote from Tina Rosenberg, *The Haunted Land: Facing Europe's Ghosts After Communism* (New York: Random House, 1995), p. 184; other quotes from Peter Raina, *Poland 1981: Toward Social Renewal* (London: George Allen & Unwin, 1985), pp. 5-7, 9.
55. Sikorski, *Full Circle,* p. 81.
56. Ascherson, *Polish August,* pp. 265; quotes from Ash, *Polish Revolution,* p. 158-159; Goodwyn, *Breaking the Barrier,* p. 296.
57. Ascherson, *The Polish August,* p. 265; Walesa quote from Ash, *Polish Revolution,* p. 164; Raina, *Poland, 1981,* pp. 98-101.
58. Michnik, *Letters,* p. 146.
59. Laba, *Roots,* pp. 88-89; Walesa quote from Potel, *Promise of Solidarity,* p. 17; Rosenberg, *Haunted Land,* pp. 138-139, 146-147, 202.
60. Rosenberg, *Haunted Land,* pp. 166, 185, 189-194.
61. Ash, *Polish Revolution,* pp. 178-182.
62. Rosenberg, *Haunted Land,* pp. 189, 192-193, 199-201.
63. Ash, *Polish Revolution,* pp. 187-189, 193-196, 203; Ost, *Solidarity,* pp. 126-127.
64. Ash, *Polish Revolution,* pp. 252-253.
65. Quotes from ibid., p. 223; Raina, *Poland, 1981,* pp. 330, 348-350, 352.
66. Maciej Lopinski, Marcin Moskit, and Mariusz Wilk, *Konspira: Solidarity Underground* (Berkeley: University of California Press, 1990), pp. 4-6.
67. Rosenberg, *Haunted Land,* pp. 205-208.
68. Stokes, *Walls Came Tumbling Down,* p. 44.
69. Lopinski et al., *Konspira,* pp. 23-24.
70. Rosenberg, *Haunted Land,* pp. 184, 197.
71. Lopinski et al., *Konspira,* pp. 40-46, 74-75.
72. Ibid., *Konspira,* pp. 59-62, 84.
73. Ibid., pp. 60-62, 93-95, 166-167, 171-173, 177-178, 180; Lawrence Wechsler, *The Passion of Poland: From Solidarity Through the State of War* (New York: Pantheon, 1984), pp. 158-161.
74. Michael H. Bernhard, *The Origins of Democratization in Poland: Workers, Intellectuals, and Oppositional Politics, 1976-1984* (New York: Columbia University Press, 1993), pp. 163-164; "simultaneous attack" and "goodwill towards" quotes from *Poland Under Jaruzelski: A Comprehensive Sourcebook on Poland During and After Martial Law,* ed. Leopold Labedz et al (New York: Charles Scribner's Sons, 1984), pp. 153, 154.
75. *Poland Under Jaruzelski,* pp. 155-157.
76. Kulerski quote from *Poland Under Jaruzelski,* pp. 158-159; Bujak quote from Lopinski et al., *Konspira,* p. 79
77. Quotes from Janine Wedel, *The Private Poland* (New York: Facts on File Publications, 1986), pp. 185-186; Weschler, *Passion of Poland,* p. 149.
78. Lopinski et al., *Konspira,* p. 104.
79. Ost, *Solidarity,* pp. 180-181; Stokes, *Walls Came Tumbling Down,* p. 122.
80. Stokes, *Walls Came Tumbling Down,* pp. 121-122.
81. Ibid., p. 124; quote from Rosenberg, *Haunted Land,* p. 233.
82. Peter Finn, "Table of History: Poles View Site of 1989 Talks that Changed Their Nation," *Washington Post,* February 12, 1999, p. A27.

83. Vaclev Havel, *The Power of the Powerless*, ed. John Keane (Armonk, NY: M.E. Sharpe, 1985), pp. 41-42.

84. Havel quote from ibid., p. 71; Bujak quote from Peter Ackerman and Christopher Kruegler, *Strategic Nonviolent Conflict: The Dynamics of People Power in the Twentieth Century* (Westport. CT: Praeger, 1994), p. 306; "We were ready" quote from Kubik, *Power of Symbols*, p. 189.

CHAPTER FOUR

1.   Alex De Jonge, *The Weimar Chronicle: Prelude to Hitler* (New York: Paddington Press, 1978), p. 85.

2.   Cyril Brown, "Ruhr Declared in State of Siege," *The New York Times,* January 12, 1923.

3.   Ibid.

4.   Ibid.

5.   Hugh Clout, *After the Ruins* (Exeter: University of Exeter Press, 1996), p. 32.

6.   Ibid., p. 33.

7.   Ibid., pp. 34-35.

8.   J. F. V. Keiger, *Raymond Poincaré,* (Cambridge: Cambridge University Press, 1997), p. 143.

9.   Stephen Schuker (Commonwealth Professor of History, University of Virginia), videotaped interview by Steve York for the documentary television series *A Force More Powerful,* Charlottesville, Virginia; December 10, 1999.

10. Ludwig Zimmerman, *Frankreichs Ruhrpolitik* (Goettingen: University of Goettingen, 1971), p. 22.

11. Klaus Tenfelde (Professor, University of the Ruhr, Bochum, Germany), videotaped interview by Steve York for the documentary television series *A Force More Powerful,* Bochum, Germany; May 26, 1999

12. Cecil John Charles Street, *Rhineland and Ruhr* (London: A. Couldrey and Co., 1923), p. 46; De Jonge, *Weimar Chronicle,* p. 77.

13. Cyril Brown, *The New York Times,* July 18, 1922.

14. Cyril Brown, "Wirth Cabinet Out on Socialists' Veto," *The New York Times,* November 13, 1922.

15. Klaus Schwabe (Professor, Historical Institute, University of Aachen), videotaped interview by Steve York for the documentary television series *A Force More Powerful,* Aachen, Germany; May 25, 1999.

16. Schuker, York interview.

17. Edwin L. James, "Poet Exudes Optimism on His 60th Birthday," *The New York Times,* November 25, 1922.

18. Cyril Brown, "Germans to Offer Passive Resistance," *The New York Times,* January 10, 1923

19. Schuker, York interview.

20. Edwin L. James, "French Army Ready at Gates of Essen as Germany is Declared in Default," *The New York Times,* January 10, 1923.

21. Schwabe, York interview.

22. Klaus Harbeck, *Das Kabinett Cuno, 22. November bis 12. August, 1923* (Boppard am Rhein: H. Boldt, 1968), pp. 316-317.

23. Ibid., p. 317.

24. Cyril Brown, "Reichstag Backs Cuno's Resistance," *The New York Times,* January 14, 1923.

25. Cyril Brown, "Berlin Takes Quick Action," *The New York Times,* January 11, 1923.

26. Harbeck, *Das Kabinett Cuno,* p. 329; quote from Gerald D. Feldman, *The Great Disorder: Politics, Economics, and Society in the German Inflation, 1914-1924* (New York: Oxford University Press, 1993), p. 636; Schuker, York interview.

27. Edwin L. James, "Anti-French Demonstrations by Workers at Essen," *The New York Times,* January 16, 1923.

28. Cyril Brown, "French Sure of Success," *The New York Times,* January 14, 1923.

29. "The Other War in the Ruhr," *The Nation,* February 21, 1923, p. 216.

30. "Wanted: A German Gandhi," *The Nation,* January 17, 1923, p. 59.

31. Ludwig Zimmermann, *Frankreichs Ruhrpolitik* (Goettingen: Universitaet Goettingen, 1971), p. 101; Edwin L. James, "Serious View of Germany's Position," *The New York Times,* January 14, 1923.

32. Edwin L. James, "Boycott of French Spreads in Germany," *The New York Times,* January 17, 1923.

33. Cyril Brown, "Complete Isolation of the Ruhr Valley Next French Step to Meet Resistance," *The New York Times,* January 23, 1923.

34. Cyril Brown, "German Magnates Confer with French," *The New York Times,* January 25, 1923.

35. Friedrich Grimm, *Vom Ruhrkrieg zur Rheinlandraeumung* (Hamburg: Hanseatische Verlagsanstalt, 1930), p. 38.

36. "Germany's Moral Equivalent for War," *The Nation,* February 7, 1923, p. 138.

37. Schuker, York interview; Schwabe, York interview.
38. Paul Wentzcke, *Ruhrkampf: Einbruch und Abwehr im Rheinischen-Westfaelischen Industriegebiet* (Berlin: R. Hobbing, 1930), p. 192.
39. Ibid., p. 193.
40. Ibid., p. 195.
41. Ibid., p. 195.
42. Ibid., p. 196.
43. Cyril Brown, "Passive Resistance Meets French Moves," *The New York Times,* January 20, 1923.
44. "Force Preferred to Coal," *The Nation,* March 14, 1923, p. 32.
45. Schuker, York interview.
46. Quote from Theo Gaudig, videotaped interview by Steve York for the documentary television series *A Force More Powerful,* Essen, Germany; May 24, 1999; Hans Schwerdner, videotaped interview by Steve York for the documentary television series *A Force More Powerful,* Essen, Germany; May 25, 1999.
47. Friedrich Muckermann, *Tragikomisches von der Ruhr* (Muenster: Matthias- Gruenewald, 1923), pp. 4, 7.
48. "In the expensive" quote from "Germany and the True France," *The Nation,* February 7, 1923, p. 18; "And everyone" quote from Cyril Brown, "French Spread Toward Cologne to Stop Gaps in Ruhr," *The New York Times,* February 4, 1923; Hans Schwerdner, York interview.
49. Wentzcke, *Ruhrkampf,* p. 216.
50. "Blood-Money," *The Nation,* January 31, 1923, p. 60; quotes from Graham Greene, *A Sort of Life* (London: Bodley Head, 1971), p. 58.
51. Lothar Erdmann, *Die Gewerkschaften im Ruhrkampfe* (Berlin: Reimar Hobbing Verlag, 1924), p. 145.
52. Peter Ackerman and Christopher Kruegler, *Strategic Nonviolent Conflict: The Dynamics of People Power in the Twentieth Century* (Westport, CT: Praeger, 1994) p. 112; Erdmann, *Die Gewerkschaften,* pp. 147-149.
53. Herman J. Rupieper, *The Cuno Government and Reparations* (Den Haag: Martinus Nijhoff, 1979), p. 170.
54. Ibid., p. 173.
55. "What else" quote from Cyril Brown, "Two Frenchmen Shot by German Police," *The New York Times,* February 13, 27, 1923; "It is true" quote from "Blood-Money," *The Nation,* January 31, 1923.
56. Cyril Brown, "Ruhr Mobs Fired On," *The New York Times,* February 5, 1923.
57. Edwin L. James, "Resistance is Stiffened by New Orders in Berlin," *The New York Times,* February 6, 1923.
58. Cyril Brown, "German Passive Resistance in Ruhr Giving Place to Active Hostility," *The New York Times,* February 18, 1923.
59. Cyril Brown, "Arrests and Riots Mark Day in Ruhr," *The New York Times,* February 12, 1923.
60. Schuker, York interview.
61. Street, *Rhineland and Ruhr,* p. 52.
62. Cyril Brown, "Miners Appeal to Cuno," *The New York Times,* March 21, 1923.
63. Quotes from "The Military Heel," *The Nation,* November 22, 1923; Harri Petras, *Der Ruhrkampf im Spiegel der Ereignisse im Hattinger Raum* (Hattingen: Stadt Hattingen, 1973) p. 178.
64. Petras, *Der Ruhrkampf,* p. 173.
65. Erdmann, *Die Gewerkschaften,* pp. 196-197; Street, *Rhineland and Ruhr,* p. 54.
66. Cyril Brown, "Mayence Workers Return," *The New York Times,* May 7, 1923.
67. Cyril Brown, "French Returns Rising Steadily in Ruhr," *The New York Times,* May 21, 1923.
68. Quote from William Manchester, *The Arms of Krupp, 1587-1968* (Boston: Little, Brown, 1968), pp. 408-409; Tenfelde, York interview; Hans Schwerdner, York interview.
69. Manchester, *Arms of Krupp,* p. 409.
70. Cyril Brown, "Cuno's Fate Depends on Acceptance," *The New York Times,* June 3, 1923.
71. Quotes from Edwin L. James, "Close-Up Bochum at 4 P. M.," *The New York Times,* March 2, 1923; Tenfelde, York interview.
72. Schuker, York interview.
73. "The 'Security' of France," *The Nation,* April 11, 1923.
74. Wentzcke, *Ruhrkampf,* p. 236.
75. Cyril Brown, "Talk of Workers' Republic in Ruhr," *The New York Times,* May 27, 1923.
76. Ibid.
77. Rupieper, *Cuno Government,* p. 108; quote from Edwin L. James, "Germans Ask for Moratorium," *The New York Times,* June 4, 1923.
78. Gaudig, York interview.

80. Edwin L. James, "Ruhr Army to be Reinforced," *The New York Times,* March 15, 1923; Schuker, York interview.
81. Cyril Brown, "3 French Ministers Investigate Ruhr," *The New York Times,* April 19, 1923.
82. Cyril Brown, "German Mark Crashes to 57,000 to Dollar," *The New York Times,* May 23, 1923.
83. Edwin L. James, "French Permit Return of Some Trained Police," *The New York Times,* May 31, 1923.
84. Erdmann, *Die Gewerkschaften,* p. 203; Schuker, York interview.
85. Edwin L. James, "French Scoff at Note," *The New York Times,* May 3, 1923.
86. Edwin L. James, "Text of Franco-Belgian Reply Refusing German Note," *The New York Times,* May 5, 1923.
87. Cyril Brown, "Guerrilla War Now Prevails in Ruhr," *The New York Times,* July 2, 1923.
88. Cyril Brown, "Cuno Repudiated," *The New York Times,* August 9, 1923.
89. Edwin L. James, "Neither Peace Nor Victory," *The New York Times,* September 27, 1923.
90. Schuker, York interview.

CHAPTER FIVE

1. John Danstrup, *A History of Denmark* (Copenhagen: Wivel, 1947), p. 169; Richard Petrow, *The Bitter Years: The Invasion and Occupation of Denmark and Norway* (New York: Morrow, 1974), p. 47.
2. Jytte Brunn, videotaped interview by Steve York for the documentary television series *A Force More Powerful,* Herfolge, Denmark; October 4, 1998.
3. Petrow, *Bitter Years,* p. 45.
4. Ibid., p. 45.
5. Ibid., pp. 46-48.
6. Ibid., pp. 47-50.
7. Ibid., pp. 48-49.
8. Ibid., p. 50.
9. Quotes from ibid., p. 51; Danstrup, *History of Denmark,* p. 171; Peter Ackerman and Christopher Kruegler, *Strategic Nonviolent Conflict: The Dynamics of People Power in the Twentieth Century* (Westport, CT: Praeger, 1994), p. 216.
10. Lennart Bergfeldt, *Experiences of Civilian Resistance: The Case of Denmark, 1940-1945* (Uppsala: University of Uppsala, 1993), p. 93.
11. Herbert Pundik, videotaped interview by Steve York for the documentary television series *A Force More Powerful,* Copenhagen; October 2, 1998.
12. John Orem Thomas, *The Giant Killers: The Story of the Danish Resistance Movement* (New York: Taplinger Publishing Co., 1976), pp. 92-93.
13. Danstrup, *History of Denmark,* pp. 178-179.
14. Ibid., p. 180; quote from Brunn, York interview.
15. Thomas, *Giant Killers,* pp. 101-102.
16. Bergfeldt, *Experiences of Civilian Resistance,* pp. 96-98.
17. Petrow, *Bitter Years,* p. 163.
18. Ibid., p. 165.
19. Thomas, *Giant Killers,* pp. 108-110.
20. Ibid., pp. 111-113.
21. Ibid., pp. 112, 114-115.
22. Ibid., pp. 116-117
23. Petrow, *Bitter Years,* pp. 188-190.
24. Ibid., pp. 190-191.
25. Thomas, *Giant Killers,* p. 120.
26. Ibid., p. 121.
27. Ibid., p. 122.
28. Bergfeldt, *Experiences of Civilian Resistance,* p. 112.
29. Thomas, *Giant Killers,* pp. 124-125.
30. Ibid., pp. 125-127.
31. Ibid., p. 128.
32. Ibid., pp. 129, 131.
33. Ibid., pp. 130, 133.
34. Ibid., p. 135.

35. Therkel Straede, *October, 1943: The Rescue of the Danish Jews from Annihilation* (Copenhagen: Royal Danish Ministry of Foreign Affairs: Museum of Danish Resistance 1940-1945, 1993), p. 12.
36. Thomas, *Giant Killers*, p. 141.
37. Ibid., pp. 142, 144.
38. Ibid., p. 145.
39. Jorgen Haestrup, *Secret Alliance* (Odense: University of Odense, 1976), p. 45.
40. Thomas, *Giant Killers*, pp. 145-146.
41. Ibid., p. 144.
42. Ibid., p. 148.
43. Ibid., p. 149.
44. Petrow, *Bitter Years*, pp. 211-212.
45. Ibid., p. 215.
46. Thomas, *Giant Killers*, p. 153.
47. Ninna Almdal, videotaped interview by Steven York for the documentary television series *A Force More Powerful*, Copenhagen; October 3, 1998.
48. Louis DeJong, *The Netherlands and Nazi Germany* (Cambridge: Harvard University Press, 1990), p. 43.
49. Ibid., pp. 52-53.
50. M. R. D. Foot, *Holland at War Against Hitler: Anglo-Dutch Relations, 1940-1945* (London: Frank Cass, 1990), p. 45.
51. Werner Warmbrunn, *The Dutch Under German Occupation, 1940-1945* (Stanford, CA: Stanford University Press, 1963), pp. 108-109.
52. This section relies for story elements and quoted statements on: Nathan Stoltzfus, *Resistance of the Heart: Intermarriage and the Rosenstrasse Protest in Nazi Germany* (New York: W.W. Norton & Company, 1996).
53. *The Gandhi Reader*, ed. Homer A. Jack (New York, Grove Press, 1994), p. 334.

CHAPTER SIX

1. William Krehm, *Democracies and Tyrannies of the Caribbean* (Westport, CT: Lawrence Hill & Co., 1984), p. 13.
2. Patricia Parkman, *Nonviolent Insurrection in El Salvador: The Fall of Maximiliano Hernandez Martinez* (Tucson: University of Arizona Press, 1988), pp. 27, 31, 43.
3. Jeffrey M. Paige, *Coffee and Power: Revolution and the Rise of Democracy in Central America* (Cambridge, MA: Harvard University Press, 1997), pp. 14-15, 53.
4. Thomas P. Anderson, *Matanza: El Salvador's Communist Revolt of 1932* (Lincoln: University of Nebraska Press, 1971), p. 7; Paige, *Coffee and Power*, pp. 44-46; Parkman, *Nonviolent Insurrection*, p. 7.
5. Anderson, *Matanza*, p. 18; Paige, *Coffee and Power*, p. 46; Parkman, *Nonviolent Insurrection*, pp. 9, 11-14.
6. Parkman, *Nonviolent Insurrection*, pp. 7-8, 11-16; Alistair White, *El Salvador* (New York: Praeger, 1973), pp. 86-88.
7. Anderson, *Matanza*, pp. 45-46; Paige, *Coffee and Power*, p. 111; Parkman, *Nonviolent Insurrection*, p. 15.
8. Krehm, *Democracies and Tyrannies*, p. 6.
9. Quote from ibid., p. 7; Parkman, *Nonviolent Insurrection*, pp. 17-18.
10. Jose Napoleon Duarte and Diana Page, *Duarte: My Story* (New York: Putnam, 1986), p. 31; Tommie Sue Montgomery, *Revolution in El Salvador: From Civil Strife to Civil Peace* (Boulder, CO: Westview Press, 1995), p. 35; Parkman, *Nonviolent Insurrection*, p. 13; Everett Wilson, "The Crisis of National Integration in El Salvador, 1919-1935," Ph.D. Diss., Stanford University, 1970, p. 243.
11. Quote from Krehm, *Democracies and Tyrannies*, p. 5; Montgomery, *Revolution in El Salvador*, p. 34; Parkman, *Nonviolent Insurrection*, p. 18.
12. Duarte and Page, *Duarte*, p. 31; Paige, *Coffee and Power*, pp. 110-111.
13. Duarte and Page, *Duarte*, p. 32; Montgomery, *Revolution in El Salvador*, p. 35; Paige, *Coffee and Power*, p. 112; Parkman, *Nonviolent Insurrection*, pp. 18, 20.
14. Anderson, *Matanza*, pp. 92-136; Montgomery, *Revolution in El Salvador*, p. 37; Parkman, *Nonviolent Insurrection*, p. 20.
15. Paige, *Coffee and Power*, pp. 101, 104, 122-124.
16. Quote from Parkman, *Nonviolent Insurrection*, p. 26; Montgomery, *Revolution in El Salvador*, p. 39.

17. Duarte and Page, *Duarte,* pp. 34-35.
18. Quote from Francisco Moran, *Las Jornadas Civicas de Abril y Mayo de 1944* (San Salvador: University of El Salvador Press, 1979), p. 23; Krehm, *Democracies and Tyrannies,* pp. 10-11; Parkman, *Nonviolent Insurrection,* pp. 17-18, 21-23.
19. Quote from Moran, *Las Jornadas Civicas,* p. 59; Parkman, *Nonviolent Insurrection,* p. 33.
20. Parkman, *Nonviolent Insurrection,* pp. 30-31.
21. Ibid., p. 27.
22. Ibid., p. 31.
23. Montgomery, *Revolution in El Salvador,* pp. 25, 39-41.
24. Parkman, *Nonviolent Insurrection,* pp. 26, 40.
25. Krehm, *Democracies and Tyrannies,* p. 10; Montgomery, *Revolution in El Salvador,* p. 40.
26. Montgomery, *Revolution in El Salvador,* p. 40; Parkman, *Nonviolent Insurrection,* p. 40.
27. Montgomery, *Revolution in El Salvador,* p. 40; Parkman, *Nonviolent Insurrection,* p. 28.
28. Parkman, *Nonviolent Insurrection,* p. 32.
29. "[T]o conduct" and "democracy is highways" quotes from Krehm, *Democracies and Tyrannies,* pp. 12, 19; "eloquent pro-democratic speech" quote from Parkman, *Nonviolent Insurrection,* p. 33.
30. Parkman, *Nonviolent Insurrection,* p. 33.
31. Ibid., pp. 34-37.
32. Krehm, *Democracies and Tyrannies,* pp. 9, 12, 34, 36-37.
33. Parkman, *Nonviolent Insurrection,* pp. 41-43.
34. Ibid., pp. 42-43, 45.
35. Ibid., pp. 47-49.
36. Moran, *Las Jornados Civicas,* pp. 33-40, 47-48.
37. Parkman, *Nonviolent Insurrection,* pp. 49-52.
38. Ibid., p. 49.
39. Ibid., pp. 50-52.
40. Krehm, *Democracies and Tyrannies,* pp. 13, 52-53.
41. Moran, *Las Jornados Civicas,* pp. 141-142; Parkman, *Nonviolent Insurrection,* pp. 49-50.
42. Parkman, *Nonviolent Insurrection,* p. 63.
43. Krehm, *Democracies and Tyrannies,* pp. 13-14; Moran, *Las Jornadas Civicas,* pp. 43, 45, 53-54, 57.
44. Moran, *Los Jornados Civicas,* pp. 61-62.
45. Parkman, *Nonviolent Insurrection,* p. 58.
46. Krehm, *Democracies and Tyrannies,* pp. 15, 58-59.
47. Ibid., p. 16.
48. "[N]ights were hideously staccato" quote from ibid., pp. 16-17; "destroy the livelihood" quote from Parkman, *Nonviolent Insurrection,* p. 59.
49. Krehm, *Democracies and Tyrannies,* p. 17; Moran, *Los Jornados Civicas,* pp. 142-144; Parkman, *Nonviolent Insurrection,* p. 59.
50. Krehm, *Democracies and Tyrannies,* p. 18; Parkman, *Nonviolent Insurrection,* p. 59.
51. Krehm *Democracies and Tyrannies,* p. 20; "Victor" quote from Moran, *Los Jornados Civicas,* p. 59.
52. Parkman, *Nonviolent Insurrection,* p. 61.
53. Ibid., pp. 90-92, 99.
54. Ibid., pp. 93-94.
55. Ibid., pp. 60-61, 65, 80.
56. Ibid., pp. 80-81.
57. Krehm, *Democracies and Tyrannies,* p. 18.
58. Parkman, *Nonviolent Insurrection,* p. 68.
59. Ibid., pp. 65-66.
60. Ibid., p. 66.
61. Ibid., pp. 67-68.
62. Ibid, pp. 68-69.
63. Krehm, *Democracies and Tyrannies,* pp. 23, 72.
64. Parkman, *Nonviolent Insurrection,* pp. 72, 73-74.
65. Ibid., p. 70.
66. Ibid., p. 72.
67. Ibid., pp. 75-76.
68. Duarte and Page, *Duarte,* p. 38.
69. Parkman, *Nonviolent Insurrection,* pp. 81-82.
70. Ibid., p. 81.
71. Ibid., pp. 74-75.

72. Ibid, p. 76.
73. Krehm, *Democracies and Tyrannies*, pp. 23, 76-77.
74. Parkman, *Nonviolent Insurrection*, pp. 72-74.
75. Krehm, *Democracies and Tyrannies*, pp. 23, 77.
76. Parkman, *Nonviolent Insurrection*, p. 78.
77. Ibid., pp. 81-83.
78. Ibid, pp. 80, 83.
79. Ibid., pp. 77-78, 84.
80. Ibid., p. 85.
81. Ibid.
82. Krehm, *Democracies and Tyrannies*, pp. 62, 85-86.
83. Parkman, *Nonviolent Insurrection*, pp. 86-87.
84. Ibid., p. 89.
85. Montgomery, *Revolution in El Salvador*, pp. 42, 102.
86. Montgomery, *Revolution in El Salvador*, pp. 37-39; Parkman, *Nonviolent Insurrection*, p. 102; Philip J. Williams and Knut Walter, *Militarization and Demilitarization in El Salvador's Transition to Democracy* (Pittsburgh, PA: University of Pittsburgh Press, 1997), pp. 10-13.
87. Parkman, *Nonviolent Insurrection*, p. 102.
88. Ibid, p. 68.

CHAPTER SEVEN

1. Jo Fisher, *Mothers of the Disappeared* (Boston: South End Press, 1989), p. 28.
2. Ibid.
3. Ibid., p. 29.
4. Alison Brysk, *The Politics of Human Rights in Argentina: Protest, Change and Democratization* (Stanford, CA: Stanford University Press, 1994), p. 26f.
5. Ibid., p. 32
6. Ibid., p. 30.
7. Ibid., p. 34.
8. Quote from Philip McManus and Gerald Schlabach, eds., *Relentless Persistence: Nonviolent Action in Latin America* (Philadelphia: New Society Publishers, 1991), p. 84; "First we will kill" quote from Brysk, *Politics of Human Rights*, p. 35.
9. Brysk, *Politics of Human Rights*, p. 38.
10. Ibid., p. 37.
11. Quote from Robert Harvey, in *The Economist*, Jan. 26, 1980, cited in Jacobo Timerman, *Prisoner Without a Name, Cell Without a Number*, trans. Toby Talbot (New York: Knopf, 1981), p. 39; Brysk, *Politics of Human Rights*, p. 39.
12. Fisher, *Mothers of the Disappeared*, p. 53.
13. Ibid.
14. Ibid.
15. Ibid., p. 55.
16. Ibid., p. 66.
17. Ibid., p. 60.
18. Ibid.
19. Ibid., p. 63.
20. Ibid., p. 68-70.
21. Marguerite Guzman Bouvard, *Revolutionizing Motherhood: The Mothers of the Plaza de Mayo* (Wilmington, DE: Scholarly Resources, 1994), pp. 80f, 81.
22. Ibid., p. 87.
23. Ibid., p. 95.
24. Mary Helen Spooner, *Soldiers in a Narrow Land: The Pinochet Regime in Chile* (Berkeley: University of California Press, 1994), p. 187.
25. Lake Sagaris, videotaped interview by Steve York, for the documentary television *series A Force More Powerful*, Santiago, Chile; October 5, 1998.
26. Spooner, *Soldiers in a Narrow Land*, p. 188.
27. Genaro Arriagada, videotaped interview by Steve York for the documentary television series *A Force More Powerful*, Washington, D.C.; October 28, 1998.

28. Pamela Constable and Arturo Valenzuela, *A Nation of Enemies: Chile Under Pinochet* (New York: W. W. Norton, 1991), p. 65

29. David Lewis et al, "Besieged But Still Strong," *Newsweek,* September 15, 1986.

30. Christian Precht, videotaped interview by Steve York for the documentary television series *A Force More Powerful,* Santiago, Chile; October 2, 1998.

31. Constable and Valenzuela, *Nation of Enemies,* p. 68.

32. Ibid., p. 230.

33. Rodolfo Seguel, videotaped interview by Steve York for the documentary television series *A Force More Powerful,* El Teniente copper mine, Rancagua, Chile; October 1, 1998.

34. Arriagada, York interview.

35. Seguel, York interview; and Spooner, *Soldiers in a Narrow Land,* p. 189.

36. Genaro Arriagada, *Pinochet: The Politics of Power,* trans. Nancy Morris et al. (Boston: Unwin Hyman, 1988), p. 58

37. Arriagada, York interview.

38. Patricia Verdugo, videotaped interview by Steve York for the documentary television series *A Force More Powerful,* Santiago, Chile; October 5, 1998.

39. Arriagada, *Pinochet,* p. 69.

40. Verdugo, York interview.

41. Arriagada, *Pinochet,* p. 70.

42. Ibid., p. 57, 62.

43. Gabriel Valdés, videotaped interview by Steve York for the documentary television series *A Force More Powerful,* Valparaiso, Chile, October 6, 1998.

44. Arriagada, *Pinochet,* p. 71.

45. Spooner, *Soldiers in a Narrow Land,* p. 198.

46. Arriagada, *Pinochet,* p. 75.

47. Ibid., p. 67.

48. Constable and Valenzuela, *Nation of Enemies,* p. 290.

49. Arriagada, *Pinochet,* p. 76.

50. Seguel, York interview.

51. Arriagada, *Pinochet,* p. 76.

52. Spooner, *Soldiers in a Narrow Land,* p. 207.

53. Arriagada, *Pinochet,* p. 76.

54. This and the next paragraphs are based on: Spooner, *Soldiers in a Narrow Land,* pp. 209-214.

55. Lewis, "Besieged But Still Strong," *Newsweek,* September 15, 1986.

56. Shirley Christian, "Chile's Army Reacting to Attack, Arrests Foes and Shuts Magazines," *The New York Times,* September 9, 1986.

57. Monica Jiménez, interview by Steve York for the documentary television series *A Force More Powerful,* Santiago, Chile; July 30, 1998.

58. This and the following paragraph are from: Ibid.

59. Arriagada, York interview.

60. Ricardo Lagos, translation of excerpt from Chilean television broadcast, Channel 13, June 29, 1988.

61. Constable and Valenzuela, *Nation of Enemies,* p. 307.

62. Jiménez, York interview.

63. Sagaris, York interview.

64. Eyewitness source (identity confidential).

CHAPTER EIGHT

1. Gandhi quote from *The Gandhi Reader,* ed. Homer Jack (New York: Grove Press, 1994), p. 314; Hancock quote from Sudarshan Kapur, *Raising Up a Prophet: The African-American Encounter with Gandhi* (Boston: Beacon Press, 1992), p. 64.

2. Ibid., p. 29.

3. *The Gandhi Reader,* p. 311, 313.

4. Ibid., pp. 310-311.

5. "[C]onquer," "we don't," and "be cool" quotes from Diane Nash, "Inside the Sit-Ins and Freedom Rides: Testimony of a Southern Student," in *We Shall Overcome: The Civil Rights Movement in the United States in the 1950's and 1960's,* ed. David J. Garrow, (Brooklyn, NY: Carlson Publishing, 1989),

p. 959; "And it was" quote from Diane Nash, videotaped interview by Steve York for the documentary television series *A Force More Powerful*, Chicago, Illinois; August 21, 1998.

6. Ibid.
7. James Lawson, videotaped interview by Steve York for the documentary television series *A Force More Powerful*, Los Angeles, California, October 26, 1998.
8. David Halberstam, *The Children* (New York: Random House, 1998), p. 49.
9. Lawson, York interview.
10. Ibid.
11. Adam Fairclough, *To Redeem the Soul of America: The Southern Christian Leadership Conference and Martin Luther King Jr.* (Athens: University of Georgia Press, 1987), pp. 27-29; Aldon D. Morris, *The Origins of the Civil Rights Movement: Black Communities Organizing for Change* (New York: The Free Press, 1984), pp. 58-60.
12. George M. Fredrickson, *Black Liberation: A Comparative History of Black Ideologies in the United States and South Africa* (New York: Oxford University Press, 1995), pp. 256-257.
13. Doug McAdam, "Tactical Innovation and the Pace of Insurgency," *American Sociological Review* 48 (December 1983). pp. 741-743.
14. Lawson, York interview.
15. Halberstam, *Children*, pp. 73-74, 151.
16. John Lewis, *Walking with the Wind: A Memoir of the Movement* (New York: Simon and Schuster, 1998), pp. 85-87; Bernard Lafayette, videotaped interview by Steve York for the documentary television series *A Force More Powerful*, Nashville, August 20, 1998; Nash, York interview.
17. Lawson, York interview; "You've got" quote from Lewis, *Walking with the Wind*, p. 84; "I thought nonviolence" quote from Nash, York interview.
18. Lawson, York interview.
19. Quote from Lewis, *Walking with the Wind*, p. 93; Lafayette, York interview; Nash, York interview.
20. Lawson, York interview.
21. Lewis, *Walking with the Wind*, pp. 94-96.
22. Lafayette, York interview.
23. Lewis, *Walking with the Wind*, pp. 99-100.
24. Ibid., p. 99.
25. Lawson, York interview; Lewis, *Walking with the Wind*, p. 99.
26. Halberstam, *Children*, p. 60.
27. Lewis, *Walking with the Wind*, pp. 102-103.
28. George Barrett, videotaped interview by Steve York for the documentary television series *A Force More Powerful*, Nashville, Tennessee; August 19, 1998; Lawson, York interview.
29. Will Campbell, videotaped interview by Steve York for the documentary television series *A Force More Powerful*, Nashville, Tennessee; August 18, 1998.
30. Lewis, *Walking with the Wind*, p. 121; Nash, York interview.
31. Lewis, *Walking with the Wind*, pp. 105-106.
32. Lawson, York interview.
33. Lewis, *Walking with the Wind*, pp. 106-107.
34. "Did you see this" quote from Nash, York interview; Lafayette quote from Lafayette, York interview; Lawson, York interview; Lewis, *Walking with the Wind*, pp. 107-108.
35. Lewis, *Walking with the Wind*, pp. 109-110.
36. Lafayette, York interview; Lawson, York interview; Nash, York interview; John Seigenthaler, videotaped interview with Steve York for the documentary television series *A Force More Powerful*, Nashville, Tennessee; August 19, 1998.
37. Lafayette, York interview.
38. Lawson, York interview; Nash, York interview.
39. Linda T. Wynn, "The Dawning of a New Day: The Nashville Sit-ins, February 13- May 10, 1960," *Tennessee Historical Quarterly* 50, no. 1 (Spring 1991), p. 50.
40. Nash, York interview.
41. Harry Hampton and Steve Fayer (with Sarah Flynn), *Voices of Freedom: An Oral History of the Civil Rights Movement from the 1950s through the1980s* (New York: Bantam Books, 1990), p. 65.
42. Lafayette, York interview.
43. All quotes are from archival news footage from the documentary television series *A Force More Powerful*; Halberstam, *Children*, p. 234; Nash, York interview.
44. Lawson, York interview; Nash, York interview.
45. Hampton and Fayer, *Voices of Freedom*, pp. 58-59.
46. McAdam, "Tactical Innovation," p. 743.

47. Fairclough, *To Redeem the Soul,* 61-62.

48. James H. Laue, *Direct Action and Desegregation, 1960-1962: Toward a Theory of the Rationalization of Protest* (Brooklyn, NY: Carlson Publishing Group, 1989), p. 90; McAdam, "Tactical Innovation," p. 739.

49. Lewis, *Walking with the Wind,* p. 133.

50. Ibid., pp. 140-144.

51. Ibid., p. 145.

52. Robert Cook, *Sweet Land of Liberty? The African-American Struggle for Civil Rights in the Twentieth Century* (London: Longman, 1998), pp. 122-123; Halberstam, *Children,* pp. 300-301.

53. Lewis, *Walking with the Wind,* pp. 158-161.

54. Ibid., pp. 169-170.

55. Cook, *Sweet Land of Liberty?,* p. 129.

56. *The Gandhi Reader,* p. 316.

CHAPTER NINE

1. Azhar Cachalia (now Secretary for Safety and Security, Government of South Africa), videotaped interview by Steve York for the documentary television series *A Force More Powerful,* Pretoria; June 8, 1999.

2. Leonard Thompson, *A History of South Africa* (New Haven, CT: Yale University Press, 1995), pp. 215- 216; Allister Sparks, *The Mind of South Africa* (New York: Alfred A. Knopf, 1990), p. 197.

3. Meredith Martin, *In the Name of Apartheid: South Africa in the Postwar Period* (London: Hamish Hamilton, 1988), p. 73.

4. *From Protest to Challenge: A Documentary History of African Politics in South Africa, 1882-1964,* vol. 2, ed. Thomas Karis and Gwendolyn M. Carter (Stanford, CA: Hoover Institution Press, 1973), pp. 403-404.

5. Joshua N. Lazerson, *Against the Tide : Whites in the Struggle Against Apartheid* (Boulder, CO: Westview Press, 1994), pp. 151-153.

6. Nelson Mandela, *Long Walk to Freedom* (London: Abacus, 1994), p. 321.

7. The account of Popo Molefe's early life, in this and subsequent paragraphs, comes from: Rose Moss, *Shouting at the Crocodile: Popo Molefe, Patrick Lekota, and the Freeing of South Africa* (Boston: Beacon Press, 1990), pp. 16-20.

8. Anthony Marx, *Lessons of Struggle: South African Internal Opposition, 1960-1990* (New York: Oxford University Press, 1992), pp. 71-72.

9. Jeremy Seekings, "The Development of Strategic Thought in South Africa's Civic Movements, 1977-1990," in *From Comrades to Citizens: The South African Civics Movement and the Transition to Democracy,* ed. Glenn Adler and Jonny Steinberg (London: Macmillan, 2000); book consulted in manuscript before final page numbers available.

10. Marx, *Lessons of Struggle,* p. 110.

11. Jeremy Seekings, "The Origins of Political Mobilisation in the PWV Townships, 1980-84," in *Popular Struggles in South Africa,* ed. William Cobbett and Robin Cohen (Trenton, NJ: Africa World Press, 1988), pp. 65-67.

12. Ibid.; *From Protest to Challenge,* vol. 5, eds. Thomas Karis and Gail Gerhart (Bloomington: Indiana University Press, 1997), p. 333.

13. Quotes from Steven Mufson, *Fighting Years: Black Resistance and the Struggle for a New South Africa* (Boston: Beacon Press, 1990), pp. 31-32; and Tom Lodge, Bill Nasson, et al, *All, Here, and Now: Black Politics in South Africa in the 1980s* (New York: Ford Foundation, 1991), p. 40.

14. Marx, *Lessons of Struggle,* pp. 108-109, 147; Robert M. Price, *The Apartheid State in Crisis: Political Transformation in South Africa, 1975-1990* (New York: Oxford University Press, 1991), p. 160.

15. Seekings, "The Development of Strategic Thought," in *Comrades to Citizens;* book consulted in manuscript before final page numbers available.

16. Ibid.

17. Marx, *Lessons of Struggle,* p. 130; Mufson, *Fighting Years,* p. 49.

18. Mufson, *Fighting Years,* pp. 50-51.

19. Ibid., pp. 47-48.

20. Marx, *Lessons of Struggle,* p. 103.

21. Lourence DuPlessis, videotaped interview by Steve York for the documentary television series *A Force More Powerful,* Port Elizabeth, South Africa; June 11, 1999.

22. Mike Xego, videotaped interview by Steve York for the documentary television series *A Force More Powerful*, Port Elizabeth, South Africa; June 14, 1999.

23. Price, *Apartheid State in Crisis*, pp. 85-90.

24. The account of events in the Vaal Triangle, in this and subsequent paragraphs, comes from: Prakash Diar, *The Sharpeville Six* (Toronto: McClelland and Stewart, 1990), pp. xv-xxvi, 3-4.

25. Mark Swilling (The Spier Leadership Institute), videotaped interview by Sara Blecher for the documentary television series *A Force More Powerful*, Stellenbosch, South Africa; June 21, 1999.

26. Mufson, *Fighting Years*, pp. 86-87, 93.

27. Ibid., pp. 82-83, 88-89; Robert Thornton, "The Shooting at Uitenhage, 1985: The Context and Interpretation of Violence," in *Political Violence and Struggle in South Africa*, ed. N. Chabani Manganyi and André du Toit (New York: St. Martin's Press, 1990).

28. Mufson, *Fighting Years*, pp. 94-95.

29. "[C]onfuse coercion" quote from Mufson, *Fighting Years*, p. 98; "harsh scrutiny of history" quote from South Africa news footage used in the documentary television series *A Force More Powerful*; "Khmer Rouge" quote from Lodge, Nasson et al, *All, Here, and Now*, p. 338.

30. Allister Sparks, *The Mind of South Africa* (New York: Alfred A. Knopf, 1990), p. 288.

31. Price, *Apartheid State in Crisis*, p. 203; Seekings, "The Development of Strategic Thought," in *Comrades to Citizens*; book consulted in manuscript before final page numbers available.

32. The account of Matthew Goniwe and civic organizing in Lingelihle, in this and subsequent paragraphs, is drawn from: Michael Tetelman, "'We Can': Black Politics in Cradock, South Africa, 1948-85," Ph.D. diss., Northwestern University, 1997, pp. 256-323.

33. Mkhuseli Jack, videotaped interview by Steve York for the documentary television series *A Force More Powerful*, Port Elizabeth, South Africa; June 10, 1999--all words of Jack in this section are taken from this interview; Lodge, Nasson, et al, *All, Here, and Now*, p. 71; DuPlessis, York interview.

34. Swilling, Blecher interview.

35. Lourence DuPlessis, videotaped interview by Steve York.

36. Tango Lamani, videotaped interview by Steve York, Randburg, South Africa; June 7, 1999.

37. Swilling quote from Swilling, Blecher interview; Molefe quote from Popo Molefe, videotaped interview by Steve York for the documentary television series *A Force More Powerful*, Johannesburg, South Africa; June 7, 1999.

38. Janet Cherry, "Hegemony, Democracy and Civil Society: Political Participation in Kwazakele Township, 1980-90," in *From Comrades to Citizens*, ed. Adler and Steinberg.

39. Janet Cherry (Professor of Sociology, University of Port Elizabeth), videotaped interview by Steve York for the documentary television series *A Force More Powerful*, Port Elizabeth, South Africa; June 11, 1999.

40. Mzwanele Mayekiso, *Township Politics: Civic Struggles in the New South Africa* (New York: Monthly Review Press, 1996), pp. 35-51, 64-65.

41. Ibid., pp. 62, 65; Mufson, *Fighting Years*, pp. 127-128.

42. Mayekiso, *Township Politics*, pp. 73-77.

43. The account of the formation of street committees in Soweto, in this and subsequent paragraphs, is drawn from: Nomavenda Mathiane, *South Africa: Diary of Troubled Times* (New York: Freedom House, 1989), pp. 26-27, 30-31, 37, 67-70, 73.

44. Lodge, Nasson, *All, Here, and Now*, pp. 336-337.

45. Quotes from Price, *Apartheid State in Crisis*, p. 208; Cherry, York interview.

46. Price, *Apartheid State in Crisis*, p. 255.

47. Ibid., pp. 256-257.

48. DuPlessis, York interview.

49. Desmond Tutu, *The Rainbow People of God* (New York: Doubleday, 1994), p. 111.

50. Stephen M. Davis, "South Africa: Antiapartheid Sanctions," in *Protest, Power and Change: An Encyclopedia of Nonviolent Action from ACT-UP to Women's Suffrage*, ed. Roger Powers, William B. Vogele et al (New York: Garland Publishing, 1997), pp. 493-495; Price, *Apartheid State in Crisis*, pp. 225-232; Timothy D. Sisk, *Democratization in South Africa: The Elusive Social Contract* (Princeton, NJ: Princeton University Press, 1995), p. 65.

51. Marx, *Lessons of Struggle*, 229; Thompson, *History of South Africa*, p. 243.

52. Sisk, *Democratization*, pp. 83-84.

53. Thompson, *History of South Africa*, pp. 254-255.

54. *From Protest to Challenge: A Documentary History of African Politics in South Africa, 1882-1964*, vol. 3, ed. Thomas Karis and Gwendolyn M. Carter (Stanford, CA: Hoover Institution Press, 1977), pp. 776-777.

55. Cherry, York interview.

56. Desmond Tutu, videotaped interview by Steve York for the documentary television series *A Force More Powerful*, Atlanta, Georgia, August 27, 1999.

CHAPTER TEN

1. Quote from Sandra Burton, *Impossible Dream: The Marcoses, the Aquinos, and the Unfinished Revolution* (New York: Warner Books, 1989), p. 113; *People Power: An Eyewitness History, The Philippine Revolution of 1986*, ed. Monina Allarey Mercada (Manila and New York: Writers and Readers Publishing with Tenth Avenue Editions, 1986), p. 11.
2. *People Power*, p. 14.
3. "If they shoot" quote from Isabelo T. Crisostomo, *Cory, Profile of a President* (Boston: Branden Publishing Co., 1987), p. 103; *"Ninoy"* quote from Mark R. Thompson, *The Anti-Marcos Struggle: Personalistic Rule and Democratic Transition in the Philippines* (New Haven, CT: Yale University Press, 1995), p. 116.
4. Lela Garner Noble, "Politics in the Marcos Era," in *Crisis in the Philippines: The Marcos Era and Beyond*, ed. John Bresnan (Princeton, NJ: Princeton University Press, 1986), pp. 72-73; Beth Day Romulo, *Inside the Palace: The Rise and Fall of Ferdinand and Imelda Marcos* (New York: G. T. Putnam's Sons, 1987), pp. 19-20.
5. Quote from Thompson, *Anti-Marcos Struggle*, pp. 34-37; Noble, "Politics in the Marcos Era," pp. 74-76.
6. Carl H. Lande, "The Political Crisis," in *Crisis in the Philippines: The Marcos Era and Beyond*, ed. John Bresnan (Princeton, NJ: Princeton University Press, 1986), pp. 126-127; Thompson, *Anti-Marcos Struggle*, pp. 37-38.
7. Thompson, *Anti-Marcos Struggle*, pp. 52, 54.
8. Crisostomo, *Cory*, p. 77.
9. Daniel Wurfel, *Filipino Politics: Development and Decay* (Ithaca, NY: Cornell University Press, 1988), pp. 159-165, 269-270; Thompson, *Anti-Marcos Struggle*, p. 61.
10. Wurfel, *Filipino Politics*, p. 20-21.
11. Thompson, *Anti-Marcos Struggle*, pp. 65-66.
12. Ibid., pp. 78-80.
13. Ibid., pp. 84-85.
14. Ibid., p. 90.
15. Ibid., p. 91.
16. Wurfel, *Filipino Politics*, p. 253.
17. Burton, *Impossible Dream*, p. 112.
18. *People Power*, p. 11.
19. Quote from *People Power*, p. 31; Stanley Karnow, *In Our Image, America's Empire in the Philippines* (New York: Random House, 1989), p. 406.
20. *People Power*, p. 314.
21. Thompson, *Anti-Marcos Struggle*, p. 124.
22. Wurfel, *Filipino Politics*, pp. 285-286.
23. Dette Pascaul, "Organizing 'People Power' in the Philippines," *Journal of Democracy* 1, no. 1 (Winter 1990), pp. 103-104; Wurfel, *Filipino Politics*, p. 284.
24. Lewis M. Simons, *Worth Dying For* (New York: William Morrow & Co., 1987), p. 112; Thompson, *Anti-Marcos Struggle*, p. 125.
25. Quotes from Crisostomo, *Cory*, p. 157; Thompson, *Anti-Marcos Struggle*, p. 141.
26. Benedict Anderson, *The Spectre of Comparisons: Nationalism, Southeast Asia and the World* (London: Verso, 1998), p. 193; Lucy Komisar, *Corazon Aquino: The Story of a Revolution* (New York: G. Braziller, 1987), pp. 30-34.
27. Crisostomo, *Cory*, pp. 113, 131-4; Karnow, *In Our Image*, p. 403.
28. Crisostomo, *Cory*, p. 174.
29. *People Power*, p. 69.
30. Ibid., pp. 68, 70-71.
31. Ibid., pp. 75-76.
32. Thompson, *Anti-Marcos Struggle*, p. 153; Lugar and Kerry quotes from "President's News Conference on Foreign and Domestic Issues," *The New York Times*, February 12, 1986; Aquino quote from Seth Mydans, "Aquino Says She's Alarmed by the Reagan Comments," *The New York Times*, February 13, 1986.

33. *People Power,* pp. 77-78.
34. Quote from *People Power,* pp. 77-8; Crisostomo, *Cory,* p. 189.
35. Crisostomo, *Cory,* p. 193.
36. Bernard Gwertzman, "U.S. Adviser to Manila Vote Observers Gives Details of Fraud," *The New York Times,* February 22, 1986.
37. PBS television series *The United States and the Philippines: In Our Image,* associated with Karnow, *In Our Image;* quotes from Crisostomo, *Cory,* p. 196.
38. Mark Fineman, "Peso Drops 10.3% in Value, Filipinos Heed Aquino's Anti-Marcos Boycott Call," *Los Angeles Times,* February 19, 1986.
39. Joseph A. Reaves, "Marcos Hints He'll Declare Martial Law to Hold Power," *Chicago Tribune,* February 19, 1986.
40. Thompson, *Anti-Marcos Struggle,* p. 108; PBS television series *The United States and the Philippines,* associated with Karnow, *In Our Image..*
41. Crisostomo, *Cory,* pp. 203-204.
42. Clyde Haberman, "At Ministry, A Calmness and Defiance," *The New York Times,* February 23, 1986.
43. Mark Fineman, "2 Leaders Renounce Marcos, Seize Bases," *The Los Angeles Times,* February 23, 1986; quotes from Crisostomo, *Cory,* p. 206.
44. *People Power,* p. 105.
45. Ibid., p. 106.
46. Ibid., p. 109.
47. Ibid., p. 110.
48. Crisostomo, *Cory,* pp. 209-210.
49. *People Power,* p. 101.
50. This and subsequent quotations and descriptive facts in this section, on the confrontation outside the military camp, are from *People Power.*
51. Crisostomo, *Cory,* p. 226.
52. *People Power,* p. 138.
53. Ibid., p. 209.
54. Karnow, *In Our Image,* p. 420.
55. Clinton quote from News Release, Office of the Press Secretary, The White House, "Remarks by President Clinton and President Ramos at State Luncheon," November 13, 1994; "diehard Marcos loyalists" quote from "Imelda Marcos Offers Prayer for Swiss Banks," Reuters Information Service, February 24, 1996.

CHAPTER ELEVEN

1. Hanan Aruri, videotaped interview by Tom Weidlinger for the documentary television series *A Force More Powerful,* Jerusalem, October 11, 1998.
2. Thomas Friedman, *From Beirut to Jerusalem* (New York: Doubleday, 1995), pp. 426-427.
3. Robert F. Hunter, *The Palestinian Uprising: A War by Other Means* (Berkeley: University of California Press, 1991), pp. 6-7.
4. Ibid., p. 8.
5. Edgar O'Ballance, *The Intifada* (New York: St. Martin's Press, 1998), p. 1.
6. Amos Elon, *The Blood-Dimmed Tide: Dispatches from the Middle East* (New York: Columbia University Press, 1997), p. 225.
7. Souad Dajani, *The Intifada* (Amman, Jordan: Center for Hebraic Studies, 1990), p. 54.
8. Ze'ev Schiff and Edud Ya'ari, *The Intifada: The Palestinian Uprising, Israel's Third Front* (New York: Simon and Schuster, 1989), p. 91.
9. Friedman, *From Beirut to Jerusalem,* p. 341.
10. Schiff and Ya'ari, *Intifada,* pp. 83-84.
11. Dajani, *Intifada,* p. 44.
12. Mary King, "Palestinian *Intifada:* A Program of Nonviolent Struggle," in *The Middle East, 9th Edition* (Washington, DC: Congressional Quarterly Press, 2000), pp. 62-63.
13. Ibid., pp. 63-64.
14. Mubarak Awad, videotaped interview by Steve York for *A Force More Powerful,* documentary television series; Washington, D.C.; December 10, 1999.
15. Dajani, *Intifada,* p. 3;.Hunter, *Palestinian Uprising,* p. 17
16. Schiff and Ya'ari, *Intifada,* p. 17.

17. Mubarak Awad, "Nonviolence and the Intifada," in *Unarmed Forces: Nonviolent Action in Central America and the Middle East*, ed. Graeme Macqueen (Toronto: Science for Peace, 1992), p. 84; Friedman, *From Beirut to Jerusalem*, p. 328.

18. Friedman, *From Beirut to Jerusalem*, 375.

19. Hunter, *Palestinian Uprising*, p. 60.

20. Quote from Tayseer Arouri, videotaped interview by Tom Weidlinger for the documentary television series *A Force More Powerful*, Ramallah, October 9, 1998; Dajani, *Intifada*, p. 67.

21. Gene Sharp, "The Intifadah and Nonviolent Struggle," *Journal of Palestine Studies* xix, no. 1 (1987), p. 7.

22. Mordechai Bar-On, *In Pursuit of Peace: A History of the Israeli Peace Movement* (Washington, DC: U.S. Institute of Peace, 1996), p. 222.

23. Hanan Aruri, Weidlinger interview.

24. Shaul Mishal and Reuben Aharoni, *Speaking Stones: Communiques from the Intifada Underground* (Syracuse, NY: Syracuse University Press, 1994), p. 53-54.

25. Amos Elon, *Blood-Dimmed Tide*, p. 136

26. Mishal, and Aharoni, *Speaking Stones*, pp. 25-29; Dajani, *Intifada*, p. 70.

27. Quote from Tayseer Arouri, videotaped interview by Tom Weidlinger for the documentary television series *A Force More Powerful*, Jerusalem, October 9, 1998.

28. Schiff and Ya'ari, *Intifada*, pp. 193-195

29. Tayseer Arouri, Weidlinger interview.

30. "[W]hite revolution" quote from King, "Palestinian Intifada," p. 60; Edy Kaufman, "Limited Violence and the Palestinian Struggle" in *Unarmed Forces*, ed. Mcqueen, pp. 96.

31. Edy Kaufman quote from Kaufman, "Limited Violence," pp. 99-101; Mubarak Awad quote from Mubarak Awad, York interview.

32. Quote from Mubarak Awad, York interview.

33. Hunter, *Palestinian Uprising*, p. 79.

34. King, "Palestinian Intifada," p. 62.

35. Union of Palestinian Medical Relief Committees, Annual Report, 1985.

36. Quote in both Bar-On, *In Pursuit of Peace*, p. 221; and Schiff and Ya'ari, *Intifada*, p. 150.

37. Elon, *Blood-Dimmed Tide*, p. 153; Schiff, and Ya'ari, *Intifada*, p. 126.

38. Tayseer Arouri, Weidlinger interview.

39. Schiff and Ya'ari, *Intifada*, p. 253.

40. Dajani, *Intifada*, p. 96

41. Aruri, Weidlinger interview.

42. Jalal Qumsiyah, "Profiles of Israelis and Palestinians Concerned with Peace," in *The Struggle for Peace: Israelis and Palestinians*, eds. Elizabeth Warnock Fernea and Mary Evelyn Hocking (Austin: University of Texas Press, 1992), pp. 210-211.

43. King, "Palestinian Intifada," p. 61.

44. Hunter, *Palestinian Uprising*, pp. 120-122.

45. Ibid., p.104.

46. Awad, York interview.

47. Schiff and Ya'ari, *Intifada*, pp. 261-2.

48. Awad, York interview.

49. Quote from Awad, York interview; King, "Palestinian Intifada," p. 64.

50. Aruri, Weidlinger interview.

51. Awad, York interview.

52. Gene Sharp, "The Role of Power in Nonviolent Struggle," Monograph Series, No. 3, The Albert Einstein Institution, 1994.

CHAPTER TWELVE

1. Han Minzhu [pseud.], *Cries for Democracy: Writings and Speeches from the 1989 Chinese Democracy Movement* (Princeton, NJ: Princeton University Press, 1990), pp. 136-137.

2. Orville Schell, *Mandate of Heaven* (New York: Simon and Schuster, 1994), p. 29.

3. On these earlier revolts, see: Howard Levy, *Biography of Huang Ch'ao* (Berkeley: University of California Press, 1961), and Jonathan Spence, *God's Chinese Son: The Taiping Heavenly Kingdom of Hong Xiuquan* (New York: W. W. Norton, 1996); quote from Schell, *Mandate of Heaven*, p. 35

4. Michel Oksenberg, Lawrence Sullivan, and Marc Lambert, eds. *Beijing Spring, 1989: Confrontation and Conflict: The Basic Documents* (Armonk. NY: M.E. Sharpe, 1990), p. xxii.
5. Han Minzhu, *Cries for Democracy*, p. 327.
6. Ibid. Han's observations were recorded on video and then used by Carma Hinton and Richard Gordon in their documentary film on the student movement entitled *The Gate of Heavenly Peace.*
7. Samuel P. Huntington, The Third Wave: Democratization in the Late Twentieth Century (Norman: University of Oklahoma Press, 1993), p. 199.
8. Timothy Brook, *Quelling the People: The Military Suppression of the Beijing Democracy Movement* (New York: Oxford University Press, 1992), p. 169.
9. Oksenberg, et al., *Beijing Spring*, p. xl.
10. "Special Report on China," *Nonviolent Sanctions: News from The Albert Einstein Institution,* Cambridge, MA, 1990, p. 3.
11. "[A] victim" quote and "the only path" quote from Michael Laris, "A Quiet Anniversary: Tiananmen Reflections Held Mostly in Private," *Washington Post,* June 4, 1999; "I think" quote from Elisabeth Rosenthal, "Memories of June 4 Fade, Stunted by Public Silence," *The New York Times,* June 4, 1999, p. 12.
12. Rosenthal, "Memories of June 4 Fade," p. 15.
13. Gorbachev quote from Michael Parks, "Gorbachev Pledges a 10% Troop Cut; Unilateral Pullback, Trims Told," *Los Angeles Times,* December 8, 1988; Vladimir Tismaneanu, *Reinventing Politics: Eastern Europe from Stalin to Havel* (New York: The Free Press, 1993), p. 188; Raymond Pearson, *The Rise and Fall of the Soviet Empire* (New York: St. Martin's Press, 1998), p. 128.
14. Christian Joppke, *East German Dissidents and the Revolution of 1989: Social Movement in a Leninist Regime* (New York: New York University Press, 1995), pp. 148-150.
15. Roland Bleiker, *Nonviolent Struggle and the Revolution in East Germany* (Cambridge, MA: The Albert Einstein Institution, 1993), pp. 11-13, 37; Karl-Dieter Opp, Peter Voss, and Christiane Gern, *Origins of a Spontaneous Revolution, 1989* (Ann Arbor: University of Michigan Press, 1995), p. 176; quotes from Joppke, *East German Dissidents,* p. 150; Gale Stokes, *The Walls Come Tumbling Down: The Collapse of Communism in Eastern Europe* (New York: Oxford University Press), p. 139.
16. Bleiker, *Nonviolent Struggle,* pp. 8, 37; Mary Fulbrook, *Anatomy of a Dictatorship: Inside the GDR, 1949- 1989* (New York: Oxford University Press, 1995), p. 253.
17. Charles S. Maier, *Dissolution: The Crisis of Communism and the End of East Germany* (Princeton, NJ: Princeton University Press, 1997), pp. 142-144; Henry Kamm, "Evolution in Europe: How a Conductor Brought Harmony to East Germany's Peaceful Revolt," *The New York Times,* April 23 1990; Timothy Garton Ash, *The Magic Lantern: The Revolution of '89 in Warsaw, Budapest, Berlin and Prague* (New York: Random House, 1990), pp. 67-68; Robert Darnton, *Berlin Journal, 1989-1990* (New York: Norton, 1991), pp. 97-99; Fulbrook, *Anatomy of a Dictatorship,* pp. 256-257; Opp et al, *Origins of a Spontaneous Revolution,* p. 138; Stokes, *Walls Came Tumbling Down,* pp. 139-140
18. Fulbrook, *Anatomy of a Dictatorship,* pp. 255-256.
19. Philip Ward, *Bulgarian Voices* (Cambridge: The Oleander Press, 1992), pp. 301-304.
20. Nigel Hawkes, ed. *Tearing Down the Iron Curtain: The People's Revolution in Eastern Europe* (London: Hodder and Stoughton, 1990), pp. 93-94.
21. Ibid., p. 95.
22. J. F. Brown, *Surge to Freedom: The End of Communist Rule in Eastern Europe* (Durham, NC: Duke University Press, 1991), pp. 195-196; R. J. Crampton, *A Concise History of Bulgaria* (Cambridge: Cambridge University Press, 1997), pp. 209-210; Stokes, *Walls Came Tumbling Down,* pp. 145, 147.
23. Michael Andrew Kukral, *Prague 1989: Theater of Revolution* (Boulder, CO: East European Monographs, 1997), pp. 36-38.
24. Janusz Bugajski, *Czechoslovakia: Charter 77's Decade of Dissent* (New York: Praeger, 1987), pp. 41, 47-48; Bernard Wheaton and Zdenek Kavan, *The Velvet Revolution: Czechoslovakia, 1988-1991* (Boulder, CO: Westview Press, 1992), pp. 25-29.
25. Kukral, *Prague 1989,* pp. 169, 177.
26. John F. N. Bradley, *Politics in Czechoslovakia, 1945-1990* (Boulder, CO: East European Monographs, 1991), p. 63; Kukral, *Prague 1989,* pp. 47-59; quotes from Wheaton and Kavan, *The Velvet Revolution,* pp. 41-47, 199-200
27. Kukral, *Prague 1989,* p. 63; Stokes, *Walls Came Tumbling Down,* p. 156; Wheaton and Kavan, *The Velvet Revolution,* pp. 49, 52-53.
28. Kukral, *Prague 1989,* pp. 65-73; Wheaton and Kavan, *The Velvet Revolution,* pp. 64-65, 72-73.
29. Wheaton and Kavan, *The Velvet Revolution,* pp. 58-60, 63, 80; Stokes, *Walls Came Tumbling Down,* p. 157.

30. "[P]ower shortages" quote from Nestor Ratesh, *Romania: The Entangled Revolution* (New York: Praeger, 1991), p. 8; "Ethiopia" quote from Joseph Rothschild, *Return to Diversity: A Political History of East Central Europe since World War II* (New York: Oxford University Press, 1993), p. 246; Stokes, *Walls Came Tumbling Down*, p. 160; Sabrina Petra Ramet, *Social Currents in Eastern Europe: The Sources and Consequences of the Great Transformation* (Durham, NC: Duke University Press, 1995), p. 145.

31. Ramet, *Social Currents*, pp. 143-145.

32. Laszlo Tokes, *With God, for the People*, as told to David Porter (London: Hodder and Stoughton, 1990), pp. 1- 2, 4, 135

33. Ratesh, *Romania*, pp. 21-31; Stokes, *Walls Came Tumbling Down*, p. 163; Tismaneanu, *Reinventing Politics*, p. 232; Larry Watts, "The Romanian Army in the December Revolution and Beyond," in *Romania After Tyranny*, ed. Daniel N. Nelson (Boulder, CO: Westview Press, 1992), p. 107.

34. Andrei Cordrescu, *The Hole in the Flag: A Romanian Exile's Story of Return and Revolution* (New York: William Morrow, 1991), pp. 203-205; Ratesh, *Romania.*, pp. 31-43; Stokes, *Walls Came Tumbling Down*, pp. 165-166; Ramet, *Social Currents*, p. 362.

35. Gene Sharp, "The Role of Power in Nonviolent Struggle," Monograph Series, No. 3, The Albert Einstein Institution, 1994.

36. Jasper Becker, *The Lost Country: Mongolia Revealed* (London: Hodder & Stoughton, 1992), p. 44.

37. Yuri Krouchkin, *Mongolia Encyclopedia* (Ulaanbaatar: Interpress, 1998), p. 515; Tomor-Ochoriin Erdenebileg, M.P. , interview by Morris Rossabi, Ulaanbaatar, May 9, 1994; L. Sumati, Director of Sant Maral Research Center, interview by Morris Rossabi, August 14, 1997.

38. Hashbat Hulan, M.P. , interview by Morris Rossabi, Ulaanbaatar, May 26, 1998.

39. Morris Rossabi, "Mongolia in the 1990s: From Commissars to Capitalists?" *Open Society in Central Eurasia Occasional Paper Series* no. 2 (August, 1997), pp. 1-2.

40. Charles R. Bawden, *The Modern History of Mongolia* (New York: Frederick A. Praeger, 1968), pp. 304-311; D. Daspurev and S. K. Soni, *Reign of Terror in Mongolia, 1920-1990* (New Delhi: South Asian Publishers, 1992), pp. 42, 49.

41. Tomor-Ochiriin Erdenebileg, interview by Morris Rossabi, Ulaanbaatar, June 21, 1998; Robert Rupen, *How Mongolia is Really Ruled: A Political History of the Mongolian People's Republic, 1900-1978* (Stanford, CA: Hoover Institution Press, 1979), pp. 79-83; William Heaton, "Mongolia 1979: Learning from 'Leading Experiences,'" *Asian Survey* 20 (1980), p. 81.

42. Quote from Alan Sanders, "Restructuring and Openness," in *Mongolia Today*, ed. Shirin Akiner (London: Kegan Paul, 1991), pp. 67-68; William Heaton, "Mongolia in 1986: New Plan, New Situation," *Asian Survey* 27 (1987):79.

43. Kenneth Jarrett, "Mongolia in 1987: Out From the Cold?," *Asian Survey* 28 (1988), p. 81.

44. Sanders, "Restructuring and Openness," pp. 70-71; Alan Sanders, "Mongolia in 1988: Year of Renewal," *Asian Survey* 29 (1989), pp. 47-48; Morris Rossabi, "Mongolia: A New Opening?," *Current History* (September, 1992), p. 279.

45. Alan Sanders, "Mongolia in 1989: Year of Adjustment," *Asian Survey* 30 (1990), p. 62.

46. Ibid., p. 66.

47. Krouchkin, *Mongolia Encyclopedia*, pp. 446-447, 451-452; quoted words from Khenmedkheviin Dashzeveg, *MUAN-in Tuukhen Temdeglel (1989-1996)* (Ulaanbaatar: Interpress, 1998), pp. 22-23.

48. Dashzeveg, *MUAN-in Tuukhen Temdeglel*, pp. 23-24; Morris Rossabi, *China and Inner Asia from 1368 to the Present Day* (London: Thames and Hudson, 1975), pp. 149-158.

49. William Heaton, "Mongolia in 1990: Upheaval, Reform, But No Revolution Yet," *Asian Survey* 31 (1991), pp. 50-51.

50. Peter Staisch and Werner M. Prohl, *Dschingis Khan Lachelt: Die Mongolei auf dem Weg zur Demokratie* (Bonn: Bouvier Verlag, 1998), p. 29; L. Sumati, interview by Morris Rossabi, Ulaanbaatar, May 19, 1998.

51. Dashzeveg, *MUAN-in Tuukhen Temdeglel*, pp. 24-25.

52. Interview, Hashbat Hulan, M.P. , interview by Morris Rossabi, Ulaanbaatar, May 26, 1998; T. Elbegdorj, M.P. , interview by Morris Rossabi, Ulaanbaatar, May 12, 1994; Dashzeveg, *MUAN-in Tuukhen Temdeglel*, p. 27; Rossabi, "Mongolia," pp. 267-268; Paul Hyer, "The Re-evaluation of Chinggis Khan: Its Role in the Sino-Soviet Dispute," *Asian Survey* 6 (1966), pp. 696-698.

53. Becker, *Lost Country*, p. 45; Oidov Enkhtuya, M.P. , interview by Morris Rossabi, Ulaanbaatar, August 24, 1997.

54. Davaadorjiin Ganbold, interview by Morris Rossabi, Ulaanbaatar, January 8, 1997; Dashzeveg, *MUAN-in Tuukhen Temdeglel*, p. 28.

55. Dashzeveg, *MUAN-in Tuukhen Temdeglel*, p. 27.

56. Becker, *Lost Country,* p. 45; quote from Tomor-Ochiriin Erdenebileg, interview by Morris Rossabi, Ulaanbaatar, May 9, 1994.
57. Dashzeveg, *MUAN-in Tuukhen Temdeglel,* p. 33; Verena Maria Fritz, "Doppelte Transition in der Mongolei unter dem Einfluss auslandischer Geber," Ph.D. diss., Hamburg University, 1998, pp. 58-62; L. Sumati, Rossabi interview.
58. Dashzeveg, *MUAN-in Tuukhen Temdeglel,* p. 34; quote from Lama Dambajav, interview by Morris Rossabi, Ulaanbaatar, May 14, 1994.
59. Staisch and Prohl, *Dschingis Khan Lachelt,* p. 31.
60. Demchigiin Molomjamts, interview by Morris Rossabi, Ulaanbaatar, May 19, 1998.
61. Staisch and Prohl, *Dschingis Khan Lachelt,* pp. 31-32.
62. Quote from Dashiin Byambasuren, interview by Morris Rossabi, Ulaanbaatar, May 6, 1994; Dashzeveg, *MUAN-in Tuukhen Temdeglel,* pp. 35-36.
63. Staisch and Prohl, *Dschingis Khan Lachelt,* pp. 31-32.
64. Heaton, "Mongolia in 1990," p. 51.
65. Byambasuren, Rossabi interview; Heaton, "Mongolia in 1990," p. 51.
66. Staisch and Prohl, *Dschingis Khan Lachelt,* p. 35-36; Dashzeveg, *MUAN-in Tuukhen Temdeglel,* p. 36; Punsalmagiin Ochirbat, President of Mongolia, interview by Morris Rossabi, Ulaanbaatar, May 15, 1994; Heaton, "Mongolia in 1990," p. 51.
67. Michael Kohn, "Democratic Leader S. Zorig Murdered," *The Mongol Messenger,* October 7, 1998, p. 2.
68. Dashzeveg, *MUAN-in Tuukhen Temdeglel,* pp. 51-54.
69. Heaton, "Mongolia in 1990," p. 52.
70. Dashzeveg, *MUAN-in Tuukhen Temdeglel,* p. 28; Staisch and Prohl, *Dschingis Khan Lachelt,* pp. 36-37; Sanjiin Bayar, interview by Morris Rossabi, Ulaanbaatar, August 18, 1997; Bat-Erdeniin Batbayar, M.P. , interview by Morris Rossabi, January 7, 1997.
71. Dashzeveg, *MUAN-in Tuukhen Temdeglel,* p. 48; Staisch and Prohl, *Dschingis Khan Lachelt,* p. 38.
72. Gotovyn Akim, Editor-in-Chief, *Il Tovchoo;* interview by Morris Rossabi, Ulaanbaatar, August 23, 1997.

CHAPTER THIRTEEN

1. Orlando Figes, *A People's Tragedy: The Russian Revolution, 1981-1924* (New York: Penguin Books, 1996), pp. 398, 400-401.
2. "[T]he naked truth" quote from Frantz Fanon, *The Wretched of the Earth* (New York: Grove Press, 1994), p. 30; Jean-Paul Sartre quote and "gangsters will light the way" quote from Hannah Arendt, *Crises of the Republic* (San Diego: Harcourt Brace & Co., 1972), pp. 114, 122, respectively.
3. S. J. Tambiah, *Sri Lanka: Ethnic Fratricide and the Dismantling of Democracy* (Chicago: University of Chicago Press, 1986), pp. 65-68.
4. Ibid., pp. 68-69, 73-74.
5. A. Jeyaratnam Wilson, *The Break-up of Sri Lanka: The Sinhalese-Tamil Conflict* (Honolulu: University of Hawaii Press, 1988), pp. 107-115.
6. A. Jeyaratnam Wilson, *S. J. V. Chelvanayakam and the Crisis of Sri Lankan Tamil Nationalism* (Honolulu: University of Hawaii Press, 1994), p. 95.
7. Alan J. Bullion, *India, Sri Lanka and the Tamil Crisis, 1976-1994* (London: Pinter, 1995), pp. 89-91.
8. Jagath P. Senaratne, *Political Violence in Sri Lanka, 1977-1990: Riots, Insurrections, Counter-Insurgencies, Foreign Intervention* (Amsterdam: VU University Press, 1997), pp. 59-72.
9. Dagmar-Hellman Rajanayagam, "The 'Groups' and the Rise of Militant Secessionism," in *The Sri Lankan Tamils: Ethnicity and Identity,* eds. Chelvadurai Manogaran and Bryan Pfaffenberger (Boulder, CO: Westview Press, 1994), pp. 172-173; Sumantra Bose, *States, Nations, Sovereignty: Sri Lanka and the Tamil Eelam Movement* (New Delhi: Sage Publications, 1994), p. 85.
10. Tony Clifton, "Lost in the Hell of War," *Newsweek,* April 5, 1999, p. 34; Tambiah, *Sri Lanka,* pp. 118-119.
11. James Reston, Jr., *The Last Apocalypse: Europe at the Year 1000 A.D.* (New York: Doubleday, 1998). pp. 112-114.
12. "The Basques," Microsoft *Encarta* Encyclopedia, 1998.
13. Robert P. Clark, *Negotiating with ETA: Obstacles to Peace in the Basque Country, 1975-1988* (Reno: University of Nevada Press, 1990), p. 19; John Sullivan, "Forty Years of ETA: Basque Homeland and Liberty," *History Today* 49, no. 4 (April 1, 1999).

14. Clark, *Negotiating with ETA*, pp. 3-4; Daniele Conversi, *The Basques, the Catalans, and Spain* (Reno: University of Nevada Press, 1997), p. 92-96.

15. Clark, *Negotiating with ETA*, pp. 9-10.

16. E. Ramon Arango, *Spain: Democracy Regained* (Boulder, CO: Westview Press, 1995), p. 226.

17. Elkarri site on the Internet: www.encomix.es/~ingles1.html.

18. "Spain and the Basques: Not Like Ireland," *The Economist*, July 18, 1998, p. 44; Stryker McGuire and John Parry, "Spain's War on the ETA," *Newsweek/Atlantic Edition*, December 15, 1997.

19. Tim Brown, "Gerry Adams Urges Madrid to Accept Overture," *The Scotsman*, October 6, 1998, p. 10.

20. Arendt, *Crises of the Republic*, p. 147.

21. Fred Weir, "Where Rebellion Is a Tradition," *The Christian Science Monitor*, December 31, 1999, pp. 1, 8.

22. Figes, *People's Tragedy*, p. 536.

23. Arendt, *Crises of the Republic*, pp. 164-165, 184.

24. Stone Sizani, videotaped interview by Steve York for the documentary television series *A Force More Powerful*, Port Elizabeth, South Africa; June 12, 1999.

CHAPTER FOURTEEN

1. Michael Ryan, "He Fights Dictators on the Internet," *Parade Magazine*, August 23, 1998.

2. Ibid.

3. "Burma: Sacrifice for Democracy," treatment and research by Steve York for the documentary television series *A Force More Powerful*; William Glaberson, "A Guerrilla War on the Internet," *The New York Times*, April 8, 1997; quote from Peter Eng, "On-line Activists Step Up Fight," *Bangkok Post*, April 29, 1998.

4. Martin Smith, *Burma: Insurgency and the Politics of Ethnicity* (London: Zed Books, 1991), pp. 8-12.

5. Ibid., pp. 14-15.

6. Quote from Gene Sharp, "Exploring Nonviolent Struggle in Thailand and Burma," from personal files, The Albert Einstein Institution, Fall 1992.

7. Greg Michaelidis, visit and consultations with the Burma Project, March 19, 1999.

8. Tiffany Danitz and Warren P. Strobel, "Networking Dissent: Burmese Cyberactivists Promote Nonviolent Struggle Using the Internet," U.S. Institute of Peace and Nonviolence International, Washington, D.C., 1998, pp. 15-16.

9. Ibid.

10. Ted Bardacke, "Burmese Risk Stiff Jail Sentences for Surfing the Internet," *Financial Times*, October 5 and 6, 1996, p. 1; quote from "Notables and Quotables," from *Burma Debate* (Internet listserve), September/October 1997, quoted in Jonathan Shapiro, "Dialogue, Democracy, and the Internet: The Struggle for Civilian Rule in Burma," Seminar Paper, Harvard University, 1998.

11. Danitz and Strobel, "Networking Dissent;" e-mail message from Htun Aung Gyaw to Gregory Michaelidis, May 23, 1999.

12. Transcript, Radio Free Asia broadcast, 1995, Poland Series, Part I.

13. Kevin Sullivan, "Army Rulers Tighten Iron Grip on Burma," *Washington Post*, May 24, 1999.

14. Htun Aung Gyaw, e-mail message.

15. Timothy Garton Ash, "In the Serbian Soup," *New York Review of Books*, April 24, 1997, p. 25.

16. Jane Perlez, "All Walks of Life Protest in Belgrade," *The New York Times*, December 31, 1996, p. A10.

17. Announcement of Women in Black's 4th Anniversary Protest: www.igc.apc.org/balkans/women/wib-st.html (ca. May 1999).

18. David S. Bennahum, "The Internet Revolution," *Wired*, April 1997.

19. Steven Erlanger, "Even Milosevic Foes Criticize Western Media," in *The New York Times*, March 31, 1999.

20. Bennahum, "Internet Revolution."

21. Ibid.

22. Ibid.

23. Tim Judah, "How Milosevic Hangs On," *New York Review of Books*, July 16, 1998, p. 45.

24. Ibid., p. 44.

25. John R. Lampe, *Yugoslavia as History: Twice There Was a Country* (Cambridge: Cambridge University Press, 1996), 297.

26. Kosovo Briefing, International Crisis Group, South Balkans Report, February 17, 1998.

27. Chris Hedges, "Kosovo Leader Urges Resistance, But to Violence," *The New York Times*, March 13, 1998.

28. "It was a sign" quote from Peter Finn and R. Jeffrey Smith, "Rebels with a Crippled Cause," *Washington Post*, April 23, 1999, p. 32; "We are through" quote from Chris Hedges, "Kosovo's Next Masters?" *Foreign Affairs*, May-June 1999.

29. Chris Hedges, "Kosovo Leader Urges Resistance, But To Violence," *The New York Times*, March 13, 1998; quotes from Hedges, "Kosovo's Next Masters?"

30. "NATO's Campaign in Yugoslavia," in *Strategic Comments*, International Institute of Strategic Studies, London, vol. 5, no. 3, April 1999.

31. Thomas L. Friedman, *The Lexus and the Olive Tree* (New York: Farrar Straus and Giroux, 1999), p. 124-127; Ash, "In the Serbian Soup," p. 27.

32. Desko Nikitovic, telephone interview with Gregory Michaelidis, June 11,1999; CSCE *Digest* (Committee for Security and Cooperation in Europe) 21, no. 12 (December 1998).

33. Richard Holbrooke, *To End a War* (New York: The Modern Library, 1999), p. 322.

34. Commission on Security and Cooperation in Europe, transcript of hearing on political turmoil in Serbia, December 12, 1996.

35. Desko Nikitovic, television appearances on *Internight with John Gibson*, MSNBC, March 28, 1999, and *Geraldo Live*, CNBC, April 16, 1999; Carolyn Lochhead, "Cost of Kosovo," *San Francisco Chronicle*, May 7, 1999.

36. Steven Erlanger, "Even Milosevic Foes Criticize Western Media" in *The New York Times*, March 31, 1999.

37. Lochhead, "Cost of Kosovo."

38. This paragraph and the following narrative relies in part on "Who Really Brought Down Milosevic?" by Roger Cohen, *The New York Times Magazine*, November 26, 2000.

39. Stanko Lazendic, videotaped interview by Steve York, Novi Sad, Yugoslavia, November 30, 2000.

40. Srdja Popovic, videotaped interview by Steve York, Belgrade, Yugoslavia, November 13, 2000.

41. Col. Robert Helvey, videotaped interview by Steve York, Belgrade, January 30, 2001; Popovic, videotaped interview by Steve York.

42. Popovic, York interview.

43. Srdjan Milivojevic, videotaped interview by Steve York, Krusevac, Yugoslavia, November 26, 2000.

44. Zoran Djindjic, videotaped interview by Steve York, Belgrade, November 13, 2000.

45. Popovic, York interview.

46. Teofil Pancic, videotaped interview by Steve York, Belgrade, November 22, 2000.

47. Vojislav Kostunica, videotaped interview by Steve York, Belgrade, February 3, 2001.

48. Zoran Sekulic, videotaped interview by Steve York, Belgrade, November 29, 2000.

49. Velimir Ilic, mayor of Cacak, videotaped interview by Steve York, Cacak, Yugoslavia, November 24, 2000; Daniel Serwer, videotaped interview by Steve York, Washington, D.C., March 7, 2001.

50. Vojislav Kostunica, videotaped interview by Steve York, Belgrade, February 3, 2001.

51. Alex Todorovic, "Serb Opposition's Risky Gambit," *Christian Science Monitor*, October 2, 2001; quote from Djindjic, videotaped interview by Steve York; "We had secret talks" quote from Cohen.

52. Velimir Ilic, York interview.

53. Popovic, York interview.

54. Ibid.

55. Ibid.

56. Sidney Tarrow, *Power in Movement: Social Movements and Contentious Politics*, 2nd ed. (New York: Cambridge University Press, 1998), p.

57. John D. McCarthy, Clark McPhail, and John Crist, "The Diffusion and Adoption of Public Order Management Systems," *Social Movements in a Globalizing World*, ed. Donatella della Porta (New York, St. Martin's Press, 1999), p. 77.

CONCLUSION

1. Bernard Wheaton and Zdenek Kavan, *The Velvet Revolution: Czechoslovakia, 1988-1991* (Boulder, CO: Westview Press, 1992), pp. 52-53.

2. Vaclev Havel, *The Power of the Powerless* (New York: M. E. Sharp, Inc., 1985), p. 42.

3. *The Gandhi Reader*, ed. Homer Jack (New York: Grove Press, 1994), p. 76.

4. Sidney Tarrow, *Power in Movement: Social Movements and Contentious Politics* (New York: Cambridge University Press), 1998.

5. Mark Swilling, videotaped interview by Sara Blecher for the documentary television series *A Force More Powerful*, Stellenbosch, South Africa; June 21, 1999.

6. Patricia Parkman, *Nonviolent Insurrection in El Salvador* (Tucson: University of Arizona Press, 1988), p. 68.

7. Steven Mufson, *Fighting Years: Black Resistance and the Struggle for a New South Africa* (Boston: Beacon Press, 1990), p. 47-48.

8. *People Power: An Eyewitness History*, ed. Monina Allarey Mercado (New York: Writers and Readers Publishing, Inc., 1986), p. 243.

9. Azhar Cachalia, videotaped interview by Steve York for the documentary television series *A Force More Powerful*, Pretoria, South Africa; June 8, 1999.

10. Henry David Thoreau, *Walden, or Life in the Woods, and On the Duty of Civil Disobedience* (New York: New American Library/Signet Classic, 1980), pp. 225, 231.

11. Martin Green, *The Challenge of the Mahatmas* (New York: Basic Books, 1978), p. 13.

12. Hannah Arendt, "On Violence," in *Crises of the Republic* (New York: Harcourt Brace & Co., 1972), pp. 155, 176.

13. Ibid., p. 139.

INDEX

Daily Telegraph (London), 218
Dastur, Aloo, 79, 97
Dayton Accords, 481-483
de la Boétie, Etienne, 11
Degoutte, Gen. Joseph, 185, 197
DeKlerk, F.W., 366-367
Demaci, Adem, 481
demands, *by nonviolent resisters,* 16-18, 21, 24-25, 33, 37, 83, 113, 118, 140, 146, 148-150, 262, 422, 444, 471
democracy, *action to promote,* 7, 489, *effect of nonviolent movements on,* 504
Democracy Wall, 422
Democratic League of Kosovo, 481
Deng Xiaoping, 422
deportations, 233-235, 418
Dereta, Miljenko, 485
Derian, Patricia, 274
Desai, Mahadev, 85
Desai, Narayan, 107
Deutsche Allgemeine Zeitung, 181, 184
De Vincente, Azucena de Villaflor de, 272-273, 276
Dharasana, nonviolent raid at, 88-90, 93
Diario de Occidente, 253
Diario Latino, El, 248, 250-251, 253
Ding Zilin, 427
Direccion de Inteligencia Nacional (DINA), 281
disappearances, 246, 268, 270-274, 276-277, 281, 436, 462
Djindic, Zoran, 478, 487-488
doctors, nonviolent action by, 234, 259-261
Draskovic, Vuk, 478
Dua, Shiva, 97
Duarte, José Jesús, 246
Duarte, José Napoleón, 258, 263
DuBois, W.E.B., 305
Duckwitz, Georg, 222-223
Duda-Gwiazda, Joanna, 136, 144
DuPlessis, Lourence, 349, 355, 357, 363
Duvalier, Jean Claude, 292
Dvorak, Antonin, 434
Dyer, Gen. Reginald, 74

East India Company, 68-69
Ebert, Friedrich, 180, 182-183, 195
Ecoglasnost, 431-432
Ecumenical Group for Human Rights, 277
Eddie Bauer, 476

Eichmann, Adolf, 222-223, 237
Einstein, Albert, Institution, xiii, 474-475
Ekstrabladet, 213
elections, as strategic opportunity, 218-219, 295-301, 378-379, 451-452, 473, 478, 487-488, 500
elkarri, 465
Enrile, Juan Ponce, 376, 385-386, 388, 393
Esquivel, Adolfo Pérez, 277
European Community, 365
Euskadi Ta Askatasuna (ETA), 459, 464-465, 467
Evdokimov, Sergei, 13-15
expulsions, 189, 196-197

Families of the Disappeared for Political Reasons, 277
Fang Lizhi, 422
Fanon, Frantz, 458, 464, 467
Farmer, James, 307
Fellowship of Reconciliation, 307-308, 310, 313
Felski, Bogdan, 138-139
financial sanctions, 52, 57, 376, 416, 488
First Baptist Church, Nashville, 317-318, 320, 324
Fisk University, 306, 312, 316, 322
Flying University, 129, 137, 168
Foch, Marshal Ferdinand, 180
Forest Brotherhood, 491
Franco, Francisco, 248, 268, 464
Frasyniuk, Wladyslaw, 167, 169
Free Burma Coalition, 475
Freedom Council, 223, 225, 227-230
Freedom House, 485
French Revolution, 458
Fresno, Juan Francisco Cardinal, 287, 289, 291
Friedman, Milton, 282

Gador, Col. Tirgo, 386
Galtieri, Gen. Leopoldo, 277
Ganbold, Davaadorjiin, 446, 451-452
Gandhi, Kasturbai, 85, 89
Gandhi, Mohandas, 3, 6-7, 61-63, 81, 110-111, 172; *in South Africa,* 63-68, 339, 368, 399; *ideas about nonviolent action,* 5, 173, 427, 494; *as a leader,* 71, 73, 75-79, 94, 102, 108-109; *contact with Tolstoy,*